American Families

"What a collection of articles! Stephanie Coontz has gathered together the writing of many of the most important scholars of our time to address one of the most important issues of our time—the growing diversity of American Families. A great choice for undergraduate classrooms and an addition to any scholar's bookshelf."
—Barbara J. Risman, author of *Gender Vertigo: American Families in Transition*

"*American Families* provides a powerful exploration of the challenges facing contemporary families. From the historical roots of inequality to tools to theorize the meanings of difference, this collection provides engaging readings that illustrate American past and present struggles, laced with hope for the future."
—Jennifer A. Reich, author of *Fixing Families: Parents, Power, and the Child Welfare System* (Routledge)

"*American Families* is a marvel—the authors have identified some of the very best and clearest new scholarship. The book affords an accurate, thoughtful and thought-provoking glimpse at family life in the US as it really is."
—Linda Gordon, author of *The Great Arizona Orphan Abduction*

With its clear conceptual focus, well-chosen essays exploring the interactions between race-ethnicity, class, gender, and sexuality in shaping family life by leading names from across the curriculum, and its comprehensive and teachable introduction, the completely updated, revised, and expanded second edition of Stephanie Coontz's *American Families* remains the best resource available on family diversity in America.

Contributors: David Wallace Adams, David L. Brunsma, Linda Burton, Patricia Hill Collins, David Cotter, Bonnie Thornton Dill, Paula England, Donna L. Franklin, Gary Gates, Kathleen Gerson, Naomi Gerstel, Evelyn Nakano Glenn, Kristen Harknett, Joan Hermsen, Pierrette Hondagneu-Sotelo, Jerry A. Jacobs, Norrece T. Jones, Jr., Nazli Kibria, Michael Kimmel, Annette Lareau, Jennifer Lee, Leigh A. Leslie, Stephen R. Marks, Sarah McLanahan, Michael A. Messner, Steven Mintz, Rachel F. Moran, Kumiko Nemoto, Rhacel Salazar Parreñas, Allison L. Pugh, Karen Pyke, Gabrielle Raley, Rayna Rapp, Beth E. Richie, Kerry A. Rockquemore, Kevin Roy, Lillian B. Rubin, Sarah Ryan, Karen Brodkin Sacks, George J. Sánchez, Natalia Sarkisian, Rickie Solinger, Thomas J. Sugrue, Barbara Wells, Min Zhou, Maxine Baca Zinn.

Stephanie Coontz is Professor of Family History at the Evergreen State College. She is the author of numerous books, including *Marriage, a History: How Love Conquered Marriage.*

Maya Parson is a doctoral candidate in Cultural Anthropology at the University of North Carolina at Chapel Hill.

Gabrielle Raley is a doctoral candidate in Sociology at the University of California, Los Angeles.

American Families

A Multicultural Reader

Second Edition

Edited by

Stephanie Coontz
with Maya Parson and Gabrielle Raley

Routledge
Taylor & Francis Group

NEW YORK AND LONDON

First edition published 1998
This edition first published 2008
by Routledge
270 Madison Ave, New York, NY 10016

Simultaneously published in the UK
by Routledge
2 Park Square, Milton Park, Abingdon, Oxon OX14 4RN

Routledge is an imprint of the Taylor & Francis Group, an informa business

© 2008 Taylor & Francis

Typeset in Minion by
RefineCatch Limited, Bungay, Suffolk
Printed and bound in the United States of America on acid-free paper by
Edwards Brothers, Inc.

Library of Congress Cataloging in Publication Data
Coontz, Stephanie.
American families : a multicultural reader / Stephanie Coontz ; with Maya Parson and Gabrielle Raley. – 2nd ed.
    p. cm.
  Includes bibliographical references and index.
  ISBN 978–0–415–95820–2 (hardback : alk. paper) – 978–0–415–95821–9 (pbk.: alk. paper) 1. Family–United States. 2. Multiculturalism–United States. 3. Ethnicity–United States. 4. Work and family–United States. I. Parson, Maya. II. Raley, Gabrielle. III. Title.
  HQ535.A583 2008
  306.85089'00973–dc22
  2007044911

ISBN10: 0–415–95820–2 (hbk)
ISBN10: 0–415–95821–0 (pbk)

ISBN13: 978–0–415–95820–2 (hbk)
ISBN13: 978–0–415–95821–9 (pbk)

Contents

Acknowledgments

The articles in the first edition of this book were selected from the readings for a small two-quarter seminar on race, class, and gender in family scholarship that Stephanie Coontz conducted at The Evergreen State College. The five students in the seminar went way beyond the requirements of the class, participating in extra meetings, doing skilled library research to locate new work on the subject, and preparing thoughtful comments on the books and articles they read. Two of the students, Gabrielle Raley and Maya Parson, were able to remain involved in the next stages of article review and editing decisions long after the class ended. The other three students were Ben Anderson, Tamara Anderson, and Beth Vail. Their assistance was invaluable.

The second edition of this book was an even greater challenge, because of the explosion of research on this topic in the intervening years. We are very grateful to the authors in this volume who updated and sometimes completely revised their contributions, and well as to the many researchers who sent us new articles and books to review or took time out from their busy schedules to suggest other sources. We have been able to include many more articles than we were able to do in the first edition, but space limitations forced us to pass over many equally good articles. We have tried to represent those in the bibliography, which was compiled for the first edition by Maya Parson and revised for the second edition by Gabrielle Raley.

We could not have reviewed so much new research without the generous assistance of colleagues and friends. We especially thank the members of the Council on Contemporary Families, who were unfailingly generous with ideas and citations. We also received very helpful suggestions from the listserve of the Sociologists for Women in Society. Among the many individuals to whom we owe debts of gratitude are Lee Lyttle, Peta Henderson, Lynda Dickson, Shondrah Tarrezz Nash, Jeanne Flavin, Donna Franklin, Jay Green, Peggy Papp, Rich Simon, Constance Ahrons, Judith Stacey, Delia Louise Lamphere, Peggy Penn, Sandra Wagner-Wright, and Craig Severance, as well as most of the authors represented in this volume.

We would also like to acknowledge the support of the administration and staff at The Evergreen State College Library. As a group, we placed a significant burden on the reference and circulation staff. Their skills and dedication enabled us to locate hard-to-find citations and receive articles under tight deadlines.

Finally, Stephanie Coontz would especially like to thank her husband, Will Reissner, for his careful editing of her introduction and his help with several other edits of articles in the book.

Stephanie Coontz
Maya Parson
Gabrielle Raley

Introduction to the Second Edition

SINCE 1970, AMERICAN FAMILIES have undergone a dramatic diversification produced by high rates of divorce, cohabitation, unwed motherhood, the new visibility of same-sex relationships, the (re)-emergence of stepfamilies and working mothers, and a sharp rise in the number of single-person households, where once married-couple households were the norm. Racial-ethnic diversity has also increased. By 2005, nearly 13 percent of Americans were foreign-born, not quite as high a percentage as a century earlier, but an unprecedented figure in the memory of Americans alive today. Unlike the overwhelmingly European immigrants of 100 years ago, today's immigrants come from around the world, including many non-white and third world countries, and they have rapidly spread beyond the big-city enclaves in which immigrants used to cluster. Coupled with expanded internal migration of African-Americans and Hispanics to the suburbs and the Sunbelt, these trends have created greater and more widely distributed cultural and racial-ethnic diversity than ever before. Whites are now a minority in almost one-third of the nation's most populous counties.[1]

As Americans attempt to adjust to these changes, our assumptions about how family life should be organized and what the future holds for the younger generation have also been impacted by a realization that postwar social scientists were wrong in predicting that class divisions would gradually recede. Instead, these divisions have deepened and in some ways become more intractable.

The revolution in women's roles since the 1970s adds further uncertainty about the future of the family. The male breadwinner family, a comparatively new family model that became a reality for most Americans only in the 1950s, is now rejected by many Americans, and is unattainable for many others who may still believe that this is the Gold Standard for family life.

The intersection of old and new types of diversity has led to much debate about the origins and consequences of contemporary family change. Some leaders of the "family values" movement suggest that family "breakdown," especially the rise of cohabitation and unwed motherhood, is now the major cause of socioeconomic inequality and childhood disadvantage in America. Kay Hymowitz of the Manhattan Institute argues that today's race and class inequities stem less from discrimination or economic change than from willful abandonment of marriage and nuclear-family commitments by people influenced by feminism and the sexual revolution. Columnist George Will claims that "what is called the race crisis is a class problem arising from dysfunctional families and destructive behaviors." He believes that a largely African-American "underclass" has rejected family commitments and the work ethic and is thus responsible for its own poverty and isolation.[2]

Other observers dispute the view that family diversity is a sign of cultural deviance or collapsing values. Some argue that dysfunctional families are the result rather than the cause of race and class inequalities. Others suggest that many "deviant" family forms are not dysfunctional at all, but are highly adaptive, flexible arrangements for coping with distinctive challenges posed by class, race, and gender injustices. These authors argue that as white, middle-class families lose access to the economic and political support systems that sustained the stable male-breadwinner families of the 1950s and 1960s, they can learn a great deal from the more flexible and inclusive family norms of other racial-ethnic groups.[3]

This volume brings together articles by leading researchers in the field of family diversity to shed light on these debates. Their work reveals that in every historical period, including the present one, several different but interconnected family systems have coexisted within a larger constellation of power relations, unequal access to resources, and struggles over ideological representations of family life. The articles in this reader examine the changing interactions between class, race, ethnicity, socioeconomic inequality and family forms, values, and definitions, as well as relations between men and women, parents and children. Because they explore diversity in family behaviors and values in the context of group differences in social power, status, and resources, we describe this book as a multicultural reader on families rather than a reader on family diversity *per se*.

There are trade-offs in this choice. We have not been able to include any of the rich research on the differing dynamics of male-breadwinner/female-homemaker, dual-earner, and remarried families, divorced or never-married parents, and cohabiting couples, whether same-sex or hetero-sexual. Nor, except for the selection by David Adams, do we examine religious diversity, despite fascinating interactions (and disconnects) between people's religious or moral beliefs and their family experiences. For example, African-Americans are more likely to disapprove of cohabitation than whites, but are also more likely to engage in it. Rates of divorce and unwed motherhood are higher in the so-called Bible Belt than in the more liberal states of the Northeast. Evangelical Christians divorce at about the same rate as atheists and agnostics, and Pentecostals have higher divorce rates than either.[4] In all these cases, socioeconomic hierarchies interact with people's belief systems in complex and contradictory ways.

We focus in this reader on patterns of difference created by conflict, accommodation, and interaction among groups of differing power, cultural acceptance, and socioeconomic status. An underlying issue is the question of how to conceptualize diversity in a way that takes account of relationships among different groups rather than studying racial, ethnic, or socioeconomic cate-gories in isolation from each other. That question even caused us to debate use of the word multicultural in the title. Two of the authors whose work we include in this volume have argued elsewhere that "multiracial" is a better term for describing the "primary and pervasive" role of race in organizing the differences in family life and gender roles within the United States.[5]

Certainly, an emphasis on culture rather than race can understate the powerful force of the color line in determining the place of families within the U.S. constellation of power and prestige. Immigrants such as Hispanics, for example, often come from countries where the concept of racial groupings has been more subtly intertwined with social class and less dichotomized by skin color than in the United States. Once they enter the United States, however, the prevailing racial ideologies in this country tend to rearrange immigrant hierarchies and opportunities on the basis of color, with darker-skinned Hispanics experiencing greater residential segregation and diminished job opportunities. Similarly, immigrants of European origin have an advantage that transcends skill differences. Germans and Poles typically receive higher incomes than more-educated Iranians or

Indians, and low-skilled Portuguese do better than Mexicans or Dominicans, even though the educational attainments of these groups are comparable.[6]

Race continues to matter for native-born Americans as well. In July 2007 the Bureau of Labor Statistics reported that the unemployment rate of African-Americans with a high school diploma was higher than that of white high-school dropouts, while blacks with a doctorate earned, on average, $12,000 less per year than whites with a comparable degree.[7]

We feared, however, that for some readers, the term "multiracial" would reinforce the myth that race is a biological fact. Evelyn Brooks Higginbotham warns that race language tends to obscure other organizing principles such as gender or class, and also "blurs and disguises, suppresses and negates its own complex interplay" with these other power relations.[8] That is why we chose to call this a multicultural reader, defining culture as the set of learned values and behaviors and the "ideological frame of reference through which people attempt to deal with the circumstances in which they find themselves"—circumstances in which racial and class hierarchies often play a pivotal role.[9]

The term multicultural has its own difficulties. Too often, multicultural studies simply serve up a buffet of different family arrangements and values, without specifying the relationships and struggles between different groups. A "celebration of diversity" may mask the differences in power and resource among groups, and overlook their symbiotic (or parasitical) relationships. John Garvey suggests that multicultural education can become a kind of managed care, offering the palliative relief of "tolerance" rather than aggressively treating the disease of oppression.[10]

Alternatively, some cultural approaches suggest that people occupy different class positions or are assigned lower places in the racial-ethnic hierarchy *because* of their shared group values. Several of our authors explicitly argue against this approach, proposing that many "cultural" differences are the product of enforced inequalities in access to resources, or emerge in the course of coping with such inequities.

Recognizing the social origins of many cultural values and family behaviors is not the same thing as a victim-model of family diversity. The rich historical traditions and creative contemporary adaptations described in this volume demonstrate the tremendous resourcefulness of "minority" families and individuals. But unless we understand how societal relations of race, gender, class, and ethnicity influence personal decision-making, we can mistake creative, even heroic, adaptations for unconstrained choice.

As Maxine Baca Zinn and Bonnie Thornton Dill write, "intersecting forms of domination produce *both* oppression *and* opportunity."[11] Domination places some families at the top of a social hierarchy and others at the bottom, shaping the choices that all families make. The hierarchy is not static, and even at the bottom, some types of oppression open up opportunities for personal action or collective organization. Yet many of the gains achieved by families or individuals remain limited by larger power and productive relations.

When a woman charms her way out of a speeding ticket, she is not demonstrating that men and women each have their own set of advantages, but rather that the stereotypes perpetuating male dominance can sometimes be manipulated to individual advantage. When an African-American or Puerto Rican woman strikes out on her own, acting independently of men in a way that white middle-class women have sometimes envied, how much of this is gender equality and how much dire necessity? When a Black defendant with a good lawyer directs attention away from damaging evidence by focusing on the racism of the police, he is not proving that African-Americans now have an advantage in the legal system. He is using to his own benefit the demonstrable fact that the justice system routinely *does* discriminate against Black men.

The key to understanding how individuals and families make choices, without denying the constraints under which they operate, is to recognize that power is never a one-way street. The slave family, for example, was not a simple imitation of the slave-owner's family nor a helpless victim of the traffic in human beings. Neither, however, was it a self-made creation free from the restraints of white owners. Yet the families of the slave-owners were *also* molded by slavery. Their internal relations were profoundly affected by external racial hierarchies and by anxieties about social control.[12]

Today, white and "minority" families both develop their strategies and perceptions in the context of growing income inequality, declining gender inequality (although created as much by a fall in men's real wages as a rise in women's), and the de-legitimization of overt racial discrimination, coupled with the persistence of de facto segregation in schools and housing. People of color have entered formerly lily-white professions and income levels in significant numbers, while a large segment of white workers, especially less-educated males, has lost ground in comparison to more educated sectors of the working class. Yet the ranks of the extremely poor are still filled largely by African-Americans and dark-skinned Latinos. Historically-constructed feelings of entitlement on the part of whites have been shaken up without really leveling the playing field.

A good example of the confusion generated by these changes is the question of whether the United States has become—or should become—a color-blind society. With statutory segregation abolished and overt racial discrimination illegal, some people believe that America has moved beyond racism. And in many ways, progress has been remarkable. African-Americans, Latinos, and Asian-Americans now occupy powerful and prestigious positions in government, business, education, and popular culture.

In personal life as well, there is much less overt racism than in the past. In 1967, interracial marriage was still illegal in many states, and as late as 1970, nearly one-half of all Americans still favored such laws. Today, only 10 percent of Americans, and only 4 percent of young adults, would favor banning interracial unions. In 1970, less than 2 percent of married couples were interracial. By 2005 that had climbed to more than 7 percent. A majority of young Americans say that they either have dated someone of another race or would be willing to do so.[13]

Black–white intermarriage remains rarer than other forms of interracial unions, however, and biracial and multiracial African-Americans have less leeway to choose among different racial categories than other multiracial individuals, in part because of the historic legacy of the segregationist rule that "one drop" of Negro blood classifies a person as Black. Some authors fear that as Asians and Hispanics are seen as being somehow closer to white, blacks may be left behind yet again.[14]

How much of this gap is caused by class and how much by race? The residential segregation of African-Americans has always been far greater than can be explained by the average difference between whites and blacks in socioeconomic status (SES). Yet those historic patterns of segregation and job discrimination have also left poor African-Americans especially vulnerable to being stuck in racially isolated areas of concentrated poverty, decaying infrastructure, and few job opportunities. Since 1990, socioeconomic status has come to explain a larger share of the segregation between whites and African-Americans than in the past.[15]

The result has been a conflation of color and class into a new, culture-coded racism that is particularly insidious precisely because it does allow for exceptions, as long as an African-American "proves" that he or she should be exempted from the default association that popular culture makes between blacks and "street" life. A black person who displays an affluent (but not ostentatious) middle-class persona and signals rejection of anything associated with "ghetto culture" may find personal and social acceptance. But those who cannot or will not do so are often perceived as part of a dangerous or dysfunctional "underclass" and discriminated against in jobs and housing.

Recently, researchers randomly assigned names associated with African-Americans or whites to fictitious resumes that were otherwise identical in qualifications. Names such as Greg and Emily received 50 percent more callbacks for interviews than names like Lakisha and Jamal. It is unclear how much of this stems from racism pure and simple, how much from a cultural chauvinism that penalizes African-Americans for celebrating a distinctive heritage, and how much from a class-biased assumption that a "black-sounding" name signals a lower-class origin.[16]

Many articles in this volume emphasize the increasing significance of class over race in explaining differences in family life. Clearly, however, even very successful African-Americans frequently find themselves subject to racial prejudice when they step outside their own circle of friends, colleagues, and peers. As Jodie Kliman and William Madsen point out, a black executive may be able to hire and fire white employees, but he often "has less *effective* class standing than subordinates when trying to hail a cab, join a country club, buy an elegant home"—or even protect his children from racial profiling by police. Ellis Cose has eloquently described the frustration of "privileged" African-Americans who are either categorized as specialists in "black" issues or face censure if they call too much attention to racial issues.[17]

Still, there are certainly new opportunities for many African-Americans and other minorities to succeed in America, while being white confers fewer guaranteed privileges than in the past. Michael Omi and Howard Winant argue that racial hierarchies once imposed primarily through coercion now rest on "a complex system of compromises, legitimizing ideologies, . . . political rules and bureaucratic regulations." Racism is no longer monolithic, despite the persistence of racial discrimination and the concentration of poverty among inner-city African-Americans and Latinos, and there are new limits to its sway over people's lives. The result is a "messy racial hegemony," marked by contradictory, conflicted, and ambiguous relationships.[18] Several articles in this book suggest that the same kind of messiness is emerging in gender relations as well.

SECTION ONE: THE LONG TRADITION OF FAMILY DIVERSITY

Many discussions of family diversity start from the assumption that the white middle-class family ideal popularized by the TV sit-coms of the 1950s was the historical norm for most families, and that diversity is a recent development in family life. This section demonstrates that there has never been a single family model in the United States and that change has been constant for all families. In all historical periods, Bonnie Thornton Dill reminds us, Anglo-American middle-class families coexisted with and were in fact dependent upon different family arrangements and definitions in other classes and racial-ethnic groups. In the nineteenth century, native-born middle-class whites would not have been able to reorganize family life to keep their children at home longer and to redirect maternal time from producing clothing and food to specializing in child-rearing without the labor of the enslaved mothers who provided cotton to the new textile mills and the immigrant children who worked in those factories or provided household help for middle-class families.[19]

The family systems of early America were forged from the interactions and clashes between three groups: the politically, economically, and militarily dominant Euro-American colonizers; the indigenous Native Americans, and the Africans brought by Europeans first as indentured servants and then as lifetime slaves. Before the arrival of European settlers, Native American family arrangements ranged from simple monogamy (usually with divorce rights) to various forms of multiple marriage. Some societies had complex descent systems traced through the maternal or the paternal lines; others were comparatively unconcerned with lineal descent rules. But the indigenous peoples of North America all organized production, distribution, and even justice through kin networks, rather than adherence to the authority of a territorial state, and did not recognize the private ownership of land by individuals or independent nuclear families. Most Native American societies had a division of labor by gender, but it differed greatly from that of the European settlers. Indeed, several Native American groups acknowledged a third gender, whose sexual orientation is not adequately described by modern dichotomous notions of heterosexuality and homosexuality.[20]

European colonization physically decimated many Native American societies through disease and war, and also magnified the role of young men at the expense of the traditional roles of elders and women. The selection from David Adams, however, shows that even after the physical conquest and relocation of Native American groups had been accomplished, Anglo-American political leaders felt compelled to destroy Native American communal values and kinship norms in a campaign of coerced "assimilation." Later in the section, Rachel Moran's article on anti-miscegenation laws details how states prohibited other forms of assimilation by forbidding marriage between whites and various racial or ethnic groups. Interracial marriage was more frequent in the first three-quarters of the nineteenth century than it became from the 1880s to the 1930s, when anti-miscegenation laws and Jim Crow policies were most widespread.[21]

The Africans brought to America to serve the white settlers also came from kinship-based societies, although some of those societies had larger status differences and more complex political institutions than were found among the indigenous people of North America. Family conditions of imported African-Americans varied depending on whether they lived in free black settlements, colonial villages where there were just a few personal slaves or servants, great cotton plantations utilizing gang labor, or small backwoods farms where one or two slaves lived and worked under a master's close supervision. But families in all these settings had to deal with their involuntary relocation to America, the loss of their languages, the brutality of slavery, and the gradual hardening of racial attitudes over the first two centuries of colonization.

Niara Sudarkasa has argued that many African-American family forms and practices, such as child exchange networks and reliance on matrifocal extended kinship ties, were a continuation of a West African heritage. This is complicated, Leith Mullings has pointed out, by the fact that some working-class Euro-American groups developed similar family strategies as a reaction to economic necessity rather than through cultural tradition. Most historians now acknowledge that slave families probably preserved and adapted some African cultural legacies, but they also stress the combination of coercion, deprivation, resistance, and accommodation that created distinctive African-American family patterns.[22]

Brenda Stevenson's now-classic work revealed that slave families were not usually nuclear, nor were slave households organized around long-term monogamous married couples. Gender imbalance on both large plantations and small farms meant that many individuals remained single, while married couples often could not reside together. Slave families were constantly broken up, not just by routine sales but also when owners died, paid off debts, or reallocated their labor force between often far-flung properties. And masters tried at every turn to preempt parental authority over children, although parents strenuously resisted. The selection by Norrece T. Jones in this volume points out that owners used the threat of sale of family members as a method of slave control and sometimes even encouraged marriage as a way of gaining leverage over individuals through their family ties. Jones also details the resourcefulness of slave families' survival tactics.[23]

By the mid-nineteenth century, there were huge class as well as racial differences in family life and family values. Steven Mintz describes these in his section on laboring children in the mid-nineteenth century. Where Mintz and Lareau (also in this volume) emphasize class differences in the experience of childhood, Ricki Solinger stresses the role of racial ideologies in creating different attitudes and policies toward fertility, birth control, and adoption over the course of American history.

Evelyn Nakano Glenn's selection points out that cultural values can never be easily disentangled from structural conditions such as racism or political and economic constraints, or from the attempts of groups to change their position in the racial-economic hierarchy. She describes how Chinese-Americans altered their family strategies over time, using their cultural resources selectively to adapt to shifting institutional pressures and opportunities.

For many groups, migration to America forged a new cultural identity through new work and residence patterns, as well as their interactions with mainstream institutions. The selection from George Sanchez stresses the diversity among Mexican families before their migration and the alternative types of adaptation afterwards. Sanchez traces the emergence of a distinctive barrio culture in portions of Los Angeles, along with a Chicano identity quite different from earlier Mexican ones.

When people look to the "Ozzie and Harriet" ideal of the 1950s as the traditional American family, not only do they ignore the existence of other family forms and values in different economic, racial, or ethnic groups, but they also forget that this was a new norm even for the white middle class. Not until the mid-nineteenth century did the white middle class adopt the ideal of protected childhood. And not until the 1920s did a majority of white children live in a family where the wife was a fulltime homemaker, instead of working beside her husband on the farm or in a small shop, and where the children went to school instead of out to work. This reorganization of family life, which was disrupted by the Great Depression and World War II, became especially widespread after the war. But the postwar male-breadwinner family model was, as I will describe later, largely a product of government-funded educational, employment, and housing policies, many of which were unavailable to non-whites. Donna Franklin's chapter suggests that just at the time when white middle-class and working-class family patterns began to converge, African-American family patterns began to diverge more sharply from those of whites.[24]

SECTION TWO: INTEGRATING RACE, ETHNICITY, CLASS AND GENDER INTO FAMILY THEORY

We learn our first lessons about who we are, why we are that way, and what we can expect for the future in our family of origin. Family dynamics, including marriage decisions and child-rearing practices, are immensely significant in determining what assumptions, habits, and capacities individuals bring to their attempts to maintain or change their position in the social structure. But the articles in this section remind us that family forms and values, along with individual habits, are also shaped by the power relations and social inequalities of the larger society, and similar dynamics often have different outcomes, depending on a family's place in the social hierarchy.

What is adaptive for a family in one socioeconomic or political setting, or one context of race relations, may be dysfunctional—or at least risky—in another. Behaviors that are judicious in a middle-class, professional environment—for example, denying a loan to a cousin because you need to buy textbooks, or saying that you can't babysit because you have to study—can be risky for lower-class individuals, because it may cut them off from the chains of obligation and practical aid described by Gerstel and Sarkisian in this volume. In a severely impoverished environment, being prudent may mean passing up a chance to leave home to go to school or get married and deciding instead to stay close to kin and neighbors whom you can count on to share material resources and favors—even if their own demands for time and resources hold you back. Conversely, the documentary "Hoop Dreams," which focuses on the attempts of two African-American schoolboys to become basketball stars, reminds us that aspirations that would reflect unrealistic fantasizing about fame or quick riches in a middle-class youth may represent a sober assessment by a lower-class individual of what offers at least a slim chance to escape an environment where the schools are poor and the few jobs available are usually dead-ends. From another angle, what is described as deferred gratification in middle-class youth (delaying paid work to pursue higher education or an unpaid internship; avoiding marriage or childbirth) may in fact be the easiest, most gratifying path to future success.

Trying to disentangle the respective influences of race relations, class, ethnicity, gender, and sexuality on people's family adaptations, struggles, and compromises is a major analytical challenge. Even defining the terms separately poses difficulties.

Class refers to people's socioeconomic roles and resources. It can be measured in several quantitative ways and it can also be conceptualized as a historical relationship among groups. Some authors define class in terms of an individual's income or educational level. Others see class as the outcome of people's relative positions in the larger economic system of production, distribution, and exchange. According to the second definition, class cannot be defined in terms of what one earns or even what one does, but only by a person's experience as a member of a group that has a historically-specific pattern of interaction with other socioeconomic and political groups or institutions.[25]

This definition, unlike the first, may put people of similar income in different class categories, because of their different experiences and customary ways of relating to others. Likewise, it calls into question the custom of lumping all people with 4-year college degrees in the same socio-economic class, especially given the recent expansion of college participation. A degree gained in four years at Yale and one achieved after seven years of part-time work at a state college have exposed the graduates to very different social networks and economic opportunities.

The editors of this volume believe that dynamic or relational definitions of class offer more insight than simple quantitative measures of income or education into why people engage in different family strategies or bring different assumptions and goals to their childrearing. But both definitions raise the issue of how class interacts with racial and ethnic categories.

Ethnicity describes people by their supposedly common ancestry, language, and cultural heritage. Race, however, is based on no distinctive cultural or linguistic legacy and no irreducible physical difference. Racialization defines and separates people on the basis of real or imagined physical differences, but the concept of race is socially constructed and constantly changing. It has no coherent biological base, and has never been shown to explain differences in human behavior. Nevertheless, ideologies and historical practices of racism have real consequences, so that acting in a "race-blind" way on an individual level may allow and even encourage the racial structuring of society to continue.[26]

Barbara Fields argues that class and race are qualitatively different concepts, which "do not occupy the same analytical space." Class is determined by the structural relationship among groups that play different roles and have different resources within the prevailing system of economic production and social control. Class is a material condition, and although it may be mediated by ideology, it can "assert itself independently of people's consciousness," as when workers who define themselves as middle class find that they have no more control over their work conditions than the blue collar employees from whom they formerly differentiated themselves. Race, by contrast, is purely ideological. Belief in race has real consequences, Fields suggests, but there is no underlying mechanism of race that can assert itself independently of what people believe about it.[27]

Racial ideologies and practices, however, can create or sharpen class differences. Douglas Massey argues that despite the huge impact of industrial restructuring on job prospects and dependency in the cities (described in this volume by Sugrue), the emergence of a socially isolated "underclass" would not have happened without the prior existence of historically enforced racial segregation. Seemingly race-neutral decisions about where to locate new businesses or build waste plants and dumps, how to fund education, and whether to incorporate low-income housing into urban renewal projects often perpetuate or exacerbate these historic disadvantages of African-Americans and other minorities.[28]

Gender roles within families are also constructed in relation to race and class. Evelyn Nakano Glenn points out that family analysis is especially useful as a corrective to theories of racial hierarchy that do not analyze how domestic labor is assigned and resources distributed within the family, as well as to theories of gender hierarchy that assume all women do the same *kinds* of reproductive labor.[29]

Rayna Rapp points out that households are where daily reproduction takes place and families are the way we recruit people into household labor. Family, she notes, is a more emotionally loaded concept than household, and she discusses some of the different meanings of family and the practice of household work for people of different race and class backgrounds. Confusing family with household co-residence can lead observers to ignore the fact that people may have strong family ties even when they live in different households. As Gerstel and Sarkisian point out (this volume), in some ethnic groups and working-class communities, more family cooperation may occur between households rather than within a single household. Many care-givers are therefore rendered invisible when we equate family with co-residential households. In African-American communities in particular, a father's absence from the household does not necessarily mean he is uninvolved in his children's lives. In all racial-ethnic groups, some "single-parent" households formed by divorce actually have two very involved parents.[30]

Like "family," motherhood is often assumed to have a universal meaning and function. Patricia Hill Collins's article illuminates the racial and ethnic differences Rapp found in the way women evaluate the family's impact on their lives. In most race, class, and ethnic groups, women are subordinate to men of the same group, and family relations often enforce that subordination. But as Nancy Cott has noted, the critique of male dominance within the family "was historically initiated by, and remains prejudiced toward, those who perceive themselves first and foremost as 'woman'," and "who can gloss over their class, racial, and other status identifications" because those affiliations are dominant in our culture and "therefore relatively invisible." Women who belong to groups where men do not have social or economic power are less likely to place the demand for gender equality at the top of their agenda, although they will often act both collectively and individually to resist abuse or maltreatment, a point Beth Richie returns to later in this volume.[31]

The brief excerpt from Karen Brodkin Sacks suggests that we need to redefine class in ways that integrate both race and gender. She argues that the working class is defined by "membership in a community that is dependent upon waged labor, but that is unable to subsist or reproduce by such labor alone." Race and ethnicity help define that community, through the discrimination that members face in finding waged labor and the constraints imposed on them in seeking other forms of subsistence and reproduction, and also by the cultural resources they can mobilize. Gender divisions of labor are integral to and also shaped by the dynamics of class, race, and ethnicity. So are parent–child relations, since class is connected not just to immediate income and social status but also to the material and even the psychic resources parents can pass on to the next generation.[32]

As Eric Wolf points out, racial constructions have typically been used to exclude some people from the job and status ladder, while the cultural construction of ethnicity has served historically to stratify. But the difference between race and ethnicity is not always clearcut. Race can divide people of the same ethnicity or it can unite people of very different ethnic traditions on the basis of the way their color is perceived and labeled by others. Latinos, for example, unlike African-Americans, are *divided* rather than united by race. Conversely, with increased immigration from Africa and the Caribbean, researchers will have to pay more attention to ways in which blacks may be divided by ethnicity even as they are united by their racial labeling.[33]

Some former racial categories have become ethnic ones over time. Numerous researchers, for example, have shown that the Irish, originally considered a non-white race, won their status as whites in large part through participation in the fabrication of color as a category that was deemed to outweigh class. A similar evolution occurred for Jews and Italians. More recently, other groups whose ethnic origins were tied to a subordinate place in the socioeconomic and cultural hierarchy of America, and who therefore struggled to shed their ethnicity in favor of a "white" identity, have now rediscovered ethnicity, as Lillian Rubin demonstrates later in this volume.[34]

Ethnicity is shaped by more than common heritage. It is a product not just of the traditions brought to this country by immigrants, but of the particular immigrant group's class origins and occupational skills interacting with the jobs, housing stock, and political conditions they encounter in the region and period they settle. Immigrants have experienced what Alejandro Portes and Cynthia Truelove call distinctive "modes of incorporation" into the United States. These modes have encouraged groups to selectively rework and sometimes actively invent aspects of their cultural "traditions." Thus immigrants frequently celebrate holidays, rituals, stories, and even dialects that were considered unimportant or actually undesirable on their home territory. Alternatively, groups that had little in common in "the old country" may be lumped together on the basis of shared traits that assume importance only in contrast to features of the new social environment. Despite a common language, for instance, Hispanic ethnicity was originally a creation for the convenience of census takers; many writers prefer the term Latino. Portes and Truelove refer to Hispanics/Latinos as "a group in formation whose boundaries and self-definition are still in a state of flux."[35]

Similarly, Asian-Americans do not come from a single culture or speak a common language. Before 1970, the Asian-American community was largely composed of three national-origins groups—Japanese, Chinese, and Filipino. Since 1990, the group known as Asian-Americans has grown to include significant numbers of more than two dozen subgroups who differ in class and cultural origins, immigration experiences, religion, physical features, language, gender roles, and intergenerational relations. As the article by Lee and Zhou in this volume demonstrates, these groups sometimes embrace a pan-ethnic Asian-American identity for their own purposes, but they must also struggle against a very different type of pan-ethnic identity set up by the myth of Asians as the "model minority," against which Latinos and African-Americans are often unfavorably compared.[36]

Karen Pyke reviews how contemporary processes of immigration challenge older theories of assimilation and acculturation. She also discusses what these processes mean for gender relations, the new generation of immigrants' children,[37] and the elderly of immigrant communities. Her work provides a vital background to section III as well as to our discussion of theoretical questions.

While much research remains to be done on the ways that ethnicity, race, class, gender, and sexuality interact in influencing family life, many contributors to this volume draw on the notion of "social location" developed by Louise Lamphere, Patricia Zavella, and Felipe Gonzales. These authors suggest that the strategies and values that families and their individual members adopt should be examined in the specific context in which "local political and economic structures interact with people's class, ethnicity, culture, and even sexual preference." In their contribution to this volume, Maxine Baca Zinn and Barbara Wells critique generalizations about Latino families that fail to take due account of social location. Their alternative analysis explains how the diverse living arrangements of Latinos have evolved and how they play out in specific situations, with differing effects on family members.[38]

Multicultural family scholarship challenges one-size-fits-all generalizations about femininity, masculinity, motherhood, fatherhood, sexuality, and family dynamics. It also undermines traditional models of oppression, in which white middle-class masculinity is the neutral starting point, and then levels of oppression are added based on working-class status, gender, race, and sexual orientation, making a black working-class lesbian "quadruply oppressed." Leigh and Stevens complete this section by directing our attention to multiple, cross-cutting, and intersecting forms of diversity, inequality, and privilege. They discuss how post-modernism, queer theory, and oppression theory deal with what happens when a person or group stands at the intersection of two identities, then provide some concrete examples of the differing outcomes of such intersections.

SECTION THREE: GLOBALIZATION AND IMMIGRATION

Contemporary worries over immigration and growing class inequality should be placed in the context of what some economists call "the great U-turn" in America's socioeconomic and political trends since the mid-1970s. The United States emerged from World War II with the strongest economy in the world, and the profits gained from its international head start over war-damaged economic rivals trickled down to many American workers. After a huge postwar strike wave, businesses bought peace by rewarding productivity increases with wage gains and keeping on as many workers as possible during contractions in the business cycle. Meanwhile, the state provided many more subsidies to young families than it does today. Forty percent of young men starting families after World War II were eligible for veterans' benefits that were much more generous than such benefits today and allowed unprecedented numbers of working-class men to gain entry into the middle class. The federal government paid for 90 percent of the interstate highway program that created secure, well-paid jobs for blue-collar workers and opened up suburbia to middle-class and union-wage Americans. It also spurred a huge expansion of home ownership by underwriting low down-payments and long-term mortgages, which had been rejected as bad business practice by private industry.[39]

As a result, many workers had a degree of job security that is increasingly elusive in the modern economy. Between 1947 and 1973, real wages rose, on average, by 81 percent, and the gap between rich and poor declined significantly. The income of the bottom 80 percent of the population grew faster than the income of the richest 1 percent, with the most rapid gains of all made by the poorest 20 percent of the population.

The postwar period was by no means idyllic. Fifty percent of African-American married-couple families lived below the poverty level in the 1950s, and poverty was widespread among white as well as black Americans. Racial segregation was legal, and enforced by daily acts of violence. Political dissidents, gays, and lesbians were subject to widespread persecution. Women were discriminated against in virtually every sphere of life, while incest, battering, and spousal rape were largely ignored.

Even the successes of the period had a down side. The subsidies that allowed many families to move to suburbia also helped create today's urban crisis. Government policy diverted funds from urban housing and public transport to building highways, parking lots, and offices for commuters without rehousing the families that were displaced by "urban renewal" and crowded into slums.

Nevertheless, economic trends gave people hope that income inequality and poverty would continue to decline. Rising wages, steady employment, government investment in education, and corporate commitment to local communities seemed secure, and the civil rights struggle of the 1950s and 1960s raised the possibility that minorities and women would be able to claim their fair share.

All that changed after the second half of the 1970s. Between 1980 and 2004, real wages stagnated for most workers, and fell slightly for the bottom 50 percent. But the real income of the richest 1 percent jumped by 135 percent.[40]

Household income rose slightly because more household members went to work or worked longer hours. In many ways, the standard of living also continued to rise. Electronic items became more affordable, exposing even low-income Americans to an expanding world of movies, music, television, mobile phones, personal computers, and the like. Cars and homes became fancier. Middle-class families gained access to an astonishing array of material goods and services that had once been luxuries reserved for the very rich.

But the sense that Americans shared the same future was eroded by rising inequality and job insecurity. The gap between rich and poor nearly tripled between 1980 and 2005, producing the greatest concentration of wealth in the hands of the super-rich since the 1920s, just before the stock market crash. The bifurcation of jobs into richly-rewarded professional work and low-wage, dead-end jobs with little long-term security has produced what Alejandro Portes and Min Zhou call an hour-glass economy, in which the proportion of people with secure middle-income jobs has been shrinking.

At the same time, some parts of the social safety net have frayed since 1980. The Earned Income Tax Credit, inaugurated in 1975, has helped many low-income families. But by 2007, the purchasing power of the federal minimum wage had fallen to its lowest level in 50 years and the real value of a welfare check had decreased by 42 percent. (If the minimum wage had grown as fast as CEO salaries between 1990 and 2005, it would have been $23.03 an hour by 2006.)[41] Government investment in infrastructure and low-income housing plummeted between 1980 and 2005. Fewer people were covered by unemployment insurance, and for shorter periods.

Sarah Ryan argues that these changes reflect a concerted campaign by employers, aided by a business-friendly government, to drive down workers' share of national income and decrease their control over working conditions. Ryan describes a loss of benefits and security over the past two decades, along with the rise of part-time work, new management techniques, and increased reliance on overtime and/or temporary workers. These trends make it harder but also more necessary for both men and women to combine work and family life. Ryan suggests that despite appeals to the "remorseless logic" of global competition, resistance is possible and necessary if workers are to develop stable family lives.

But Lillian Rubin concludes that many white working-class Americans have come to accept racially-charged, value-laden explanations for their economic difficulties. In the early 1990s, Rubin revisited the working-class families that she first studied in the 1970s. She found that over the ensuing two decades, many women had gained a heightened sense of competence and self-esteem after they entered the labor force or improved their jobs, but that this was offset by new time stresses and family instabilities connected to the decline in union-wage jobs and benefits available to their husbands.[42] In her interviews with white working-class families, she found that their lack of a class analysis often led them to translate their economic and family frustrations into racial or anti-immigrant hostility. Even minority groups, she points out, are sometimes drawn in to this search for scapegoats.

Some observers might describe the families Rubin interviewed as trying to hang on to their "white skin privilege." But many white working people are hard-pressed to see themselves as privileged when they compare their existence to consumerist visions of a white, middle-class "lifestyle." A better way to describe their racial and ethnic prejudices might be as a search for "leverage" or "traction." They seek something to brace themselves against as they feel themselves slip downward on the American social ladder, or find themselves stuck while people above them draw further away.

One result has been growing anti-immigrant sentiment. The rest of this section explores the diversity of contemporary immigrant family life, illustrating several of the points made earlier by Pyke, and challenging many common stereotypes about immigrant families.

We begin with a case study by Rhacel Parreñas of how changes in the global economy create an internationalization of reproductive labor, as women from poorer nations such as the Philippines leave their own families to fill the demand for care-givers created by the labor-market entry of women in wealthier "host" countries. Parreñas uses the case of Filipina women, who are employed in more than 130 countries, to illustrate how household reproductive and care-giving activities have been divided among three different groups of women: middle-class women in the host nations; immigrant domestic workers (many with higher educational and professional qualifications than is commonly supposed); and women too poor to migrate, who then take over some of the family care-giving that the Filipina migrants cannot provide at home. Christine Ho argues that in many cases, international family networks have become more central in people's identity, exchange networks, and even child-rearing practices than geographically-specific households.[43]

Lee and Zhou's article shows how negative racial stereotyping and the supposedly positive image of "the model minority" have each created numerous challenges for Asian-American youth in forming their own identity and carving out a cultural niche in America. The larger book from which this excerpt is taken explores the cultural adaptations and resistance of Asian-American youth in greater detail.

As Pyke discussed earlier, and Patricia Pessar and Nancy Foner have also shown, women's status often improves when whole families immigrate to America together. This stands in sharp contrast to the situation 100 or 150 years ago, when women who moved to America often had less access to the outside world and less social respect for their roles than in the Old Country. Today, however, daughters gain access to education that confers new freedoms; wives who work outside the home gain an independent source of income that often increases their leverage in the family; and some women learn to utilize laws against domestic violence, which may not have existed in their homeland, to curtail male abuse.[44]

Transformations in gender patterns proceed in uneven and complex ways. In the popular press, middle-class white, native-born men are typically portrayed as most enlightened in adjusting to their wives' entry into the workforce. Yet contrary to stereotypes about Latino "machismo" and African-American "hypermasculinity," gender relations in minority families are extremely variable and complex. Scott Coltrane, Ross Parke, and Michele Adams report that fathers who identify themselves as Mexican are more likely to do childcare than more assimilated or acculturated Latino fathers. And employed African-American men do more housework and childcare than employed white men. In their selection, Pierrette Hondagneu-Sotelo and Michael Messner argue that the white middle-class picture of the enlightened "New Man" often confuses style with substance, ignoring deeper and more important changes in gender relations taking place among other segments of the population.[45]

But Nazil Kibria adds another layer of complexity to the issue of gender relations in immigrant communities. In some immigrant groups, women begin to openly challenge patriarchal traditions. Kibria found, however, that Vietnamese immigrant women often adopt a strategy of maneuvering within the comparatively traditional restraints of their culture. Rather than seeking access to roles outside the home or directly confronting traditional ideologies, they use familial values selectively to emphasize their husbands' and children's obligations to support them.

Interestingly, Susan Ostrander has described a similar pattern of acceptance of tradition within the top segment of the U.S. native-born upper class. Unlike Kibria's subjects, the willingness of upper-class women to accept more traditional roles has little to do with personal vulnerability, since many have their own inherited wealth. Rather, Ostrander argues, they see significant class advantages to a gendered division of labor that keeps them subordinate to husbands but puts them in charge of regulating access to high-status social institutions. Forsaking their gendered sphere of activity might jeopardize the monopoly of status and power enjoyed by the class to which they belong.[46]

SECTION FOUR: FAMILIES AND EXTREME POVERTY

The United States is unique among industrial countries in the proportion of its population that enjoys a standard of every-day living once confined to a much narrower section of the very wealthy. Today, for the first time ever, the wealthiest 20 percent of the population takes in more than half of all earned income.[47] The top 2 percent is still light years ahead of the rest of this group in total wealth, but there is now a truly large layer of people who can afford luxuries and services that were once out of reach for all but a tiny few. The orientation of advertisers and the mass media to this large and fortunate group leads many to overlook the fact the United States is also unique among affluent nations in the extent and depth of poverty.

America has the highest or near-highest poverty rates for families, children, and even individual adults among 31 industrial countries studied by the Luxembourg Income Study. Between 30 and 40 million Americans live in families that earn poverty-level wages. The earnings of another 30 to 40 million are so close to the poverty level that any setback to their health, their personal relationships, or their access to transportation can drive them into severe poverty virtually overnight. In July 2007, the Department of Housing and Urban Development reported that growing numbers of poor families spend more than half their income on rent. An analysis of 2005 census figures conducted by the McClatchy newspaper chain in 2007 found that the number of poor Americans who live in "severe" poverty had reached a 32-year high. Yet of the 31 countries in the Luxembourg study, only Mexico and Russia devote a smaller share of their gross domestic products to funding anti-poverty programs.[48]

So a large and highly visible group of super-consumers sets the standard for what families "ought" to be able to provide for their members, while an equally large group of Americans has trouble meeting their monthly bills. Every major metropolitan area has seas of stunning affluence. But the extremely poor live in neighborhoods surrounded by boarded-up abandoned buildings, corner stores offering inferior produce at higher prices, and an array of payday lenders, "instant cash" establishments and other predatory financial institutions prepared to charge them heavily to help them get through the periodic shortfalls of income that create a constant sense of crisis in their lives. As Sugrue shows in this section, jobs are scarce and offer few opportunities for upward mobility. A study of job seekers in Oakland found that there were 209 applicants for 46 jobs when a new fast-food restaurant opened there in 1994.[49]

Some people believe that America's extremes of wealth and poverty have little to do with the economic changes described here and in Ryan's selection, but instead result from a self-perpetuating mix of bad values and irresponsible habits that has created "a permanent underclass" in our cities. Conservative and libertarian think tanks such as The Heritage Foundation, the American Enterprise Institute, and the Cato Institute argue that individual and family pathologies are what prevent people from taking advantage of the many routes to social mobility provided by the American economy.

It is undeniable that the support systems, community cohesion, and informal methods of social control have been gravely eroded in many poverty-stricken neighborhoods over the past three decades. And the instability of many inner-city families and individuals is indeed a serious problem. But the articles in this section argue that blaming poverty on people's "deviant values" is a massive oversimplification. Thomas Sugrue traces the deterioration of urban neighborhoods after 1979 and explains how this process gave traction to a new group of social scientists who wished to discredit the social programs of the 1960s and promulgate the views of the think tanks mentioned above. He shows how the welfare reforms of 1996 incorporated their views and suggests that this is why they have failed to eradicate poverty or ameliorate inequality. His article, like the following three, reveals how poverty, social isolation, racial discrimination, and political marginalization interact with contemporary cultural pressures to frustrate people's ability to build family lives that accord with mainstream values.

Many studies demonstrate that most of the poor hold similar values and aspirations—for better and for worse—as other Americans, but the conditions of their lives make it harder to act upon or be rewarded for their better values. Socioeconomic pressures often lead people to behave in ways that help them cope with their immediate situation but undermine their ability to engage in effective planning for the future. Researchers Kathryn Edin *et al.* use the term "efficacy" to describe a person's ability to put together a sequence of actions that may be burdensome and time-consuming in the short run but promote long-term self-improvement or family betterment.[50] In different ways, these articles show that developing and maintaining such efficacious behaviors in deprived and marginalized communities is especially difficult and that long-range, goal-oriented behavior is seldom rewarded even when people manage to sustain it.

Gabrielle Raley takes on the issue of unwed motherhood, often said to be the result of "underclass" teenage behaviors and the cause of most childhood poverty in America. In fact, most unmarried births today are not to teens but to women in their 20s and 30s. Some of these women consciously choose single motherhood and manage to lead comfortable, stable lives. They may be unwilling or unable to marry, either because they are heterosexuals whose biological clocks are ticking without a stable relationship on the horizon or because they are lesbians. Rosanna Hertz has described in detail the decision-making processes such women go through as they plan for the birth of their child and then construct support networks among friends, co-workers, and family.[51] Very different dynamics lead to unwed births among impoverished unwed teens or women just out of their teens, and Raley discusses misapprehensions about this topic that she believes distort our political conversations and our social policy.

In their article, Kevin Roy and Linda Burton discuss how impoverished single mothers in African-American communities try to build social support networks in neighborhoods that have few resources—including few stably employed or "marriageable" men. Many attempt to "kinscript" fathers or father figures into their children's lives. They face serious challenges in doing so, but as Waldo Johnson has noted, unwed African-American fathers, contrary to racial stereotypes, are more likely than white unwed fathers to give material aid to their children or their children's mother and to maintain at least some level of involvement with their children.[52]

Based on studies of impoverished families in Oakland, California, Alison Pugh's article offers insight into parenting behaviors that might strike many middle-class observers as a reflection of poor judgment and inconsistent discipline but flow rather from poverty and unpredictable resources. When money is constantly tight and only comes in irregularly, if a family gets a small windfall, it often seems pointless to save it. Experience teaches that it will just drain away to pay for some new crisis next week. So parents who have been unable to keep promises they have made to their children in the past are often tempted to "squander" the windfall by buying something expensive for the kids when they receive an unexpected bit of cash. Such behavior doesn't help their children develop the habit of planning for the future, but when a loving parent's plans have gone awry enough times and no stability is on the horizon, it's easy to understand why she might seize the chance to give a moment's pleasure, even when an outside observer might label it irresponsible.[53]

SECTION FIVE: INTEGRATING RACE AND CLASS INTO CONTEMPORARY ISSUES OF FAMILY LIFE, GENDER, AND SEXUALITY

The articles in this section deal with a wide variety of contemporary family topics. But each illustrates how our understanding of an issue changes when we take class and/or race or ethnicity into account. For example, media portrayals of working mothers often focus on the dilemmas of a small segment of affluent, predominantly white, wives and mothers. It is frequently asserted that these women are spear-heading an "opt-out revolution," rejecting their mothers' or grandmothers' feminism and dropping out of high-powered careers to become stay-at-home moms. Their "choice" to stay home is contrasted with the plight of low-income women who want to stay home but cannot do so.

The article by Cotter, England, and Hermsen reveals that this picture is distorted by lack of historical perspective and by failure to look closely at class differences. Except for a tiny sliver of the wives of the highest earning men in the country, highly-educated and high-earning females are more likely to continue working after they become mothers than other American women. The largest group of stay-at-home moms—though not necessarily by choice—is the group of women married to men who are in the lowest 25 percent of the earnings distribution.

Similarly, Michael Kimmel argues that media reports about a "boy crisis" deform our under-standing of recent changes in gender roles and behaviors, because these reports do not pay attention to variations by race, class, and ethnicity. He finds that what is often called a "boy crisis" brought on by some recent "feminization" of American culture is in fact a race and class crisis exacerbated by the retention of traditional ideals of masculinity.

Gary Gates draws our attention to the racial and class diversity of gay and lesbian families. He argues that media stereotypes about affluent, urban-dwelling lesbians and gay men keep us from seeing the urgent issues facing low-income homosexual families. In confirming the high proportion of gay and lesbian families in various racial-ethnic groups, Gates's article challenges minority com-munities to stop seeing gay issues as a "white thing" and to confront anti-gay prejudices in their midst.[54]

Beth Richie points out that advocates for victims of domestic violence often downplay race and class differences in an attempt to show that "it can happen to anyone." But this universalistic approach, she suggests, can make it more difficult to construct a movement that meets the needs of abused women of color. Other researchers have shown that forms of intervention against domestic violence that have some impact on the behavior of married, middle-class men may backfire when they are applied to other men.[55]

We can understand contemporary parenting dilemmas better, argues Annette Lareau, if we recognize that differing parenting behaviors and ideals have their roots in different class experiences, needs, and expectations. She contrasts the middle-class parenting doctrine of "concerted cultivation" of children to the working-class belief in "natural growth," and notes that racial differences in parenting seem to be less clear-cut than class differences. David Lancey argues elsewhere that the middle-class obsession with "playing" educational games with one's children is a historically unprecedented approach to childrearing that may be connected to parents' efforts to groom their children for highly competitive jobs in the information age economy.[56]

Middle-class parenting often imparts a sense of entitlement and self-confidence that can be a big advantage to middle-class children who are already expected by society to succeed (although Lareau suggests that this child-rearing can also create self-centeredness). But parents with little social power of their own have a harder time instilling such traits in their children, and see less advantage in doing so. Even when they succeed, there is some evidence than when low-income children, especially African-American boys, act with the same self-assurance as their white middle-class peers, their behavior may be interpreted as a challenge by teachers and other authorities rather than as a charming sign of precociousness.[57]

Like Lareau, Gerstel and Sarkisian (this volume) also find that class trumps culture in most of the family patterns they studied. But it is important to remember that cultural traditions do differ. In contrast to the Anglo-European tradition, which has long viewed obligations to children as part of a package deal, contingent upon marriage and blood relatedness, many cultures have long-standing traditions of sharing child-rearing beyond the nuclear family. In Ghana, the Caribbean, and the Polynesian islands, children are often "loaned" to other households in exchanges that extend ties of affection and mutual aid beyond the nuclear family household. In Hawaii, even today (and across class lines), children are taught to address all elders as "auntie" and "uncle," implying a more inclusive and flexible definition of family than prevails in much of modern America. And a recent study of African-American households found that children from mother–grandmother or mother–other relative households (unlike whites) had no greater risk of behavior problems than children from married-couple households.[58]

Finally we turn to an encouraging sign of declining racial and ethnic prejudices—the growth of interracial marriage and the cultural acceptability of multiracial individuals. But Kumiko Nemoto suggests that the attraction of some individuals to another racial group may be intertwined with racial and socioeconomic inequities.

The National Academy of Sciences estimates that the multiracial population in the United States could top 20 percent by the year 2050.[59] Kerry Ann Rockquemore and David Brunsma explore the different ways that children of interracial unions develop a sense of their own racial and cultural identity. Sometimes a young person takes on an identity that is then challenged by others. In the late nineteenth century, Southern states ruled that "one drop" of Negro blood made a person Black, even if they identified as white and appeared that way to others. Today, by contrast, some observers question whether certain prominent biracial individuals are "black enough." But many young people are resisting pressures from family, friends, and the outside world and constructing a variety of identities and self definitions that reflect their individual needs. Maria P. P. Root suggests elsewhere that these young people need a "bill of rights" acknowledging their right to choose their own identities, develop loyalties that extend beyond a single group identity, and even change their identities and affiliations over time.[60]

CONCLUSION: SECTION SIX: WORKING WITH DIVERSITY, ENCOURAGING SOLIDARITY

How can we recognize and accommodate diversity in American family life while building the kind of solidarity that can help all families win the social supports they need? Many of the social programs needed by modern families cross the boundaries of race and class. But a recurring issue is the extent to which we can or should take account of racial and class differences in the programs we seek, especially when it comes to economic support systems.

Roger Lawson and William Julius Wilson have suggested that people should work for a universal family support program, to avoid stigmatizing poor families, especially those of color, and to counter the backlash against social welfare. There is much to be said for this. Linda Gordon and Gwendolyn Mink have shown how poor women of color have been disadvantaged by the development of a two-tier welfare system, where the stably employed get aid in the form of "entitlements" and those who are marginally employed or held back by family obligations, such as single mothers, get "charity" and are labeled the undeserving poor.[61]

But Stephen Steinberg argues that a universalist program (and by implication, even an affirmative action program based on diversity *per se*) ignores the unique, historical oppression of African-Americans and Indians in America. He believes that these groups need special attention if we are to avoid the oft-noted historical cycle in which Blacks and Native Americans get continually pushed off the job ladder while other ethnic groups climb onto the bottom rungs. Steinberg reminds us that diversity is not just about adding color and dialect to the sights and sounds of America; it is also about power relations and questions of economic justice.[62]

If we implemented affirmative action on the basis of prior oppression, where would we rank Puerto Rican and Mexican-American families in the hierarchy of disadvantage? And what about the impoverishment of groups such as the Hmong? But if we use universalistic criteria, how do we take into account the historical weight of slavery and Jim Crow in hindering the ability of African-Americans to achieve intergenerational economic stability, especially in terms of accumulated assets and inherited wealth? Even among African-Americans and whites who earn equal pay, the median worth of household assets among the whites is, on average, twelve times higher than among the Blacks. Without some sort of racial redistribution or affirmative action, this economic gap may perpetuate itself.[63]

Researchers and policy-makers will continue to debate the correct balance between addressing the historical legacy of past injustices to specific groups and uniting around issues that apply to all workers today, such as stagnating wages, increasing job insecurity, and the erosion of medical benefits and pension plans. But our final two articles suggest that once we acknowledge the differences in patterns of work and family life, we can construct policies that meet all families' needs. Gerstel and Sarkisian revisit the debate over whether minorities have stronger family ties than whites and conclude that the answer depends on what kinds of family ties one emphasizes. They show that African-Americans and Latinos tend to rely more on extended family members for help, while whites look more to the nuclear family, in large part, they suggest, because of historically-constructed class differences between these three groups. But they warn against romanticizing the extended family networks of low-income people and deluding ourselves that strong extended families can substitute for anti-poverty programs.

Jerry Jacobs and Kathleen Gerson investigate class and racial-ethnic differences in time pressures on workers. They find that the restructuring of work in America has affected different groups of workers in diametrically opposed ways—and in ways that reverse the pattern of the past, when blue-collar workers labored six days a week and professionals kept what we used to call "bankers" hours. Today it is salaried professionals who are most often forced to work too many hours. Meanwhile, low-paid, less-skilled workers often cannot work enough hours to provide security for their families. For both these groups, work policies, school hours, medical programs, and childcare arrangements are out of sync with their family needs. In addition, the expansion of two-earner families and single-parent households is a source of work-family stress that cuts across class lines. Jacobs and Gerson propose family-friendly policies that could help alleviate the stresses of all these different kinds of families.

Taken together, these articles show us the urgent need for family-friendly social policies. Unemployed or underemployed parents need jobs with adequate medical benefits; working parents need flexitime, quality childcare, and an end to forced overtime; young people need protections against racial and ethnic discrimination and low-income teens need more options for apprentice-type work programs. Surely the United States can afford to institute subsidized parental leave, as every other affluent industrial nation has done, so that staying home with one's children does not become a class or race privilege. We could certainly decide to invest as much in childcare, pre-school, and parks programs as we do in space programs or bail-outs to failed companies. We could also reorganize school hours or expand after-school programs to bring school schedules into sync with parents' work hours. We should offer parents and other care-givers the option of cutting hours and pay with no loss of health benefits or seniority, and with the rapid aging of our population, this should apply to individuals caring for aging parents as well as those with dependent children. With such support systems, our diverse families can meet the challenges of the 21st century and our society can avoid further racial and class polarization. In the process, we may be able to move past debates over "family values" and learn how to truly value families—in all their shapes and colors.[64]

Stephanie Coontz, Olympia, WA
September 30, 2007

NOTES

1. Sam Roberts, "Minorities Now Form Majority in One-Third of Most-Populous Counties," *The New York Times*, August 9, 2007.
2. David Blankenorn, *Fatherless America* (New York: Basic Books, 1995); George Will, "The 'Race' Problem," *The Olympian*, April 16, 1995, p. A9; Kay Hymowitz, *Marriage and Caste in America: Separate and Unequal Families in a Post-Marital Age* (Chicago: Ivan R. Dee, 2006).
3. Margaret Crosbie-Barnett and Edith Lewis, "Use of African-American Family Structures and Functioning to Address the Challenges of European-American Postdivorce Families," *Family Relations* 42 (1993), 243–248.
4. For a discussion of these differences in marital attitudes and behaviors, see Stephanie Coontz, *Marriage, A History: How Love Conquered Marriage* (New York: Viking, 2006). In these cases, the most likely cause of the divergence in beliefs and behaviors is connected to class. But religious differences and institutions affect families in other ways as well. For example, Jennifer Hirsch points out that the greater distance between the Catholic Church and women's daily lives in America, as opposed to Mexico, greatly changes the reproductive and sexual behavior of Mexican women in transnational communities. Jennifer Hirsch, *A Courtship After Marriage: Sexuality and Love in Mexican Transnational Families* (Berkeley: University of California Press, 2003). See also Shondrah Nash's study of how two

formerly abused Christian wives came to reinterpret Biblical teachings, "The Changing of the Gods," *Qualitative Sociology* 29 (2006a), 195–209. On the role of religion for new immigrant groups, see Alejandro Portes and Ruben G. Rumbaut, *Immigrant America: A Portrait,* third edition (Berkeley: University of California Press, 2006).

5.   Maxine Baca Zinn and Bonnie Thornton Dill, "Theorizing Difference from Multiracial Feminism," *Feminist Studies* 22 (1996), p. 324.

6.   E. Douglas Massey, Ruth Zambrano, and Sally Alonzo Bell, "Contemporary Issues in Latino Families," in Ruth Zambrano, ed., *Understanding Latino Families: Scholarship, Policy, and Practice* (Thousand Oaks, CA: Sage, 1995), p. 194; Roger Waldinger and Greta Gilbertson, "Immigrants' Progress: Ethnic and Gender Differences Among U.S. Immigrants in the 1980s," *Sociological Perspectives* 37 (1994), p. 441.

7.   DeWayne Wickham, "A Tough Sell," *USA Today,* August 21, 2007.

8.   Evelyn Brooks Higginbotham, "African-American Women's History and the Metalanguage of Race," *Signs* 17, 1992, p. 255.

9.   Leith Mullings, *On Our Own Terms: Race, Class, and Gender in the Lives of African-American Women* (Routledge, 1997), p. 80.

10. John Garvey, "My Problem with Multicultural Education," in Noel Ignatiev and John Garvey, eds., *Race Traitor* (Routledge, 1996), pp. 25–30.

11. Zinn and Dill, "Theorizing Difference," p. 327.

12. See, for example, Stephanie McCurry, *Masters of Small Worlds: Yeoman Households, Gender Relations, and the Political Culture of the Antebellum South Carolina Low Country* (New York: Oxford University Press, 1995).

13. Michael Rosenfeld, *The Age of Independence: Interracial Unions, Same-Sex Unions, and the Changing American Family* (Cambridge, MA: Harvard University Press, 2007).

14. Zhenchao Qian and Daniel Lichter, "Social Boundaries and Marital Assimilation: Interpreting Trends in Racial and Ethnic Intermarriage," *American Sociological Review* 72 (2007), 63–94; Lee, Bean, and Sloane, "Beyond Black and White," *Contexts* 2:3 (2003), 26–33.

15. John Ireland and Rima Wilkes, "Does Socioeconomic Status Matter? Race, Class, and Residential Segregation," *Social Problems* 53 (2006).

16. Eduardo Bonilla-Silva, " 'New Racism,' Color-Blind Racism, and the Future of Whiteness in America," in Susan Ferguson, ed., *Mapping the Social Landscape* (Boston: McGraw Hill, 2008); John Solomon and Les Black, *Racism and Society* (Basingstoke, 1996); Marianne Bertrand and Sendhill Mullaination, "Are Emily and Fred More Employable than Lakisha and Jamal?", *The American Economic Review* 94 (2004), 991–1014.

17. Jodie Kliman and William Madsen, "Social Class and the Family Life Cycle," in Betty Carter and Monica McGoldrick, eds., *The Changing Family Life Cycle* (Boston: Allyn and Bacon, in press); Ellis Cose, *The Rage of a Privileged Class* (New York: Harper Collins, 1995).

18. Michael Omi and Howard Winant, *Racial Formation in the United States: From the 1960s to the 1990s* (New York: Routledge, 1994).

19. Mary Ryan, *Cradle of the Middle Class*; Leith Mullings, *On Our Own Terms: Race, Class, and Gender in the Lives of African-American Women* (Routledge, 1997).

20. For more references on Native American diversity see Stephanie Coontz, *The Social Origins of Private Life: A History of American Families, 1600–1900* (London: Verso, 1988); Brian Schnarch, "Neither Man Nor Woman: Berdache— A Case for Non-Dichtomous Gender Construction," *Anthropologica* XXXIV (1992), pp. 106–121.

21. Aaron Gullickson, "Black/White Interracial Marriage Trends, 1850–2000," *Journal of Family History* (3), 2006.

22. Niara Sudarkasa, "Intepreting the African Heritage in Afro-American Family Organization," in Harriette Pipes McAdoo, *Black Families* (Thousand Oaks: Sage, 1988); Mullings, *On Our Own Terms,* p. 82; Andrew T. Miller, "Social Science, Social Policy, and the Heritage of African-American Families," in Michael Katz, ed., *The Underclass Debate* (Princeton: Princeton University Press, 1993); Mary Benin and Verna Keith, "The Social Support of Employed African American and Anglo Mothers," *Journal of Family Issues* 16 (1995), 275–297.

23. Brenda Stevenson, *Life in Black and White* (New York: Oxford University Press, 1996).

24. On the origins of the 1950s male breadwinner family, see Stephanie Coontz, *The Way We Never Were: American Families and the Nostalgia Trap* (New York: BasicBooks, 1992). For a discussion of the historical differences in black and white family structures, which became more pronounced after the 1940s, see Steven Ruggles, "The Origins of African-American Family Structure," *American Sociological Review* 59 (1994), 136–152.

25. For further discussion of the relational aspect of class, see E. P. Thompson, *The Making of the English Working Class* (New York: Vintage, 1963), p. 9.

26. Michael Omi and Howard Winant, *Racial Formation in the United States* (Routledge, 1994).

27. Barbara J. Fields, "Ideology and Race in American History," in J. Morgan Kousser and James M. McPherson, eds., *Region, Race, and Reconstruction: Essays in Honor of C. Vann Woodward* (Oxford University Press, 1982), pp. 150–151.

28. Douglas Massey, "American Apartheid: Segregation and the Making of the Underclass," *American Journal of Sociology* 96 (1990), 329–357; Cedric Herring, "Is Job Discrimination Dead?", in Jeff Goodwin and James Jasper, *The Contexts Reader* (New York: Norton, 2008).

29. Evelyn Nakano Glenn, "From Servitude to Service Work: Historical Continuities in the Racial Division of Paid Reproductive Labor," *Signs* 18 (1992). For more on the intersection of gender with other forms of inequalities, see Patricia Hill Collins, *Black Feminist Thought: Knowledge, Consciousness, and the Politics of Empowerment* (Boston: Unwin Hyman, 1990).

30. Andrew Billingsley, *Climbing Jacob's Ladder: The Enduring Legacy of African-American Families* (New York: Touchstone, 1992); Sandra Danziger and Norma Radin, "Absent Does Not Equal Uninvolved: Predictors of Fathering in Teen Mother Families," *Journal of Marriage and the Family* 52 (1990). On the variety of family forms and practices across cultures see Coontz, "The Evolution of Matrimony," *Annals of the American Psychotherapy Association* 30 (Winter 2006) and chapter 9 of Coontz, *The Way We Never Were*.

31. Nancy Cott, *The Grounding of Modern Feminism* (New Haven: Yale University Press, 1987); bell hooks, *Feminist Theory From Margin to Center* (Boston: South End Press, 1984), pp. 1–2, 18.

32. Joan Acker, "Class, Gender, and the Relations of Distribution," *Signs* 13 (1988).

33. Eric Wolf, *Europe and the People Without History* (Berkeley: University of California Press, 1982); Douglas Massey, Ruth Zambrana, and Sally Alonzo Hall, "Contemporary Issues in Latino Families: Future Directions for Research, Policy, and Practice," in Ruth Zambrana, ed., *Latino Families: Laying a Foundation for Research, Policy, and Practice* (Sage, 1995).

34. David Roediger, *The Wages of Whiteness: Race and the Making of the American Working Class* (London: Verso, 1988); Noel Ignatiev, *How the Irish Became White* (New York: Routledge, 1995).

35. Alejandro Portes and Cynthia Truelove, "Making Sense of Diversity: Recent Research on Hispanic Minorities in the United States," *Annual Review of Sociology* 13 (1987), 359–385.

36. Min Zhou and Yang Sao Xiong, "The Multifaceted American Experiences of the Children of Asian Immigration," *Ethnic and Racial Studies* 28 (2005). See also Michael Omi and Howard Winant, "Contesting the Meaning of Race in the Post-Civil Rights Movement Era," in Pedraza and Rumbaut, *Origins and Destinies*, p. 472; Sucheng Chan, *Asian Americans: An Interpretive History* (Boston: Twayne, 1991); Masako Ishii-Kuntz, "Chinese American Families," in Mary Kay DeGenova, ed., *Families in Cultural Perspective* (San Francisco: Mayfield, 1997); Masako Iishi-Kuntz, "Japanese American Families," in DeGenova, *Families*; Iishi-Kuntz, "Intergenerational Relationships among Chinese, Japanese, and Korean Americans," *Family Relations* 46 (1997), pp. 23–32; Harry Kitano and Roger Daniels, *Asian Americans: Emerging Minorities* (Englewood Cliffs: Prentice-Hall, 1988); Laura Uba, *Asian Americans: Personality Patterns, Identity, and Mental Health* (New York: Guilford, 1994).

37. For more on immigrant youth and children, see Carola Suarez-Orozco and Marcelo Suarez-Orozco, *Children of Immigration* (Cambridge, MA: Harvard University Press, 2001).

38. Louise Lamphere, Patricia Zavella, and Felipe Gonzales with Peter B. Evans, *Sunbelt Working Mothers: Reconciling Family and Factory* (Cornell University Press, 1993), p. 4.

39. The points in this and the following paragraphs are documented in my books, *The Way We Never Were: American Families and the Nostalgia Trap* (New York: Basic Books, 1992) and *The Way We Really Are: Coming to Terms with America's Changing Families* (New York: Basic Books, 1997). For a comparison of contemporary veteran's benefits with those of earlier decades, see Stephen Manning, "Vets find GI bill fails college-tuition test," *Seattle Times*, May 10, 2007. On real wages from 1947–1973, see Paul Krugman, "Wages, Wealth, and Politics," *The New York Times*, August 18, 2006.

40. For this and the next two paragraphs, see Krugman, "Wages, Wealth, and Politics"; Robert Frank, *Falling Behind: How Rising Inequality Harms the Middle Class* (Berkeley: University of California Press, 2007); "The Inequality Economy," *New York Times Magazine*, June 10, 2007; Louis Uchitelle, "The Richest of the Rich," *New York Times*, July 15, 2007; Alejandro Portes and Min Zhou, "The New Second Generation: Segmented Assimilation and its Variants," *Annals of the American Academy of Political and Social Science* 530 (1993); Lori Montgomery, "The Growing Rich–Poor Gap," *The Washington Post National Weekly Edition*, February 5–11, 2007; Jane Bryant Quinn, "The Economic Perception Gap," *Newsweek*, November 20, 2006.

41. Jeanne Sahadi, "CEO Pay, Sky High Gets Even Higher," August 30, 2005, CNN/Money; Jeanne Sahadi, "CEO Paycheck, $42,000 a day," June 21, 2006, CNN/Money. Retrieved September 12, 2007.

42. The original study appeared as *Worlds of Pain: Life in the Working-Class Family* (New York: Basic Books, 1992, first published 1976).

43. Grace Chang, "Global Exchange: The World Bank, 'Welfare Reform,' and the Global Trade in Filipina Workers," in Coontz, Parson, and Raley, *American Families: A Multicultural Reader*, first edition (New York: Routledge, 1999); Christine Ho, "The Internationalization of Kinship and the Feminization of Caribbean Migration: The Case of Afro-Trinidadian Immigrants in Los Angeles," *Human Organization* 52 (1993), pp. 32–40.

44. Patricia Pessar, "Gender and Family," in Mary Waters and Reed Ueda, eds, with Helen Morrow, *The New Americans: A Guide to Immigration Since 1965* (Cambridge, MA: Harvard University Press, 2007); Nancy Foner, *In a New Land: A Comparative View of Immigration* (New York: New York University Press, 2005); Hirsch, *A Courtship After Marriage*.

45. Beth Anne Shelton and Daphne John, "Ethnicity, Race, and Difference: A Comparison of White, Black, and Hispanic Men's Household Labor Time," in Jane Hood, ed., *Men, Work, and Family* (Thousand Oaks, CA: Sage, 1997); Stephanie Coontz and Maya Parson, "Complicating the Contested Terrain of Work\Family Intersections," *Signs* 22 (1997), pp. 440–452; Scott Coltrane, Ross Parke, and Michele Adams, "Complexity of Father Involvement in Low-Income Mexican-American Families," *Family Relations* 53:2 (2004).

46. Susan Ostrander, *Women of the Upper Class* (Philadelphia: Temple University Press, 1984), p. 152.

47. Marca R. della Cava, "Spending is Hotter than the 4th of July," *USA Today*, July 3, 2007; Richard Wolfe, "Poverty Drops as Nation's Median Income Climbs; More People are Working Longer," *USA Today*, August 29, 2007.

48. Fred Brooks, "The Living Wage Movement: Potential Implications for the Working Poor," *Families in Society* 88 (2007); Tony Pugh, "U.S. Economy Leaving Record Numbers in Severe Poverty," McClatchy Newspapers, February 24, 2007; Tony Pugh, "Nation's Poor Spend Most of Earnings on Rent," Centredaily.com, July 15, 2007.

49. Carol Stack, "Coming of Age in Oakland," in J. Goode and J. Maskovsky, eds., *The New Poverty Studies* (New York: NYU Press, 2001).

50. Kathryn Edin, Paula England, Emily Fitzgibbons Shafer, and Joanna Reed, "Forming Fragile Families: Was the Baby Planned, Unplanned, or In Between?," in Paula England and Kathryn Edin, eds., *Unmarried Couples with Children* (New York: Russell Sage, 2007).

51. Rosanna Hertz, *Single by Chance, Mothers by Choice* (New York: Oxford University Press, 2006).

52. Waldo Johnson, "Parental Involvement among Unwed Fathers," *Children and Youth Services Review* 23 (2001); personal communication, August 9, 2007.

53. It's also interesting to consider the race and class prejudices that come into play when we think about responsible planning. While politicians heap censure on poor women who fail to plan for their child's support and expect to be bailed out by government, they take it for granted that people who build expensive homes on a flood plain or in a known hurricane path should be bailed out when the inevitable disaster occurs.

54. On contemporary diversity and the need to deal with the special issues of prejudice in minority communities, see Juan Battle and Natalie Bennett, "Striving for Place: Lesbian, Gay, Bisexual and Transgender People," in Alton Honsby, ed., *A Companion to African-American History* (New York: Blackwell, 2005); E. S. Morales, "Ethnic Minority Families and Minority Gays and Lesbians," in F. W. Bozett and M. B. Sussmen, *Homosexuality and Family Relations* (NY: Harrington Park Press, 1990), pp. 217–39 and Beverley Greene and Nancy-Boyd Franklin, "African-American Lesbians," in Joan Laird and Robert-Jay Green, *Lesbians and Gays in Couples and Families* (San Francisco: Jossey-Bass, 1996).

55. Berk, R. A., A. Campbell, *et al.*, "The Deterrent Effect of Arrest in Incidents of Domestic Violence: A Bayesian Analysis of Four Field Experiments," *American Sociological Review* 57 (1992); Buzawa, E. S., *Domestic Violence: The Criminal Justice Response* (Thousand Oaks, CA: Sage, 2003). For more on domestic violence and class, race and ethnicity, see Natalie Sokoloff and Christina Pratt, eds., *Domestic Violence at the Margins: Readings on Race, Class, Gender, and Culture* (New Brunswick, NJ: Rutgers University Press, 2005); Kimberly Crenshaw, "Mapping the Margins: Intersectionality, Identity Politics, and Violence Against Women of Color," in M. Fineman and R. Mykitiuk, eds., *The Public Nature of Private Violence* (New York: Routledge, 1994).

56. David Lancy, *The Anthropology of Childhood: Cherubs, Chattels, Changelings* (Cambridge: Cambridge University Press, 2008).

57. Ann Ferguson, *Bad Boys: Public Schools in the Making of Black Masculinity* (Ann Arbor: University of Michigan Press, 2000).

58. Carol Stack, "Cultural Perspectives on Child Welfare," in Martha Minow, ed., *Family Matters: Readings on Family Lives and the Law* (New York: The New Press, 1993), pp. 344–349; E. Alan Howard, Robert Heighton, Cathie Jordan, and Ronald Gallimore, "Traditional and Modern Adoption Patterns in Hawaii," in Vern Carroll, ed., *Adoption in Eastern Oceania* (Honolulu: U of Hawaii Press, 1970), pp. 21–51; Jean Peterson, "Generalized Extended Family Exchange: A Case From the Philippines," *Journal of Marriage and the Family* 55 (1993); Kate Porter Young, "Notes on Sisterhood, Kinship, and Marriage in an African American South Carolina Island Community," *Center for Research on Women, Working Paper 6*, August 1992, p. 12; Leslie Gordon Simons *et al.*, "Parenting Practices and Child Adjustment in Different Types of Households," *Journal of Family Issues* 27 (2006).

59. Jennifer Lee, Frank Bean, and Kathy Sloane, "Beyond Black and White," *Contexts* 2 (2003), 26–33.

60. Maria P. P. Root, ed., *The Multiracial Experience: Racial Borders as the New Frontier* (Thousand Oaks: Sage, 1996).

61. William Julius Wilson, "Poverty, Social Rights, and the Quality of Citizenship," in Katherine McFrate, Roger Lawson, and William Julius Wilson, *Poverty, Inequality and the Future of Social Policy* (New York: Russell Sage, 1995); Linda Gordon, *Pitied but Not Entitled: Single Mothers and the History of Welfare* (New York: Free Press, 1994); Gwendolyn Mink, *The Wages of Motherhood: Inequality in the Welfare State, 1917–1942* (Ithaca: Cornell University Press, 1995).

62. Stephen Steinberg, "The Case for a Race Specific Policy," *New Politics* (1995).

63. Richard America, ed., *The Wealth of Race: The Present Value of Benefits from Past Injustices* (Westport: Greenwood, 1990); Melvin Oliver and Thomas Shapiro, *Black Wealth/White Wealth: A New Perspective on Racial Inequality* (New York: Routledge, 1995).

64. For more on these issues and what other industrial countries are doing to help families, see Sheila Kamerman, "Gender Role and Family Structure Changes in the Advanced Industrial West," in Katherine McFate, Roger Lawson, and William Julius Wilson, eds., *Poverty, Inequality, and the Future of Social Policy* (New York: Russell Sage, 1995); Barbara Bergmann, *Saving Our Children from Poverty: What the United States Can Learn from France* (New York: Russell Sage, 1996); Jody Heymann, Alison Earle, and Jeffrey Hayes, "A Study of Work Policies in 180 countries: U.S. compares well with others in protecting individual workers against discrimination, but ranks low in protecting workers' family lives," briefing paper prepared for the Council on Contemporary Families, February 1, 2007. Go to *www.contemporaryfamilies.org*.

I

WHO WE WERE: DIVERSITY AND INEQUALITY IN AMERICAN FAMILY HISTORY

1

Fictive Kin, Paper Sons, and Compadrazgo
Women of Color and the Struggle for Family Survival

BONNIE THORNTON DILL

RACE HAS BEEN FUNDAMENTAL to the construction of families in the United States since the country was settled. People of color were incorporated into the country and used to meet the need for cheap and exploitable labor. Little attention was given to their family and community life except as it related to their economic productivity. Upon their founding, the various colonies that ultimately formed the United States initiated legal, economic, political, and social practices designed to promote the growth of family life among European colonists. As the primary laborers in the reproduction and maintenance of families, White[1] women settlers were accorded the privileges and protection considered socially appropriate to their family roles. The structure of family life during this era was strongly patriarchal, denying women many rights, constraining their personal autonomy, and making them subject to the almost unfettered will of the male head of the household. Nevertheless, women were rewarded and protected within patriarchal families because their labor was recognized as essential to the maintenance and sustenance of family life.[2] In addition, families were seen as the cornerstone of an incipient nation, and thus their existence was a matter of national interest.

In contrast, women of color experienced the oppression of a patriarchal society but were denied the protection and buffering of a patriarchal family. Although the presence of women of color was equally important to the growth of the nation, their value was based on their potential as workers, breeders, and entertainers of workers, not as family members. In the eighteenth and nineteenth centuries, labor, and not the existence or maintenance of families, was the critical aspect of their role in building the nation. Thus they were denied the societal supports necessary to make their families a vital element in the social order. For women of color, family membership was not a key means of access to participation in the wider society. In some instances, racial-ethnic families were seen as a threat to the efficiency and exploitability of the work force and were actively prohibited. In other cases, they were tolerated when it was felt they might help solidify or expand the work force. The lack of social, legal, and economic support for the family life of people of color intensified and extended women's work, created tensions and strains in family relationships, and set the stage for a variety of creative and adaptive forms of resistance.

AFRICAN AMERICAN SLAVES

Among students of slavery, there has been considerable debate over the relative "harshness" of American slavery, and the degree to which slaves were permitted or encouraged to form families. It is generally acknowledged that many slave owners found it economically advantageous to encourage family formation as a way of reproducing and perpetuating the slave labor force. This became increasingly true after 1807, when the importation of African slaves was explicitly prohibited. The existence of these families and many aspects of their functioning, however, were directly controlled by the master. Slaves married and formed families, but these groupings were completely subject to the master's decision to let them remain intact. One study has estimated that about 32 percent of all recorded slave marriages were disrupted by sale, about 45 percent by death of a spouse, about 10 percent by choice, and only 13 percent were not disrupted (Blassingame 1972). African slaves thus quickly learned that they had a limited degree of control over the formation and maintenance of their marriages and could not be assured of keeping their children with them. The threat of disruption was one of the most direct and pervasive assaults on families that slaves encountered. Yet there were a number of other aspects of the slave system that reinforced the precariousness of slave family life.

In contrast to some African traditions and the Euro-American patterns of the period, slave men were not the main providers or authority figures in the family. The mother-child tie was basic and of greatest interest to the slave owner because it was essential to the reproduction of the labor force.

In addition to the lack of authority and economic autonomy experienced by the husband-father in the slave family, use of rape of women slaves as a weapon of terror and control further undermined the integrity of the slave family.

> It would be a mistake to regard the institutionalized pattern of rape during slavery as an expression of white men's sexual urges, otherwise stifled by the specter of the white womanhood's chastity. . . . Rape was a weapon of domination, a weapon of repression, whose covert goal was to extinguish slave women's will to resist, and in the process, to demoralize their men. (Davis 1981:23–24)

The slave family, therefore, was at the heart of a peculiar tension in the master-slave relationship. On the one hand, slave owners sought to encourage familiarities among slaves because, as Julie Matthaei (1982:81) states, "These provided the basis of the development of the slave into a self-conscious socialized human being." They also hoped and believed that this socialization process would help children learn to accept their place in society as slaves. Yet the master's need to control and intervene in the family life of the slaves is indicative of the other side of this tension. Family ties had the potential to become a competing and more potent source of allegiance than the master. Also, kin were as likely to socialize children in forms of resistance as in acts of compliance.

It was within this context of surveillance, assault, and ambivalence that slave women's reproductive labor[3] took place. They and their men-folk had the task of preserving the human and family ties that could ultimately give them a reason for living. They had to socialize their children to believe in the possibility of a life in which they were not enslaved. The slave woman's labor on behalf of the family was, as Angela Davis (1971) has pointed out, the only labor in which the slave engaged that could not be directly used by the slave owner for his own profit. Yet, it was crucial to the reproduction of the slave owner's labor force, and thus a source of strong ambivalence for many slave women. Whereas some mothers murdered their babies to keep them from being slaves, many sought within the family the autonomy and creativity that were denied them in other realms of the society. The maintenance of a distinct African American culture is testimony to the ways in which slaves maintained a degree of cultural autonomy and resisted the creation of a slave family that only served the needs of the master.

Herbert Gutman (1976) gives evidence of the ways in which slaves expressed a unique African American culture through their family practices. He provides data on naming patterns and kinship ties among slaves that fly in the face of the dominant ideology of the period, which argued that slaves were immoral and had little concern for or appreciation of family life. Yet Gutman demonstrates that, within a system that denied the father authority over his family, slave boys were frequently named after their fathers, and many children were named after blood relatives as a way of maintaining family ties. Gutman also suggests that after emancipation a number of slaves took the names of former owners in order to reestablish family ties that had been disrupted earlier. On plantation after plantation, Gutman found considerable evidence of the building and maintenance of extensive kinship ties among slaves. In instances where slave families had been disrupted, slaves in new communities reconstituted the kinds of family and kin ties that came to characterize Black family life throughout the South. The patterns included, but were not limited to, a belief in the importance of marriage as a long-term commitment, rules of exogamy that excluded marriage between first cousins, and acceptance of women who had children outside of marriage. Kinship networks were an important source of resistance to the organization of labor that treated the individual slave, and not the family, as the unit of labor (Caulfield 1974).

Another interesting indicator of the slaves' maintenance of some degree of cultural autonomy has been pointed out by Gwendolyn Wright (1981) in her discussion of slave housing. Until the early 1800s, slaves were often permitted to build their housing according to their own design and taste. During that period, housing built in an African style was quite common in the slave quarters. By 1830, however, slave owners had begun to control the design and arrangement of slave housing and had introduced a degree of conformity and regularity to it that left little room for the slaves' personalization of the home. Nevertheless, slaves did use some of their own techniques in construction, often hiding them from their masters.

> Even the floors, which usually consisted of only tamped earth, were evidence of a hidden African tradition: slaves cooked clay over a fire, mixing in ox blood or cow dung, and then poured it in place to make hard dirt floors almost like asphalt. . . . In slave houses, in contrast to other crafts, these signs of skill and tradition would then be covered over. (Wright 1981:48)

Housing is important in discussions of family because its design reflects sociocultural attitudes about family life. The housing that slave owners provided for their slaves reflected a view of Black family life consistent with the stereotypes of the period. While the existence of slave families was acknowledged, they certainly were not nurtured. Thus, cabins were crowded, often containing more than one family, and there were no provisions for privacy. Slaves had to create their own.

> Slave couples hung up old clothes or quilts to establish boundaries; others built more substantial partitions from scrap wood. Parents sought to establish sexual privacy from children. A few ex-slaves described modified trundle beds designed to hide parental love-making. . . . Even in one room cabins, sexual segregation was carefully organized. (Wright 1981:50)

Perhaps most critical in developing an understanding of slave women's reproductive labor is the gender-based division of labor in the domestic sphere. The organization of slave labor enforced considerable equality among men and women. The ways in which equality in the labor force was translated into the family sphere are somewhat speculative. Davis (1981:18), for example, suggests that egalitarianism between males and females was a direct result of slavery: "Within the confines of their family and community life, therefore, Black people managed to accomplish a magnificent feat. They transformed that negative equality which emanated from the equal oppression they suffered as slaves into a positive quality; the egalitarianism characterizing their social relations."

It is likely, however, that this transformation was far less direct than Davis implies. We know, for example, that slave women experienced what has recently been called the "double day" before most other women in this society. Slave narratives (Jones 1985; White 1985; Blassingame 1977) reveal that women had primary responsibility for their family's domestic chores. They cooked (although on some plantations meals were prepared for all the slaves), sewed, cared for their children, and cleaned house after completing a full day of labor for the master. John Blassingame (1972) and others have pointed out that slave men engaged in hunting, trapping, perhaps some gardening, and furniture making as ways of contributing to the maintenance of their families. Clearly, a gender-based division of labor did exist within the family, and it appears that women bore the larger share of the burden for house-keeping and child care.

In contrast to White families of the period, however, the division of labor in the domestic sphere was reinforced neither in the relationship of slave women to work nor in the social institutions of the slave community. The gender-based division of labor among the slaves existed within a social system that treated men and women as almost equal, independent units of labor.[4] Thus Matthaei (1982:94) is probably correct in concluding that

> whereas the white homemaker interacted with the public sphere through her husband, and had her work life determined by him, the enslaved Afro-American homemaker was directly subordinated to and determined by her owner. . . . The equal enslavement of husband and wife gave the slave marriage a curious kind of equality, an equality of oppression.

Black men were denied the male resources of a patriarchal society and therefore were unable to turn gender distinctions into female subordination, even if that had been their desire. Black women, on the other hand, were denied support and protection for their roles as mothers and wives, and thus had to modify and structure those roles around the demands of their labor. Reproductive labor for slave women was intensified in several ways: by the demands of slave labor that forced them into the double day of work; by the desire and need to maintain family ties in the face of a system that gave them only limited recognition; by the stresses of building a family with men who were denied the standard social privileges of manhood; and by the struggle to raise children who could survive in a hostile environment.

This intensification of reproductive labor made networks of kin and fictive kin important instruments in carrying out the reproductive tasks of the slave community. Given an African cultural heritage where kinship ties formed the basis of social relations, it is not at all surprising that African American slaves developed an extensive system of kinship ties and obligations (Gutman 1976; Sudarkasa 1981). Research on Black families in slavery provides considerable documentation of participation of extended kin in child rearing, childbirth, and other domestic, social, and economic activities (Gutman 1976; Blassingame 1972; Genovese and Miller 1974).

After slavery, these ties continued to be an important factor linking individual household units in a variety of domestic activities. While kinship ties were also important among native-born Whites and European immigrants, Gutman (1976:213) has suggested that these ties were comparatively more important to Afro-Americans than to lower-class native white and immigrant Americans, the result of their distinctive low economic status, a condition that denied them the advantages of an extensive associational life beyond the kin group and the advantages and disadvantages resulting from mobility opportunities.

His argument is reaffirmed by research on African American families after slavery (Shimkin et al. 1978; Aschenbrenner 1975; Davis 1981; Stack 1974). Niara Sudarkasa (1981:49) takes this argument one step further, linking this pattern to the African cultural heritage.

> Historical realities require that the derivation of this aspect of Black family organization be traced to its African antecedents. Such a view does not deny the adaptive significance of consanguineal networks. In fact, it helps to clarify why these networks had the flexibility they had and why they, rather than conjugal relationships, came to be the stabilizing factor in Black families.

In individual households, the gender-based division of labor experienced some important shifts during emancipation. In their first real opportunity to establish family life beyond the controls and constraints imposed by a slave master, Black sharecroppers' family life changed radically. Most women, at least those who were wives and daughters of able-bodied men, withdrew from field labor and concentrated on their domestic duties in the home. Husbands took primary responsibility for the fieldwork and for relations with the owners, such as signing contracts on behalf of the family. Black women were severely criticized by Whites for removing themselves from field labor because they were seen to be aspiring to a model of womanhood that was considered inappropriate for them. The reorganization of female labor, however, represented an attempt on the part of Blacks to protect women from some of the abuses of the slaves system and to thus secure their family life. It was more likely a response to the particular set of circumstances that the newly freed slaves faced than a reaction to the lives of their former masters. Jacqueline Jones (1985) argues that these patterns were "particularly significant" because at a time when industrial development was introducing a labor system that divided male and female labor, the freed Black family was establishing a pattern of joint work and complementarity of tasks between males and females that was reminiscent of preindustrial American families. Unfortunately, these former slaves had to do this without the institutional supports given White farm families and within a sharecropping system that deprived them of economic independence.

CHINESE SOJOURNERS

An increase in the African slave population was a desired goal. Therefore, Africans were permitted and even encouraged at times to form families, as long as they were under the direct control of the slave master. By sharp contrast, Chinese people were explicitly denied the right to form families in the United States through both law and social practice. Although male laborers began coming to the United States in sizable numbers in the middle of the nineteenth century, it was more than a century before an appreciable number of children of Chinese parents were born in America. Tom, a respondent in Victor Nee and Brett de Bary Nee's book, *Longtime Californ'*, says: "One thing about Chinese men in America was you had to be either a merchant or a big gambler, have lot of side money to have a family here. A working man, an ordinary man, just can't!" (1973:80).

Working in the United States was a means of gaining support for one's family with an end of obtaining sufficient capital to return to China and purchase land. This practice of sojourning was reinforced by laws preventing Chinese laborers from becoming citizens, and by restrictions on their entry into this country. Chinese laborers who arrived before 1882 could not bring their wives and were prevented by law from marrying Whites. Thus, it is likely that the number of Chinese American families might have been negligible had it not been for two things: the San Francisco earthquake and fire in 1906, which destroyed all municipal records, and the ingenuity and persistence of the Chinese people, who used the opportunity created by the earthquake to increase their numbers in the United States. Since relatives of citizens were permitted entry, American-born Chinese (real and claimed) would visit China, report the birth of a son, and thus create an entry slot. Years later, since the records were destroyed, the slot could be used by a relative or purchased by someone outside the family. The purchasers were called "paper sons." Paper sons became a major mechanism for increasing the Chinese population, but it was a slow process and the sojourner community remained predominantly male for decades.

The high concentration of males in the Chinese community before 1920 resulted in a split household form of family. As Evelyn Nakano Glenn observes:

> In the split household family, production is separated from other functions and is carried out by a member living far from the rest of the household. The rest—consumption, reproduction and socialization—are carried out by the wife and other relatives from the home village.... The split household form makes possible maximum exploitation of the workers.... The labor of prime-age male workers can be bought relatively cheaply, since the cost of reproduction and family maintenance is borne partially by unpaid subsistence work of women and old people in the home village. (1983:38–39)

The Chinese women who were in the United States during this period consisted of a small number who were wives and daughters of merchants and a larger percentage who were prostitutes. Lucia Cheng Hirata (1979) has suggested that Chinese prostitution was an important element in helping to maintain the split household family. In conjunction with laws prohibiting intermarriage, it helped men avoid long-term relationships with women in the United States and ensured that the bulk of their meager earnings would continue to support the family at home.

The reproductive labor of Chinese women, therefore, took on two dimensions primarily because of the split household family. Wives who remained in China were forced to raise children and care for in-laws on the meager remittances of their sojourning husbands. Although we know few details about their lives, it is clear that the everyday work of bearing and maintaining children and running a household fell entirely on their shoulders. Those women who immigrated and worked as prostitutes performed the more nurturant aspects of reproductive labor, that is, providing emotional and sexual companionship for men who were far from home. Yet their role as prostitutes was more likely a means of supporting their families at home in China than a chosen vocation.

The Chinese family system during the nineteenth century was a patriarchal one and girls had little value. In fact, they were considered temporary members of their father's family because when they married, they became members of their husband's family. They also had little social value; girls were sold by some poor parents to work as prostitutes, concubines, or servants. This saved the family the expense of raising them, and their earnings became a source of family income. For most girls, however, marriages were arranged and families sought useful connections through this process. With the development of a sojourning pattern in the United States, some Chinese women in those regions of China where this pattern was more prevalent would be sold to become prostitutes in the United States. Most, however, were married to men whom they saw only once or twice in the twenty- or thirty-year periods during which these men sojourned in the United States. A woman's status as wife ensured that a portion of the meager wages her husband earned would be returned to his family in China. This arrangement required considerable sacrifice and adjustment by wives who remained in China and those who joined their husbands after a long separation.

Maxine Hong Kingston tells the story of the unhappy meeting of her aunt, Moon Orchid, with her husband, from whom she had been separated for thirty years: "For thirty years she had been receiving money from him from America. But she had never told him that she wanted to come to the United States. She waited for him to suggest it, but he never did" (1977:144). His response to her when she arrived unexpectedly was to say: " 'Look at her. She'd never fit into an American house-hold. I have important American guests who come inside my house to eat.' He turned to Moon Orchid, 'You can't talk to them. You can barely talk to me.' Moon Orchid was so ashamed, she held her hands over her face" (1977:178).

Despite these handicaps, Chinese people collaborated to establish the opportunity to form families and settle in the United States. In some cases it took as long as three generations for a child to be born on U.S. soil.

> In one typical history, related by a 21 year old college student, great-grandfather arrived in the States in the 1890s as a "paper son" and worked for about 20 years as a laborer. He then sent for the grandfather, who worked alongside great-grandfather in a small business for several years. Great-grandfather subsequently returned to China, leaving grandfather to run the business and send remittance. In the 1940s, grandfather sent for father; up to this point, none of the wives had left China. Finally, in the late 1950s father returned to China and brought his wife back with him. Thus, after nearly 70 years, the first child was born in the United States. (Glenn 1983:14)

CHICANOS

Africans were uprooted from their native lands and encouraged to have families in order to increase the slave labor force. Chinese people were immigrant laborers whose "permanent" presence in the country was denied. By contrast, Mexican Americans were colonized and their traditional family life was disrupted by war and the imposition of a new set of laws and conditions of labor. The hardships faced by Chicano families, therefore, were the results of the U.S. colonization of the indigenous Mexican population, accompanied by the beginnings of industrial development. The treaty of Guadalupe Hidalgo, signed in 1848, granted American citizenship to Mexicans living in what is now called the Southwest. The American takeover, however, resulted in the gradual displacement of Mexicans from the land and their incorporation into a colonial labor force (Barrera 1979). Mexicans who immigrated into the United States after 1848 were also absorbed into that labor force.

Whether natives of northern Mexico (which became part of the United States after 1848) or immigrants from southern Mexico, Chicanos were a largely peasant population whose lives were defined by a feudal economy and a daily struggle on the land for economic survival. Patriarchal families were important instruments of community life, and nuclear family units were linked through an elaborate system of kinship and godparenting. Traditional life was characterized by hard work and a fairly distinct pattern of sex-role segregation.

> Most Mexican women were valued for their household qualities, men by their ability to work and to provide for a family. Children were taught to get up early, to contribute to their family's labor to prepare themselves for adult life.... Such a life demanded discipline, authority, deference—values that

cemented the working of a family surrounded and shaped by the requirements of Mexico's distinctive historical pattern of agricultural development, especially its pervasive debt peonage. (Saragoza 1983:8)

As the primary caretakers of hearth and home in a rural environment, Chicana's labor made a vital and important contribution to family survival. A description of women's reproductive labor in the early twentieth century may be used to gain insight into the work of the nineteenth-century rural women.

> For country women, work was seldom a salaried job. More often it was the work of growing and preparing food, of making adobes and plastering houses with mud, or making their children's clothes for school and teaching them the hymns and prayers of the church, or delivering babies and treating sickness with herbs and patience. In almost every town there were one or two women who, in addition to working in their own homes, served other families in the community as *curanderas* (healers), *parteras* (midwives), and school-teachers. (Elasser et al. 1980:10)

Although some scholars have argued that family rituals and community life showed little change before World War I (Saragoza 1983), the American conquest of Mexican lands, the introduction of a new system of labor, the loss of Mexican-owned land through the inability to document ownership, and the transient nature of most of the jobs in which Chicanos were employed resulted in the gradual erosion of this pastoral way of life. Families were uprooted as the economic basis for family life changed. Some people immigrated from Mexico in search of a better standard of living and worked in the mines and railroads. Others, who were native to the Southwest, faced a job market that no longer required their skills. They moved into mining, railroad, and agricultural labor in search of a means of earning a living. According to Albert Camarillo (1979), the influx of Anglo[5] capital into the pastoral economy of Santa Barbara rendered obsolete the skills of many Chicano males who had worked as ranch hands and farmers prior to the urbanization of that economy. While some women and children accompanied their husbands to the railroad and mining camps, many of these camps discouraged or prohibited family settlement.

The American period (after 1848) was characterized by considerable transiency for the Chicano population. Its impact on families is seen in the growth of female-headed households, reflected in the data as early as 1860. Richard Griswold del Castillo (1979) found a sharp increase in female-headed households in Los Angeles, from a low of 13 percent in 1844 to 31 percent in 1880. Camarillo (1979:120) documents a similar increase in Santa Barbara, from 15 percent in 1844 to 30 percent by 1880. These increases appear to be due not so much to divorce, which was infrequent in this Catholic population, as to widowhood and temporary abandonment in search of work. Given the hazardous nature of work in the mines and railroad camps, the death of a husband, father, or son who was laboring in these sites was not uncommon. Griswold del Castillo (1979) reports a higher death rate among men than women in Los Angeles. The rise in female-headed households, therefore, reflects the instabilities and insecurities introduced into women's lives as a result of the changing social organization of work.

One outcome, the increasing participation of women and children in the labor force, was primarily a response to economic factors that required the modification of traditional values. According to Louisa Vigil, who was born in 1890, "The women didn't work at that time. The man was supposed to marry that girl and take care of her. . . . Your grandpa never did let me work for nobody. He always had to work, and we never did have really bad times" (Elasser et al. 1980:14).

Vigil's comments are reinforced in Mario Garcia's (1980) study of El Paso. In the 393 households he examined in the 1900 census, he found 17.1 percent of the women to be employed. The majority of this group were daughters, mothers with no husbands, and single women. In Los Angeles and Santa Barbara, where there were greater work opportunities for women than in El Paso, wives who were heads of household worked in seasonal and part-time jobs, and lived from the earnings of children and relatives in an effort to maintain traditional female roles.

Slowly, entire families were encouraged to go to railroad work camps and were eventually incorporated into the agricultural labor market. This was a response both to the extremely low wages paid to Chicano laborers and to the preferences of employers, who saw family labor as a way of stabilizing the work force. For Chicanos, engaging all family members in agricultural work was a means of increasing their earnings to a level close to subsistence for the entire group and of keeping the family unit together. Camarillo provides a picture of the interplay of work, family, and migration in the Santa Barbara area in the following observation:

> The time of year when women and children were employed in the fruit cannery and participated in the almond and olive harvest coincided with the seasons when the men were most likely to be engaged in seasonal migratory work. There were seasons, however, especially in the early summer when the entire family migrated from the city to pick fruit. This type of family seasonal harvest was evident in Santa Barbara by the 1890s. As walnuts replaced almonds and as the fruit industry expanded, Chicano family labor became essential. (1979:93)

This arrangement, while bringing families together, did not decrease the hardships that Chicanas had to confront in raising their families. We may infer something about the rigors of that life from Jesse Lopez de la Cruz's description of the workday of migrant farm laborers in the 1940s. Work conditions in the 1890s were as difficult, if not worse.

> We always went to where the women and men were going to work, because if it were just the men working it wasn't worth going out there because we wouldn't earn enough to support a family. . . . We would start around 6:30 a.m. and work for four or five hours, then walk home and eat and rest until about three-thirty in the afternoon when it cooled off. We would go back and work until we couldn't see. Then I'd clean up the kitchen. I was doing the housework and working out in the fields and taking care of two children. (Quoted in Goldman 1981:119–120)

In the towns, women's reproductive labor was intensified by the congested and unsanitary conditions of the barrios in which they lived. Garcia described the following conditions in El Paso:

> Mexican women had to haul water for washing and cooking from the river or public water pipes. To feed their families, they had to spend time marketing, often in Ciudad Juarez across the border, as well as long, hot hours cooking meals and coping with the burden of desert sand both inside and outside their homes. Besides the problem of raising children, unsanitary living conditions forced Mexican mothers to deal with disease and illness in their families. Diphtheria, tuberculosis, typhus and influenza were never too far away. Some diseases could be directly traced to inferior city services. . . . As a result, Mexican mothers had to devote much energy to caring for sick children, many of whom died. (1980:320–321)

While the extended family has remained an important element of Chicano life, it was eroded in the American period in several ways. Griswold del Castillo (1979), for example, points out that in 1845 about 71 percent of Angelenos lived in extended families, whereas by 1880, fewer than half did. This decrease in extended families appears to be a response to the changed economic conditions and the instabilities generated by the new sociopolitical structure. Additionally, the imposition of American law and custom ignored, and ultimately undermined, some aspects of the extended family. The extended family in traditional Mexican life consisted of an important set of family, religious, and community obligations. Women, while valued primarily for their domesticity, had certain legal and property rights that acknowledged the importance of their work, their families of origin, and their children. In California, for example,

> equal ownership of property between husband and wife had been one of the mainstays of the Spanish and Mexican family systems. Community-property laws were written into the civil codes with the intention of strengthening the economic controls of the wife and her relatives. The American government incorporated these Mexican laws into the state constitution, but later court decisions interpreted these statutes so as to undermine the wife's economic rights. In 1861, the legislature passed a law that allowed the deceased wife's property to revert to her husband. Previously it had been inherited by her children and relatives if she died without a will. (Griswold del Castillo 1979:69)

The impact of this and similar court rulings was to "strengthen the property rights of the husband at the expense of his wife and children" (Griswold del Castillo 1979:69).

In the face of the legal, social, and economic changes that occurred during the American period, Chicanas were forced to cope with a series of dislocations in traditional life. They were caught between conflicting pressures to maintain traditional women's roles and family customs, and the need to participate in the economic support of their families by working outside the home. During this period the preservation of traditional customs—such as languages, celebrations, and healing practices—became an important element in maintaining and supporting familial ties.

According to Alex Saragoza (1983), transiency, the effects of racism and segregation, and proximity to Mexico aided in the maintenance of traditional family practices. Garcia has suggested that women were the guardians of Mexican cultural traditions within the family. He cites the work of anthropologist Manuel Gamio, who identified the retention of many Mexican customs among Chicanos in settlements around the United States in the early 1900s.

> These included folklore, songs, and ballads, birthday celebrations, saints' days, baptisms, weddings, and funerals in the traditional style. Because of poverty, a lack of physicians in the barrios, and adherence to traditional customs, Mexicans continued to use medicinal herbs. Gamio also identified the maintenance of a number of oral traditions, and Mexican style cooking. (Garcia 1980:322)

Of vital importance to the integrity of traditional culture was the perpetuation of the Spanish language. Factors that aided in the maintenance of other aspects of Mexican culture also helped in sustaining the language. However, entry into English-language public schools introduced the children and their families to systematic efforts to erase their native tongue. Griswold del Castillo reports that in the early 1880s there was considerable pressure against speakers of Spanish in the public schools. He also found that some Chicano parents responded to this kind of discrimination by helping support independent bilingual schools. These efforts, however, were short-lived.

Another key factor in conserving Chicano culture was the extended family network, particularly the system of *compadrazgo* (godparenting). Although the full extent of the impact of the American period on the Chicano extended family is not known, it is generally acknowledged that this family system, though lacking many legal and social sanctions, played an important role in the preservation of the Mexican community (Camarillo 1979). In Mexican society, godparents were an important way of linking family and community through respected friends or authorities. Participants in the important rites of passage in the child's life, such as baptism, first Communion, confirmation, and marriage, godparents had a moral obligation to act as guardians, to provide financial assistance in times of need, and to substitute in case of the death of a parent. Camarillo (1979) points out that in traditional society these bonds cut across class and racial lines.

The rite of baptism established kinship networks between rich and poor, between Spanish, mestizo and American Indian, and often carried with it political loyalty and economic-occupational ties. The leading California patriarchs in the pueblo played important roles in the *compadrazgo* network. They sponsored dozens of children for their workers or poorer relatives. The kindness of the *padrino* and *madrina* was repaid with respect and support from the *pobladores* (Camarillo 1979: 12–13).

The extended family network, which included godparents, expanded the support groups for women who were widowed or temporarily abandoned and for those who were in seasonal, part- or full-time work. It suggests, therefore, the potential for an exchange of services among poor people whose income did not provide the basis for family subsistence. Griswold del Castillo (1979) argues that family organization influenced literacy rates and socioeconomic mobility among Chicanos in Los Angeles between 1850 and 1880. His data suggest that children in extended families (defined as those with at least one other relative living in a nuclear family household) had higher literacy rates than those in nuclear families. He also argues that those in larger families fared better economically and experienced less downward mobility. The data here are too limited to generalize to the Chicano experience as a whole, but they do reinforce the actual and potential importance of this family form to the continued cultural autonomy of the Chicano community.

CONCLUSION

Reproductive labor for African American, Chinese American, and Mexican American women in the nineteenth century centered on the struggle to maintain family units in the face of a variety of assaults. Treated primarily as workers rather than as members of family groups, these women labored to maintain, sustain, stabilize, and reproduce their families while working in both the public (productive) and private (reproductive) spheres. Thus, the concept of reproductive labor, when applied to women of color, must be modified to account for the fact that labor in the productive sphere was required to achieve even minimal levels of family subsistence. Long after industrialization had begun to reshape family roles among middle-class White families, driving White women into a cult of domesticity, women of color were coping with an extended day. This day included subsistence labor outside the family and domestic labor within the family. For slaves, domestics, migrant farm laborers, seasonal factory workers, and prostitutes, the distinctions between labor that reproduced family life and labor that economically sustained it were minimized. The expanded workday was one of the primary ways in which reproductive labor increased.

Racial-ethnic families were sustained and maintained in the face of various forms of disruption. Yet the women and their families paid a high price in the process. High rates of infant mortality, a shortened life span, and the early onset of crippling and debilitating disease give some insight into the costs of survival.

The poor quality of housing and the neglect of communities further increased reproductive labor. Not only did racial-ethnic women work hard outside the home for mere subsistence, they worked very hard inside the home to achieve even minimal standards of privacy and cleanliness. They were continually faced with disease and illness that resulted directly from the absence of basic sanitation. The fact that some African women murdered their children to prevent them from becoming slaves is an indication of the emotional strain associated with bearing and raising children while participating in the colonial labor system.

We have uncovered little information about the use of birth control, the prevalence of infanticide, or the motivations that may have generated these or other behaviors. We can surmise, however, that no matter how much children were accepted, loved, or valued among any of these groups of people, their futures were precarious. Keeping children alive, helping them to understand and participate in a system that exploited them, and working to ensure a measure—no matter how small—of cultural integrity intensified women's reproductive labor.

Being a woman of color in nineteenth-century American society meant having extra work both inside and outside the home. It meant being defined as outside of or deviant from the norms and values about women that were being generated in the dominant White culture. The notion of separate spheres of male and female labor that developed in the nineteenth century had contradictory outcomes for Whites. It was the basis for the confinement of upper-middle-class White women to the household and for much of the protective legislation that subsequently developed in the workplace. At the same time, it sustained White families by providing social acknowledgment and support to women in the performance of their family roles. For racial-ethnic women, however, the notion of separate spheres served to reinforce their subordinate status and became, in effect, another assault. As they increased their work outside the home, they were forced into a productive labor sphere that was organized for men and "desperate" women who were so unfortunate or immoral that they could not confine their work to the domestic sphere. In the productive sphere, racial-ethnic women faced exploitative jobs and depressed wages. In the reproductive sphere, they were denied the opportunity to embrace the dominant ideological definition of "good" wife or mother. In essence, they were faced with a double-bind situation, one that required their participation in the labor force to sustain family life but damned them as women, wives, and mothers because they did not confine their labor to the home.

Finally, the struggle of women of color to build and maintain families provides vivid testimony to the role of race in structuring family life in the United States. As Maxine Baca Zinn points out:

> Social categories and groups subordinate in the racial hierarchy are often deprived of access to social institutions that offer supports for family life. Social categories and groups elevated in the racial hierarchy have different and better connections to institutions that can sustain families. Social location and its varied connection with social resources thus have profound consequences for family life. (1990:74)

From the founding of the United States, and throughout its history, race has been a fundamental criterion determining the kind of work people do, the wages they receive, and the kind of legal, economic, political, and social support provided for their families. Women of color have faced limited economic resources, inferior living conditions, alien cultures and languages, and overt hostility in their struggle to create a "place" for families of color in the United States. That place, however, has been a precarious one because the society has not provided supports for these families. Today we see the outcomes of that legacy in statistics showing that people of color, compared with whites, have higher rates of female-headed households, out-of-wedlock births, divorce, and other factors associated with family disruption. Yet the causes of these variations do not lie merely in the higher concentrations of poverty among people of color; they are also due to the ways race has been used as a basis for denying and providing support to families. Women of color have struggled to maintain their families against all of these odds.

NOTES

Acknowledgments: The research in this study was an outgrowth of my participation in a larger collaborative project examining family, community, and work lives of racial-ethnic women in the United States. I am deeply indebted to the scholarship and creativity of members of the group in the development of this study. Appreciation is extended to Elizabeth Higginbotham, Cheryl Townsend Gilkes, Evelyn Nakano Glenn, and Ruth Zambrana (members of the original working group), and to the Ford Foundation for a grant that supported in part the work of this study.

1. The term "White" is a global construct used to characterize peoples of European descent who migrated to and helped colonize America. In the seventeenth century, most of these immigrants were from the British Isles. However, during the time period covered by this article, European immigrants became increasingly diverse. It is a limitation of this chapter that time and space do not permit a fuller discussion of the variations in the White European immigrant experience. For the purposes of the argument being made herein and of the contrast it seeks to draw between the experiences of mainstream (European) cultural groups and those of racial-ethnic minorities, the differences among European settlers are joined and the broad similarities emphasized.
2. For a more detailed discussion of this argument and the kinds of social supports provided these families, see an earlier version of this paper: "Our Mothers' Grief: Racial-Ethnic Women and the Maintenance of Families," *Journal of Family History* 13 (4) (1988): 415–431.
3. The term "reproductive labor" is used to refer to all of the work of women in the home. This includes, but is not limited to, the buying and preparation of food and clothing, provision of emotional support and nurturance for all family members, bearing children, and planning, organizing, and carrying out a wide variety of tasks associated with socialization. All of these activities are necessary for the growth of patriarchal capitalism because they maintain, sustain, stabilize, and reproduce (both biologically and socially) the labor force.
4. Recent research suggests that there were some tasks assigned primarily to males and some others to females. Whereas some gender-role distinctions with regard to work may have existed on some plantations, it clear that slave women were not exempt from strenuous physical labor.
5. This term is used to refer to White Americans of European ancestry.

REFERENCES

Aschenbrenner, Joyce. 1975. *Lifelines: Black Families in Change.* New York: Holt, Rinehart, and Winston.
Baca Zinn, Maxine. 1990. "Family, Feminism and Race in America." *Gender and Society* 4 (1) (March): 68–82.
Barrera, Mario. 1979. *Race and Class in the Southwest.* Notre Dame, Ind.: Notre Dame University Press.
Blassingame, John. 1972. *The Slave Community: Plantation Life in the Antebellum South.* New York: Oxford University Press.
———. 1977. *Slave Testimony: Two Centuries of Letters, Speeches, Interviews, and Autobiographies.* Baton Rouge: Louisiana State University Press.
Camarillo, Albert. 1979. *Chicanos in a Changing Society.* Cambridge, Mass.: Harvard University Press.
Caulfield, Mina Davis. 1974. "Imperialism, the Family, and Cultures of Resistance." *Socialist Review* 4 (2) (October): 67–85.
Davis, Angela. 1971. "Reflections on the Black Woman's Role in the Community of Slaves." *Black Scholar* 3 (4) (December): 2–15.
———. 1981. *Women, Race, and Class.* New York: Random House.
Degler, Carl. 1980. *At Odds.* New York: Oxford University Press.
Elasser, Nan, Kyle MacKenzie, and Yvonne Tixier Y. Vigil. 1980. *Las Mujeres.* New York: The Feminist Press.
Garcia, Mario T. 1980. "The Chicano in American History: The Mexican Women of El Paso, 1880–1920—A Case Study." *Pacific Historical Review* 49 (2) (May): 315–358.
Genovese, Eugene D., and Elinor Miller, eds. 1974. *Plantation, Town, and County: Essays on the Local History of American Slave Society.* Urbana: University of Illinois Press.
Glenn, Evelyn Nakano. 1983. "Split Household, Small Producer, and Dual Earner: An Analysis of Chinese-American Family Strategies." *Journal of Marriage and the Family* 45 (1) (February): 35–46.
Goldman, Marion S. 1981. *Gold Diggers and Silver Miners.* Ann Arbor: University of Michigan Press.
Griswold del Castillo, Richard. 1979. *The Los Angeles Barrio: 1850–1890.* Los Angeles: University of California Press.
Gutman, Herbert. 1976. *The Black Family in Slavery and Freedom, 1750–1925.* New York: Pantheon.
Hirata, Lucia Cheng. 1979. "Free, Indentured, Enslaved: Chinese Prostitutes in Nineteenth Century America." *Signs* 5 (Autumn): 3–29.
Jones, Jacqueline. 1985. *Labor of Love, Labor of Sorrow.* New York: Basic Books.
Kennedy, Susan Estabrook. 1979. *If All We Did Was to Weep at Home: A History of White Working-Class Women in America.* Bloomington: Indiana University Press.
Kessler-Harris, Alice. 1981. *Women Have Always Worked.* Old Westbury, N.Y.: The Feminist Press.
———. 1982. *Out to Work.* New York: Oxford University Press.
Kingston, Maxine Hong. 1977. *The Woman Warrior.* New York: Vintage Books.
Matthaei, Julie. 1982. *An Economic History of Women in America.* New York: Schocken Books.
Nee, Victor G., and Brett de Bary Nee. 1973. *Longtime Californ'.* New York: Pantheon Books.

Saragoza, Alex M. 1983. "The Conceptualization of the History of the Chicano Family: Work, Family, and Migration in Chicanos." In *Research Proceedings of the Symposium on Chicano Research and Public Policy*. Stanford, Calif.: Stanford University, Center for Chicano Research.

Shimkin, Demetri, E. M. Shimkin, and D. A. Frate, eds. 1978. *The Extended Family in Black Societies*. The Hague: Mouton.

Spruill, Julia Cherry. 1972. *Women's Life and Work in the Southern Colonies*. New York: W. W. Norton. (First published Chapel Hill: University of North Carolina Press, 1938).

Stack, Carol S. 1974. *All Our Kin: Strategies for Survival in a Black Community*. New York: Harper & Row.

Sudarkasa, Niara. 1981. "Interpreting the African Heritage in Afro-American Family Organization." In *Black Families*, Harriette Pipes McAdoo, ed. Beverly Hills, Calif.: Sage.

White, Deborah Gray. 1985. *Ar'n't I a Woman? Female Slaves in the Plantation South*. New York: W. W. Norton.

Wright, Gwendolyn. 1981. *Building the Dream: A Social History of Housing in America*. New York: Pantheon.

Zaretsky, Eli. 1978. "The Effects of the Economic Crisis on the Family." In *U.S. Capitalism in Crisis*, edited by Crisis Reader Editorial Collective. New York: Union of Radical Political Economists.

2

excerpts from

Education for Extinction
American Indians and the Boarding School Experience, 1875–1928

David Wallace Adams

In retrospect it is not surprising that reformers should look to schools as central to the solution of the Indian problem. As an instrument for fostering social cohesion and republicanism, no institution had been more important in the spread of the American system. In the case of Indians, the challenge facing educators was particularly difficult: the eradication of all traces of tribal identity and culture, replacing them with the common-place knowledge and values of white civilization. Reformers believed that the school's capacity to accomplish this transformation would determine the long-term fate of the Indian race, for if the doctrine of historical progress and the story of westward expansion taught anything, it was the incompatibility of white civilization and Indian savagism. The former must inevitably supplant the latter. Fortunately, Indians need not perish as a race. Once they shed their attachment to tribal ways—that is to say, their Indianness— and joined the march of American progress, their continued existence in the nation's future was assured. Schools would show them the way.

Boarding schools, especially the off-reservation variety, seemed ideally suited for this purpose. As the theory went, Indian children, once removed from the savage surroundings of the Indian camp and placed in the purified environment of an all-encompassing institution, would slowly learn to look, act, and eventually think like their white counterparts. From the daily regimentation and routine, Indian children would learn the need for order and self-discipline. In the half-day schedule devoted to academics they would master the fundamentals of English, take to heart the moral maxims of McGuffey, and from their history textbook appreciate the meaning of 1492. Balancing the academic side would be classes in industrial training and domestic science, a rotating system of institutional chores, and outing assignments, all designed to prepare them for the path ahead. Sunday sermons, midweek prayer meetings, holiday ceremonies, patriotic drills, and football contests, all in their own way, would contribute to the students' cultural metamorphosis. When it was all over, the onetime youthful specimens of savagism would be thoroughly Christianized, individualized, and republicanized, fit candidates for American citizenship and ideal agents for uplifting an older generation still stranded in the backwaters of barbarism—"a little child shall lead them."

Judged by the ambitious scope of their assimilationist vision, reformers clearly failed to achieve their objective. Beyond the fact that congressional parsimony never allowed the educational assault to be waged with the intensity that reformers envisioned, the reasons for their failure go much deeper. Underlying the reform program was the presupposition that the acculturation process was a relatively simple matter of exchanging one cultural skin for another. The possibility that Indians, either as students or returnees, once having been exposed to the white man's cultural system would react in any manner other than complete embracement, that the acculturation process itself could involve various forms of selective incorporation, syncretization, and compartmentalization, was beyond their comprehension. [But] Indian students were anything but passive recipients of the curriculum of civilization. When choosing the path of resistance, they bolted the institution, torched buildings, and engaged in a multitude of schemes to undermine the school program. Even the response of accommodation was frequently little more than a conscious and strategic adaptation to the hard rock of historical circumstance, a pragmatic recognition that one's Indianness would increasingly have to be defended and negotiated in the face of relentless hegemonic forces.

If the boarding school failed to fulfill reformers' expectations, it still had a profound impact on an Indian child's psychological and cultural being. Returning students, whatever their disposition toward their late experience, could not help but be affected by their sustained exposure to white ways of knowing and living during which time they inevitably acquired new attitudes, values, skills, prejudices, desires, and habits of behavior. Like it or not, most returned students were agents of cultural change, and over time white education would constitute one of the major acculurative forces shaping Indian society. On the other hand, one of the chief consequences for students attending an off-reservation facility was an enlarged sense of identity as "Indians." At schools like Carlisle and Haskell, Sioux children were regularly thrown into intimate association with Comanche and Navajo. At Sherman Institute, Hopi slept, ate, drilled, and played alongside Cahuilla and Serrano. At such institutions students learned that the "Great Father" made no allowances for tribal distinctions; Indians were simply Indians. Ironically, the very institution designed to extinguish Indian identity altogether may have in fact contributed to its very persistence in the form of twentieth-century pan-Indian consciousness.

In the final analysis, the boarding school story constitutes yet another deplorable episode in the long and tragic history of Indian-white relations. For tribal elders who had witnessed the catastrophic developments of the nineteenth century—the bloody warfare, the near-extinction of the bison, the scourge of disease and starvation, the shrinking of the tribal land base, the indignities of reservation life, the invasion of missionaries and white settlers—there seemed to be no end to the cruelties perpetrated by whites. And after all this, the schools. After all this, the white man had concluded that the only way to save Indians was to destroy them, that the last great Indian war should be waged against children. They were coming for the children.

INSTITUTION

The boarding school, whether on or off the reservation, was the institutional manifestation of the government's determination to completely restructure the Indians' minds and personalities. To understand how it functioned in this regard one must attempt to understand how Indian students actually came to know and experience it. And this effort must necessarily begin at that point in time when Indian youths left behind the familiar world of tribal ways for the unfamiliar world of the white man's school. For philanthropists, of course, the journey of Indian children to boarding school was that first step out of the darkness of savagery into the light of civilization. For most Indian youths it meant something entirely different. In any event, the day they left for boarding school could never be forgotten.

For a young Lakota Sioux named Ota Kte, or Plenty Kill—later named Luther Standing Bear—the idea of attending the white man's school first presented itself in the fall of 1879, when he and a friend noticed a crowd gathering around one of the agency buildings at Rosebud. Curious, the two boys approached the building and peered through a window. The room was mostly filled with Sioux, but there were also a few whites among them.

> When they saw us peeping in at the window, they motioned for us to come inside. But we hesitated. Then they held out some sticks of candy. At this, we ran away some little distance, where we stopped to talk over this strange proceeding. We wondered whether we had better go back again to see what the white people really wanted. They had offered us candy—and that was a big temptation. So we went back and peeped in at the window again. This time the interpreter came to the door and coaxed us inside. He was a half-breed named Charles Tackett. We called him Ikubansuka, or Long Chin. We came inside very slowly, a step at a time, all the time wondering what it meant.[1]

From Long Chin, Plenty Kill learned that the whites had come to collect children for a school in the East (the man in charge of the white party was Captain Pratt, recruiting his first volunteers for Carlisle). If Plenty Kill wanted to go to the white man's school, Long Chin explained, he must bring his father, Standing Bear, to the agency to enter his son's name in the ledger. Plenty Kill was both suspicious and intrigued with the proposal. After giving the matter some thought, however, he decided he wanted to go with the captain. As for his reasons, he later recalled:

> When I had reached young manhood the warpath for the Lakota was a thing of the past. The hunter had disappeared with the buffalo, the war scout had lost his calling, and the warrior had taken his shield to the mountain-top and given it back to the elements. The victory songs were sung only in the memory of the braves. So I could not prove that I was a brave and would fight to protect my home and land. I could only meet the challenge as life's events came to me. When I went East to Carlisle School, I thought I was going there to die; . . . I could think of white people wanting little Lakota children for no other reason than to kill them, but I thought here is my chance to prove that I can die bravely. So I went East to show my father and my people that I was brave and willing to die for them.[2]

The next day, Plenty Kill, the other recruits, and a number of parents left for the Missouri, where the final parting would take place as the children boarded a steamer to take them south. The final farewell was emotional. The children had no sooner boarded the steamer than both parents and children began to sob. "It was a sad scene," Plenty Kill recalls. "I did not see my father or stepmother cry, so I did not shed any tears. I just stood over in a corner of the room we were in and watched the others all crying as if their hearts would break."[3]

The next day, the steamer pulled into shore whereupon the recruits were directed to a "long row of little houses standing on long pieces of iron which stretched away as far as we could see." Each house had a little stairway. Instructed to climb up into the "little houses," the Indians found them to be lined with cushioned seats.

> I took one of these seats, but presently changed to another. I must have changed my seat four or five times before I quieted down. We admired the beautiful room and the soft seats very much. While we were discussing the situation, suddenly the whole house started to move away with us. We boys were in one house and the girls in another. We expected something terrible would happen. We held our blankets between our teeth, because our hands were both busy hanging to the seats, so frightened were we.

As the locomotive picked up speed, Plenty Kill noticed the line of telegraph poles passing by. "It seemed to me that the poles almost hit the windows, so I changed my seat to the other side."[4]

When the train pulled into Sioux City, Iowa, the Indians were informed that they would be taken from the train to one of the city's restaurants. Not knowing what to expect, some of the older boys placed feathers in their hair and painted their faces. Just three years after the Custer debacle, this act further excited a crowd of spectators who were on hand to see firsthand the sons and daughters of Sitting Bull's Sioux. Indeed, as Pratt ushered the Indians through the mob of onlookers, they heard frightening imitations of the Sioux war whoop. "We did not like this," recalls Plenty Kill, "and some of the children were naturally very much frightened. I remember how I tried to crowd into the protecting midst of the jostling boys and girls." Once in the restaurant, the Indians noticed a crowd of whites pressing their faces against the window. Too upset to eat, the Indians scooped up the food in their blankets and took it back to the train.[5]

By the next day, the "iron road" had taken them as far as "Smoky City," or Chicago. "Here we saw so many people and such big houses that we began to open our eyes in astonishment. The big boys said, 'The white people are like ants; they are all over—everywhere.' " Since the layover in Chicago was a long one, the Indians were placed in a large waiting room where they entertained themselves by dancing. Back on the train, "the big boys began to tell us little fellows that the white people were taking us to the place where the sun rises, where they would dump us over the edge of the earth, as we had been taught that the earth was flat, with four corners, and when we came to the edge, we would fall over." On the second night out of Chicago the anxiety was at fever pitch.

> Now the full moon was rising, and we were traveling toward it. The big boys were singing brave songs, expecting to be killed any minute. We all looked at the moon, and it was in front of us, but we felt that we were getting too close to it for comfort. We were very tired, and the little fellows dozed off. Presently the big boys woke everybody. They said they had made a discovery. We were told to look out the window and see what had happened while we were dozing. We did so, and the moon was now behind us! Apparently we had passed the place where the moon rose![6]

After a journey of several days, the train finally arrived at Carlisle, Pennsylvania. A two-mile walk brought the travel-weary recruits to the great gate that served as the entrance to the Carlisle barracks. Plenty Kill would later lay claim to a very special distinction: "I was the first Indian boy to step inside the Carlisle Indian school grounds."[7]

Such is Plenty Kill's remembrance. It is, of course, just one story. How others experienced the journey depended on several factors. Younger children, for instance, must have felt the pain of being separated from family and community more severely than older ones. Those coerced into attending school were surely more bitter than those who went voluntarily and with their parents' blessing. Children who had attended a day school, which constituted a sort of intermediate introduction to white schooling, must have found it easier than those taken directly from the camp. Moreover, it must have been much more difficult for the first generation of children, who had no idea of what lay ahead, than it was for later recruits, who had the benefit of learning from returned students what to expect. Finally, because different tribes had been exposed to white ways with varying intensity, it stands to reason that those children coming from cultures where there had been sustained contact with whites would find both the idea and necessity of schooling more comprehensible than those to whom the school was the first taste of white civilization.

But regardless of these differing circumstances, leaving for boarding school was almost always a painful affair, as evidenced by an account left by Hoke Denetsosie, a Navajo, who, at the age of six, was carted off to a reservation boarding school in 1926. In this instance the departure occurred after an all-night ceremony of ritualistic praying and singing, an apparent effort by parents to protect their children against any evil that might lie ahead.

Early in the morning, after we had eaten, the police assembled us near . . . two old black Model "T" Fords. They started to warm up the cars, and the machines just shook all over. Altogether there were 14 boys and girls, all taller than I was. Some of the parents gathered around talking to their kids. Some were weeping. There was a wave of sadness all around. All of us wore our hair long, tied into bundles behind our necks. Just before we climbed into the cars some of the girls' parents got shears, and cut off the hair bundles and kept them. As we moved out everyone wept again, and we all waved good-bye; then we were on our way.[8]

The Assault on Cultural Identity

From the policymakers' point of view, the civilization process required a twofold assault on Indian children's identity. On the one hand, the school needed to strip away all outward signs of the children's identification with tribal life, that is to say, their savage ways. On the other, the children needed to be instructed in the ideas, values, and behaviors of white civilization. These processes— the tearing down of the old selves and the building of new ones—could, of course, be carried out simultaneously. As the savage selves gave way, so the civilized selves would emerge. As a "total institution," the boarding school was designed to systematically carry out this mission.[9]

For boys the stripping away process began when the school sheared off their long hair. Shortly after arriving at Carlisle, Luther Standing Bear noticed "some white men come inside the school grounds carrying big chairs." The interpreter informed the boys that the men had come to cut their hair. While sitting in class Standing Bear noticed that one by one the boys were being quietly removed: first, Ya Slo; then, Whistler. Each returned looking strange in his short hair. When it came to Standing Bear's turn, he comments that "it hurt my feelings to such an extent that the tears came into my eyes." All the short-cropped Sioux boys felt strange. "We still had our Indian clothes, but were all 'bald-headed.' None of us slept well that night; we felt so queer. I wanted to feel my head all the time."[10]

The short-hair policy was rooted in two considerations. First, it made it easier to control the problem of head lice. Head lice were by no means universal among recruits, but a general policy of short hair made dealing with the problem much simpler. Frank Mitchell, a Navajo, recalls that after bathing and having his hair cut, a "blue ointment" was immediately applied "to kill the bugs." After this, "they checked our heads every now and then and would give us treatments. They kept us clean by bathing us every so often. And of course, finally, they got rid of all of those scabs and sores."[11]

But the reason for short haircuts went deeper than cleanliness. At the heart of the policy was the belief that the children's long hair was symbolic of savagism; removing it was central to the new identification with civilization. It is interesting that Standing Bear rejects the idea that cleanliness was the primary reason for the short-hair policy: "The fact is that we were to be transformed, and short hair being the mark of gentility with the white man, he put upon us the mark." This motivation can clearly be seen in an incident recalled in a letter from S. M. McCowan to a former student at Fort Mohave Boarding School. McCowan, who had been superintendent of the institution, recalled:

I can remember when I first took you into the Ft. Mojave school and what a time I had in cutting your hair for the first time. I can see now all the old Mojave women standing around crying, while you covered your long hair with your arms and told me that I wouldn't dare to cut that hair off, but the hair was cut in spite of all your efforts and the direful predictions of the Mojave women. I compelled you to have your hair cut off, not because of any objections to the long hair in itself, but merely because the long hair was a symbol of savagery.[12]

The haircutting exercise, in addition to being a traumatic experience, could also spark deep resentment and occasionally even resistance. Commissioner Morgan made note of this fact after witnessing a haircutting session involving Hopi boys. "The boys had beautiful, glossy, black, long straight hair," reports Morgan, "but unfortunately it did not bear close examination, and when they had submitted their hair to the scissors and their locks were thrown into the fire there was, . . . a great destruction of the innocents." Morgan went on to confess that a number of school super-intendents were having difficulty keeping older boys in school, in part because of their aversion to losing their hair.[13]

Perhaps the most serious rebellion occurred at the opening of Pine Ridge Boarding School. Anticipating that the Sioux would not take kindly to having their braids cut off, the plan of operation was for each child to be called individually into a room where a teacher and a matron, supplied with a pair of scissors, would carry out the hair removal beyond the view of the anxious onlookers who were outside pressing against shade-drawn windows. But just as the first child was seated, a breeze swept aside the window shades, revealing the horrible sight of the matron about to slice off a long braid. According to one account:

> Like a war whoop rang out the cry: "*Pahin Kaksa, Pahin Kaksa!*" The enclosure rang with alarm, it invaded every room in the building and floated out on the prairie. No warning of fire or flood or tornado or hurricane, not even the approach of an enemy could have more effectively emptied the building as well as the grounds of the new school as did the ominous cry. "They are cutting the hair!" Through doors and windows the children flew, down the steps, through the gates and over fences in a mad flight toward the Indian villages, followed by the mob of bucks and squaws as though all were pursued by a bad spirit. They had been suspicious of the school from the beginning; now they knew it was intended to bring disgrace upon them.[14]

According to Luther Standing Bear, a revolt against Pratt's haircutting order by Carlisle's first recruits nearly occurred as well. On the evening after the boys were informed that their hair must be cut, they held a secret "council." Standing Bear remembers Robert American Horse proclaiming, "If I am to learn the ways of the white people, I can do it just as well with my hair on." Almost to a person, the assembled boys shouted "Hau," signifying their agreement. But this resolve weakened the next day as, one by one, they were summoned to the barber's chair. The question remained whether any of the boys would actually make a stand.[15]

Pratt knew nothing about any of this. Instead, thinking that all was going smoothly with the barbers, he left for a scheduled trip to Indian Territory, leaving the school under Mrs. Pratt's charge. It was after his departure that one of the older boys steadfastly refused to have his braids removed. Wishing to avoid an incident, Mrs. Pratt sent the barbers away, declaring that the fate of the one holdout would be resolved upon her husband's return. Late that night, however, Mrs. Pratt and the white staff were awakened suddenly by a general commotion. The long-haired recalcitrant had undergone a change of heart. Securing a knife, he had walked out on the parade ground to publicly cut off his braids. Since by Sioux tradition the cutting off of hair was always associated with mourning, the boy's dramatic act spontaneously evoked a characteristic response from those in the barracks. Boys and girls alike now filled the night air with a shrill wailing that was both eerie and not a little unsettling to the staff. Mrs. Pratt feared that the nearby residents of Carlisle might be aroused, provoking even a worse situation. Finally, however, order was restored.[16]

The second step in the civilization process called for changing the students' dress. It made little difference whether students arrived wearing elegant buckskin or threadbare trade blankets; shortly after their arrival, their traditional clothing was exchanged for the standard school uniform. Indian service regulations held that each boy should be provided with two plain suits, with an extra pair of trousers, and each girl with three dresses. In some instances, boys also received a Sunday suit of better quality. The annual clothing ration also included the necessary underwear, nightclothes, and finally, boots.[17]

In spite of such standards, considerable variability in the quality of clothing existed among schools. Generally speaking, students at off-reservation schools were better provided for, in part because such schools were showcases for the government's Indian policy. Another factor was that these schools possessed large sewing and tailoring classes, where capable students were expected to turn out sufficient uniforms and dresses to meet the school's needs. A number of schools—Carlisle, Haskell, Genoa, Phoenix, and others—were well-known for their handsome and smart-looking dress. At Carlisle, for instance, the shoulders of the boys' dark blue uniforms were decorated with red braid, with student officers sporting red stripes as well. Carlisle girls, meanwhile, had their dark blue cloaks lined in bright red. In 1893, the superintendent of the boarding school at Albuquerque reported that since the Indian girls had recently taken to comparing their own dress with the pervading style of white girls, they had been allowed to adorn their school dresses with a few ruffles and a bit of lace. This change, it was noted, had "made a vast difference in the general feeling among the girls, who are much more willing and cheerful."[18]

The situation was decidely different at remote reservation schools. Students often had to make do with tattered clothes, oversized boots, and beaten hats, while an overworked seamstress patched, mended, and prayed daily for a new clothing allotment. "Wearing mended clothes may implant habits of economy and be of some practical value," one agent complained in 1897, "but the wearing of crownless, brimless, and otherwise illshapen hats, and the continued wear of boots and shoes long after they have served their purpose, lessens the wearer's self-respect, lowers the school in his estimation, and in short, creates a formidable barrier to the attainment of the end and aim of education." Sometimes, students gave up a finer quality of clothing than what they received in return. One Hopi boy, for instance, recalls being separated from a "beautiful new blanket with colored stripes" that his grandfather had specially woven for him in exchange for the standard school issue—in this case, a blue shirt, mustard-colored pants, and heavy shoes. As for the fate of the blanket, "I saw it later, in the possession of the wife of the superintendent."[19]

Students reacted differently to this aspect of their transformation. According to one school official: "A school uniform is a great cross to Indian pupils. One Indian never likes to appear like any other." Besides going against the grain of Indian youngsters' individuality, some articles of white clothing were resented simply because they were uncomfortable. Stiff boots and woolen underwear were clearly in this class. And of course many students must have seen the emphasis on uniform dress for what it was: yet another aspect of the school's design to turn Indians into carbon copies of their white overseers. Still, it appears that this aspect of the transformation process was less traumatic than the haircutting policy. Indeed, some appear to have experienced a certain excitement in dressing up like whites, even though, as we see below, the occasion was sometimes marked by a good deal of confusion.

How proud we were with clothes that had pockets and boots that squeaked! We walked the floor nearly all that night. Many of the boys even went to bed with their clothes all on. But in the morning, the boys who had taken off their pants had a most terrible time. They did not know whether they were to button up in front or behind. Some of the boys said the open part went in front; others said, 'No, it goes at the back.' There is where the boys who had kept all their clothes on came in handy to look at. They showed the others that the pants buttoned up in front and not at the back. So here we learned something again.[20]

Yet another assault on tribal identity came in the form of new names. The policy of renaming students was motivated by several concerns. First, many students arrived at school with names the teachers could neither pronounce nor memorize. Most teachers had little patience with such names as Ain-dus-gwon, John Sang-way-way, Wah-sah-yah, Min-o-ke-shig, and Mah-je-ke-shig. As one Indian Office official observed at a national educational conference, "a teacher would be at a disadvantage in trying to be either affectionate or disciplinary with an eight-syllabled girl like Sah-gah-ge-way-gah-bow-e-quay." Second, some students had names that, once translated, were perceived to be ridiculous and occasionally humiliating—such as Mary Swollen Face, Nancy Kills-a-Hundred, Sam Slow-Fly, John Bad-Gum, Ada Parts-His-Hair, and Lizzie-Looks-Twice.[21]

Finally, renaming students was part of a conscious government policy to give Indians surnames. As Indians became property owners and thoroughly imbued with the values of possessive individualism, it would be virtually impossible to fix lines of inheritance if, for example, the son of Red Hawk went by the name Spotted Horse. "When Indians become citizens of the United States under the allotment act," Commissioner Morgan informed agents and school superintendents, "the inheritance of property will be governed by the laws of the respective states, and it will cause needless confusion and, doubtless, considerable ultimate loss to the Indians if no attempt is made to have the different members of a family known by the same family name on the records and by general reputation." For this reason, Indian Office employees in the field were instructed to move forward with the renaming process. The work proceeded slowly, and although most of the responsibility fell to the Indian agent, school officials also played a vital role, particularly in the early years.[22]

The renaming process followed several patterns. One pattern was to use the original untranslated Indian name, although sometimes in shortened form, as a surname. When practical, this was the preferred policy of the Indian Office. In a circular issued in 1890, Commissioner Morgan admitted that in many instances "the Indian name is difficult to pronounce and to remember," but then went on to say that "in many other cases the Indian word is as short and as euphonious as the English word that is substituted." Fourteen years later, an Indian Office official reiterated the point by saying: "Let the Indian keep both his personal and race identity . . . for the sake of his property it is necessary that he adopt our system of family names, but that is no reason why we should ruthlessly thrust upon him our English names when his own will answer just as well, even better. We want to educate the Indian—lead him on, not stamp him out."[23] By this liberal policy, if it may be termed as such, a Kiowa man with the name of Richard Sitahpetale or a Navajo woman called Ruth Chesehesbega could make their way in civilized society as easily as a Richard Smith or a Ruth Miller.

Another pattern was to use the translated Indian name as a surname. Under this system a Robert Redhawk or a William Swiftriver would do nicely. But such translations were not always workable. As noted earlier, some Indian names, once translated, appeared to be ridiculous and even uncouth, others were too long, and many simply could not be translated without losing their original meaning. As Alice Fletcher pointed out, the translated Dakota name Young-Man-Afraid-of-His-Horses conveyed little of the meaning behind the original, which actually meant "the young man whose valor is such that even the sight of his horses brings fear to his enemies." In such instances, if the Dakota original was short and pronounceable, it would be retained. Otherwise, it would be abandoned.[24]

A third pattern was to give children completely new names. At this point, agents and superintendents were presented with several options. One approach, recommended by John Wesley Powell, was to select from the tribal vocabulary names for geographical forms and animal life with which Indians could readily identify. For instance, the Sioux word for "roan horse" might be received with greater enthusiasm than Miller or Erickson. Another option was simply to randomly bestow common American names such as Smith, Brown, and Clark. Still another method, and one practiced for many years with conscious intent, was to rename students after famous historical figures. Harriet Patrick Gilstrap tells us that when her father, the agent at Sac and Fox Agency, gave the Indians new names, "first came the names of the presidents, then the vice-presidents, then prominent people of the day."[25]

But the Indian Office increasingly frowned on such ridiculous changes, and some schools made a conscious effort to retain at least a modicum of the Indian name. Thus, Hampton Institute was critical of the fact that two of its new transfer students had arrived with the names Julius Caesar and Henry Ward Beecher. Such names were nonsensical, declared the *Southern Workman*. A more humane approach was the Hampton method. When a boy arrived at the school with the name Hehakaavita (Yellow Elk), an inquiry about the boy's father's name evoked the response "Good Wood." Hence, the boy's new name became Thomas Goodwood. On another occasion, the son of an old chief, Medicine Bull, was given the new name of Samuel M. Bull. Such alterations, Hampton held, met the necessity of assigning a new name yet recognized the individuality, if not the heritage, of the student. Besides, renaming alone would not civilize savages: "Old Sitting Bull would be nonetheless a savage were he to take to himself the most honorable name we know . . . George S. Bull Washington."[26]

Whatever process superintendents used in bestowing new names, the fact remains that it constituted a grave assault on Indian identity. This is true for two reasons. First, as George A. Pettit has made clear in his landmark study *Primitive Education in North America*, traditional Indian names and the naming process itself were fundamentally connected to the process of cultural transmission and served a variety of educational purposes: as a stimulus to self-improvement, as a reward for a special achievement, and finally, as a means of transferring the traits of a revered relative or tribal figure to a member of a new generation. Because some Indian youth were sometimes given a series of names in the course of their development, and since the giving of names was frequently ritualized in elaborate ceremony, tribal naming practices were clearly central to the perpetuation of cultural outlook.[27] Second, as already discussed, a major justification for changing names was the argument that assigning surnames was an essential step in transforming Indians into self-reliant property owners. Thus, the renaming process was pregnant with cultural significance.

It is difficult to judge how students actually experienced the renaming process or what meanings they ascribed to it, but three instances from Carlisle are suggestive. Luther Standing Bear recalls that after a few days at Carlisle the interpreter announced: "Do you see all these marks on the blackboard? Well, each word is a white man's name. They are going to give each one of you one of these names by which you will hereafter be known." The first boy stepped forward and with a long pointer touched one of the names, which was written on a piece of tape and attached to the back of his shirt.

> When my turn came, I took the pointer and acted as if I were about to touch an enemy. Soon we all had the names of white men sewed on our backs. When we went to school, we knew enough to take our proper places in the class, but that was all. When the teacher called the roll, no one answered his name. Then she would walk around and look at the back of the boys' shirts. When she had the right name located, she made the boy stand up and say "Present." She kept this up for about a week before we knew what the sound of our new names was.[28]

Another boy at Carlisle was given the name "Conrad."

Dear Captain Pratt:

I am going to tell you something about my name. Captain Pratt, I would like to have a new name because some of the girls call me Cornbread and some call me Cornrat, so I do not like that name, so I want you to give me a new name. Now this is all I want to say.   Conrad[29]

Jason Betzinez, an Apache youth from Geronimo's band, was more fortunate. Shortly after arriving at Carlisle,

Miss Low selected for me the name of Jason. She said that Jason was some man who hunted the golden fleece but never found it. I thought that was too bad but it didn't mean anything to me at that time so I accepted the name. In the intervening years I believe that the story of Jason and his search for the golden fleece has set a pattern for my life.[30]

In this instance the name "Jason" served the same instructional function that many tribal names had served in traditional Indian life; it gave meaning and guidance to his life. The object of Betzinez's search and that of the famous mythological figure were, of course, altogether different. The Jason of Greek lore sought the golden fleece; Jason, an Apache thrown into the strange world of the white man, would seek something far more precious, his very identity. Still, the Carlisle Apache's new name could serve as a metaphor for his life, and for that matter, for countless other Indians as well.

Adjustments to New Surroundings

Meanwhile, students were adjusting to their new physical surroundings. Since the overriding purpose of the boarding school was to bring about the student's civilization, it logically followed that the physical environment should approximate a civilized atmosphere as closely as possible. At the very least, physical facilities should be of firm structure, should be large enough to house the students enrolled, and should reflect a mindful consideration for sanitation and hygiene. This was the ideal. Unfortunately, it was not always achieved. In 1882, Indian Commissioner Price lectured Congress: "Children who shiver in rooms ceiled with canvas, who dodge the muddy drops trickling throughout worn-out dirt roofs, who are crowded in ill-ventilated dormitories, who recite in a single school-room, three classes at a time, and who have no suitable sitting-rooms nor bath-rooms, are not likely to be attracted to or make rapid advancement in education and civilization." According to Price, the Indian Bureau was currently forced to use facilities "which long ago should have been condemned as unserveable and even unsafe."[31]

In the next decade living conditions improved markedly, especially at off-reservation schools. Touring several schools in 1892, Special Indian Agent Merial A. Dorchester found that the best ones provided each girl with a single bed, washstand, towel, bowl and pitcher, and brush and comb. Some dormitories had sliding curtains between the beds, "making a retired place for each girl, which helps her on the line of modesty." Others were divided into small rooms where the girls "are taught how to arrange and beautify them in a pretty and hygienic manner." Superintendent of Indian Schools William Hailmann also stressed the progress being made when he addressed the Lake Mohonk Conference in 1897. In school after school, he explained, the kerosene lamp was giving way to the electric light, the wood stove to steam heat, the bathtub to the "needle bath." At remote reservation schools, however, such renovations were slow in coming. Just a year after Hailmann's optimistic assessment, Commissioner William Jones admitted that too many schools suffered from a "deplorable deficiency" in providing Indian youth with acceptable living facilities.[32]

Adjusting to a new physical environment also meant adjusting to new conceptions of space and architecture.[33] The boarding school, the new recruits quickly learned, was a world of lines, corners, and squares. Rectangular dormitories and dining rooms and square classrooms were filled with beds, tables, and desks—all carefully arranged in straight rows. Whites, Indians surmised, largely conceived of space in linear terms. This was no mean observation, especially for students who came from cultures where definitions of space and the meanings assigned to it were radically different. For Lakota students, for instance, the essential touchstones of cultural reality—the sky, the sun, the moon, the tepee, the sundance lodge, and the "sacred hoop"—were all circular phenomena. Thus, an old Lakota, Black Elk, would tell John Neihardt in 1931: "You will notice that everything the Indian does is in a circle. Everything that they do is the power from the sacred hoop." But now, Black Elk would lament, his people were living in houses. "It is a square. It is not the way we should live. . . . Everything is now too square. The sacred hoop is vanishing among the people. . . . We are vanishing in this box."[34] Although the circle held less symbolic significance in other cultures than it did for the Sioux, the larger point should not be missed: conceptions of space are not neutral.

The same could be said for the layout of school grounds. "Our sense of place—of space—is largely determined by the manner in which we see ourselves in relation to nature," writes Jamake Highwater. In the landscaping of school grounds, Indian students received another lesson on white civilization's attitude toward space and nature. In his annual report in 1898, Commissioner William Jones informed superintendents that in order to impress upon the minds of Indian youths a new conception of "order," "system," and "the beautiful," they should attempt to reconstruct "unsightly banks and rugged hillsides so as to make them more pleasing to the eye." Elsewhere, superintendents were instructed, "The grounds around the buildings must receive proper attention, insofar that agreeable designs in landscaping be improvised, diversified with flowers, shrubs, and trees and swarded areas, producing pleasing and attractive surroundings." In other words, weeds, cactus, and earth must give way to manicured lawns, pruned trees, and contoured gardens. The lesson in all this was clear: nature existed to serve man's ends. In the interest of symmetry and order, the wild must be tamed, just as the Indian must be civilized.[35]

Adjusting to the white man's food—and the lack of it—was another challenge. According to official policy as stated in 1890, "Good and healthful provisions must be supplied in abundance; and they must be well cooked and properly placed on the table." Moreover, schools were urged to offer a varied menu and to use the school farm and dairy to furnish the necessary amount of fruits, vegetables, and dairy products. Although coffee and tea could be served on occasion, milk was deemed preferable. In those instances where school farms produced great amounts of fresh produce and where dairy, stock raising, and poultry departments were going concerns, the stipulated standards were met. One Navajo boy who attended the school at Fort Defiance recalls: "When I entered school there was plenty to eat there, more food than I used to get at home. . . . So I was happy about that; I was willing to go to school if they were going to feed me like that."[36]

But most would remember this aspect of boarding school life with considerable bitterness. Sometimes this displeasure stemmed from being forced to abandon traditional foods for those of the white man. Others complained about the way the food was cooked. Perhaps the most serious complaint was that they left the table half-starved. A Klamath Indian, who was detailed as a meat cutter at his boarding school, recalls that the best cuts went to the employees, while the children got only the necks and ribs. He remembers, "I learned to steal at school to keep from going hungry." [. . .]

As students soon learned, they were not only expected to eat new foods but to eat them in a special manner. In short, they must acquire the food rites of civilized society. Enter the world of knives, forks, spoons, tablecloths, and napkins. In the finer schools, tin plates and cups would eventually give way to glassware and white china. Thus equipped, the school dining room became a classroom for instructing Indians in the rudiments of middle-class table manners. Frank Mitchell recalls:

> One of the problems we faced . . . was that we did not know how to eat at a table. We had to be told how to use the knife, fork and spoons. And when we started eating, we were so used to eating with our fingers that we wanted to do it that way at school, and we had to be taught. Although we had things there to eat with, like a fork, we had never used them at home, so we did not know what they were or how to use them; so we always wanted to stick our fingers in our food. Of course, it took some time before we got used to how we were to conduct ourselves with these different things.[37]

Food not only had to be eaten in a certain manner but it had to be eaten at precise intervals in the day, which typified another distinctive feature of boarding school life—the relentless regimentation. As every new recruit soon discovered, nearly every aspect of his day-to-day existence—eating, sleeping, working, learning, praying—would be rigidly scheduled, the hours of the day intermittently punctuated by a seemingly endless number of bugles and bells demanding this or that response. As one school official observed, the Indian "knew he was coming to a land of laws, but his imagination could never conceive of such a multiplicity of rules as he now finds thrown about them; bells seem to be ringing all the time, and the best he can do is to follow his friendly leader." [. . .]

Why were schools organized like military training camps? Part of the answer lies in the sheer organizational problems created by having to house, feed, teach, and, most significantly, control several hundred "uncivilized" youths. Good health, neatness, politeness, the ability to concentrate, self-confidence, and patriotism were also attributed to military regimen. The superintendent of Haskell even reported in 1886 that by organizing the school into a battalion of five companies, he had managed to break up persisting tribal associations; forcing students to sleep in dormitories and to sit in the mess hall by their assigned companies required them to converse in English.[38]

But there were deeper reasons for the military atmosphere, reasons related to policymakers' perceptions of the "wildness" of Indian children. Indian children, it was argued, were products of cultures almost entirely devoid of order, discipline, and self-constraint, all prized values in white civilization. It was a well-known fact, according to Commissioner Morgan, that Indian parents "generally exercise very little control over their children and allow them the utmost freedom." Part of the problem, policymakers surmised, stemmed from Indians' unfamiliarity with the white man's clock and, once exposed to it, their general disdain for it. From a less ethnocentric perspective, anthropologist Bernard Fontana has made a similar observation, namely, that Indian and white societies have historically subscribed to different conceptions of time. Whereas white society has increasingly become governed by "clock time," Indians have traditionally been oriented to "natural time." "In devising a mechanical means of arbitrarily segmenting the day into regularly spaced units," writes Fontana, white society has "made an artifact of time. . . . Our notion of time and our methods of time-keeping are the very underpinnings of our entire industrial system." Indians, on the other hand, have traditionally lived out their lives in accordance with natural phenomena. Fontana makes an important point. The cultural and psychological distance separating the two orientations was immense, as this Arapaho remembrance makes clear:

> It was a long time before we knew what the figures on the face of a clock meant, or why people looked at them before they ate their meals or started off to church. We had to learn that clocks had something to

do with the hours and minutes that the white people mentioned so often. Hours, minutes, and seconds were such small divisions of time that we had never thought of them. When the sun rose, when it was high in the sky, and when it set were all the divisions of the day that we had ever found necessary when we followed the old Arapaho road. When we went on the hunting trip or to a sun dance, we counted time by sleeps.[39]

Until the students' concept of natural time was supplanted by that of clock time, school authorities reasoned, it would be next to impossible to develop in them an appreciation for the importance of promptness and punctuality, key values in civilized life. "Make the most of time," one school newspaper exhorted. "You have no right to waste your own time; still less, then, the time of others. Be punctual in the performance of all your duties." By constantly marching and drilling, the clocklike, mechanical movements on the drill field would hopefully carry over to other areas of student behavior. As students internalized the measured units of the clock, so too would they come to discipline and regulate their bodies and lives. "Be punctual to the minute. Even a little beforehand is preferable to being behind time. Such a habit . . . no doubt will mean a great deal to you in the after life"—that is, life after boarding school.[40] [. . .]

Students entered boarding school with vastly different religious backgrounds. Some came already converted to Christianity. In this regard, schools were reaping the harvest of missionary efforts across Indian country. Thus, shortly after a group of Dakota children arrived at Hampton in 1879, they sang for the student body "Nearer My God to Thee," although in a language unrecognizable to all but a few.

> Mita Wakantanka,
> Nikiyedan,
> Kakix mayanpi xta,
> He taku ani;
> Nici waun wacin,
> Mita Wakantanka,
> Nikiyedan.

"My thoughts went to and fro," reported one observer of the scene, "and when I looked at their beaming faces and knew that they understood the words they were singing, for they sang in their own language, I felt that they were nearer to Him at that hour."[41]

Most, however, came from cultures still permeated by a traditional religious outlook. What were the common denominators of this worldview?[42] First, traditional Indian cultures were so thoroughly infused with the spiritual that native languages generally had no single word to denote the concept of religion. It would have been incomprehensible to isolate religion as a separate sphere of cultural existence. For the Kiowa, Hopi, or Lakota, religion explained the cosmological order, defined reality, and penetrated all areas of tribal life—kinship relations, subsistence activities, child raising, even artistic and architectural expression. The theistic structures of native religions differed greatly. Some religious systems were polytheistic, but others, as Joseph Epes Brown observes, represented "a form of theism wherein concepts of monotheism and polytheism intermingle and fuse without being confused." Thus, the Lakota universe, to cite just one example, was populated by a pantheon of gods, spirits, and personalities, but pervading all was *Wakan-Tanka*, or the "Great Mysterious." Hence, Brown quotes Black Elk, "Wakan-Tanka, you are everything, and yet above everything." The spirit world pervaded all.[43]

A second theme was man's fundamental interrelatedness with nature. Unlike Christianity where God and man stood apart—really above—nature, Indians lived in ecological harmony with their environment, approached it with reverential humility, and ultimately, ascribed to it a spiritual significance unknown to European-Americans. According to the Indian worldview, all creatures—the buffalo, the eagle, the spider—and the inanimate world as well, possessed their own unique soul or spiritual essence. In such a world nature was filled with spiritual lessons, to be read and interpreted just as the white man read his Jesus book. Nature, moreover, was not something to be objectified and conquered, nor to be seen as merely a source of sustenance and shelter; it was, rather, a profound source of spiritual awareness from whence man could reaffirm his elemental relationship with all living things.[44]

A third characteristic was the richness and variety of religious expression. On one level this manifested itself in elaborate tribal ceremonies—the sun dance of the Plains peoples, the kachina dances of the Pueblo, the Midewiwin of the Objibwa, the chantways of the Navajo, to name just a few. Added to these are the culturally prescribed provisions for individual religious expression. Particularly noteworthy in this regard are the role of dreams and the almost ubiquitous vision quest. In the latter instance the supplicant sought direct communication with the supernatural, which might appear in the form of a hawk, a fox, an ant, or perhaps a "thundering being." The knowledge and power gained from such an experience often shaped the entire life course and personality of the vision seeker. Also, most cultures singled out those significant transitions in the life cycle—birth, puberty, marriage, and death—for public ceremonial recognition although, again, the manner of expression differed greatly from one culture to another. Finally, each religious system possessed its own songs, dances, myths, and ritual dramas.[45]

Fourth, and by way of comparison to Christianity, Native American religions tended not to conceive of personal morality or ethics as the special domain of religion. Although it is true that all cultures certainly knew of "evil" and possessed their own definition of proper social behavior, the social regulation of interpersonal behavior had its source in the larger social fabric of tribal existence. This, of course, was in direct contradiction to Christianity, which, from the Indians' perspective, seemed preoccupied with "sin" and provided a biblical prescription for nearly all aspects of social relations. It was for this reason that Indians who had converted to Christianity soon discovered they had embraced not only a new God but an entirely new way of life. An extension of the morality issue was the whites' conception of heaven as the exclusive destiny of the righteous, as compared with the Indians' view of the afterlife, which was rarely as restrictive. What Henry Warner Bowden says of northeastern cultures applies to Indians generally: "They thought the gods would punish sacrilegious acts almost immediately, just as socially destructive behavior met with swift communal justice. But they assumed that everyone would eventually reside in the same place after death."[46]

If Christianity and traditionalism were the polar extremes of Indian religious belief, by the turn of the century other forms of religious expression had come upon the scene. By the 1880s, for instance, some tribes in the Northwest were converting to Shakerism, which took its name from the fact that its followers frequently achieved a trembling, trancelike state in the course of praying, singing, and dancing—in all, a ritualized synthesis of white and native religious expression. An even more powerful movement was the rapid spread of the so-called peyote religion, later designated the Native American Church. The most sensational aspect of this new faith involved chewing peyote buttons, which produced powerful and transcendent visions wherein the worshiper achieved an enhanced sense of self, power, and spiritual consciousness. Beyond this, the new religion proved to be a highly flexible configuration of native and Christian traditions: core elements included the worship of a supreme being (the "Great Spirit" or God); the belief in both white and Indian spirits (angels, the devil, the thunderbird), the fusion of Christian ethics with native values, and the blending of native and Christian ritualistic practices. Finally, discussion must include the brief but ill-fated ghost dance religion that swept across the Central and High Plains in the late 1880s, culminating in the tragic episode at Wounded Knee in December 1890. Given the brevity of the movement, its long-term influence on Indian youth is questionable. Still, some students home for the summer surely observed relatives swept up in the fervor of the moment, observed the dancing and ritualized trances, and heard firsthand accounts from dancers who told of seeing the utopian world to come, a world without whites, where Indians would be reunited with fallen warriors and the prairies once again would be teeming with bison.[47]

[. . .]

It was in this context that boarding school superintendents waged an aggressive campaign of Christianization. By the 1890s Indian Office rules stipulated, "Pupils of Government schools shall be encouraged to attend the churches and Sunday-schools of their respective denominations." Even though local churches were encouraged to open their doors to Indian students, schools also were expected to develop a systematic program of religious instruction. A typical week's activities included Sunday morning, afternoon, and evening services, daily morning and evening prayers, and a special Wednesday evening prayer meeting. [. . .]

An inordinate amount of time was spent on moral training. In the eyes of educators, Indian children were products of cultures that placed little emphasis on "virtue," at least as it was understood in the context of Christian ethics. In the words of one Indian agent, "The Indians are simple children of nature, and many things condemned as immoral among whites are with them without offense."[48] In particular, Indian children needed to be taught the moral ideals of charity, chastity, monogamy, respect for the Sabbath, temperance, honesty, self-sacrifice, the importance of pure thoughts and speech—indeed, an almost endless array of personal characteristics important to the formation of "character."

Fundamental to this aim was implanting the idea of sin and a corresponding sense of guilt. [. . .]

The evidence about student's reaction to conversion efforts is sketchy at best. But most students, like Helen Sekaquaptewa, probably went through the motions, kept their counsel, and endured the hours of preaching and praying as best they could.

> I remember one preacher especially, although they were all about the same. I couldn't understand a thing he was talking about but had to sit and listen to a long sermon. I hated them and felt like crying. If I nodded my head going to sleep, a teacher would poke me and tell me to be good. It seemed as if this preacher would talk all night. He put a great deal of emotion into his sermons. He would work himself up to a climax talking loud and strong, and then calm down to a whisper, and I would think, "Now he is going to stop." But no, he would start all over again and go on and on.[49]

How many students simply rejected the school's conversion efforts outright? Again, the evidence is sketchy. Helen Sekaquaptewa relates that the various missionaries "were always urging and bribing us with little presents to join their church," and then goes on to say: "It didn't appeal to me and I didn't join any of them." Even more suggestive is a missionary newspaper's account of Pratt's effort at a school assembly to extract from students a public declaration of their religious inclinations. When asked how many were already Christian, thirty-four students stood. When asked how many were "trying" to become Christians, another seventy-two rose from their seats. Interestingly, this account was presented as evidence that the school's missionary program was rapidly winning converts. But it also provides an indication of the number who remained skeptical of the Christian message; the vast majority had remained seated.[50]

[. . .]

Parents' Opposition to Boarding Schools

The opposition of Indian parents to white schooling was both deeply felt and widespread. "The Indians have a prejudice against schools," the agent at Sac and Fox Agency reported in 1882, and another agent complained, "The Crows are bitterly opposed to sending their children to school and invent all kinds of excuses to get the children out or keep from sending them." Similarly, the Lemhi in Idaho were said to be "constantly at rebellion against civilizing elements," the school being a prime irritant. The problem, the agent lamented, was that the Indians in his charge had "not yet reached that state of civilization to know the advantages of education, and consequently look upon school work with abhorrence." Frustrated over recruitment problems, the superintendent of one school could only conclude that the average Indian had as much regard for education "as a horse does for the Constitution."[51]

When parents refused to enroll their children in school, agents normally resorted to either withholding rations or using the agency police. When one agent at Fort Peck met with resistance, he sent the police to round up the children, denied rations to the parents, and then, to drive the point home, locked several of the most intractable fathers in the agency guardhouse. In any event, the forced procurement of children was usually unpleasant business.[52] In 1886, the agent to the Mescalero Apache reported:

> Everything in the way of persuasion and argument having failed, it became necessary to visit the camps unexpectedly with a detachment of police, and seize such children as were proper and take them away to school, willing or unwilling. Some hurried their children off to the mountains or hid them away in camp, and the police had to chase and capture them like so many wild rabbits. This unusual proceeding created quite an outcry. The men were sullen and muttering, the women loud in their lamentations, and the children almost out of their wits with fright.[53]

Resistance to the annual fall roundup took a number of forms. Most dramatic were those instances when an entire village or tribal faction refused to turn over their children. Sometimes parents simply slipped away from the main camp for several weeks until the pressure for students had let up. Another response was to offer up orphans or children living on the fringe of extended kinship circles. Occasionally, resistance took the form of bargaining. This occurred on those reservations where the school-age population was in excess of dormitory space, thus allowing tribal leaders and agents to negotiate a family quota until the school was filled. In other instances, the whole matter was simply dropped in the lap of tribal policemen, who in turn might put the agonizing question to a mother—which child to give up, which to hold back? In his memoirs, Frank Mitchell readily admits that he was the first child to be given over because he was the "black sheep" of the family. Indeed, he argues that when Navajo policemen were looking for children, they consciously avoided taking the "prime." Rather, "they took those who were not so intelligent, those the People thought could be spared because of their physical conditions, and those who were not well taken care of."[54]

Even after children were enrolled, parents still found ways to oppose the school. In the face of a particularly obnoxious school policy, or in time of crisis, parents were known to withdraw their children en masse or to encourage runaways. Sending delegations to the agency, drawing up petitions to Washington, and catching the ear of an inspector were other methods of protest. From the Indian Office's point of view, the most insidious form of resistance was the conscious efforts of tribal elders to undermine the school's teachings during vacation periods by enculturating youth in the curriculum of traditional culture, a phenomenon that, it may be remembered, was one of the major reasons for policymakers' preference for off-reservation schools. And finally, after 1893 some parents took full advantage of their legal right to deny the transfer of older students to off-reservation institutions.

What prompted such resistance? In part, the answer lies in the distinction Edward Dozier makes between "forced" and "permissive" acculturation. "The forceful imposition of religion, ideologies and behavior patterns by the dominant society on a subordinate one appears to be met in every case with resistance and rejection," writes Dozier. On the other hand, when cultural interchange takes place free of compulsion in a "permissive contact situation," then "the resultant product is a new cultural whole where the cultural traits of both groups are fused harmoniously in both meaning and form."[55] To be sure, Dozier's distinction overstates the case; forced acculturation need not always result in resistance. Still, the argument is sound in the main. Conquered and colonized, Native Americans were hardly of a mind to view government policies, including that of compulsory education, as benign.

If nothing else, the policy of forced acculturation exacerbated an age-old characteristic of native life, tribal factionalism.[56] "Upon close study," Hamlin Garland observed in 1902,

> each tribe, whether Sioux, or Nävajo, or Hopi will be found to be divided, . . . into two parties, the radicals and the conservatives—those who are willing to change, to walk the white man's way; and those who are deeply, sullenly skeptical of all civilizing measures, clinging tenaciously to the traditions and lore of their race. These men are often the strongest, and bravest of their tribe, the most dignified and the most intellectual. They represent the spirit that will break but will not bow. And, broadly speaking, they are in the majority. Though in rags, their spirits are unbroken; from the point of view of their sympathizers, they are patriots.[57]

Although Garland's analysis fails to do justice to the complexity of tribal opinion, it does offer a major motivation for resistance, namely, that a significant body of tribal opinion saw white education for what it was: an invitation to cultural suicide. If white teachings were taken to heart, almost every vestige of traditional life would be cast aside. At the very least, whites expected Indians—and here, of course, the extent of the list differed with cultures—to abandon their ancestral gods and ceremonies; redefine the division of labor for the sexes; abolish polygyny; extinguish tribal political structures; squelch traditions of gift giving and communalism; abandon hunting and gathering; and restructure traditional familial and kinship arrangements. Across campfires, tribal elders weighed the issues. And many, like this Papago parent, asked:

> Now, are we a better people than we were years ago when we sang our own songs, when we spoke to the Great Spirit in our own language? We asked then for rain, good health and long life. Now what more do we want? What is that thought so great and so sacred that cannot be expressed in our own language, that we should seek to use the white man's words?[58]

When such attitudes translated into a complete indictment of white ways, the agent's call for students was almost certain to meet with staunch resistance.

But opposition to schools did not always spring from a comprehensive rejection of white ways. It might just as well represent opposition to some selective aspect of the school program: punishing children for speaking their native tongue, pressuring them to convert to Christianity, forcing them to perform manual labor. Especially obnoxious to some was the school's manner of disciplining Indian children, and even more, the practice of dressing and drilling them like soldiers.[59] One of the reasons given by Spotted Tail for withdrawing his children from Carlisle in 1880 was his discovery that Pratt had turned the school into "a soldier's place."[60]

NOTES

1. Luther Standing Bear, *My People, the Sioux* (1928; reprint, Lincoln: University of Nebraska Press, 1975), 123.
2. Standing Bear, *Land of the Spotted Eagle* (Boston: Houghton Mifflin Company, 1933), 68–69, 230–31. Also, Standing Bear, *My People, the Sioux*, 124, 128.
3. Standing Bear, *My People, the Sioux*, 187.
4. Ibid., 128–29.
5. Standing Bear, *Land of the Spotted Eagle*, 231–32; and Standing Bear, *My People, the Sioux*, 129–30.
6. Standing Bear, *My People, the Sioux*, 130–32.
7. Ibid., 133.
8. "Hoke Denetsosie" in *Stories of Traditional Navaho Life and Culture*, ed. Broderick H. Johnson (Tsaile, Ariz.: Navajo Community College Press, 1977), 81. For other accounts see "Max Hanley," in ibid., 36–37; Frank Mitchell, *Navajo Blessingway Singer: The Autobiography of Frank Mitchell, 1881–1967*, ed. Charlotte J. Frisbie and David A. McAllester (Tucson: University of Arizona Press, 1978), 57–61; Albert Yava, *Big Falling Snow: A Tewa-Hopi Indian's Life and Times and the History and Traditions of His People*, ed. Harold Courlander (Albuquerque: University of New Mexico Press, 1978), 14–18; Richard Henry Pratt, *Battlefield and Classroom: Four Decades with the American Indian, 1867–1904*, ed. Robert M. Utley (New Haven: Yale University Press, 1964), 203–4; Clark Wissler, *Indian Cavalcade or Life on the Old-time Indian Reservations* (New York: Sheridan, 1938), 183–84; and *Southern Workman*, August 1881, 85. For an excellent analysis of autobiographical accounts of leaving for school see Michael C. Coleman, *American Indian Children at School, 1850–1930* (Jackson: University Press of Mississippi, 1993), chap. 4.
9. According to Erving Goffman total institutions include the following characteristics. "First, all aspects of life (eating, sleeping, playing, working, learning) are conducted in the same place and under the same single authority. Second, each phase of a member's daily activity is carried out in the immediate company of a large batch of others, all of whom are treated alike and required to do the same thing together. Third, all phases of the day's activities are tightly scheduled, with one activity leading at a pre-arranged time into the next, the whole circle of activities being composed from above through a system of explicit, formal rules and a body of officials. Finally, the contents of the various enforced activities are brought together as parts of a single, overall, rational plan purportedly designed to fulfill the official aims of the institution." By Goffman's definition, examples of total institutions include concentration camps, mental hospitals, army barracks, prisons, and work camps. See Erving Goffman, "The Characteristics of Total Institutions," in *Complex Organizations: A Sociological Reader*, ed. Amitai Etzioni (New York: Holt, Rinehart, and Winston, 1961), 313–14; also see Goffman, *Asylums: Essays on the Social Situation of Mental Patients and Other Inmates* (Chicago: Aldine Publishing, 1961), 3–124, and C. A. McEwen, "Continuities in the Study of Total and Nontotal Institutions," *Annual Review of Sociology* 6 (1980): 143–85. Historians have applied the concept with varying degrees of accuracy and insight. One of the most important results of this discussion has been the recognition that there are great differences between total institutions—for instance, concentration camps and prisons—in their capacity to shape and control behavior. Slavery historians, for instance, have argued that the concept is of limited use in understanding the "peculiar institution." See, for instance, John W. Blassingame, *The Slave Community: Plantation Life in the Antebellum South* (New York: Oxford University Press, 1972), appendix. Other applications include David Rothman, *The Discovery of the Asylum* (Boston: Little, Brown, 1971); George Harwood Phillips, "Indians and the Breakdown of the Spanish Mission System in California," *Ethnohistory* 21 (Fall 1974): 291–302; and Thomas James, *Exile Within: The Schooling of Japanese Americans, 1942–1945* (Cambridge: Harvard University Press, 1987), 92. Were Indian boarding schools total institutions? They clearly fulfill the requirements of Goffman's definition and even appear to go beyond it when he states that "total institutions do not substitute their own unique culture for something already formed. We do not deal with acculturation as assimilation but with something more restricted than these. In a sense, total institutions do not look for cultural victory" (Goffman, "The Characteristics of Total Institutions," 317). Boarding schools, of course, existed for the express purpose of achieving "cultural victory." It is also suggestive that in 1891 Commissioner Morgan compared boarding schools to juvenile asylums and houses of correction. ARCIA, 1891, 62–63. Still, as this book later shows, the boarding school's control over Indian students was not absolute.
10. Standing Bear, *My People, the Sioux*, 140–41.
11. Mitchell, *Navajo Blessingway Singer*, 62.
12. Standing Bear, *Land of the Spotted Eagle*, 189. McCowan is quoted in Lorraine M. Scherer, "Great Chieftains of the Mohave Indians," *Southern California Quarterly* 48 (March 1966): 18.
13. ARCIA, 1892, 615.
14. Julia B. McGillycuddy, *McGillycuddy, Agent: A Biography of Dr. Valentine T. McGillycuddy* (Stanford: Stanford University Press, 1941), 205–6.

15. Standing Bear, *My People, the Sioux*, 140.
16. Pratt, *Battlefield and Classroom*, 232.
17. ARCIA, 1890, cli; and U.S. Office of Indian Affairs, *Rules for the Indian School Service* (Washington, D.C.: Government Printing Office, 1898), 31.
18. Carnelita S. Ryan, "The Carlisle Indian Industrial School" (Ph.D. dissertation, Georgetown University, 1962), 42; and ARCIA, 1893, 429.
19. ARCIA, 1897, 161; and Helen Sekaquaptewa (as told to Louise Udall), *Me and Mine: The Life Story of Helen Sekaquaptewa* (Tucson: University of Arizona Press, 1969), 32.
20. Frederick Riggs, "Peculiarities of Indian Education," *Southern Workman*, February 1901, 69; and Standing Bear, *My People, the Sioux*, 142.
21. ARCIA, 1904, 424; ARCIA, 1890, clx; and U.S. Office of Indian Affairs, *Rules for the Indian School Service*, 1898, 26.
22. ARCIA, 1890, clx. See Daniel F. Littlefield, Jr., and Lonnie E. Underhill, "Renaming the American Indian: 1890–1913," *American Studies* 12 (Fall 1971): 33–45.
23. ARCIA, 1890, clx-xlxi; and ARCIA, 1904, 424.
24. ARCIA, 1904, 426.
25. ARCIA, 1890, clxi; and Harriet Patrick Gilstrap, "Memories of a Pioneer Teacher," *Chronicles of Oklahoma* 38 (Spring 1960): 23.
26. *Southern Workman*, May 1889, 55.
27. George A. Pettit, *Primitive Education in North America* (Berkeley: University of California Press, 1946), 59–74.
28. Standing Bear, *My People, the Sioux*, 137.
29. Quoted in Pratt, *Battlefield and Classroom*, 293.
30. Jason Betzinez, *I Fought with Geronimo*, ed. Wilber S. Nye (Harrisburg, Pa.: Stackpole Company, 1959), 154.
31. ARCIA, 1882, p. 30. Agents continually complained of conditions. See ARCIA, 1886, 222, 230; ARCIA, 1887, 148; ARCIA, 1888, 77; ARCIA, 1889, 343–44; and ARCIA, 1900, 266.
32. ARCIA, 1892, 605; LMC, 1897, 36; and ARCIA, 1898, 18.
33. For contrasting definitions of Indian and white concepts of space see Bernard L. Fontana, "The Melting Pot that Wouldn't: Ethnic Groups in the American Southwest Since 1846," *American Indian Culture and Research Journal* 1 (1974): 21; Jamake Highwater, *The Primal Mind: Vision and Reality in Indian America* (1981; reprint, New York: New American Library, 1982), chap. 5; Peter Nabokov and Robert Easton, *Native American Architecture* (New York: Oxford University Press, 1989); and Joseph Epes Brown, *The Spiritual Legacy of the American Indian* (New York: Crosswood Publishing, 1982), 50–52.
34. Raymond J. DeMallie, ed., *The Sixth Grandfather: Black Elk's Teachings Given to John G. Neihardt* (Lincoln: University of Nebraska Press, 1984), 290–91. Also see George W. Linden, "Dakota Philosophy," *American Studies* 18 (Fall 1977): 33; and John (Fire) Lame Deer and Richard Erdoes, *Lame Deer: Seeker of Visions* (1972; reprint, New York: Washington Square Press, 1976), 96–97, 100–101.
35. Highwater, *The Primal Mind*, 119; ARCIA, 1898, 20; and U.S. Office of Indian Affairs, *Rules for the Indian School Service*, 1898, 25.
36. ARCIA, 1890, cli; and Mitchell, *Navajo Blessingway Singer*, 62.
37. ARCIA, 1890, cli; ARCIA, 1892, 604–5; and Mitchell, *Navajo Blessingway Singer*, 63.
38. ARCIA, 1898, 357; E. P. Grinstead, "Value of Military Drills," *Native American*, 21 March 1914, 151–52; and ARCIA, 1886, 224.
39. ARCIA, 1892, 616; Fontana, "The Melting Pot that Wouldn't," 20; and Althea Bass, *The Arapaho Way: A Memoir of an Indian Boyhood* (New York: Clarkson N. Potter, 1966), 6.
40. *Sherman Bulletin*, 21 December 1910, 1; and Grinstead, "Value of Military Drills," 153.
41. *Southern Workman*, January 1897, 7.
42. For an introduction to this aspect of Indian societies, see Brown, *The Spiritual Legacy of the American Indian*; Ake Hultkrantz, *Belief and Worship in Native North America* (Syracuse, N.Y.: Syracuse University Press, 1981); Hultkrantz, *The Religions of the American Indians* (Berkeley: University of California Press, 1979); Hartley Burr Alexander, *The World's Rim: Great Mysteries of the North American Indians* (Lincoln: University of Nebraska Press, 1953); and Sam D. Gill, ed., *Native American Religions: An Introduction* (Belmont, Calif.: Wadsworth Publishing, 1982).
43. See Brown, *Spiritual Legacy of the American Indian*, x, 69.
44. Ibid., 38–40, 53–54, 71–72, 124; Christopher Vecsey, "American Indian Environmental Religions," in *American Indian Environments: Ecological Issues in Native American History*, ed. Christopher Vecsey and Robert W. Venables (Syracuse, N.Y.: Syracuse University Press, 1980), 1–37; Hultkrantz, *Belief and Worship in Native North America*, chap. 7; and N. Scott Momaday, "Native American Attitudes to the Environment," in *Seeing with a Native Eye: Essays on Native American Religion*, ed. Walter Holden Capps (New York: Harper and Row, 1976), chap. 6.
45. See works cited in note 42.
46. Henry Warner Bowden, *American Indians and Christian Missions: Studies in Cultural Conflict* (Chicago: University of Chicago Press, 1981), 121.
47. Homer G. Barnett, *Indian Shakers: A Messianic Cult of the Pacific Northwest* (Carbondale: Southern Illinois University Press, 1957); James S. Slotkin, *The Peyote Religion: A Study in Indian-White Relations* (Glencoe, Ill.: Free Press, 1956); Weston LaBarre, *The Peyote Cult* (New York: Schocken Books, 1969); Omer C. Stewart, *Peyote Religion: A History* (Norman: University of Oklahoma Press, 1987); James Mooney, *The Ghost-Dance Religion and the Sioux Outbreak of 1890*, Fourteenth Annual Report of the Bureau of American Ethnology, 1892–1893, pt. 2 (Washington, D.C.: Gov-

ernment Printing Office, 1896); and Robert M. Utley, *The Last Days of the Sioux Nation* (New Haven: Yale University Press, 1963), chap. 5.

48.   ARCIA, 1884, 68.
49.   Sekaquaptewa, *Me and Mine*, 129.
50.   Ibid. and *Iapi Oaye: The Word Carrier*, February 1882, 15.
51.   ARCIA, 1882, 152; ARCIA, 1890, 307; ARCIA, 1897, 164; and ARCIA, 1900, 220. Also see ARCIA, 1881, 188; ARCIA, 1884, 100; ARCIA, 1895, 278; ARCIA, 1899, 168, 202; and ARCIA, 1906, 237.
52.   ARCIA, 1886, 318; and ARCIA, 1887, 226–27.
53.   ARCIA, 1886, 417.
54.   Mitchell, *Navajo Blessingway Singer*, 57.
55.   Edward Dozier, "Forced and Permissive Acculturation," *The American Indian* 7 (Spring 1955): 38.
56.   On the role of factionalism see Richard P. Metcalf, "Who Should Rule at Home? Native American Politics and Indian-White Relations," *Journal of American History* 61 (December 1974): 651–65; and Robert B. Berkhofer, Jr., *Salvation and the Savage: An Analysis of Protestant Missions and American Indian Response 1787–1862* (New York: Atheneum, 1972), chap. 7.
57.   Hamlin Garland, "The Red Man's Present Needs," *North American Review* 174 (April 1902): 479.
58.   Quoted, LMC, 1901, 76.
59.   See for example ARCIA, 1882, 223–24; Alford, *Civilization*, 90; ARCIA, 1879, 124; ARCIA, 1887, 321; ARCIA, 1888, 253; and LMC, 1893, 1025.
60.   For an account of Spotted Tail's visit to Carlisle see George E. Hyde, *A Sioux Chronicle* (Norman: University of Oklahoma Press, 1956), 51–57; and Pratt, *Battlefield and Classroom*, 236–40.

3

excerpt from

Born a Child of Freedom, Yet a Slave

"The Threat of Sale: The Black Family as a Mechanism of Control"

Norrece T. Jones Jr.

The fundamental principles upon which the system is based, are simply these: That all living on the plantation, whether colored or not, are members of the same family, and to be treated as such—that they all have their respective duties to perform, and that the happiness and prosperity of all will be in proportion to the fidelity with which each member discharges his part. I take occasion to inculcate repeatedly that, as the patriarch (not tyrant) of the family, my laws, when clearly promulgated, must be obeyed—that, as patriarch, it is my duty to protect their rights, to feed, clothe and house them properly—to attend to them carefully when sick—to provide for all their proper wants—to promote peace, harmony and good feeling, as so far as practicable, their individual comfort. *On the other hand, the servants are distinctly informed that they have to work and obey my laws, or suffer the penalty.* (Emphasis added.)

Southern planter, 1853[1]

Mother, is Massa gwine to sell us tomorrow?

Slave folk song[2]

THE PLANTOCRACY OF SOUTH CAROLINA attempted various methods of pacification and repression to cow African-American slaves into submission, but the most effective long-term mechanism of control was the threat of sale. Blacks feared the realization of that portentous suggestion more than any other mode of punishment, for while they could endure the pain of chastisement through whipping, it was more difficult to suffer the grave psychological injuries that stemmed from the severance of familial bonds through sale. Memories of that traumatic experience would linger long after the wounds of a sadistic beating had healed. Parents who were sold would worry about the welfare of children growing up without a mother and a father. Slave men and women heard frightening tales from masters about the dangers of life in other states or in other parts of the same state where they might be sold.[3] Charles Ball, for instance, who was sold more than once before he was transported from Maryland to a South Carolina plantation in 1805, recalled:

I shall never forget the sensations which I experienced this evening on finding myself in chains, in the state of South Carolina. From my earliest recollections, the name of South Carolina had been little less terrible to me than that of the bottomless pit. In Maryland, it had always been the practice of masters and mistresses, who wished to terrify their slaves, to threaten to sell them to South Carolina; where, it was represented, that their condition would be a hundred fold worse than it was in Maryland.[4]

The removal of recalcitrant and incorrigible bondsmen was a time-tested and widespread custom. As one judge said in 1833, "The owners of slaves frequently send them off from amongst their kindred and associates as a punishment, and it is frequently resorted to, as the means of separating a vicious negro from amongst others exposed to be influenced and corrupted by his example."[5] One planter who owned about one hundred and thirty-five slaves was so pleased with this method of chastening blacks that he urged his heirs to continue the practice. He left instructions in an 1855 will that the "young negroes be kept on one of his plantations, and . . . to sell any of them that are turbulent or otherwise troublesome."[6]

Reliance on punitive sales had long been a tactic used by masters to rid themselves of non-compliant slaves. In 1740 the wealthy South Carolinian Robert Pringle sold "a Very Likely Young Wench" to Portugal for the sole reason that "she had a practice of going frequently to her Father and Mother, who Live at a Plantation I am Concern'd in about Twenty Miles from Town from whence there was no Restraining her from Running away there & Staying every now & then."[7] This savage and brutal mode of disciplining "execrable," "indifferent," or simply "bad" slaves was employed throughout the antebellum period and was even quite common during the Civil War.[8] Such sales were sanctioned by almost all in the white community and received particular approval from the religious sector.[9] With the exception of the Society of Friends, every denomination in the South had compromised with slavery until by midway in the nineteenth century religious leaders were either silent or offered divine justification for the traffic in human chattels.[10] One prominent Presbyterian preacher and slaveowner in South Carolina argued that nothing human was being sold, only the right to "labor and service." "When we buy and sell them," he declared, "it is not *human flesh and blood* that we buy and sell, but we buy and sell a *right*, established by Providence, and sanctioned by Scripture, to *their labor and service for life*."[11] (Emphasis in the original.)

Slaves knew that much more was at stake than the sale of labor. Susan Hamlin, who was born in 1833, recounted after she was freed the heartrending sorrows and screams of slaves who were torn from loved ones and of others who had discovered that a sale was coming. Hamlin, who had been a house servant at the Charleston home of Edward Fuller, told of a couple who were married one night and learned the next morning that the wife had been sold: "De gal ma got in de street an' cursed de [owner] fur all she could find. . . . De police took her to de Work House . . . an' what become of 'er, I never hear."[12]

It is crucial to note that not only familial ties but also the land on which black men and women had toiled, loved, borne children, and buried their dead acted as a powerful centripetal force that made the prospect of sale all the more horrifying. Many observers, both before and during the war, remarked about the magnetism of African-American birth and burying places.[13] Charles Nordhoff, for example, said that ex-slaves displayed "the same strong local attachment . . . characteristic of the black freedmen in the British West Indies."[14] When Union forces evacuated Edisto Island, just off the coast of South Carolina, in 1862, Laura Towne, the Northern schoolteacher who had come to teach liberated blacks, recorded: "A few old people had determined not to leave the home they loved so much, and they waited on shore till the last moment and then came hurrying down."[15] It is understandable, therefore, that most newly freed slaves returned to the area they had lived in while in bondage.[16] Funeral rites and burial grounds hold great importance in African-American culture. As late as the 1950s, some descendants of slaves arranged to have their remains interred on the plantations where their forebears rested.[17] Referring to blacks who had been slaves held by her relative R. F. W. Allston, Patience Pennington commented:

> Every year more hands leave the plantation [at Chisora Wood] and flock to the town, and every year more funerals wend their slow way from the town to the country; for though they all want to live in town, none is so poor but his ashes must be taken "home"; that is, to the old plantation where his parents and grandparents lived and died and lie waiting the final summons. . . . The whole family unite and "trow een" to make up the sum necessary to bring the wanderer home; and even the most careless and indifferent of the former owners respect the feeling and consent to have those who have been working elsewhere for years, and who perhaps left them in the lurch on some trying occasion, laid to rest in the vine-covered graveyard on the old plantation.[18]

Such attachments were in all likelihood stronger before emancipation. An individual sold might be separated not only from the birthplace and burial grounds so important to black Carolinians, but removed perhaps forever from parents, cousins, aunts, uncles, grandparents, siblings, and friends. Bitter memories of such separations remained for years. The pain could still be seen in the tears of aging men and women who recalled lost kin and in the invectives expressed by ex-slaves and their descendants about the whites who commanded the inhuman domestic and international slave trade.[19] At least for slaves, their disdain of masters as a whole often inspired a blanket distrust of whites in general.[20] A slave whose master or mistress did everything possible to prevent sales and to minimize lashings was still a slave. Resentment of this reality contributed to the steady flow of errant slaves streaming into distant states. So extensive was the influx of "undesirable" slaves into the Palmetto State that in 1847 a group of citizens from Charleston appealed to the legislature to limit admission of "vicious slaves." Their petition demonstrates how widespread that market had become as well as how prevalent the belief that "docile" local slaves were prodded to mischief by recalcitrant outsiders. Their appeal stated in part:

> Your petitioners . . . shew That the persevering efforts, in some parts of our Union, to intermeddle injuriously with our slave population furnish increased motives for vigilance on our part, not only in repelling interference from abroad, but in a stricter government of our slaves at home is liable to mischievous disturbance from the importation of vicious or criminal slaves from other states. That as laws have been passed by the states South West of us prohibiting the importation of slaves into those states merely for Sale and not the property of residents or immigrants passing through them. [*sic*]
>
> This State and the City of Charleston in particular, have become the common place of meeting between the slave dealer from places north of us and the purchaser South West of us. That the motive of the Slave dealer is not only to approach as near as he can to his buyer, but to remove the slave as far from his old range and from notorious bad character, as possible. That while on sale here many vicious slaves are palmed upon careless or confiding citizens among us, and their mixture with our own has had a sensible influence upon the docility and usefulness of our slaves. That your petitioners are not to be confounded with those inimical to Southern interests who oppose the removal of slaves from state to state under any circumstances. *We propose* to confine the admission of Slaves into this State, to those brought here by their owners, residents in this State and those the property of emigrants passing into or through this State and we propose to prohibit under proper sanctions the introduction of slaves into this state *merely for sale*. . . .[21] (Emphasis in the original.)

Most masters chose not to accept the fact that blacks who were native-born and free from "outside forces" could be refractory. They continued to delude themselves that they could preserve the purity and peacefulness of their slaves by keeping out all troublemakers. Slaveholders continued exercising, therefore, the powerful lever of deportation not only to accomplish this objective, but to warn bondsmen that they were not the subjects of idle threats.[22] To be sure, the mere presence of non-South Carolinian slaves proved the seriousness of remote planters, but the departure of local, native-born neighbors who failed to heed their owners' warnings was evidence of the sudden uprooting *all* slaves could face. The consequences of R. F. W. Allston's orders, for instance, would not have missed the attention of blacks:

> Appropos of sales you enquire what Brass is to do. I sent him up to split Rails, and told him upon his repeated failure that he must go to the vendue table [auction block], whenever he could not do this. Now if any one about you is going to Charleston, give Brass a new shirt and send to Robertson Blacklock and Co. to be turn'd into money, forthwith. It is the best thing to be done with Brass. There must be no fuss about it, or noise, or notice.[23]

Needless to say, sales, either effected or threatened, would have been less meaningful to someone who lacked the bonds of friendship and family. South Carolinian enslavers learned this lesson early when, as a cost-saving measure in 1714, they experimented with deportations instead of their traditional solution of executions of slaves who committed crimes. Within three years, slave-holders revoked the law establishing the policy of deportations after they discovered that it prompted slaves "to commit great numbers of robberies, burglaries and other felonies, well knowing they were to suffer no other punishment for their crimes, but transportation, which to them was rather an encouragement to pursue their villanies."[24] In a black population largely male and single, planters during the first quarter of the eighteenth century had to find other methods of control.[25] The next century, however, brought new life to an old experiment.

By 1800, Africans and African-Americans generally had enmeshed themselves in an intricate and extensive network of kinship ties that commanded a loyalty so powerful that the atmosphere was ripe for masters to impose more successfully a compliance based on slave fears of banishment. Indeed, until the Confederacy lost its war, the prospect of being sold, whether for profit or punishment, hovered over all those in chains. This most-feared possibility was made real in innumerable ways. Not only did planters threaten to sell slaves who persistently refused to comply, but they saw to it that insubordinate slaves, as well as other bondpeople, constantly witnessed auctions and the endless processions of human chattels driven by diverse whites to distant destinies in captivity.[26] While one could choose not to watch such scenes, there very likely were black neighbors who had traveled on and remembered well each step of that route.

Jacob, a slave who belonged to Charles Manigault, would not have taken lightly the message from his master delivered to him after he had spent three weeks in solitary confinement while in jail and received a whipping for being "a bad disposed Nigger." Manigault's "compliments" were to be given to Jacob with notice that if he did not change for the better, New Orleans would be his destination—a marketplace, Jacob was reminded, where "several of the gang" had already been sent for "their misconduct, or their running away for no cause."[27] Although it is not possible to determine the exact number of punitive sales, virtually all sources indicate that the communication network among blacks was so efficient and extensive that most slaves were probably aware of those that did occur. As former slave Isaiah Butler declared, everyone knew the meaning of "I'll put you in my pocket, sir!"[28]

During the summer of 1863 some men owned by Plowden C. J. Weston, a planter on the Waccamaw River near Georgetown, tried to escape to Union forces. As a result of this "bad conduct," Weston decided to "dispose of them" because "he could never consider them as his people again." Elizabeth Collins, the English companion of Mrs. Weston, said about that event: "They were each sold to different people,—sold from their wives, poor things, who felt it very much at first; but the contented mind of the black people causes them soon to forget."[29] In grave contrast to the impression Miss Collins had of their mnemonic abilities, African-American slaves retained lucid memories of relatives and friends torn away from them and the circumstances under which they occurred. Newly freed slaves spoke constantly of "transported" family members, and the authors of slave autobiographies were frequently most graphic when describing how loved ones were lost to the notorious "trader."[30] Charles Ball, for example, wrote mournfully of witnessing his mother "dragged . . . towards the place of sale" after he was "snatched . . . from her arms." Years later, he wrote, "Young as I was, the horrors of that day sank deeply into my heart, and even at this time, though half a century has elapsed, the terror of the scene returns with painful vividness upon my memory."[31] In a different way, but with the same effect, Caleb Craig, born in 1851 on a Blackstock, South Carolina, plantation, recalled, "My mammy name Martha. Marse John soon give us chillun to his daughter, Miss Marion. In dat way us separated from our mammy. Her was a mighty pretty colored woman and I has visions and dreams of her, in my sleep, sometime yet."[32]

Craig was not unique in experiencing lurid flashbacks of sales and family separations: other ex-slaves—both in the nineteenth and the twentieth centuries—expressed similar sentiments and emotions.[33] Sylvia Cannon was eighty-five in 1937 when she cried about the unknown fate of her brothers sold while in bondage. Mrs. Cannon said: "I see em sell some slaves twice fore I was sold en I see de slaves when dey be traveling like hogs to Darlington. Some of dem be women folks looking like dey gwine to get down dey so heavy."[34] A large number of slaves would have had cause to weep over some relative who had vanished in the interregional slave trade. Despite such losses, the black family survived as an institution, for the ideas and principles guiding it were anchored in traditions so deep-seated and binding that they could endure even after familial links had been severed. To understand its survival and the full impact of sales, one must examine concepts of kinship in Africa as well as in North America, which made the black family the single most powerful source of support among slaves.

Sidney Mintz and Richard Price suggest in their brilliant anthropological study that "certain widespread fundamental ideas and assumptions about kinship in West Africa" may have been retained and shared by enslaved Africans landing in the Americas. The two scholars noted also that "the aggregate of newly-arrived slaves, torn from their own local kinship networks, would have continued to view kinship as the normal idiom of social relations."[35] Such beliefs could have been passed on easily to the descendants of indigenous Africans held captive in South Carolina, for on many plantations generations of particular slave families lived and flourished.[36] This was especially true in the district of Georgetown because after the 1780s "very few slaves [were] brought in from outside" its borders and apparently fewer were exported to foreign parts than in other areas.[37] Numerous sources indicate that native-born Africans were often the transmitters of social norms and history both to their progeny and to members of the broader society.[38]

One such African evidently so inspired his daughter, for many years later her young mistress remembered, "Often we children would . . . listen with rapt absorption to Maum Hetty's tales of the Guinea Negroes of whom her father was one before he was brought as a slave to Carolina. Sometimes she taught us scraps of native African songs, and when we were able to count to ten in African we concluded that our education was complete indeed."[39] What the Maum Hettys of the South added to their lessons to blacks in private, however, was a different story. Collectively, they instilled in black children and young adults familial obligations that reached far beyond the typical white American nuclear family. These and other norms—particularly those dictating what were acceptable marital bonds—distinguished slaves from members of the planter class. In his massive study of the black family, Herbert Gutman found that slaves adhered to rigid rules of exogamy in their selection of mates, while the men and women of the slave-holding elite often married first cousins. Because he found similar patterns, mores, and norms among slaves on quite disparate plantations, Gutman concluded that those patterns were influenced neither by slaves' occupation nor by the type of planter on the estate. He therefore discarded the ever-popular "mimetic theories of Afro-American culture."[40] It is my belief that because of the strength of the black family, sale and the threat of sale acted as a major determinant of slave behavior. Sold slaves not only disseminated and unified slave culture, but graphically demonstrated the reality behind each threat of sale.

Sidney Mintz was correct in arguing that "within the structure of a slave society the slaves were required to engineer styles of life that might be preserved in the face of terible outrage."[41] The black family did engineer such survival strategies. It was an extremely cohesive and resilient unit that demanded from its members numerous obligations and infinite devotion. Slave parents, for example, played certain economic roles, such as vegetable gardening and hunting, that were essential to the procurement of adequate food for their offspring. Moreover, although other relatives gave some assistance, fathers and mothers were responsible for the bulk of their children's socialization. So intense was loyalty to one's family that Union officers found it difficult initially to recruit blacks into the army because they feared to leave loved ones unprotected. Once freedmen did enlist, it was difficult sometimes to retain them because, as one observer noted, "A negro thinks to go and see his family the height of happiness."[42] Thus, the magnetism of African-American kinship ties sometimes irritated the self-proclaimed friends of the slave, just as it infuriated his adversaries almost perennially.

The family was, ironically, not only at the base of masters' most effective control mechanism, it was the source also of their most persistent aggravation, the runaway. Contemporary publications and correspondence are replete with cases of absconding blacks who were thought to have deserted in order to reunite with relatives.[43] Such knowledge must have simply added to the frustration of many masters, for it did not always help in retrieving their property. "A black fellow named Ned," for instance, was still evading capture almost a year later despite his master's careful listing in a runaway advertisement of "relations" that the thirty-two-year-old plowman and wagoner had living "at Mrs. Bird's, at the Rocks, at Dr. Wilson's, on the State Road, and at Moorer's in St. Mathews Parish."[44] Half a century earlier, John Davis recalled about his travels in South Carolina:

> The Charleston papers abound with advertisements for fugitive slaves. I have a curious advertisement now before me.—"Stop the runaway! Fifty dollars reward! Whereas my waiting fellow, Will having eloped from me last Saturday, *without any provocation*, (it being known that I am a *humane master*) . . . *Will may be known by the incisions of the whip on his back*; and I suspect has taken the road to *Coosohatchie*, where he has a wife and five children, whom I sold last week to Mr. Gillespie."[45] (Emphases in the original.)

Analogous suspicions about why and where bondsmen ran were expressed throughout the antebellum period. In 1829 monetary compensation was offered for the apprehension of "George, Celia, and Sarah." Their owner declared that "there is every reason to suppose the wenches are harboured on John's Island, from whence they came, and where they have connexions . . . and that the fellow George, who has runaway since has joined them, the whole being of one family."[46] There was, of course, no single reason for slave desertions, but it is interesting that members of the immediate family often escaped together.[47]

Enslaved husbands, wives, daughters, and sons shipped great distances from each other rarely forgot those left behind and frequently pursued every method of ending the separation. In an effort to join family members in South Carolina a Samuel Tayler wrote the following letter to his former mistress:

> My Dear Mistress I have been in this City about three years and belong at present to Mr. Sam'l Jerques, merchant. I was sold for $1,900. He is remarkably kind and gives me a fair opportunity of making pocket money. But still my mind is always dwelling on home, relations, & friends which I would give the world to see. As times now are, I suppose I may be purchased for about 10 or $11 hundred dollars. If you my Dear Mistress, can buy me, how happy I would be to serve you and your heirs; I beg you will write me how *all* my relations are, and inform them that I have enjoyed uninterrupted health since I came here. Rember me also to Sarah, my ma ma, and Charlotte, my old fellow servant & Amy Tayler.
>
> I would be glad to belong to my young mistress, Mrs. Parker in case you should not feel disposed to take me.[48]

Some slaves never gave up the hope of reuniting with loved ones many miles away. Pitiful efforts were still being made long after Emancipation. Black newspapers well into the 1870s and 1880s were filled with "Information Wanted" sections carrying appeals from mothers, fathers, sisters, brothers, and children who refused to abandon the glimmer of hope that they might yet find family members who had been torn from them in bondage.[49] Charles Gatson pleaded for "information of his children, Sam and Betsy Gatson" in 1870. He wrote, "They formerly belonged to Washington Fripp, of Newhaw, South Carolina; were carried to Charleston and there sold by a trader to go far South, it is supposed to Mississippi or Louisiana. They are now about twenty-two to twenty-five years old, and were taken away in 1861."[50]

The behavior of blacks during the Civil War offers further testimony to the strength and binding character of African-American kinship ties. In the face of tremendous odds, which ranged from possible sale to Cuba[51] to murder, whole familes, not merely individuals, were the most common venturers to Union lines. Charles Nordhoff observed in 1863, "They have strong affection for their children. It is well known that few men run away to us alone; as a rule they come off bringing with them their wives and little ones—often from great distances, and at frightful risks."[52] Almost all Northerners who visited Port Royal, the place of convergence for thousands of contrabands, commented similarly and noted the great skill and diligence with which freedmen sought relatives sold off or by some other means taken from them while in servitude.[53] Although for the first time in their lives these slaves could feel secure in keeping their families intact, many nevertheless sacrificed all and hazarded possible permanent separation by joining the Union Army's fight against their oppressors.

African-American men in the army continued to demonstrate a role as providers and as heads of families while they served. The soldiers in Thomas Higginson's black regiment in South Carolina, for example, "intrusted him, when they were paid off, with seven hundred dollars, to be transmitted by him to their wives, and this besides what they had sent home in other ways,—showing the family-feeling to be active and strong in them."[54] It appears that the overriding concern of black patriarchs, whether in fighting in the Yankee army or while serving as cooks, body servants, and laborers for Confederate troops, was the care and future welfare of their families. One Stephen Moore wrote this while accompanying his officer-owner in the Confederate ranks:

> Dear Wife   I take the present opportunity of writing you a few lines to let you know how I am getting on. I am as well as common and hope these few lines may find you all well. I was rite smartly vext til Minus come here. He said you was all well and that gave me satisfaction. Tell Minuses Mother that he is in a half mile of me. I can see him any time I want too. He is well. I will try to come

home in 2 or 3 weeks if I can get off. You and Elihue must gather me about 40 chickens when I come home. I will have the money to pay for them. I am making money every day. Tell Numer and Ransom they must sea to my children & sea that they mind theirs mother & tell Elihu like wise . . .

Tell Synthy and Chany I am very much ablige to them for the word they sent me by Minus. Tell Lizabeth, Nelly and Gracy I thank them for this compliments they sent. Tell Mother I will send her money as soon as an oppertunity will admit. Tell Mr. Hill [overseer] I want to see him as well as any body else. Tell him to please take this letter & read it to Rachel. I will thank you to take this letter and read it to all my people. Tell Rachel I have bought a fine watch for her [but] I have no way to send it & will keep it and bring it when I come. . . . Tell Rachel if she needs any money to write to me when Elihew write. The money is not to be made it is all ready made. I have 3 meals of victuals to cook a day and the rest of the time is mine. If you don't spend the money I send you keep it for me when I come hom. Rachel pay Gracy 30 cts for me, pay Noah 25 cts for me, pay Numer one dollar & a half & I will settle the balance when I come. Write sone.[55]

The role slave mothers and, particularly, slave fathers played in the acquisition of food for their families made the threat of sale all the more intimidating. While most scholars do stress the adequacy of slaves' diet, few note or address the significance of why and how it became so sufficient.[56] Planters in South Carolina generally furnished only a peck of corn per week to each slave to be ground into grits or meal. All sources indicate that this quantity was constant between 1800 and 1865. Other staples, such as potatoes or rice, were sometimes substituted for corn and a small portion of salt was allotted on occasion.[57] Masters rarely provided any meat other than bacon, and that usually not weekly. Although there is some scant evidence that the amount of meat given during this period increased slightly from about a pound per week to three, no data have been uncovered to establish that there was any change throughout the years under examination in the sporadic and infrequent distribution of that luxury.[58] At least on seventeen plantations, it was not until the 1851 death of the proprietor, Nathaniel Heyward, that the more than one thousand bondsmen on these estates began receiving *any* form of meat, and this was due to the benevolence of the new master, Charles Heyward.[59]

Historians of U. B. Phillips's caliber never failed to cite the rules for management of planters like James Henry Hammond, who left instructions that workers be given "three pounds of bacon or pickled pork every week."[60] Unfortunately, Mr. Hammond kept no records that would indicate whether these orders were in fact carried out and, if so, how often. Documents of this nature would, of course, be the most definitive. The present writer, however, studied the detailed accounts of meat distribution for three South Carolinians over periods of nine, six, and eight months.

William Ervin Sparkman, of Springwood plantation in Georgetown District, possessed one hundred and two laborers in 1845.[61] Between March 31 and December 25, 1844, he furnished meat to blacks on three occasions: July 28, August 18, and September 8. He specified the amount allotted for the week of July 28 alone, at which time appeared the entry "3 lbs meat a piece." The type of viand was described simply as "meat," except on the 18th of August, when "bacon" was designated. On December 26, undoubtedly as part of the Christmas celebrations, slaves received "10 lbs Beef, 1 pt. lasses, & tobacco." For an interval of nine months, workers received meat from their master during four weeks only.[62]

The eleven slaves owned by Dr. J. Rhett Motte, of Exeter Plantation in St. John's, Berkeley, were supplied with meat once a month for all but two months, January and April, during a six-month period ending June 30, 1850. Dr. Motte gave no quantities and referred simply to "meat" on all but one occasion, when he cited "bacon" as part of the provisions on June 16.[63] John Milliken, the proprietor of Mulberry Plantation, "one of the oldest establishments on Cooper River,"[64] kept complete food-allotment records from December 1853 to March 1854 and from January to April 1857. During this time, excluding January 1857, he gave a monthly meat allowance of unknown measure and twice presented a "big pot," probably containing some meat. It is interesting that there was no mention of a "big pot" in 1857 and that, beginning in February of the same year, the weekly distribution of corn, rice, or potatoes was reduced to only three weeks during each month.[65] All slaveholders were looking constantly for ways to trim the costs of feeding laborers, and perhaps this was one method. An 1856 "Bill to alter and amend the Law in relation to the trial of owners . . . for not furnishing their slaves with sufficient clothing or food" indicates that planters of this type were prevalent enough to warrant this retention and expansion of the 1740 Act penalizing such behavior.[66]

Slaveowners may possibly have distributed such sparse rations because they believed blacks had different nutritional needs from whites; some, at least, used this as their rationale.[67] James Henry Hammond explained on November 6, 1847, that they needed fat and salt and strong drink:

> Negroes must be kept hardy; they will not *bear* fine treatment; if they were furnished with fine houses and feather beds they would often sleep out at night and thus danger of exposure would be greatly increased. The food of negros should be strong and stimulating; their nature requires stimulants Fat and salty. bacon is the best meat they can get. Fresh meat is poisonous in summer.
>
> Strong drinks are good for negros; they require something to stimulate them.[68] (Emphasis in the original.)

Not all South Carolinians were satisfied with the type of food slaves received. One planter wrote, "It is only necessary to inquire of the physician, or to consult any medical work, to be convinced that an improper attention to diet, is one of the most prolific causes of disease among our negroes."[69] Ironically, H. Perry Pope, a medical student in Charleston, presented a thesis one year later urging masters to add meat to slave provisions. As a positive incentive to this policy, he noted the substantial superiority in growth of domestics' children, who ate generally the remains of meals in the Big House, over that of field hands' offspring, who survived on the comestibles supplied by owners and whatever their parents could produce.[70]

Obviously, planters differed in their views about slave food. But the most crucial judges are those who had to subsist on it. Jacob Stroyer, born in 1849 on a large plantation near Columbia, South Carolina, recalled bitterly the "mush" children were fed at the summer residence of their owner. He and all other children "too small to work" were taken each May or June to that vacation home and separated from family members who remained to labor on the plantation about four miles away. What "the slaves called mush" was corn flour; it was served usually with either "a gill of sour milk" or molasses. That "seldom changed diet," as well as loneliness, no doubt, made the children "anxious for Sundays to come, when our mothers, fathers, sisters and brothers would bring something from the plantation, which, however poor, we considered very nice, compared with what we had during the week. . . . Among the many desirable things our parents brought us, the most delightful was cow pease, rice, and a piece of bacon, cooked together," a mixture they called "hopping John."[71]

While such supplements pleased the young Jacob, a plethora of evidence indicates that most slaves considered their food allotment insufficient and complained frequently about its quality and quantity—particularly the paucity of meat.[72] John Jackson, who was enslaved by Robert English in Sumter district, said he was fed "twice a day," but protested:

All we got to eat then was three corn cake dumplins and one plate of soup. No meat unless there happened to be a rotten piece in the smoke house. This would be given to us to make our soup. Why the dogs got better eating than we poor colored folks.[73]

Another former slave declared that the males on his plantation in Beaufort District "didn't have time to frolic 'cause they had to fin' food for the family; master never give 'nough to las' the whole week."[74] An awareness of these conditions enables one to understand why the struggle for food is such a consistent theme in African-American folklore. As Charles Joyner observed, blacks "like folk groups everywhere, remembered what they found memorable, used what they found usable, and forgot what they found forgettable."[75]

In order to make their daily fare adequate, American bondsmen demonstrated remarkable resourcefulness and industry. Slaves were the de facto owners of garden patches around their homes and/or on other parts of the plantation where a wide assortment of vegetables were grown. Planters sanctioned and encouraged this practice universally in South Carolina and even allowed men they did not own to keep and farm such land on their estates if their wives were there.[76] Others foraged for wild greens. And many raised poultry, or sometimes hogs, which they either saved for family consumption or sold in order to procure certain luxury food items. But the principal method of obtaining the much-coveted meat and fish in their diet was by hunting and fishing by which the men procured rabbits, raccoons, oysters, shad, trout, and clams. Both males and females appropriated foodstuffs from their masters, but they also acquired delicacies through "legal" pursuits, such as the manufacture and sale of baskets, bowls, ladles, and the like, and through paid labor during free time which enabled them to purchase many of the desired articles not furnished by slaveholders.[77] Charles Pinckney was not far from correct when he said of the enslaved worker: "When his owner is barbarian enough to withhold the necessary food, he has always intellect, and generally opportunity to supply the deficiency."[78]

It is clear that slave parents supplied a large percentage, if not the bulk, of their families' food. The fulfillment of this vital function explains why mothers and fathers were particularly apprehensive about threatened sale. They would have been tempted inevitably to ask, "Will our children be provided for as well if either of us is sold?" In view of the dreaded day that they might be separated, parents began instructing children early in certain techniques and stratagems of survival. The first lessons taught to young bondsmen were strict obedience to elders and silence unless spoken to or addressed in some manner. Laura Towne did not think blacks were "harsh" to their offspring, but commented that, "They have a rough way of ordering them that sounds savage. When you speak to a child who does not answer, the others say, 'Talk, talk. Why you not talk?'—in the most ordersome tone to the silent one."[79] Growing accustomed to imperious commands was part and parcel of being a slave. Moreover, it was imperative that each child learn how to hold his or her tongue, for a careless slip could bring down the wrath of masters on all. This was probably the reason bondsmen did not "allow their children under certain ages to enter into conversations with them."[80] In the eyes of the enslaved, the home was the safest training ground for teaching these modes of combating white repression.

There is some evidence that slaves instructed their youngest progeny to view masters as evil and powerful adversaries with whom they should have as little contact as possible. In reference to his former owner, John Collins recalled, "De slaves whisper his name in fear and terror to de chillun when they want to hush them up. They just say to a crying child: 'Shet up or old Nick will ketch you!' Dat child sniffle but shet up pretty quick."[81] Contemporary travelers observed frequently that slave children were afraid of whites and would run away at their approach.[82] A native South Carolinian, fearful about how outsiders might view this, suggested that

> Young servants should not be suffered to run off and hide when the master comes up, or any other white person; they should be taught to stand their ground, and speak when *spoken to*, in a polite manner; have them well clothed and this thing is more easily accomplished. A lot of ragged little negroes always gives a bad impression to strangers, and is often the cause of their running away and being hard to manage when grown. Talk to them; take notice of them; it soon gives them confidence and adds greatly to their value.[83] (Emphasis in the original.)

As young laborers grew older, their parents entrusted them with the more difficult and dangerous lessons of prevarication and appropriation. Juvenile blacks were such good students that one of the major impetuses among planters for the religious proselytizing of young slaves was the hope that it would neutralize their "negative" home influences. The ruling class was not very successful, however, for the descendants of slaves continued to internalize antiservile characteristics. To inculcate various stratagems, mores, and values, African-American slaves relied heavily on a didactic, as well as an entertaining, folklore.[84] In this regard things do not appear to have changed greatly when Julia Peterkin early in the twentieth century became mistress of an Orangeburg District plantation once owned by Langdon Cheves. She observed:

> The training of children is concerned chiefly with self-preservation in this world and preparation for the life to come. They are taught to provide for the needs of their bodies, to save their souls and to abide by the ancient customs, beliefs and rules of conduct handed down from generation to generation by word of mouth. In the hot summer evenings when they sit on cabin doorsteps with their parents, or in the winter time around fires that burn in the wide chimneys, time not whiled away with singing is often spent listening to the old folk tales which are rich in negro philosophy, and sparkle with negro ideas of wit and repartee. Many of these tales teach some simple moral lesson. The people who treasure these stories have no books, have never seen a play or moving picture, have never read a newspaper; but whether the stories are of men or of beasts, they invariably portray the same human traits and problems that make worth-while literature and plays and moving pictures.[85]

In much the same fashion, slave children learned not only how to "lib on de fat uv de land," but how to share with fellow blacks. They were instilled with principles of cooperation and assistance, illustrated most dramatically during the Civil War when, as a result of the benevolence of blacks, few orphans went uncared for. In addition, slaves generally were taught to treat elders with great reverence and to address them with honorific titles such as "Daddy" and "Maumer." Blacks of the same age group referred to each other as "Bro" (brother), "Titty" (sister), or "Co" (cousin), which caused Northerners trying to discern actual blood ties no small confusion. These traditions and mores stemmed most likely from the efforts of African-Americans to assure the well-being of children who might be separated from *real* parents.[86] Gutman states that "fictive, or quasi, kin" bound

> *unrelated adults to one another* and thereby [infused] enlarged slave communities with conceptions of obligation that had flowed initially from kin obligations rooted in blood and marriage. The obligations to a brother or a niece were transformed into the obligations toward a fellow slave or a fellow slave's child, and behavior first determined by familial and kin obligation became enlarged social obligation. Just as the fictive aunts and uncles may have bound children to quasi kin, so, too, the ties between a child and its fictive adult kin may have bound children's parents to their fictive aunts and uncles.[87] (Emphasis in the original.)

Such attitudes and beliefs undoubtedly helped more than anything else to preclude the divisive tendencies inherent in an excessive loyalty to *particular* families, especially when one's own might be sold.

Obviously, young slaves were learning more than simply what adults demanded of them: they also began to perceive what adults expected of each other. It would have been difficult to miss the great importance older blacks placed on inquiries about one's family as part of all greetings. Similarly, children gradually would have learned that those who best provided for their families, and who verbally thrashed and even physically assaulted a mysterious and amorphous group known simply as "buckra" or "whites," were for some as yet undetermined reason considered pillars of the community.[88] To be sure, much was unclear to the young, but these early messages no doubt had an impact.[89] So, too, must the names and titles slaves gave one another, for once entering interracial settings the pervasive "Sirs," "Madames," "Mrs.," and "Mr.'s," whom black youth both knew and admired, were reduced—despite age and status—to "boy," "girl," or a generic "nigger."[90] The psychic damage done could not be erased, but in a multitude of ways prior to this awakening, young blacks had been subtly, explicitly, and continuously taught that, regardless of their status in the broader society, there would be dignity and respect among themselves.

Another way of instilling self-esteem in a humbling environment was in selecting the names of children. Recent scholarship has established the tremendous role those name choices played in cultivating individuality and distinctiveness.[91] Tragically for fresh African arrivals, however, a psychological denuding occurred with the expunction of their names at purchase. According to Gabriel Manigault, whose grandfather owned over two thousand slaves:

> Upon naming a negro a card upon which it was written was tied around his neck and it was a common thing to see a planter in his fields, go up to a field hand, whether man or woman and insert his forefinger under the collar of the shirt to draw out the card . . . This of course was only done for a short time, and became unnecessary as soon as the darkey could pronounce his name.[92]

Not all imports learned so quickly. It is not by chance that eighteenth-century runaway advertisements were replete with African names—some cited beside the English names that certain fugitives had doggedly rejected.[93] Even later, many held tenaciously to their African names or adopted surnames equally symbolic of an independence and identity long repressed. Toward the end of the antebellum period, young Jacob Stroyer recalled his father's having a surname "he could not use in public" because the last name of his owner was Singleton. What made the elder Stroyer's act illegal, his son discovered, was "that to allow him to use his own name would be sharing an honor which was due only to his master, and that would be too much for a negro, *said they*, who was nothing more than a servant."[94] (Emphasis in the original.)

Black fathers and mothers throughout South Carolina and elsewhere broke the law; they did so not only to preserve a measure of autonomy for themselves, but also to instill in their children a spirit of independence. These unlettered but driven educators hoped that this spirit and the various techniques of survival they taught would one day congeal among the young into a base from which yet another generation could launch their people's seemingly endless struggle for freedom. In their thinking, the key prerequisite for that legacy was knowledge. As a result, they labored continually to learn as much about the world around and beyond them as possible. The postwar mania of freedmen for learning was no less real during slavery. Those responsible for the control of slaves were confronted too often with slaves who could read, decipher, and convey craftily their findings. Southern controllers watched closely any setting in which a dangerous "progress and diffusion of knowledge" might occur.[95]

In 1838 more than three hundred South Carolinians from the districts of Abbeville and Edgefield lashed out against the proposal of a missionary to preach to blacks. They argued:

> Some of the negroes will attend your meetings for religious improvement; others from idle curiosity; and a few of the more daring and intelligent, with restless spirits, to impart to each other every whisper that reaches them of the progress of Abolition, and the glowing prospect of their liberation. . . . When the last census was taken, the black population exceeded the white upwards of sixty-one thousand five hundred. We consider the common adage true, that "knowledge is power." . . . Intelligence and slavery have no affinity for each other.[96]

With the last view in mind, lawmakers repeatedly passed legislation prohibiting the written instruction of slaves. The recurrence of such laws and the uncovering recently of extensive correspondence by ex-slaves fighting in the Civil War make it clear that neither threats of maimings nor severe beatings prevented some slaves from becoming literate.[97] Most, of course, never did, but masters feared those who succeeded because they sometimes aided escapes and other illegal travels by forging passes and obtaining information belying planter myths about the impossibility of blacks surviving as free men and women. That slaves could escape, survive, and overcome a hostile white world were insights not a few black adults had acquired. Young blacks were both the beneficiaries of this knowledge and the ones who could make the most troublesome use of it. The enslaved thus taught their owners a bitter lesson: while they with relative ease could maintain a predominantly illiterate mass beneath them, it was far more difficult to keep an ignorant one.

Although slave elders succeeded in capturing some autonomous space and the minds of most among them, they did so under a complex system of controls that made each unservile move a serious risk. In such a setting, they could ill afford to shield their children indefinitely from the looming dangers. Consequently, children received many perplexing, contradictory, and paradoxical messages. Two family histories provide stark insights on the contradictions in slave responses to danger. George Cato, the great-great-grandson of Cato, leader of the Stono Rebellion of 1739, described the risks his ancestor had been willing to take:

> As it come down to me, I thinks de first Cato take a darin' chance on losin' his life, not so much for his own benefit as it was to help others. . . . Long befo' dis uprisin', de Cato wrote passes for slaves and do all he can to send them to freedom. He die but he die for doin' de right, as he see it.[98]

But the descendants of Robert Nesbit, who had been acquitted of insurrection charges during the Denmark Vesey conspiracy of 1822, learned why their forebear failed to help Vesey, though he was his friend and fellow "property-owner." Israel Nesbit wrote:

> My great-granddaddy never take no part in de plannin', 'cause he tried all de time to show Vesey he was headin' to a fall and was playin' wid dynamite. . . . Granddaddy say dat de loyalty of de slave to his master was so deep under de skin of de slave, dat it was even stronger than de long dream of freedom.[99]

Obviously, young slaves in the transition from childhood to adolescence had much to question and to resolve. How, for example, would they have reconciled tales of their people's courage and strength with the lacerated backs of so many among them? Some explanation, too, had to be forthcoming when loved ones were sold, slave rebels killed, or everyone in the quarters punished. Was it worth emulating slave and free black heroes if it meant death or shipment to worse circumstances? The discord and ambiguity such questions raised is reflected in the testimony of ex-slaves who were still children at the outbreak of the Civil War. Reuben Rosborough said, "My marster was a kind and tender man to slaves. You see a man love hosses and animals? Well, dat's de way he love us, though maybe in bigger portion." Still, he had to concede that his master "was good enough to buy my old gran' mammy Mary, though she never could do much work."[100] With similar reasoning, Ellen Renwick concluded her owner was "good": he "didn't whip . . . much."[101]

While distinguishing between "good" and "bad" masters implicitly seems to legitimize planter rule, most slaves never sanctioned the authority of slave ownership. They lived and usually died, however, in a war zone that made accurate comparative assessments of their oppressors vital. An owner who fed more, parted family members less, and left wider channels open for autonomy had to be preferred over one who often did the opposite. Differences were always on the minds of those in chains, yet despite variations in treatment, a slave was a slave. This was the crucial constant. Through their words and actions, the unfree consistently brought that point home. Rarely did they allow any kindness or humoring to blur the reality that the principal objective and motive of planters was the enrichment of their pockets and their power. Nor is it coincidental that ex-slaves so often referred to themselves as beasts of burden when they described their former owners' behavior. One former slave could not resist adding a pungent note to her recollections of slave food: "Us had all us need to eat. . . . Marse like to see his slaves fat and shiny, just like he want to see de carriage hosses slick and spanky when he ride out to preachin' at Ainswell."[102]

However ignorant planters might be of such sentiments in the slave community, they were keenly aware of slaves' devotion to their families and cognizant of how effectively that affinity could be exploited. Adele Petigru Allston settled on the following plan to control workers after three children of "a highly favoured servant"[103] had absconded toward the end of the Civil War.

> I think Mary and James should be taken up and sent to some secure jail in the interior and held as hostages for the conduct of their children. And they should understand that this is done by the police of the country, who require that the older negroes should endeavour to influence the younger ones to order and subordination while this war lasts, and that they will be held responsible for the behavior of their children. For this course to have the best effect it ought to be universal, and ought to be required by the police of the country. I wish you to show this letter to Col. Francis Heriot and consult him as to what course he thinks best. If he thinks it best to make an example among the old people whose children have deserted, then let a cart or wagon be ready as soon as the search of the houses is over, and Mary and James sent off. Some place of confinement would be the best . . . letting them understand they would have to remain there until the end of the war, and desertion or rebellion in any of their children would be laid at their door. If this is done let them not have a day or an hour on the place after it is fixed on. Let them have no communication with any of their family except in presence of a white person, and put their children who have never learnt to work at once to learn. It does not seem to me reasonable or right to leave negroes in the enjoyment of privileges and ease and comfort, whose children go off in this way. I am persuaded it is done with their knowledge and connivance.[104]

Members of the plantocracy realized also the conservative effect of marriage and, for the most part, encouraged such unions.[105] Holland McTyeire, a Baptist minister who supported this policy observed that

> Local as well as family associations . . . are strong yet pleasing cords binding him to his master. His welfare is so involved in the order of things that he would not for any consideration have it disturbed. He is made happier and safe; put beyond discontent, or temptations to rebellion and abduction; for he gains nothing in comparison with what he loses. His comforts cannot be removed with him, and he will stay with them.[106]

The gravitational pull of the connubial relations of slaves was revealed most vividly to Captain and Mrs. Basil Hall while traveling through South Carolina in 1828. They witnessed a slave coffle of about twenty-five individuals, two of whom were "bolted together." When one of the men was asked the reason for the chains, he replied quite happily, "Oh sir, they are the best things in the world to travel with." His companion said nothing. Upon further inquiries, Captain Hall learned that the silent bondsman had a wife on a neighboring plantation whose owner refused to sell her and, thereby, caused their separation. To prevent desertion, "the wretched husband was . . . shackled to a young unmarried man, who, having no such tie to draw him back, might be more safely trusted on the journey."[107] If the single male were to wed, he would undoubtedly remember the distraught partner en route to his new home and very likely behave without misconduct so as to avoid following in those shackled footsteps.

American planters were not the first enslavers to recognize the pacifying influence of conjugal and other family attachments. As early as 1527 Spanish authorities had enacted a measure to promote marriage among slaves. They reasoned that this "would calm them down," decrease the number of runaways, and prevent "unrest."[108] The Jamaican ruling class also noted the greater manageability of blacks who were married and, significantly, often placed indigenous Africans with Creole families during their "sea-soiling" process. Referring to this practice, Bryan Edwards, author of an 1801 study on the British West Indies, stated that within eight or ten months "new people . . . begin to get well established in their families, their houses and provision-grounds; and prove in all respects as valuable as the native or creole negroes." He described further the great desire of creole slaves to bring the "raw" Africans into their families and observed that:

> The strangers too were best pleased with this arrangement, and ever afterwards considered themselves as the adopted children of those by whom they were thus protected, calling them parents, and venerating them as such; and I never knew an instance of the violation of a trust thus solicited and bestowed.[109]

Slaveholders in the United States directed recent purchases, both domestic and foreign, to reside with families in their possession, but there is no way of determining whether this was done for reasons of control or of economic convenience. Whatever the case, the consequences were the same: slaves forged pseudo-kinship bonds quickly and adjusted rapidly to the ways of the plantation.[110] When Charles Ball arrived in South Carolina he was told to live at the home of Nero, a slave with a wife and five children. The following excerpt from *Fifty Years in Chains*, illustrates how swiftly one could become "part of the family."

> I could make wooden bowls and ladles, and went to work with a man who was clearing some new land about two miles off—on the second Sunday of my sojourn here, and applied the money I earned in purchasing the tools necessary to enable me to carry on my trade. I occupied all my leisure hours, for several months after this, in making wooden trays, and such other vessels as were most in demand. These I traded off, in part to a storekeeper . . . and for some of my work I obtained money. Before Christmas, I had sold more than thirty dollars worth of my manufactures; but the merchant with whom I traded, charged such high prices for his goods, that I was poorly compensated for my Sunday toils, and nightly labours; nevertheless, by these means, I was able to keep *our family* supplied with molasses, and some other luxuries, and at the approach of winter, I purchased three coarse blankets, to which Nero added as many, and we had all these made up into blanket-coats for Dinah, ourselves, and the children.[111] (Emphasis added.)

Although the black family was the source of the planters' most effective control mechanism, it was also, for slaves, the greatest mitigation of the harshness and severity of bondage. John Jackson spoke angrily of the many sadistic and humiliating beatings he received as a slave, but stressed the following turning point during "those horrible times": "I growed up and married when I was very young, and I loved my little girl wife. Life was not a burden then. I never minded the whippings I got. I was happy."[112] The kinship networks created by African-Americans helped shield bondsmen from the dehumanization inevitable in any slave society. Slaves could depend on familial relations—both real and fictive—when in need, and however futile it may have been, protection sometimes from white oppressors.[113] Yet the family served as a pacifying institution as well. Gutman suggests that slave women bore children in part because they were aware that evidence of their fertility might persuade masters not to exchange them for more "profitable" servants.[114] Because a slave, once informed of the owner's decision to sell, could do little to alter the decision other than to appeal to the owner or practice self-mutilation,[115] many slaves sought to prevent separation from loved ones by abiding by the rules of the plantation. Not a few slaves regarded obedience as a fair price to pay for keeping their families intact.

Some slave elders, without any *direct* external pressure, taught their progeny lessons that can be classified as "internal controls," in the sense that they kept community members "out of trouble" and "peaceful."[116] Aaron Ford, a former slave, recalled these guidelines and instructions he received from his grandfather throughout his sixteen years of servitude:

> I remember my grandfather all right. He de one told me how to catch otters. Told me how to set traps. Heard my grandfather tell bout whippin slaves for stealin. Grandfather told me not to take things dat were not mine. If a pile of corn was left at night, I was told not to bother it. In breakin corn, sometimes people would make a pile of corn in de grass en leave it en den come back en get it in de night. Grandfather told me not to never bother nothin bout people's things.[117]

One slaveholder, David Golightly Harris, received help from his slaves when he "had difficulty with Matt," one of his slaves.

> I tied him [Matt] up and gave him a gentle admonition in the shape of a good whipping. I intended to put him in jail and keep him there until I sold him but he seemed so penitent & promised so fairly & *the other negroes promising to see that he would behave himself in future* that I concluded that I would try him once more.[118] (Emphasis added.)

For exactly two months, Matt's neighbors, some of whom were certainly his relatives, were able apparently to constrain him, but, finally, he was converted into cash. Harris noted that Matt himself "was willing to be sold."[119]

Perhaps the most telling statement on the role of the family came in 1863 from Jim, a slave captured by Union forces with his master on Bailey's Island in South Carolina. Laura Towne described Jim as "sad" and recorded his declaration that "he would not give up the wife and children now on the Main for all the freedom in the world."[120] Familial bonds militated against and sometimes prevented revolutionary fervor. The difference in the number of men and women who ran away reflects this phenomenon indirectly. According to one scholar, at least 80 percent of all runaways were males between the ages of sixteen and thirty-five. He posited that mothers were more unwilling to defect because of their stronger attachment to children, whereas many young men had yet to assume the responsibilities of marriage and fatherhood and therefore felt less obligated to stay.[121] Although some bondsmen fled to the North, the majority simply remained "out" near their homes and often for remarkably long periods of time through the assistance of their families and friends.[122] While this was a constant annoyance to planters, it did not hurt their pockets as much as the loss of captive laborers who obtained permanent freedom above the

Mason-Dixon line. Again, African-Americans' family ties guaranteed and protected the property interests of the ruling class.

It is not difficult to imagine the influence masters had over slaves with mates and kin on other plantations: they had the power to withhold the passes that bondsmen were required to carry when absent from the estates of their owners. Although most blacks probably did not wait for such "permission," they still would have needed, on occasion, the sanction of planters, and good behavior was undoubtedly a major criterion.[123] Mrs. Benjamin Perry, for example, promised the visiting mother of Delia, a fifteen-year-old servant, that Delia could visit her at Christmas "if" she was "a good girl."[124] Members of the plantocracy did help slaves sometimes to see relatives and to keep their families together,[125] and it is highly unlikely that such aid was unappreciated or forgotten by blacks. In the eyes of the enslaved, kinship ties were of paramount importance and worthy of infinite sacrifice. In this lay the force of masters' threats to sell. Not surprisingly, those slaveholders who made it a habit of "transporting" unruly and incorrigible blacks were known to have "well-ordered people" who gave "little trouble."[126] The threat of sale was the most effective long-term mechanism of control.

NOTES

1. Foby, "Management of Servants," *SC*, XI (August 1853), 226.
2. George P. Rawick, ed., *The American Slave: A Composite Autobiography*, Supplement, Series 1 (Westport, Conn.: Greenwood Press, 1977), 11, p. 283.
3. Bobby Frank Jones, "A Cultural Middle Passage: Slave Marriage and Family in the Ante-Bellum South" (Ph.D. dissertation, University of North Carolina, 1965), pp. 6–7; J. G. Clinkscales, *On the Old Plantation: Reminiscences of His Childhood* (New York: Negro Universities Press, 1969), pp. 37–38 (originally published in 1916); George P. Rawick, ed., *The American Slave: A Composite Autobiography* (Westport, Conn.: Greenwood Publishing Company, 1972), III, iii, pp. 218–20, II, ii p. 77; Jacob Stroyer, *My Life in the South* (Salem, Mass.: Observer and Job Print, 1885), pp. 42–43; A. M. French, *Slavery in South Carolina and the Ex-Slaves; Or, the Port Royal Mission* (New York: Negro Universities Press, 1969), p. 94 (originally published in 1862).
4. Charles Ball, *Fifty Years in Chains*, with an introduction by Philip S. Foner (New York: Dover Publications, 1970), p. 68 (originally published in 1837).
5. Nowel v. O'Hara, 1 Hill 150, April 1833. (151), in Helen T. Catterall, ed., *Judicial Cases Concerning American Slavery and the Negro* (Washington, D.C.: Carnegie Institute of Washington, 1929), II, p. 352.
6. Hinton v. Kennedy, 3 S.C. 459, November 1871. Will, 1855: (480), in Ibid., p. 477.
7. Robert Pringle, Charles Town, to Edward & John Mayne & Co., Lisbon, September 19, 1740, in Walter B. Edgar, ed., *The Letterbook of Robert Pringle* (Columbia: The University of South Carolina Press, 1972), I, p. 247.
8. Plantation Book of Charles Cotesworth Pinckney and Successors, 1812–1861, "Slave List," pp. 1–11, The Pinckney Family Papers, LC; John Chesnut, Camden, to Charles Chesnut, Philadelphia, September 25, 1835, Williams-Chesnut-Manning Papers, SC; James R. Sparkman Plantation Book, 1845, II, Sparkman Family Papers, SHC; Douglass v. Price, 4 Rich. Eq. 322, May 1852. (326), in Catterall, *Judicial Cases*, II, p. 433; David Golightly Harris Farm Journals, June 9, 11, 1860 (microfilm), SHC; Elizabeth Collins, *Memories of the Southern States* (Taunton: Barnicott, 1865), p. 71; William Elliot, Adam's Run, to William Elliot, Jr., August 25, 1862, Elliot-Gonzales Papers, SHC; "State vs. Frank, Hannah, and Matilda, slaves of Charles J. Colcock, Beaufort District, S.C.," June 16, 1862, Francis W. Pickens and Milledge L. Bonham Papers, LC; William Capers, Gowrie Plantation, to Charles Manigault, Charleston, S.C., September 15, 28, 1863, in Ulrich B. Phillips, ed., *Plantation and Frontier Documents, 1649–1863: Illustrative of Industrial History in the Colonial & Ante-Bellum South* (Cleveland: The Arthur H. Clark Company, 1909), II, pp. 32–33.
9. Charles C. Jones, *The Religious Instruction of the Negroes* (New York: Negro Universities Press, 1969), p. 133 (originally published in 1842); "Religious Instruction of Slaves," *DR*, o.s., XXVI (January 1859), 108; Rev. Andrew Flinn Dickson, *Plantation Sermons, or Plain and Familiar Discourses for Instruction of the Unlearned* (Philadelphia: Presbyterian Board of Publication, 1856), pp. 13–14.
10. H. Shelton Smith, *In His Image, But . . . Racism in Southern Religion, 1780–1910* (Durham, N.C.: Duke University Press, 1972), pp. 43–47, 53–55, 59–60, 69, 138.
11. John B. Adger, *The Christian Doctrine of Human Rights and Slavery* (Columbia, S.C., 1849), p. 15, quoted in Ibid., p. 138.
12. Rawick, *The American Slave*, II, ii, pp. 234–35.
13. Una Pope-Hennessy, *The Aristocratic Journey: Being the Outspoken Letters of Mrs. Basil Hall Written During a Fourteen Months' Sojourn in America, 1827–1828* (New York: G. P. Putnam's Sons, 1931), p. 210; John C. Calhoun,

Cane Brake (Edgefield County, S.C.), to Thomas Green Clemson, Brussels, December 13, 1845, Calhoun Family Typescripts; Frederick Douglass, *Life and Times of Frederick Douglass* (1962), p. 97, cited in Herbert G. Gutman, *The Black Family in Slavery & Freedom, 1750–1925* (New York: Pantheon Books, 1976), pp. 357–58; *Preliminary Report Touching the Condition and Management of Emancipated Refugees; Made to the Secretary of War, by the American Freedmen's Inquiry Commission, June 30, 1863* (New York: John F. Trow, 1863), p. 13; Elizabeth Hyde Botume, *First Days Amongst the Contrabands* (New York: Arno Press and The New York Times, 1968), pp. 84, 209–10 (originally published in 1892); Elizabeth Ware Pearson, ed., *Letters From Port Royal, 1862–1868* (New York: Arno Press and The New York Times, 1969), p. 97 (originally published in 1906); Ray Allen Billington, ed., *The Journal of Charlotte L. Forten: A Free Negro in the Slave Era* (New York: Collier Books, 1961), p. 211.

14. Charles Nordhoff, "The Freedmen of South-Carolina," in Frank Moore, ed., *Papers of the Day* (New York: Charles T. Evans, 1863), p. 11.

15. Rupert Sargent Holland, ed., *Letters and Diary of Laura M. Towne: Written From the Sea Islands of South Carolina, 1862–1884* (Cambridge: Riverside Press, 1912), pp. 74–75.

16. Joel Williamson, *After Slavery: The Negro in South Carolina During Reconstruction, 1861–1877* (Chapel Hill: The University of North Carolina Press, 1965), pp. 39–44; Guion Griffis Johnson, *A Social History of the Sea Islands: With Special Reference to St. Helena Island, South Carolina* (Chapel Hill: The University of North Carolina Press, 1930), p. 190; Julia Peterkin, *Roll, Jordan, Roll. Photographic Studies by Doris Ulmann* (New York: Robert O. Ballou, 1933), p. 28.

17. Elsie Clews Parsons, *Folk-Lore of the Sea Islands, South Carolina* (Cambridge, Mass.: The American Folk-Lore Society, 1923), pp. 213–16; "Memoirs of S. W. Ferguson: Family History and Boyhood," April 26, 1900 (typescript), pp. 15, 20, Heyward and Ferguson Family Papers (typescript and microfilm), SHC; Anne Sinkler Fishburne, *Belvidere: A Plantation Memory* (Columbia: University of South Carolina Press, 1949), pp. 106–7; Leon Stone Bryan, Jr., "Slavery On a Peedee River Rice Plantation, 1825–1865" (M.A. thesis, Johns Hopkins University, 1963), p. 186.

18. Patience Pennington (E. W. A. Pringle), *A Woman Rice Planter* (Cambridge: The Belknap Press of Harvard University Press, 1961), p. 59, quoted in Bryan, "Slavery On a Peedee River Rice Plantation," pp. 183–84, 186.

19. George Rogers, Jr., *The History of Georgetown County, South Carolina* (Columbia: University of South Carolina Press, 1970), p. 328; Gutman, *The Black Family*, pp. 357–58; Austin Bearse, *Reminiscences of Fugitive-Slave Law Days* (Boston: Warren Richardson, 1880), pp. 8–10; Abream Scriven to Dinah Jones, Savannah (Ga.), September 19, 1858, Charles Colcock Jones Papers, Special Collections Division, Tulane University Library, New Orleans, in Robert S. Starobin, ed., *Letters of American Slaves* (New York: New Viewpoints, 1974), p. 58; French, *Slavery in South Carolina*, p. 125; Rawick, *The American Slave*, II, i, pp. 180, 188; E. C. L. Adams, *Nigger to Nigger* (New York: Charles Scribner's Sons, 1928), pp. 235–36.

20. Thomas Wentworth Higginson, *Army Life in a Black Regiment* (Boston: Beacon Press, 1962), pp. 52–53 (originally published in 1869).

21. "Petition of Certain Citizens of Charleston Praying to Prohibit the Introduction of Slaves Merely for Sale and for Certain Other Amendments of the Law in Relation to Slaves," 1847, (Folder 64), Slavery Files, SCA.

22. "Memoirs of S. W. Ferguson," p. 3, Heyward and Ferguson Family Papers, SHC; Harriet Martineau, *Society in America* (London: Saunders and Otley, 1837), II, pp. 333–34; William P. Harrison, ed., *The Gospel Among the Slaves* (Nashville: Publishing House of the M. E. Church, South, 1893), p. 359.

23. Robert F. W. Allston, Plantersville, to Adele Petigru Allston, April 10, 1863, in J. H. Easterby, ed., *The South Carolina Rice Plantation as Revealed in the Papers of Robert F. W. Allston* (Chicago: University of Chicago Press, 1945), p. 184.

24. Thomas Cooper and David J. McCord, eds., *The Statutes at Large of South Carolina* (Columbia, 1836–41), VII, p. 370, quoted in Peter Wood, *Black Majority: Negroes in Colonial South Carolina From 1670 Through the Stono Rebellion* (New York: Alfred A. Knopf, 1974), p. 280.

25. Wood, *Black Majority*, pp. 25–26, 140, 159–60.

26. Rawick, *The American Slave*, sup., 11, pp. 132–33; Gutman, *The Black Family*, pp. 145–46, 148–49, 153, 357–58; Leslie Howard Owens, *This Species of Property: Slave Life and Culture in the Old South* (New York: Oxford University Press, 1976), pp. 184–85; "Memoirs," n.d. (typescript), pp. 66–67, 77, John O'Neale Papers, PL.

27. Manigault Letter Book, 1846–1848 (typescript), Charles Izard Manigault, Paris, to Mr. Haynes, (Savannah River), March 1, 1847, pp. 26–27, Charles Manigault Papers, SC.

28. Rawick, *The American Slave*, II, i, p. 159.

29. Collins, *Memories of the Southern States*, p. 71.

30. Ray Allen Billington, ed., *The Journal of Charlotte L. Forten: A Free Negro in the Slave Era* (New York: Collier Books, 1961), pp. 151–52, 160; Holland, *Letters and Diary of Laura M. Towne*, p. 28; Stroyer, *My Life in the South*, pp. 43–44; Thomas H. Jones, *The Experience and Personal Narrative of Uncle Tom Jones: Who Was for Forty Years a Slave; also, the Surprising Adventures of Wild Tom, a Fugitive Negro from South Carolina* (New York: G. C. Holbrook, 1854), pp. 7–8, cited in Stanley Feldstein, "The Slave's View of Slavery" (Ph.D. dissertation, New York University, 1969), p. 35.

31. Ball, *Fifty Years in Chains*, pp. 17–18.

32. Rawick, *The American Slave*, II, i, pp. 229–30.

33. Stroyer, *My Life in the South*, pp. 42–44; Rawick, *The American Slave*, II, i, pp. 65–67, II, ii, pp. 144–45; Orland Kay Armstrong, *Old Massa's People: The Old Slaves Tell Their Story* (Indianapolis: Bobbs-Merrill Company, 1931), pp. 258–59.

34. Rawick, *The American Slave*, II, i, pp. 180, 188.

35. Sidney Mintz and Richard Price, *An Anthropological Approach to the Afro-American Past: A Caribbean Perspective* (Philadelphia: Institute for the Study of Human Issues, 1976), p. 34.

36. Arney Robinson Childs, ed., *The Private Journal of Henry William Ravenel, 1859–1887* (Columbia: University of South Carolina Press, 1947), p. 240; George W. Williams, ed., *Incidents In My Life: The Autobiography of the Rev. Paul Trapier, S.T.D. With Some of His Letters* (Charleston: Dalcho Historical Society, 1954), p. 32; Charles I. Manigault Book Containing Loose Papers, 1776–1872 (typescript) p. 17, Charles Manigault Papers, SC.

37. Rogers, *History of Georgetown County*, pp. 328, 343; Charles W. Joyner, "Slave Folklife of the Waccamaw Neck: Antebellum Black Culture in the South Carolina Lowcountry" (Ph.D. dissertation, University of Pennsylvania, 1977), p. 30.

38. Armstrong, *Old Massa's People*, pp. 44–45; Rawick, *The American Slave*, III, iii, p. 14; Billington, *Journal of Charlotte Forten*, pp. 160, 178; Fredrika Bremer, *The Homes of the New World: Impressions of America*, trans. Mary Howitt (New York: Harper & Brothers, 1868), I, p. 394; Holland, *Letters and Diary of Laura M. Towne*, p. 177.

39. Fishburne, *Belvidere*, p. 25.

40. Herbert G. Gutman, *The Black Family in Slavery & Freedom, 1750–1925* (New York: Pantheon Books, 1976), pp. 36, 45–46, 52, 88, 93, 101–2, 154, 196–97, 199, 217–18, 220.

41. Sidney Mintz, *Caribbean Transformations* (Chicago: Aldine Publishing Company, 1974), p. 77.

42. Pearson, *Letters From Port Royal*, pp. 44, 97, 133–35; Holland, *Letters and Diary of Laura M. Towne*, pp. 45–54.

43. "150 Reward," The Charleston *Mercury*, January 6, 1829; Thomas L. Shaw, "Ten Dollars Reward," Georgetown *Gazette*, December 16, 1825; "Forty Dollars Reward," The Charleston *Mercury*, January 6, 1829; "Absconded," The Charleston *Courier*, July 27, 1829; *American Slavery As It Is: Testimony of A Thousand Witnesses* (New York: American Anti-Slavery Society, 1839), p. 23; J. S. Buckingham, *The Slave States of America* (London: Fisher, Son, & Co., 1842), I, p. 571; Langdon Cheves, Pendleton, to Langdon Cheves, Jr., Savannah, May 2, 1844, Cheves Family Papers, SCHS; Anderson *Gazette*, June 5, 1846, III, p. 3.

44. The Charleston *Courier*, February 17, 1849.

45. John Davis, *Travels of Four Years and a Half in the United States of America: During 1798, 1799, 1800, 1801, and 1802* (London: 1803), pp. 92–93.

46. "John's Island," The Charleston *Mercury*, July 1, 1829.

47. Frances Lance, "Ranaway on the 29th," *The Southern Patriot*, April 18, 1829; *American Slavery As It Is*, p. 63; Jno. Cothran, "$20 Reward!" Greenville *Mountaineer*, September 21, 1838; Anne King Gregorie, *History of Sumter County, South Carolina* (Sumter: Library Board of Sumter County, 1954), p. 144; Henry Sills, "$30.00 Reward," Cheraw *Intelligencer and Southern Register*, March 5, 1824.

48. Samuel Tayler, Mobile, Ala., to Mrs. Elizabeth Blythe, [Georgetown], September 2, 1838, R. F. W. Allston Papers, SCHS.

49. "Information Wanted," *South Carolina Leader*, May 12, 1866, I, n.pag.; Leon F. Litwack, *Been in the Storm So Long: The Aftermath of Slavery* (New York: Vintage Books, 1979), pp. 230–32.

50. "Information Wanted," *New Era*, July 28, 1870, I, n.pag.

51. Cuba, like other sugar-producing societies, was feared by North American slaves as a destination little worse than hell. Not only did rumors abound of unrelenting labor, but of masters whose brutality made American slaveholders seem benign. See Holland, *Letters and Diary of Laura M. Towne*, pp. 53–54.

52. Nordhoff, "Freedmen of South-Carolina," p. 20.

53. "Testimony of Col. Higginson," American Freedmen's Inquiry Commission (microfilm), Reel 200, File III, p. 192, NA; Holland, *Letters and Diary of Laura M. Towne*, pp. 45–46, 49, 53–54, 107; Billington, *Journal of Charlotte L. Forten*, pp. 165–66, 178, 182; Botume, *First Days Amongst the Contrabands*, pp. 54–57, 68, 154, 163. While ministering among the contrabands, the Reverend Mansfield French declared that blacks' herculean search for relatives was a "sacred work" that deserved every possible assistance. Unfortunately, as Leon Litwack discovered, neither the extraordinary skill of blacks in tracking down each clue and rumor, nor their steadfast determination to remain on trails that "suddenly appeared to vanish," led many to find their families. See French, *Slavery in South Carolina*, p. 27, and Litwack, *Been in the Storm So Long*, pp. 230–31.

54. Edward L. Pierce, "Freedmen at Port Royal," *AM*, XII (September 1863), 311.

55. Stephen Moore, Camp on James Island, to Rachel, July 8, 1862, Thomas John Moore Papers, SC.

56. Ulrich B. Phillips, *American Negro Slavery: A Survey of the Supply, Employment and Control of Negro Labor As Determined by the Plantation Regime*, with a foreword by Eugene Genovese (Baton Rouge: Louisiana State University Press, 1966), pp. 264–68, 279, 286; Kenneth M. Stampp, *The Peculiar Institution: Slavery in the Ante-Bellum South* (New York: Vintage Books, 1956), pp. 282–89; Eugene D. Genovese, "Rejoinder," *SL*, 6 (November-December 1966), 58, 61; Robert W. Fogel and Stanley L. Engerman, *Time On the Cross: The Economics of American Negro Slavery* (Boston: Little, Brown and Company, 1974), I, pp. 109–17. In challenging the Fogel and Engerman thesis that "slavery provided a better diet for blacks than did freedom for most whites," Richard Sutch argues: "The slave *diet* may have generally been nutritionally balanced even when the *ration* provided by the master was not," for slaves, despite their masters, made it so. See Richard Sutch, "The Care and Feeding of Slaves," in Paul A. David et al., *Reckoning With Slavery: A Critical Study in the Quantitative History*, with an introduction by Kenneth M. Stampp (New York: Oxford University Press, 1976), pp. 268, 281–82.

57. Ball, *Fifty Years in Chains*, p. 194; George W. Knepper, ed., *Travels in The Southland, 1822–1823: The Journal of Lucius Versus Bierce* (Columbus: Ohio State University Press, 1966), p. 81; William L. McCaa, "Observations on the Manner of Living and Diseases of the Slaves on the Wateree River, S.C." (Sr. thesis, University of Pennsylvania, 1823), p. 1,

WHL; Moses Roper, *A Narrative of the Adventures and Escape of Moses Roper From American Slavery* (New York: Negro Universities Press, 1970), p. 60 (originally published in 1838); H. Perry Pope, "A Dissertation on the Professional Management of Negro Slaves" (Sr. thesis, Medical College of the State of South Carolina, 1837), pp. 3–4, MU; *American Slavery As It Is*, p. 28; Henry William Ravenel, "Recollections of Southern Plantation Life," *TYR*, XXV (June 1936), 753; Nordhoff, "Freedmen of South Carolina," p. 5; French, *Slavery in South Carolina*, pp. 67, 118–20.

58.   Charles M. Clark, "Plantation Overseers in South Carolina, 1820–1860" (M.A. thesis, University of South Carolina, 1966), p. 30; Ball, *Fifty Years in Chains*, pp. 205–7, 262–63; William E. Sparkman Plantation Record, 1844–1866, March 31, 1844, to December 29, 1844, SHC; Dr. J. Rhett Motte's Exeter Plantation Work Book, St. Johns, Berkeley, January 1, 1850, to July 7, 1850, I, Motte Family Papers, SC; Mulberry Journal for 1853–1857, December 3, 1853, to April 25, 1857, Mulberry Plantation Journals, 1853–1889, SCHS; Knepper, *Travels in the Southland*, p. 81; Ravenel, *TYR*, 751; Roper, *A Narrative*, p. 60; Manigault Letter Book, Charles Izard Manigault, Naples, to Mr. J. F. Cooper, Gowrie, January 10, 1848, pp. 59–60, Charles Manigault Papers, SC.

59.   Duncan Clinch Heyward, *Seed From Madagascar* (Chapel Hill: The University of North Carolina Press, 1937), pp. ix, 182; Gutman, *The Black Family*, p. 237.

60.   Phillips, *American Negro Slavery*, p. 265.

61.   Chalmers Gaston Davidson, *The Last Foray: The South Carolina Planters of 1860, A Sociological Study* (Columbia: University of South Carolina Press, 1971), p. 252; Sparkman Plantation Record, January 1, 1845, SHC.

62.   Sparkman Plantation Record, March 31, 1844, to December 26, 1844, SHC.

63.   Dr. Motte's Work Book, January 1, 1850, to June 30, 1850, I, Motte Family Papers, SC.

64.   Helen G. McCormack, "A Provisional Guide to Manuscripts in the South Carolina Historical Society," *SCHM*, 47 (July 1946), 173.

65.   Mulberry Journal, December 3, 1853, to April 25, 1857, Mulberry Plantation, Journals, SCHS.

66.   "Report of the Committee on Colored Population," December 4, 1856 (Folder 217), Slavery Files, SCA.

67.   Clark, "Plantation Overseers," p. 30; Stampp, *The Peculiar Institution*, pp. 283–84; Robert [Cox?], Head Quarters, [Sullivan's Island], 20th Regt. S.C.V., to Brother, September 29, 1862, I, Cox Papers (typescript), p. 167, SC; H. D. McCloud, "Hints on the Medical Treatment of Negroes" (Sr. thesis, Medical College of South Carolina, 1850), pp. 15–16, MU.

68.   Farmer's Club (ABC Farmer's Club) Records, 1846–1893, Beech Island, Aiken County, November 6, 1847 (typescript), p. 45, SC.

69.   A Planter, "Notions on the Management of Negroes, &c.," *SA*, IX (November 1836), 582; Dr. Roderick Murchison, New York, to Elizabeth Murchison, Orangeburg, S.C., February 1, 1817, Bruce, Jones, and Murchison Papers, SC.

70.   H. Perry Pope, "A Dissertation on the Professional Management of Negro Slaves," pp. 3–4, MU.

71.   Stroyer, *My Life in the South*, p. 11.

72.   Ball, *Fifty Years in Chains*, pp. 54, 207, 262–63, 323; Roper, *A Narrative*, p. 60; *Anti-Slavery Advocate*, II (February 1, 1862), 498–99, in John W. Blassingame, ed., *Slave Testimony: Two Centuries of Letters, Speeches, Interviews and Autobiographies* (Baton Rouge: Louisiana State University Press, 1977), p. 359; "Rosa Barnwell to the Editor," *Liberator*, November 7, 1862, in Blassingame, *Slave Testimony*, p. 698; Billington, *Journal of Charlotte Forten*, p. 149; Nordhoff, "Freedmen of South Carolina," p. 5; French, *Slavery in South Carolina*, pp. 118–19; Rawick, *The American Slave*, III, iii, pp. 8–10, 272; Dorothy Sterling, *Captain of the Planter, The Story of Robert Smalls* (New York, 1958), pp. 16, 24, 29–31, cited in Willie Lee Rose, *Rehearsal for Reconstruction: The Port Royal Experiment* (New York: Vintage Books, 1964), p. 131.

73.   Rochester *Union and Advertiser*, August 9, 1893, in Blassingame, *Slave Testimony*, pp. 511–12.

74.   Rawick, *The American Slave*, II, i, p. 125.

75.   Joyner, "Slave Folklife," pp. 158–59, 162–64, 321.

76.   John Drayton, *A View of South Carolina, As Respects Her Natural and Civil Concerns* (Charleston: W. P. Young, 1802), p. 145; Ball, *Fifty Years in Chains*, p. 194; Bremer, *Homes of the New World*, I, p. 297; Ravenel, *TYR*, 762; D. E. Smith, *A Charlestonian's Recollections, 1846–1913* (Charleston: Carolina Art Association, 1950), pp. 27, 29; Rawick, *The American Slave*, III, iii, pp. 8–10, 272; Joyner, "Slave Folklife," pp. 194, 321; Lawton v. Hunt, 4 Rich. Eq. 233, January, 1852. (234), in Catterall, *Judicial Cases*, pp. 431–32.

77.   Sutch, "Care and Feeding of Slaves," p. 282; Charles Joyner, *Down by the Riverside: A South Carolina Slave Community* (Urbana: University of Illinois Press, 1984), p. 99; Adam Hodgson, *Remarks During a Journey Through North America in the Years 1819, 1820, and 1821 . . .* (New York: Samuel Whiting, 1823), p. 117; Bremer, *Homes of the New World*, I, pp. 297, 305; Charles A. Raymond, "The Religious Life of the Negro Slave," *HNM*, XXVII (September 1863), 676; Alice R. Huger Smith, *A Carolina Rice Plantation of the Fifties . . . With Chapters From the Unpublished Memoirs of D. E. Huger Smith* (New York: William Morrow and Company, 1936), pp. 71–72; Holland, *Letters and Diary of Laura M. Towne*, pp. 27–28; Rawick, *The American Slave*, III, iii, pp. 200–1, II, i, p. 244, II, ii, p. 76; Jones, "A Cultural Middle Passage," pp. 126, 131; Ball, *Fifty Years in Chains*, pp. 194–95, 205, 257, 274–75; Kneppler, *Travels in the Southland*, p. 81; Nordhoff, "Freedmen of South Carolina," pp. 5–16, 18; Heyward, *Seed From Madagascar*, p. 182.

78.   Charles Cotesworth Pinckney, *An Address Delivered in Charleston Before the Agricultural Society of South-Carolina . . . The 18th August, 1829* (Charleston: A. E. Miller, 1829), p. 4.

79.   Holland, *Letters and Diary of Laura M. Towne*, p. 25.

80.   Stroyer, *My Life in the South*, pp. 23–24; "Have Manners: Grandma Kit and Aunt Maria Heywood," (D-4–33a), Federal Writers' Project, S.C.: Folklore MSS (typescript), SC; Jones, "A Cultural Middle Passage," p. 107.

81.   Rawick, *The American Slave*, II, i, pp. 224–25.

82. William Howard Russell, *My Diary North and South* (New York: Harper & Brothers, 1863), p. 55; Collins, *Memories of the Southern States*, p. 31; Rawick, *The American Slave*, III, iii, pp. 261–62.

83. W. W. Gilmer, "Management of Servants," *FP*, III (July 1852), 110.

84. "Report on Management of Slaves, Duty of Overseers, and Employers to Darlington County Agricultural Society," August 1852, pp. 1–2, Thomas Cassels Law Papers, SC; Bremer, *Homes of the New World*, I, pp. 291–92; Charles I. Manigault Book Containing Loose Papers, p. 16, Charles Manigault Papers, SC; Armstrong, *Old Massa's People*, p. 200; Pinckney, *An Address*, pp. 10–12; Charles Cotesworth Pinckney, El Dorado, to William Capers, January 23, 1835, Conference Papers, Methodist Collection, Wofford College, quoted in Rogers, *History of Georgetown County*, pp. 352–53; Joyner, "Slave Folklife," pp. 159–75; E. C. L. Adams, *Nigger to Nigger* (New York: Charles Scribner's Sons, 1928), pp. 175–76; Parsons, *Folk-Lore of the Sea Islands*, pp. xvii, 22–23, 97, 102; Charles C. Jones, *Negro Myths From the Georgia Coast* (Columbia: The State Company, 1925), pp. 53–54.

85. Julia Peterkin, *Roll, Jordan, Roll. Photographic Studies by Doris Ulmann* (New York: Robert O. Ballou, 1933), p. 231; Archie Vernon Huff, *Langdon Cheves of South Carolina* (Columbia: University of South Carolina Press, 1977), pp. 192, 194–96.

86. Rawick, *The American Slave*, II, i, p. 220, III, iii, pp. 77–99, 145, 153; Ravenel, *TYR*, 757, 761, 764; Pearson, *Letters From Port Royal*, p. 215; Joyner, "Slave Folklife," pp. 167, 169; Jones, *Negro Myths*, pp. 53–54; Holland, *Letters and Diary of Laura M. Towne*, pp. 107, 148, 150; Botume, *First Days Amongst the Contrabands*, pp. 48–49, 68–69, 139, 190, 237–43; "Manners Will Carry You," (D-4-331), Federal Writers' Project, S.C., SC; William Francis Allen and others, *Slave Songs of the United States* (New York: A. Simpson & Co., 1867), pp. xxix–xxx, 39; Mintz, *An Anthropological Approach*, pp. 35, 37; Gutman, *The Black Family*, pp. 154, 216–18, 226–28.

87. Gutman, *The Black Family*, p. 220.

88. Joyner, "Slave Folklife," p. 169; Hodgson, *Remarks*, p. 130; Botume, *First Days Amongst the Contrabands*, p. 36; Thomas L. Webber, *Deep Like the Rivers: Education in the Slave Quarter Community, 1831–1865* (New York: W. W. Norton and Company, 1978), pp. 19, 221, 225, 318; John W. Blassingame, "Status and Social Structure in the Slave Community: Evidence From New Sources," in Harry P. Owens, ed., *Perspectives and Irony in American Slavery* (Jackson: University Press of Mississippi, 1976), p. 147.

89. Thomas Webber argues, for instance, that by the time slaveholders began any serious efforts to shape the worldview of slave youths, the latter already had learned how "to adopt the roles required by plantation etiquette *without an identification with* the reality suggested by the role." (Emphasis added.) See Webber, *Deep Like the Rivers*, p. 261.

90. Hodgson, *Remarks*, p. 130; Smith, *Carolina Rice Plantation*, p. 71.

91. Stephen Gudeman, "Herbert Gutman's The Black Family in Slavery and Freedom, 1750–1925: An Anthropologist's View," *SSH*, 3 (October 1979), 60–61; Cheryll Ann Cody, "Naming, Kinship, and Estate Dispersal: Notes on Slave Family Life on a South Carolina Plantation, 1786 to 1833," *WMQ*, XXXIX (January 1982), 202–3; John C. Inscoe, "Carolina Slave Names: An Index to Acculturation," *JSH*, XLIX (November 1983), 553–54.

92. Autobiography of Gabriel Manigault, 1836–1899 (typescript), pp. 44–45, SC.

93. Inscoe, *JSH*, 533; South-Carolina *Gazette*, September 27, 1773, in Lathan A. Windley, *Runaway Slave Advertisements: A Documentary History from the 1730s to 1790* (Westport, Conn.: Greenwood Press, 1983), III, pp. 329–30.

94. Stroyer, *My Life in the South*, p. 16.

95. Ibid., pp. 33–34; James Henry Hammond to John C. Calhoun, May 10, 1844, John C. Calhoun Papers, Clemson University, quoted in Drew G. Faust, "Culture, Conflict and Community: The Meaning of Power on an Antebellum Plantation," *JOSH*, 14 (Fall 1980), 92, 96; Pope-Hennessy, *The Aristocratic Journey*, p. 221; "Remonstrance," Greenville *Mountaineer*, November 2, 1838.

96. "Remonstrance," Greenville *Mountaineer*, November 2, 1838. The concerns expressed by those citizens probably explain the great exertions taken to assure that slaves received no information on military formations and organization. See "An Ordinance to Amend an Ordinance Passed to Prevent Slaves or Free Persons of Color from Assembling at Military Parades," in George B. Eckhard, *A Digest of the Ordinances of the City Council of Charleston, From the Year 1783 to Oct. 1844* (Charleston: Walker & Burke, 1844), p. 175.

97. Condy, *Digest of the Laws*, pp. 170, 180; *The Suppressed Book About Slavery!* (New York: Carleton, 1864), p. 245; James Lardner, "Liberating Lessons of War," Washington *Post*, January 12, 1982, B 1, 11; Rawick, *The American Slave*, III, iii, p. 14, III, iv, pp. 5, 165.

98. Rawick, *The American Slave*, sup., 11, pp. 98, 100.

99. Ibid., pp. 261–62.

100. Rawick, *The American Slave*, III, iv, p. 45.

101. Ibid., p. 9.

102. Ibid., II, i, p. 235.

103. Adele Petigru Allston to Colonel Francis Heriot, July 1864, in Easterby, *South Carolina Rice Plantation*, pp. 199–200.

104. Adele Petigru Allston to Jesse Belflowers, July 16, 1864, in Easterby, *South Carolina Rice Plantation*, p. 292.

105. An Inhabitant of Florida, Zaphaniah Kingsley, *A Treatise on the Patriarchal, or Co-operative System of Society as it Exists in Some Governments . . . Under the Name of Slavery, With Its Necessity and Advantages*, 2d ed. (Freeport, N.Y.: Books for Libraries Press, 1970), p. 9 (originally published in 1829); Jones, "A Cultural Middle Passage," pp. 76–78; Plantation Manual of James H. Hammond of Beech Island, South Carolina, circa 1834 (typescript), p. 4, WHL.

106. Quoted in Gutman, *The Black Family*, pp. 79–80.

107. Basil Hall, *Travels in North America, in the Years 1827 and 1828* (Edinburgh: Cadell and Co., 1829), III, pp. 128–29.

108.   Richard Konetzke, ed., *Colección de Documentos para la historia de la formación social de Hispanoamerica, 1493–1810* (Madrid, 1962), Real Cedula, February 1, 1570, vol. 1, p. 451, quoted in Gwendolyn Midlo Hall, *Social Control in Slave Plantation Societies: A Comparison of St. Domingue and Cuba* (Baltimore: The Johns Hopkins Press, 1971), p. 94.

109.   Bryan Edwards, *The History, Civil and Commercial of the British Colonies in the West Indies* (London: John Stockdale, 1801), 2, pp. 155–56; John Stewart, *A View of the Past and Present State of the Island of Jamaica* . . . (New York: Negro Universities Press, 1969), p. 281 (originally published in 1823); A Gentleman, *An Account of Jamaica, and Its Inhabitants* (London: Longman, Hurst, Rees, and Orme, 1808), p. 250.

110.   Gutman, *The Black Family,* p. 154.

111.   Ball, *Fifty Years in Chains,* pp. 142, 192, 195.

112.   Rochester *Union and Advertiser,* August 9, 1893, in Blassingame, *Slave Testimony,* p. 512.

113.   Botume, *First Days Amongst the Contrabands,* pp. 55–57, 179–80; Lloyd v. Monpoey, 2N. and McC. 446, May 1820, in Catterall, *Judicial Cases,* II, p. 315; Watson v. Hamilton, 6 Richardson 75, November 1852, in Catterall, *Judicial Cases,* II, pp. 434–35; "State vs Eddy (a Negro Slave)," August 8, 1849, (Case 97), Spartanburg Court of Magistrates and Freeholders Records (microfilm), SCA; William Wyndham Malet, *An Errand to the South in the Summer of 1862* (London: Richard Bentley, 1863), pp. 203–5; "Testimony of Harry McMillan," American Freedmen's Inquiry Commission, pp. 128–29, NA; Pierce, *AM,* 302–3; Jolliffe v. Fanning, 10 Richardson 428, May 1856, in Catterall, *Judicial Cases,* p. 451; E. Perry, Greenville, to B. F. Perry, November 29, 1843, Benjamin F. Perry Papers (typescript), p. 2, SC; George I. Crafts, Thebes, to Miss Maria [R. Campbell?], January 1, 1847, George I. Crafts Correspondence, 1846–1847 (typescript), CLS; Holland, *Letters and Diary of Laura M. Towne,* pp. 224–25; Rawick, *The American Slave,* II, i, p. 110; Pearson, *Letters From Port Royal,* pp. 55–56; Eric Perkins, *Roll, Jordan, Roll: A 'Marx' for the Master Class,"* *RHR,* 3 (Fall 1976), 48–49.

114.   Gutman, *The Black Family,* pp. 75–76.

115.   John Gabriel Guignard, II, Evergreen, to James Sanders Guignard, I, November 24, 1829, Guignard Family Papers, SC; Caldwell v. Wilson, 2 Speers 75, December 1843. (77), in Catterall, *Judicial Cases,* II, p. 387; Bryan v. Robert, 1 Strob. Eq. 334, May 1847, in Catterall, *Judicial Cases,* II, p. 403; Owens v. Simpson, 5 Rich. Eq. 405, May 1853, in Catterall, *Judicial Cases,* II, p. 438; Young ads. Plumeau, Harper (second edition), 543, March 1827, in Catterall, *Judicial Cases,* II, p. 336.

116.   Jones, "A Cultural Middle Passage," pp. 211–18; Stroyer, *My Life in the South,* pp. 19–23.

117.   Rawick, *The American Slave,* II, ii, pp. 75–76.

118.   Harris Farm Journals, January 6, 1858, SHC.

119.   Ibid., March 6, 1858.

120.   Holland, *Letters and Diary of Laura M. Towne,* pp. 109–10.

121.   Eugene D. Genovese, *Roll, Jordan, Roll: The World The Slaves Made* (New York: Pantheon Books, 1974), pp. 648–49.

122.   Peter Lewis, "50 Dollars Reward," The Georgetown *Gazette,* November 19, 1800; "Petition of Edward Brailsford," November 26, 1816, General Assembly Petitions, SCA; James Sanders Guignard, I, Columbia, to John Gabriel Guignard, II, December 9, 1833, Guignard Family Papers, SC; "The State vs. Negro Jim," October 10, 1849, (Case 109), Spartanburg Court Records, SCA; (Case 252), May 19, 1852, Pendleton/Anderson District Court of Magistrates and Freeholders Records (microfilm), SCA; Deloach v. Turner, 6 Richardson 117, January 1853. (119), in Catterall, *Judicial Cases,* II, p. 435; Stroyer, *My Life in the South,* pp. 64–68; Philo Tower, *Slavery Unmasked: Being a Truthful Narrative of a Three Years' Residence and Journeying in Eleven Southern States* (Rochester: Darrow & Brothers, 1856), pp. 119–21; (Case 231), October 11, 1860, Spartanburg Court Records, SCA; Rawick, *The American Slave,* II, ii, p. 36.

123.   Jones, "A Cultural Middle Passage," p. 52; Cloud v. Calhoun, 10 Rich. Eq. 358, November 1858. (363), in Catterall, *Judicial Cases,* II, p. 461; Plowden C. J. Weston, "Rules and Management for the Plantation, 1859," cited in Collins, *Memories of the Southern States,* pp. 104–5.

124.   E. Perry, Greenville, to B. F. Perry, November 29, 1843, Benjamin Perry Papers, p. 2, SC.

125.   William Jones, Goshen, Ga., to Langdon Cheves, Charleston, S.C., June 18, 1830, Cheves Family Papers, SCHS; Caldwell v. Wilson, 2 Speers 75, December 1843. (77), in Catterall, *Judicial Cases,* II, p. 387; Bryan v. Robert, 1 Strob. Eq. 334, May 1847, in Catterall, *Judicial Cases,* II, p. 403; John Bratton, Camp near Richmond, to Bette Bratton, January 27, 1865, John Bratton Correspondence, 1861–1865 (typescript), p. 200, SHC.

126.   *Proceedings of the Meeting in Charleston, S.C., May 13–15, 1845, on the Religious Instruction of the Negroes Together With the Report of the Committee, and the Address to the Public* (Charleston: Published by Order of the Meeting, 1845), pp. 53–55; Manigault Letter Book, Charles Izard Manigault, Paris, to Anthony Barclay Esqr, British Consul, New York, April 15, 1847, p. 36, Charles Manigault Papers, SC.

4

Split Household, Small Producer, and Dual Wage Earner
An Analysis of Chinese-American Family Strategies

Evelyn Nakano Glenn

Most research on family patterns of black and other urban poor minorities points to the decisive impact of larger institutional structures. Particular attention has been paid to structures that lock certain classes of people into marginal employment and/or chronic unemployment (Drake and Cayton, 1962; C. Valentine, 1968). It has been argued that many characteristics of family organization—for example, reliance on female-based kinship networks—represent strategies for coping with the chronic poverty brought about by institutional racism (Stack, 1974; Valentine, 1978). Structural factors are considered sufficiently powerful to outweigh the influence of cultural tradition, especially in the case of blacks.[1]

Chinese Americans, despite their historical status as an economically exploited minority, have been treated in almost exactly opposite terms. Studies of the Chinese-American family have largely ignored social and economic conditions. They focus on purely cultural determinants, tracing characteristics of family life to Chinese values and traditions. The resulting portrayal of the Chinese-American family has been highly favorable; the family is depicted as stable and problem-free—low in rate of divorce (Huang, 1976), delinquency (Sollenberger, 1968), and welfare dependency (Light, 1972). These virtues are attributed to the family-centered values of Chinese society.

Given this positive assessment, the absence of challenge to the cultural approach is understandable. Still, the case of the Chinese cannot be disengaged from controversies involving other minority groups. The apparent fortitude of the Chinese has been cited as evidence supporting the view of black and Hispanic families as disorganized. Along with other "model" minorities, notably the Japanese and Cubans, the Chinese seem to have offered proof that some groups possess cultural resources that enable them to resist the demoralizing effects of poverty and discrimination. By implication, the difficulties experienced by blacks and Hispanics are due in some measure to the cultural weaknesses of these groups.

On the basis of an historical review and informant interviews,[2] this study argues that a purely cultural analysis does not adequately encompass the historical realities of Chinese-American family life. It argues, furthermore, that a fuller understanding of the Chinese-American family must begin with an examination of the changing constellation of economic, legal, and political constraints that have shaped the Chinese experience in America. When followed by an analysis of the strategies adopted to cope with these constraints, such an examination reveals the many institutionally created problems the Chinese have confronted in forming and maintaining family life, and the variety of strategies they have used to overcome limitations. By positing a more or less passive cultural determinism and a continuity of Chinese culture, the cultural approach used up to now by many writers tends to obscure not only the problems and struggles of Chinese-American families but also their heterogeneity over time.

CULTURAL VS. INSTITUTIONAL APPROACHES TO THE CHINESE-AMERICAN FAMILY

The cultural approach grows out of the dominant assimilative perspective in the race- and ethnic-relations field (Gordon, 1964; Park, 1950). This perspective focuses on the initial cultural and social differences among groups and attempts to trace the process of assimilation over time; much literature on Chinese Americans is framed in these terms (Hirata, 1976). The rather extreme emphasis on traditional *Chinese* culture, however, seems to require further explanation. The emphasis may be due in part to the prevailing conception of the Chinese as perpetual foreigners or "strangers" (Wolff, 1950). The image of the Chinese as strange, exotic and different seems to have preceded their actual arrival in the United States (Miller, 1969). Since arriving, their marginal position in the larger society, combined with racist ideology, has served to perpetuate and popularize the image. First, laws excluding the Chinese from citizenship and preventing them from bringing over spouses and children ensured that for over 130 years a large proportion of the Chinese-American population consisted of non-English-speaking alien residents. Second, discriminatory laws and practices forced the Chinese to congregate in ethnic ghettos and to concentrate in a narrow range of enterprises such as laundries, restaurants, and tourist-oriented businesses (Light and Wong, 1975) that simultaneously reinforced and exploited their foreignness. Moreover, because of distinctive racial features, Americans of Chinese ancestry have been lumped together in the public mind with Chinese foreign nationals and recent immigrants, so that third-, fourth- or even fifth-generation Americans are assumed to be culturally as well as racially Asian. It is not surprising, therefore, to find that until recently studies of Chinese Americans interpreted social and community organizational patterns as products of Chinese culture rather than as responses to economic and social conditions in the United States (Lyman, 1974, is an exception; see also Hirata, 1976; and Kwong, 1979 for related critiques).

Studies of family life follow in this same mold. Authors typically begin by examining traditional Chinese family patterns, then attempt to show how these patterns are expressed in a new setting and undergo gradual change through acculturation (e.g., Hsu, 1971; Haynor and Reynolds, 1937; Kung, 1962; Sung, 1971; Weiss, 1974). The features identified as typical of Chinese-American families and as evidence of cultural continuity are (a) stable family units as indicated by low rates of divorce and illegitimacy; (b) close ties between generations, as shown by the absence of adolescent rebellion and juvenile delinquency; (c) economic self-sufficiency, demonstrated by avoidance of welfare dependency; and (d) conservatism, expressed by retention of Chinese language and customs in the home.

Each of these characteristics is interpreted in terms of specific aspects of Chinese culture. For example, the primacy of the family unit over the individual in Chinese society is credited for the rarity of divorce. Similarly, the principles of Confucianism (filial piety, respect for elders, and reverence for tradition) are cited as the philosophical bases for close control over children by parents and retention of Chinese language and customs in the home; and the family-based production system in the Chinese agricultural village is seen as the precedent for immigrants' involvement in family enterprise and economic self-sufficiency.

An institutional approach starts at a different point, looking not at Chinese society but at conditions in the United States. More specifically, it focuses on the legal and political restrictions imposed on the Chinese, particularly with respect to immigration, citizenship, residential mobility, and economic activity. The Chinese were the first group excluded on racial grounds from legally immigrating, starting in 1882 and continuing until the mid-1950s. When they were allowed entry, it was under severe restrictions which made it difficult for them to form and maintain families in the United States. They also were denied the right to become naturalized citizens, a right withheld until 1943. This meant that for most of their 130-year history in the United States, the Chinese were categorically excluded from political participation and entrance into occupations and professions requiring citizenship for licensing (see Konvitz, 1946). In addition, during the latter part of the nineteenth century and through the early twentieth, California and other western states in which the Chinese were concentrated imposed head taxes and prohibited Chinese from carrying on certain types of businesses. The Chinese were routinely denied most civil rights, including the right to testify in court, so they had no legal recourse against injury or exploitation (Wu, 1972; Jacobs and Landau, 1971). Having initially worked in railroad building, agriculture, and mining, the Chinese were driven out of smaller towns, rural areas, and mining camps during the late nineteenth century and were forced to congregate in urban ghettos (Lyman, 1977). The effect of these various restrictions was to keep the Chinese in the status of alien guests or commuters going back and forth between China and America. In addition, the restrictions led to a population made up disproportionately of male adults, concentrated in Chinatowns, and limited to a few occupations and industries.

These circumstances provide an alternative explanation for some of the features previously described as originating in Chinese culture: (a) low divorce rates result when spouses are forced to stay together by the lack of economic options outside of family enterprises; (b) low delinquency rates may reflect the demographic composition of the population which, up to the mid-1950s, contained few adolescents who, therefore, could be more effectively controlled by community sanctions; (c) avoidance of welfare is necessitated by the illegal status of many immigrants and the lack of access to sources outside the community; (d) retention of Chinese language and custom is a logical outcome of ghetto life and denial of permanent membership in American society.

Being able to generate plausible explanations does not itself constitute support for one approach over the other. However, in addition to offering alternative interpretations, the two approaches lead to quite different expectations regarding the degree of types of changes which the Chinese-American family has undergone over time. By tracing family patterns to a specific cultural system, the *cultural approach* implies a continuity in family organization over time, with change occurring gradually and linearly via acculturation. By connecting family patterns to contemporaneous institutional structures, the *institutional approach* implies that family organization could and probably would undergo dramatic change with alteration in external constraints. A related point is that the cultural approach suggests that Chinese-American family patterns are unique to this group, while the institutional approach suggests that other groups with differing cultural traditions might display similar patterns under parallel conditions.

The analysis that follows tests these expectations against the historical evidence by documenting the existence of qualitatively different family forms among Chinese Americans in different historical periods, with occasional reference to similar family forms among other groups in comparable circumstances. Three distinct family types are identified, corresponding to three periods demarcated by shifts in institutional constraints.

THE SPLIT-HOUSEHOLD FAMILY

For the first seventy years of Chinese presence in the United States, from 1850 to 1920, one can hardly speak of family life, since there were so few women or children (Lyman, 1968; Nee and Nee, 1974). As Table 4.1 shows, from the late nineteenth to the early twentieth century, the ratio of males to females ranged from 13:1 to 20:1. In 1900 less than 4% of the Chinese population consisted of children fourteen years and under, compared to 37.4% of the population of whites of native parentage (U.S. Census, 1902).

The first thirty-two years, from 1850 to 1882, was a period of open immigration, when over 300,000 Chinese left Guangdong Province to work in California and the West (Lyman, 1974). Most were able-bodied young men, recruited for labor on the railroads and in agriculture, mining and manufacturing. Although some men of the merchant class came and brought wives or concubines, the vast majority of immigrants were laborers who came alone, not intending to stay; over half left wives behind in China (Coolidge, 1909). Many were too impoverished to pay for passage and came on the credit ticket system, which obligated them to work for a fixed term, usually seven years, to pay for transport (Ling, 1912). These "birds of passage" labored to send remittances to relatives and to accumulate capital to enable them to acquire land in China. Two-thirds apparently succeeded in returning, as there were never more than 110,000 Chinese in the United States at any one time.

It is possible that, like other Asian immigrants, Chinese laborers eventually would have sent for wives, had open immigration continued. The passage of the Chinese Exclusion Act of 1882 precluded this possibility. The Act barred laborers and their relatives but exempted officials, students,

Table 4.1 Chinese Population in the United States, by Sex, Sex Ratio, Percentage Foreign Born, and Percentage Under Age 15, 1860–1970

Year	Total	Male	Female	Male/Female Ratio	% Foreign Born	% Aged 14 or Under
1860	34,933	33,149	1,784	18.58		
1870	63,199	58,633	4,566	12.84	99.8	
1880	105,465	100,686	4,779	21.06	99.0	
1890	107,475	103,607	3,868	26.79	99.3	
1900	89,863	85,341	4,522	18.87	90.7	3.4
1910	71,531	66,856	4,675	14.30	79.3	a
1920	61,639	53,891	7,748	6.96	69.9	12.0
1930	74,954	59,802	15,152	3.95	58.8	20.4
1940	77,504	57,389	20,115	2.85	48.1	21.2
1950	117,140	76,725	40,415	1.90	47.0	23.3
1960	236,084	135,430	100,654	1.35	39.5	33.0
1970	431,583	226,733	204,850	1.11	46.9	26.6

Source: U.S. Censuses for the years 1872, 1883, 1895, 1902, 1913, 1922, 1933, 1943, 1953, 1963, and 1973. List of specific tables available upon request.

Note: [a] Figures for California, Oregon, and Washington—which together had a somewhat lower male-female ratio (11.33) than the United States as a whole—show 7.0% of the Chinese population to be under age 15 in those states.

tourists, merchants, and relatives of merchants and citizens. Renewals of the Act in 1892 and 1902 placed further restrictions on entry and return. Finally, the Immigration Act of 1924 cut off all immigration from Asia (Wu, 1972). These acts achieved their aim, which was to prevent the Chinese from settling in the United States. With almost no new immigration and the return of many sojourners to China, the Chinese population dwindled from a high of 107,000 in 1890 to 61,000 in 1920. Chinese men of the laboring class—faced with an unfavorable sex ratio, forbidden as non-citizens from bringing over wives, and prevented by laws in most western states from marrying whites—had three choices: (a) return permanently to China; (b) if single, stay in the United States as bachelors; or (c) if married, remain separated from families except for occasional visits.

Faced with these alternatives, the Chinese nevertheless managed to take advantage of openings in the law; if they had not, the Chinese population in the United States would have disappeared. One category for which entry was still allowed was relatives of citizens. Men born in the United States could return to China, marry, and father children, who were then eligible for entry. The 1906 earthquake and fire in San Francisco that destroyed most municipal records proved a boon for the large Chinese population of that area. Henceforth, residents could claim American birth without officials being able to disprove the contention (Sung, 1971). It became common practice for American-born Chinese (actual or claimed) to visit China, report the birth of a son, and thereby create an entry slot. Years later the slot could be used by a relative, or the papers could be sold to someone wanting to immigrate. The purchaser, called a "paper son," simply assumed the name and identity of the alleged son.

Using these openings, many families adopted a strategy of long-term sojourning. Successive generations of men emigrated as paper sons. To ensure loyalty to kin, young men were married off before leaving. Once in America they were expected to send money to support not only wives and children but also parents, brothers, and other relatives. In some villages overseas remittances constituted the main source of income. It has been estimated that between 1937 and 1940 overseas Chinese remitted more than $2 billion, and that an average of $7 million per annum was sent from the United States in the years between 1938 and 1947 (Lyman, 1968; Sung, 1971). In one typical family history, recounted by a 21-year-old college student, great-grandfather arrived in the United States in the 1890s as a paper son and worked for about twenty years as a laborer. He then sent for the grandfather, who helped great-grandfather run a small business. Great-grandfather subsequently returned to China, leaving grandfather to carry on the business and forward remittances. In the 1940s grandfather sent for father. Up to this point, none of the wives had left China; finally, in the late 1950s, father returned to China and brought back his wife, so that after nearly seventy years, a child was finally born in the United States.

The sojourning strategy led to a distinctive family form, the *split-household family*. A common sociological definition of a family is: a group of people related by blood or marriage, cooperating to perform essential domestic tasks such as production, consumption, reproduction, and socialization. In the split-household family, production would be separated from other functions and carried out by a member living far away (who, of course, would be responsible for his own consumption needs). The other functions—reproduction, socialization, and the rest of consumption—would be carried out by the wife and other relatives in the home village. The family would remain an interdependent, cooperative unit, thereby fulfilling the definition of a family, despite geographical separation. The split-household form made possible the maximum exploitation of the worker. The labor of prime-age male workers could be bought relatively cheaply, since the cost of reproduction and family maintenance was borne partially by unpaid subsistence work of women and old people in the village. The sojourner's remittances, though small by U.S. standards, afforded a comfortable standard of living for family members in China.

The split household is not unique to the Chinese and, therefore, cannot be explained as a culturally preferred pattern. Sojourning occurs where there are (a) large differences in the level of economic development of receiving vs. sending regions, and (b) legal/administrative barriers to integration of the sending group. Three examples of the phenomenon are guest workers in Western Europe (Castles and Kosack, 1973); gold-mine workers in South Africa (Boserup, 1970); and Mexican braceros in the American Southwest (Power, 1979). In all three cases, prime-age workers from disadvantaged regions are issued limited-duration permits to reside in regions needing low-wage labor but are prevented from bringing relatives or settling permanently. Thus, the host country benefits from the labor of sojourners without having to incorporate them into the society. Although the persistence of sojourning for several generations makes the Chinese somewhat unusual, there is evidence that legal restrictions were critical to maintaining the pattern. Other societies to which the Chinese immigrated did not prohibit intermarriage or limit economic competition—for example, Peru and the Philippines. In these societies a high proportion of the Chinese intermarried with the native population (Wong, 1978; Hunt and Walker, 1974).

The life of the Chinese sojourner in the United States has been described in sociological and historical studies (see Nee and Nee, 1974; Lyman, 1977). Employed as laborers or engaged in small enterprises, the men lived in rented rooms alone or with other "bachelors." In place of kin ties, they relied on immigrant associations based on fictive clan relationships. As is common in predominantly male societies, many sojourners found outlets in gambling, prostitution, and drugs. Those successful enough or frugal enough to pay for passage returned periodically to China to visit and to father more children. Others, as a result of bad luck or personal disorganization, could never save enough to return. Even with movement back and forth, many sojourners gradually came to feel remote from village ties, and attached to life in the Chinese-American colony. Thus, they ended up staying in the United States more or less by choice (Siu, 1952).

The situation of wives and relatives in China has not been documented in the literature. According to informants, wives generally resided with in-laws; and remittances were sent to the husband's kin, usually a brother or son, to insure that wives remained chaste and subject to the ultimate control of their husbands. Despite the lack of formal authority, most wives had informal influence and were consulted on major decisions. An American-born informant, the daughter of an herbalist and his concubine, was sent as a young girl to be raised by her father's first wife in China. This first wife never wanted to join her husband, as she lived quite comfortably in the village; with remittances from her husband, she maintained a large house with two servants and oversaw substantial landholdings and investments. The father's concubine led an arduous life in the United States, raising several children, running the household, and working long hours in the shop.

Parent-child relations were inevitably affected by separation. The mother-child tie was strengthened by the absence of the father. The mother's tie with her eldest son, normally an important source of leverage within an extended-kin household, became particularly close. In contrast, prolonged absence made the father's relationship with his children more formal and distant. The long periods between visits meant that the children were spaced far apart, and the father was often middle-aged or elderly by the time the youngest child was born. The age gap between fathers and later children added to the formality of the relationship.

THE SMALL-PRODUCER FAMILY

Despite obstacles to family formation, the presence of families was evident in the major U.S. Chinatowns by the 1920s. As Table 4.1 shows, the male-female ratio fell, and the proportion of children nearly doubled between 1920 and 1930. These early families were started primarily by small entrepreneurs, former laborers who had accumulated enough capital to start a small business alone or in partnership. Due to occupational restrictions and limited capital, the enterprises were confined to laundries, restaurants, groceries, and other small shops. Once in business they could register as merchants, return to China, and bring over wives and children. There was an economic incentive to bring over families; besides providing companionship and affection, women and children were a source of free labor for the business.

The number of families grew steadily, then jumped dramatically during the 1950s due to changes in immigration regulations. The first small opening was created in 1943 with the repeal of the Chinese Exclusion Act. In recognition of China's position as an ally in World War II, a token quota of 105 entrants per year was granted, and permanent residents were declared eligible for citizenship. A larger opening was created by the "Brides Act" of 1946, which permitted entry to wives and children of citizens and permanent residents, and by the Immigration Act of 1953, which gave preference to relatives of citizens (Lee, 1956; Li, 1977b). For the first time in over sixty years, sizable legal immigration flowed from China; and for the first time in history, the majority of entrants were women. The women fell into two general categories: wives separated from their husbands for periods ranging up to thirty years or more, and brides of servicemen and other citizens who took advantage of the 1946 and 1953 laws to visit China and get married (Lee, 1956). The marriages were usually arranged hastily; Chinese families were eager to have eligible daughters married to Americans, so the men had no problem finding prospects on short notice. At the same time, parents of American-born men often preferred Chinese-born brides (Lee, 1956). An American-born woman explained why; she once had an engagement broken off because her fiancé's parents objected to the marriage:

> They thought American girls will be bossy; she'll steal the son and go out freely. They said, "She will ruin your life. She'll be free spending with money." Also, she won't support the parents the rest of their life. They want a typical Chinese girl who will do what the father wants. [Interview with subject]

At his parents' urging, the fiancé later visited China and brought back a wife.

During the period from about 1920 to the mid-1960s, the typical immigrant and first-generation family functioned as a productive unit in which all members, including children, worked without wages in a family business. The business was profitable only because it was labor-intensive and members put in extremely long hours. Often, for reasons of thrift, convenience, or lack of options, the family's living quarters were located above or behind the shop; thus, the workplace and home were physically joined.

Some flavor of the close integration of work and family life is seen in this description of the daily routine in a family laundry, provided by a woman who grew up in Boston's Chinatown during the 1930s and 1940s. The household consisted of the parents and four children. The work day started at 7:00 in the morning and did not end until midnight, six days a week. Except for school and a short nap in the afternoon, the children worked the same hours as the parents, doing their homework between midnight and 2:00 A.M. Each day's routine was the same. All items were marked or tagged as they were brought in by customers. A commercial cleaner picked up the laundry, washed it, and brought it back wet. The wet laundry was hung to dry in a back room heated by a coal burner. Next, items were taken down, sprinkled, starched, and rolled for ironing. Tasks were allocated by age and sex. Young children of six or seven performed simple tasks such as folding socks and wrapping parcels. At about age ten they started ironing handkerchiefs and underwear. Mother operated the collar and cuff press, while father hand-ironed shirts and uniforms. Only on Sunday did the family relax its hectic regimen to attend church in the morning and relax in the afternoon.

This family may have been unusually hard working, but this sort of work-centered family life was common among the generation that grew up between 1920 and 1960. In fact, the close-knit small-business family was portrayed in several popular autobiographies covering this period (Lowe, 1943; Wong, 1950; Kingston, 1976). These accounts describe a life of strict discipline, constant toil, and frugality. Family members constantly interacted, but communication tended to revolve around concrete details of work. Parents directed and admonished the children in Chinese as they worked, so that the American-born Chinese became fluent in Chinese as well as in English, which they learned in school. Education was stressed, so that children's time was fully occupied by studying, working, and caring for younger siblings. Not so apparent in these accounts was the high incidence of disease, including tuberculosis, due to overcrowding and overwork (Lee et al., 1969).

The small-producer family had several distinct characteristics. First was the lack of any clear demarcation between work and family life. Child care, domestic maintenance, and income-producing activities occurred simultaneously in time and in the same location. Second was the self-contained nature of the family as a production and consumption unit. All members contributed to family income and domestic maintenance, including the children. Third was the division of labor by age and gender, with gradations of responsibility according to capacity and experience. Elder siblings were responsible for disciplining and taking care of younger siblings, who in turn were expected to defer to their older brothers and sisters. Finally, there was an emphasis on the collectivity over the individual. With so many individuals working in close quarters for extended periods of time, a high premium was placed on cooperation. Self-expression, which might engender conflict, had to be curbed.

While these features are in some way similar to those found in Chinese peasant families, they do not necessarily represent carryovers of Chinese patterns; they can be attributed equally to the particular material and social conditions arising from the family's involvement in small enterprise, an involvement dictated by limited economic options. There is evidence that these features are common to small-producer families in various societies and times (see, for example, Demos's 1970 account of the early Puritan families of the Massachusetts Bay Colony). Moreover, the Chinese-American small-producer family had some features that differed from those of rural Chinese families due to circumstances of life in America. Of great significance was the family's location in a society whose dominant language and customs differed greatly. Children had the advantage in this regard. Once they started school, children quickly learned to speak and write English, while parents were rarely able to acquire more than rudimentary English. The parents came to depend on their children to act as mediators in relation to the outside society. As a result children gained a great deal of status at an early age, in contrast to the subordinate position of children in China. American-born Chinese report that, starting at age eight or nine, they helped their parents in business and domestic matters by reading documents and contracts, accompanying them to the bank to fill out slips, negotiating with customers, and translating notices in stores.

A second circumstance was the age composition of immigrant communities, which were made up primarily of childbearing-aged men, and later, women. In the initial period of family formation, therefore, there were no grandparents; and households tended to be nuclear in form. In China the preferred pattern was for sons to live with parents, and wives were required to defer to mothers-in-law. The young immigrant mother, however, did not have to contend with in-laws. As a result of this, and the fact that she was an equal producer in the family economy, the wife had more autonomy. Many informants recall their mothers as the disciplinarians and central figures in the household.

THE DUAL WAGE EARNER FAMILY

Following World War II, particularly after the Civil Rights Movement of the 1960s, discrimination against Asian Americans eased. College-educated Chinese Americans were able to enter white-collar occupations and industries formerly barred to them and to move into previously restricted neighborhoods. Among these socially mobile families, the parents still shop and visit friends in Chinatown; but their children tend not to have ties there. The lowering of barriers also speeded the integration of the so-called scholar-professional immigrants. Educated in Hong Kong, mainland China or Taiwan, many are Mandarin-speaking, in contrast to the Cantonese-speaking resident population. The older segment of this group arrived as students in the 1940s and 1950s and stayed, while the younger segment entered under the 1965 immigration act, which did away with national quotas and gave preference to relatives of citizens and permanent residents and to those in needed occupations. Employed as professionals, this group tends to live in white neighborhoods and to have little connection with Chinatown. Thus, for the socially mobile American-born and the scholar/professional immigrants, the trend has been toward assimilation into the mainstream of American society.

At the same time, however, there has been a countertrend that has re-Sinicized the Chinese-American population. The same immigration law that brought in professionals and scholars has brought in an even larger influx of working-class Chinese. Under the liberalized law, over 20,000 Chinese have entered the United States each year since 1965, primarily via Hong Kong (U.S. Department of Justice, 1977).[3] About half the immigrants can be classified as working class, having been employed as service workers, operatives, craftsmen, or laborers in Hong Kong (Nee and Nee, 1974). After arrival, moreover, a significant proportion of professional, managerial and white-collar immigrants experience a drop in occupational status into blue-collar and service jobs because of language and licensing difficulties (U.S. Department of Health, Education and Welfare, 1974).

Unlike the earlier immigrants who came over as individuals, most new immigrants come over in family groups—typically a husband, wife and unmarried children (Li, 1977a). The families have pulled up stakes in order to gain greater political security, economic opportunity, and educational advantages for their children. Since the law gives preference to relatives, most families use kinship ties with previous immigrants to gain entry. Frequently, the ties are used in a chainlike fashion (Li, 1977b). For example, a couple might sponsor the wife's sister, her husband and children; the sister's husband in turn sponsors his parents, who later bring over one of their children, and so forth. In this way an extended-kin network is reunited in the United States.

Initially, the new immigrants usually settle in or near Chinatown so that they can trade in Chinese-speaking stores, use bilingual services, and find employment. They are repopulating and stimulating growth in Chinatowns at a time when these communities are experiencing declines due to the mobility of American-born Chinese (Hong, 1976). The new immigrants have less dramatic adjustments to make than did earlier immigrants, having lived for some years in an urban society that exposed them to Western goods and lifestyles. In addition, although bilingual social services are frequently inadequate, municipal and country agencies now provide medical care, advice on immigration problems, family counseling, and the like. The immigrants rely on these public services rather than on the clan associations which, thus, have lost their old influence.

Despite the easier adjustment and greater opportunities for mobility, problems of language, and discrimination in small trade, construction and craft unions still affect immigrants who are not professionally trained. Having given up property, businesses or jobs, and having exhausted their resources to pay for transportation and settlement, they must quickly find a way to make a living and establish their families in a highly industrialized economy. The strategy most families have adopted is for husband and wife to find employment in the secondary labor market, the labor-intensive, low-capital service and small manufacturing sectors. The wage each earns is low, but by pooling income a husband and wife can earn enough to support a family. The typical constellation is a husband, who works as a waiter, cook, janitor, or store helper, and a wife who is employed in a small garment shop (Nee and Nee, 1974; Ikels and Shiang, 1979; "Tufts' lease . . .," 1981; cf. Lamphere, Silva and Sousa, 1980 for parallels with Azorean immigrants).

Although many women have been employed in Hong Kong, for most it is a new experience to juggle fulltime work outside the home with child care and housework. In Hong Kong mothers could do piecework at home, stitching or assembling plastic flowers during spare hours (Ikels and Shiang, 1979). In the United States employment means a long complicated day involving dropping off children at school, going to work in a shop for a few hours, picking up children from school, preparing food, and returning for a few more hours of work in the shop. Another change in many families is that the women's earnings comprise a greater share of family income in the United States. The pay differential between men and women, which is large in Hong Kong, becomes less or even reversed because of the downward shift in the husband's occupation (Hong, 1980). Wives and husbands become more or less coequal breadwinners.

Perhaps the most striking feature of the dual-worker family is the complete segregation of work and family life. As a result, in contrast to the round-the-clock togetherness of the small-producer family, parents and children in the dual-worker family are separated for most of the day. While apart they inhabit totally different worlds. The parents' lives are regulated by the discipline of the job, while children lead relatively unstructured and unsupervised lives, often in the company of peers whose parents also work (Nee and Nee, 1974). Furthermore, although mothers are usually at home by early evening, the father's hours may prevent him from seeing the children at all. The most common shift for restaurant workers runs from 2:00 in the afternoon until 11:00 at night. The sons and daughters of restaurant workers reported that they saw their fathers only on their days off.

The parents' fatigue, the long hours of separation, and the lack of common experiences combine to undermine communication. Children complain that their parents are not around much and, when they are, are too tired to talk. One young student notes, "We can discuss things, but we don't talk that much. We don't have that much to say." In addition, many parents suffered serious trauma during World War II and the Chinese Revolution, which they refuse to discuss. This refusal causes blocks to intimacy between parents and children since certain topics become taboo. For their part parents complain that they have lost control over their children. They attribute the loss of influence to the fact that children adjust to American ways and learn English much more quickly than parents. Over a period of years, a language barrier frequently develops. Since parents are not around to direct and speak to children in Chinese, the children of wage-earning parents lose the ability (or willingness) to speak Chinese. When they reach adolescence, moreover, children can find parttime employment, which gives them financial independence as well as money to spend on outside recreation.

The absence of a close-knit family life among dual-worker families has been blamed for the eruption of youth rebellion, delinquency, and gang violence in Chinatowns during the 1960s and 1970s (Lyman, 1974; Nee and Nee, 1974). While the change in family patterns undoubtedly has been a factor, other demographic and social changes have contributed to the surfacing of youth problems (Light and Wong, 1975). Adolescents make up a higher proportion of the new immigrants than they did in previous cohorts, and many immigrants arriving as adolescents encounter difficulties in school because of the language barrier. When they leave school they face unemployment or the prospect of low-wage service jobs. Similar obstacles were faced by the early immigrants, but they take on a new meaning in the present era when expectations are higher and when there is more awareness of institutional racism.

In a similar vein, dual-worker families are beset by the chronic difficulties that plagued Chinese-American families in the past—rundown crowded housing, low incomes, immigration problems, and language difficulties; but their impact is different now that the family faces them in a less unified fashion. Social workers employed in Chinatown report that the immigrant family is torn by a multiplicity of problems.[4] Ironically, the resilience of the Chinese-American family until recently has retarded efforts at relief. It has taken the visible outbreak of the youth unrest mentioned above to dramatize the fact that the Chinese-American family cannot endure any and all hardships without support. For the first time, social services, housing programs, and other forms of support are being offered to Chinese-American families.

SUMMARY AND CONCLUSIONS

This sociohistorical examination of the Chinese-American immigrant family has emphasized three main points: first, throughout their history in the United States, Chinese Americans have faced a variety of economic, social and political constraints that have had direct effects on family life. Second, Chinese-American families have displayed considerable resourcefulness in devising strategies to overcome structural obstacles and to take advantage of the options open to them. Third, the strategies adopted have varied according to the conditions prevailing during given historical periods, resulting in three distinct family types.

The characteristics and differences among the family types, discussed in the previous sections, are summarized in Table 4.2. Each type can be characterized in terms of six major dimensions: the economic strategy, the make-up of the household(s), the nature of the relation between production or work and family life, the division of labor in the household, conjugal roles, and relations between generations.

The split-household type, prevalent until 1920, adopted the strategy of sending married men abroad to specialize in income-producing activities. This created two separate households, one in the United States consisting of a primary individual—or, in some cases, a pair of related males such as a father and son—and another in China, consisting of the relatives of the sojourner—wife, children, parents, and brothers and their wives. Production was separated from the rest of family life, with the husband/father engaging in paid work abroad while the other relatives engaged in subsistence activities (e.g., small-scale farming) and carried out other domestic functions. Husband and wife, therefore, led completely separate existences, with the husband's relation to parents taking precedence over his relation to his wife, and the wife forming her primary attachment with children.

The small-producer type succeeded the split-household type around 1920 and became more common after the late 1940s when women were allowed to join their spouses in the United States. The economic strategy was to engage in small-scale enterprises that relied on the unpaid labor of

Table 4.2 Characteristics of Three Types of Chinese Immigrant Families

Characteristics	Split Household	Small Producer	Dual Wage
Historical period[a]	c. 1882–1920	c. 1920–1965	c. 1965–present
Economic strategy	male sojourning	family business	individual wage work
Household composition	two households:(a) in United States—primary individual; (b) in China—extended	nuclear	nuclear
Work and family life	separated	fused	separated
Division of labor	husband/father—paid work; wife/ other relatives—unpaid domestic and subsistence work	husband, wife and children— unpaid production work	husband and wife— paid and unpaid work; children—unpaid domestic work
Conjugal roles	segregated	joint or shared	symmetrical
Intergenerational relations	strong mother-child tie; weak father-child tie	strong parent-child tie	attenuated parent-child tie

Note: [a] The occurrence of each type is not exclusive to one period but is more prominent during the designated period.

husband, wife, and children. The nuclear household was the basic unit, with no separation between production and family life, and was focused around work. Close parent-child relations resulted from the enforced togetherness and the constant interaction required to carry on the business. The economic roles of husband and wife were basically parallel, and most daily activities were shared in common.

Finally, the dual-wage type, which has predominated among immigrants arriving after 1965, is based on a strategy of individual wage work, with husband and wife engaged in low-wage employment. The pooling of two wages provides sufficient income to support the family. The household is primarily nuclear, with production and family life separate, as is common in industrial society. The clearest division of labor is between parents and children, with parents specializing in income-producing activities while children are economically inactive. The roles of husband and wife are symmetrical; that is, they engage in similar proportions of paid and unpaid work but in separate settings (cf. Young and Wilmott, 1973). Because parents' employment schedules often keep them away from home, there is little shared activity. The parent-child tie becomes attenuated, with children involved in a separate world of peers.

The existence of three distinctly different family types corresponding to different historical periods calls into question the adequacy of purely cultural explanations of Chinese-American family patterns. If cultural patterns were the sole or primary determinants, we would expect to find greater continuity in family patterns over time; instead, we find discontinuities associated with shifts in institutional conditions. These discontinuities underline the importance of the larger political economic structures in which the family is embedded.

At the same time, the family is shown as actively striving to survive and maintain ties within the constraints imposed by these structures. The persistence of ties and the variety of strategies adopted by Chinese-American families testify to their resilience and resourcefulness in overcoming obstacles. Further insights into the relationships among and between culture, larger institutional structures, and family strategies might be gained through comparative historical analysis of different racial and ethnic groups.

NOTES

The author is grateful to Gloria Chun, Judy Ng and Yee Mei-Wong for discussions that provided valuable insights; and to Ailee Chin, Gary Glenn, Larry Hong, Charlotte Ikels, Peter Langer, S. M. Miller, T. Scott Miyakawa, and Barbara Vinick for comments on earlier drafts. A previous version of this paper was presented at the meetings for the Study of Social Problems, Toronto, August, 1981.

1. Although some scholars (e.g., Herskovitz, 1958; Levine, 1977) have argued for the continuity of African cultural patterns among American blacks, family sociologists have not systematically explored the possible influence of an autonomous black culture with African roots. This is true even for those who depict the black family as strong and resilient (e.g., Billingsley, 1968; Hill, 1971). Those who characterize it as weak and disorganized (e.g., Frazier, 1939; Moynihan, 1965) have relied on a particular type of cultural formulation, one that views the culture as degraded, a legacy of past economic and social deprivation.
2. The analysis is based on review of the English-language literature on Chinese Americans and informant interviews of twenty-nine individuals of varying ages, nativity, and family status, mainly residing in the Boston area. Informants were interviewed about family immigration histories, economic activities, household composition, residence, and relations among family members. Social and community workers provided broader information on typical tensions and problems for which help was sought.
3. Although the immigrants enter via Hong Kong, they mostly originate from the same region of southern China as the earlier immigrants. They or their parents fled Guangdong during the Sino-Japanese War or during the land reform following the Communist victory. Hence, they tend to have kinship ties with earlier immigrants.
4. According to community workers and government agencies, the most common problems are low, though not poverty-level, family income; substandard and dilapidated housing; language difficulties; legal problems with immigration; and unresolved past traumas, including separation between family members.

REFERENCES

Billingsley, A. 1968. *Black Families in White America.* Englewood Cliffs, NJ: Prentice-Hall.
Boserup, E. 1970. *Women's Role in Economic Development.* New York: St. Martin's Press.
Castles, S. and Kosack, G. 1973. *Immigrant Workers and Class Structure in Western Europe.* London: Oxford University Press.
Coolidge, Mary. 1909. *Chinese Immigration.* New York: Henry Holt.
Demos, John. 1970. *A Little Commonwealth.* London: Oxford University Press.
Drake, S. C. and Cayton, H. R. 1962. *Black Metropolis* (rev. ed.). New York: Harper and Row.
Frazier, E. F. 1939. *The Negro Family in the United States* (rev. ed.). New York: Macmillan.
Gordon, M. M. 1964. *Assimilation in American Life: The Role of Race, Religion, and National Origin.* New York: Oxford University Press.
Haynor, N. S. and Reynolds, C. N. 1937. "Chinese family life in America." *American Sociological Review* 2:630–637.
Herskovitz, M. 1958. *The Myth of the Negro Past.* Boston: Beacon Press.
Hill, R. A. 1971. *The Strengths of Black Families.* New York: Emerson Hall.
Hirata, L. C. 1976. "The Chinese American in sociology." Pp. 20–26 in E. Gee (Ed.), *Counterpoint: Perspectives on Asian Americans.* Los Angeles: Asian American Studies Center, University of California, Los Angeles.
Hong, L. K. 1976. "Recent immigrants in the Chinese American community: issues of adaptations and impacts." *International Migration Review* 10 (Winter):509–514.
———. 1980 Personal communication.
Hsu, F. L. K. 1971. *The Challenge of the American Dream: The Chinese in the United States.* Belmont, CA: Wadsworth.
Huang, L. J. 1976. "The Chinese American family." Pp. 124–147 in C. H. Mindel and R. W. Habenstein (Eds.), *Ethnic Families in America.* New York: Elsevier.
Hunt, C. I. and Walker, L. 1974. "Marginal trading peoples: Chinese in the Philippines and Indians in Kenya." Ch. 4 in *Ethnic Dynamics: Patterns of Intergroup Relations in Various Societies.* Homewood, IL: Dorsey Press.
Ikels, C. and Shiang, J. 1979. "The Chinese in Greater Boston." Interim Report to the National Institute of Aging.
Jacobs, P. and Landau, S. 1971. *To Serve the Devil, Volume II: Colonials and Sojourners.* New York: Vintage Books.
Kingston, M. H. 1976. *The Woman Warrior.* New York: Knopf.
Konvitz, M. G. 1946. *The Alien and Asiatic in American Law.* Ithaca, NY: Cornell University Press.
Kung, S. W. 1962. *Chinese in American Life: Some Aspects of Their History, Status, Problems, and Contributions.* Seattle, WA: University of Washington Press.
Kwong, P. 1979. *Chinatown, New York: Labor and Politics, 1930–1950.* New York: Monthly Review Press.

Lamphere, L., Silva, F. M. and Sousa, J. P. 1980. "Kin networks and family strategies; working class Portuguese families in New England." Pp. 219–245 in L. S. Cordell and S. Beckerman (Eds.), *The Versatility of Kinships*. New York: Academic Press.

Lee, L. P., Lim, A. and Wong, H. K. 1969. Report of the San Francisco Chinese Community Citizen's Survey and Fact Finding Committee (abridged ed.). San Francisco: Chinese Community Citizen's Survey and Fact Finding Committee.

Lee, R. H. 1956. "The recent immigrant Chinese families of the San Francisco-Oakland area." *Marriage and Family Living* 18 (February):14–24.

Levine, L. W. 1977. *Black Culture and Black Consciousness*. New York: Oxford University Press.

Li, P. S. 1977a. "Occupational achievement and kinship assistance among Chinese immigrants in Chicago." *Sociological Quarterly* 18(4):478–489.

——. 1977b. "Fictive kinship, conjugal tie and kinship claim among Chinese immigrants in the United States." *Journal of Comparative Family Studies* 8(1):47–64.

Light, I. 1972. *Ethnic Enterprise in America*. Berkeley and Los Angeles: University of California Press.

Light, I. and Wong, C. C. 1975. "Protest or work: dilemmas of the tourist industry in American Chinatowns." *American Journal of Sociology* 80:1342–1368.

Ling, P. 1912. "The causes of Chinese immigration." *Annals of the American Academy of Political and Social Sciences* 39 (January):74–82.

Lowe, P. 1943. *Father and Glorious Descendant*. Boston: Little, Brown.

Lyman, S. M. 1968. "Marriage and the family among Chinese immigrants to America, 1850–1960." *Phylon* 29(4):321–330.

——. 1974. *Chinese Americans*. New York: Random House.

——. 1977. "Strangers in the city: the Chinese in the urban frontier." In *The Asians in North America*. Santa Barbara, CA: ABC Clio Press.

Miller, S. C. 1969. *The Unwelcome Immigrant: The American Image of the Chinese, 1785–1882*. Berkeley: University of California Press.

Moynihan, D. P. 1965. *The Negro Family: The Case for National Action*. Washington, DC: U.S. Department of Labor, Office of Planning and Research (reprinted in Lee Rainwater and William Yancey, *The Moynihan Report and the Politics of Controversy*. Cambridge, MA: MIT Press, 1967).

Nee, V. G. and Nee, B. 1974. *Longtime Californ'*. Boston: Houghton Mifflin.

Park, R. E. 1950. *Race and Culture*. Glencoe, IL: The Free Press.

Power, J. 1979. *Migrant Workers in Western Europe and the United States*. Oxford: Pergamon Press.

Siu, P. C. T. 1952. "The sojourners." *American Journal of Sociology* 8 (July):32–44.

Sollenberger, R. T. 1968. "Chinese American childbearing practices and juvenile delinquency." *Journal of Social Psychology* 74 (February):13–23.

Stack, C. B. 1974. *All Our Kin: Strategies for Survival in a Black Community*. New York: Harper and Row.

Sung, B. L. 1971. *The Story of the Chinese in America*. New York: Collier Books. "Tufts' lease on two Kneeland Street buildings threatens over 600 jobs in Chinatown." *Sampan* (May 1981).

U.S. Bureau of the Census 1872. Ninth Census. Vol. I: The Statistics of the Population of the United States. Washington, DC: Government Printing Office.

——. 1883. Tenth Census. Statistics of the Population of the United States. Washington, DC: Government Printing Office.

——. 1895. Eleventh Census. Report on Population of the United States, Part I. Washington, DC: Government Printing Office.

——. 1902. Twelfth Census of the United States Taken in the Year 1900. Census Reports, Vol. II: Population, Part II. Washington, DC: United States Census Office.

——. 1913. Thirteenth Census of the United States Taken in the Year 1910, Vol. I: Population, General Report and Analysis. Washington, DC: Government Printing Office.

——. 1922. Fourteenth Census Taken in the Year 1920, Volume II: Population, General Report and Analytic Tables. Washington, DC: Government Printing Office.

——. 1933. Fifteenth Census of the United States: 1930. Population, Vol. II: General Report, Statistics by Subject. Washington, DC: Government Printing Office.

——. 1943. Sixteenth Census of the Population: 1940. Population Characteristics of the Non-White Population by Race. Washington, DC: Government Printing Office.

——. 1953. U.S. Census of the Population: 1950. Vol. IV: Special Reports, Part 3, Chapter B, Non-White Population by Race. Washington, DC: Government Printing Office.

——. 1963. U.S. Census of the Population: 1960. Subject Reports. Nonwhite Population by Race. Final Report PC(2)–1C. Washington, DC: Government Printing Office.

——. 1973. Census of Population: 1970. Subject Reports. Final Report PC(2)–1G, Japanese, Chinese and Filipinos in the United States. Washington, DC: Government Printing Office.

U.S. Department of Health, Education and Welfare. 1974. A Study of Selected Socioeconomic Characteristics of Ethnic Minorities Based on the 1970 Census, Vol. II: Asian Americans. HEW Publication No. (OS) 75–121. Washington, DC: U.S. Department of Health, Education and Welfare.

U.S. Department of Justice. 1977. Immigration and Naturalization Service Annual Report. Washington, DC: U.S. Department of Justice.

Valentine, B. L. 1978. *Hustling and Other Hard Work*. New York: The Free Press.

Valentine, C. 1968. *Culture and Poverty: Critique and Counter-proposals*. Chicago: University of Chicago Press.

Weiss, M. S. 1974. *Valley City: A Chinese Community in America*. Cambridge, MA: Schenkman.

Wolff, K. 1950. *The Sociology of Georg Simmel.* Glencoe, IL: The Free Press.

Wong, B. 1978. "A comparative study of the assimilation of the Chinese in New York City, and Lima, Peru." *Comparative Studies in Society and History* 20 (July):335–358.

Wong, J. S. 1950. *Fifth Chinese Daughter.* New York: Harper and Brothers.

Wu, C. 1972. *"Chink": A Documentary History of Anti-Chinese Prejudice in America.* New York: Meridian.

Young, M. and Wilmott, P. 1973. *The Symmetrical Family.* London: Routledge and Kegan Paul.

5

excerpt from

Huck's Raft
"Laboring Children"

Steven Mintz

Lucy Larcom, the ninth child in a family of ten, was eleven when she went to work in a Lowell, Massachusetts, textile mill in 1836. Her father, a sea captain, had died a year earlier, and Lucy's mother, a boardinghouse proprietor, was barely able to support the family. Lucy felt "it would be a pleasure to feel that I was not a trouble or burden or expense to anyone," so she and an older sister applied to be mill girls. The mill had one job available; because Lucy was taller than her sister, she received the job.

Initially Lucy enjoyed the sense of independence and peer-group companionship she experienced in the mill. She and half a dozen girls changed the bobbins on the machines every three-quarters of an hour, and spent the rest of the time frolicking amid the machinery, "teasing and talking to the older girls, or entertaining ourselves with games and stories in a corner, or exploring" the mill's mysteries. Soon, however, she felt frustrated by the low pay (two dollars for a week's work), the long hours (from five o'clock in the morning till seven at night, with a half-hour for breakfast and dinner, six days a week), and the abysmal working conditions (the windows nailed shut, the dim light, the dust and fabric fibers that filled the air). Above all, she complained about the lack of educational opportunities, the noise, and routine. "The buzzing and hissing whizzing of the pulleys and rollers and spindles and flyers," she later recalled, "often grew tiresome . . . When you do the same things twenty times—a hundred times a day—it is so dull!" She remained in the mill for ten years, then left for Illinois with a married sister.

Capitalist expansion and growth carried far-reaching consequences for children's lives. For the urban middle class, increasing economic affluence allowed parents to provide an extended, protected childhood; but for the laboring classes, a sheltered childhood was impossible. The demands of a market economy made their children indispensable economic resources, whose labor could be exploited in new ways. Unlike their middle-class counterparts, children in laboring families were expected to repay their parents' sacrifices by contributing to the family economy. These children worked not because their parents were heartless, but because their labor was essential to their family's survival.

The wrenching social and economic changes of the nineteenth century—the explosive growth of cities and industry, the rapid movement into the trans-Mississippi West, the sharp increase in foreign immigration, and the expansion of commercial agriculture and tenant farming—produced patterns of schooling, play, and work that differed dramatically by class, ethnicity, gender, race, and region. Indeed, at no point in American history was childhood as diverse as it was in the mid and late nineteenth century. The experiences of Lucy Larcom and two other girls—Lai Chow and Ann McNabb—offer useful examples. Lai Chow was only twelve years old when she was sold by her family in China and smuggled along with two dozen other young girls in crates marked "dishware" on a vessel bound for San Francisco, where she was forced into prostitution. Ann McNabb, who migrated from Ireland to Philadelphia in the 1860s, worked as a live-in cook. Yet these girls' diverse experiences were the product of interconnected economic developments. The early stages of industrialization generated a voracious demand for child labor at the same time that it disrupted rural household industries, stimulating a massive migration from farms and rural villages in Europe and the eastern United States to rapidly growing cities and factory towns. Growing middle-class affluence created intense demand for domestic servants, most of whom were teenaged or even younger. Meanwhile the growth of an integrated national market propelled hundreds of thousands of migrants—including 400,000 pioneers and more than a quarter-million Chinese immigrants—to the Far West.

Several shared realities cut across the boundaries of class, ethnicity, gender, or region, especially a high incidence of child mortality. As late as 1895, 18 percent of children—one in six—died before their fifth birthday. While mortality was greatest among the poor, most affluent families with five or six children experienced the death of at least one child. Another commonality was heavily gendered expectations for sons and daughters. Girls were much more likely to be sheltered in the house, to take part in housework, and to hand over all their earnings to their parents, while boys were more likely to be encouraged to move into the outside world and explore its possibilities. But regional and especially class differences remained the defining feature of family life, work, schooling, and play in the United States throughout the century. It was not until the mid-twentieth century that educators and self-described "child savers" succeeded in universalizing the middle-class norm of an extended, protected childhood.

During the nineteenth century, only a small minority of children experienced the middle-class ideal of maturation taking place gradually, in carefully calibrated steps, within institutions segregated from adult society. The vast majority of families living in urban working-class neighborhoods, in mill and mining towns, and in the rural Northeast, South, Midwest, and Far West continued to rely heavily on children's labor and earnings. On farms, children as young as five or six pulled weeds and chased birds and cattle away from crops. By the time they reached eight, many tended livestock, milked cows, churned butter, fed chickens, collected eggs, hauled water, scrubbed laundry, and harvested crops. In urban areas, working-class children ran errands, scavenged, participated in street trades, or took part in outwork, forms of manufacturing that took place in the home.

As for schooling, its amount varied starkly by ethnicity, social class, and geographic location. While the amount of grammar school education increased sharply for all groups—with enrollment reaching half of all young people aged five to nineteen in 1850 and almost 60 percent in 1870—enrollment was much higher in the Northeast, Midwest, and Far West than in the South, where fewer than half of all children attended school as late as 1890. In rural areas the school year was much shorter than elsewhere because of seasonal labor needs. While urban students typically began their education around the age of seven, attended school nine months a year, and completed a year of high school, rural children went to school six months a year for less than five years. Schooling differed not only in length but in content and form. Urban students attended schools with age-graded classrooms, a standardized curriculum, and trained educators, while rural students attended one-room schools containing a wide range of ages with teachers lacking formal preparation. Class and region also heavily influenced the age of school leaving. In increasing numbers, the urban middle class enrolled in high school and remained there until the age of sixteen or seventeen. In contrast, around puberty, farm children went off temporarily to work as hired laborers, while the urban working-class entered regular employment at "apprentice" or "youth" wages.

The settings in which children played varied widely, as did the games they played and the toys they had. By the 1870s middle-class children had a growing number of store-bought, manufactured toys and board games, designed to inculcate moral values and gender norms and prepare boys for future careers. In one popular board game, The Mansion of Happiness, players passed by "Honesty" and "Idleness" before reaching "Happiness." Working-class and farm children, in contrast, played with homemade toys—dolls made from corncobs, balls made from socks, or jacks from corn kernels—and amused themselves not in nurseries or playrooms but in rural fields or city streets. Compared with their urban middle-class counterparts, working-class and farm children enjoyed much less privacy inside the home, but greater freedom from parental oversight outside the home. After 1870 urban middle-class children participated in adult-organized youth groups and team sports, while urban working-class children enjoyed commercial amusements, notably penny arcades, dance halls, and amusement parks.

The expansion of a market economy and the growth of industry had paradoxical effects on children's lives. Middle-class children were excluded from the world of work while the economic value of working-class and farm children expanded and their labor potential became more essential to their family's economic well-being. The earnings of children between the ages of ten and fifteen often amounted to 20 percent of a family's income and spelled the difference between economic well-being and destitution. A teenage son's income frequently exceeded his father's. Accumulating a savings account or purchasing a house required sons and daughters to subordinate their personal wishes to larger family considerations. Key decisions—about the length of schooling or the age of entry into the workforce—were based on family needs rather than individual choice. Among many ethnic groups it was common for daughters to leave school at an early age and enter work so that their brothers could continue their education. It was also customary for a daughter to remain unmarried and to care for younger siblings or aging parents. The cooperative family economy made decisionmaking a by-product of collective needs rather than of individual preferences.

While the Industrial Revolution did not invent child labor, it did make child labor more visible by removing child and teenage workers from domestic settings. The first textile mill in the United States, Samuel Slater's mill in Pawtucket, Rhode Island, which opened in 1790, had a workforce consisting of seven boys and two girls, ages seven to twelve, who operated the factory's seventy-two spindles. Slater soon discovered that children, "constantly employed under the immediate inspection" of a supervisor, could produce three times as much as whole families working without supervision in their own homes. To keep the children alert and awake, Slater whipped them with a leather strap and sprinkled them with water. On Sundays the children attended a special school established by Slater.

During the early phases of industrialization, textile mills and agricultural tool, metal goods, nail, and rubber factories had a ravenous appetite for cheap, tractable teenage laborers. In many mechanized industries, from a quarter to half the workforce was under the age of twenty. Generally child and teenage laborers were hired not by the mill or factory owner, but by a skilled adult worker, who was responsible for their discipline. Child workers were disciplined by ridicule and taunting as well as by physical punishments, including slaps, ear boxing, and whippings.

Even before the rise of the factory system, the significance of child labor had grown. During the late eighteenth century the growth of household industries greatly increased young children's economic value. Merchant capitalists distributed raw materials to individual households, which then manufactured finished goods. Dexter Whittemore, the owner of a country store in rural Fitzwilliam, New Hampshire, distributed palm leaves to local farm families. Family members braided the leaves into hats in exchange for credits on the store's ledgers. For cash-strapped farm families, the opportunity to earn cash was a godsend. The money was used to pay off debts, finance farm improvements, purchase household goods, or send children to school. Domestic industries provided work for thousands of rural children, and the quantity of goods they produced was staggering. In 1809 farm families near Philadelphia produced more than 230,000 yards of cloth for sale, four times the amount produced by the area's textile mills. Massachusetts farm households produced more than 100,000 pairs of shoes—more than all the nation's professional shoemakers combined. After 1820, however, household industries declined and were replaced by manufacturing in city shops and factories.

Apprenticeship, like domestic manufacturing, also diminished. Until the early nineteenth century, apprenticeship was how boys were trained in skilled trades. More than a system of labor, apprenticeship was also a way to deal with potentially disruptive adolescents. Like the system of indentured servitude it resembled, the apprenticeship system provided a foster home for youths in their teens. Compared with its rigidly regulated European counterpart, the American system of apprenticeship was an "anemic institution," providing a much briefer experience. Nevertheless, apprenticeship was a major part of the process of growing up in early America, with apprentices usually living in the master's house under his watchful eye.

Following the American Revolution, however, the apprenticeship system disintegrated as teenagers obtained new opportunities to enter trades. The Revolution itself was partly responsible for the system's demise, as many youths were no longer willing to display the deference that the master-apprentice relationship required. Economic uncertainties contributed as well. Faced by sharp fluctuations in demand for the goods they produced, masters shortened the terms of apprenticeships, preferring simply to hire workers when demand was high. The introduction of labor-saving machinery and an influx of immigrants from Europe accelerated the institution's demise. In trades such as printing, mechanization produced a glut of skilled artisans, and "slop shops" offered employment to young men with a minimum of skills. By the 1850s most apprentices were no more than semiskilled workers or machine tenders. Meanwhile, manuals, printed guides, and lectures and demonstrations at mechanics' institutes allowed young men to learn craft skills on their own without going through a formal apprenticeship.

By the mid-nineteenth century, apprenticeship resembled most other employment relationships. Instead of living in a master's home, apprentices received cash wages and resided in boarding-houses in distinct working-class neighborhoods. The paternalistic view of a master who supervised behavior and provided for an apprentice's welfare was replaced by a new conception of labor as a commodity that could be acquired or disposed of according to the laws of supply and demand. No longer did masters advertise in newspapers for the return of runaway apprentices; instead they simply hired new employees. As the apprenticeship system declined, male teenagers were pushed out of the skilled trades and into unskilled labor. In Newark, New Jersey, the proportion of white males between the ages of fifteen and twenty in the skilled trades fell by over a third, while the proportion who were jobless or in school rose from 7 to 27 percent. In the future, teenage workers would be used primarily as helpers, messengers, or unskilled laborers.

As the close, highly ritualized master-apprenticeship bonds disappeared, advice books, self-help manuals, mechanics' institutes, apprentice libraries, and lyceums proliferated to help young men navigate the difficult transition away from home during the teen years and the increasing choices, opportunities, and possible roadblocks they faced. Apprenticeship's decline also encouraged educational reformers to devise the modern high school as an instrument to fill the void left by the end of this system of labor.

The demise of apprenticeship coincided with a shift in authority relations within the working-class family. In certain respects the apprenticeship system had reinforced paternal power, by giving a father a formal say in a son's career choice. Under common law, a son remained under his father's control until the age of twenty-one. Fathers had a legal right to their sons' earnings and had the power of consent over their sons' decision to leave an apprenticeship and assume a new one. By the mid-nineteenth century, increasing numbers of sons were contesting their father's authority to dictate their choice of a career. At the same time a growing number of the sons of skilled laborers and prosperous commercial farmers, convinced that apprenticeships were no longer a secure route to a promising career, were staying at home longer and attending school beyond the middle elementary grades in order to pick up the skills necessary to become a clerk or a broker. For these young men, ties between parents and children were intensified and prolonged, yet paternal authority was giving way to maternal counseling and peer companionship.

The breakdown of the apprenticeship system produced a class division tied to decisions made at puberty. Especially after the economic panic of 1837, young men either entered a factory between the ages of twelve and fourteen, a choice that doomed them to a life of unskilled or semiskilled labor, or remained in school into their mid-teens before entering a clerkship or another salaried position in their late teens or early twenties. Those who pursued school had the care and shelter of the middle-class home. Those who went to work in factories developed a very different and distinctive urban working-class youth culture. Cash incomes made possible the advent of young "dandies," who patronized theaters and music halls, paraded through city streets in ostentatious dress, and promenaded with young women. Barber shops, boardinghouses, firehouses, saloons, and theaters provided settings where young working-class men could socialize. Prizefights, horse races, and politics played an important role in the new peer culture. In the early 1850s the bitterly nativist Know Nothing political party overwhelmingly drew its most ardent supporters from these same youths in their teens and twenties.

Many young unskilled laborers and factory operatives spent their free time congregating on street corners, committing petty theft, or seeking entertainment in bowling alleys, tippling shops, gaming houses, and theaters. Seeking a sense of belonging, identity, and excitement, they were particularly likely to join volunteer fire companies that allowed them to don hats, badges, and uniforms, and fight fires at close range, or join sports teams, or youth gangs, which engaged in the ethnic, racial, and religious rioting that plagued mid-nineteenth-century cities. In the deadliest riot of the nineteenth century, the New York City Draft Riots of 1863, most of those arrested were under twenty-one.

Whatever the gains in personal freedom and flexibility that came with apprenticeship's demise, there were also losses. Apprenticeship had allowed young men to gain self-respect, independence, competence, and maturity while remaining connected to adults who had an obligation to them. It provided a balance between youthful independence and adult mentoring that has since been lost. The initiation rites, parades, and other rituals that signaled a young person's entrance into a particular trade and the world of adulthood were swept away. Instead urban adolescents either attended high school and remained in the parental home or else were cast adrift to make their way as best they could. Some—like the young Samuel Clemens, who arranged informal apprenticeships as a printer and later as a riverboat pilot—gradually found their way to a successful adulthood. But many others did not; caught in the tide of a modern market economy, they became delinquents, joined gangs, or drifted into a life of poverty and unskilled labor, joining America's growing underclass of the chronically unemployed or underemployed.

The same economic developments that transformed the experience of teenage males also drastically altered the lives of young working-class women. For young women, the early stages of the Industrial Revolution increased employment opportunities beyond the traditional options of domestic service and clothesmaking. Young unmarried women made up a majority of the workforce in cotton textile mills and a substantial minority of workers in factories manufacturing ready-made clothing, furs, hats, shoes, and umbrellas. Some, like Lucy Larcom, found the new opportunities exhilarating. Unlike farm work or domestic service, employment in a mill offered female companionship and an independent income. Wages (which could be as little as $1.45 a week) were twice what a young woman could make as a seamstress, tailor, or schoolteacher, and mill girls were able to spend their free time attending lectures, participating in sewing groups and literary improvement circles, and producing their own publications such as the *Lowell Offering*. What made mill work tolerable was the fact that employment was a temporary expedient before marriage. Most worked in the mills fewer than four years and frequently interrupted their stints in the mills for several months at a time with trips back home.

By the 1830s, however, increasing competition caused deteriorating working conditions that drove native-born girls out of the mills. Employers cut wages, lengthened the workday, and required mill workers to tend four looms instead of two. Hannah Borden, a young Fall River, Massachusetts, textile worker, was required to have her looms running at five in the morning. She was given an hour for breakfast and half an hour for lunch. Her workday ended at half past seven, fourteen and a half hours after it had begun. For a six-day work week she received between $2.50 and $3.50. Such labor was destructive of health and well-being. The mill girls militantly protested the wage cuts and worsening work environment. In 1834 and again in 1836, they went on strike. Eleven-year-old Harriet Hanson described her role in the 1836 walkout: "When the day came on which the girls were to turn out . . . the girls in my room stood irresolute, uncertain what to do . . . I, who began to think they would not go out, after all their talk, became impatient, and started on ahead, saying . . . 'I don't care what you do, I am going to turn out whether anyone else does or not.' " As a result of her participation in the strike, Harriet's mother, a widow who ran a boardinghouse in Lowell, was fired. She was told: "You could not prevent the older girls from turning out, but your daughter is a child and her you could control." During the 1840s fewer young native-born women were willing to work in the mills. "Slavers"—long, black wagons that crisscrossed the Vermont and New Hampshire countryside in search of mill hands—arrived empty in Rhode Island and Massachusetts mill towns. Increasingly they were replaced with a new class of permanent factory operatives, immigrant women from Ireland.

More common than factory employment for teenage girls was domestic service. Servants, who had previously been regarded as quasi-family members and been referred to as "help," were now considered paid employees. A servant's life was onerous and burdensome. Live-in servants were on call six and a half or even seven days a week. Their day began at half past four or five in the morning, and their responsibilities included cooking and serving meals, washing up, trimming and filling lamps, cleaning, placing coal and wood in fireplaces and stoves, cleaning, doing laundry, and caring for children. Even though domestic service paid better than factory work and the physical conditions were far superior, young women considered household service the most demeaning form of labor because of the psychological abuse and often the sexual abuse.

In rapidly growing urban areas, many young working-class women took on outwork, manufacturing shoes, clothing, or other household items inside their own home or a boardinghouse. By the 1830s a highly visible group of young women used their earnings to participate in the expanding urban working-class youth culture. The "Bowery gal" challenged Victorian notions of propriety by promenading down city streets wearing flashy clothes. But most urban working-class young women, especially the daughters of skilled workers, eschewed fancy clothes and gave their wages to their parents. They worked at home or stayed in school in a working-class version of domesticity.

In the poorest families, especially those headed by widows or single mothers, children's ability to earn their keep provided the indispensable margin of subsistence. They toted water up stairs, helped out with cooking, cleaning, and laundry, and ran errands. Poor families living in cellars or garrets also depended on children to perform various kinds of outwork. Young children cut and glued boxes, dipped matchsticks, or sewed seams and buttons. They also carried goods back and forth to a shop. Poor children too young for wage work scavenged for wood or coal and scoured the docks for tea, coffee, sugar, flour, and other goods that could be used at home. They hawked newspapers, held horses, blackened boots, and even caught butterflies for canary growers. Poor children participated in the informal economy, selling fruit or matches on street corners and scrub brushes and other household goods door-to-door, or peddling loose cotton, old rope, shreds of canvas and rags, bits of hardware, and bottles and broken glass to junk dealers and to papermakers, foundries, and glassmakers.

Scavenging produced considerable dismay among public authorities, who regarded it as a form of petty theft. Most of the child scavengers came from single-parent homes that depended on their labor and expected children to earn their keep. "Of the children brought before me for pilfering," wrote a police magistrate in 1830, "nine out of ten are those whose fathers are dead, and who live with their mothers, and are employed in this way." When children refused to contribute to the family economy, poorer parents turned to public authorities for help. William Codman's mother placed her son in a New York asylum in 1853 "because he would not work, and she could not support him." Working-class families held a very different view of childhood from the middle class. Far less sentimental in their conception of childhood, they did not believe that parents should make economic sacrifices for their children without reciprocal labor from their offspring.

During the nineteenth century an increasing proportion of working-class children were the daughters and sons of immigrants. Many came from Germany, Ireland, and Scandinavia, pushed from their homelands by famine, political unrest, and the destruction of traditional handicrafts by factory enterprise. In addition, 288,000 Chinese immigrants arrived in the United States between 1854 and 1883. Although most immigrants were adult males, one group—Irish Catholics—included significant numbers of children and teens, many of whom arrived in the United States alone.

Fifteen-year-old Diarmuid O'Donovan Rossa of County Cork was one of the many Irish children to suffer grievously from the potato famine. In 1846 he and a brother dug "over two hundred yards of a piece of a ridge, and all the potatoes I could pick . . . would not fill a skillet. They were no larger than marbles." The *Illustrated London News* described conditions in Diarmuid's county. Whole families subsisted on wild weeds, and "15,000 persons . . . are destitute; of this 5000 are entirely dependent on casual charity . . . The deaths . . . now average 25 daily!!" Altogether around 150,000 people in County Cork died during the famine years 1845–1847, including Diarmuid's father. Evicted from their small farm, Diarmuid's mother, sister, and two brothers emigrated to Philadelphia. Only Diarmuid, now seventeen, remained. "I supposed they thought I was old enough to take care of myself," he later said. His family's departure remained etched in his memory. "The cry of the weeping and wailing of that day rings in my ears still," he recalled.

During the summer of 1845 a "blight of unusual character" devastated Ireland's potato crop, the basic staple in the Irish diet. A few days after potatoes were dug from the ground, they turned into a slimy, decaying, blackish "mass of rottenness." Expert panels, convened to investigate the blight's cause, suggested that it was a result of "static electricity" or the smoke that billowed from railroad locomotives or "mortiferous vapours" rising from underground volcanoes. In fact the cause was a fungus that had traveled from America to Ireland. In 1846 the potato crop was just one-fifth as large as it had been two years earlier. Half a million Irish were evicted from their cottages, and "famine fever"—dysentery, typhus, and infestations of lice—soon spread through the Irish countryside. Observers reported seeing children crying with pain and looking "like skeletons, their features sharpened with hunger and their limbs wasted, so that there was little left but bones, their hands and arms." Masses of bodies were buried without coffins, a few inches below the soil.

Over the next five years, 750,000 Irish died, and approximately a million Irish migrated to the United States. Freighters offered fares as low as $17 to $20 between Liverpool and Boston—fares subsidized by English landlords eager to be rid of the starving peasants. The journey to the United States took five to ten weeks, and conditions aboard the "famine ships" were abominable. Steerage compartments were only about five feet high and contained two tiers of bunks, with each berth holding at least four people. On one vessel, only a pound of meal or bread was allotted as a daily ration for each adult, half a pound for each child under the age of fourteen, and a third of a pound for those under seven years, along with a pint of water. As many as 10 percent of the emigrants perished while still at sea. In 1847, 40,000 (or 20 percent) of those who set out from Ireland died along the way. "If crosses and tombs could be erected on water," wrote the U.S. commissioner for emigration, "the whole route of the emigrant vessels from Europe to America would long since have assumed the appearance of a crowded cemetery."

Lacking the money to move elsewhere, most Irish immigrants remained near the port cities where they landed. Often whole families crowded into a single room. Nativist Protestant reformers stigmatized immigrant family life as disorganized, denouncing the prevalence of drinking, youth gangs, domestic violence, and the number of children institutionalized in almshouses, houses of refuge, and reformatories. In fact the biggest contributor to family instability among Irish immigrants was the high death rate among unskilled Irish Catholic workers. "It is well established," one Irish American noted, "that the average length of life of the emigrant after landing here is six years; and many insist it is much less." Harsh outdoor labor, reported another observer, meant that "a man who labours steadily for 10 to 12 years in America is of very little use afterwards."

Many young people arrived in America by themselves and took whatever jobs were available. Some girls, like Ann McNabb, who migrated to Philadelphia, became live-in household servants, an occupation that native-born girls shunned. As late as 1900, three-fifths of all Irish-born women in the United States were domestic servants. Other young Irish women did piecework in factories or their own apartments, making nine shirts a week for a total of about ninety cents. In the second generation, many became schoolteachers or nurses, while many boys worked as laborers, constructing streets or canals or sewers, or toiling on the docks. Al Smith, the grandson of an Irish immigrant, was born in 1873 in Hell's Kitchen on New York's Lower East Side. He took his first job selling newspapers when he was eleven. After his father's death when he was thirteen, he left school and took a series of jobs, including unloading barrels of fish at New York's Fulton Fish Market, where his days began at three in the morning.

Migration to America profoundly altered Irish families. For the first and second generations of immigrants, the stresses of emigration, poverty, and unskilled labor sometimes resulted in severe family tension and disruption, weakening the role of the father and husband and widening the division between male and female spheres. Widowhood and single-parent female-headed households were much more common in the United States than in Ireland as a result of the high male mortality rate, frequent on-the-job accidents, and desertion. One son whose father deserted his family was the dramatist Eugene O'Neill, and as a result his "family always was ill-fed and poorly-clad." Single-parent families were more common among the Irish than any nineteenth-century ethnic group except African Americans. Migration enhanced sons' economic significance and gave daughters greater responsibilities and independence.

The childhood of Anne Sullivan, the "miracle worker" who gained international renown as Helen Keller's teacher, illustrates the problems of poverty and family instability in extreme form. Born to desperately poor and troubled immigrant parents in 1866, she had a father with a drinking problem and a mother suffering from tuberculosis. At the age of five Anne contracted trachoma, an eye disease associated with filthy living conditions. When she was eight, Anne's mother died. A sister and brother were sent to live with relatives, while Anne remained home to care for her father. When she was ten, her father deserted Anne, and she and her brother were placed in the Massachusetts almshouse at Tewksbury, where her brother died of tuberculosis. Anne's experience underscored the stresses and family tensions that migration imposed on many children of immigrants.

During the nineteenth century, as many families made their livelihoods from mining coal or minerals from the earth as worked in the nation's iron and steel mills. In eastern Pennsylvania alone, mining engaged more than 100,000 families. After his family emigrated from Lithuania to the coalfields near Scranton, Pennsylvania, nine-year-old Joseph Miliauska earned seventy cents for a ten-hour day as a breaker boy, separating coal from the slate and rocks. If his boss caught a boy slipping up and letting slate pass by, Joseph recalled, "you'd get it in the back with a broom."

Coalmining families endured a particularly harsh existence. Employment was grueling, dangerous, and erratic, and annual earnings were extremely low. At the end of the nineteenth century, when one state survey estimated that it took a yearly income of $754 to provide food, clothing, and shelter for a family of five, 60 percent of the adult miners in eastern Pennsylvania anthracite fields earned less than $450. To supplement the father's income, sons entered the mines as soon as they were physically able. Boys as young as nine or ten started out as door boys, driver boys, or breaker boys. Door boys sat for hours in the darkness of the mine to open and shut the doors that permitted the mule-drawn mine cars to pass. Driver boys dumped coal from the cars, after which it descended through processing machines to the breaker boys, who cleaned and inspected it and separated rocks and slate from the coal. Breaker boys covered their mouths with handkerchiefs to keep out the coal dust, but they were forbidden to wear gloves, even in the coldest weather, because doing so impaired their finger movement and sense of touch. "If we were discovered wearing gloves," remembered one breaker boy, "the boss would strike our knuckles with a long stick he carried." As a result, for the first few weeks the sulfur on the coal irritated the boys' skin and caused their fingers to swell, crack open, and bleed, causing a condition called "red tips." Until their fingers hardened, mothers applied goose grease to their sons' fingers every night.

The heavy reliance on child labor and wages meant that few boys could stay in school very long. Most boys had no more than five years of formal education, and half were out of school by their twelfth birthday. Coalminers' daughters typically assisted their mothers in such tasks as manufacturing handicrafts or taking in laundry or boarders or gardening. As late as 1924, over half of West Virginia's mining families planted gardens and kept cows, pigs, and poultry. "Miners couldn't always depend upon the mine," one later recalled; "therefore we would have to raise a garden to make sure we always ate."

Much as industrialization generated enormous demand for unskilled child labor in mills and mines, and growing middle-class affluence created a growing hunger for household servants, the commercialization of agriculture made children's farm labor more valuable than ever before. The lure of commercial agriculture led some 400,000 pioneering families to venture westward to settle in California, Oregon, and the Great Plains. Nancy Kelsey was eighteen years old and already a mother when she migrated westward on the first wagon train to California in 1841. "We were then out of provisions, having killed and eaten all our cattle," she recalled. "I walked barefeeted until my feet were blistered and lived on roasted acorns for two days." This first party of sixty-nine pioneers endured almost inconceivable hardships. They were forced to abandon their wagons and eat their pack animals, "half roasted, dripping with blood."

It took Americans a century and a half to expand as far west as the Appalachian Mountains, a few hundred miles from the Atlantic coast. It took another fifty years to push the frontier to the Mississippi River. By 1830, fewer than 100,000 pioneers had crossed the Mississippi. But during the 1840s, tens of thousands of Americans ventured beyond the Mississippi, and by 1850 they had pushed the edge of settlement to California and the Oregon country of the Pacific Northwest. The journey west was a tremendous test of human endurance. Thirteen-year-old Mary Murphy lost her mother and five other relatives to starvation. "I hope I shall not live long, for I am tired of this troublesome world and want to go to my mother," she wrote. That was in 1847. Murphy was a survivor of the infamous Donner party, which became snowbound in the Sierra Nevada and resorted to cannibalism to survive.

[. . .]

Some 40,000 children faced blizzards, desert heat, massacres and epidemics on the way west between 1841 and 1865. On the overland trail, pioneer children bore responsibilities that were crucial to their families' survival. They cared for livestock, hunted and fished, cooked, stood guard, scouted for camping spots, nursed the sick and injured, and buried the dead. Girls got up before dawn and collected wood and buffalo chips (animal dung used for fuel), hauled water, kindled campfires, kneaded dough, and milked cows. They also tended younger children. On the westward trail, it proved impossible to maintain a rigid age or sexual division of labor. Boys and girls drove or maintained wagons and livestock, stood guard duty, and hunted buffalo and antelope for extra meat. Childhood accidents and diseases were an ever-present danger. Young children fell out of wagons and under wagon wheels.

[. . .]

The frontier could not have been settled without children's labor. They provided game and wild plants for their families' tables as well as the fuel to cook their food. They cut hay, herded cattle and sheep, burned brush, gathered eggs, and churned butter. They also broke sod, planted, weeded, and harvested. Farmers on the plains could not afford to delay their offspring's entry into the family workforce. A Kansas father bragged that his two-year-old son could "fetch up cows out of the stock fields, or oxen, carry in stove wood and climb in the corn crib and feed the hogs and go on errands." Improved plows and other farm machinery allowed young sons and daughters to assist with plowing, planting, and harvesting. An Oklahoma father gave each of his children a knife to hack the soil and "make a seed bed for a garden and the first crop of kaffir corn." Fannie Eisele was only ten years old when she began to plow her family's Oklahoma fields, and Helen Brock at fifteen was branding calves and erecting fences.

[. . .]

In contrast to their urban middle-class counterparts, frontier children were not subjected to close supervision in the vast outdoors. Instead they were encouraged to act independently and to assume essential family responsibilities at an early age. An entry in the diary of a twelve-year-old Helena, Montana, girl underscores the degree to which a frontier childhood could be exposed to adult realities: "At two o'clock in the morning a highway Robber was hung on a large pine tree. After breakfast we went to see him. At ten o'clock preaching, at one o'clock a large auction sale of horses and cattle. At two o'clock Sunday school. At three o'clock a foot race. At seven o'clock preaching. The remainder of the time spent by hundreds of miners in gambling and drinking." [. . .]

Although a frontier childhood encouraged a youth of self-reliance, inner-directedness, and early independence, many western children experienced youths of withering poverty, dispiriting routine, and personal entrapment. [. . .]

Of the 400,000 families that took advantage of the Homestead Act to start a farm, fewer than a third managed to "prove up" the land to which they laid claim. During the late nineteenth century drought, grasshoppers, fire, hail, blizzards, and floods devastated farms from Texas to the Dakotas, leaving many families destitute. A Minnesota girl described her family's plight to the state governor: "We have no money now[,] nothing to sell to get any more clothes with as the grasshoppers destroyed all of our crops what few we had for we have not much land broke yet . . . We . . . almost perish here sometimes with the cold." For many children, the western adventure was a nightmare from which they longed to awaken.

The Industrial Revolution had radical effects on children's experiences. For the middle class, growing affluence allowed parents to provide their children a sheltered childhood, free from work responsibilities and devoted to education and play. For working-class, immigrant, and farm children, the growth of industry and the expansion of commercial agriculture increased parents' dependence on child labor. As a result, two divergent conceptions of childhood emerged. One conception, the useful childhood, was based on the premise that all family members, including children, should contribute to a family's support. Rooted in the experience of farm, artisanal, and frontier families, this idea took on heightened significance in an urban and industrial context, where low wages and frequent bouts of unemployment made children's earnings essential for a family's well-being. As a result, many working-class and immigrant parents expected that their economic sacrifices should be matched by sacrifices and labors from their offspring. The other conception was a protected childhood, sheltered from the stresses and demands of the adult world. First adopted by the rapidly expanding urban middle class, this ideal proved highly attractive to working-class and farm families as well. In the late nineteenth century, a central demand of labor unions was the "family wage," which would allow a male breadwinner to support his family without the economic contributions of his wife and children. Meanwhile, in rural areas, the more prosperous farmers began to substitute hired labor for children's labor whenever possible, and in the urban North, African-American parents struggled to keep their children in school and prolonged their children's education despite economic pressures.

6

excerpts from

Becoming Mexican American
Ethnicity, Culture, and Identity in Chicano Los Angeles, 1900–1945

GEORGE J. SÁNCHEZ

FAMILY LIFE AND THE SEARCH FOR STABILITY

As GUADALUPE SALAZAR LOOKED out of her train window, her mind was full of images of the past and questions about the future. Heading from Chicago to Los Angeles, she realized that her life in the United States had not turned out as she had hoped. It was the middle of the Great Depression, and Guadalupe had just ended a marriage that had lasted only a few years. Her ex-husband, Arcadio Yñiguez, had crossed the border in 1913 as a teenager from Nochistlán, Zacatecas, fleeing the violence of the Mexican Revolution. Working at a variety of odd jobs, he finally settled in Chicago during the 1920s, and there met and married Guadalupe. When the two split up, Arcadio returned to Nochistlán, while Guadalupe and their five-year-old son left for California. She was determined to start a new life in Los Angeles, where her father resided, although she had not seen him since his impressment into military service during the revolution twenty years earlier. A single female parent in 1931, Guadalupe Salazar saw her immigrant dream fade into a painful reality of insecurity.[1]

The generation of scholars who wrote during the post-World War II decades about European immigrant family life would not have been surprised by Salazar's experience. Their work emphasized the sharp discontinuities between traditional family relations in Old World peasant villages and the life immigrants encountered in modern, industrial cities after migration. Rooted in an unbending model of modernization, their studies found family disintegration to be an unfortunate, but inevitable consequence of the immigrants' undeniable break with their past. Guadalupe's failed marriage might easily have been portrayed by this school of immigration history as the result of a futile attempt to construct an orthodox union in a new and hostile environment. As Oscar Handlin put it: "Roles once thoroughly defined were now altogether confounded."[2]

Yet Guadalupe's story defied such characterization. Reunited with her father, she built a new life in Los Angeles out of which emerged a remarkable family. Her second husband, Tiburcio Rivera, had been a band musician in Mexico. He knew Guadalupe from Chicago, where he briefly owned a pool hall. They did not court until he too moved to California. In addition to Guadalupe's son, the couple had four daughters, all of whom grew up in East Los Angeles. The family endured the Depression, frequent bouts with overt discrimination, and hazardous work conditions. In spite of these hardships Guadalupe and Tiburcio provided their children a stable working-class family life.

Fifty-five years after her arrival in the city, Guadalupe Salazar received the "Mother of the Year" award from the senior citizen clubs in East Los Angeles. Mother of five, grandmother of 28, and great-grandmother of 10, she had become the respected elder of an extended family that totaled more than 200. Asked about her success, she responded: "You have to have family unity."[3]

Critics of the "Handlin school" of immigration history have pointed to the stability and resiliency of immigrant families such as Guadalupe Salazar's. Their depiction of immigrant adaptation stresses the retention of traditional values and the durability and adaptability of social relationships, all of which helped Mexican Americans to withstand the changes wrought by migration, settlement, and adjustment. In particular, these historians understand the critical role of kinship networks which allowed Salazar to reestablish herself in Los Angeles. Her relationship with her father, though strained because of the separation in Mexico, was rebuilt in the United States. In fact, this family was strengthened by Salazar's decision to call upon kin in time of need. As revisionist historian Virginia Yans-McLaughlin has pointed out, "immigrants put their Old World family ties to novel uses in America," essentially putting "new wine in old bottles."[4]

Just as historians of immigration debated the degree of cultural persistence inherent in immigrant family life, Chicano social scientists were examining the dynamics of the Mexican immigrant family. These scholars depicted *la familia* as warm and nurturing, an environment of support and stability in times of stress. They surmised that since roles and expectations continued to be circumscribed in the traditional manner, conflict within the family was kept to a minimum. From this perspective, *machismo* was not so much a maladaptive response which solidified male dominance, but rather represented an appropriate mechanism to insure the continuation of Mexican family pride and respect. Although noted in the literature, the oppression of women within the family was dismissed as a necessary evil in order to maintain family stability and tradition.[5]

Ironically, this approach had much in common with another, older body of sociological literature that depicted the Mexican family as pathological. These psychoanalytically oriented studies were the product of decades of stereotypical accounts examining "the problem" of the Mexican. They viewed Mexican families as authoritarian and *macho*-dominated, impeding individual achievement and independence while promoting passivity and familial dependence. Thus, the same values that some Chicano scholars characterized as positive were viewed as "a tangle of pathology" by Anglo American social scientists.[6] What both groups shared was a unidimensional view of the Mexican family, a caricature suspended in time and impervious to the social forces acting upon it. Such a perspective found any acculturated family to be atypical.

When placed in historical context, both characterizations of the Mexican immigrant family are problematic. First, and most important, they ignore the great diversity among Mexican immigrant families. Although many Mexicans migrated from rural villages, others came from cities. Many families migrated as entire units, while others were involved in chain migration. Some immigrants settled in largely Mexican communities along the border; others ventured further inland where the Anglo American population dominated. Before 1940, thousands of families and individual family members were in this country only temporarily. Perhaps the majority came as single migrants, and reconstituted their families in the United States. These families were often mixtures of Mexicans born on both sides of the border and occasionally included non-Mexican spouses. Moreover, individual families acculturated and adapted to American life in a multitude of ways.

Second, both conflict and consensus existed within each family. Individual members of a family might disagree over a particular family decision. Over time, positions would reverse themselves as other situations arose. Difficult periods of maturation, like a child's adolescence, could prove to be times of family conflict, while family unity might be invoked during periods of crisis and abrupt change, such as the death of a parent or a new marriage. Moreover, while Mexican family members often gave highest priority to the welfare of the family, specific family decisions could mask the range of compromises made by individuals involved in that resolution.

Finally, every Mexican who came to the United States made adjustments. Though most families did not disintegrate under the weight of changing circumstances, they certainly acclimated. The nature of this acculturation varied, depending on the setting, and different strategies were developed to fit the needs of the historical moment. A new identity was continuously being formed.

To understand the diversity of family experiences among Mexican immigrants in Los Angeles, we must examine critically assumptions regarding family life in turn-of-the-century Mexico in regions that contributed migrants to the United States. Most interpretations characterize Mexican families as hierarchical, rigidly patriarchal, solidified by age-old customs rooted in peasant values and Catholic tradition. Mexicans were characterized as having large, extended family structures in which gender roles were strictly separated, reinforced by stern parental discipline and community pressure. Each individual village usually consisted of a few extended families linked to each other through generations of intermarriage and other kin relationships, including *compadrazgo*, the interlocking bond created by parents and godparents of a child.

Recent studies challenge this interpretation of Mexican family life, depicting much more flexibility within family patterns. By the turn of the century, economic challenges brought about by the penetration of market capitalism into all but the most isolated villages during the Porfiriato forced families to adapt. As land prices were driven up, families were forced to send members, usually adolescent boys and young husbands, into the wage economy. Women were also swept into the cash-based economy. Some marketed surplus food raised on family plots, while others sewed for profit utilizing Singer technology. Central markets in most villages became more active points of economic exchange. A family's own land was increasingly attended to by those outside this cash nexus, usually by women and children closer to home or those who returned from various forms of wage labor in time to complete a harvest.

Rigid gender roles could hardly be maintained under these circumstances. The Mexican family showed that it was capable of flexibility and adaptability, even under the most distressing circumstances. In addition to migration brought about by economic conditions, most villages contained families that had experienced the death of their male heads of household. Widows were often able to maintain a family's well-being, aided by older adolescents or nearby relatives. Female-headed households, the result of either death or desertion, were not uncommon at the turn of the century, although marriage continued to be the preferred societal norm for all adult women.

Most families participated in economic migration in order to maintain a life that they identified as rooted in traditional values. Working for the railroad or in the mines was intended as a short-term solution to an emergency. Yet the Mexican government's economic and social policies around the turn of the century transformed these strategies into a way of life. Porfirian economics demanded a large, growing wage labor pool, as did economic developments in the United States. Families found themselves caught in a cycle of economic uncertainty, necessitating the flexibility of "traditional" roles and norms for survival.

After 1910, the Mexican Revolution only intensified these patterns. Geographic mobility increased, often forcing entire families to flee their native villages to avoid the danger of incoming troops. More often, male family members were sent scurrying, either to avoid conscription or to join one of the military factions. It was common, in the absence of men, for women to perform most day-to-day economic functions related to a family's property and sustenance. If not touched directly by the fighting, families found that destruction of neighboring fields, markets, or transportation could force them to engage in more extensive migration to market their goods or earn wages for their labor.

Mexicans who migrated to the United States generally came from families that had already engaged in years of creative adaptation to adversity. Unlike European immigrant families, whose movement into American society could best be described as chain migration, Mexican families were much more likely to be involved in a pattern of circular migration. Although most European immigrant groups also had high rates of return migration, ranging from 25 to 60 percent, only Mexicans exhibited a pattern of back-and-forth movement that would continue for years.[7] Men ventured north across the border to engage in seasonal labor, then returned south for a period of a few months or a couple of years. If economic circumstances once again necessitated extra cash, the circular pattern began anew. During World War I and up until 1921, the United States government contributed to this pattern by giving entrance visas to temporary workers in order to regulate their movement back into Mexico at the end of a season.

Changes in U.S. immigration policy, however, made it more difficult to engage in this practice after 1921. An enlarged border patrol, enforced literacy tests, and higher visa fees made back-and-forth migration more risky and more expensive during the 1920s. Workers who had grown accustomed to legal, relatively easy passage across the border were now faced with the prospect of venturing north illegally or being held up indefinitely in border cities. Increasingly, Mexicans were forced to decide where they wanted to reside permanently. While many returned to Mexico, the large increase in the Mexican population of Los Angeles during the 1920s suggests that a significant proportion determined to make their homes in the north. For single, independent migrants, the decision meant a reorientation to the experience of working and living in the United States. Heads of households were required to move whole families across the border.

The process of family migration was often tortuous. It was likely to involve careful decision-making concerning which family members should be on which side of the border, taking place over several years. Economic opportunities and emotional attachments had to be weighed. Individual preferences could not always be ignored for the sake of the family good. Others besides immediate family members were often involved in the move; some provided resources while others provided short- and long-term care of minors.

The experience of one family, accessible to us through archived transcripts of the Board of Special Inquiry of the Immigration Service, may serve as an example of the complex process of family migration to Los Angeles.[8] On August 25, 1917, three individuals—María López de Astengo, her twelve-year-old son, José Jr., and Mrs. María Salido de Villa—presented themselves to American immigration authorities in Nogales, Arizona. Mrs. Astengo and her son had ventured north from Rosario, Sinaloa, on the western coast of Mexico. María's husband, José Sr., had fled their ranch two years earlier to avoid the danger associated with the revolution and to earn income for the family. A bookkeeper in Mexico, he used his experience to gain employment as an office clerk in Los Angeles, earning $2.50 a day. Mrs. Astengo did not intend to cross into the United States herself; rather, she was sending her son with a friend of her family, Mrs. Villa, who was going north to visit her own two children who lived in Los Angeles. Mrs. Villa's son had married in the United States and had lived in Los Angeles for the last five years. Her daughter arrived in Los Angeles in 1915. Mrs. Villa intended to return to Mexico in November or December when "the weather gets cold."

The following spring Mrs. Astengo sent Enrique, her next eldest son, to live with his father. He traveled with three other young Mexicans from Rosario, none family members. María Valdez, age twenty-seven, headed the group, guarding everyone's money during the passage. María, accompanied by her fourteen-year-old brother Jesús, came north to see her younger sister Josefina, who had been in the United States for about a year. Josefina was single and supported herself by working as a laundress. She lived in Los Angeles with a widowed second cousin. Josefina had been instructed by her mother in Rosario to put young Jesús in an American public school. María herself intended to stay only for about six months before returning to Rosario.

The fourth member of the group was Jesús Cambreros, a seventeen-year-old girlfriend from Rosario, who came to Los Angeles to live with her married sister Elisa, also a laundress. Elisa's husband, Luis Martinez, worked for Wells Fargo Express, earning seven or eight dollars a week. Since coming to the United States as a boy from Chihuahua, Martinez had also been a baker and a foundry worker. The couple had a baby and lived in a six-room house in the downtown area, renting out space to two other adults.

A few months later, Mrs. Astengo and the rest of her family joined her husband and sons in Los Angeles. But the migration of relatives did not end there. That summer, José Astengo urged his sister in Rosario to send her son to Los Angeles to attend school, rather naïvely noting that the city was "very clean . . . perfectly safe and pleasant" with "no saloons, gambling houses, or houses of prostitution." At the beginning of July, Carlos Osuna made the trip through Nogales, accompanied by José's brother. Both planned on living with José's family while attending school. Another brother, Jesús, was also reportedly working in Los Angeles.

These reports of three distinct border crossings suggest the intricate nature of Mexican family migration to the United States. The Astengos first sent their husband north as a temporary measure. Younger male sons followed, once José had established himself in Los Angeles. María Astengo and the youngest children were the last to leave the homeland. Complicating the picture, brothers of José and a nephew also ventured northward when opportunities presented themselves for work or education. The Astengos sent family members north via train, but each trip was facilitated by other relatives or hometown friends who accompanied the travelers. Regular communication between family members on both sides of the border, including periodic visits and oral messages sent through family friends, enabled José to monitor the migration process. It is more difficult to assess the decision-making power of María, since we are not privy to their personal correspondence. One son reported that María maintained a family store in Rosario while José was in the United States, a fact which indicates some level of economic autonomy. Although the Astengos were better off than the average Mexican family, their experiences with immigration characterize many of the ways Mexicans took advantage of economic opportunity.

Other families who emigrated illustrate the many dimensions of familial migration. Older adolescents and young adults formed the bulk of the permanent emigrants. In particular, single men ventured north to find work, often aided by relatives or friends when they arrived. Young women also moved north, but were invariably accompanied by other family members and had relatives waiting for them in Los Angeles. The migration of these young adults' parents was often more problematic, but many visited their children, at least until the tightening of restrictions during the years from 1921 to 1924.

Single male migrants served as initiators of most Mexican migration. Although many European immigrant groups displayed high levels of family migration, the Mexican pattern seems to be similar to that of Italians, whose single migrant rate was around 75 percent. Among male Mexican immigrants who chose to naturalize in Los Angeles, in fact, only 10 percent had first ventured to the United States as married men. As in the Italian case, single Mexican migrants were also more likely to return to their homeland than those who were married and accompanied by their spouses.[9] Single migrants, like those married but traveling alone, generally remained in touch with their families in Mexico. As long as those ties remained strong, a high proportion of single males returned.

For single male migrants through the mid-1920s, the central Plaza area of Los Angeles remained the most important area of introduction to the city. Although this area also contained recently arrived families, single men dominated community life. Theatres, restaurants, bars, dancing clubs, and pool halls nearby catered to this male clientele. The Plaza itself was often used as an employment recruitment site, and on the weekends served as a locus for political discussions. Rental housing, including boarding houses for single men, was the norm in the barrio around the Plaza. Upon arriving in Los Angeles with eight other single men, Arturo Morales, a twenty-eight-year-old from Acatlán, Jalisco, remembered being directed to a rooming house run by a woman from his home state. Within a week, all had obtained work, sharing two rooms in the boarding house between the eight of them.[10] Although other ethnic newcomers to Los Angeles increasingly flocked to the Plaza in the 1920s, most notably Italians and Chinese, Mexicans remained the largest group in the historic Mexican pueblo plaza area.

Many, if not most, of these single Mexican men stayed in Los Angeles only temporarily. Often they entered the city with the idea of earning money quickly, then returning to their families in Mexico. Living in the central Plaza area made this plan more possible. A male worker traveling alone could find employment through the various employment agencies with offices near the Plaza, or simply stand around in the early morning and wait for a prospective employer's call. Housing, though crowded and often unsanitary, was relatively cheap in the district and was tolerated by laborers hoping to stay only briefly in the city. With images of loved ones waiting across the border in need, many single men found Los Angeles to be a relatively easy place to find a job and earn extra cash before returning home.

On the other hand, the loosening of ties with the Mexican family of origin was crucial in generating a permanent immigrant population in Los Angeles. Although exact figures are not available, a significant number of single male migrants, who formed the vast majority of the transient Mexican population in the city, reoriented themselves toward permanent residency in the United States. While family considerations were fundamental to Mexicans who contemplated leaving their homeland, breaking those connections was crucial if a migrant was to stay in the United States. This process was aided by the restrictive immigration requirements which originated in 1917. But other factors were also important in solidifying this pattern.

The regional and state origins of immigrants were important factors which determined whether a newcomer planted roots in Los Angeles or not. According to Manuel Gamio's pathbreaking study, migrants from Mexico's agricultural central plateau were much more likely to send money back to their families. Although Los Angeles's Mexican population contained a considerable portion of members from this region, equally significant were migrants from urban areas and northern Mexico. These individuals were less likely to be supporting family members in Mexico. Familiarity with the United States and U.S.-Mexico border communities made it much more likely that single men migrating from northern border areas settled in Los Angeles permanently. Urban migrants were less likely to be involved in the supplemental cash economy which allowed many migrants to retain their agricultural land in Mexico.

The passage of time itself, of course, loosened ties to Mexico. Although many migrants no doubt originally intended a short visit to Los Angeles, thousands never achieved their goals. More often than not, Mexicans could not save much from the meager wages they received. It was easy to postpone a return to Mexico until the ever-elusive extra dollar was earned. As Estanislao Gómez, an immigrant from Guadalajara, put it: "I had always considered returning to Mexico, but the months and years went by, along with the fact that since I earn very little I can't save much."[11] Furthermore, Los Angeles was not a border community, and conditions there made regular contact difficult. Urban jobs, unlike agricultural employment, were less likely to be seasonal and were inflexible in providing time to visit relatives in Mexico. Periodic visits also required surplus cash which many migrants were never able to accrue.

Ironically, it was often the establishment of new family ties which broke a single male's connection to his family of origin. When marriage occurred in the United States, ties to families of origin immediately became secondary. As stays in the United States were lengthened, the likelihood increased dramatically that a young single man would encounter a woman to marry in this country. This turn of events changed the orientation of Mexican men living in the United States from that of expatriates temporarily working here to heads of households formed in the United States.

Unlike men, Mexican migrant women in this period rarely ventured to Los Angeles unattached to their families or unaccompanied by relatives. Even if their family of origin remained in Mexico, they lived in Los Angeles with extended family—siblings, cousins, uncles, or aunts. Most came to the city with their family unit, either as wives or children, directly from Mexico or from another part of the American Southwest. Those single adult women who came north migrated only after some personal or family tragedy. Juana Martínez, for example, migrated from Mazatlán, Sinaloa, with her mother and two sisters only after her divorce and the death of her father. Leova González de López also left Mazatlán, but only to escape the slanderous talk that surrounded her decision to raise her brother's son as a single parent. Tellingly, González was an orphan herself and migrated to Los Angeles under the guidance of her aunt.[12]

From the start, women's orientation toward the United States was formed in the confines of a Mexican family, not as single, independent migrants living alone. Eventually, many of the Chicanas who migrated to Los Angeles as children, whether Mexican or American-born, found employment as young adults to help support their families and often to provide themselves with independent income. A small minority tried to live alone or with girlfriends, away from the watchful eye of intruding relatives.

Perhaps because the largest single concentration of unmarried men lived in the crowded housing around the Plaza, this area was strictly off limits to most women living alone. Instead, the majority lived in the adjacent metropolitan areas to the south and west of the Plaza. Unlike the barrios developing east of the river, housing alternatives to the single-family home emerged. Small apartments, a few boarding houses for women, and households willing to take in a non-related young female were much more common in this part of the city than in other areas populated by Mexican immigrants. Close to downtown, these households provided easy access to both the industrial labor and white-collar employment available to young Mexican women.[13]

The areas west of the river were also home to the communities most integrated with other working-class ethnic groups and, with the exception of the Plaza, least solidly Mexican/Chicano in their cultural orientation. Women and men who lived here were exposed to the cultural practices of myriad ethnic groups, even as they enjoyed the anonymity of living in a big city. "Here no one pays any attention to how one goes about, how one lives," declared Elenita Arce, pleased at the greater freedoms allowed unmarried women.[14] These areas also seemed to provide a haven for immigrants who went against traditional Mexican family practice. Knowledge and use of effective birth control, for example, seemed concentrated in a small group of Mexican women living in these downtown communities.[15] Also, most single Mexican immigrant men and women lived west of the Los Angeles River, while Chicano family life was increasingly centered east of the river during the 1920s. Over three-quarters of all the single migrants sampled lived in the barrios west of the river. Of the single migrants over age twenty-nine—and therefore much less likely to ever marry—most also lived west of the river.[16]

Marriage, however, continued to be part of the expected practice for both Mexican women and men. In Los Angeles, a wide range of possible marriage partners was available. Not only did immigrants from a variety of different Mexican locales reside in the city, but a rapidly growing group of American-born Chicanos provided other potential partners. Non-Mexicans were also potential marriage partners, although prejudice and limited contact kept their numbers relatively small. Still, both native-born Anglo Americans and foreign-born whites were listed among the husbands and wives of Mexican immigrants who applied for naturalization before 1940.

An examination of marriage patterns between Mexican immigrants and other groups reveals figures similar to those offered by earlier historians and social scientists.[17] Almost 83 percent of the marriages involving Mexican immigrants in a sample of 1,214 marriages took place within the Mexican/Chicano community. Some 209 marriages, or 17.2 percent, were between Mexican immigrants and non-Chicanos. Not surprisingly, intermarriage was significantly more prevalent among Mexican immigrant women who chose to naturalize, involving one-third of those in the sample.[18] Marriage to non-Chicanas born outside the United States accounted for only 1.9 percent of the marriages of Mexican men, yet Mexican immigrant women married more foreign-born Anglo American men than American-born ones (see Table 6.1).

A profile of the Mexican immigrant men who married Anglos uncovers some revealing patterns. Mexican men who married non-Chicanas were more likely to have migrated to the United States before age twenty and to have come from larger urban areas in Mexico. Four-fifths of the Mexican immigrant men who intermarried arrived in this country before age twenty, while men in the sample who married Mexican immigrant women were more likely to have come as adults.[19] Most of the future spouses in intermarried couples came as children to the United States and therefore grew up in similar conditions to American-born Chicanos.

Additionally, urban areas, and to a lesser extent coastal areas, were more likely to produce immigrants who intermarried, largely because they were more familiar with American culture and urban life. Señora María Rovitz Ramos, for example, married a young, bilingual Anglo American. She had grown up in Mazatlán, where her father was owner of a hotel catering to European and American tourists.[20] Immigrants born in Mexico City were particularly likely to intermarry. In fact,

Table 6.1 Marriage Patterns of Mexican Immigrants in Los Angeles

Background of spouse	Men		Women		Total	
	Number	Percent	Number	Percent	Number	Percent
Mexican immigrant	670	60.7	47	42.4	717	59.1
Mexican American	261	23.7	27	24.3	288	23.7
Total Chicano	931	84.4	74	66.7	1,005	82.8
Anglo American	151	13.7	18	16.2	169	13.9
Foreign-born Anglo	21	1.9	19	17.1	40	3.3
Total Anglo	172	15.6	37	33.3	209	17.2
Total	1,103	100.0	111	100.0	1,214	100.0

Source: Analysis of naturalization documents, National Archives, Laguna Niguel, California.

the sample revealed that more immigrants from the Mexican capital married Anglo Americans in Los Angeles (38 percent) than married other Mexican immigrants (24 percent).

Non-Chicanos who married Mexican immigrants also shared certain characteristics. Typically, they were also migrants to Los Angeles, often coming as adults. Mexican immigrant women were just as likely to marry foreigners as they were men born in the United States. For Mexican immigrant men, intermarriages most often were made with newcomers from the Midwest or East, although many of these spouses were American-born offspring of Italian or Irish Catholic immigrants.[21] Like Mexican women, these Anglo spouses also tended to marry young—age twenty-two on average. As recent arrivals to Los Angeles, they shared with their Mexican spouses the disruption of family ties and the need to acclimate to life in Los Angeles.

Not surprisingly, intermarried couples were less likely to live in the barrios around the Plaza area and in East Los Angeles. In fact, well over half of all intermarried couples lived in the larger metropolitan area to the south and west of the Plaza, compared to only one-third of the all-Mexican couples in my sample. Many reasons account for this distribution. According to contemporary observers, Mexicans who intermarried were generally lighter-skinned, and thus more easily able to move into areas restricted from dark-skinned Mexicans.[22] Entry was usually eased by a non-Chicano spouse.

Second, many intermarried couples were better off financially and could afford to live outside the barrio. One well-to-do immigrant couple saw three of their Mexican-born children marry Anglo Americans, even though the father felt the spouses "didn't belong to [our] society." The rest of the family, including four other unmarried children, lived in Hollywood, where most of their relations were with Americans. A successful real estate broker, a light-skinned intermarried Mexican woman, admitted: "Although I like my people very much I don't want to live with them, especially on the East Side, because they are very dirty there, there are many robberies and one can't live at ease."[23]

The area west of the river and south of the Plaza provided shelter for Mexican immigrants who were searching for greater cultural freedom, independence from their families, or interaction with other ethnic groups. Still solidly working-class, this community was a secondary one for many different European and Asian groups. It also housed, along Central Avenue, the largest community of blacks in Los Angeles. A substantial number of Mexican immigrants lived here, in more integrated surroundings than in other parts of the city. This integration occurred, however, largely separate from the city's Anglo American middle class. Here was a neighborhood of ethnic mixture, a polyglot zone of working-class people from around the globe.

For Mexicans, this community was more than a haven for intermarried couples and single women living alone. It represented the social freedom found in the United States, especially for women who were caught between the restrictive practices of Mexican families and the more liberal views of Anglo Americans. One representation of this battle within the family was over issues of dress and appearance of young daughters. Angelita V., for example, asserted her independence from her family of origin upon getting married at age nineteen:

> The first thing I did was to bob my hair. My father would not permit it and I have wanted to do [it] for a
> long time. I will show my husband that he will not boss me the way my father has done all of us.[24]

Other families exhibited tensions over a daughter's refusal to wear a rebozo as head covering or whether makeup would be permitted.[25]

Another aspect of that independence was less supervision over young single women, a situation that provided greater opportunities for young men and women of all nationalities to meet. This greater liberty allowed for more widespread sexual experimentation and subtle changes in sexual mores. Tellingly, almost one-third of the women involved in cross-cultural marriages had conceived a child before marriage, compared with one-fifth of first births among all-Mexican couples. When both partners had been born in Mexico, strict cultural prescriptions against sex before marriage seemed to prevail.[26] On the other hand, more than half the Mexican immigrant women sampled who married American citizens, Chicano or Anglo, had already given birth or were pregnant at marriage (see Table 6.2).

Despite the increase in premarital sex among women who did not marry Mexican men, widespread cultural values shared in both Chicano and Anglo communities encouraged men and women to marry if pregnancy occurred. In every group, less than 20 percent of births occurred outside of marriage, and only two single women in the sample had children. Many of the Chicano couples who contributed to the 20 percent were probably common-law marriages that were legalized in preparation for naturalization. While American officials and social workers often saw common-law marriages as evidence of moral decay, the Mexican immigrant community viewed these unions as legitimate.[27]

Experimentation among Mexican immigrants living in Los Angeles also led to an increase in married women who worked outside the home. Both Mexican and American cultures designated men as the principal family wage earners. Whether or not a newly married woman worked for wages was often a source of discussion and consternation, although many families found the income generated by wives essential. Among the married women sampled where information concerning employment status was known, about 40 percent were engaged in wage labor outside the home.[28] While this figure is similar to the proportion of married Chicanas found working in other studies of southern California communities in this period, it seems to be a higher rate than that found among married women along the border.[29] This proportion of working Chicana married women is much higher than that of other married women, including most immigrant women. In 1920 nationwide, only 6.3 percent of married native white women worked for wages outside the home, while 7.2 percent of foreign-born wives were in the work force. Only the proportion of black wives who were paid laborers, 32.5 percent, was similar to that found for Chicanas in Los Angeles.[30]

In contrast to earlier historical arguments, Mexican-born women were more likely to be employed than American-born Chicanas. Almost half of those women were working for wages, as

Table 6.2 Marriage and Conception Among Mexican Immigrants

| Type of marriage (husband/wife) | First Birth | | | | |
	Outside of marriage	Conceived before marriage	In first 3 years of marriage	After 3 years of marriage	Total
All-Mexican immigrants	51 (14.5%)	20 (5.7%)	219 (62.2%)	62 (17.6%)	352 (100%)
Mexican/Mex. Am.	30 (14.9%)	33 (16.3%)	112 (55.4%)	27 (13.4%)	202 (100%)
Mexican/Anglo	13 (14.9%)	11 (12.7%)	44 (50.6%)	19 (21.8%)	87 (100%)
Mex. Am./Mexican	4 (20.0%)	7 (35.0%)	9 (45.0%)	0 (0.0%)	20 (100%)
Anglo/Mexican	3 (20.0%)	6 (40.0%)	6 (40.0%)	0 (0.0%)	15 (100%)
Total	101 (14.9%)	77 (11.4%)	390 (57.7%)	108 (16.0%)	676 (100%)

Source: Analysis of marriage dates and birthdates of eldest children from naturalization documents, National Archives, Laguna Niguel, California.

compared with only 20 percent of the American-born Chicana population. These figures call into question Richard Griswold del Castillo's argument for the nineteenth century that Mexican women "had a more traditional frame of reference" and therefore were less likely than native-born women to enter the job market.[31] One reason for this discrepancy may be that different cultural prescriptions were at work during the early twentieth century that made immigrant women more likely to engage in wage labor after marriage. The flexibility demanded of the Mexican immigrant family for survival in a rapidly changing economy overrode "traditional" frames of reference. The shift had begun in Mexico, where women in migrant families were called upon to head households temporarily while men looked for work elsewhere. In Los Angeles, many Mexican immigrant women entered the labor force when their husbands were unable to find employment, were temporarily laid off, or when family expenses became burdensome.[32]

Although much of the change in women's roles occurred to the west of the Los Angeles River, repercussions were felt throughout Chicano Los Angeles. Young Chicanas living in East Los Angeles with their parents increasingly challenged the elders' notions of dating and courtship, even as they maintained a deferential attitude toward them in other areas. Moreover, many of the skilled workers who bought homes in the east-side neighborhoods of Lincoln Heights and Brooklyn Heights during the 1920s were able to do so because their wives continued to work after marriage, thereby increasing family income.

Family life in the barrios of Los Angeles ranged from conventional to experimental, and often these families lived in close proximity to one another. Even within a family, certain members could exhibit behavior that others might consider inappropriate or "un-Mexican."[33] Freedom could be positive or negative depending on one's position in the family. One Mexican mother, living with her unmarried children west of the Plaza, enjoyed the freedom to go wherever she wanted without restriction. In Mexico, she had felt oppressed by prescriptive social customs. Nevertheless, she did not like the behavior of young women in this country. "Liberty," she stated, had been "contagious" to her daughters, and this bothered her a great deal.[34]

The creation during the 1920s of a more concentrated Mexican community east of the river, however, offered an opportunity to reassert certain family practices deemed traditional in a wholly different setting. The settlement of Mexican families in East Los Angeles implied a permanency which was not characteristic of Mexican communities west of the river. The stability of permanent settlement in the United States, for example, allowed opposition to married women working to regain ascendancy. Married women living east of the river in Belvedere and Boyle Heights were less likely to be employed than those elsewhere. Having achieved a sense of stability through the extra earnings of female employment, many married women left their jobs after moving to an east-side neighborhood.[35]

This process of claiming certain family practices as traditional in a new setting is crucial to understanding Chicano culture. Migration itself inevitably disrupted the family, often forcing members on both sides of the border to adjust to a new constellation of individuals. As migrants reached important life stages, however, they had the opportunity to influence their own "culture"—shaped, of course, by their conception of tradition. This process was influenced by the fact that widespread segregation of Mexicans in the American Southwest kept many cultural practices insulated from those of the Anglo American majority.[36]

Marriage, and the related practice of courtship, was one life stage in which Chicanos were able to alter cultural practices. The age at which men and women married is one indication of this transformation. Migration itself had tended to delay marriage, particularly for women. The average age at marriage for men sampled was approximately 26.3 years. Women married at a substantially younger age, 23. Men who married in Mexico averaged just over 25.7 years of age and women's average age was barely over 21 years. Even more interesting, however, is the fact that those who migrated from Mexico as children married younger than all other groups. Men who had migrated under the age of 15 married at approximately 24.5 years of age, while women who were child migrants married, on the average, under age 20.[37]

These figures suggest that Mexican immigrants did not delay marriage even after being exposed to the American custom of later marriage. The instability of the migratory process itself caused many young adult migrants to postpone marriage until settled. But once established in the new environment, Mexicans who grew up in American society were likely to marry younger than their counterparts in Mexico. Perhaps the erroneous assumption by Mexican parents that Mexicans in the homeland married very young encouraged them to urge their children—particularly the girls— to marry early.[38]

For children seeking greater independence, young marriages provided an escape from strict immigrant parents. Henrietta from Belvedere, age eighteen, expressed anger that "as soon as I was sixteen my father began to watch me and would not let me go anywhere or have my friends come home. He was born in old Mexico but he has been here long enough to know how people do things."[39] This strict discipline could backfire, ironically leading some young women to flee to their own marriage in order to be free of their parents. Concha, also from Belvedere, used her knowledge of Mexican mores to make her own marital decision:

> My father would not let Joe come to the house. He said when it was time for me to get married, he would have something to say about who my husband would be. So Joe and I fixed that. I ran off with him and stayed with his family. We knew that my father would make us get married then.[40]

Single migrants who lived west of the river often moved to East Los Angeles once they were married. This act usually involved a conscious decision to live in the barrios of the east side, among the growing community of Chicanos. It symbolized the reassertion of community life, this time in the context of an American barrio. It also signaled the passing from a migrant to a more settled mode of existence. For some, particularly women, it could also mean the surrender of freedoms gained through work outside the home and living beyond the cultural dictates of family.

If the communities to the south and west of the Plaza were more conducive to ethnically intermarried couples, Mexican immigrants who married American-born Chicanos congregated in East Los Angeles. These mixed-nativity couples found the barrios east of the river, particularly Belvedere and Boyle Heights, particularly appealing. Over one-third of the families in these two neighborhoods displayed this foreign-born/native-born marriage pattern, as compared with one-quarter of the total sample. As these communities grew during the 1920s, they gradually became the locus of Chicano cultural development. Since integration of the Mexican immigrant population with American-born Chicanos contributed to the creation of a distinctive barrio culture, both Belvedere and Boyle Heights became important settings for the definition of Chicano life in California during the twentieth century.

Like those who intermarried, almost all Mexican immigrants who married American-born Chicanos arrived in the United States before the age of twenty. Unlike the intermarried, however, their places of origin in Mexico were more broadly representative of the entire immigrant group. Border states consistently produced immigrants who married second-generation Chicanos, with 40 percent of immigrants from Sonora, Chihuahua, and Nuevo León engaging in this marriage pattern. Obviously, the interaction of the Mexican population living along the American-Mexican border gave immigrants from this area a sense of common purpose and tradition that fostered intergenerational marriage.

Other immigrants, however, refused to consider marriage to Mexican Americans. Juana Martínez, who had migrated to Los Angeles with her sisters and mother after a failed marriage and the death of her father, worked as a dance-hall employee in the Plaza area. She felt strongly that if she remarried, it would be with a fellow immigrant. "The Americans are very dull and very stupid. They let the women boss them. I would rather marry an American than a *pocho*, however." ("Pocho" refers to the American offspring of Mexican immigrant parents.) A fellow coworker, Gloria Navas, agreed, saying that she preferred immigrant men because "they know how to behave, they are not as 'rough-neck' as the *pochos*."[41]

Many Mexican immigrant men refused to consider marrying American citizens because American-born Chicanas appeared to exercise greater independence from their husbands. "Here the old women want to run things and the poor man has to wash the dishes while the wife goes to the show," exclaimed thirty-year-old Ignacio Sandoval from Fresnillo, Zacatecas. Another man who had lived in the United States for twenty-five years had remained single because he felt that women in this country were "very unrestrained." He surmised that "they are the ones who control their husband and I nor any other Mexican won't stand for that." He argued that even Mexican women who migrated to the United States took advantage of laws protecting women and became like American women.[42]

Unions between Mexican immigrants and American-born Chicanos, however, did occur often, but could result in continued tensions. One Mexican-born husband expressed resentment that his American-born "wife does not want to stay home and take care of the baby. She learned how to work in a beauty parlor and now she wants to start a beauty parlor and make money."[43] In another cross-generational couple, it was the American-born wife who had complaints:

> My husband is a good man but—too many kids. I am twenty-three years old and I have five. American women do not look old and tired when they are twenty-three. They are still girls. Look at me. My father picked out this husband for me, but he should have sent to Mexico for a girl for him if he wanted to have one.[44]

Although most Mexican immigrants were married to other Mexican immigrants in Los Angeles, only about one-quarter of these marriages involved individuals from the same Mexican state of origin. In light of all the various possible unions in the city, then, no more than 15 percent of Mexican marriages in Los Angeles possibly involved immigrants from the same state in Mexico. Compared with Italians in San Francisco, for example, 65 percent of whom married immigrants from the same commune, the figure for Mexicans is exceedingly low.[45] One possible explanation is that in Los Angeles racism set all Mexicans apart from American society and obfuscated cultural divisions that had existed in Mexico. Sustaining allegiance to a certain area in Mexico became much less important than beginning a new life as an ethnic family in the United States. A more generic form of Chicano identity—different from that of other ethnic groups in America—began to dominate Mexican American cultural life in Los Angeles.[46]

The act of marriage, of course, only began the process of redefining cultural values within the family. The actual nature of the union between husbands and wives varied tremendously, depending on the individuals' perspectives. Recent attempts to describe the Chicano family have portrayed it as an institution closely paralleling that of other immigrant families, something akin to a "father-dominated but mother-centered" family life.[47] Countering the image of the traditional

Mexican family as a rigid patriarchy, these interpretations have stressed the flexibility of roles in given social and economic circumstances. Some have begun to place emphasis on the mother-centeredness of the Chicano family, while others have continued to examine the implications of male domination.[48]

One aspect of family life which had profound impact on the relationship between husband and wife was the pattern of childbearing. The number of children a couple had often reflected cultural values regarding family life. However, some immigrant historians have noted substantial variation between immigrant groups from agricultural backgrounds who settled in America's urban centers. For example, Dino Cinel has argued for Italians in San Francisco that "the crucial point is not the transition from rural to urban life, but the way people perceive the transition."[49] Mexican immigrants to Los Angeles exhibited an assortment of birthrate patterns which corroborate Cinel's assertion.

Mexican immigrant families sampled had an average of 2.62 children, with the largest families containing eleven children. The relatively low average number of children—compared with popular notions of Mexican family size—is undoubtedly a result of the youth of the group which applied for naturalization. Many were couples who had only recently married. Stark differences can be noted in the average number of children, however, when one compares all-Mexican marriages with those involving one non-Mexican immigrant (see Table 6.3).

Intermarriage with an American-born or foreign-born Anglo resulted in an average of only 1.29 children, as compared with all-Mexican marriages which averaged 3.17 children per family. Marriages involving one Mexican immigrant and an American-born Chicano fell between these two extremes, with 2.59 children per family. Mexican immigrant women who married a man born in the United States, whether a Chicano or an Anglo, were likely to bear substantially fewer children than if they married a man born in Mexico. Mexican immigrant men, on the other hand, were likely to have large families as long as they married within the Chicano community. Only marriages to Anglo women substantially reduced the size of families of Mexican immigrant men.

Not surprisingly, large families were more readily found in East Los Angeles than west of the Los Angeles River. Every barrio east of the river averaged at least 2.8 children per family, while the average west of the river was under 2.5. Given the prevalence of single migrants to the south and west of the Plaza, along with smaller families in these communities, children were a more dominant

Table 6.3 Number of Children for Various Types of Marriages

Type of marriage (husband/wife)	No children	1–2 children	3–5 children	6–8 children	Over 8 children	Number (Average)
All-Mexican immigrant	66 (15.8%)	129 (30.9%)	140 (33.5%)	72 (17.2%)	11 (2.6%)	418 (3.17)
Mexican/Mex. Am.	34 (14.4%)	100 (42.2%)	77 (32.5%)	20 (8.4%)	6 (2.5%)	237 (2.71)
Mexican/Anglo	44 (33.9%)	59 (45.4%)	25 (19.2%)	2 (1.5%)	0 (0.0%)	130 (1.36)
Mex. Am./Mexican	7 (25.9%)	15 (55.6%)	5 (18.5%)	0 (0.0%)	0 (0.0%)	27 (1.52)
Anglo/Mexican	18 (54.5%)	11 (33.3%)	3 (9.1%)	1 (3.0%)	0 (0.0%)	33 (1.00)
Total	169 (20.0%)	314 (37.2%)	250 (29.6%)	95 (11.2%)	17 (2.0%)	845[a] (2.63)

Source: Analysis of naturalization documents, National Archives, Laguna Niguel, California.

Note: [a]403 marriages in the sample contained no information on children.

presence in the barrios on the east side than they had been in the more integrated, working-class neighborhoods around downtown.

Despite variance in the eventual sizes of families, marriage invariably led to childbirth for women in all possible unions in the sample. Between two-thirds and three-quarters of all women had given birth within eighteen months of marriage. Childrearing continued to be the main expectation for married women of this period, even if they continued to work after marriage. The differences that did exist in child-bearing practices between families reflect the spacing between births and the curtailment of childbearing among mature unions. The age of marriage and the interval between marriage and first birth were the same for all types of married couples.

As east-side barrios began to grow, the construction of family ties proved a strong basis upon which to promote a sense of community. Powerful religious sanctions against marital breakup kept the numbers of female-headed households low. Despite widespread male migration and the cultural breakdown historians have attributed to both European and black newcomers to the cities, no more than 55 marriages out of 1,249 unions in this sample were affected by divorce or separation. This 4.4 percent rate of divorce is low by American standards in the period, since a 1916 study found one divorce for every five marriages in Los Angeles. More than one-third of these separations occurred between Mexican immigrants who had married Anglos, even though less than 20 percent of the unions in the total sample were intermarriages.[50]

Moreover, three-fourths of these breakups occurred during the 1930s and the instability of the Great Depression. Although it is impossible to know for certain, it does appear that the economic crisis, and the accompanying stress it placed on families, was a direct cause of many of these divorces and desertions. Unemployed men sometimes found it easier to abandon their families than to watch helplessly as their loved ones struggled. Many relief organizations concentrated aid to families with no male head, and perhaps some fathers may have discerned leaving as the best option.

The liberal divorce practices in the United States did provide an alternative generally unavailable in Mexico for women caught in bad marriages. Exercising this option, however, often forced a confrontation with deeply held beliefs concerning proper family relations. Minnie Ortiz, who spent years tolerating her husband's philandering and lack of economic ambition, finally had enough after her husband struck her. A lawyer advised her to apply for a divorce. She did so promptly, but remembered "crying my eyes out, thinking of my shattered home life and of my fatherless girls."[51]

Tellingly, more Chicano families were broken up by death than by divorce or desertion. Sixty-six spouses in my sample were widowed while living in Los Angeles, a rate of 5.3 per 100. Dangerous conditions at work made men more at risk. Some women who lost their husbands moved in with relatives, but most were able to continue as heads of their households. Men who lost their wives often asked relatives to raise their children, since most Chicanos believed that female nurturing was crucial to childrearing. Whatever the situation, family and community networks were called upon in time of family tragedy. As one local Anglo American official acknowledged: "The Mexicans respond to appeals on the basis of their responsibility toward children, on the duties of sisters, aunts, uncles, etc. This is not so in the case of Americans, who are more individualistic."[52]

Many observers who disagree on the strengths and weaknesses of the Chicano family agree that Mexicans are familistic in orientation.[53] Critics of this family orientation accuse the Mexican American family of retarding individual development. These observers blame economic reverses on a family life which encourages members to seek semiskilled jobs with immediate, though circumscribed, rewards. Moreover, familism is often blamed for the lack of a strong sense of public duty, particularly the tendency of Chicanos to dissociate themselves from American politics and public organizations. When emphasis is placed so strongly on the family, they allege that there is little time for contemplating the needs of society.

A strong sense of family, however, enabled Mexican immigrants to survive in a hostile American environment, and contributed to a strengthening of community sentiment inside the barrio. Lack of economic opportunity and outright racial discrimination were at the root of limited mobility, and strong family networks allowed Mexicans to persevere in difficult economic times. As following chapters will make clear, even those who eschewed family solidarity rarely moved up the economic ladder. If anything, familism contributed to slow, but steady, economic advancement, and it was often a family tragedy or widespread economic misfortune which sidetracked Mexican immigrants and Mexican Americans in their quest for greater economic security.

In the period directly following migration, Mexicans were unable to settle down because they could rarely count on the extended family networks available in their native villages. As individuals, they had only their own limited economic resources. Unemployment often led to more migration. Even so, many called upon cousins, distant relatives, and friends from hometowns to aid in this difficult period of transition.[54] As immigrants married, particularly if they married American-born Chicanos, they established roots in a new community which they hoped would bring greater stability to their lives. In time, these barrios came to serve as places which made other newcomers to the city feel welcome.

Creative, adaptative strategies predominated among Mexican immigrants who settled in Los Angeles. Only strong, flexible family ties insured the survival of all members. Certain individuals chose to go it alone, and others left the barrio altogether. Yet, for most immigrants, family and community came together in the emerging neighborhoods east of the river. At times, the barrio was for some a stifling, restrictive environment. Strong cultural norms were enforced which kept the community at least outwardly familiar to most newcomers from Mexico. More often than not, however, the barrio provided a haven for Mexican immigrants and American-born Chicanos. There they could adapt to American society while still retaining in their daily lives much of the flavor of Mexico.

NOTES

1. Marita Hernández and Robert Montemayor, "Mexico to U.S.—a Cultural Odyssey," *Los Angeles Times*, 24 July 1983, pp. 1, 18.
2. Oscar Handlin, *The Uprooted: The Epic Story of the Great Migrations That Made the American People*, 2nd ed., enlarged (1951; Boston: Little, Brown, 1973), 210. Virginia Yans-McLaughlin refers to the body of work portraying immigrant family life in this fashion as a "disorganization" school in *Family and Community: Italian Immigrants in Buffalo, 1880–1930* (Ithaca: Cornell Univ. Press, 1971), 19.
3. Hernández and Montemayor, "Odyssey," 1, 18–21.
4. Yans-McLaughlin, *Family and Community*, 61, 64. For a historical account of the Mexican immigrant family from this perspective, see Mario T. García, "La Familia: The Mexican Immigrant Family, 1900–1930," in *Work, Family, Sex Roles and Language*, Mario Barrera, Alberto Camarillo, and Francisco Hernández, eds. (Berkeley: Tonatiuh-Quinto Sol, 1980), 117–39.
5. David Alvirez and Frank D. Bean, "The Mexican American Family," in *Ethnic Families in America*, Charles H. Mindel and Robert W. Haberstein, eds. (New York: Elsevier, 1976); Miguel Montiel, "The Social Science Myth of the Mexican American Family," *El Grito: A Journal of Contemporary Mexican American Thought* 3 (1970), 56–63; Nathan Murillo, "The Mexican American Family," in *Chicanos: Social and Psychological Perspectives*, Nathaniel N. Wagner and Marsha J. Haug, eds. (St. Louis: C.V. Mosby, 1971), 97–108; Octavio Ignacio V. Romano, "The Anthropology and Sociology of the Mexican-Americans: The Distortion of Mexican-American History," *El Grito* 2:1 (Fall 1968), 13–26. For an overview of this literature, see Alfredo Mirandé, "The Chicano Family: A Reanalysis of Conflicting Views," *Journal of Marriage and the Family* 39 (1977), 750–51. An excellent summary of various theoretical approaches to family

history and their possible application to Chicano history is provided by Richard Griswold del Castillo in chapter 1 of *La Familia: Chicano Families in the Urban Southwest, 1848 to the Present* (Notre Dame: Univ. of Notre Dame Press, 1984), 1–9.

6.   Mirandé, "The Chicano Family," 748–51.

7.   For a description of widespread European return migration, see John Bodnar, *The Transplanted: A History of Immigrants in Urban America* (Bloomington: Indiana Univ. Press, 1985), 53–54.

8.   The following account is derived from transcripts of interviews conducted by a Board of Special Inquiry at Nogales, Arizona, from 25 August 1917 to 1 July 1918, Records of the Immigration and Naturalization Service, RG 85, Box 250, Folder 54281/36B, National Archives, Washington, D.C. These interviews were conducted beginning in 1917 when entrance to the United States was requested by children under the age of sixteen unaccompanied by their parents. Their purpose was to determine whether the child was likely to become a public charge, therefore detailed information regarding the child's family situation in Mexico and the United States was obtained.

9.   Dino Cinel, *From Italy to San Francisco: The Immigrant Experience* (Stanford: Stanford Univ. Press, 1982), 168; Naturalization Records, RG 21, National Archives, Laguna Niguel, California.

10.   "Interview with Arturo Morales," No. 11, p. 1, interview by Luis Felipe Recinos, 8 April 1927, Biographies & Case Histories III folder, Z-R5, Manuel Gamio collection, Bancroft Library, University of California, Berkeley.

11.   "Vida de Estanislao Gómez," 1, interview by Luis Felipe Recinos, 2 April 1927, Biographical & Case Studies II folder, Gamio collection.

12.   See "Vida de Leova López," 1, interview by M. Robles, 19 April 1927, Biographies & Case Histories II folder; and "Interview with Juana Martínez," No. 102, p. 1, interview by Luis Felipe Recinos, 6 April 1927, Biographies & Case Histories I folder, Gamio collection.

13.   For descriptions of the growth of the central business district and nearby factories, see Robert M. Fogelson, *The Fragmented Metropolis: Los Angeles, 1850–1930* (Cambridge, Mass.: Harvard Univ. Press, 1967), 147–51; Scott L. Bottles, *Los Angeles and the Automobile: The Making of the Modern City* (Berkeley: Univ. of California Press, 1987), 200–201; and Howard J. Nelson, "The Vernon Area, California—A Study of the Political Factor in Urban Geography," *Annals of the Association of American Geographers* 42 (1952), 177–91. For the continuation of these patterns as late as 1940, see Eshref Shevky and Molly Lewin, *Your Neighborhood: A Social Profile of Los Angeles* (Los Angeles: Haynes Foundation, 1949), 24–26.

14.   "The Arce (Galván) family," 8, interview by Luis Felipe Recinos, 8 April 1927, Biographies & Case Histories III folder, Gamio collection.

15.   See "Interview with Gloria Navas," No. 56, p. 4, interview by Luis Felipe Recinos, 16 April 1927, Biographies & Case Histories I folder; and "Interview with Elisa Morales," No. 53, pp. 3, 5, interview by Luis Felipe Recinos, 16 April 1927, Biographies & Case Histories II folder, Gamio collection. Joanne Meyerowitz describes similar responses to urban environments by these "women adrift" in "Women and Migration: Autonomous Female Migrants to Chicago, 1880–1930," *Journal of Urban History* 13 (1987), 147–68.

16.   Analysis of naturalization documents, National Archives, Laguna Niguel, California.

17.   Constantine Panunzio found a 17 percent rate of exogamous marriages among Mexicans in "Intermarriage in Los Angeles, 1924–1933," *American Journal of Sociology* 48 (1942), 698, 701. Griswold del Castillo finds similar figures in *Familia*, 106–7. See Edward Murguia, *Chicano Intermarriage: A Theoretical and Empirical Study* (San Antonio: Trinity Univ. Press, 1982), for comparisons with other regions over time.

18.   This figure is skewed by the fact that the number of Mexican immigrant women who naturalized was small—involving only 111 marriages—and that Mexican women who married Mexican men were probably less likely to naturalize than those who married Anglo American men.

19.   The pattern is similar for women, although there are many fewer in the sample.

20.   "Interview with Sra. María Rovitz Ramos," No. 7, pp. 1, 4, interview by Luis Felipe Recinos, 2 April 1927, Biographies & Case Histories I folder, Gamio collection.

21.   From survey of Anglo American spouses in naturalization documents. The argument that ethnic groups tend to intermarry within religious groupings has been made by Milton Gordon in *Assimilation in American Life: The Role of Race, Religion, and National Origins* (New York: Oxford Univ. Press, 1964). Edward Murguia makes a similar argument specifically for Chicanos in *Chicano Intermarriage*, 35. According to at least one local official, Jewish-Mexican intermarriage was rare, despite substantial interaction, because Russian Jews felt that Mexicans were "filthy and godless and without sex morality because of their public courtship." See "Interview with Dr. Miriam Van Waters, Referee of Juvenile Court, Hall of Justice, Los Angeles, California," 2–512, American Officials folder, 74/187c, Paul S. Taylor collection, Bancroft Library, University of California, Berkeley.

22.   For examples of lighter-skinned Mexicans intermarrying, see "José Robles," "Sra. Ruhe López," and "Sr. Campos" in Manuel Gamio, *The Life Story of the Mexican Immigrant* (1931; rpt., New York: Dover, 1971), 226–37.

23.   "Interview with the Santaella family," No. 45, pp. 2–3, interview by Luis Felipe Recinos, 15 April 1927, Biographies & Case Histories II folder, Gamio collection. "Interview with María Rovitz Ramos," 6. See also Richard Romo, *East Los Angeles: History of a Barrio* (Austin: Univ. of Texas Press, 1983), 85. One quantitative analysis of the 1940 U.S. census suggests that significant rates of intermarriage between Mexican women and non-Mexican men occurred in the Southwest during this period, often leading to relatively higher economic standing for these women. Brian Gratton, F. Arturo Rosales, and Hans DeBano, "A Sample of the Mexican-American Population in 1940," *Historical Methods* 21 (1988), 83–85.

24.   Quoted in Mary Lanigan, "Second Generation Mexicans in Belvedere" Master's thesis, University of Southern California, 1932), 20.

25.   Ibid., 18–21.

26.   Knowledge, let alone use, of effective birth control methods besides abstinence does not appear to have been widespread in the Mexican immigrant community. In addition to strict cultural sanctions against birth control emanating from the Catholic Church, legal restrictions against dispensing birth control information still existed. Mexican women were unlikely to have access to the occasional private physician who might be willing to give such advice. The one exception to this generalization seems to have been the small group of Mexican women who regularly worked as dance hall girls in the Plaza area. See "Interview with Gloria Navas," p. 4; and "Interview with Elisa Morales," No. 53, pp. 3, 5, interview by Luis Felipe Recinos, 16 April 1927, Biographies & Case Histories II folder, Gamio collection.

27.   Analysis of birth and marriage dates in naturalization documents, National Archives, Laguna Niguel, California. To place marriage patterns in Los Angeles in a larger historical context, see John D'Emilio and Estelle B. Freedman, *Intimate Matters: A History of Sexuality in America* (New York: Harper and Row, 1988), chap. 5, esp. 89–90.

28.   The vast majority of the married couples sampled do not list any information for wives because that question was not asked of husbands applying for naturalization until the second phase of the process. The figures do reflect, however, the labor status of the 142 married women who took out first papers, along with wives of men who got to the second level of the process. This percentage therefore is tentative, as it is based only on 187 total couples in the overall sample of 1,249 (15.0%). In addition, this group would tend to represent those most settled in the United States.

29.   Albert Camarillo, *Chicanos in a Changing Society: From Mexican Pueblos to American Barrios in Santa Barbara and Southern California, 1848–1930* (Cambridge: Harvard Univ. Press, 1979), 220; Douglas Guy Monroy, "Mexicanos in Los Angeles, 1930–1941: An Ethnic Group in Relation to Class Forces" (Ph.D. diss., University of California, Los Angeles, 1978), 77; and Mario T. García, *Desert Immigrants: The Mexicans of El Paso, 1880–1920* (New Haven: Yale Univ. Press, 1981), 75, 200.

30.   Carl Degler, *At Odds: Women and the Family in America from the Revolution to the Present* (New York: Oxford Univ. Press, 1980), 384. See also Yans-McLaughlin, *Family and Community*, 173; and Bodnar, *Translated*, 78–80.

31.   Griswold del Castillo, *Familia*, 63.

32.   See Paul S. Taylor, "Mexican Women in Los Angeles Industry in 1928," *Aztlán* 11 (1980), 104–5.

33.   See "The Arce (Galván) family," Gamio collection.

34.   "Interview with Santaella family," 4, Gamio collection.

35.   Analysis of naturalization documents, National Archives, Laguna Niguel, California. See also Taylor, "Industry," 106–8.

36.   See Alex M. Saragoza, "The Conceptualization of the History of the Chicano Family," in *The State of Chicano Research in Family, Labor and Migration Studies*, Armando Valdez, Albert Camarillo and Tomás Almaguer, eds. (Stanford: Stanford Center for Chicano Research, 1983), 119–20.

37.   Naturalization documents, National Archives, Laguna Niguel, California. Other areas of the Southwest also produced early marriages among more stable populations. Sarah Deutsch reports that from 1860 to 1910, Chicanas married in New Mexico between the ages of 15 and 21, while men tended to marry between age 19 and 26. See "Culture, Class, and Gender: Chicanas and Chicanos in Colorado and New Mexico, 1900–1940" (Ph.D. diss., Yale University, 1985), 83.

38.   See figures for Mascota, Jalisco, in Carlos B. Gil, *Life in Provincial Mexico: National and Regional History Seen from Mascota, Jalisco, 1867–1972* (Los Angeles: UCLA Latin American Studies Center Publications, 1983), 95–98.

39.   Lanigan, "Second Generation," 25–26.

40.   Ibid., 26.

41.   "Interview with Juana Martínez," 3–4; "Interview with Gloria Navas," 7, Gamio collection.

42.   "Interview with Ignacio Sandoval," 5; "Interview with Luis Aguiñaga," 1–2, Gamio collection.

43.   Lanigan, "Second Generation," 34.

44.   Ibid., 33.

45.   Cinel, *From Italy*, 177.

46.   In contrast, see ibid., 177–78, or Yans-McLaughlin, *Family and Community*, 256–57, for Italians. See Abraham Cahan, *The Rise of David Levinsky* (1917; rpt., New York: Harper and Row, 1960), 106, for Jews.

47.   This terminology was first used to describe the southern Italian family by two anthropologists. See Leonard W. Moss and Walter H. Thomson, "The South Italian Family: Literature and Observation," *Human Organization* 18 (1959), 38.

48.   See Deutsch, "Culture," 90, for an analysis which stresses the flexibility of the sexual division of labor within the Chicano family. For studies of the contemporary Chicano family which stress flexibility, see Griswold del Castillo, *Familia*, 118–19; Maxine Baca Zinn, "Marital Roles, Marital Power and Ethnicity: A Study of Changing Families" (Ph.D. diss., University of Oregon, 1978); and Lea Ybarra, "Conjugal Role Relationships in the Chicano Family" (Ph.D. diss., University of California, Berkeley, 1977).

49.   Cinel, *From Italy*, 188.

50.   Analysis of marital status information from naturalization documents, National Archives, Laguna Niguel, California. See Elaine Tyler May, *Great Expectations: Marriage and Divorce in Post-Victorian America* (Chicago: Univ. of Chicago Press, 1980), 9, for comparative data for the rest of Los Angeles.

51. "Manuela 'Minnie' Ortiz," interview by J. Isaac Aceves, 14 June 1937, p. 330, Field Continuity, Mexican Population, San Diego Project, Federal Writers Project collection, Department of Special Collections, University of California, Los Angeles.

52. "Interview with Dr. Miriam Van Waters, Referee of Juvenile Court, Hall of Justice, Los Angeles, California," 1–511, Taylor collection.

53. See Mirandé, "The Chicano Family," 751.

54. See Susan E. Keefe and Amado Padilla, *Chicano Ethnicity* (Albuquerque: Univ. of New Mexico Press, 1987), especially chaps. 9 and 10, for a modern account of this process in southern California.

7

excerpt from

Interracial Intimacy: The Regulation of Race & Romance

"Antimiscegenation Laws and the Enforcement of Racial Boundaries"

RACHEL F. MORAN

ANY HISTORY OF antimiscegenation laws must begin with the regulation of black–white intimacy, but it must not end there. Laws barring sex and marriage between blacks and whites had the longest history and the widest application in the United States. As one historian of intermarriage has pointed out, however, antimiscegenation "laws were enacted first—and abandoned last—in the South, but it was in the West, not the South, that the laws became most elaborate. In the late nineteenth century, western legislators built a labyrinthine system of legal prohibitions on marriages between whites and Chinese, Japanese, Filipinos, Hawaiians, Hindus, and Native Americans, as well as on marriages between whites and blacks."[1] At one time or another, thirty-eight states adopted laws regulating interracial sex and marriage. All of these laws banned black–white relationships, but fourteen states also prohibited Asian–white marriages and another seven barred Native American–white unions.[2] No state ever officially banned Latino–white intermarriage, though, presumably because treaty protections formally accorded former Spanish and Mexican citizens the status of white persons.

Antimiscegenation laws have played an integral role in defining racial identity and enforcing racial hierarchy.[3] To understand the distinctive ways in which antimiscegenation statutes were used to establish norms about race, it is essential to focus on the two groups that suffered the most onerous legal burdens: blacks and Asians. For blacks, the laws identified them as diminished persons marked with the taint of slavery and inferiority, even after they were nominally free. Although the statutes formally limited the freedom of blacks and whites alike, the restrictions clearly functioned to block black access to the privileges of associating with whites. For Asians, antimiscegenation laws confirmed their status as unassimilable foreigners. Already marked as racially distinct and unfit for citizenship by federal immigration laws, state constraints on intermarriage prevented Asian male immigrants from integrating into communities by thwarting their sexuality, hindering them from developing ties to the United States through marriage, and deterring them from having children who would be American citizens by birth. For both blacks and Asians, segregation in sex, marriage, and family was a hallmark of intense racialization and entrenched inequality.

THE BLACK EXPERIENCE: DRAWING THE COLOR LINE AND KEEPING IT IN PLACE

The regulation of sex and marriage played a singularly important role in drawing the color line between whites and blacks. Antimiscegenation laws in the South laid a critical foundation for securing the full personhood of whites and entrenching the diminished status of blacks. Whenever racial ambiguity threatened the established social order, statutory restrictions on interracial sex and marriage were imposed to keep the color line firmly in place. During the colonial era, Southern states faced special challenges in drawing racial boundaries and establishing sexual norms. In New England, settlers were mostly farmers and artisans who arrived with families, settled in towns, and had strong religious traditions. In these homogeneous communities, same-race families were the norm and sex outside of marriage was relatively rare.[4] By contrast, in the Chesapeake world of Virginia and Maryland, settlers came from a wide range of backgrounds. Many arrived alone as indentured servants, who had contracted to work until they paid for their passage to America. No sense of community based on shared origins, townships, or religious beliefs bound the newcomers together. Men outnumbered women by four to one. In addition, the scarcity of marriageable women was exacerbated because indentured female servants could not marry until they completed their terms of service. Under these circumstances, rates of extramarital sex and out-of-wedlock pregnancy soared despite laws punishing fornication, adultery, and rape.[5]

When slavery began to replace indentured servitude as the primary source of labor in the upper South during the last decades of the seventeenth century, white indentured servants often worked in close proximity to black slaves. In some instances, coworkers became sexual intimates, and interracial sex and marriage began to blur the color line.[6] Antimiscegenation laws became a way to draw a rigid boundary between slave and free, black and white. Maryland enacted the first antimiscegenation statute in 1661, and Virginia followed suit one year later. Even before that, Virginia authorities in the 1630s and 1640s had whipped and publicly humiliated those who participated in interracial sexual liaisons.[7]

By punishing interracial sex severely, authorities in Maryland and Virginia sent a clear message that whites were not to adopt the sexual practices of slaves. Slaves typically did not enjoy access to the formal institution of marriage, although they did conduct their own slave marriage rituals. Some slaves practiced polygamy or polygyny, and many did not condemn premarital intercourse. Without social stigma, a woman might have sex and even bear children by a man before having been recognized by other slaves as "married" to him.[8] Legislation prohibiting interracial intimacy clearly condemned these alternative sexual and marital practices as heathen and unfit for right-minded, white Christians.

In the early settlement years, interracial marriage had been tolerated, presumably because of the uncertain racial status of blacks and the shortage of women. As the institution of slavery was consolidated in the late seventeenth century, marriages across the color line became anomalous and dangerous exceptions to the emerging racial hierarchy. Interracial unions enabled black women to control access to their sexuality through marriage, and it enabled black men to occupy a superior position to white women in a patriarchal institution that treated the husband as master. Marriages across the color line could give blacks and their mixed-race offspring access to white economic privileges by affording them the property protections that marriage and inheritance laws offered.[9] Black–white marriages threatened the presumption that blacks were subhuman slaves incapable of exercising authority, demonstrating moral responsibility, and capitalizing on economic opportunity. If whites could share their emotional lives and economic fortunes with blacks, how could blacks be anything less than full persons?

The Chesapeake colonies enacted statutes to ensure that, rather than benefit blacks, interracial marriages would simply degrade Whites. Under Virginia's 1691 law, a white spouse was to be banished from the colony within three months of an interracial wedding. In 1705, Virginia authorized jail sentences of six months for whites married to blacks or mulattoes. In Maryland, "freeborne English women" who married "Negro slaves" were required to serve their husbands' masters during their husbands' lifetimes.[10] These laws stripped whites of racial privileges based on their intimacy with blacks.

Despite these harsh sanctions, some whites paid the price to marry across the color line. In Maryland in 1681, Nell Butler, known as "Irish Nell," fell in love with a slave known as "Negro Charles." When Nell, an indentured servant, informed Lord Baltimore, her master, of the planned marriage, he warned her that she and all her descendants would live as slaves. Unswayed and defiant, Nell replied that she would rather marry Charles than Lord Baltimore himself. She did marry Charles and spent the rest of her life working for his masters, probably as an indentured servant. Had she not married Charles, her contract of servitude with Lord Baltimore would have ended in four or five years. Nell reportedly died "much broken and an old woman." Still, Lord Baltimore was wrong about Nell's offspring. In the eighteenth century, a Maryland court held that neither Nell nor her descendants could be slaves. Subsequently, masters complained of runaway mulatto slaves who claimed to be "descendants of the famous Nell Butler."[11]

As the story of Irish Nell suggests, the problem of mulatto offspring was a serious one in a slave economy predicated on a clearcut boundary between whites and blacks. Despite laws punishing interracial sex, one-fifth of children born out of wedlock at the end of the seventeenth century were mulattoes.[12] Whether slave or free, these mulattoes complicated the enforcement of slavery and compromised its claims to moral authority. Mulatto slaves who could pass as white were considered particularly risky property because they could easily run away and escape detection. In 1835 in Virginia, whites refused to bid on one male slave because he was "too white" and might "too easily escape from slavery and pass himself as a free man." Later on, light-skinned mulatto slaves were used to call into question the very propriety of slavery. A favorite theme of abolitionist literature was the "white slave," who reminded white audiences that they too might be held in bondage.[13]

With widespread interracial sex that threatened the color line, the Virginia legislature had to define and ultimately confine the relevance of the mulatto. A 1705 law classified a mulatto as "the child of an Indian and the child, grandchild, or great grandchild of a negro."[14] During the Revolutionary era, high rates of emancipation coupled with Virginia's "one-fourth black" rule allowed some free mixed-race individuals to claim the privileges of whites, although they obviously had some African ancestry. Officials concluded that "[m]ulattoes must be made black, and the unfreedom of blacks must be defined and made universal."[15] To this end, the upper South adopted a one-drop rule, which defined as black any person with traceable African ancestry.

The adoption of a rule of hypodescent kept blacks from transmitting special privileges to the next generation through interracial sex or marriage. This racial tax on offspring precluded them from gaining official recognition of their white ancestry. By erasing their white heritage, the racial classification scheme converted mulattoes into blacks by a type of parthenogenesis: It was almost as though the child had been generated by a single parent without intercourse across the color line. As slavery hardened the lines between whites and blacks, the racial tax on mulattoes increased. Their curtailed privileges clearly identified them as nonwhite, and even the lightest mulattoes were denied the privileges of whiteness.

The imperative of consolidating racial boundaries was so great that Chesapeake authorities were willing to undo the legal tradition of paterfamilias. A long-standing English rule mandated that a child's status follow that of the father. Given the initial scarcity of white women in the Chesapeake, most interracial sex probably took place between white men and black women. As a result, the majority of mulatto offspring were free under the English approach. In 1662, Virginia departed from tradition by making a child's status follow that of the mother.[16] Under this matrilineal approach, children like Irish Nell's would be free, but most mulattoes would be slaves. Even mulattoes born to white mothers enjoyed only tenuous liberties. Under a 1691 Virginia law, they could still be sold as servants until the age of thirty. Mulattoes could not hold public office, and by 1723, free mulattoes were stripped of many of the privileges—including voting and the unrestricted right to bear arms—that white citizens enjoyed.[17] Virginia authorities also were concerned that doting white fathers might subvert laws that made their mulatto offspring slaves by emancipating them. To discourage manumission of mulatto offspring, masters had to send their freedmen out of the colony, and authorities were encouraged to eliminate roving bands of "negroes, mulattoes, and other slaves [perhaps Indians]."[18] In 1723, Virginia made private emancipation even more difficult.[19] Restricting the liberty of racially ambiguous mulattoes was essential to ensuring their definition as nonwhite.

Despite formal, legal restrictions, an influential and powerful white father sometimes could rely on his privileged position to win local—albeit fragile and informal—acceptance of a mixed-race child. In 1805 in Campbell County, Virginia, Robert Wright, the mulatto son of a wealthy white landowning father and black slave mother, inherited his father's estate and became a well-to-do planter. Robert's father, a lifelong bachelor, was estranged from his white brothers and sisters and determined to pass on his substantial holdings to his beloved only son. With his father's support and guidance, Robert learned to manage the land and gained entry into the uppermost echelons of Campbell County's white society. One year after inheriting his father's property, Robert married a white woman. Although the county clerk and minister never recorded the marriage because of its illegality, Robert and his wife lived openly as a married couple and had a child together without being ostracized by their white neighbors.

Robert's troubles began when his wife ran away with a white man. In petitioning Virginia legislators for divorce so that he could marry another white woman, Robert sought formal accept-ance of his white privilege, but the jerry-built, informal status of his father's making could not survive legal scrutiny. In his petition, Robert emphasized that he, his wife, and her lover were all free. He argued that despite the ban on interracial marriage, the union was "to all intents and purposes valid and binding between the parties" because they had obtained a marriage license and been married by a clergyman. Even if the minister had destroyed the marriage certificate, the marriage clearly had been recognized as valid for approximately a decade in the Campbell County community. White citizens in the community wrote in support of Robert's petition, noting his propriety, kindness to his wife, and reputation as "an honest, upright, and good citizen."[20]

Despite Robert's status in Campbell County, the state of Virginia could not permit its official ban on interracial marriage to be subverted. The Virginia House of Delegates decisively rejected Robert's divorce petition, making clear that "Robert Wright could be married to a white woman in his community, [but] he could not be married to her in law."[21] With the illusion of his whiteness destroyed, Robert lost standing in Campbell County. On tax rolls, his designation was changed from "White" to "M," for mulatto. When he persisted in living with the white woman he had hoped to wed, many of his neighbors condemned his public adultery. Humiliated and ostracized, Robert died at the age of 38, two years after the House of Delegates stripped away the pretense of his whiteness.[22]

Robert Wright's story is remarkable primarily because it demonstrates the privileges that white fathers could confer on mulatto offspring even in the face of antimiscegenation laws. Robert's father demonstrated his power as a white landowner in the community by subverting the legal restrictions on his mulatto son's ability to manage a white man's estate, mingle with the white elite, and marry a white woman. Yet even someone as influential as Robert's father could not create a foolproof escape from restrictions on personhood and identity that were essential to the preservation of racial inequality. Once Robert's wife left him for a white lover, the mulatto's manliness and his entitlement to the privileges of whiteness were called into question. Robert was no longer free to marry the woman of his choice, and his neighbors ceased to think of him as morally deserving or racially white. Robert's despoiled identity as mulatto was marked by incursions on his autonomy to associate with whites as he pleased.

In other instances, though, informal recognition of mulatto children reinforced racial hierarchy and subverted sexual mores that condemned incest and adultery. For example, in antebellum Loudon County, Virginia, a quadroon slave woman named Ary lived with her white paternal uncle. There she became the concubine of her young master, who also was her cousin. Far from challenging racial privilege, Ary's circumstances reinforced it: She avoided associating too closely with blacks, perhaps remembering her master's admonition not to get involved with "colored men" because they "weren't good enough" for her.[23] Nor did the situation trigger outrage at her sexual exploitation: Ary insisted that she was her father's favorite child, and she proudly described her elite white heritage and her young master's attentions to her. The price of Ary's sense of superiority to blacks was a complete dependency on white male relatives for validation of her racial and sexual worth. Because of their racial privilege, these men could define Ary's identity wholly in relation to their sexual needs, regardless of their relationship to her as father, uncle, or cousin.

In general, interracial relationships were tolerated only insofar as they left norms of racial and sexual privilege intact. By deprecating white women who cohabited or had intercourse with blacks, the affairs could be dismissed as indecent and depraved. According to historian Martha Hodes, local communities regularly turned a blind eye to black or mulatto men and poor white women who lived together as man and wife, so long as they remained on the outskirts of white society. These long-term liaisons as well as brief sexual encounters could be explained by characterizing the women as low-class and licentious.[24] For instance, in North Carolina in 1825, Polly Lane, a white indentured servant, accused Jim, a slave, of rape. Although Jim pleaded innocent, he was convicted and sentenced to death. As Jim awaited execution, white neighbors noted that Polly appeared to be pregnant, and they became suspicious of her claim of rape.[25] Four doctors submitted a statement that "without an excitation of lust, or the enjoyment of pleasure in the venereal act, no conception can probably take place."[26] When Polly gave birth to a child declared to be of "mixed blood," Jim was eventually pardoned "in part by invoking the white woman's bad reputation, thereby demonstrating that a poor and transgressing white woman could be worth less to elite whites than the profitable labor of a slave."[27]

Where the pressure to consolidate racial and sexual norms was less intense, sex across the color line was commonplace despite its racially ambiguous consequences. White men enjoyed ready and open access to black and mulatto women as a mark of their untrammeled freedom and privilege. In the lower South, for example, free mulattoes were rare and posed little threat to the system of slavery. The issue of interracial sex was openly debated in newspapers in South Carolina in the 1730s, and one anonymous poet wondered: "Kiss me black or white, why need it trouble you?"[28] This laissez-faire attitude toward sex across the color line allowed wealthy white planters regularly to indulge their appetite for black and mulatto women. In New Orleans and Charleston, there was a profitable "fancy trade" in mulatto women, who brought twice the price of a prime field hand. Free mulatto women went to quadroon balls in New Orleans to meet wealthy white men. Under a system of concubinage known as "placage," the men could make formal arrangements to support the women for a few years or for life in exchange for sexual services.[29] Without fear of social reprisal, plantation owners set up special residences for black and mulatto mistresses, and some slave owners even went so far as to bring concubines into their own homes, where their white wives had to endure the humiliation in silence.[30] At a time when the New England colonies and upper South frowned on extramarital sexuality, planters in the lower South openly flouted the norm of fidelity in marriage. Tolerance of concubinage commodified black and mulatto women, but it also damaged the status of white women. One northern visitor to the South in 1809 remarked that the "dull, frigid insipidity, and reserve" of southern women was one of the most insidious costs of slavery.[31]

The lower South's tolerance for interracial relationships was linked to an unwillingness to adopt hard and fast legal definitions of blackness. As Judge William Harper wrote in 1835:

> We cannot say what admixture of negro blood will make a colored person. The condition of the individual is not to be determined solely by distinct and visible mixture of negro blood, but by reputation, by his reception into society, and his having commonly exercised the privileges of a white man. . . . [I]t may be well and proper, that a man of worth, honesty, industry, and respectability, should have the rank of a white man, while a vagabond of the same degree of blood should be confined to the inferior caste.[32]

A flexible classification scheme permitted mulattoes to earn the privileges of whiteness through personal accomplishments and social connections. This reward system enhanced the mulattoes' value to whites as racial mediators: Mulattoes would not identify too closely with blacks, for fear of jeopardizing the benefits associated with their White heritage. Tolerance for mulattoes was so great in some parts of the lower South that they were able to establish themselves as a separate elite. In Louisiana, mulattoes amassed large estates and slaves to work their properties, educated their children abroad, and developed their own elegant, cultural traditions. Labeled "Creoles," these highly successful mulattoes kept their social distance from both whites and blacks by adopting a norm of endogamy, or in-marriage.[33]

By the 1850s, the industrial revolution had transformed the textile industry, and the demand for cotton had grown dramatically. Southern planters needed a growing number of slaves, and the proportion of mulattoes in bondage increased. As the slave population became "lighter," the free mulatto population seemed increasingly anomalous and dangerous. Grand juries were convened to identify the hazards associated with free mulattoes. As one jury concluded, "We should have but two classes, the Master and the slave, and no intermediate class can be other than immensely mischievous to our peculiar institution."[34] When the lower South found it necessary to rigidify racial boundaries, it followed the lead set in the upper South. States punished interracial sexual contacts, encouraged free people of color (of whom 75 percent were mulatto) to leave the jurisdiction, and adopted a one-drop rule that denied the relevance of mixed-race origins altogether. Vigilantes reinforced these legal changes by punishing those who had interracial sex and by threatening free people of color with violence.[35]

Although the one-drop rule had been consolidated in the South before the Civil War, the war and its aftermath threatened to undo racial boundaries. Nothing was better calculated than the prospect of interracial sex and marriage to stir up fears that the color line was crumbling completely. For this reason, when calling for emancipation, orthodox abolitionists shunned the issue of sex and marriage across racial boundaries. Indeed, when freethinker Francis Wright established an interracial community and called for amalgamation of the races, she was promptly dubbed the "priestess of Beelzebub" and dropped by mainstream abolitionists who feared her radicalism would hurt the movement.[36] Similarly, after the war, most Reconstruction efforts focused on "political" equality, such as the right to vote, sit on juries, and hold office. Republican reformers deflected concerns that political equality would lead to "social" equality, as typified by race-mixing in integrated communities. When southern Democrats coined the term *miscegenation* to ridicule the quest for racial equality during Reconstruction, Republicans chided their opponents for implying that cross-racial sexual liaisons were even tempting.[37] The distinction between political and social equality made clear that the races would remain separate and distinct. Blacks would be formally rehabilitated as full persons before the law, but they would remain subordinate in informal and intimate spheres of life.

Although a few southern states did eliminate antimiscegenation laws after the Civil War, black–white intermarriage dropped sharply. The decline is particularly striking because of the strong incentives for white women to cross the color line. The ranks of white males had been decimated by the bloody conflict, and black men enjoyed newfound status and freedom of movement. Yet only in places with a particularly liberal view of race relations like New Orleans did some white women become involved with black men.[38] Presumably, the harsh pressures of public opinion prevented white women and black men from crossing the color line. Many white southerners blamed their defeat on the corrupting influence of miscegenation:

> It does seem strange that so lovely a climate, and country, with a people in every way superior to the Yankees, should be overrun and destroyed by them. But I believe that God has ordered it all, and I am firmly of the opinion . . . that it is the judgment of the Almighty because the human and brute blood have mingled to the degree it has in the slave states. Was it not so in the French and British Islands and see what has become of them.[39]

To prevent further transgressions, self-appointed vigilante groups delivered swift and terrible punishment to black men suspected of consorting with white women. The Ku Klux Klan formed at about this time, and it sometimes lynched freedmen prominent in Reconstruction politics under the guise of retribution for the mistreatment of white women.[40] Through this clandestine attack on interracial relations, whites were able to send a clear message that political equality would not dismantle the color line. Restrictions on sex, marriage, and family would continue to be a cornerstone in defining racial difference.

Although black men suspected of having sex with white women could be lynched,[41] black women were unable to fend off the advances of white men. Ironically, once slavery ended, black and mulatto women found it more difficult than during the antebellum period to limit their sexual availability to only one white male. As a result, the number of mulatto offspring increased after emancipation. Reconstruction legislators did try to protect black and mulatto women from sexual exploitation. Efforts to outlaw concubinage failed, but some states adopted bastardy statutes that enabled black and mulatto women to file paternity suits so that white men would be forced to support their illegitimate mulatto children. These bastardy statutes eventually were repealed.[42]

Even though interracial marriages were exceedingly rare during Reconstruction, white southern males promptly reinstated antimiscegenation laws when they regained control of state legislatures in the post-Reconstruction era. With the one-drop rule of racial classification in place,[43] the color line could once again be officially consolidated by regulating sex and marriage. Under this regime, antimiscegenation laws became critical to conserving the integrity and purity of the white race. Without these prohibitions, blacks could gain access to white wealth and privilege through marriage. After all, in black–white marriages, the one-drop rule dictated that the heirs to white fortunes would be black.

Interracial sexuality outside of marriage became a means of establishing racial power and domination. White men could enjoy the sexual favors of black women with impunity, but black men would pay with their lives for sexual contact with white women. When white men impregnated black women, the offspring were illegitimate and generally could not even seek support from their fathers. The children of these black–white relationships threatened neither white identity nor privilege. By contrast, if black men had adulterous relations with married white women, any resulting offspring threatened the racial integrity of white men's families. After Reconstruction, then, antimiscegenation laws reaffirmed antebellum definitions of racial identity and reasserted the superiority of whites as marital partners. White men expressed their sexual dominance by policing access to white women and enjoying the favors of black women without obligations of marriage or support.

THE CHINESE AND JAPANESE EXPERIENCE: RACIAL UNASSIMILABILITY AND SEXUAL SUBORDINATION

Although antimiscegenation laws were used to draw racial boundaries between whites and blacks during the colonial era and early years of nationhood, the color line was well-established by the time Chinese and Japanese began to immigrate to the United States in substantial numbers during the mid to late nineteenth century.[44] Definitions of blackness evolved through state legislation, but for Asians, federal immigration law made their status as nonwhite wholly unambiguous. Much of the racialization of Asians took place as successive waves of immigrants were labeled nonwhite, unassimilable, and unfit for citizenship. The Chinese were the first to arrive, coming in substantial numbers after 1848 when gold was discovered in California.[45] Early on, the U.S. government made plain that the Chinese were not white. Under a 1790 naturalization law, only "free white persons" were eligible for citizenship.[46] When Chan Yong applied for citizenship in 1854, a federal district court denied his application because he did not qualify as white, although newspaper accounts at the time stated that he was lighter-skinned than most Chinese.[47]

After the Civil War, race relations in America were contested. Congress amended the naturalization law to permit "aliens of African nativity" and "persons of African descent" to petition for citizenship. When the naturalization law was codified in 1875, the reference to "free white person" was dropped, leaving open the possibility that the Chinese could naturalize. Chinese immigrants quickly capitalized on the statutory uncertainty by filing petitions for naturalization in San Francisco.[48] Shortly thereafter, a federal court made clear that as nonwhites, Chinese immigrants continued to be ineligible for citizenship.[49]

A few years later, the federal government went even further in defining the Chinese as undesirable nonwhite aliens. In 1882, by an overwhelming margin, Congress passed the Chinese Exclusion Act, the first statute to ban a group from immigrating to the United States based solely on race or ethnicity. The Act prohibited any Chinese laborer or miner from entering the United States, and it barred any state or federal court from naturalizing any Chinese.[50] After passage of the Act, the Chinese population in the United States declined precipitously.[51] Periodically renewed and strengthened by Congress,[52] the law remained in force until 1952 when the McCarran-Walter Act nullified racial restrictions and substituted a quota system for immigration based on national origin.[53]

The Japanese began to arrive in the United States about twenty years after the Chinese. Most Japanese emigrated to Hawaii to work in the sugar industry, and their numbers were small because of restrictive Japanese emigration policies.[54] After 1890, two important changes in Japanese immigration occurred. First, the number of immigrants increased substantially so that by 1910, the Japanese outnumbered the Chinese; and second, Japanese immigrants began to arrive in the western continental United States, particularly California, to replace the dwindling numbers of Chinese laborers and to escape low wages and poor working conditions in Hawaii.[55] Having observed the mistreatment of the Chinese, the Japanese struggled to avoid occupying the same place in the racial hierarchy by distinguishing themselves from the Chinese under federal naturalization policy. Although the 1790 law permitted only whites to become citizens, the Chinese Exclusion Act of 1882 withheld the privilege of naturalization only from the Chinese. Several hundred Japanese successfully petitioned for citizenship in lower federal courts on the ground that they were not covered by legislation targeting the Chinese.[56] The federal government soon moved to clarify the status of the Japanese as nonwhite. In 1905, the U.S. attorney general informed President Theodore Roosevelt that the Japanese were and always had been ineligible for naturalization based on their race. One year later, the attorney general issued a formal opinion to that effect.[57]

Despite this setback, the Japanese continued to try to win favorable treatment under immigration laws by highlighting their capacity to assimilate to an American way of life. In a 1922 case, Takao Ozawa asked that his petition for naturalization be granted because the word *free* was more important than the word *white* in determining eligibility of "free white persons" for citizenship. Ozawa insisted that even though he was nonwhite, he should be allowed to naturalize because he could successfully shoulder the responsibilities of democratic freedom.[58] Despite Ozawa's proofs of good moral character and individual accomplishment, the U.S. Supreme Court denied his eligibility for citizenship. According to the Court, Ozawa's status as nonwhite barred him from naturalization, regardless of his ability to conform to an American way of life.[59] Race was a categorical stigma, one that did not permit individuals to escape through acculturation and achievement.

The federal government's treatment of immigrants from India cemented the racialization of Asians.[60] Unlike the Chinese and Japanese, Asian Indians were treated as Caucasian under the prevailing scientific taxonomy. Even so, the U.S. attorney general refused to find that Asian Indians qualified as "free white persons,"[61] but several federal district courts reached a different conclusion.[62] To remedy the confusion, the U.S. Supreme Court made clear in its 1923 decision in *United States v. Thind*[63] that Asian Indians were ineligible for citizenship because they were non-white. According to *Thind*, Congress used the term *white* rather than *Caucasian* because it was relying on popular, not scientific, conceptions of race. As the Court explained: "It may be true that the blond Scandinavian and the brown Hindu have a common ancestor in the dim reaches of antiquity, but the average man knows perfectly well that there are unmistakable and profound differences between them today. . . ."[64] Just as personal accomplishments could not save the Japanese, science could not save the Asian Indian from racialization. All Asians—whether Chinese, Japanese, or Asian Indian—had been definitively categorized as nonwhite. Any claims of racial ambiguity were decisively laid to rest by Congress, the attorney general, and the Supreme Court.

By labeling Asian immigrants unassimilable and unfit for citizenship, the federal government made them easy targets for racial discrimination in the western states where they settled. Bans on intermarriage were one of a number of state restrictions on Asian immigrants' liberties, all of which were designed to mark them as inferior and undesirable. With the color line clearly drawn by federal immigration laws, the statutes reinforced the temporary status of Asian sojourners, who came to the United States to work and then return to their home countries. Antimiscegenation laws marked the newcomers' marginal and subordinate status, prevented them from developing permanent ties to America through marriage and family, and severely restricted sexual options for Asian men in bachelor communities.

The racialized imagery that informed federal immigration policy dominated debates about the personhood of Asians. Popular accounts analogized the Chinese to blacks because of their willingness to work in conditions akin to slavery, their incapacity to handle freedom, and their distinctive physical appearance.[65] One politician compared the Chinese to Native Americans and recommended their removal to reservations.[66] These racial images in turn were linked to a degraded sexuality. One California magazine confirmed the depravity of Chinese women by noting that their physical appearance was "but a slight removal from the African race."[67] As early as 1854, the *New York Tribune* characterized the Chinese as "lustful and sensual in their dispositions; every female is a prostitute of the basest order."[68] Other journals claimed that debauched Chinese males went to Sunday school only to ravage white female teachers. Readers were warned that Chinese men could not be left alone with children, especially little girls. Sexual anxieties about the Chinese were exacerbated by religious differences, as Christian missionaries sought to proselytize a people characterized as base and lecherous pagans.[69]

California's laws were particularly important because so many Asian immigrants resided there. During the convention to draft the 1879 California constitution, the chairman of the Committee on the Chinese warned: "Were the Chinese to amalgamate at all with our people, it would be the lowest, most vile and degraded of our race, and the result of that amalgamation would be a hybrid of the most despicable, a mongrel of the most detestable that has ever afflicted the earth."[70] To address these concerns, the delegates proposed an 1878 constitutional amendment to restrict intermarriage of Chinese and whites: "The intermarriage of white persons with Chinese, negroes, mulattoes, or persons of mixed blood, descended from a Chinaman or negro from the third generation, inclusive, or their living together as man and wife in this State, is hereby prohibited. The Legislature shall enforce this section by appropriate legislation."[71] The California electorate ratified the provision the following year, and the California legislature quickly moved to enact antimiscegenation statutes. The California Civil Code was amended in 1880 to prohibit the issuance of marriage licenses authorizing the union of "a white person with a negro, mulatto, or Mongolian."[72]

Although levels of interracial sex and marriage among whites and Chinese were quite low, the California legislature criminalized Chinese–white intermarriage in 1901.[73] That same year, the legislation was held unconstitutional based on a procedural defect.[74] California did not re-enact the statute until 1905, primarily in response to intensified concerns about amalgamation with a new group of Asian immigrants, the Japanese.[75] As with the Chinese, Americans feared what they presumed to be Japanese immigrants' alien racial identity and unbridled sexual impulses. When the Japanese government successfully lobbied for its nationals to be exempted from laws that segregated the Chinese, political leaders warned of the dangers of white girls "sitting side by side in the school rooms with matured Japs, with their base minds, their lascivious thoughts, multiplied by their race and strengthened by their mode of life."[76] California's 1905 antimiscegenation law reflected fears of both racial difference and sexual deviance. The statute addressed eugenic concerns that Asian immigrants were a threat to the "self-preservation of [the white] race"[77] as well as anxieties about the lawless sexuality of Japanese immigrants.[78]

Even with state antimiscegenation laws in place, concerns about Asian intermarriage persisted. In 1907, Congress had passed an Expatriation Act,[79] which stripped American women of their citizenship if they married foreign nationals. In 1922, in response to protests from women's groups, Congress passed the Cable Act. In general, the Act did away with the practice of treating a woman's nationality as derivative of her husband's, thereby assuring a wife the freedom to choose her own allegiance. In the area of race, though, women who crossed the color line to marry Asian immigrants remained disempowered. The Cable Act continued to strip American women of their citizenship if they married aliens ineligible to naturalize. The marital autonomy of white women was sacrificed to preserve racial distinctions.

Moreover, the Cable Act made it more difficult than before for American men, usually native-born Chinese, to bring their wives from China. Because a woman's nationality was now independent of her husband's, the U.S. Supreme Court interpreted the Act as barring Chinese women from entering the country based on marriage to an American citizen. Previously, the women had been able to come to the United States but not naturalize. These provisions remained in effect for ten years.[80] Unable to bring wives from China and barred by antimiscegenation laws from marrying white women, even American-born Chinese had limited marital options. Citizenship by birth did not spare them from the adverse consequences of racial difference.

Restrictive immigration policies and state bans on intermarriage had particularly harsh consequences for the Chinese, who were denied access to wives of any race. Federal policy treated the Chinese as sojourners—temporary male workers who would eventually return to their homelands after fulfilling their labor contracts. Poor, unable to speak English, and unfamiliar with American customs, Chinese immigrants were ill-equipped to challenge their isolation. Many of them could not even afford their wives' additional passage. These obstacles were compounded by cultural tradition, which dictated that Chinese women join their husbands' extended families. This practice cemented the family's expectation that the men would return someday and send remittances in the meantime.[81]

Given this combination of federal policy, limited resources, and cultural traditions, the number of Chinese women coming to the United States during the nineteenth century was minuscule. In 1852, of 11,794 Chinese, only 7 were female. By 1870, Chinese men outnumbered Chinese women in the United States by 14 to 1. These severe imbalances in turn led to images of sexual deprivation and degradation. Men living without women in bachelor communities seemed deviant and dangerous. The few Chinese women in the United States were vulnerable to sexual exploitation, which reinforced the image of sojourners as predatory and debauched. According to the 1870 census, 61 percent of Chinese women were "prostitutes," while only 21 percent were "housekeepers."[82] Chinese women regularly worked in the sex trade after having been lured to the United States with promises of marriage, abducted, or sold into indentured servitude by needy families.

Antimiscegenation laws arguably played a more significant role in sending messages of racial inferiority than in thwarting interracial relationships. Anxieties about lustful Chinese bachelors harming white women appear to have been largely unfounded. Although interracial sex between blacks and whites remained relatively commonplace even under antimiscegenation laws, Chinese men were unlikely to cross the color line to cohabit and procreate with white women. During the early decades of Chinese migration, only the most affluent and powerful Chinese might dare to take a white wife or mistress.[83] The linguistic and cultural isolation of the Chinese, their segregation in immigrant enclaves, and their vulnerability to deportation—all of these factors undoubtedly made affairs with white women an unlikely prospect, and Chinese men frequently remained childless bachelors. Indeed, even as late as the 1920s and 1930s, many Chinese men chose to remain single rather than intermarry. According to Los Angeles County marriage records for 1924–1933, of the Chinese who married, only 23.7 percent had a non-Chinese spouse. Given that there were nine Chinese men for every two Chinese women at the time, the majority of Chinese men must have remained alone.[84] Although there is little evidence that the Chinese pursued white women for sex and marriage, western states continued to threaten the immigrants with criminal prosecution under antimiscegenation laws.

Far from alleviating the problems of bachelor communities, Congress consistently enacted immigration policies that worsened the gender imbalances. In 1875, the Page Law barred Chinese prostitutes from entering the country. Tough interrogation techniques were used to enforce the ban. In fact, the law was so intimidating that the number of Chinese women coming to the United States dropped by 68 percent between 1876 and 1882.[85] Shortly after the Chinese Exclusion Act was passed, a federal court in 1844 held that Chinese women assumed the status of their laborer husbands and were barred from entry. Only the wives of lawfully domiciled merchants could enter the United States.[86] Immigration laws were so effective in deterring family creation that, in 1890, only 8.7 percent of the Chinese in the United States were native born.[87] Restrictive immigration policies coupled with antimiscegenation laws confirmed the sojourner's status as a dehumanized and degraded laborer: "Permitted neither to procreate nor to intermarry, the Chinese immigrant was told, in effect, to re-emigrate, die out—white America would not be touched by his presence."[88]

The only relief that the Chinese had from harsh immigration policies came with the 1906 San Francisco earthquake. Because official records had been destroyed, Chinese men claimed to be native-born citizens who could bring their wives from China to the United States. Between 1907 and 1924, ten thousand Chinese women entered the country. By contrast, before 1900, only slightly more than forty-five hundred Chinese women lived in America.[89] This loophole was closed in 1924 when Congress restricted entry of Chinese women to students and wives of clergymen, professors, and government officials.[90] One year later, the U.S. Supreme Court upheld the law, even though it barred native-born Chinese from bringing their spouses to America.[91] The Chinese themselves felt the bitter sting of the federal government's efforts to restrict female immigration: "We were beginning to repopulate a little now so they passed this law to make us die out altogether."[92]

In contrast to the Chinese, Japanese immigrants were able to build same-race families in the United States. Although the Japanese also arrived as *dekaseginin*, or "men who go out to work," they soon were converted to *teiju*, or "permanent residents abroad."[93] Arriving in California in the midst of anti-Chinese hysteria, the Japanese quickly concluded that sojourner status would subordinate and humiliate them. With the support of the Japanese government, the newcomers embarked on a strategy of settlement to ensure economic independence, social standing, and self-respect.[94] Integral to this strategy was the immigration of Japanese women, who could help to build stable, self-sufficient families and communities. When the United States moved to restrict immigrant labor from Japan, a 1908 "Gentleman's Agreement" permitted Japanese residents to bring members of their immediate family to the United States.[95] The agreement protected the Japanese from the hardships of bachelor communities. In 1905–8, 16 percent of Japanese immigrants were women, but by 1909–14, the proportion exceeded 50 percent.[96] The ongoing arrival of Japanese women rapidly rectified gender imbalances in the immigrant community. In 1900, there were almost five Japanese men for every Japanese woman. By 1910, the ratio had dropped to 3.5 to 1, and by 1920, it was only 1.6 to 1. Moreover, nearly every adult Japanese female was married.[97]

Despite these important differences between the Chinese and Japanese immigrant experiences, both groups triggered anxieties about race-mixing. Fears associated with bachelor communities persisted for the Chinese, but the fears surrounding the Japanese arguably should have dissipated by the 1920s. The Japanese had built prosperous families and communities in the United States. Carefully screened by the Japanese government, immigrants arrived with higher rates of literacy and more material resources than their counterparts from Europe.[98] A number of Japanese became entrepreneurs, running successful farms and small businesses. In addition to their economic accomplishments, Japanese immigrants were able to forge stable, same-race families due to the steady influx of women from their home country.

Because the Japanese represented the anomaly of nonwhites with material resources, however, their self-contained communities sparked conflicting anxieties about their sexual and marital proclivities among whites. Some whites concluded that the Japanese settlements were proof of the immigrants' unassimilability and chauvinism. As one witness from California testified before the Senate Committee on Immigration in 1924:

> [W]ith great pride of race, they have no idea of assimilating in the sense of amalgamation. They do not come to this country with any desire or intent to lose their racial or national identity. They come here specifically and professedly for the purpose of colonizing and establishing here permanently the proud Yamato race. They never cease to be Japanese. They have as little desire to intermarry as have the whites, and there can be no proper amalgamation, you will agree, without intermarriage. In Hawaii, where there is every incentive for intermarriage, the Japanese have preserved practical racial purity. . . .[99]

At the same time, the Japanese immigrants' ability to establish farms and businesses raised fears that they would try to convert their economic success into sexual and marital privilege. One farmer worried that property and wealth would lead Japanese men to covet white wives with disastrous consequences:

> Near my home is an eighty-acre tract of as fine land as there is in California. On that tract lives a Japanese. With that Japanese lives a white woman. In that woman's arms is a baby. What is that baby? It isn't Japanese. It isn't white. I'll tell you what that baby is. It is a germ of the mightiest problem that ever faced this state; a problem that will make the black problem of the South look white.[100]

Concerns about the Japanese immigrants' sexuality were magnified by their integration into white schools and communities. Anti-Japanese propaganda warned that the Japanese were "casting furtive glances at our young women. They would like to marry them."[101]

Despite widespread fears that prosperous Japanese men would prey on white women, the rate of outmarriage among first-generation Japanese, or *Issei*, was quite low. Los Angeles County marriage records between 1924 and 1933 indicate that of *Issei* women who married, only 1.7 percent wed non-Japanese men; of the *Issei* men who married, fewer than 3 percent had non-Japanese brides. This was the lowest rate of outmarriage for any racial group in the area. By comparison, of blacks who married, 11.3 percent had nonblack spouses, and of Chinese who married, 23.7 percent wed non-Chinese.[102] Nor is there any evidence that the Japanese regularly evaded antimiscegenation laws through extramarital affairs with whites that produced illegitimate offspring.

The self-sufficiency and success of Japanese communities presented a singular challenge in interpreting the significance of antimiscegenation laws. Although bans on intermarriage could be interpreted as an unequivocal mark of racial subordination for blacks and Chinese, the same was not true for the Japanese. By building prosperous, autonomous communities, Japanese immigrants appeared to be exercising the freedom to forge a separate but equal society in the shadow of racial restrictions. Confronted with a nonwhite population that defied easy categorization as inferior or dependent, whites could no longer assume that low intermarriage rates automatically signaled a diminished status. To preserve a sense of white superiority, the lack of Japanese–white relationships had to be attributed either to Japanese chauvinism or to thwarted sexuality. Although the Chinese and Japanese generally abided by restrictions on intermarriage, one group of Asian immigrants refused to accept race-based limits on their sexual and marital autonomy. Unlike other Asian immigrants, Filipinos arrived in the United States steeped in the American democratic tradition. Convinced of their entitlement to full personhood, Filipinos fought vigorously for the freedom to date and marry as they saw fit.

Filipinos arrived on the West Coast, particularly California, in the 1920s and 1930s.[103] Like the Chinese, most Filipino immigrants were male: In 1930, there were 40,904 Filipino men but only 1,640 women. By 1940, of the Filipinos in the United States, there were still seven men for every woman.[104] They, too, formed bachelor communities and sparked fears of miscegenation.[105] Popular accounts portrayed the Filipinos as lascivious dandies with a taste for white women. One anti-Filipino spokesman described the immigrants as "little brown men attired like 'Solomon in all his glory,' strutting like peacocks and endeavoring to attract the eyes of young American and Mexican girls."[106] The president of the Immigration Study Commission warned of race-mingling between "Filipino coolie fathers and low-grade white mothers," whose numerous offspring could become "a serious burden."[107] Sexual anxieties reached such a pitch that race riots broke out in 1930 when white men became angry at Filipino men who were socializing with white women.[108]

Filipinos reacted defiantly to efforts to control their sexuality. Unique among Asian immigrants, Filipinos arrived not from a foreign country but from an American territory. As a result, they had been educated in American schools, spoke English, and were familiar with American history and civics. They felt that their discriminatory treatment betrayed the ideals taught in their classrooms: "In school in the Islands we learn from the Declaration of Independence that all men are created equal. But when we get over here we find people treating us as if we were inferior."[109] Filipinos confounded their critics by reveling in their depiction as sexually powerful and threatening. In 1936, a San Francisco municipal court judge wrote in *Time* magazine that Filipinos "have told me bluntly and boastfully that they practice the art of love with more perfection than white boys."[110] The Philippine Resident Commissioner responded dryly: "[T]he Judge admits that Filipinos are great lovers."[111] Another Filipino wrote to *Time* that "We, Filipinos, however poor, are taught from the cradle up to respect and love our women. . . . If to respect and love womenfolks is savagery, then make the most of it, Judge. We plead guilty."[112]

Filipinos in California strongly resisted the application of antimiscegenation laws. Most of California's Filipino population resided in Los Angeles County. California forbade marriages between whites and Mongolians, but the Los Angeles City Council announced in 1921 that Filipinos were exempt because they were not Mongolian. Eight years later, the California attorney general issued a contrary opinion, concluding that the term *Mongolian* included Filipinos as well as Chinese and Japanese.[113] Nevertheless, county clerks in Los Angeles continued to issue marriage licenses to Filipino–white couples.[114] In 1930, a lawsuit was filed to force the clerks to cease issuing licenses to Filipinos who were marrying whites. When a superior court judge held that the California attorney general's opinion was binding,[115] the Filipino community reacted with outrage.[116]

Filipino leaders promptly spearheaded efforts to fight the decision. By 1931, four cases were pending in Los Angeles superior courts on the legality of Filipino–white marriages.[117] Reversing itself after only one year, the superior court held that the term *Mongolian* did not include Filipinos. The California court of appeals agreed, affirming the lower court decision by a 3–3 vote. According to the court of appeals, the California legislature had not intended to cover Filipinos under the antimiscegenation law because anthropologists typically classified Filipinos as "Malays," not "Mongolians," and the legislature presumably had adopted this usage. Moreover, the original legislative debate was focused on Chinese, not Filipinos. The court added that the legislature could always amend the statute if it wanted to bar marriages between Filipinos and whites.[118] The California legislature did not take long to act on this suggestion. Nine days before the court's decision, a state senator introduced a bill that would amend the antimiscegenation statute to preclude Filipino–white marriages. Within a few months, California had adopted a new law to cover "negroes, Mongolians, members of the Malay race, or mulattoes."[119] The 1933 provision remained in effect until the California Supreme Court declared it unconstitutional fifteen years later.[120]

Faced with the ban on intermarriage, Filipinos did not concede defeat. Instead, they evaded California's antimiscegenation law by leaving the state to marry. Efforts to close this loophole met with limited success. In 1936, a California court of appeals ruled that a Filipino–white marriage that took place in New Mexico was valid in California. In that case, a white woman sought to annul her marriage on the ground that her Filipino husband had falsely represented himself to be "of Spanish Castilian descent." She testified that she would not have married him had she known he was Filipino because the marriage was illegal in California. The judge held that marriages between whites and Filipinos were legal in New Mexico, so "the ethnological status of the parties was not a ground of annulment."[121] In 1938, the California legislature passed a resolution calling on Utah to prevent whites and Filipinos from going there to evade the ban on miscegenation. Utah obliged by outlawing white–Filipino marriages that same year. Still dissatisfied, a California legislator introduced a bill to void interracial marriages that took place outside the state if they would be illegal in California. The bill died in committee.[122]

In addition to circumventing the law by going out of state, Filipinos married Mexican, Chinese, Japanese, and Eskimo women. In fact, most mixed couples in Los Angeles were Filipino–Mexican. There were some cultural affinities between Filipino immigrants and Mexican women because Spain had at one time colonized the Philippines. Consequently, many Filipinos spoke Spanish and were devout Catholics. Although Mexican-origin women were formally classified as white under California law, registrars seldom stood in the way of a marriage between a Mexican woman, particularly one who was dark skinned, and a Filipino man.[123] The prevalence of intermarriage among Filipinos was so great that by 1946, over half of the immigrants' children were biracial.[124] Far from accepting their relegation to bachelor communities, Filipino immigrants drew on their familiarity with American law and culture to challenge the ban on intermarriage. Unlike the Japanese who relied on separate settlements, Filipinos invoked their rights to freedom and equality before the law. When Filipino demands for recognition of their full personhood failed, they asserted their autonomy by using loopholes to circumvent racial restrictions.

CONCLUSION

Although antimiscegenation laws were identical in form, they served different functions at different times and for different groups. In the colonial era and during the early years of nationhood, bans on intermarriage were critical to drawing the color line between indentured white servants and blacks. Once the color line was in place, the statutes became a way to enforce racial hierarchy by barring blacks from assimilating through marriage to whites. Interracial sex continued to occur on a widespread basis, but it did not threaten white identity and privilege because the one-drop rule classified any illegitimate offspring as black. Nor did the extramarital liaisons jeopardize white superiority since white men could have their way with black women, but black men faced severe sanctions for having sex with white women.

Asian immigrants were subject to harsh restrictions on intermarriage, although their racial identities already were clear from federal immigration law. The use of antimiscegenation laws to subordinate the Chinese was in some ways harsher than their use to subordinate blacks. Blacks could form same-race families, but Chinese men often remained single and childless for life because of the shortage of Chinese women. Although forced to live in bachelor communities, Chinese men did not cross the color line to procreate. Linguistically, culturally, and economically isolated, Chinese men were ill-equipped to pursue extramarital liaisons with white women. Their emasculation reinforced their powerlessness, even as they were portrayed as sexually degraded and lascivious. The penalties for whites who became involved with the Chinese also were in certain respects more severe than for those who became involved with blacks. Although a white spouse in a black–white marriage remained white, American women who wed Chinese immigrants were stripped of their nationality, thereby taking on some of their spouses' unassimilable, alien qualities.

Enforcing racial subordination was particularly critical where the prosperous Japanese were concerned. The ability of Japanese immigrants to build stable, successful businesses, families, and communities threatened a sense of white superiority. In response, nativists insisted that the Japanese could not assimilate through naturalization or intermarriage, whatever their personal accomplishments. At the same time, though, nativists feared that Japanese racial pride made them spurn assimilation to a white way of life. While intermarriage remained a daunting prospect, the possibility that the Japanese might choose to remain a separate people also threatened white superiority. Just when proof of racial subordination was most urgently needed, antimiscegenation laws could no longer offer unambiguous evidence of white desirability and unattainability.

Although the Chinese and Japanese generally complied with antimiscegenation laws, Filipino immigrants defied the statutes. Rather than simply evade the restrictions through illicit liaisons, Filipinos demanded the right to cross the color line to date and marry women of their choice. Explicitly linking their masculinity to romantic and marital freedom, Filipinos were unwilling to forgo intimacy as the price of admission to the American workforce. Though economically marginal, Filipinos were not hampered by the linguistic and cultural isolation that doomed the Chinese to perennial bachelorhood. Often able to communicate in English and aware of American political ideals, Filipinos had a well-developed sense of democratic entitlement and acted on it. Their collective, confrontational approach to restrictions on sexual and marital freedom is unique in the annals of antimiscegenation law.

NOTES

1. Peggy Pascoe, "Race, Gender, and Intercultural Relations: The Case of Interracial Marriage," 12 *Frontiers* 5, 6 (1991).
2. Robert J. Sickels, *Race, Marriage, and the Law* 64 (1972); Paul R. Spickard, *Mixed Blood: Intermarriage and Ethnic Identity in Twentieth-Century America* 374–75 (1989).
3. For a collection of historical essays that describe interracial relationships and their impact on race relations, see Martha Hodes (ed.), *Sex, Love, Race: Crossing Boundaries in North American History* (1999).
4. Fewer than 10 percent of brides in colonial New England were pregnant when they married. John D'Emilio and Estelle B. Freedman, *Intimate Matters: A History of Sexuality in America* 9–10 (1988).
5. As many as one-third of all brides in the Chesapeake were pregnant when they married. Id. at 9–13.
6. A. Leon Higginbotham Jr., *In the Matter of Color: Race and the American Legal Process: The Colonial Period* 22 (paperback ed. 1980) ("Some scholars have argued that for at least half a century the status of blacks in America remained incompletely defined—socially somewhere at the bottom of the white servant class perhaps, but nowhere near chattel slaves.").
7. H. R. McIlwaine (ed.), *Minutes of the Council and General Court of Colonial Virginia, 1622–1632, 1670–1676 with Notes and Excerpts from Original Council and General Court Records, into 1683, Now Lost* 477, 479 (1924) (citing *Re Davis* (Sept. 1630)); I Helen Tunnicliff Catterall (ed.), *Judicial Cases concerning American Slavery* 77–78 (1926); Joel Williamson, *New People: Miscegenation and Mulattoes in the United States* 7–10 (1980); Higginbotham, *In the Matter of Color* at 23–24.
8. D'Emilio and Freedman, *Intimate Matters* at 13. For differing views of the nature of black families under slavery and the impact of slavery on contemporary black family structure, see Herbert G. Gutman, *The Black Family in Slavery and Freedom, 1750–1925* (1976); John Blassingame, *The Slave Community: Plantation Life in the Ante-Bellum South* (1972); Eugene Genovese, *Roll, Jordan, Roll: The World the Slaves Made* (1974); Robert Fogel and Stanley Engerman, *Time on the Cross: The Economics of American Negro Slavery* (1974); E. Franklin Frazier, *The Negro Family in the*

United States (1939); Abram Kardiner and Lionel Oresey, *The Mark of Oppression: Explorations in the Personality of the American Negro* (1951); Kenneth Stampp, *The Peculiar Institution in the Ante-Bellum South* (1964); Stanley Elkins, *Slavery: A Problem in American Institutional and Intellectual Life* (1968).

9. For discussions of how antimiscegenation laws deprived unmarried sexual partners and their children of the benefits of marriage and inheritance law, see Virginia R. Dominguez, *White by Definition: Social Classification in Creole Louisiana* 56–84 (1986); Emily Field Van Tassel, "Personal Liberty and Private Law: 'Only the Law Would Rule between Us': Antimiscegenation, the Moral Economy of Dependency, and the Debate over Rights after the Civil War," 70 *Chi.-Kent L. Rev.* 873, 876, 895, 904–9 (1995).

10. Williamson, *New People* at 8–10.

11. Martha Hodes, *White Women, Black Men: Illicit Sex in the Nineteenth-Century South* 19–38 (1997).

12. D'Emilio and Freedman, *Intimate Matters* at 14.

13. Hodes, *White Women, Black Men* at 120; Martha Elizabeth Hodes, "Sex across the Color Line: White Women and Black Men in the Nineteenth Century American South" 10–36 (Ph.D. diss., 1991).

14. Williamson, *New People* at 10.

15. Id. at 14.

16. Id. at 8; Higginbotham, *In the Matter of Color* at 43–44.

17. Williamson, *New People* at 8, 10; Higginbotham, *In the Matter of Color* at 45, 47.

18. Williamson, *New People* at 9–10; see also Higginbotham, *In the Matter of Color* at 47–48.

19. Higginbotham, *In the Matter of Color* at 48.

20. Thomas E. Buckley, S.J., "Unfixing Race: Class, Power, and Identity in an Interracial Family," 102(3) *Va. Magazine of History and Biography* 349, 361 (July 1994).

21. Id. at 363.

22. Id. at 364–67.

23. Brenda E. Stevenson, *Life in Black & White: Family and Community in the Slave South* 241 (1996).

24. D'Emilio and Freedman, *Intimate Matters* at 103–4; Hodes, *White Women, Black Men* at 48–50, 65; Hodes, "Sex across the Color Line," at 63–66.

25. Hodes, *White Women, Black Men* at 38–48.

26. Id. at 48.

27. Id. at 61.

28. Williamson, *New People* at 17.

29. Id. at 22–23; D'Emilio and Freedman, *Intimate Matters* at 102–3.

30. Williamson, *New People* at 67–71; D'Emilio and Freedman, *Intimate Matters* at 102. By contrast, penalties for sex across the color line were imposed on white male servants, white males who did not own slaves, and white women. Higginbotham, *In the Matter of Color* at 158–59.

31. D'Emilio and Freedman, *Intimate Matters* at 94.

32. II Helen Tunnicliff Catterall (ed.), *Judicial Cases Concerning American Slavery* 269, 359 (1929); Williamson, *New People* at 18.

33. Williamson, *New People* at 20–22. For a description of racial tensions that arose over the use of the term *Creole* in Louisiana to identify both blacks and whites, see Dominguez, *White by Definition* at 140–48.

34. Williamson, *New People* at 22–23.

35. Id. at 71–75; Hodes, *White Women, Black Men* at 148–65; Hodes, "Sex across the Color Line," at 177–79.

36. D'Emilio and Freedman, *Intimate Matters* at 113–14.

37. Hodes, *White Women, Black Men* at 143–48, 166–75; Hodes, "Sex across the Color Line," at 188–96.

38. Williamson, *New People* at 88–91; F. James Davis, *Who Is Black?: One Nation's Definition* 49 (1991); Ernest Porterfield, *Black and White Mixed Marriages* 12, 32–33 (1978).

39. Williamson, *New People* at 92, quoting letter from William Howard to James Gregorie, Jan. 12, 1868, *Gregorie-Elliott Papers*, Southern Historical Collection, University of North Carolina, Chapel Hill.

40. Hodes, *White Women, Black Men* at 148–59; Hodes, "Sex across the Color Line," at 196–212.

41. Donna L. Franklin, *Ensuring Inequality: The Structural Transformation of the African-American Family* 64 (1997); D'Emilio and Freedman, *Intimate Matters* at 220–21.

42. D'Emilio and Freedman, *Intimate Matters* at 106–7.

43. Williamson, *New People* at 96–98.

44. See Ronald Takaki, *Strangers from a Different Shore* 12–15 (paperback ed. 1989). This chapter focuses on groups like the Chinese and Japanese who arrived in substantial numbers before World War II. Because restrictions on intermarriage began to disappear after World War II, the experience of groups like Koreans, Samoans, and Indochinese, who mainly arrived after 1945, are not discussed. Sil Dong Kim, "Interracially Married Korean Women Immigrants: A Study in Marginality" 61–63, 64–66 (Ph.D. diss., 1979); Lee Houchins and Chang-Su Houchins, "The Korean Experience in America, 1903–24," in *The Asian American: The Historical Experience* 129–56 (Norris Hundley Jr. ed., 1976); Verona Gordon, "Culturally Sensitive Nursing Care for Indochinese Refugees," in *Asian and Pacific American Experiences: Women's Perspectives* 206 (Nobuya Tsuchida ed., 1982).

45. Three Chinese arrived in California in 1848; by 1852, about twenty-five thousand resided there. Chinese laborers were imported to work on the railroads in the 1860s, and the Chinese comprised one-fourth of the state's workforce by 1870. Takaki, *Strangers from a Different Shore* at 79. The population of Chinese in the United States grew from 34,933 in 1860 to 107,488 in 1890. Megumi Dick Osumi, "Asians and California's Anti-Miscegenation Laws,"

in *Asian and Pacific American Experiences* (Tsuchida ed.), at 1, 2–3; Kim, "Interracially Married Korean Women Immigrants," at 58–59.

46. Act of March 26, 1790, ch. 3, 1 Stat. 103. For a fuller discussion of the role of race in the naturalization process, see generally Ian Haney López, *White By Law: The Legal Construction of Race* (1996).

47. Corrine K. Hoexter, *From Canton to California: The Epic of Chinese Immigration* 44 (1976). For an article focusing on Asian efforts to obtain citizenship, see Charles J. McClain, "Tortuous Path, Elusive Goal: The Asian Quest for American Citizenship," 2 *Asian L.J.* 33 (1995).

48. Charles J. McClain, *In Search of Equality: The Chinese Struggle against Discrimination in Nineteenth-Century America* 70–73 (1994).

49. *In re Ah Yup*, 1 F. Cas. 223, 223–25, 5 Sawy. 155, 157–59 (1878) (No. 104). A congressman from California also introduced a bill to make clear that no Chinese could become a citizen, but the need for the bill was obviated by the federal court's decision. Twenty years later, the U.S. Attorney General's Office issued opinions that cast doubt on the citizenship of Chinese who received certificates of naturalization before their ineligibility for citizenship was settled. 21 Op. Att'y Gen. 37 (1898).

50. Act of May 6, 1882, ch. 126, 22 Stat. 58, §§ 1, 14, 15; McClain, *In Search of Equality* at 147–50, 191–92, 201–3; Elmer Sandmeyer, *The Anti-Chinese Movement in California* 93–95 (1939). The U.S. Supreme Court upheld the Chinese Exclusion Act in 1889 based on Congress's plenary power to regulate immigration. Chinese Exclusion Case, *Chae Chan Ping v. United States*, 130 U.S. 581, 608–10 (1889). Later, a federal court reinforced the racial categorization of Chinese under the law by denying entry to British nationals from Hong Kong because they were still "laborers of the Chinese race." *In re Ah Lung*, the Chinese Laborer from Hong Kong, 18 F. 28 (C.C.D. Cal. 1883). For a description of events leading up to the *Ah Lung* decision, see McClain, *In Search of Equality* at 155–56.

51. Takaki, *Strangers from a Different Shore* at 111–12.

52. Act of May 6, 1882, ch. 126, 22 Stat. 58, §§ 1, 14, 15; McClain, *In Search of Equality* at 147–50, 191–92, 201–3; Sandmeyer, *The Anti-Chinese Movement in California* at 93–95.

53. Immigration and Nationality Act, Pub. L. No. 414, 66 Stat. 163 (1952), *as amended*, 8 U.S.C. §§ 1101 et seq.

54. Kim, "Interracially Married Korean Women Immigrants," at 59–60; Osumi, "Asians and California's Anti-Miscegenation Laws," in *Asian and Pacific American Experiences* (Tsuchida ed.), at 9.

55. Kim, "Interracially Married Korean Women Immigrants," at 60; Osumi, "Asians and California's Anti-Miscegenation Laws," in *Asian and Pacific American Experiences* (Tsuchida ed.), at 9; Takaki, *Strangers from a Different Shore* at 180–81.

56. See *Ozawa v. United States*, 260 U.S. 178, 183 (1922) (argument on behalf of petitioner citing early instances of Japanese naturalization); see also Bradford Smith, *Americans from Japan* 148 (1948) (describing how some Japanese successfully petitioned for citizenship in the mid- to late 1850s, sometimes by capitalizing on their military service records).

57. Letter to President Theodore Roosevelt from U.S. Attorney General William H. Moody, July 19, 1905; 21 Op. Att'y Gen. 37,581 (1906). Eager to cultivate good relations with Japan, President Roosevelt pressed for legislation that would permit the Japanese to naturalize. His efforts were unsuccessful, however. Raymond A. Esthus, *Theodore Roosevelt and Japan* 147 n. 3 (1966).

58. *Ozawa v. United States*, 260 U.S. 178 (1922).

59. Id. at 198; Takaki, *Strangers from a Different Shore* at 208–9; Smith, *Americans from Japan* at 148.

60. Asian Indians began arriving in the United States in 1907. Unfavorable immigration policies kept their numbers small. In 1909, Congress restricted immigration from India, and less than a decade later, immigration was banned altogether. Takaki, *Strangers from a Different Shore* at 62.

61. Letter from U.S. Secretary of Commerce and Labor Oscar Straus to U.S. Attorney General Charles J. Bonaparte, Jan. 9, 1907; letter from Bonaparte to Straus, Jan. 11, 1907; letter from U.S. Attorney Robert T. Devlin to Bonaparte, Aug. 8, 1907; letter from Bonaparte to Devlin, Aug. 14, 1907; letter from Professor W. F. Willcox to Bonaparte, Sept. 13, 1907; letter from Bonaparte to Willcox, Sept. 16, 1907; letter from Willcox to Bonaparte, Sept. 24, 1907; letter from Bonaparte to Willcox, Sept. 27, 1907.

62. *United States v. Balsara*, 180 F. 694 (2d Cir. 1910); *In re Mozumdar*, 207 F. 115 (E.D. Wash. 1913). For a general discussion of the controversy surrounding the classification of Asian Indians, see Joan M. Jensen, *Message from India: Asian Indian Immigrants in North America* 248–49 (1988); Gary Hess, "The Forgotten Asian Americans: The East Indian Community in the United States," in *The Asian Americans*, at 169–70.

63. 261 U.S. 204 (1923).

64. Id. at 209. For an article criticizing the Court for judging East Indians by "the 'blueness' of [their] Caucasian blood" rather than their personal accomplishments in the United States, see Gurdial Singh, "East Indians in the United States," 30 *Soc. & Soc. Res.* 208, 212 (Jan.–Feb. 1946).

65. Takaki, *Strangers from a Different Shore* at 35–36, 100–101; Dan Caldwell, "The Negroization of the Chinese Stereotype in California," 53 *S. Calif. Q.* 123 (1971).

66. See, e.g., 13 *Cong. Rec.* 3268 (1882) (statement of Senator John Tyler Morgan of Alabama) (likening the problems of assimilating the Chinese and the Indians and arguing for restrictive immigration policies); see generally Takaki, *Strangers from a Different Shore* at 102.

67. Caldwell, "The Negroization of the Chinese Stereotype in California," 53 *S. Calif. Q.* at 128, quoting Hutching's *California Magazine*, vol. I, at 387 (March 1857).

68. Stuart Miller, *The Unwelcome Immigrant: The American Image of the Chinese, 1785–1882* at 169 (1969), quoting *N.Y. Tribune*, Oct. 2, 1854.

69. Osumi, "Asians and California's Anti-Miscegenation Laws," in *Asian and Pacific American Experiences* (Tsuchida ed.), at 6–7; see also Takaki, *Strangers from a Different Shore* at 101.

70. I *Debates and Proceedings of the Constitutional Convention of California 1878–9* at 632 (1880) (E. B. Willis and P. K. Stockton official stenographers).

71. Id. at 225.

72. California Statutes, 23d Scss., ch. 74, §1, p. 121 (1880) (amending § 69). Significantly, the legislature did not move immediately to make intermarriage illegal, although it easily could have amended a law banning marriages between whites and blacks or mulattoes to include the Chinese. At least one scholar has argued that legislators were concerned about the possibility that such an amendment would void retroactively all marriages between whites and Chinese. Osumi, "Asians and California's Anti-Miscegenation Laws," in *Asian and Pacific American Experiences* (Tsuchida ed.), at 6.

73. California Statutes, 34th Sess., ch. 157, § 20, pp. 335–36 (1901) (amending §§ 60, 69).

74. *Lewis v. Dunne*, 134 Cal. 291, 66 P. 478 (1901) (declaring 1901 amendments to Civil Code invalid for failure to comply with the constitutional requirement of being "re-enacted and published at length as revised" and the requirement that an act's title deal with a definite subject).

75. California Statutes, 36th Sess., ch. 414, § 2, p. 554 (1905) (amending § 60). For a general discussion of the California legislature's efforts to deal with miscegenation among Chinese and whites, see Osumi, "Asians and California's Anti-Miscegenation Laws," in *Asian and Pacific American Experiences* (Tsuchida ed.), at 9, 11, 13–14.

76. Franklin Hichborn, *Story of the Session of the California Legislature of 1909* at 207 n. 90 (1909), quoting Assemblyman Johnson's speech regarding a bill to mandate that the Japanese attend segregated schools.

77. Roger Daniels, *The Politics of Prejudice: The Anti-Japanese Movement in California and the Struggle for Japanese Exclusion* 49 (1978), quoting Chester Harvey Rowell, owner and editor of the *Fresno Republican*.

78. See *Reports of the Senate Immigration Commission, Immigrants in Industries—Part 25: Japanese and Other Immigrant Races in the Pacific Coast and Rocky Mountain States*, 61st Cong., 2d Sess. at vol. 1, pp. 162–63 (1911) (noting strong antipathy to Japanese intermarriage in the western United States).

79. Act of Mar. 2, 1907, ch. 2534, 34 Stat. 1228–29, §3. See generally Candice Lewis Bredbenner, *A Nationality of Her Own: Women, Marriage, and the Law of Citizenship* 16 (1998).

80. Cable Act of 1922, Pub. L. No. 67–346, 42 Stat. 1021–22, *amended by* Act of July 3, 1930, Pub. L. No. 71–499, 46 Stat. 849, *repealed by* Act of Mar. 3, 1931, Pub. L. No. 71–829, 46 Stat. 1511–12; *Chang Chan v. Nagle*, 268 U.S. 346, 353 (1925) (concluding that Chinese women could not rely on marriage to a citizen husband to enter the United States). See also Sucheng Chan, "The Exclusion of Chinese Women, 1870–1943," in *Chinese Immigrants and American Law* 36 (Charles J. McClain ed., 1994); Bredbenner, *A Nationality of Her Own* at 124–29, 134–35 (describing denationalization of American women under principle of "derivative citizenship").

81. Takaki, *Strangers from a Different Shore* at 36–37; Chan, "The Exclusion of Chinese Women," in *Chinese Immigrants and American Law* (McClain ed.), at 2–5.

82. D'Emilio and Freedman, *Intimate Matters* at 135; Takaki, *Strangers from a Different Shore* at 121–23.

83. For an account of a wealthy and successful Chinese businessman who entered into a contract with his white female lover that pledged their lifelong allegiance to one another, although interracial marriages were illegal, see Lisa See, *On Gold Mountain: The One-Hundred-Year Odyssey of My Chinese-American Family* 56 (paperback ed. 1995). Meanwhile, unbeknownst to his white "wife," the Chinese businessman had a wife in China. He justified the arrangement on the ground that he had seen his Chinese wife only once, their marriage had never been consummated, and some men in his home country kept country wives to care for aging parents and city wives for companionship. Id. at 55.

84. Spickard, *Mixed Blood* at 47–48.

85. Act of March 3, 1875, ch. 141, 18 Stat. 477–78; see generally George Anthony Peffer, "Forbidden Families: Emigration Experiences of Chinese Women Under the Page Law, 1875–1882," 6 *J. American Ethnic History* 28 (1986); Chan, "The Exclusion of Chinese Women," in *Chinese Immigrants and American Law* (McClain ed.), at 97–109.

86. Case of the Chinese Wife, *In re Ah Moy*, 21 F. 785 (1884), *writ of error dismissed as moot*, 113 U.S. 216 (1885) (wife of Chinese laborer); for cases dealing with the rights of the wives of Chinese merchants, see *In re Chung Toy Ho and Wong Choy Sin*, 42 F. 398 (D. Or. 1890); *United States v. Chung Shee*, 71 F. 277 (S.D. Cal. 1895); *United States v. Gue Lim*, 83 F. 136 (N.D. Wash. 1897), aff'd, 176 U.S. 459 (1900); *Ex parte Chan Shee*, 236 F. 579 (N.D. Cal. 1916); *Chew Hoy Quong v. White*, 244 F. 749 (9th Cir. 1917), rev'd and remanded, 249 F. 869 (1918). For a description of these cases, see Chan, "The Exclusion of Chinese Women," in *Chinese Immigrants and American Law* (McClain ed.), at 18–26.

87. Osumi, "Asians and California's Anti-Miscegenation Laws," in *Asian and Pacific American Experiences* (Tsuchida ed.), at 8; Takaki, *Strangers from a Different Shore* at 254.

88. Osumi, "Asians and California's Anti-Miscegenation Laws," in *Asian and Pacific American Experiences* (Tsuchida ed.), at 8.

89. Takaki, *Strangers from a Different Shore* at 234–35.

90. Act of May 26, 1924, ch. 190, 43 Stat. 153, §§ 3–4.

91. *Cheung Sum Shee v. Nagle*, 268 U.S. 336 (1925) (merchants); *Chang Chan v. Nagle*, 268 U.S. 346 (1925) (native-born Chinese). Congress later amended the law in response to vigorous lobbying by native-born Chinese. House Comm. on Immigration and Naturalization, *Hearings on H.R. 2404, H.R. 5654, H.R. 10524*, 71st Cong., 2d Sess. 544–46

(1930) (testimony of Kenneth F. Fung, Executive Secretary, Chinese American Citizens' Alliance, and Florence P. Kahn, Representative from California). The new law allowed native-born Chinese to bring their wives to the United States if the marriage had been consummated before 1924. Act of June 13, 1930, ch. 476, 46 Stat. 581.

92. Takaki, *Strangers from a Different Shore* at 234–35.

93. Spickard, *Mixed Blood* at 26–27.

94. Yuji Ichioka, *The Issei: The World of the First Generation Japanese Immigrants, 1885–1924* at 60–61, 146–50 (1988); Takaki, *Strangers from a Different Shore* at 197–98; Spickard, *Mixed Blood* at 27. For a description of one Japanese colony of farmers in the San Joaquin Valley that was founded by a businessman and publisher who strongly endorsed the development of ethnic enclaves, see Kesa Noda, *Yamato Colony, 1906–1960* (1981).

95. Spickard, *Mixed Blood* at 27–28; Takaki, *Strangers from a Different Shore* at 46, 202–3; Osumi, "Asians and California's Anti-Miscegenation Laws," in *Asian and Pacific American Experiences* (Tsuchida ed.), at 14. The agreement remained in place until 1921 when a "Ladies' Agreement" was reached to prohibit emigration of "picture brides," that is, women from Japan chosen for arranged marriages with immigrant husbands. In effect, the Ladies' Agreement stopped the flow of Japanese immigration altogether. Takaki, *Strangers from a Different Shore* at 208.

96. Spickard, *Mixed Blood* at 26–27; see also Takaki, *Strangers from a Different Shore* at 46–47.

97. Spickard, *Mixed Blood* at 28–29.

98. Takaki, *Strangers from a Different Shore* at 47.

99. Senate Committee on Immigration, *Japanese Immigration Legislation: Hearings on S. 2576*, 68th Cong., 1st Sess. 5 (1924) (statement of Mr. V. S. McClatchy of Sacramento, California).

100. Id.

101. Osumi, "Asians and California's Anti-Miscegenation Laws," in *Asian and Pacific American Experiences* (Tsuchida ed.), at 13, quoting *Grizzly Bear*, July 1923, at 27.

102. Spickard, *Mixed Blood* at 47–48.

103. By 1930, there were 45,208 Filipinos in the United States, of whom 30,470 resided in California. Osumi, "Asians and California's Anti-Miscegenation Laws," in *Asian and Pacific American Experiences* (Tsuchida ed.), at 16, citing 1930 U.S. Census, vol. III, pt. 1, at 120.

104. Id. at 23; Takaki, *Strangers from a Different Shore* at 58.

105. For a personal account of life in the Filipino bachelor communities, see Carlos Bulosan, *America Is in the Heart* (1946).

106. Manuel Buaken, *I Have Lived with the American People* 169–70 (1948), quoting *Evening Pajaronian*, Jan. 8, 1930.

107. C. M. Goethe, "Filipino Immigration Viewed as a Peril," *Current History* 353, 354 (June 1931), reprinted in *Letters in Exile: An Introductory Reader on the History of Filipinos in America* 72 (1976). Elsewhere, the author characterized white women who involved themselves with Filipino men as "near-moron[s]." Id.

108. H. Brett Melendy, *Asians in America: Filipinos, Koreans, and East Indians* 52–55 (1977) (describing the application of antimiscegenation laws to Filipinos and race riots in California).

109. Takaki, *Strangers from a Different Shore* at 326.

110. Sylvain Lazarus, "Lovers' Departure," *Time*, Apr. 13, 1936, at 17.

111. Takaki, *Strangers from a Different Shore* at 329.

112. Ernest Ilustre, "Great Lovers," *Time*, Apr. 27, 1936, at 4.

113. California Office of the Attorney General, Opinion No. 5641 (June 8, 1926).

114. Osumi, "Asians and California's Anti-Miscegenation Laws," in *Asian and Pacific American Experiences* (Tsuchida ed.), at 18–19.

115. *Robinson v. Lampton*, No. 2496504 (Sup. Ct. L.A. County 1930).

116. For a Filipino's personal account of the tensions surrounding the California courts' treatment of intermarriage, see Bulosan, *America Is in the Heart* at 143.

117. *Roldan v. Los Angeles County*, 129 Cal. App. 267, 18 P.2d 706 (1933); *Visco v. Los Angeles County*, No. 319408 (Sup. Ct. L.A. County 1931) (holding that California law did not bar marriage of a Filipino to a "Mexican Indian girl" and noting in dictum that a Filipino could also marry a white woman); *Laddaran v. Laddaran*, No. 095459 (Sup. Ct. L.A. County 1931) (upholding validity of Filipino–white intermarriage); *Murillo v. Murillo*, No. D97715 (Sup. Ct. L.A. County 1931) (same). For an article chronicling these legal decisions and concluding that efforts to stop race-mixing would prove futile, see Nellie Foster, "Legal Status of Filipino Intermarriages in California," 16 *Soc. & Soc. Res.* 441 (May–June 1932).

118. *Roldan v. Los Angeles County*, 129 Cal. App. 267, 18 P.2d 706 (1933).

119. Calif. Stat., 50th Sess., ch. 104, pp. 561–62 (1933) (amending §§ 60, 69).

120. *Perez v. Sharp*, 32 Cal. 2d 711, 198 P.2d 17 (1948). See chapter 5 for a discussion of the California Supreme Court's decision to strike down the state's antimiscegenation law.

121. *People v. Godines*, 17 Cal. App. 2d 721, 62 P.2d 787 (1936).

122. Osumi, "Asians and California's Anti-Miscegenation Laws," in *Asian and Pacific American Experiences* (Tsuchida ed.), at 22; see also "Anti-Miscegenation Laws and the Filipino," in *Letters in Exile* at 63.

123. Leti Volpp, "American Mestizo: Filipinos and Anti-Miscegenation Laws in California," 33 *U.C. Davis L. Rev.* 795 (2000) (nothing that relations between Filipino men and Mexican women did not prompt serious opposition and that in one case in Los Angeles, a court permitted a Filipino–Mexican marriage because the Mexican wife was denied her status as a white woman).

124. Takaki, *Strangers from a Different Shore* at 341–43.

8

Race, Class, and Reproductive Politics in American History

RICKIE SOLINGER

IN THE LATE TWENTIETH CENTURY, women's rights advocates known as Second Wave feminists devised the term "reproductive politics" to describe late-twentieth-century struggles over contraception and abortion, race and sterilization, class and adoption, women and sexuality, and other related subjects. "Reproductive politics" is a useful term because it captures the way that questions about power are at the heart of these debates. For example: who has the power to make decisions about keeping or ending a pregnancy? The pregnant woman, a physician, or a state legislator? Who has the power to define a *legitimate* mother, that is, a woman who has the right to raise her own child? A city welfare official, a congressman, an adoption agency, a Supreme Court judge, or the mother herself? "Reproductive politics" refers most basically to the questions, *Who has power over matters of pregnancy and its consequences, and how is that power exercised and contested?*

But these power struggles are not just between legislators, courts, and all women as a single category. Different groups of women have different kinds of reproductive concerns and have been subjected to different kinds of reproductive control. Consider, for example, an enslaved African woman, a Cherokee woman, an unmarried white school teacher, and the wife of a Philadelphia merchant in 1850. Why might each of these women have cared to encourage or discourage pregnancy? What population concerns, consumption issues, labor needs, and racial prejudices inclined authorities to exercise what kinds of control over the reproductive lives of the various groups of fertile women in society? What were the consequences for these different groups of women of trying to control pregnancies or of becoming pregnant and a mother? How would the answers to these questions be different if we were investigating the experiences of an African-American woman, a Cherokee woman, or a white merchant's wife in 1950 instead of 1850? Or in 2010?

In order to explore these matters, I will introduce several different examples of reproductive politics across U.S. history, each of which illustrates how a woman's reproductive life was shaped by the interaction between her race and class and the historical moment in which she had heterosexual sex and got pregnant. Together, these examples reveal that there is no single history of reproductive politics in the United States. Laws and policies have changed over time. The meanings of race and class in relation to reproduction have changed over time. Women's reproductive intentions and their reproductive responsibilities to their families and communities have changed over time. But the laws and policies of the United States have consistently valued the reproductive activity and "choices" of some women more than others.

RACE, SLAVERY, AND MOTHERHOOD IN THE NINETEENTH CENTURY

Throughout the era of American slavery, white law makers and law enforcers used control over reproduction as a strategy for enforcing the distinction between races, establishing the "legal meanings of racial difference," enforcing the degradation of non-white women, and in general for facilitating white supremacy.[1] The reproductive capacity of African-American women was the resource whites relied on to produce an enslaved labor force, to produce and transmit property and wealth across generations, to consolidate white control over land in North America, and to produce a class of human beings who, in their ineligibility for citizenship, underwrote the exclusivity and value of white citizenship.

After the international slave trade was outlawed in 1808 and before the 13th Amendment to the Constitution ended slavery in the United States in 1865, slave owners faced the task of increasing their capital investment in slaves and, at the same time, increasing their labor force. Eager to maximize slave reproduction, owners devised "breeding schemes" to achieve their goals, especially during the time of booming cotton profits after 1820. Many owners personally impregnated enslaved girls and women, often through rape. Some also denied enslaved persons the right to choose to live in monogamous marital relationships, demanding instead that enslaved men and women have several or serial sexual partners "to promote the rapid birth of slave children."[2] Thomas Jefferson spoke directly about the benefits to owners of an enslaved and fecund woman: "I consider a woman who brings a child every two years as more profitable than the best man on the farm; what she produces is an addition to capital."[3] Jefferson didn't comment here on another principle he relied on: that the slave owner regularly maximized profits by exercising his right to liquidate the "additional capital" that enslaved women produced. That is, the slave owner could and did sell away the enslaved woman's children whenever he deemed such a sale beneficial to his interests.

In the nineteenth century, at the same time as slave owners exploited enslaved women sexually and reproductively, white motherhood was invested with "a new glory." The Victorian "empire of the mother" wrapped white women in a sentimental halo of love, tenderness, "rigor and bliss," and domestic power.[4] White cultural authorities constructed the African-American woman as the sexualized, negligent, super-fertile "counterimage" against whom the white Victorian mother was defined and set above. The privileges this comparison conferred on white women, who were in other ways constrained by their reproductive roles, helps us understand why cross-class and cross-race coalitions of women have been so difficult to create and sustain.

RACE AND FERTILITY CONTROL IN THE MID-TWENTIETH CENTURY

Little more than half a century after the end of slavery, in the early twentieth century, the descendants of enslaved women were still the targets of "breeding schemes." But this time, the goal was to produce a more *eugenically fit* population by restricting the reproduction of "unfit races." Eugenicists claimed that if poor women continued to reproduce while middle class women made more prudent reproductive decisions, then poverty would persist and spread, and the population of the country would be degraded to the point where democracy could not flourish. Eugenicists typically supported immigration restrictions, deportations, and sterilization to protect the "quality" of *American* babies and the jobs of *American* workers, targeting Mexican workers, Chinese immigrants, and African-Americans.

Even after the decline of the organized eugenics movement by the early 1960s, politicians, policy makers, and welfare agency personnel updated policies aimed to *limit* the number of African-American babies. In the midst of the Civil Rights era, many politicians still refused to address housing and job discrimination, the deficiencies of the education system, and other large structural causes of poverty and inequality. Instead, they argued that the unrestrained "breeding" of African-American women and other women of color was the source of all social problems. So they pressed such women to do their duty: to use birth control, get sterilized, abstain from sex, or to suffer public policy punishments for having "too many children."

At the same time, white women, always defined as precious reproducers of valuable new white citizens, were gaining access to the new valued status of *choicemakers*. According to the nineteenth-century cult of domesticity, white women had to stay home and replenish the white race. But now legislators allowed them to choose the birth control pill and other contraceptive methods—not a duty, as it was for African-American, Chicana, and Native American women, but as *a right*, a choice, a symbol of "liberation," and a mark of modern womanhood. Birth control was introduced as a mass commodity in the mid-twentieth century in a thoroughly racialized fashion.

The story of sterilization in the mid-twentieth century is similarly racialized. In the early 1970s, after decades of forbidding white, middle-class women to undergo sterilization, doctors largely stopped interfering when these women asked to be sterilized. Sterilization became another liberating "choice" a modern woman might make and pay for. The white-feminist-inspired Arkansas Family Planning Act, legislated in 1973, for example, allowed physicians to distribute birth control information and devices to anyone who asked, and legalized voluntary sterilization of anyone over eighteen (and for anyone under eighteen who was married), without any waiting period.

Because they had different histories and because medical authorities and others assigned different values to their pregnancies, white middle class women and poor women of color often had diametrically opposed responses to the new popularity of sterilization. Many white women did not understand why poor women of color saw sterilization as a dangerous medical option and why they called for laws that mandated thirty-day waiting periods before a doctor could carry out a sterilization.

In the early 1970s, sterilization was the most common form of contraception among women over the age of twenty-five in the United States, but black women and poor women generally were sterilized at twice the rate of white, middle-class women, and many women of color felt that this was not entirely voluntary.[5] Doctors, social workers, social commentators and others were very likely to pressure poor women (but not middle-class women) to undergo sterilization. One survey showed that 33 percent of the public hospitals studied obtained consent for sterilization while women were in labor—hardly a time when women were capable of informed consent.[6]

An obstetrician about to perform a Caesarian section delivery on Jovita Rivera, a Mexican woman in Los Angeles, pressed her—after she had been sedated—to accept sterilization. Rivera reported that her doctor "told her she should have her 'tubes tied' because her children were a burden to the government." Rivera testified as part of a group of women, all of whom had been pressured in the same way to have their tubes tied. None of these women was a recipient of public assistance, but doctors in Los Angeles and elsewhere assumed that women who looked like Jovita Rivera were on welfare and should therefore curtail their fertility permanently.[7]

SINGLE MOTHERHOOD, ADOPTION, AND RACE IN MID-TWENTIETH CENTURY AMERICA

In the mid-twentieth century, before "single motherhood" became a normalized status (or another "choice") in the United States, an unmarried, pregnant woman's fate depended almost entirely on her race. If an African-American young woman got pregnant in the 1950s without having a husband, she was very likely to keep and raise her baby, often within the home of her original family. Her parents might have been sorry that their daughter had a child before finishing school or before getting married, but they did not question that this child was part of the family.

But proponents of school segregation, restrictive public housing, and enforced sterilization—as well as exclusionary welfare policies—all used the issue of relatively high rates of out-of-marriage pregnancies and childbirth among African-American women to support their campaign to resist integration. In 1956 the *New York Times* reported on a hearing in the U.S. House of Representatives on the desegregation of schools in Washington, DC. The prevalence of unwed mothers among black schoolgirls was a rallying cry for southern segregationists, the paper observed. And the House sub-committee majority triumphantly wrote its report recommending that segregation be restored, in part to protect the chastity of white girls by shielding them from proximity to the pregnancies of their African-American peers. Many states passed laws excluding unwed mothers from access to public assistance.[8]

To justify their punitive attitude, officials argued that such women didn't have babies out of maternal feelings or out of the desire to make a family, or even because they lacked contraceptives. They had babies, the officials claimed, in order to get welfare. If we deny them welfare, officials argued, we will halt their reproductive adventures. We will reduce welfare costs, reduce taxes, and slow the population growth of minorities in the United States.[9]

Unmarried white girls and women who became unwillingly pregnant in these same years had quite a different experience. On the one hand, their families were generally far less willing to embrace their babies. But on the other hand, their communities and lawmakers were far less interested in publicizing the fact that white women also got pregnant "out of wedlock" or passing punitive laws to deal with these situations. These girls and women, if they could not or would not seek an illegal abortion, were frequently shunned by their parents and communities and hidden away in maternity homes or the homes of distant relatives. And for the first time in American history, unmarried mothers were pressured to give their babies up for adoption. In fact, in the post-World War II years, we see the *invention of* (white) *adoption*, a development that depended on the transformation of the white "bastard child" into a valuable, sought-after commodity.

The new adoption system also depended on selling the idea that a white woman's sexual and reproductive mistakes could be fixed. For the first time, the white unwed mother was encouraged to give away her baby, forget all about the unfortunate episode, and go back to high school or college, back to her job, back on the dating market, escaping social stigma. She could marry and have "real" children, a "real" family all her own, and no one would ever know her secret.

The invention of adoption underscored the racialized differences between the "value" of the white baby and the "value" of babies of color. Politicians, the media, and other cultural forces defined "illegitimate" babies of poor women of color as lacking value and as creating expense for white taxpayers. These babies were consigned to their own poor mothers. White babies born to unwed mothers were, at the very same time, defined as prizes, worth great sums of money and great quantities of love to thousands of white, often infertile, couples competing with each other to have such a child for their own, to complete their family.[10]

By the early 1970s, with the legalization of abortion, some women ended their untimely, unwed pregnancies. Among the ones who stayed pregnant, fewer and fewer white, unmarried girls and women were willing to listen to those who claimed that without husbands, they could not be legitimate mothers. "If I can decide whether or not to stay pregnant," many figured, "surely I can decide whether or not to be the mother of the child I give birth to." Reasoning this way, white women began refusing to relinquish their babies for adoption. Quite suddenly the "adoption market" in white babies dried up, just when hundreds of thousands of prospective adoptive parents had come to think that adoption was another valid, modern choice for building families.

Since the early 1970s, potential adopters have had to look around the world for adoptable children, most often in areas of desperate poverty where many babies are born to women too poor to take care of them. Adoption, a choice for affluent women that is in large part created by the "choicelessness" of other women in a faraway country, continues to divide women by race and resources.

ABORTION: CREATING THE CONTOURS OF "CHOICE"

Most Americans don't know that abortion was legal in the United States for most of the nation's first one hundred years. Then, in the second half of the nineteenth century, state by state, the newly established American Medical Association, concerned about solidifying the status and clientele of physicians, worked with state legislators to outlaw abortion and the midwives who traditionally performed the procedure. From the middle of the nineteenth century until approximately the middle of the twentieth century, abortion and most methods of contraception were illegal. Women were officially ordered to live their lives without any control over their reproductive capacity, deepening their vulnerability in a culture where females had less social power and almost no political and economic power compared to men.

All over the country, however, women passed information among each other, mother to daughter, friend to friend, about how to limit fertility and where to turn for help when homemade methods failed. No matter what the laws said, women were determined to shape their reproductive lives and the size of their families to the extent possible. Experts estimate that in the years before legalized abortion, the number of abortions performed every year in this country (mostly in secret, sometimes under legal conditions in hospitals, as a response to health emergencies) was approximately seventy percent of the number performed in the first years after *Roe v. Wade*.[11]

When the Supreme Court legalized abortion in 1973, women all over the country spoke out about how the *Roe v. Wade* decision changed their lives. One woman explained how having the legal right to manage her own fertility helped her be a responsible mother: "My job on the assembly line at the plant was going well and I needed that job desperately to support the kids. Also I had started night school to improve my chances to get a better job. I just couldn't have another baby—five kids were enough for me to support."[12] Many spoke about the relief they felt being able to get the procedure performed in a legal clinic, without fear of breaking the law, without having to sneak around.

A Native American woman put it this way: "Personally, legal abortion allowed me the choice as a teenager living on a very poor Indian Reservation to finish growing up and make something of my life."[13] In this era of "women's liberation," women of all races and economic statuses strongly associated the ability to manage fertility and family-formation with being able to go to school and earn a living unimpeded by unexpected pregnancies and babies. Women reported then, and report in retrospect, that reproductive rights finally made women into full citizens. But within a couple of years after the Supreme Court decision, Congress and the Supreme Court clarified the meaning of "abortion rights," making this "right" available only to women who had enough money to pay for an abortion.

Roe v. Wade had seemed, at first, to protect women's access to abortion against both religious objections and financial tests. But in 1977 Congress passed the Hyde Amendment, which denied this kind of protection to poor women and only to poor women. Henry Hyde, Republican representative from Illinois, explained his strategy: "I certainly would like to prevent, if I could legally, anybody having an abortion, a rich woman, a middle-class woman, or a poor woman. Unfortunately, the only vehicle available is the HEW Medicaid bill."[14] Hyde was probably aware that restricting the access of poor women could eventually impact the access of all women. As one physician presciently observed in 1978, "Denial of abortion to low-income women jeopardizes their availability to all women. Private insurers may now decide to not reimburse for abortions. Anti-abortion forces will be encouraged to pursue further means of undermining the Supreme Court rulings of 1973, now that Congress has led the way."[15]

In the abortion funding cases that were argued before the Supreme Court between 1976 and 1980, the Court backed away from viewing abortion as a medical service to which all women had a right. Now abortion became just another discretionary service that a consumer could or could not purchase, depending on how much money she had.

Since 1977 the federal government's decision to deny funding for abortions and reproductive counseling services for poor women—the Hyde Amendment—has mandated "forced motherhood" for unwillingly pregnant girls and women who don't have enough money to pay for private services. In recent years, the government has limited public access to information about abortion services and education about reproductive biology by funding "abstinence-only" curricula. At the same time, the government has backtracked on granting women access to birth control materials. As a result of these public policies, many women, especially low-income women dependent on public healthcare facilities, become pregnant and give birth against their will or better judgment.[16]

THE LEGACY

Reproductive politics has a long and complicated—and racially and economically conditioned—history in the United States. And clearly reproductive politics is still evolving, still one of the most intense sites for public debate about power relations in this country.

Women are no longer enslaved in the United States, so there are no more slave owners to sell the children of unfree mothers. Unmarried white mothers are no longer coerced to give their babies away for adoption. More women than ever are becoming mothers without husbands, although the teenage pregnancy rate has been falling for more than a decade. Single mothers today define their own status in a variety of ways, and the outcomes of their pregnancies are far less likely than in the mid-twentieth century to be dictated by their race. But since the replacement of the seventy-year-old Aid to Dependent Children program in 1996 with Temporary Assistance to Needy Families, poor women are no longer guaranteed public assistance while they have young children to support. Neither are they guaranteed access to the information or services they'd need to manage their fertility.

Once we've accepted that reproductive politics has a history—that the meanings and consequences of sex, pregnancy, motherhood and satellite issues change over time—we still need to underscore the fact that there is no single history of reproductive politics that can be traced from the eighteenth century to the twenty-first century in the United States. No one set of experiences can describe the conditions of fertility or sex-and-pregnancy for all women. In this multi-ethnic, multi-racial, class-structured society, we need different, sometimes overlapping, often completely distinct histories of reproductive politics to describe the experiences of demographically diverse groups of women. Reproductive politics has been important to the dynamic process of defining race since the beginning of the nation, and we continue to grapple with the legacy of this history in our debates about welfare and child policy, reform of the medical system, and immigration laws. "Choice" doesn't begin to describe the complicated range of options and constraints that confront different groups of fertile and heterosexually active women in contemporary America.

NOTES

1. Kathleen M. Brown, *Good Wives, Nasty Wenches, and Anxious Patriarchs* (Chapel Hill, NC: University of North Carolina Press, 1996), 207.
2. Brenda Stevenson, "Distress and Discord in Virginia Slave Families," in Vicki L. Ruiz and Ellen Carol DuBois, eds., *Unequal Sisters: A Multicultural Reader in U.S. Women's History*, 3rd ed. (New York: Routledge, 2000), 51; also see Deborah Gray White, *"Aren't I a Woman?": Female Slaves in the Plantation South* (New York: Oxford University Press, 1985).
3. Adrienne Dale Davis, "Don't Let Nobody Bother Yo' Principle: The Sexual Economy of American Slavery," in Sharon Harley and The Black Women and Work Collective, eds., *Sister Circle: Black Women and Work* (New Brunswick, NJ: Rutgers University Press, 2002), 109–110.
4. Mary Ryan, *Womanhood in America: From Colonial Times to the Present*, 2nd ed. (New York: New Viewpoints, 1979), 98; White, *Ar'n't I a Woman?*, 29.
5. Michael Sullivan DeFine, "A History of Govenmentally Coerced Sterilization: The Plight of the Native American Woman," 2; Jennifer Nelson, *Women of color and the Reproductive Rights Movement* (New York: New York University Press, 2003), Chapter 2.
6. Stephen Trombley, "Sterilization and Informed Consent in the 1960s," in *The Right to Reproduce: A History of Coercive Sterilization* (London: Weidenfeld and Nicholson, 1988), 175–213.
7. Elena Rebecca Guitterrez, "The Racial Politics of Reproduction: The Social Construction of Mexican-Origin Women's Fertility," Ph.D. diss, Sociology, University of Michigan, 1999, 204.
8. Bell, *ADC*, 97–99; Rickie Solinger, *Wake Up Little Susie: Single Pregnancy and Race before Roe v. Wade* (New York: Routledge, 2000), Chapters 1–2.
9. See, for example, The Congressional Record, 82d Cong., 1st sess., September 26, 1951, 97, pt. 9, "Fraud and Waste in Public Welfare Programs."
10. See Rickie Solinger, " 'Race and Value:' Black and White Illegitimate Babies in the U.S.A." *Gender & History* 4 (1992): 343–63.
11. Christopher Tietze, "Two years' experience with a liberal abortion law: Its impact on fertility trends in New York City," *Family Planning Perspectives* 5(1): 36–41, 1973. Stanley Henshaw, sociologist and Senior Fellow at The Alan Guttmacher Institute, writes, "I think the 70% figure is reasonable nationally. Other studies of national trends came to similar conclusions." Email to author, August 24, 2007.
12. Paltrow brief.
13. Paltrow brief.
14. *Congressional Record*—House, Vol. 123, Pt. 16, June 17, 1977, 19698–19715.
15. Lawrence Berger, M.D., "Abortions in America: The Effects of Restrictive Funding," *New England Journal of Medicine*, June 29, 1978.
16. Ehrenreich, "Surrogacy and Abortion Funding," 1395.

9

excerpt from

Ensuring Inequality: The Structural Transformation of the African-American Family
"World War II and its Aftermath"

Donna L. Franklin

So comprehensive and fundamental are the changes brought by war, and so closely is the family interrelated with larger society, that there is perhaps no aspect of family life unaffected by war.
Ernest Burgess, "The Effect of War on the American Family"

WORLD WAR II HAD a profound effect on American society. For the United States, it lasted twice as long as World War I, brought over fourteen million men and women into the armed forces, and added another ten million to the labor force. Family life, considered as an institution, began a period of significant change. As Arthur Marwick has argued, war always tests existing institutions, and sometimes leads to their transformation or collapse.[1] The severe strain World War II placed on African-American families involved two major challenges: the consequences of wartime disruption, and an exodus from the South that was twice as large as the one that occurred between 1910 and 1930. During the 1940s, 1.5 million blacks left the South. By the end of the decade, the proportion of blacks in urban areas would finally exceed those in rural areas—a shift that had been made by whites some thirty years before.[2]

WARTIME MIGRATION AND URBAN DISCONTENT

During the war more than fifteen million Americans, whites as well as blacks, migrated in search of better job opportunities in urban areas where the industrial economy was growing. Whereas blacks had migrated to the North during the 1930s to escape economic, social, and political oppression in the South, their migration in the 1940s—like that of millions of whites—was spurred by the revival of the nation's economy. For blacks, however, an additional combination of factors contributed to their patterns of northward migration, and their numbers in many northern cities grew to such an extent that in 1940 "new migrants outnumbered the original Negro dwellers eight to one."[3] As Gunnar Myrdal predicted in 1944, there was "bound to be a redefinition of the Negro's status in America" as a result of this war.[4]

One major factor in the northward movement of blacks was the decline in opportunities for agricultural workers caused largely by problems of soil depletion. As white tenant farmers migrated to urban areas in the South, competition between blacks and whites arose where none had existed before. In earlier decades, black workers had occupied a clearly defined niche in the labor market in southern cities: They held the jobs that white men did not want. When young whites moved in from the rural areas and started taking these jobs, blacks were at a distinct disadvantage in competing for them.

The displaced black workers of the South represented an ideal labor pool for the North, with its burgeoning economic activity. For northern industries, the black migrants of this second wave were more than willing to take bottom-level jobs at low wages, which were nonetheless higher than those they had previously received.[5] They fit Karl Marx's description of wage workers who did not own property: those who "bear the burdens of society without enjoying its advantages, are excluded from society and forced into the most resolute opposition to all other classes."[6]

THE ROOTS OF RACIAL UNREST

Although blacks were migrating in greater numbers to the North, with its promise of unprecedented opportunity, the same sort of Jim Crow laws that separated the races in the South were still on the books in many states in the North.[7] Government offices and military establishments were segregated, as were most public and private facilities, such as hotels, restaurants, railroad and bus stations, libraries, parks, and museums. When blacks sought legal redress, they found that the aim of Supreme Court decisions was to require more equality within separation, not to end the separation.[8]

The issue of equality versus separation was most clearly illustrated in the case of Arthur Mitchell of Chicago, the only African-American to serve in Congress during the 1940s. Mitchell sued after he was forced to move from his Pullman berth into a day coach when the train on which he was traveling crossed into Arkansas. The Supreme Court ruled that he should have been provided with all-black Pullman accommodations just as comfortable as those he had been forced to leave, but not that his rights had been violated when he was separated from the white passengers on the train. The Court said that the issue was "not a question of segregation but of equality of treatment." Mitchell praised the Court's decision as the "greatest advance in civil rights in my lifetime."[9]

As blacks migrated northward in greater numbers and found themselves excluded from expanding job opportunities, they became increasingly discontent and bitter. The migration itself was viewed with increasing alarm and soon attracted mounting opposition in the North. Racial clashes broke out in factories, schools, and neighborhoods in cities both large and small. In the big cities, especially in New York, a wave of violent crimes by young blacks against whites spread fear and panic throughout the white neighborhoods.

One of the problems that continued to plague black families was the difficulty of securing adequate housing. The construction of new homes during the war years was for the most part limited to white neighborhoods. When public housing for blacks was proposed, political battles generally erupted over location and funding. In the winter of 1940/1941, race riots—replete with bombings and burnings—broke out in Dallas in response to the white community's attempts to stop what it believed was a black neighborhood's encroachment on an all-white area. In 1942 riots broke out in Detroit when the Sojourner Truth Housing Project was built in a white area. Hundreds of whites beat and stoned blacks, and police assisted by turning their clubs on the blacks. When the skirmish ended, the twenty people injured and the one hundred arrested were all black.[10]

With the racial conflict escalating, A. Philip Randolph, president of the Brotherhood of Sleeping Car Porters, the first black trade union group in organized labor, decided to provide the leadership for a protest march for equal employment opportunity. Supported by the NAACP and the National Urban League, Randolph put out an appeal throughout the country, urging infuriated black Americans to march on Washington and demand their right to wartime jobs.[11]

THE PRESIDENTIAL REMEDY: EXECUTIVE ORDER 8802

In June 1941, President Franklin Roosevelt, seeing the distinct possibility that one hundred thousand blacks might march on Washington, issued Executive Order 8802 establishing the Committee on Fair Employment Practices (FEPC). This order mandated that federal contracts would be awarded only to those industries that would hire black and white workers on an equal basis. Nothing in the executive order banned segregation; it simply insisted on equality. Even with this narrowly circumscribed power, FEPC did not develop a strong record in settling complaints. Twenty-six of the thirty-five nondiscrimination compliance orders issued to employers in 1945 were simply ignored. In addition, nine of ten unions cited for discrimination by FEPC declined to follow compliance orders.[12]

In spite of this weak enforcement, government pressure and wartime labor shortages led to increased hiring of blacks in defense industries. Indeed, political pressure was basically all that Executive Order 8802 could provide. Compliance could be ordered by FEPC officials, and in theory government contractors who did not heed the order could lose their contracts. However, both the government officials and those they regulated knew that Congress and the public would never allow any major contract to be canceled.

In an effort to bring public attention to the grave difficulties blacks were having in securing employment, members of the FEPC used the meager funds appropriated to them to hold public hearings across the nation, at which employers were brought in and asked to give their reasons for hiring only a few blacks or none at all.[13] This process simply frustrated most members of the black community. They had already heard the reasons firsthand from employers; they wanted jobs, not publicity. In spite of their lack of faith in FEPC's ability to make substantive changes in the hiring practices of white employers, during the five-year period following the implementation of the Executive Order 8802, blacks filed fourteen thousand complaints of continued hiring discrimination.[14]

In 1944 blacks won an important victory in the judicial arena. In *Smith* v. *Allwright*, the Supreme Court ruled that excluding blacks from voting in Democratic Party primaries in the South was an unconstitutional infringement of their civil rights. Paradoxically, this victory led to more incidents of violence against southern black voters, thereby increasing the migration of blacks to the North.[15]

THE AFRICAN-AMERICAN MALE AND MILITARY SERVICE

While FEPC was directing attention to discrimination in industry, the question of who would put an end to discrimination in the military remained unanswered. Black organizations such as the NAACP and the National Urban League, founded in 1909 and 1911 respectively, were just beginning to formulate their organizational policies when America entered World War I in 1917. The Selective Service Act of May 1917 did not exclude blacks, and almost three million were registered under the Act. They were accepted for service in the four black army regiments, but once those regiments were filled, they were turned away.[16]

By 1939, the United States Army had only 3,640 black regular soldiers and only five black officers, three of whom were chaplains. African-Americans were excluded entirely from the Marine Corps and the Army Air Corps, and the navy and the Coast Guard were permitting blacks to participate only on a limited basis.[17] With the war imminent, black men wanted to demonstrate their patriotism through military service. But they also wanted to bring an end to segregation by participating fully and equally in the armed forces. Neil Wynn, a historian who has studied blacks in World War II, asserts that "military service thus became central to the whole campaign for civil rights."[18]

Significant changes in the black community between World Wars I and II had increased the chance that racial restrictions on military service could be eliminated. Not only was the black community more urbanized, but its greater sophistication and race consciousness were reflected in the growing circulation of black newspapers and increased membership in civil rights organizations. By 1940, the NAACP had a membership approaching ninety thousand and a budget of over $60,000, and the combined circulation of more than 150 black newspapers totaled 1,276,600.[19]

African-American organizational efforts were most clearly evident in the Committee for the Participation of Negroes in National Defense, created specifically to ensure black participation in the war effort. With primary sponsorship from the *Pittsburg Courier*, an influential black newspaper, and under the leadership of Rayford W. Logan, a veteran of World War I, the committee begin a campaign to end discrimination. With the primary goal of changing military policies, the committee set out to coordinate the efforts of individuals and organizations during the years 1939 through 1941.

In 1941 local draft boards were inducting black men, but only when necessary to meet their quotas; only two thousand blacks were drafted during the first year of Selective Service. By December 1941, however, one hundred thousand black soldiers had enlisted in the army, in that enlisting was easier than waiting to be drafted. The army still held to its policy of segregated units, however, and hospitals, mess halls, and recreational facilities—including theatres, post exchanges, and canteens on the bases—were roughly equal but always separate. The policy that was most offensive to black men, however, was the one that prevented them from serving in combat units.[20]

Racial violence erupted at army bases, and both black and white soldiers were left dead and wounded as blacks begin to demand greater opportunities within the military establishment. In a typical incident, reported in the *New York Times* on April 3, 1942, three soldiers were killed and five others wounded after an argument between black and white soldiers over who would have first use of a telephone booth. A racial outburst in Fayetteville, North Carolina, in August 1941 left two soldiers dead and five wounded. At another army post an hour-long gun battle, between an entire company of black soldiers and a company of military police, left a dozen dead and wounded. Ironically, the first man in the United States Army to be killed in World War II was a black sergeant, brought down by a U.S. M-1 rifle.[21]

BLACK WOMEN SEIZE ECONOMIC OPPORTUNITIES

As local economies expanded and large numbers of men went into the armed services, the ensuing labor shortage opened up many traditionally male fields to women.[22] Aware of women's potential contributions to national goals, four state legislatures enacted equal pay laws during the war, and a number of states passed laws protecting married women from discrimination in employment. For the first time, Congress considered an equal pay bill and an equal rights amendment to the Constitution.[23]

The wartime expansion of the economy brought important changes in the labor force participation of both black and white females. The employment of black women increased from 1.5 million
to 2.1 million between 1940 and 1944, but their share of the total female labor force declined from
13.8 to 12.5 percent. These changes reflect three primary factors:

1. Before the war, the labor force participation of black women was relatively higher than that of
   white women.
2. The war economy improved the the employment prospects of black men, thereby decreasing the
   need for black women to go into the labor market.[24]
3. Black women entered the labor force much more slowly because of the persistence of racial
   discrimination.[25]

Although a 1943 poll found that black women were more willing to accept unappealing jobs than
white women, they were still at a distinct disadvantage in the burgeoning labor market for several
reasons.[26] Charles S. Johnson noted that black women remained in "the most marginal position of
all classes of labor."[27]

First, because of the kinds of jobs created in the defense industries, employers had a clear
preference for male workers, and even in the face of critical labor shortages, they were reluctant to
hire women to fill jobs that had traditionally been held by men.[28] When women were actually hired
to fill such positions, they were expected to retain their "femininity"; and since black women were
perceived as less "feminine" than white women, they were generally given the most demanding and
lowest-paying jobs. Denying black women jobs in the newly opened war industries was one means
of "keeping them in their place."[29]

Second, many employers were unwilling to integrate the working areas inside their plants and
often defended their actions by claiming that were not enough black women workers to warrant
setting up separate facilities. Work stoppages did occur in many plants where black women were
hired; but Karen Anderson has noted that when union–management education efforts among
whites were coupled with a firm commitment by employers, the result was a smooth integration of
black workers.[30]

Finally, black women went into the newly created war industries in such large numbers that
nearly half of all white housewives lost their black domestics. One domestic who left work for a
higher-paying factory job put it this way: "Lincoln freed the Negroes from cotton picking and Hitler
was the one that got us out of the white folks' kitchen."[31] The black domestics who were still willing
to work in white households during the war charged twice as much, were less willing to live in, and
refused to do many of the chores (such as window washing) they had done before the war. Susan
Hartmann has noted that domestic workers who found better-paying jobs in factories, offices, and
service industries "enjoyed the higher wages and better conditions as well as the independence,
social contacts, and 'self-respect' that attended their new occupations."[32]

Although the war opened up new areas of employment to black women (Figure 9.1), racial
discrimination kept them at a disadvantage in their competition with white women. They had
difficulty getting admitted to training programs, and found that even training courses did not
remove the difficulty of getting hired. For instance, in Cape Girardeau, Missouri, ten black women
applied for jobs at a clothing plant that made WAC uniforms. Because their previous experience had
been in domestic service and home sewing, plant officials refused to hire them on the grounds that
they had no experience with power sewing machines. Yet when another group of black women in
St. Louis completed 200 to 600 hours of training on power sewing machines, they were nevertheless
refused jobs by firms producing military uniforms. (Three of them found work in a cartridge plant,

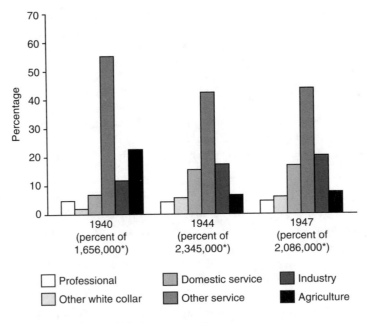

* Total number of black woman workers

Figure 9.1 Black women's employment patterns, by type of employment, 1940–1947. (From D'Ann Campbell, *Women at War with America: Private Lives in a Patriotic Era* [Cambridge, Mass.: Harvard University Press, 1984], 240)

where their training was irrelevant.) The managers of the St. Louis firms defended their actions by pointing to work stoppages that had occurred in other midwestern plants when black women were employed.[33]

After an FEPC investigation found that the highest salaried black employee in one federal agency was the director's chauffeur, and that only 2 percent of another agency's employees were black, the federal government undertook an aggressive campaign to recruit for black employees.[34] Between 1940 and 1942, a large number of black women were hired for federal clerical positions, though they were segregated from white clerks.[35] When black women were recruited and hired for certain positions, they had found it harder to get promotions than white women. In a survey that followed blacks and whites with similar efficiency ratings, it was found that whites received promotions six times more often than blacks.[36]

As noted earlier, black women who were lucky enough to be hired were assigned to the hardest, least desirable jobs. For example, the Pennsylvania Railroad in Baltimore hired about fifty black women in 1943 for work that was sweltering, burdensome, and sometimes hazardous: Some served as water and fire tenders, keeping up the fire and steam in the locomotives, and others did various kinds of unskilled physical labor. Similarly, a black woman interviewed by the Women's Bureau in Baltimore reported that her job as a loader at the arsenal entailed lifting fifty-five-pound boxes of TNT all day for the meager wage of $18 a week. Although their participation in factory work quadrupled, black women were heavily concentrated in positions of janitors, sweepers, and material handlers.[37]

Although the federal government had established FEPC to safeguard employment opportunities for racial minorities, government agencies themselves were often guilty of discrimination. For example, the War Department allowed the supervisors of armories, plants, and warehouses under its supervision to refuse jobs to black women. In 1943, an advertisement was reportedly posted in the Pentagon cafeterias and dining rooms for "competent white female help." In Cincinnati, Ohio, black women who applied to the United States Employment Service for work indicated that they were either ignored or referred to domestic or maintenance jobs.[38]

The challenges that black women faced in the workplace during the war years were not ameliorated by the domestic propaganda campaigns engaged in by the Office of War Information (OWI). In films, newsreels, newspapers, and magazines, the OWI sought to boost home-front morale and encourage industry to deal with labor shortages equitably, in part by hiring more women. According to Maureen Honey, this propaganda improved the images of white women as workers but did nothing for blacks:

> In wartime stories, no blacks appeared as heroes or heroines, and they were cast in the lowest occupational ratings of all groups surveyed. Furthermore, they (along with Jews) were the only group to possess more disapproved than approved character traits. In short, . . . the war had no positive impact on the fictional treatment of black people.[39]

MARRIAGE AND MARITAL DISSOLUTION DURING THE WAR

During the economic crisis of the 1930s, many marriages had been postponed. In 1946 more than 2.2 million couples said their vows, twice as many as in any year before the war, and set a nuptial record that was not equaled for 33 years.[40] And while the economic boom brought in by the war was the catalyst for a rush to the altar for blacks and whites, Figure 9.2 demonstrates that the marriage rates were even higher for black males than for white males. Although the marriage rates for black males were considerably higher prior to the war, both black and white males had similar increases from 1939 to 1941 (about 16 percent). In 1942, however, with the increased tempo of the draft and the favorable opportunity for black male employment for the first time in war industries, the rise in the marriage rate was much more significant for blacks than for whites.

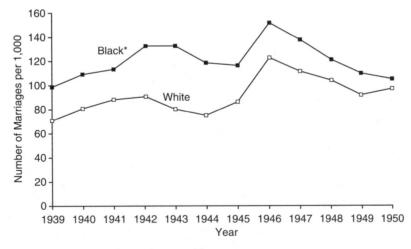

*Figures for blacks are for non-whites

Figure 9.2 Marriages per 1,000 eligible males, 1939–1950. Marriage eligibles represent single men fifteen years or older and all divorced or widowed men, as of July 1 of each year. (From Paul Jacobson, *American Marriage and Divorce* [New York: Rinehart, 1959], 102)

Clearly, the marriage boom reflected the influence of the war. Many young people married in order to experience marital intimacy before the husband was shipped overseas. While some married to avoid the draft, others wed to acquire the benefits provided to dependents of military personnel.[41] For example, a monthly allotment check of $50 and a life insurance policy of $10,000 was given to the wife of each enlisted man. Women who married for these reasons were sometimes referred to as "Allotment Annies."[42] The marriage rates were highest for blacks and whites, however, during 1946 and 1947, when soldiers were returning home from the war.

Black marriage rates were increasing for another reason. With the enlistment of black men in the armed services and the increase in the total number of employees required for the booming war industries, the black male employment rate rose sharply almost overnight. Equally important, the new jobs were no longer confined to semiskilled work; thousands of blacks were now integrated into the manufacturing and industrial sector of the economy as skilled laborers. Black men had employment opportunities that were unparalleled at any other time in American history.[43]

While the war and the growth it created in the economy was an impetus for marriage, the opening up of higher-paying jobs to women narrowed the gap in income levels between males and females and created more tension in marital relationships. According to one study that examined the effects of working wives on family power relationships, the stresses were greater in working-class households than in middle-class ones.[44]

Even though a disproportionate number of black marriages would be classified as working-class, two different patterns emerged among blacks, both placing strain on their marriages. First, black males made greater economic gains than black females during the war years, thereby enhancing their authority within the family; this shift decreased the marital power of many black women who had previously "controlled the purse strings." Second, many black women were able to move up from domestic work to higher-paying industrial jobs, thereby increasing further their economic independence and paradoxically placing additional strain on the marriages.

In a minority of the black families, stressful marriages were rejuvenated as the result of the war. Before the war, the Brown family lived in Des Moines, Iowa. Howard Brown was an unemployed porter, with a wife and three children, who yearned for a law degree that seemed far beyond his reach. Sarah Brown became the sole provider of the family and amassed a great deal of anger and resentment toward Howard and became emotionally distant from him. She turned to her children both for help in the home and for the companionship her husband failed to give. She also came to enjoy the freedom and independence her job gave her. Sarah did not seek a divorce, however, "for the sake of the children." Howard enlisted in the army and spent his military years in New York, where he was drawn into the excitement of the Harlem scene. He wrote long letters home, full of longing for Sarah and dreams for the future. The new mood continued upon his return to Des Moines, and he enrolled in a local college on the GI bill to pursue his dream of becoming a lawyer. In addition, he spent much more time in the home being helpful to Sarah and playing with the children.[45]

In many cases wartime brides and grooms hardly got to know each other before the husband left for active duty; many such marriages were predictably undone when the veterans returned home. In the late 1930s, 85 marriages in 10,000 had ended in divorce, whereas between 1941 and 1945 the figure rose to 114. And in 1946 and 1947, the years when many veterans returned from the war, the annual rate climbed to 158 per 10,000, the same years in which marriage rates skyrocketed.[46]

When we look at the number of divorces per one thousand married males by race, however, somewhat different patterns emerge. The divorce rate for both black and white males hit its peak in

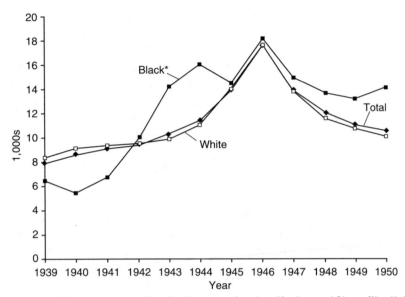

Figure 9.3 Divorces per 1,000 married males. (From Paul Jacobson, *American Marriage and Divorce* [New York: Rinehart, 1959], 102)

1946, at 18.7 and 18.1 per thousand, respectively; but the rates for whites dropped every year thereafter until 1950 (Figure 9.3), while for blacks, although the divorce rates declined somewhat, from 1948 to 1950 there was very little change. In 1939 white males had a divorce rate of 8.6 per thousand, compared to 6.6 for black males. By 1950 this rate had climbed to 13.9 for black males and had stabilized at 9.8 for white males.

As these figures suggest, divorce among black males was relatively infrequent during the early part of the century: Until the war years, desertion or informal separation were still the accepted means of dissolving a marriage. This was especially the case in the rural South, and these practices were probably carried to urban centers as blacks migrated north. Paul Jacobson has maintained that the "relatively greater upswing" in the black divorce rate since World War II has also been due in large measure to economic factors. As black males gained more financial security vis-à-vis black women during the 1940s, they emulated the practice of white males by retaining lawyers and filing divorce petitions to safeguard their earnings from their separated wives.[47]

THE DESTABILIZATION OF THE BLACK FAMILY

During the 1940s, several developments were drawing attention to the metamorphosis of the American family. Births to single women doubled during the decade, and there was a dramatic increase in juvenile delinquency.[48] A sample of eighty-three municipal courts showed an increase in cases from 65,000 to 75,500 between 1940 and 1942. Delinquency increased twice as fast among white girls as black girls and three times as fast among white boys as black boys. Delinquency reached a peak in 1943, the year in which the most mothers were employed.[49]

Obviously, the prolonged separation of husbands from wives was a major disruptive factor. In 1948, John Durand tabulated the percentage of husbands absent from their wives and controlled for race. He found that in 1944, in the age category 20–24, 19.3 percent of white women and 19.4

percent of black women had an absent spouse. In the age categories 25–29 and 30–34, however, these percentages dropped sharply for white women to 13.3 and 13.1; for black women, however, they declined only slightly to 16.1 and 18.4, respectively.[50]

These higher rates of absence encouraged infidelity of both spouses.[51] But the double standard prevailed: Infidelity on the part of a soldier/husband was viewed as natural and inevitable, but a wife's infidelity was harshly censured. For example, an army chaplain, Captain H. A. Robinson, wrote a column in the *Baltimore Afro-American* in which he warned that servicemen's wives who were not faithful to their husbands could have their allotments terminated or be divorced by their husbands.[52]

World War II brought about unprecedented opportunities for extramarital and premarital experiences, by facilitating the shift to urban living and providing youth with more economic autonomy and freedom from adult supervision. As many young men left home to join the armed services, many young women left home in search of jobs. During the 1940s, moral reformers were most concerned with the behavior of "victory girls" or "good-time Charlottes," whereas during World War I their attention had been focused on the dangers presented to young men by prostitution.[53]

The moral reformers were likewise alarmed at the skyrocketing birthrates to unmarried women. In 1940, the rate for unmarried white women in the 15–44 age group was 3.6 per thousand, but it increased to 5.1 in 1945 and stabilized at 5.8 in 1950. For unmarried blacks, the rate was 39.7 in 1940, then 45.3 in 1945; and 69.1 in 1950. Thus, births to unmarried black women, already much higher, increased dramatically from 1945 to 1950, a time when births to unmarried white women were stabilizing.[54]

Among unmarried black women, the age cohort that had the highest increase were the adolescents. When Cutright conducted a more detailed analysis of trends in births to unmarried black teenagers aged 14, 15–17, and 18–19, he found that among those aged 14 and under the rate increased by about six per thousand between 1940 and 1950, whereas for whites the change was insignificant. In addition, for blacks in the age category 15–17, the rate increased from 38 to 53 per thousand, and for whites the rate rose from four to five. During the 1940s there was a precipitous increase in adolescent childbearing among unmarried blacks, although it would not be formally identified as a social problem until the 1970s.[55]

On the positive side, African-Americans benefited in at least two ways during the war years. First, the average income of black families more than doubled between 1939 and 1945, even though it still fell far below that of whites.[56] A study conducted by the Harlem Children's Center in 1942 found that the number of black households on public welfare, as well as the number of undernourished children, had diminished. It also claimed that better employment opportunities had given black men a new measure of self-respect, which it viewed as having a positive influence on family relationships.[57]

Second, maternal and infant mortality rates took an especially sharp plunge in the 1940s, for blacks and whites alike. While the drop was due in part to the increasing incidence of hospital delivery and new medical procedures, another factor was congressional authorization of the Emergency Maternity and Infant Care (EMIC) program in 1943. Through this program, the federal government subsidized the cost of medical care for the wives and infants of enlisted men.[58] The rates of infant and maternal mortality for blacks plummeted in the 1940s, although the maternal mortality rate for black women remained three times higher than the rate for white women.[59] These gains for black women were a direct result of their having husbands in the military; the risks in pregnancy and childbearing for all other black women remained unchanged.[60]

POSTWAR ADJUSTMENT

After the defeat of Germany and the surrender of Japan, employment in defense industries was cut in half. Within a year of Japan's surrender in August 1945, nine million servicemen and women were discharged, and the government canceled war contracts worth more than $35 billion. In 1946 the weakening position of African-American workers became more precarious when Congress refused to appropriate funds for FEPC. President Truman refused to establish another such commission but instead ordered the inclusion of nondiscrimination clauses in defense contracts.

The limited protection FEPC had provided was sorely needed in the aftermath of the war, for various blatant forms of discrimination reappeared. A report published in 1947 by the National Committee on Segregation in the Nation's Capital found that discrimination remained as prevalent as ever.[61] In a particularly flagrant example, federal agencies that had aggressively recruited black clerical workers during the war now posted flyers listing clerical job openings for "whites only."[62]

Blacks remained optimistic, however, that during these postwar years black women would be able to retreat to their homes and take care of their families. In March 1947, an editorial in *Ebony* entitled "Goodbye Mammy, Hello Mom," pointed out that black women had never historically had the opportunity to devote their full attention to their families, but now for the first time "since 1619" they would enjoy the benefits derived from their husbands' high wages. The article ended by noting that "the cooking over which the 'white folks' used to go into ecstasies is now reserved for her own family and they really appreciate it."[63]

What this writer did not anticipate, however, was that the stressors that had burdened the black family "since 1619" would finally take their toll, and many black women would retreat to homes without husbands and the benefits derived from their wages. By 1950, African-American mothers were single parents at twice the rate of white women: In that year 17.6 percent of black families were headed by a woman, compared to 8.5 percent of white families.[64]

Not only were black women more likely to be without husbands, but the war had done little to enhance their position in the labor force. By the end of the decade, black women continued to be the lowest paid workers, with incomes lagging behind both white women and black men. Whereas black women continued to earn less than half the income of white women, the income of black men relative to white men grew from just 41 percent in 1939 to 61 percent by 1950. Even with husbands present, 30.2 percent of black wives worked, compared to only 19.6 percent of their white counterparts.[65]

The wartime labor shortage did make it possible for black women to prove their capabilities in skilled and semiskilled jobs that had once been closed to them, but most of them were not able to hold on to those jobs.[66] In 1950 the percentage of black women in domestic service was greater than it had been in 1940, and their labor force participation remained steady at about 37 percent.[67] In contrast, the rate for white women rose from 24.5 to 28.4 percent. In most major northern cities, the jobless rate for black women was three to four times higher than for foreign-born white women.[68]

During the postwar years, black migrants continued to flow into the northern cities, where white neighborhoods used restrictive real estate covenants and acts of violence to keep them confined to certain sections of town. The declining conditions in the ghettos, coupled with tenuous access to adequate health care, increased the prevalence of disease among blacks and pushed mortality rates for blacks higher in the cities than in rural areas.

Stanley Lieberson has found that between 1930 and 1950 there was "substantial deterioration in the unemployment situation of blacks" compared to whites, both immigrant and native. And while he found "no deterioration in the black educational position in the North through 1930," he has shown that by the 1950s the relatively favorable educational position of blacks compared to new immigrants had largely eroded.[69]

Perhaps the assault on black families during the postwar years is most clearly reflected in the divorce and separation rates for black couples, which were four times as high as whites'. This greater incidence of marital disruption was directly related to the high rate of black male unemployment.[70] And, of course, the problems of black families were exacerbated by a fertility rate much higher than that reported for whites.[71]

Many black women expressed an unwillingness to return to domestic service after having worked in industry. Here are the reasons given by one of them:

[Some people say] they can't be as bad as they seem to me—these women I have worked for as a domestic . . . so overbearing, so much a slavedriver, so unwilling to grant us even a small measure of human dignity. But I have had three years of experience in at least a dozen households to bear eloquent witness to the contrary.

Take this matter of inconsiderateness, of downright selfishness. No other women workers have the slave hours we domestics have. We usually work twelve and fourteen hours a day, seven days a week, except for our pitiful little "Thursday afternoon off . . ." See how your legs ache after being on them from 7:00 a.m. to 9:00 p.m., when you are finishing the last mountain of dishes in the pantry!

. . . It is not only the long hours, the small pay, and the lack of privacy—we often have to share a room with the children—that we maids find hardest to bear. It is being treated most of the time as though we are completely lacking in human dignity and self respect. During my first years at this work I was continually hopeful. But now I know that when I enter the service elevator I should park my self-respect there along with the garbage that clutters it.[72]

With few alternatives available to them, many destitute black mothers applied to ADC for financial assistance. (After 1950, ADC became AFDC, or Aid to Families with Dependent Children.) There was likewise a precipitious increase in the number of black adolescent mothers applying for AFDC, in that adolescent childbearing among blacks proliferated for the first time during the 1950s. As the welfare rolls expanded, the late 1940s had brought violent pervasive attacks on ADC. As Harold Silver of Detroit noted in his address to the Family Service Association of America in 1950, "the headlines and impressions created by the press were that from 30 to 50 percent of the AFDC program's clientele were 'fraud' and 'chiselers,' that millions of dollars of tax funds were being wasted through carelessness and negligence of administration." Silver then points out that in 1948, an exhaustive investigation of the Department of Public Welfare in Detroit had found that only two warrants for fraud had been issued, and that neither one had resulted in conviction.[73]

CONCLUSION

World War II placed severe strains on all American families, but its heaviest impact was felt by the African-American family, weakened by slavery, sharecropping, and the northern migration. During the 1940s, twice the number of blacks migrated to the North than had relocated there between 1910 and 1930. By the end of the postwar decade, the proportion of blacks in urban areas would finally exceed those in rural areas—a shift that had been made by whites some 30 years before.

The war catalyzed an unprecedented tide of migration for whites as well. The federal government's efforts to remedy shortages in housing and schools were not only inadequate but were aimed primarily at white communities. And occasional attempts to assist the black community were met with strong resistance from whites. Race riots broke out in many cities when black neighborhoods were perceived as encroaching on all-white areas. In these skirmishes, blacks were invariably the ones injured or arrested.

With FEPC abandoned and defense industries shutting down, discrimination in the labor market proliferated, and black employment rates plummeted. By the end of the war, the proportion of black women in domestic service was greater than it had been in 1941. The jobless rate for black women was three to four times greater than for foreign-born white women. By 1948 most of the gains that blacks had made during the wartime boom had been wiped out, and labor analysts predicted that the security of the black worker would depend almost entirely on a strong economy.

Facing a weakened economy without the social controls once provided by the communal aspects of southern life, black marriages disintegrated, and out-of-wedlock births proliferated, especially among adolescents. Although clearly disadvantaged in their competition with white women for jobs in the labor market, many black women opted not to return to the paltry wages and irregular hours of the domestic service jobs they had held before the war. In an effort to cope with their much higher rates of desertion, separation, and divorce from black men, and with the difficulty of securing support from the financially beleaguered fathers, black mothers became more reliant on welfare.

In the postwar political climate of patriotic fervor and obsession with the threat of communism, government programs to help the poor were often criticized as "creeping socialism," and were attacked with little abatement until the presidential election of 1952. Although many of these attacks were groundless and inaccurately documented, welfare leaders found it difficult to rebut them, because the real problem was not the socialistic nature of government programs but the failure of black family patterns, with all their handicaps, to conform to mainstream norms. Unfortunately, public ignorance about the complexity of these handicaps would persist for decades, and the plight of poor black families would become increasingly distinct and desperate.

NOTES

1. Arthur Marwick, *War and Social Change in the Twentieth Century* (New York: St. Martin's Press, 1974), 6–14.
2. Reynolds Farley, *The Growth of the Black Population* (Chicago: Markham, 1970), 42. Jack T. Kirby, "The Southern Exodus, 1910–60: A Primer for Historians," *Journal of Southern History* 49 (November 1983): 585–600. Kirby argues that the earlier migration was partly responsible for the direction and volume of the larger migration that followed, because it established "interregional networks of family and friends" (592).
3. Robert C. Weaver, *Negro Labor: A National Problem* (New York: Harcourt, Brace & Co, 1946), 91. Although some social analysts had argued that this boom in the nation's economy spurred the migration patterns for blacks as well as whites, a closer analysis revealed that it applied only to whites. See Harold B. Myers for the argument that the 1930s was a "depression" migration and the 1940s was an "economic boom" migration, making no distinctions between blacks and whites, "Defense Migration and Labor Supply," *Journal of the American Statistical Association* 37 (March 1942). This analysis was challenged by Daniel M. Johnson and Rex R. Campbell, *Black Migration in America: A Social Demographic History* (Durham, N.C.: Duke University Press, 1981), ch. 8. For figures on the growth of black migration to the North, see Robert C. Weaver, *Negro Labor: A National Problem* (New York: Harcourt, Brace, 1946), 91. On the competition between whites and blacks for jobs in southern cities, see T. J. Woofter, Jr., "Southern Population and Social Planning," *Social Forces* 14(October 1935): 609–18.
4. Gunnar Myrdal, *An America Dilemma* (New York: Harper, 1944), 997.
5. For further details on migration to areas with a sizable number of defense industries, see Department of Commerce, Census Bureau, *Current Population Reports*, series P-23, no. 42, *The Social and Economic Status of the Black Population in the United States, 1971* (Washington, D.C.: Government Printing Office, 1972), 18. See also Weaver, *Negro Labor*.
6. Quoted in T. B. Bottomore, *Karl Marx* (Glencoe, Ill.: Free Press, 1950), 64.
7. As late as 1949, only eighteen states had passed laws that would make it illegal to discriminate on the basis of race in public facilities, and even those laws were limited in application. For a closer examination of the various forms of segregation in most states and the laws that enforced them, see Richard Bardolph, ed., *The Civil Rights Record: Black Americans and the Law, 1849–1970* (New York: Crowell, 1970).

8.   Blacks did not accept the social humiliation of segregation passively. When more forceful forms of opposition were blocked, they used other means, like placing "out of order" signs on white restrooms (to force whites to use the same facilities) or painting over the signs designating "colored" or "white." See Benjamin Muse, *American Negro Revolution* (Bloomington: University of Indiana Press, 1968); Frank A. Aukofer, *City With a Chance: A Case History of Civil Rights Revolution* (Milwaukee: Bruce, 1968).

9.   Quoted in Geoffrey Perrett, *Days of Sadness, Years of Triumph: The American People 1939–1945* (New York: Coward, McCann & Geoghegan 1973) 148.

10.   Karen Tucker Anderson, *Wartime Women: Sex Roles, Family Relations and the Status of Women During WW II* (Westport, Conn., Greenwood Press, 1981), 80. Perrett, *Days of Sadness,* 312.

11.   For a discussion on social action taken by blacks during the wartime period for jobs, see Herbert Garfinkel, *When Negroes March: The March on Washington Movement in the Organizational Politics for FEPC* (Glencoe, Ill.: Free Press, 1959). For a discussion of the role of FEPC and the leadership of A. Philip Randolph, see Louis C. Kesselman, *The Social Politics of FEPC: A Study in Reform Movements* (Chapel Hill: University of North Carolina Press, 1948).

12.   Kesselman, *Social Politics of FEPC,* 23n; Harvard Sitkoff, *A New Deal for Blacks: The Emergence of Civil Rights as a National Issue* (New York: Oxford University Press, 1978).

13.   On the efforts of local black workers to put pressure on FEPC, see Lester B. Granger, "A Hopeful Sign in Race Relations," *Survey Graphic* 23 (November 1944), 355–56; William H. Harris, "Federal Intervention in Union Discrimination: FEPC and West Coast Shipyards during World War II," *Labor History* 22 (Summer 1981): 325–47; John C. Walter, "Frank R. Crosswaith and Labor Unionization in Harlem, 1939–45," *Afro-Americans in New York Life and History 7* (July 1983): 47–58.

14.   It should be noted that black women filed more than one of every four discrimination complaints heard by FEPC between July 1943 and December 1944. But even when black women were hired, they were the first to be laid off. These FEPC figures are taken from George E. Demar, "Negro Women Are American Workers, Too," *Opportunity: Journal of Negro Life* 21 (April 1943): 41–42. On the complaints filed for continued discrimination and the challenges that the FEPC faced as it endeavored to settle complaints, see Malcolm Ross, *All Manner of Men* (New York: Reynal and Hitchcock, 1948) and Philip S. Foner, *Organized Labor and the Black Worker, 1916–1973* (New York: Praeger, 1973).

15.   For a closer examination of the struggle for black voting rights in the South during the 1940s, see John Hope Franklin, *From Slavery to Freedom,* 7th ed. (New York: Knopf, 1994); Thomas R. Brooks, *Walls Come Tumbling Down: A History of the Civil Rights Movement 1940–1970* (Englewood Cliffs, N.J.: Prentice-Hall, 1994).

16.   For an analysis of the black experience in World War I, from the perspective of the black soldier, see Kingsley Moses, "The Negro Comes North," and John Richards, "Some Experiences with Colored Soldiers," in *World War I at Home: Readings on American Life, 1914–1920,* ed. David F. Trask (New York: Wiley, 1970). The problems the black men faced in the army during World War I were aggravated by an Army Signal Corps film entitled *Training of Colored Troops,* which presented stereotypic images of blacks. This film, a dramatized portrayal of a black soldier from induction to training, contributed further to the negative image of the black soldiers by highlighting a watermelon-eating and dancing competition; National Archives Film Library, NA 111H–1211–PPSA-1.

17.   Ulysses G. Lee, *The Employment of Negro Troops: The U.S. Army in World War II* (Washington, D.C., Center for Military History, U.S. Army 1966), 29–38; Richard M. Dalfiume, "The Forgotten Years of the Negro Revolutions," in *The Negro in Depression and War,* ed. Bernard Sternsher (Chicago: Quadrangle Books, 1969); John W. Davis, "The Negro in the United States Navy, Marine Corps, and Coast Guard," *Journal of Negro Education* 12 (Summer 1943): 345–349.

18.   Neil A. Wynn, *The Afro-American Experience and the Second World War,* rev. ed. (New York: Holmes & Meier, 1993), 21. On the status of black servicemen during the war, see also W. Y. Bell, Jr., "The Negro Warrior's Home Front," *Phylon* 5 (Third Quarter 1944): 271–78; Mary Frances Berry and John W. Blassingame, *Long Memory: The Black Experience in America* (New York: Oxford University Press, 1992): 320–30.

19.   Langston Hughes, *Fight for Freedom: The Story of the NAACP* (New York, 1962), 197–98; Wynn, *Afro-American Experience,* 19. In 1943 the NAACP received over $5,000 from servicemen, and by the end of the war donations from soldiers amounted to $25,000, and some fifteen thousand had joined the organization.

20.   One survey found that all blacks were not opposed to segregation. As many as 40 percent thought separate post exchanges were a good idea, 48 per cent thought them a poor idea, and 12 percent were undecided. Thirty-eight percent of those questioned favored racially separate units, 36 percent wanted integrated ones, and 26 percent were undecided; Wynn, *Afro-American Experiences,* 28–29.

21.   Perrett, *Days of Sadness,* 153.

22.   For a review of the changing opportunity structure for women during the Second World War, see Joan Ellen Trey, "Women in the War Economy," *Review of Radical Political Economics* 4 (July 1972); Eleanor Straub, "Government Policy toward Civilian Women during World War II" (Ph.D. diss., Emory University, 1973); Leila Rupp, *Mobilizing Women for War: German and American Propaganda, 1939–1945* (Princeton: Princeton University Press, 1978); William Chafe, *The American Woman: Her Changing Social, Economic, and Political Roles, 1920–1970* (New York: Oxford University Press, 1972); D'Ann Campbell, *Women at War with America: Private Lives in a Patriotic Era* (Cambridge, Mass.: Harvard University Press, 1984); Susan M. Hartmann, *The Home Front and Beyond: American Women in the 1940s* (Boston: Twayne Publishers, 1982).

23.   Hartmann, *Home Front and Beyond,* 22.

24. A Florida survey found that "since the war started the Negro men had higher incomes and they could afford to have a higher standard of living. Therefore, their wives and children no longer had to cook for the whites." For the Florida survey results in their entirety see Howard W. Odum, *Folk, Region, and Society* (Chapel Hill: University of North Carolina Press, 1964), 63.

25. Nora R. Tucker and Thomasina W. Norford, "Ten Years of Progress: The Negro Woman in the Labor Force," in *Women United*, Souvenir Year Book (National Council of Negro Women, 1951); Mary S. Bedell, "Employment and Income of Negro Workers—1940–52," *Monthly Labor Review* 76 (June 1953): 596–601; Department of Labor, Women's Bureau *Negro Women War Workers*, Bulletin no. 202 (Washington, D.C., 1945). For a comprehensive analysis of black women's employment experiences during World War II, see Jacqueline Jones, *Labor of Love, Labor of Sorrow, Black Women's Work and the Family from Slavery to the Present* (New York: Basic Books, 1985), ch. 7; Karen Tucker Anderson, "Last Hired, First Fired: Black Women Workers During World War II," *Journal of American History* 69 (June 1982): 82–97.

26. A Roper poll found that three out of four black women were willing to take factory jobs, whereas only one in eight white women found factory work acceptable. Factory work was also acceptable to those with only an elementary education (37 percent), in contrast to its rejection by better-educated women (2 percent). Education and socio-economic/racial status clearly overlapped, in that most black women had attained less education than white women. The analysis of variance demonstrated that both race and class had a strong independent effect; Roper-*Fortune* poll 35, May 1943, Roper Center, Williams College.

27. Quoted in Philip S. Foner, *Women and the American Labor Movement: From World War I to the Present* (New York: Free Press, 1980), 344.

28. Campbell, *Women at War*, chapter 4 provides an excellent overview of attitudes and practices of male employers and workers.

29. For popular attitudes regarding women and employment during the 1930s and 1940s, see Rupp, *Mobilizing Women for War*, Lois Scharf, *To Work and to Wed: Female Employment, Feminism, and the Great Depression* (Westport, Conn.: Greenwood Press, 1980); Mary Kelly, ed., *Woman's Being, Woman's Place: Female Identity and Vocation in American History* (Boston: Hall, 1979).

30. Straub, "Government Policy toward Civilian Women," pp. 297–300; Anderson, "Last Hired, First Fired," 7.

31. Quoted in Odum, *Folk, Region, and Society*, 63.

32. Hartmann, *Home Front and Beyond*, 90

33. Straub, "Government Policy toward Civilian Women," 302.

34. For examples of discrimination in federal agencies during the pre- and postwar years, see Samuel Krislov, *The Negro in Federal Employment: The Quest for Equal Opportunity* (Minneapolis: University of Minnesota Press, 1967); L.J.W. Hayes, *The Negro Government Worker* (Washington, D.C.: Howard University Graduate School, 1941); Dorothy K. Newman, Nancy J. Amidei, Barbara Carter, *Protest, Politics, and Prosperity: Black Americans and White Institutions 1940–75* (New York: Pantheon, 1978).

35. A group of black secretaries entering a government lunchroom in 1945 found all the tables full except one partly occupied by white men. When they took the empty seats, their lunch trays were swept to the floor by one of the men, who insisted that no blacks were going to eat at his table; Newman, *Protest, Politics, and Prosperity*, 306.

36. Kenesaw M. Landis, *Segregation in Washington: A Report of the National Committee on Segregation in the Nation's Capital* (Chicago:, 1948), 60–74.

37. Karen Anderson, *Wartime Women: Sex Roles, Family Relations, and the Status of Women during World War II* (Westport, Conn.: Greenwood Press, 1981), 35–39; Alice Kessler-Harris, *Out to Work: a History of Wage-Earning Women in the United States* (New York: Oxford University Press, 1982), 273–99.

38. Anderson, "Last Hired, First Fired," 82–97; Hartmann, *Home Front and Beyond*.

39. Maureen Honey, *Creating Rosie the Riveter: Class, Gender, and Propaganda during World War II* (Amherst: University of Massachusetts Press, 1984), 28–29, 83. For a more in-depth discussion of the propaganda on African-Americans generated during the war, see Bernard Berelson and Patricia J. Salter, "Majority and Minority Americans: An Analysis of Magazine Fiction," *Public Opinion Quarterly* 10 (Summer 1946): 168–97.

40. Landon Y. Jones, *Great Expectations: America and the Baby Boom Generation* (New York: Coward, McCann & Geoghegan, 1980), 11. According to an analysis conducted by Thomas Espenshade, as of 1940–45, white women were spending 49.4 percent of their total lifetime married, compared to 41.9 percent for black women. For 1945–50 this figure increased to 53.7 percent for white women and decreased to 40.2 for black women. The percent of time in a first marriage increased for both groups in 1945–1950. However, for whites the percent of time in remarriages increased in 1945–50, but it dropped precipitously for blacks during the same time frame. The proportion of their lifetime that black women can expect to spend in an intact marriage or a remarriage was analyzed in 1975–1980 and the percentage had declined from 40 percent at the rates prevalent in 1945–1950 to 22 percent; "The Recent Decline of American Marriage: Blacks and White in Comparative Perspective," in *Contemporary Marriage*, eds. Kingsley Davis and Amyra Grossbard-Schechtman (New York: Russell Sage Foundation, 1986), 56–64.

41. Men with dependents were deferred until 1942. It should be noted that this was not as much the case for black couples; for the most part, black men voluntarily enlisted in that many were being overlooked by their local draft boards.

42. For more information on Allotment Annies, see Ronald H. Bailey, *The Home Front: U.S.A.* (Alexandria, Va.: 1978), 51.

43.   On the growth of blacks in industry and the conflicts they experienced as they made attempts to join forces with organized labor in the 1940s, see Neil Lichtenstein, *Labor's War at Home: The CIO in World War II* (New York: Cambridge University Press, 1982); Sumner M. Rosen, "The CIO Era, 1935–55," in *The Negro and the American Labor Movement* ed. Julius Jacobson (Garden City, N.Y.: Anchor/Doubleday, 1968); August Meier and Elliott Rudwick, *Black Detroit and the Rise of the UAW* (New York: Oxford University Press, 1979); Alma Herbst, *The Negro in the Slaughtering and Meat-Packing Industry in Chicago* (New York: Arno Press, 1971); Herbert R. Northrup, *Organized Labor and the Negro* (New York: Harper, 1944). The labor force participation of black men simultaneously declined during this period. William J. Wilson analyzed a similar pattern during the postwar years through the early 1980s and has asserted that "the increasing delay of first marriage and the low rate of remarriage among black women seem to be directly tied to the increasing labor force problems of men"; *The Truly Disadvantaged: The Inner City, the Underclass, and Public Policy* (Chicago: University of Chicago Press), 84.

44.   Mirra Komarovsky, *Blue-Collar Marriage* (New York: Random House, 1967), 70–74.

45.   Reuben Hill and Elise Boulding, *Families Under Stress: Adjustment to the Crises of War Separation and Reunion* (New York: Harper Brothers, 1949), 275–77.

46.   Frances E. Merrill, *Social Problems on the Home Front* (New York: Harper & Row, 1948), chap. 2; Paul H. Jacobson, "Differentials in Divorce by Duration of Marriages and Size of Family," *American Sociological Review* 15 (April 1950): 235–44.

47.   Paul H. Jacobson, *American Marriage and Divorce* (New York: Rinehart, 1959), 102.

48.   Abbott L. Ferris, *Indicators of Trends in the Status of Women* (New York: Russell Sage Foundation, 1971), 351. In 1940 single women bore children at the rate of 7.1 per thousand women aged 15–44; by 1950 the rate had reached 14.1.

49.   Campbell, *Women at War*, 203; Hartmann, *The Home Front and Beyond*, 179. Social scientists and experts on the family, not surprisingly, identified the working mothers as one of the primary causes. For comprehensive analyses of social problems and the role of women, see Merrill, *Social Problems*; Chafe, *American Woman*; Glick, *American Families* (New York: Wiley, 1957).

50.   John Durand, *The Labor Force in the United States, 1890–1960* (New York: Gordon and Breach, 1948): 224–26.

51.   When Drake and Cayton studied the changes in the marital status among African-Americans living in poverty during the war, they found that about forty out of every hundred black women were "available" in the sense that they did not have husbands. They also found that nearly all of the men reported themselves as "single" even though in many cases they may have been previously married. They noted that individuals from the ranks of the "sixty per cent married" were continuously dropping into the ranks of the "forty per cent available," and vice versa; *The Black Metropolis* (New York: Harcourt, Brace, 1945) 585; St. Clair Drake, "The Negro in the North During Wartime Chicago," *Journal of Educational Sociology* 17 (January, 1944): 266.

52.   Quoted in Anderson, *Wartime Women*, 81.

53.   For an analysis of the sexual norms during the 1940s, see John D'Emilio and Estelle B. Freedman, *Intimate Matters: A History of Sexuality in America* (New York: Harper & Row), 260–62; Allan M. Brandt, *No Magic Bullet: A Social History of Venereal Disease in the United States since 1880* (New York: Oxford University Press 1985), 164, 167–68.

54.   Phillips Cutright, "Illegitimacy in the United States: 1920–1968," in *Demographic and Social Aspects of Population Growth*, ed. Charles F. Westoff and Robert Parke, Jr., U. S. Commission on Population Growth and the American Future, Research Reports, vol. 1 (Washington, D.C.: Government Printing Office, 1972), 381–438. It should also be noted that when out-of-wedlock ratios are calculated by the number of births rather than the number of women, in 1940 the figure was 40.3 per thousand for all births and by 1950 that figure was 40.9 births, reflecting no growth. However, when these figures are broken down by race some differences emerge. For whites the ratios were 19.8 in 1940 and 23.6 in 1945 but dropped to 17.5 by 1950, whereas for blacks the ratios were 166.4 in 1940 and 179.3 in 1945, and they held constant in 1950 at 179.5.

55.   Ibid.

56.   Figures on the employment gains of black men: Susan Hartmann, *Home Front and Beyond*, 5. Figures on the income increase for black families: Campbell, *Women at War*, 218. For a distribution of employees in the auto industry during the war years by gender and race see Ruth Milkman, "Redefining 'Women's Work': Organizing the Sexual Division of Labor: Historical Perspectives on 'Women Work' and the Am. Labor Movement", *Socialist Review* 49 (Jan–Feb, 1980): 128–33; Alan Clive, "Women Workers in World War II: Michigan as a Test Case," *Labor History* 20 (Winter, 1979): 44–69; Meier and Rudwick, *Black Detroit*.

57.   Reported in George Gregory, Jr., "Wartime Guidance for Tomorrow's Citizens," *Opportunity* 21 (April 1943): 70–71, 90–91.

58.   Martha M. Eliot and Lillian R. Freedman, "Four Years of the EMIC Program," *Yale Journal of Biology and Medicine* 19 (March 1947): 621–35.

59.   Sam Shapiro, Edward R. Schlesinger, and Robert E. L. Nesbit, Jr., *Infant, Perinatal, Maternal and Childhood Mortality in the United States* (Cambridge, Mass.: Harvard University Press, 1968), 248, 329; Richard C. Wertz and Dorothy C. Wertz, *Lying-In: A History of Childbirth in America* (New York: Free Press, 1977), 164–73.

60.   The difference in mortality rates between blacks and whites can be explained in part by the persistence of midwifery and home deliveries in southern black communities. For example, in 1942 in a small town in Mississippi 119 black babies were delivered by midwives and 37 by physicians, and of those 37 deliveries by physicians, 26 were delivered at home. In 1941 and 1942 in Alabama and South Carolina, 62 percent and 80 percent of the black babies were delivered by midwives, respectively; Campbell, *Women at War*, 179.

61. President's Committee on Civil Rights, *To Secure These Rights* (Washington, D.C.: Government Printing Office, 1947), 58.

62. Newman, *Protest, Politics, and Prosperity*, 103. See also Thomas Richardson, "Negro Discrimination by Uncle Sam," *March of Labor* 1 (July 1949): 22.

63. *Ebony* March, 1947, 36.

64. Department of Commerce, Census Bureau, "Characteristics of Single, Married, and Widowed/Divorced Persons in 1947" *Current Population Reports*, series P-20, no. 10 (Washington, D.C.: Government Printing Office, 1948).

65. Hartmann, *Home Front and Beyond*, 5–6.

66. The proportion of women of all races employed in domestic service was reduced again, by more than half a million—from nearly 20 percent to 10 percent. White women gained more from this shift than black women. For information on changes in black and white women's occupational status during the 1940s, see Department of Labor, Women's Bureau, "Changes in Women's Occupations, 1940–1950," *Bulletin* no. 153 (Washington, D.C.: Government Printing Office, 1954); C. Arnold Anderson and Mary Jean Bowman, "The Vanishing Servant and the Contemporary Status System of the American South," *American Journal of Sociology* 59 (November 1953). Figures on the median income of black women compared to white women are from George E. Demar, "Negro Women are American Workers, Too," *Opportunity: Journal of Negro Life* 21 (April 1943): 41–42.

67. A black woman who preferred her job as a machine operator in a can company was "beginning to accept the fact that Negro women will be forced to return to domestic work." For in-depth interviews with black women who were employed as domestics during the 1940s and sought to reconcile their jobs with their feelings of dignity and self-worth, see Bonnie Thornton Dill, "Across the Barriers of Race and Class: An Exploration of the Relationship between Work and Family among Black Female Domestics" (Ph.D. diss., New York University, 1979); Robert Hamburger, *A Stranger in the House* (New York: Collier, 1978).

68. Phyllis A. Wallace, *Black Women in the Labor Force* (Cambridge, Mass.: MIT Press, 1980), 44; Valerie Kincaide Oppenheimer, *The Female Labor Force in the United States: Demographic and Economic Factors Governing Its Growth and Changing Composition* (Westport, Conn.: Greenwood Press, 1970), 78–79.

69. Stanley Lieberson, *A Piece of the Pie: Blacks and White Immigrants Since 1880* (Berkeley: University of California Press, 1980), 200–250.

70. For a comprehensive discussion and analysis, see Phillips Cutright, "Components of Change in the Number of Female Family Heads Aged 15–44: United States, 1940–1970," *Journal of Marriage and the Family* 36 (November 1974): 714–22; La Frances Rodgers-Rose, "Some Demographic Characteristics of Black Women: 1940 to 1975," in *The Black Woman*, ed. La Frances Rodgers-Rose (Beverly Hills: Sage Publications, 1980).

71. In the early 1940s black organizations had cooperated with the Planned Parenthood Federation in campaigns to make contraceptives available to black families, but to little avail. When researchers surveyed 357 black women in rural Maryland in 1950 and 1951 they found that just one in five practiced birth control. See Christopher Tietze and Sarah Lewit, "Patterns of Family Limitation in a Rural Negro Community," *American Sociological Review* 18 (October 1953): 563–64; Myrdal, *America Dilemma*, 178–81.

72. Quoted in Herbert Aptheker, ed., *A Documentary History of the Negro People in the United States*, vol. 3, *From the Beginning of the New Deal to the End of the Second World War, 1933–1945* (Secaucus, N.J.: Citadel Press, 1974), 382–84.

73. Quoted in Winifred Bell, *Aid to Dependent Children* (New York: Columbia University Press, 1965), 62.

II

RACE, ETHNICITY, CLASS, AND GENDER IN FAMILY THEORY

10

Shifting the Center
Race, Class, and Feminist Theorizing about Motherhood

PATRICIA HILL COLLINS

I dread to see my children grow, I know not their fate. Where the white boy has every opportunity and protection, mine will have few opportunities and no protection. It does not matter how good or wise my children may be, they are colored.

an anonymous African-American mother in 1904, reported in Lerner 1972, p. 158.

FOR NATIVE AMERICAN, African-American, Hispanic, and Asian-American women, motherhood cannot be analyzed in isolation from its context. Motherhood occurs in specific historical situations framed by interlocking structures of race, class, and gender, where the sons and daughters of white mothers have "every opportunity and protection," and the "colored" daughters and sons of racial ethnic mothers "know not their fate." Racial domination and economic exploitation profoundly shape the mothering context, not only for racial ethnic women in the United States, but for all women.[1]

Despite the significance of race and class, feminist theorizing routinely minimizes their importance. In this sense, feminist theorizing about motherhood has not been immune to the decontextualization of Western social thought overall.[2] While many dimensions of motherhood's context are ignored, the exclusion of race and/or class from feminist theorizing generally (Spelman 1988), and from feminist theorizing about motherhood specifically, merits special attention.[3]

Much feminist theorizing about motherhood assumes that male domination in the political economy and the household is the driving force in family life, and that understanding the struggle for individual autonomy in the face of such domination is central to understanding motherhood (Eisenstein 1983).[4] Several guiding principles frame such analyses. First, such theories posit a dichotomous split between the public sphere of economic and political discourse and the private sphere of family and household responsibilities. This juxtaposition of a public, political economy to a private, noneconomic and apolitical, domestic household allows work and family to be seen as separate institutions. Second, reserving the public sphere for men as a "male" domain leaves the private domestic sphere as a "female" domain. Gender roles become tied to the dichotomous constructions of these two basic societal institutions—men work and women take care of families. Third, the public/private dichotomy separating the family/household from the paid labor market shapes sex-segregated gender roles within the private sphere of the family. The archetypal white, middle-class nuclear family divides family life into two oppositional spheres—the "male" sphere of economic providing and the "female" sphere of affective nurturing, mainly mothering. This normative family household has, as its ideal head, a working father who earns enough to allow his spouse and dependent children to withdraw from the paid labor force. Due in large part to their superior earning power, men as workers and fathers exert power over women in the labor market and in families. Finally, the struggle for individual autonomy in the face of a controlling, oppressive, "public" society, or the father as patriarch, comprises the main human enterprise.[5] Successful adult males achieve this autonomy. Women, children, and less successful males, namely those who are working-class or from racial ethnic groups, are seen as dependent persons, as less autonomous, and therefore as fitting objects for elite male domination. Within the nuclear family, this struggle for autonomy takes the form of increasing opposition to the mother, the individual responsible for socializing children by these guiding principles (Chodorow 1978; Flax 1978).

Placing the experiences of women of color in the center of feminist theorizing about motherhood demonstrates how emphasizing the issue of father as patriarch in a decontextualized nuclear family distorts the experiences of women in alternative family structures with quite different political economies. While male domination certainly has been an important theme for racial ethnic women in the United States, gender inequality has long worked in tandem with racial domination and economic exploitation. Since work and family have rarely functioned as dichotomous spheres for women of color, examining racial ethnic women's experiences reveals how these two spheres actually are interwoven (Glenn 1985; Dill 1988; Collins 1990).

For women of color, the subjective experience of mothering/motherhood is inextricably linked to the sociocultural concern of racial ethnic communities—one does not exist without the other. Whether because of the labor exploitation of African-American women under slavery and its ensuing tenant farm system, the political conquest of Native American women during European acquisition of land, or exclusionary immigration policies applied to Asian-Americans and Hispanics, women of color have performed motherwork that challenges social constructions of work and family as separate spheres, of male and female gender roles as similarly dichotomized, and of the search for autonomy as the guiding human quest. "Women's reproductive labor—that is, feeding, clothing, and psychologically supporting the male wage earner and nurturing and socializing the next generation—is seen as work on behalf of the family as a whole, rather than as work benefiting men in particular," observes Asian-American sociologist Evelyn Nakano Glenn (1986, p. 192). The locus of conflict lies outside the household, as women and their families engage in collective effort to create and maintain family life in the face of forces that undermine family integrity. But this "reproductive labor" or "motherwork" goes beyond ensuring the survival of one's own biological children or those of one's family. This type of motherwork recognizes that individual survival, empowerment, and identity require group survival, empowerment, and identity.

In describing her relationship with her "Grandmother," Marilou Awiakta, a Native American poet and feminist theorist, captures the essence of motherwork:

> Putting my arms around the Grandmother, I lay my head on her shoulder. Through touch we exchange sorrow, despair that anything really changes.

Awiakta senses the power of the Grandmother and of the motherwork that mothers and grandmothers do:

> But from the presence of her arms I also feel the stern, beautiful power that flows from all the Grandmothers, as it flows from our mountains themselves. It says, "Dry your tears. Get up. Do for yourselves or do without. Work for the day to come." (1988, p. 127)

Awiakta's passage places women and motherwork squarely in the center of what are typically seen as disjunctures, the places between human and nature, between private and public, between oppression and liberation. I use the term "motherwork" to soften the existing dichotomies in feminist theorizing about motherhood that posit rigid distinctions between private and public, family and work, the individual and the collective, identity as individual autonomy and identity growing from the collective self-determination of one's group. Racial ethnic women's mothering and work experiences occur at the boundaries demarking these dualities. "Work for the day to come," is motherwork, whether it is on behalf of one's own biological children, or for the children of one's own racial ethnic community, or to preserve the earth for those children who are yet unborn. The space that this motherwork occupies promises to shift our thinking about motherhood itself.

SHIFTING THE CENTER: WOMEN OF COLOR AND MOTHERWORK

What themes might emerge if issues of race and class generally, and understanding of racial ethnic women's motherwork specifically, became central to feminist theorizing about motherhood? Centering feminist theorizing on the concerns of white, middle-class women leads to two problematic assumptions. The first is that a relative degree of economic security exists for mothers and their children. The second is that all women enjoy the racial privilege that allows them to see themselves primarily as individuals in search of personal autonomy, instead of as members of racial ethnic groups struggling for power. It is these assumptions that allow feminist theorists to concentrate on themes such as the connections among mothering, aggression, and death, the effects of maternal isolation on mother-child relationships within nuclear family households, maternal sexuality, relationships among family members, all-powerful mothers as conduits for gender oppression, and the possibilities of an idealized motherhood freed from patriarchy (Chodorow and Contratto 1982; Eisenstein 1983).

While these issues merit investigation, centering feminist theorizing about motherhood in the ideas and experiences of African-American, Native American, Hispanic, and Asian-American women might yield markedly different themes (Andersen 1988; Brown 1989). This stance is to be distinguished from one that merely adds racial ethnic women's experiences to preexisting feminist theories, without considering how these experiences challenge those theories (Spelman 1988). Involving much more than simply the consulting of existing social science sources, the placing of ideas and experiences of women of color in the center of analysis requires invoking a different epistemology. We must distinguish between what has been said about subordinated groups in the dominant discourse, and what such groups might say about themselves if given the opportunity. Personal narratives, autobiographical statements, poetry, fiction, and other personalized statements have all been used by women of color to express self-defined standpoints on mothering and motherhood. Such knowledge reflects the authentic standpoint of subordinated groups. Therefore, placing these sources in the center and supplementing them with statistics, historical material, and other knowledge produced to justify the interests of ruling elites should create new themes and angles of vision (Smith 1990).[6]

Specifying the contours of racial ethnic women's motherwork promises to point the way toward richer feminist theorizing about motherhood. Themes of survival, power, and identity form the bedrock and reveal how racial ethnic women in the United States encounter and fashion motherwork. That is, to understand the importance of working for the physical survival of children and community, the dialectical nature of power and powerlessness in structuring mothering patterns, and the significance of self-definition in constructing individual and collective racial identity is to grasp the three core themes characterizing the experiences of Native American, African-American, Hispanic and Asian-American women. It is also to suggest how feminist theorizing about motherhood might be shifted if different voices become central in feminist discourse.

MOTHERWORK AND PHYSICAL SURVIVAL

When we are not physically starving we have the luxury to realize psychic and emotional starvation.

(Cherrie Moraga 1979, p. 29)

Physical survival is assumed for children who are white and middle-class. The choice to thus examine their psychic and emotional well-being and that of their mothers appears rational. The children of women of color, many of whom are "physically starving," have no such choices however. Racial ethnic children's lives have long been held in low regard: African-American children face an infant mortality rate twice that for white infants; and approximately one-third of Hispanic children and one-half of African-American children who survive infancy live in poverty. In addition racial ethnic children often live in harsh urban environments where drugs, crime, industrial pollutants, and violence threaten their survival. Children in rural environments often fare no better. Winona LaDuke, for example, reports that Native Americans on reservations often must use contaminated water. And on the Pine Ridge Sioux Reservation in 1979, 38 percent of all pregnancies resulted in miscarriages before the fifth month, or in excessive hemorrhaging. Approximately 65 percent of all children born suffered breathing problems caused by underdeveloped lungs and jaundice (1988, p. 63).

Struggles to foster the survival of Native American, Hispanic, Asian-American, and African-American families and communities by ensuring the survival of children comprise a fundamental dimension of racial ethnic women's motherwork. African-American women's fiction contains numerous stories of mothers fighting for the physical survival both of their own biological children and of those of the larger Black community.[7] "Don't care how much death it is in the land, I got to make preparations for my baby to live!" proclaims Mariah Upshur, the African-American heroine of Sara Wright's 1986 novel *This Child's Gonna Live* (p. 143). Like Mariah Upshur, the harsh climates which confront racial ethnic children require that their mothers "make preparations for their babies to live" as a central feature of their motherwork.

Yet, like all deep cultural themes, the theme of motherwork for physical survival contains contradictory elements. On the one hand, racial ethnic women's motherwork for individual and community survival has been essential. Without women's motherwork, communities would not survive, and by definition, women of color themselves would not survive. On the other hand, this work often exacts a high cost for large numbers of women. There is loss of individual autonomy and there is submersion of individual growth for the benefit of the group. While this dimension of motherwork remains essential, the question of women doing more than their fair share of such work for individual and community development merits open debate.

The histories of family-based labor have been shaped by racial ethnic women's motherwork for survival and the types of mothering relationships that ensued. African-American, Asian-American, Native American and Hispanic women have all worked and contributed to family economic well-being (Glenn 1985; Dill 1988). Much of their experiences with motherwork, in fact, stems from the work they performed as children. The commodification of children of color, starting with the enslavement of African children who were legally "owned" as property, to the subsequent treatment of children as units of labor in agricultural work, family businesses, and industry, has been a major theme shaping motherhood for women of color. Beginning in slavery and continuing into the post-World War II period, Black children were put to work at young ages in the fields of Southern agriculture. Sara Brooks began full-time work in the fields at the age of eleven, and remembers, "we never was lazy cause we used to really work. We used to work like men. Oh, fight sometime, fuss sometime, but worked on" (Collins 1990, p. 54).

Black and Hispanic children in contemporary migrant farm families make similar contributions to their family's economy. "I musta been almost eight when I started following the crops," remembers Jessie de la Cruz, a Mexican-American mother with six grown children. "Every winter, up north. I was on the end of the row of prunes, taking care of my younger brother and sister. They would help me fill up the cans and put 'em in a box while the rest of the family was picking the whole row" (de la Cruz 1980, p. 168). Asian-American children spend long hours working in family businesses, child labor practices that have earned Asian Americans the dubious distinction of being "model minorities." More recently, the family-based labor of undocumented racial ethnic immigrants, often mother-child units doing piecework for the garment industry, recalls the sweatshop conditions confronting turn-of-the-century European immigrants.

A certain degree of maternal isolation from members of the dominant group characterizes the preceding mother-child units. For women of color working along with their children, such isolation is more appropriately seen as reflecting a placement in race- and class-stratified labor systems than as a result of a patriarchal system. The unit may be isolated, but the work performed by the mother-child unit closely ties the mothering experiences to wider political and economic issues. Children, too, learn to see their work and that of their mother not as isolated from wider society, but as essential to their family's survival. Moreover, in the case of family agricultural labor or family businesses, women and children work alongside men, often performing the same work. If isolation occurs, the family, not the mother-child unit, is the focus of such isolation.

Children working in close proximity to their mothers receive distinctive types of mothering. Asian-American children working in urban family businesses, for example, report long days filled almost exclusively with work and school. In contrast, the sons and daughters of African-American sharecroppers and migrant farm children of all backgrounds have less access to educational opportunities. "I think the longest time I went to school was two months in one place," remembers Jessie de la Cruz. "I attended, I think, about forty-five schools. When my parents or my brothers didn't find work, we wouldn't attend school because we weren't sure of staying there. So I missed a lot of school" (de la Cruz 1980, pp. 167–8). It was only in the 1950s, in fact, that Southern school districts stopped the practice of closing segregated Black schools during certain times of the year so that Black children could work.

Work that separated women of color from their children also framed the mothering relationship. Until the 1960s, large numbers of African-American, Hispanic, and Asian-American women worked in domestic service. Even though women worked long hours to ensure their children's physical survival, that same work ironically denied mothers access to their children. Different institutional arrangements emerged in these mothers' respective communities to resolve the tension between maternal separation due to employment and the needs of dependent children. The extended family structure in African-American communities endured as a flexible institution that mitigated some of the effects of maternal separation. Grandmothers are highly revered in Black communities, often because grandmothers function as primary caretakers of their daughters' and daughter-in-laws' children (Collins 1990). In contrast, exclusionary immigration policies that militated against intergenerational family units in the United States led Chinese-American and Japanese-American families to make other arrangements (Dill 1988).

Some mothers are clearly defeated by the demands for incessant labor that they must perform to ensure their children's survival. The magnitude of their motherwork overwhelms them. But others, even while appearing to be defeated, manage to pass on the meaning of motherwork for survival to their children. African-American feminist June Jordan remembers her perceptions of her mother's work:

> As a child I noticed the sadness of my mother as she sat alone in the kitchen at night. . . . Her woman's work never won permanent victories of any kind. It never enlarged the universe of her imagination or her power to influence what happened beyond the front door of our house. Her woman's work never tickled her to laugh or shout or dance. (Jordan 1985, p. 105)

But Jordan also sees her mother's work as being essential to individual and community survival:

> She did raise me to respect her way of offering love and to believe that hard work is often the irreducible factor for survival, not something to avoid. Her woman's work produced a reliable home base where I could pursue the privileges of books and music. Her woman's work invented the potential for a completely new kind of work for us, the next generation of Black women: huge, rewarding hard work demanded by the huge, different ambitions that her perfect confidence in us engendered. (Jordan 1985, p. 105)

MOTHERWORK AND POWER

Jessie de la Cruz, a Mexican-American migrant farm worker, experienced firsthand the struggle for empowerment facing racial ethnic women whose daily motherwork centers on issues of survival:

> How can I write down how I felt when I was a little child and my grandmother used to cry with us 'cause she didn't have enough food to give us? Because my brother was going barefooted and he was cryin' because he wasn't used to going without shoes? How can I describe that? I can't describe when my little girl died because I didn't have money for a doctor. And never had any teaching on caring for sick babies. Living out in labor camps. How can I describe that? (de la Cruz 1980, p. 177)

A dialectical relationship exists between efforts of racial orders to mold the institution of motherhood to serve the interests of elites, in this case, racial elites, and efforts on the part of subordinated groups to retain power over motherhood so that it serves the legitimate needs of their communities (Collins 1990). African-American, Asian-American, Hispanic, and Native American women have long been preoccupied with patterns of maternal power and powerlessness because their mothering experiences have been profoundly affected by this dialectical process. But instead of emphasizing maternal power in dealing with father as patriarch (Chodorow 1978; Rich 1986), or with male dominance in general (Ferguson 1989), women of color are concerned with their power and powerlessness within an array of social institutions that frame their lives.

Racial ethnic women's struggles for maternal empowerment have resolved around three main themes. First is the struggle for control over their own bodies in order to preserve choice over whether to become mothers at all. The ambiguous politics of caring for unplanned children has long shaped African-American women's motherwork. For example, the widespread institutionalized rape of Black women by white men, both during slavery and in the segregated South, created countless biracial children who had to be absorbed into African-American families and communities (Davis 1981). The range of skin colors and hair textures in contemporary

African-American communities bears mute testament to the powerlessness of African-American women in controlling this dimension of motherhood.

For many women of color, choosing to become a mother challenges institutional policies that encourage white, middle-class women to reproduce, and discourage or even penalize low-income racial ethnic women from doing so (Davis 1981). Rita Silk-Nauni, an incarcerated Native American woman, writes of the difficulties she encountered in trying to have additional children. She loved her son so much that she only left him to go to work. "I tried having more after him and couldn't," she laments.

> I went to a specialist and he thought I had been fixed when I had my son. He said I would have to have surgery in order to give birth again. The surgery was so expensive but I thought I could make a way even if I had to work 24 hours a day. Now that I'm here, I know I'll never have that chance. (Brant 1988, p. 94)

Like Silk-Nauni, Puerto Rican and African-American women have long had to struggle with issues of sterilization abuse (Davis 1981). More recent efforts to manipulate the fertility of women dependent on public assistance speaks to the continued salience of this issue.

A second dimension of racial ethnic women's struggles for maternal empowerment concerns the process of keeping the children that are wanted, whether they were planned for or not. For mothers like Jessie de la Cruz, whose "little girl died" because she "didn't have money for a doctor," maternal separation from one's children becomes a much more salient issue than maternal isolation with one's children within an allegedly private nuclear family. Physical and/or psychological separation of mothers and children, designed to disempower individuals, forms the basis of a systematic effort to disempower racial ethnic communities.

For both Native American and African-American mothers, situations of conquest introduced this dimension of the struggle for maternal empowerment. In her fictional account of a Native American mother's loss of her children in 1890, Brant explores the pain of maternal separation:

> It has been two days since they came and took the children away. My body is greatly chilled. All our blankets have been used to bring me warmth. The women keep the fire blazing. The men sit. They talk among themselves. We are frightened by this sudden child-stealing. We signed papers, the agent said. This gave them rights to take our babies. It is good for them, the agent said. It will make them civilized. (1988, p. 101)

A legacy of conquest has meant that Native American mothers on "reservations" confront intrusive government institutions such as the Bureau of Indian Affairs in deciding the fate of their children. For example, the long-standing policy of removing Native American children from their homes and housing them in reservation boarding schools can be seen as efforts to disempower Native American mothers. For African-American women, slavery was a situation where owners controlled numerous dimensions of their children's lives. Black children could be sold at will, whipped, or even killed, all without any recourse by their mothers. In such a situation, getting to keep one's children and raise them accordingly fosters empowerment.

A third dimension of racial ethnic women's struggles for empowerment concerns the pervasive efforts by the dominant group to control the children's minds. In her short story, "A Long Memory," Beth Brant juxtaposes the loss felt by a Native American mother in 1890 whose son and daughter had been forcibly removed by white officials, to the loss that she felt in 1978 upon losing her daughter in a custody hearing. "Why do they want our babies?" queries the turn-of-the-century mother. "They want our power. They take our children to remove the inside of them. Our power" (Brant 1988, p. 105). This mother recognizes that the future of the Native American way of life lies in retaining the power to define that worldview through the education of children. By forbidding children to speak their native languages, and in other ways encouraging children to assimilate into Anglo culture, external agencies challenge the power of mothers to raise their children as they see fit.

Schools controlled by the dominant group comprise one important location where this dimension of the struggle for maternal empowerment occurs. In contrast to white, middle-class children, whose educational experiences affirm their mothers' middle-class values, culture, and authority, the educational experiences of African-American, Hispanic, Asian-American and Native American children typically denigrate their mothers' perspective. For example, the struggles over bilingual education in Hispanic communities are about much more than retaining Spanish as a second language. Speaking the language of one's childhood is a way of retaining the entire culture and honoring the mother teaching that culture (Moraga 1979; Anzaldua 1987).

Jenny Yamoto describes the stress of continuing to negotiate with schools regarding her Black-Japanese sons:

> I've noticed that depending on which parent, Black mom or Asian dad, goes to school open house, my oldest son's behavior is interpreted as disruptive and irreverent, or assertive and clever. . . . I resent their behavior being defined and even expected on the basis of racial biases their teachers may struggle with or hold. . . . I don't have the time or energy to constantly change and challenge their teachers' and friends' misperceptions. I only go after them when the children really seem to be seriously threatened. (Yamoto 1988, p. 24)

In confronting each of these three dimensions of their struggles for empowerment, racial ethnic women are not powerless in the face of racial and class oppression. Being grounded in a strong, dynamic, indigenous culture can be central to these women's social constructions of motherhood. Depending on their access to traditional culture, they invoke alternative sources of power.[8]

"Equality, per se, may have a different meaning for Indian women and Indian people," suggests Kate Shanley. "That difference begins with personal and tribal sovereignty—the right to be legally recognized as people empowered to determine our own destinies" (1988, p. 214). Personal sovereignty involves the struggle to promote the survival of a social structure whose organizational principles represent notions of family and motherhood different from those of the mainstream. "The nuclear family has little relevance to Indian women," observes Shanley. "In fact, in many ways, mainstream feminists now are striving to redefine family and community in a way that Indian women have long known" (p. 214).

African-American mothers can draw upon an Afrocentric tradition where motherhood of varying types, whether bloodmother, othermother, or community othermother, can be invoked as a symbol of power. Many Black women receive respect and recognition within their local communities for innovative and practical approaches not only to mothering their own "blood" children, but also to being othermothers to the children in their extended family networks, and those in the community overall. Black women's involvement in fostering Black community development forms the basis of this community-based power. In local African-American communities, community othermothers can become identified as powerful figures through their work in furthering the community's well-being (Collins 1990).

Despite policies of dominant institutions that place racial ethnic mothers in positions where they appear less powerful to their children, mothers and children empower themselves by understanding each other's position and relying on each other's strengths. In many cases, children, especially daughters, bond with their mothers instead of railing against them as symbols of patriarchal power. Cherrie Moraga describes the impact that her mother had on her. Because she was repeatedly removed from school in order to work, by prevailing standards Moraga's mother would be considered largely illiterate. But she was also a fine storyteller, and found ways to empower herself within dominant institutions. "I would go with my mother to fill out job applications for her, or write checks for her at the supermarket," Moraga recounts.

> We would have the scenario all worked out ahead of time. My mother would sign the check before we'd get to the store. Then, as we'd approach the checkstand, she would say—within earshot of the cashier— "oh, honey, you go 'head and make out the check," as if she couldn't be bothered with such an insignificant detail. (1979, p. 28)

Like Cherrie Moraga and her mother, racial ethnic women's motherwork involves collaborating to empower mothers and children within structures that oppress.

MOTHERWORK AND IDENTITY

Please help me find out who I am. My mother was Indian, but we were taken from her and put in foster homes. They were white and didn't want to tell us about our mother. I have a name and maybe a place of birth. Do you think you can help me?

(Brant 1988, p. 9)

Like this excerpt from a letter to the editor, the theme of lost racial ethnic identity and the struggle to maintain a sense of self and community pervade many of the stories, poetry and narratives in Beth Brant's volume, *A Gathering of Spirit*. Carol Lee Sanchez offers another view of the impact of the loss of self. "Radicals look at reservation Indians and get very upset about their poverty conditions," observes Sanchez.

> But poverty to us is not the same thing as poverty is to you. Our poverty is that we can't be who we are. We can't hunt or fish or grow our food because our basic resources and the right to use them in traditional ways are denied us. (Brant 1988, p. 165)

Racial ethnic women's motherwork reflects the tensions inherent in trying to foster a meaningful racial identity in children within a society that denigrates people of color. The racial privilege enjoyed by white, middle-class women makes unnecessary this complicated dimension of the mothering tradition of women of color. While white children can be prepared to fight racial oppression, their survival does not depend on gaining these skills. Their racial identity is validated by their schools, the media, and other social institutions. White children are socialized into their rightful place in systems of racial privilege. Racial ethnic women have no such guarantees for their children; their children must first be taught to survive in systems that oppress them. Moreover, this survival must not come at the expense of self-esteem. Thus, a dialectical relationship exists between systems of racial oppression designed to strip subordinated groups of a sense of personal identity and a sense of collective peoplehood, and the cultures of resistance extant in various racial ethnic groups that resist the oppression. For women of color, motherwork for identity occurs at this critical juncture (Collins 1990).

"Through our mothers, the culture gave us mixed messages," observes Mexican-American poet Gloria Anzaldua. "Which was it to be—strong or submissive, rebellious or conforming?" (1987, p. 18). Thus women of color's motherwork requires reconciling contradictory needs concerning identity. Preparing children to cope with and survive within systems of racial oppression is extremely difficult because the pressures for children of racial ethnic groups to assimilate are pervasive. In order to compel women of color to participate in their children's assimilation, dominant institutions promulgate ideologies that belittle people of color. Negative controlling images infuse the worlds of male and female children of color (Tajima 1989; Collins 1990; Green 1990). Native American girls are encouraged to see themselves as "Pocahontases" or "squaws"; Asian-American girls as "geisha girls" or "Suzy Wongs"; Hispanic girls as "Madonnas" or "hot-blooded whores"; and African-American girls as "mammies," "matriarchs," and "prostitutes." Girls of all groups are told that their lives cannot be complete without a male partner, and that their educational and career aspirations must always be subordinated to their family obligations.

This push toward assimilation is part of a larger effort to socialize racial ethnic children into their proper, subordinate places in systems of racial and class oppression. Since children of color can never be white, however, assimilation by becoming white is impossible despite the pressures. Thus, a second dimension of the mothering tradition involves equipping children with skills to confront this contradiction and to challenge systems of racial oppression. Girls who become women believing that they are only capable of being maids and prostitutes cannot contribute to racial ethnic women's motherwork.

Mothers make varying choices in negotiating the complicated relationship of preparing children to fit into, yet resist, systems of racial domination. Some mothers remain powerless in the face of external forces that foster their children's assimilation and subsequent alienation from their families and communities. Through fiction, Native American author Beth Brant again explores the grief felt by a mother whose children had been taken away to live among whites. A letter arrives giving news of her missing children:

> This letter is from two strangers with the names Martha and Daniel. They say they are learning civilized ways. Daniel works in the fields, growing food for the school. Martha is being taught to sew aprons. She will be going to live with the schoolmaster's wife. She will be a live-in girl. What is live-in girl? I shake my head. The words sound the same to me. I am afraid of Martha and Daniel. These strangers who know my name. (Brant 1988, pp. 102–103)

Other mothers become unwitting conduits of the dominant ideology. Gloria Anzaldua (1987, p. 16) asks:

> How many times have I heard mothers and mothers-in-law tell their sons to beat their wives for not obeying them, for being *hociconas* (big mouths), for being *callajeras* (going to visit and gossip with neighbors), for expecting their husbands to help with the rearing of children and the housework, for wanting to be something other than housewives?

Some mothers encourage their children to fit in, for reasons of survival. "My mother, nursed in the folds of a town that once christened its black babies Lee, after Robert E., and Jackson, after Stonewall, raised me on a dangerous generation's old belief," remembers African-American author Marita Golden.

> Because of my dark brown complexion, she warned me against wearing browns or yellow and reds . . . and every summer I was admonished not to play in the sun "cause you gonna have to get a light husband anyway, for the sake of your children." (Golden 1983, p. 24)

To Cherrie Moraga's mother:

> On a basic economic level, being Chicana meant being "less." It was through my mother's desire to

protect her children from poverty and illiteracy that we became "anglocized"; the more effectively we could pass in the white world, the better guaranteed our future. (1979, p. 28)

Despite their mothers' good intentions, the costs to children taught to submit to racist and sexist ideologies can be high. Raven, a Native American woman, looks back on her childhood:

I've been raised in the white man's world and was forbade more or less to converse with Indian people. As my mother wanted me to be educated and live a good life, free from poverty. I lived a life of loneliness. Today I am desperate to know my people. (Brant 1988, p. 221)

To avoid poverty, Raven's mother did what she thought best, but ultimately, Raven experienced the poverty of not being able to be who she was.

Still other mothers transmit sophisticated skills to their children, enabling them to appear to be submissive while at the same time to be able to challenge inequality. Willi Coleman's mother used a Saturday-night hair-combing ritual to impart a Black women's standpoint to her daughters:

Except for special occasions mama came home from work early on Saturdays. She spent six days a week mopping, waxing and dusting other women's houses and keeping out of reach of other women's husbands. Saturday nights were reserved for "taking care of them girls' " hair and the telling of stories. Some of which included a recitation of what she had endured and how she had triumphed over "folks that were lower than dirt" and "no-good snakes in the grass." She combed, patted, twisted and talked, saying things which would have embarrassed or shamed her at other times. (Coleman 1987, p. 34)

Historian Elsa Barkley Brown captures this delicate balance that racial ethnic mothers negotiate. Brown points out that her mother's behavior demonstrated the "need to teach me to live my life one way and, at the same time, to provide all the tools I would need to live it quite differently" (1989, p. 929).

For women of color, the struggle to maintain an independent racial identity has taken many forms: All reveal varying solutions to the dialectical relationship between institutions that would deny their children their humanity and institutions that would affirm their children's right to exist as self-defined people. Like Willi Coleman's mother, African-American women draw upon a long-standing Afrocentric feminist worldview, emphasizing the importance of self-definition, self-reliance, and the necessity of demanding respect from others (Terborg-Penn 1986; Collins 1990).

Racial ethnic cultures, themselves, do not always help to support women's self-definition. Poet and essayist Gloria Anzaldua, for example, challenges many of the ideas in Hispanic cultures concerning women. "Though I'll defend my race and culture when they are attacked by non-*mexicanos*, . . . I abhor some of my culture's ways, how it cripples its women, *como burras*, our strengths used against us" (1987, p. 21). Anzaldua offers a trenchant analysis of the ways in which the Spanish conquest of Native Americans fragmented women's identity and produced three symbolic "mothers." *La Virgen de Guadalupe*, perhaps the single most potent religious, political and cultural image of the Chicano people, represents the virgin mother who cares for and nurtures an oppressed people. *La Chingada (Malinche)* represents the raped mother, all but abandoned. A combination of the other two, *La Llorona* symbolizes the mother who seeks her lost children. "Ambiguity surrounds the symbols of these three 'Our Mothers,' " claims Anzaldua.

In part, the true identity of all three has been subverted—*Guadalupe*, to make us docile and enduring, *la Chingada*, to make us ashamed of our Indian side, and *la Llorona* to make us a long-suffering people. (1987, p. 31).

For Anzaldua, the Spanish conquest, which brought racism and economic subordination to Indian people, and created a new mixed-race Hispanic people, simultaneously devalued women:

> No, I do not buy all the myths of the tribe into which I was born. I can understand why the more tinged with Anglo blood, the more adamantly my colored and colorless sisters glorify their colored culture's values—to offset the extreme devaluation of it by the white culture. It's a legitimate reaction. But I will not glorify those aspects of my culture which have injured me and which have injured me in the name of protecting me. (Anzaldua 1987, p. 22)

Hispanic mothers face the complicated task of shepherding their children through the racism extant in dominant society, and the reactions to that racism framing cultural beliefs internal to Hispanic communities.

Many Asian American mothers stress conformity and fitting in as a way to challenge the system. "Our parents are painted as hard workers who were socially uncomfortable and had difficulty expressing even the smallest opinion," observes Japanese-American Kesaya Noda, in her auto-biographical essay "Growing Up Asian in America" (1989, p. 246). Noda questioned this seeming capitulation on the part of her parents: " 'Why did you go into those camps,' I raged at my parents, frightened by my own inner silence and timidity. 'Why didn't you do anything to resist?' " But Noda later discovers a compelling explanation as to why Asian-Americans are so often portrayed as conformist:

> I had not been able to imagine before what it must have felt like to be an American—to know absolutely that one is an American—and yet to have almost everyone else deny it. Not only deny it, but challenge that identity with machine guns and troops of white American soldiers. In those circumstances it was difficult to say, "I'm a Japanese-American." "American" had to do. (1989, p. 247)

Native American women can draw upon a tradition of motherhood and woman's power inherent in Native American cultures (Allen 1986; Awiakta 1988). In such philosophies, "water, land, and life are basic to the natural order," claims Winona LaDuke.

> All else has been created by the use and misuse of technology. It is only natural that in our respective struggles for survival, the native peoples are waging a way to protect the land, the water, and life, while the consumer culture strives to protect its technological lifeblood. (1988, p. 65)

Marilou Awiakta offers a powerful summary of the symbolic meaning of motherhood in Native American cultures. "I feel the Grandmother's power. She sings of harmony, not dominance," offers Awiakta. "And her song rises from a culture that repeats the wise balance of nature: the gender capable of bearing life is not separated from the power to sustain it" (1988, p. 126). A culture that sees the connectedness between the earth and human survival, and sees motherhood as symbolic of the earth itself, holds motherhood as an institution in high regard.

CONCLUDING REMARKS

Survival, power, and identity shape motherhood for all women. But these themes remain muted when the mothering experiences of women of color are marginalized in feminist theorizing. Feminist theorizing about motherhood reflects a lack of attention to the connection between ideas and the contexts in which they emerge. While such decontextualization aims to generate universal "theories" of human behavior, in actuality, it routinely distorts, and omits huge categories of human experience.

Placing racial ethnic women's motherwork in the center of analysis recontextualizes mother-hood. While the significance of race and class in shaping the context in which motherhood occurs remains virtually invisible when white, middle-class women's mothering experiences assume prominence, the effects of race and class on motherhood stand out in stark relief when women of color are accorded theoretical primacy. Highlighting racial ethnic mothers' struggles concerning their children's right to exist focuses attention on the importance of survival. Exploring the dialectical nature of racial ethnic women's empowerment in structures of racial domination and economic exploitation demonstrates the need to broaden the definition of maternal power. Emphasizing how the quest for self-definition is mediated by membership in different racial and social class groups reveals how the issues of identity are crucial to all motherwork.

Existing feminist theories of motherhood have emerged in specific intellectual and political contexts. By assuming that social theory will be applicable regardless of social context, feminist scholars fail to realize that they themselves are rooted in specific locations, and that the specific contexts in which they are located provide the thought-models of how they interpret the world. While subsequent theories appear to be universal and objective, they actually are partial perspec-tives reflecting the white, middle-class context in which their creators live. Large segments of experience, specifically those of women who are not white and middle-class, have been excluded (Spelman 1988).

Feminist theories of motherhood are thus valid as partial perspectives, but cannot be seen as *theories* of motherhood generalizable to all women. The resulting patterns of partiality inherent in existing theories, such as, for example, the emphasis placed on all-powerful mothers as conduits for gender oppression, reflect feminist theorists' positions in structures of power. These theorists are themselves participants in a system of privilege that rewards them for not seeing race and class privilege as being important.

Theorizing about motherhood will not be helped by supplanting one group's theory with that of another; for example, by claiming that women of color's experiences are more valid than those of white, middle-class women. Varying placement in systems of privilege, whether race, class, sexuality, or age, generates divergent experiences with motherhood; therefore, examination of motherhood and mother-as-subject from multiple perspectives should uncover rich textures of difference. Shifting the center to accommodate this diversity promises to recontextualize motherhood and point us toward feminist theorizing that embraces difference as an essential part of commonality.

NOTES

1. In this essay, I use the terms "racial ethnic women" and "women of color" interchangeably. Grounded in the experiences of groups who have been the targets of racism, the term "racial ethnic" implies more solidarity with men involved in struggles against racism. In contrast, the term "women of color" emerges from a feminist background where racial ethnic women committed to feminist struggle aimed to distinguish their history and issues from those of middle-class, white women. Neither term captures the complexity of African-American, Native American, Asian-American and Hispanic women's experiences.

2. Positivist social science exemplifies this type of decontextualization. In order to create scientific descriptions of reality, positivist researchers aim to produce ostensibly objective generalizations. But because researchers have widely differing values, experiences, and emotions, genuine science is thought to be unattainable unless all human characteristics except rationality are eliminated from the research process. By following strict methodological rules, scientists aim to distance themselves from the values, vested interests, and emotions generated by their class, race, sex, or unique situation. By decontextualizing themselves, they allegedly become detached observers and manipulators of nature. Moreover, this researcher decontextualization is paralleled by comparable efforts to remove the objects of study from their contexts (Jaggar 1983).

3. Dominant theories are characterized by this decontextualization. Boyd's (1989) helpful survey of literature on the mother-daughter relationship reveals that while much work has been done on motherhood generally, and on

the mother-daughter relationship, very little of it tests feminist theories of motherhood. Boyd lists two prevailing theories, psychoanalytic theory and social learning theory, that she claims form the bulk of feminist theorizing. Both of these approaches minimize the importance of race and class in the context of motherhood. Boyd ignores Marxist-feminist theorizing about motherhood, mainly because very little of this work is concerned with the mother-daughter relationship. But Marxist-feminist analyses of motherhood provide another example of how decontextualization frames feminist theories of motherhood. See, for example, Ann Ferguson's *Blood at the Root: Motherhood, Sexuality, and Male Dominance* (1989), an ambitious attempt to develop a universal theory of motherhood that is linked to the social construction of sexuality and male dominance. Ferguson's work stems from a feminist tradition that explores the relationship between motherhood and sexuality by either bemoaning their putative incompatibility or romanticizing maternal sexuality.

4. Psychoanalytic feminist theorizing about motherhood, such as Nancy Chodorow's groundbreaking work, *The Reproduction of Mothering* (1978), exemplifies how decontextualization of race and/or class can weaken what is otherwise strong feminist theorizing. Although I realize that other feminist approaches to motherhood exist—see Eisenstein's (1983) summary, for example—I have chosen to stress psychoanalytic feminist theory because the work of Chodorow and others has been highly influential in framing the predominant themes in feminist discourse.

5. The thesis of the atomized individual that underlies Western psychology is rooted in a much larger Western construct concerning the relation of the individual to the community (Hartsock 1983). Theories of motherhood based on the assumption of the atomized human proceed to use this definition of individual as the unit of analysis, and then construct theory from this base. From this grow assumptions based on the premise that the major process to examine is that of freely choosing, rational individuals engaging in bargains (Hartsock 1983).

6. The narrative tradition in the writings of women of color addresses this effort to recover the history of mothers. Works from African-American women's autobiographical tradition, such as Ann Moody's *Coming of Age in Mississippi*, Maya Angelou's *I Know Why the Caged Bird Sings*, Linda Brent's *Narrative in the Life of a Slave Girl*, and Marita Golden's *The Heart of a Woman* contain the authentic voices of Black women centered on experiences of motherhood. Works from African-American women's fiction include Sarah Wright's *This Child's Gonna Live*, Alice Walker's *Meridian*, and Toni Morrison's *Sula* and *Beloved*. Asian-American women's fiction, such as Amy Tan's *The Joy Luck Club* and Maxine Kingston's *Woman Warrior*, and autobiographies such as Jean Wakatsuki Houston's *Farewell to Manzanar* offer a parallel source of authentic voice. Connie Young Yu (1989) entitles her article on the history of Asian-American women "The World of Our Grandmothers," and proceeds to recreate Asian-American history with her grandmother as a central figure. Cherrie Moraga (1979) writes a letter to her mother as a way of coming to terms with the contradictions in her racial identity as a Chicana. In *Borderlands/La Frontera*, Gloria Anzaldua (1987) weaves autobiography, poetry and philosophy together in her exploration of women and mothering.

7. Notable examples include Lutie Johnson's unsuccessful attempt to rescue her son from the harmful effects of an urban environment in Ann Petry's *The Street*; and Meridian's work on behalf of the children of a small Southern town after she chooses to relinquish her own child, in Alice Walker's *Meridian*.

8. Noticeably absent from feminist theories of motherhood is a comprehensive theory of power and explanation of how power relations shape theories. Firmly rooted in an exchange-based marketplace, with its accompanying assumptions of rational economic decision-making and white, male control of the marketplace, this model of community stresses the rights of individuals, including feminist theorists, to make decisions in their own self-interests, regardless of the impact on larger society. Composed of a collection of unequal individuals who compete for greater shares of money as the medium of exchange, this model of community legitimates relations of domination either by denying they exist or by treating them as inevitable but unimportant (Hartsock, 1983).

REFERENCES

Allen, Paula Gunn. 1986. *The Sacred Hoop: Recovering the Feminine in American Indian Traditions*. Boston: Beacon.

Andersen, Margaret. 1988. "Moving Our Minds: Studying Women of Color and Reconstructing Sociology." *Teaching Sociology* 16 (2), pp. 123–132.

Anzaldua, Gloria. 1987. *Borderlands/La Frontera: The New Mestiza*. San Francisco: Spinsters.

Awiakta, Marilou. 1988. "Amazons in Appalchia." In Beth Brant, ed., *A Gathering of Spirit*. Ithaca, NY: Firebrand, pp. 125–130.

Boyd, Carol J. 1989. "Mothers and Daughters: A Discussion of Theory and Research." *Journal of Marriage and the Family* 51, pp. 291–301.

Brant, Beth, ed. 1988. *A Gathering of Spirit: A Collection by North American Indian Women*. Ithaca, NY: Firebrand.

Brown, Elsa Barkley. 1989. "African-American Women's Quilting: A Framework for Conceptualizing and Teaching African-American Women's History." *Signs* 14 (4), pp. 921–929.

Chodorow, Nancy. 1978. *The Reproduction of Mothering*. Berkeley, CA: University of California Press.

——, and Susan Contratto. 1982. "The Fantasy of the Perfect Mother." In Barrie Thorne and Marilyn Yalom, eds., *Rethinking the Family: Some Feminist Questions*. New York: Longman, pp. 54–75.

Coleman, Willi. 1987. "Closets and Keepsakes." *Sage: A Scholarly Journal on Black Women* 4 (2), pp. 34–35.

Collins, Patricia Hill. 1990. *Black Feminist Thought: Knowledge, Consciousness and the Politics of Empowerment.* New York: Unwin Hyman/Routledge.

de la Cruz, Jessie. 1980. "Interview." In Studs Terkel, ed., *American Dreams: Lost and Found.* New York: Ballantine.

Davis, Angela Y. 1981. *Women, Race, and Class.* New York: Random House.

Dill, Bonnie Thornton. 1988. "Our Mothers' Grief: Racial Ethnic Women and the Maintenance of Families." *Journal of Family History* 13 (4), pp. 415–431.

Eisenstein, Hester. 1983. *Contemporary Feminist Thought.* Boston: G. K. Hall.

Ferguson, Ann. 1989. *Blood at the Root: Motherhood, Sexuality, and Male Dominance.* New York: Unwin Hyman/Routledge.

Flax, Jane. 1978. "The Conflict between Nurturance and Autonomy in Mother-Daughter Relationships and within Feminism." *Feminist Studies* 4 (2), pp. 171–189.

Glenn, Evelyn Nakano. 1985. "Racial Ethnic Women's Labor: The Intersection of Race, Gender and Class Oppression." *Review of Radical Political Economics* 17 (3), pp. 86–108.

——. 1986. *Issei, Nisei, War Bride: Three Generations of Japanese American Women in Domestic Service.* Philadelphia: Temple University Press.

Green, Rayna. 1990. "The Pocahontas Perplex: The Image of Indian Women in American Culture." In Ellen Carol DuBois and Vicki Ruiz, eds., *Unequal Sisters.* New York: Routledge, pp. 15–21.

Hartsock, Nancy. 1983. *Money, Sex and Power.* Boston: Northeastern University Press.

Jordan, June. 1985. *On Call.* Boston: South End Press.

LaDuke, Winona. 1988. "They always come back." In Beth Brant, ed., *A Gathering of Spirit.* Ithaca, NY: Firebrand, pp. 62–67.

Lerner, Gerda. 1972. *Black Women in White America.* New York: Pantheon.

Moraga, Cherrie. 1979. "La Guera." In Cherrie Moraga and Gloria Anzaldua, eds., *This Bridge Called My Back: Writings By Radical Women of Color.* Watertown, MA: Persephone Press, pp. 27–34.

Noda, Kesaya E. 1989. "Growing Up Asian in America." In Asian Women United of California, eds., *Making Waves: An Anthology of Writings By and About Asian American Women.* Boston: Beacon, pp. 243–50.

Rich, Adrienne. 1986 [1976]. *Of Woman Born: Motherhood as Institution and Experience.* New York: W. W. Norton.

Shanley, Kate. 1988. "Thoughts on Indian Feminism." In Beth Brant, ed., *A Gathering of Spirit.* Ithaca, NY: Firebrand, pp. 213–215.

Smith, Dorothy E. 1990. *The Conceptual Practices of Power: A Feminist Sociology of Knowledge.* Boston: Northeastern University Press.

Spelman, Elizabeth V. 1988. *Inessential Woman: Problems of Exclusion in Feminist Thought.* Boston: Beacon Press.

Tajima, Renee E. 1989. "Lotus Blossoms Don't Bleed: Images of Asian Women." In Asian Women United of California, eds., *Making Waves: An Anthology of Writings By and About Asian American Women.* Boston: Beacon, pp. 308–317.

Terborg-Penn, Rosalyn. 1986. "Black Women in Resistance: A Cross-Cultural Perspective." In Gary Y. Okhiro, ed., *In Resistance: Studies in African, Caribbean and Afro-American History.* Amherst: University of Massachusetts Press, pp. 188–209.

Wright, Sarah. 1986. *This Child's Gonna Live.* Old Westbury, NY: Feminist Press.

Yamoto, Jenny. 1988. "Mixed Bloods, Half Breeds, Mongrels, Hybrids . . ." In Jo Whitehorse Cochran, Donna Langston, and Carolyn Woodward, eds., *Changing Our Power: An Introduction to Women's Studies.* Dubuque, IA: Kendall/Hunt, pp. 22–24.

Yu, Connie Young. 1989. "The World of Our Grandmothers." In Asian Women United of California, eds., *Making Waves: An Anthology of Writings By and About Asian American Women.* Boston: Beacon, pp. 33–41.

11

Family and Class in Contemporary America

Notes Toward an Understanding of Ideology*

Rayna Rapp

This paper is grounded in two contexts, one political and one academic. The political context is that of the Women's Movement, in which a debate seems always to be raging concerning the future of the family. Many of us have been to an archetypical meeting in which someone stands up and asserts that the nuclear family ought to be abolished because it is degrading and constraining to women. Usually, someone else (often representing a Third World position) follows on her heels, pointing out that the attack on the family represents a White, middle-class position, and that other women need their families for support and survival. Evidently both speakers are, in some senses, right. And just as evidently they aren't talking about the same families.

The archetypical political debaters arguing over the meaning of the family aren't talking about the same families. Neither are the social scientists. We need to make a distinction between families and households, and to examine their relation to one another. The entities in which people actually live are not families, but households (as any census-taker, demographer, or fieldworking anthropologist will tell you). Households are the empirically measurable units within which people pool resources and perform certain tasks. Goody analyzes them as units of production, reproduction and consumption.[1] They are residential units within which personnel and resources get distributed and connected. Households may vary in their membership composition, and also in their relation to resource allocation, especially in a system such as our own. That is, they vary systematically in their ability to hook into, accumulate, and transmit wealth, wages, or welfare. This seems a simple unit to define.

Families, on the other hand, are a bit more slippery. In English we tend to gloss "family" to mean household. But analytically, the concept means something else. For all classes of Americans, the word has at least two levels of meaning.[2] One is normative: husbands, wives and children are a set of relatives who should live together (that is, the nuclear family). The other meaning includes a more extended network of kin relations which people may activate selectively. That is, the American family includes the narrower and broader webs of kin ties that are "the nuclear family" and all relations by blood and marriage. The concept of family is presumed in America to carry a heavy load of affect. We say, "blood is thicker than water," "till death do us part," "you can choose your friends, but not your relatives," etc. What I will argue in this paper is that the concept of family also carries a heavy load of ideology.

The reason for this is that the family is the normative, correct way in which people get recruited into households. It is through families that people enter into productive, reproductive, and consumption relations. The two genders enter them differently. Families organize households, and it is within families that people experience the absence or presence, the sharing or witholding, of basic poolable resources. "Family" (as a normative concept in our culture) reflects those material relations; it also distorts them. As such, the concept of family is a socially necessary illusion which simultaneously expresses and masks recruitment to relations of production, reproduction and consumption—relations that condition different kinds of household resource bases in different class sectors. Our notions of family absorb the conflicts, contradictions and tensions that are actually generated by those material, class-structured relations that households hold to resources in advanced capitalism. "Family," as we understand (and misunderstand) the term, is conditioned by the exigencies of household formation, and serves as a shock-absorber to keep households functioning. People are recruited and kept in households by families in all classes, yet the families they have (or don't have) are not the same.

Having asserted that households and families vary by class, we now need to consider that third concept, class. If ever a concept carried a heavy weight of ideology, it is the concept of class in American social science. We have a huge and muddled literature which attempts to reconcile objective and subjective criteria, to sort people into lowers, uppers and middles, to argue about the relation of consciousness to material reality.[3] I will say only the following: "social class" is a shorthand for a process, and not a thing. That process is the one by which different social relations to the means of production are inherited and reproduced under capitalism. As the concept is developed by Marx, the process of capital accumulation generates and constantly deepens relations between two categories of people: those who are both available and forced to work for wages because they own no means of production, and those who control those means of production. The concept of class expresses a historical process of expanding capital. In the process, categories of people get swept up at different times and places, and deposited into different relations to the means of production, and to one another. People then get labeled "blue-collar" or "white-collar"; they may experience their social existence as mediated by ethnicity or the overwhelming legacy of slavery and racism. Yet all of these categories must be viewed in the light of the historic process of capitalist accumulation in the United States. To a large extent, what are actually being accumulated are changing categories of proletarians. Class formation and composition is always in flux; what gets accumulated in it are relationships. Under advanced capitalism, there are shifting frontiers which separate poverty, stable wage-earning, affluent salaries, and inherited wealth. The frontiers may be crossed by individuals, and in either direction. That is, both upward and downward mobility are real processes. The point is, "class" isn't a static place which individuals inhabit. It is a process determined by the relationships set up in capital accumulation.

Returning to the initial distinction between family and household, I want to explore how these two vary among differing class sectors in contemporary America and to draw a composite picture of the households formed around material relations by class, and the families which organize those households. I will argue that those families mean different things by class, and by genders as well, because classes and genders stand in differing material relations to one another. I'll further argue that their meanings are highly ideological.

I'd like to begin with a review and interpretation of the studies done on the working-class family. There are studies which span the post-war decades from the late 1940s to the present. They are regionally diverse, and report on both cities and suburbs. The data provided by researchers such as Berger, Gans, Komarovsky, Howell, Rubin, and others reveal a composite portrait.[4] The most salient characteristic of household organization in the working class is dependency on hourly wages. Stable working-class households participate in relations of production, reproduction and consumption by sending out their labor-power in exchange for wages. "Sending out" is important: there is a radical split between household and workplace, yet the resources upon which the household depends come from participation in production outside of itself. How much labor-power a working-class household needs to send out is determined by many things: the cost of reproducing (or maintaining) the household, the work careers and earning trajectories of individual members, and the domestic cycle (that is, the relations between the genders and the generations, which specify when and if wives and adolescent children are available to work outside the home). Braverman[5] estimates that the average working-class household now sends out 1.7 full-time equivalent workers. That figure tells us that a high percentage of married women and teenaged children are contributing their wages to the household. In many ways, the work patterns for 19th century European capitalism described by Tilly and Scott[6] still leave their mark on the contemporary American working-class household: it is not only male heads of household upon whom survival depends.

What the working class sends out in exchange for basic resources is labor-power. Labor-power is the only commodity without which there can be no capitalism. It is also the only commodity for which the working class controls its own means of production.[7] Control over the production of labor-power undoubtedly affected women's experiences historically, as it still does today.[8] In the early stages of industrialization, it appears that working-class households literally produced a lot of babies (future labor-power) as their strategy for dealing with a market economy.[9] Now workers produce fewer children, but the work of servicing them (social reproduction) is still a major process that goes on in the household. Households are the basic units in which labor-power is reproduced and maintained. This takes place in a location radically removed from the workplace. Such relations therefore appear as autonomous from capital, but of course they are not: without wages, households are hard to form and keep functioning; without the production of a disciplined labor force, factories cannot produce and profit.

The work that gets done in households (primarily by women) is not simply about babies. Housework itself has recently been rediscovered as work, and its contribution to arenas beyond the household is clear.[10] At the very least, housework cuts the reproduction costs of wage-workers. Imagine if all those meals had to be bought at restaurants, those clothes cleaned at laundry rates, those beds made by hotel employees! Housework is also what women do in exchange for access to resources which are bought by their husbands' wages. As such, it is a coin of exchange between men and women. As housework is wageless, it keeps its workers dependent on others for access to commodities bought with wages. It makes them extremely vulnerable to the work conditions of their men. When women do work (as increasingly they do), their primary definition as house-workers contributes to the problems they encounter in entering the paid labor force. They are available for part-time (or full-time) work in the lowest paid sectors of the labor market, in jobs which leave them less economically secure than men. Participation in the "sexregated" labor market then reinforces dependency upon the earnings of other household members, and the continued importance of women's domestic labor.[11]

Of course, these rather abstract notions of "household participation" in the labor market or in housework are experienced concretely by family members. Working-class families are normatively nuclear. They are formed via marriage, which links men and women "for love" and not "for money."[12] This relation is of course both real, and a socially necessary illusion. As such, it is central to the ideology of the family. The cultural distinction between love and money corresponds to the distinction between private family life in the home, and work life outside the home. The two are experienced as opposite; in fact they are interpenetrating. The seeming autonomy to exchange love at home expresses something ideological about the relation between home and work: one must work for the sake of the family, and having a family is the "pay-off" for leading a good life. Founding a family is what people do for personal gratification, for love and for autonomy. The working-class family literature is full of life-histories in which young women saw "love" as the way to get out of their own, often difficult families. Rubin's interviews, for example, are full of teenaged girls who said, "When I grow up, I'll marry for love, and it will be better than my parents' marriage." You may marry for love, but what you mainly get is babies; 40–60 percent of teenaged pregnancies are conceived premaritally, and approximately 50 percent of working-class women marry in their teen years.[13] It's a common experience to go from being someone's child to having someone's child in under a year. This is not exactly a situation which leads to autonomy.

For men, the situation is complementary. As one of the young working-class men in Rubin's study puts it:

> I had to work from the time I was thirteen and turn over most of my pay to my mother to help pay the bills. By the time I was nineteen, I had been working for all those years and I didn't have anything—not a thing. I used to think a lot about how when I got married, I would finally get to keep my money for myself. I guess that sounds a little crazy when I think about it now because I have to support the wife and kids. I don't know *what* I was thinking about, but I never thought about that then.[14]

What you get from the romance of love and marriage is in fact not simply a family, but a household, and that's quite another matter. Romance is implicated in gender identity and ideology. We are all aware of the cultural distinction made between the sexual identity of a good and a bad girl; a good girl is one who accumulates her sexual resources for later investment. Autonomy means escaping your childhood family to become an adult with your own nuclear family. For young men, the identity process includes the cultural role of wild boy—one who "sows some wild oats," hangs out on street corners, perhaps gets in trouble with the police, and drinks.[15] Ideally, the good girl domesticates the wild boy; she gives him love, and he settles down and goes out to work. Autonomy means becoming an adult with your own nuclear family as an escape. But of course, autonomy is illusive. The family is classically seen as an escape from production, but in fact it is what sends people into relations of production, for they need to work to support their families. The meaning of production is simultaneously denied and experienced through family relations; working-class wives say of a good husband that he works steadily, provides for the kids, and never harms anyone in the family. The complementary statement is uttered by working-class husbands, who define a good wife as one who keeps the kids under control when he comes home from a hard day's work, and who runs the household well.[16] To exchange love is also to underwrite both the necessity and the ability to keep on working. *This* is the heritage that working-class families pass on, in lieu of property, to their children.

The family expresses ideology in another sense as well—the distinction between norms and realities. The norms concerning families are that people should be loving and sharing within them, and that they should be protective. The reality is too often otherwise, as the recent rising consciousness of domestic violence indicates. Even without domestic violence, there are more commonplace stresses to which families are often subjected. Rubin found in her study that 40 percent of the adults she interviewed had an alcoholic parent.[17] Fifty percent had experienced parental desertion or divorce in their childhood. National statistics confirm these figures.[18] About half the adults in her study had seriously destabilizing experiences within their families. The tension generated by relations to resource base can often tear households apart. Under these conditions, to label the working-class personality "authoritarian" seems a cruel hoax. When the household is working, it expresses work discipline.

Ideology is expressed in gender role in families in another sense as well. Throughout the urban kinship literature, across classes and ethnic groups, the work of reproducing families is in part undertaken by larger kinship groups (the family in the broader sense of relatives). Family networks in this larger sense are women-centered and tend to be serviced by women. There exists a large literature on women-centered kinship networks in which it is usually assumed that women minister to kinship because they minister to families in general. Sylvia Yanagisako suggests that there is also a symbolic level to the kinship work which women do: ideologically, women are assigned to "inside, home, private" domains, while men are seen to represent the outside world.[19] Nuclear families are under cultural constraints to appear as autonomous and private. Yet they are never as private in reality as such values might indicate. The ideal autonomy of an independent nuclear family is constantly being contradicted by the realities of social need, in which resources must be pooled, borrowed, shared. It is women who bridge the gap between what a household's resources really are, and what a family's position is supposed to be. Women exchange babysitting, share meals, lend small amounts of money. When a married child is out of work, his (or her) nuclear family turns to the mother, and often moves in for a while. The working-class family literature is filled with examples of such pooling.[20] To the extent that women "represent" the family, they facilitate the pooling which is needed at various points in the domestic cycle. Men maintain, at least symbolically, the autonomy of their families. Pooling is a norm in family behavior, but it's a hard norm to live with, to either meet or ignore. To comply with the demands of the extended family completely is to lose control over material and emotional resources; to refuse is very dangerous, as people know they will need one another. The tightrope act which ensues is well characterized in the classic mother-in-law story, which usually concerns a young wife and her husband's mother. The two women must figure out a way to share the small services, the material benefits, and the emotional satisfactions which one man brings to them both in their separate roles of mother and wife. The autonomy of the younger woman is often compromised by the elder's needs; the authority of the mother is sometimes undermined by the demands of the wife. Women must constantly test, strain, and repair the fibers of their kinship networks.

Such women-centered networks are implicated in a process which has not yet been discussed. We have spoken of production and reproduction as they affect the working-class household and family. We ought briefly to mention consumption as well. As a household function, consumption includes turning an amount of wages into commodities so that labor-power may be reproduced. This is often women's work. And work it really is. Weinbaum and Bridges tell us that the centralization and rationalization of services and industry under advanced capitalism may be most efficient from the point of view of capital, but it leaves a lot of unrewarding, technical work to be done by women in supermarkets, in paying bills, in dealing with huge bureaucracies.[21] Women experience the pay packet in terms of the use values it will buy. Yet their consumption work is done in the world of exchange value. They mediate the tension between use and exchange, as exemplified in the classic tales concerning domestic quarrels over money in which the man blames the woman for not making his pay check stretch far enough. In stable working-class neighborhoods, the consumption work is in part done by women united by family ties who exchange services, recipes, sales information, and general lifestyle skills. Kinship networks are part of "community control" for women. As Seifer notes, working-class women become involved in political issues that threaten the stability of their neighborhoods.[22] Perhaps one reason is that their neighborhoods are the locus of extended families within which both work needs and emotional needs are so often met.

When everyone submits to the conditions described here "for the sake of the family," we see the pattern that Howell labels "settled living."[23] Its opposite, in his words, is "hard living," a family lifestyle which includes a lot of domestic instability, alcohol, and rootlessness. I want to stress that I am here departing from a "culture of poverty" approach. The value of a label like "hard living" is that it stresses a continuum made up of many attributes. It is composed of many processes with which the working class has a lot of experience. Given the national statistics on alcoholism, desertion, divorce, premarital pregnancy, etc., everyone's family has included such experiences, either in its own domestic cycle, or in the wider family network.[24] Everyone had a wild brother, or was a bad girl, or had an uncle who drank too much, or cousins who got divorced. In each of such cases, everyone experienced the pooling of resources (or the lack of pooling) as families attempted to cope with difficult, destabilizing situations. In a sense, the hard livers keep the settled livers more settled: the consequences of leaving the normative path are well-known and are not appealing. This, too, is part of the working-class heritage. In studies by Seifer, Howell and Rubin, young women express their hopes of leaving a difficult family situation by finding the right man to marry. They therefore marry young, with little formal education, possibly about to become parents, and the cycle begins again.

Of course, hard living is most consistently associated with poverty in the urban family literature. For essentially political reasons, Black poverty has more frequently been the subject of social science analysis than has white poverty, but the pattern is found across races. Black Americans have survived under extremely difficult conditions; many of their household and family patterns have evolved to deal with their specific history, while others are shared with Americans of similar class and regional backgrounds. The problems of household formation under poverty conditions are not unique to any group of people; some of the specific, resilient solutions to those problems may be. Because we know far more about Black families in poverty than we do about whites, I'll draw a composite picture of households and families using studies that are primarily Black.[25] Even when talking about very poor people, analysts such as Liebow, Hannerz, Valentine, and Stack note that there are multiple household types, based on domestic cycles and the relative ability to draw on resources. Hannerz, for example, divides his Black sample into four categories.[26] Mainstreamers live in stable households composed of husband, wife and children. The adults are employed, and either own their own homes or aspire to do so. Their households don't look very different from the rest of the working class. Swingers (Hannerz's second type) are younger, single persons who may be on their way into mainstream life, or they may be tending toward street-families (type three), whose households are headed by women. It is this type which is most important for our study. The fourth category is composed of street men who are peer-oriented, and predominantly hard-core unemployed or underemployed. They are similar to the men of *Tally's Corner*.[27] While Hannerz and Liebow both give us a wealth of information about what men are doing, they don't analyze these men's domestic arrangements in detail. It is Carol Stack,[28] who did her field work from the perspective of female-centered households, who most clearly analyzes household formation of the very poor. She presents us with domestic networks: extremely flexible and fluctuating groups of people committed to resource pooling, to sharing, to mutual aid, who move in and out from under one another's roofs.

Given the state of the job market, welfare legislation, and segregated slum housing, households are unstable. These are people essentially living below socially necessary reproduction costs. They therefore reproduce themselves by spreading out the aid and the risks involved in daily life. For the disproportionally high numbers who are prevented from obtaining steady employment, being part of what Marx called the floating surplus population is a perilous endeavor. What this means in human terms is not only that the poor pay more (as Caplowitz tells us),[29] but that the poor share more as well. Stack's monograph contains richly textured descriptions of the way that food, furniture, clothing, appliances, kids, and money make the rounds between individuals and households. She subtitles one chapter, "What Goes Round Comes Round," and describes the velocity with which pooling takes place. People try to give what they can and take what they need. Meeting consumption requirements is hard work under these conditions, and domestic networks get the task done. The pleasures and pressures of such survival networks are predominantly organized around the notion of family.

Meyer Fortes tells us that "domestic groups are the workshops of social reproduction."[30] Whatever else they do, the families that organize domestic networks are responsible for children. As Ladner and Stack[31] remind us, poverty, low levels of formal education, and early age for first pregnancy are highly correlated: a lot of young girls have children while they are not fully adults. Under these circumstances, at least among Black families, there is a tremendous sharing of the children themselves. On the whole, these are not kids who grow up in "isolated nuclear families." Stack, for example, found that 20 percent of the A.D.C. (Aid to Dependent Children) children in her study were being raised in a household other than that which contained the biological mother. In the vast majority of cases, the household was related through the biological mother's family. Organizing kinship networks so that children are cared for is a primary function of families. Men, too, often contribute to child-rearing. Like women, they share out bits and pieces of whatever they have. While some men make no contribution, others may be simultaneously contributing to sisters, to a mother and aunt, as well as to wives or lovers. They may sleep in one household, but bring groceries, money, and affection to several others.[32] Both Stack and Ladner analyze the importance of a father's recognition of his children, by which act he links the baby to his own kinship network. It is family in the broader sense of the term that organizes social reproduction.

Family may be a conscious construction of its participants. Liebow, Stack, Ladner and others describe fictive kinship, by which friends are turned into family. Since family is supposed to be more reliable than friendship, "going for brothers," "for sisters," "for cousins," increases the commitment of a relationship, and makes people ideally more responsible for one another. Fictive kinship is a serious relationship. Stack (who is white) describes her own experience with Ruby, a Black woman with whom she "went for sisters." When Ruby's child was seriously ill, Stack became deeply involved in the crisis. When the baby was admitted to the hospital, she and Ruby rushed over for visiting hours. They were stopped by a nurse, who insisted that only the immediate family could enter. Ruby responded, "Caroline here is my sister, and nothing's stopping her from visiting this baby." And they entered, unchallenged. Ruby was correct; under the circumstances, white Caroline was her sister.[33]

Liebow notes that fictive kinship increases the intensity of relationships to the point where they occasionally explode: the demands of brothers and sisters for constant emotional and material aid may lead to situations that shatter the bonds. Fictive kinship is a prime example of family-as-ideology. In this process, reality is inverted. "Everybody" gets a continuous family, even though the strains and mobility associated with poverty may conspire to keep biological families apart. The idiom of kinship brings people together despite centrifugal circumstances.

It is important not to romanticize this pattern. It has enormous benefits, but its participants also pay high costs. One of the most obvious costs is leveling: resources must be available for all, and none may get ahead. Variations in the chance for survival are smoothed out in domestic networks via sharing. Stack tells the story of a couple, Calvin and Magnolia, who unexpectedly inherit a sum of money. While the money might have enabled them to insure their own security, it is gone within a few months. It disappears into the network, of which Calvin and Magnolia are the central couple, to pay off bills, buy clothing for children, allow people to eat better.[34] Similar stories are told by Hannerz, Liebow, and Howell. No one gets ahead because individual upward mobility can be bought only at the price of cutting off the very people who have contributed to one's survival. Upward mobility becomes a terribly scarring experience under these circumstances. To get out, a person must stop sharing, which is unfamilial, unfriendly, and quite dangerous. It also requires exceptional circumstances. Gans[35] speaks of the pain which working-class children face if they attempt to use school as a means to achieve mobility, for they run into the danger of being cut off from their peer-group. The chance for mobility may occur only once or twice in a lifetime—for example, at specific moments in a school career, or in marriage. People rarely get the occasion, and when they do, to grasp it may simply be too costly. The pressures to stay in a supportive and constraining network, and to level out differences may be immense. These pressures contribute to the instability of marriage and the normative nuclear family, for the old networks compete with the new unit for precious resources.

The family as an ideological construction is extremely important to poor people. Many studies show that the poor don't aspire to less "stable families," if that term is understood as nuclear families. They are simply much more realistic about their life-chances. Ties to family, including fictive family, are the lifelines that simultaneously hold together and sustain individuals. My guess is that among the poor, families do not exhibit the radical split between "private, at home" and "public, at work" which is found in families of the stable working class. Neither work relations nor household relations are as continuous, or as distinct. What is continuous is the sharing of reproduction costs throughout a network whose resources are known to all. There can be no privatization when survival may depend on rapid circulation of limited resources. In this process, women don't "represent" kinship to the outside world. They become the nodal points in family nets which span whatever control very poor people have over domestic and resource-getting arrangements. Families are what make the huge gap between norm and reality survivable.

It is particularly ironic that the ideology of family, so important to poor people, is used by ruling class ideologues to blame the poor for their own condition. In a society in which *all* Americans subscribe to some version of the normative nuclear family, it is cruelty to attack "the Black family" as pathological. Mainstream culture, seeing the family as "what you work for" (and what works for you), uses "family language" to stigmatize those who are structurally prevented from accumulating stable resources. The very poor have used their families to cement and patch tenuous relations to survival; out of their belief in "family" they have invented networks capable of making next-to-nothing go a long way.[36] In response, they are told that their notion of family is inadequate. It isn't their notion of family that is deficient, but the relationship between household and productive resources.

If we now return to the political debate which opened this paper, I believe we can see that there are two different concepts of family at work. To achieve a normative family is something many categories of Americans are prevented from doing because of the ways that their households plug into tenuous resource bases. And when normative families are achieved, it is at substantial and differential costs to both men and women.

Having considered the meaning of family and household among class sectors with regular or unstable relations to wages, we should now consider those sectors with more affluent resource bases. Analyzing the family and household life of the middle class is a tricky business. The term "middle class" is ambiguous; a majority of Americans identify themselves as part of it whenever they answer questionnaires, and the category obviously carries positive connotations. Historically, we take the notion from the Marxian definition of the petty bourgeoisie: that category of people who own small amounts of productive resources, and have control over their working conditions in ways that proletarians do not. The term signifies a stage in proletarianization in which small-scale entrepreneurs, tradesfolk, artisans, and professionals essentially stand outside the wage-labor/capital relation. That stage is virtually over: there are ever fewer small-scale proprietors or artisans working on their own account in post-World War II America. We now use the term to refer to a different sector—employees in corporate management, government and organizational bureaucrats of various kinds, and professionals, many of whom work directly or indirectly for big business, the state and semi-public institutions. On the whole, this "new middle class" is dependent on wages; as such, it bears the mark of proletarianization. Yet the group lives at a level that is quite different from the wage levels of workers.[37] Such a category is obviously hard to define; like all class sectors, it must be historically situated, for the middle class of early 20th century America differs markedly from that of our own times. To understand what middle class means for the different groups, we need to know not only their present status, but also the ethnic and regional variations in class structure within which their families entered America.

In a sense, the middle class is a highly ideological construction which pervades American culture; it is, among other things, the perspective from which mainstream social scientists approach the experiences of all the other sectors they attempt to analyze. To analyze the middle class's household formations and family patterns, we have to examine not only the data available on all the people who claim to be middle class, but also explore the biases inherent in much of social science. This is a task beyond the scope of the present paper. Instead, I merely suggest a few tentative ideas as notes toward future research.

Households among the middle class are obviously based on a stable resource base which allows for some amount of luxury and discretionary spending. When exceptional economic resources are called for, nonfamilial institutions usually are available in the form of better medical coverage, expense accounts, pension plans, credit at banks, etc. Such households may maintain their economic stability at the cost of geographical instability; male career choices may move households around like pieces on a chessboard. When far from family support networks, such households may get transitional aid from professional moving specialists, or institutions like the Welcome Wagon.[38] Middle-class households probably are able to rely on commodity-forms rather than on kinship processes to ease both economic and geographic transitions.

The families which organize such households are commonly thought to be characterized by egalitarian marriages.[39] Rubin comments that "egalitarian marriage" may be a biased gloss for a communication pattern in which the husband's career is in part reflected in the presentation of his wife.[40] To entertain intelligently, and instill the proper educational and social values in the children, women may need to know more about the male world. They represent the private credentials of family to the public world of their men at work. If this is the case, then "instrumental communication" might be a more appropriate term.

I am not prepared at this point to offer an analysis of middle-class kinship patterns, but I have a few hunches to present:

1) At this level, kinship probably shifts from the lateral toward the lineal. That is, resources (material and economic) are invested lineally, between parents, children, and grandchildren, and not dispersed into larger networks, as happens with working-class and poor families. Such a pattern would of course vary with geographical mobility, and possibly with ethnicity. There is usually a greater investment across generations, and a careful accumulation within them. This kind of pattern

can be seen, for example, in the sums invested in children's educations, setting up professional practices, wedding gifts (in which major devolvement of property may occur), etc.

2) Perhaps friendship, rather than kinship, is the nexus within which the middle class invests its psychic and "familial" energies. Friendship allows for a great deal of affective support and exchange, but usually does not include major resource pooling. It is a relation which is consistent with resource accumulation, rather than dispersal. If the poor convert friendship into kinship to equalize pooling, it seems to me that the middle class does the converse: it reduces kinship exchanges, and replaces them with friendship, which protects them from pooling and leveling.[41]

There is one last sector of the American class system whose household and family patterns would be interesting to examine—the upper class, sometimes identified as the ruling class, or the very rich. Once again, I limit myself to a few tentative observations. As one sociologist (either quite naive or quite sardonic) commented, "We know so little about the very wealthy because they don't answer our questionnaires." Indeed! They fund them, rather than answer them. The few studies we do have (by authors such as Domhoff, Amory, Baltzell, Veblen) are highly suggestive. The upper class, they tell us, appears to hang together as a cultural phenomenon. They defend their own interests corporately, and have tremendous ideological importance.

We know very little about the household structure of the very rich. They are described as having multiple households which are recomposed seasonally[42] and filled with service workers, rather than exclusively with kin and friends. While there is a general tendency toward "conspicuous consumption," we have no basic information on the relation of their resource bases to domestic arrangements.

When we turn to the family structure of the very rich, some interesting bits and pieces emerge (which may possibly be out of date). Families are described as extremely lineal, and concerned with who they are, rather than what they do. People have access to one another through their control of neighborhoods, schools, universities, clubs, churches, and ritual events. They are quite ancestor-oriented, and conscious of the boundaries which separate the "best" families from all others. Families are obviously the units within which wealth is accumulated and transmitted. Yet the link between wealth and class is not so simple; some of the "best" families lose fortunes but remain in the upper class. Mobility is also possible. According to Baltzell,[43] under certain circumstances it is possible for nonmembers to enter the class via educational and work-related contacts. What emerges from the literature is a sketch of a group which is perhaps the only face-to-face subculture that America contains.

Women serve as gatekeepers of many of the institutions of the very rich.[44] They launch children, serve as board members at the private schools, run the clubs, and facilitate the marriage pools through events like debuts and charity balls. Men also preside over exclusive clubs and schools, but different ones. The upper class appears to live in a world which is very sex-segregated. Domhoff mentions several other functions that very rich women fulfill. These include: (1) setting social and cultural standards, and (2) softening the rough edges of capitalism by doing charity and cultural work. While he trivializes the cultural standards that women establish for things like dress and high art, I think he has alerted us to something more important. In the upper class, women "represent" the family to the outside world. But here, it is an outside world that is in many senses created by their own class (in the form of high cultural institutions, education, social welfare, and charity). Their public presence is an inversion of reality: they appear as wives and mothers, but it is not really their family roles but their class roles which dictate those appearances. To the extent that "everyone else" either has a wife/mother or is a wife/mother, upper-class women are available to be perceived as something both true and false. What they can do because of their families (and ultimately, for their families) is utterly, radically different from what other women who "represent" their families can do. Yet what everyone sees is their womanness as family members, rather than as class members. They influence our cultural notions of what feminine and familial behavior should be. They simultaneously become symbols of domesticity and of public service to which others may aspire. The very tiny percentage of very wealthy women who live in a sex-segregated world and have no need to work are thus perceived as benevolent and admirable by a much larger group of women whose relation to sex-role segregation and work is not nearly so benign. "Everybody" can yearn for a family in which sex-role segregation is valued; nobody else can have a family in which it is valued quite as highly as theirs. In upper-class families, at least as they present themselves to "the public," we see a systematic confusion of cultural values with the values of family fortunes. We have here an excellent illustration of how the ideas of the ruling class become part of the ruling ideas of society.

* * *

At each level of American society, households vary systematically as to resource base, and their ability to tap wealth, wages, and welfare. Households are organized by families (which means relatives both distant and close, imaginary and real). Families both reflect and distort the material relations within which households are embedded. The working-class and middle-class household may *appear* isolated from the arenas in which production takes place. But in fact, their families are formed to generate and deepen relations to those work processes that underwrite their illusion of autonomy. Women's experience with "the family" varies systematically by class because class expresses the material and social relations upon which their household bases rest. We need to explore their transformative potential as well as the constraints that differential family patterns provide.

Women have structurally been put in the position of representing the contradictions between autonomy and dependence, between love and money, in the relations of families to capitalism. The ideological role that women have played needs to be demystified as we struggle toward a future in which consumption and reproduction will not be determined by capitalist production, in which households will have access to more even resource bases, and in which women will neither symbolically nor in their real relations be forced to bridge the gap between affective norms and contradictory realities under the name of love. To liberate the notion of voluntary relations which the normative family is supposed to represent, we have to stop paying workers off in a coin called love.**

NOTES

* Social analysis is always a collective endeavor, even when individually presented. This paper builds quite directly on the published work of many people cited in the text, and the unpublished work and discussion of many others. The University of Michigan's Women Studies Program called this paper into being, gave it a first airing, and contributed a stimulating set of discussions. Subsequent presentation of these ideas at the New School for Social Research, the URPE. Spring conference on Public Policy, and the Anthropology Department of the University of Northern Colorado provided invaluable feedback. I especially want to thank Jill Cherneff, Ingelore Fritsch, Susan Harding, Mike Hooper, Janet Siskind, Deborah Jay Stearns, Batya Weinbaum and Marilyn Young for their comments. The women of Marxist-Feminist Group II posed the questions which led me to write this paper; they supplied, as always, the supportive context within which the meaning of my work has been discussed. Above all, Gayle Rubin deserves my thanks for her general intellectual aid, and the specific editorial work she did in turning my primary process into a set of written ideas.
** This paper was first presented to the University of Michigan's Women's Studies Research on Women Seminar sponsored by Grant #E.H. 2–5643–76–772 from the National Endowment for the Humanities. It is reprinted with grateful acknowledgement from the Special Issue of the University of Michigan Papers in Women's Studies, June 1978.

    1.   Jack Goody, "The Evolution of the Family," in *Household and Family in Past Time*, Peter Laslett and Richard Wall, eds. (Cambridge, 1972).

2. Ibid. Also see David M. Schneider and Raymond T. Smith, *Class Differences and Sex Roles in American Kinship and Family Structure* (Englewood Cliffs, 1973).
3. There is a vast literature on this subject. Its mainstream interpretations in relation to family research are reviewed in Luther B. Otto, "Class and Status in Family Research," *Journal of Marriage and the Family*, 1975, 37: 315–332. Marxist perspectives are presented in Charles H. Anderson, *The Political Economy of Social Class* (Englewood Cliffs, 1974); Anderson, *Toward a New Sociology*, revised edition (Homewood, Ill., 1974); Alfred Szymanski, "Trends in the American Class Structure," *Socialist Revolution*, July–August 1972, No. 10; and Harry Braverman, *Labor and Monopoly Capital: The Degradation of Work in the Twentieth Century* (New York, 1974).
4. This composite is drawn from the works of Bennett Berger, *Working Class Suburb: A Study of Auto Workers in Suburbia* (Berkeley, 1968); Herbert J. Gans, *The Urban Villagers* (New York, 1962); Gans, *The Levittowners* (New York, 1967); Louise Kapp Howe, ed., *The White Majority: Between Poverty and Affluence* (New York, 1970); Joseph Howell, *Hard Living on Clay Street* (New York, 1973); Mirra Komarovsky, *Blue Collar Marriage* (New York, 1962); Lillian Rubin, *Worlds of Pain* (New York, 1976); Joseph A. Ryan, ed., *White Ethnics: Life in Working Class America* (Englewood Cliffs, 1973); Nancy Seifer, "Absent From the Majority: Working Class Women in America," Middle America Pamphlet Series, National Project on Ethnic America; *American Jewish Committee*, 1973; Seifer, *Nobody Speaks for Me: Self-Portraits of American Working Class Women* (New York, 1976); Arthur B. Shostak, *Blue Collar Life* (New York, 1969); Richard Sennett and Jonathan Cobb, *The Hidden Injuries of Class* (New York, 1972); Patricia Cayo Sexton and Brendan Sexton, *Blue Collars and Hard Hats* (New York, 1971); and Studs Terkel, *Working* (New York, 1972).
5. Braverman, *Labor and Monopoly Capital*.
6. Louise Tilly and Joan Scott, "Women's Work in Nineteenth Century Europe." *Comparative Studies in Society and History*, 1975, 17: 36–64.
7. See Ira Gerstein, "Domestic Work and Capitalism," *Radical America*, 1973, 7: 101–130.
8. Linda Gordon, *Women's Body, Women's Right: A Social History of Birth Control in America* (New York, 1976).
9. Louise Tilly, "Reproduction, Production and the Family among Textile Workers in Roubaix, France," paper presented at the Conference on Social History, February 1977.
10. The economic value of housework has been the subject of vigorous debate in Marxist literature in recent years. The debate was begun with the publication of Mariarosa Dalla Costa, "Women and the Subversion of the Community," *Radical America*, 1972, 6: 67–102; and continued by Wally Secombe, "The Housewife and Her Labour Under Capitalism," *New Left Review*, 1974, 83: 3–24; Jean Gardiner, "Women's Domestic Labour," *New Left Review*, 1975, 89: 47–71; Lise Vogel, "The Earthly Family," *Radical America*, 1973, 7: 9–50; Gerstein, "Domestic Work and Capitalism"; and others. See also Heidi I. Hartmann, "Capitalism and Women's Work in the Home, 1900–1930." Ph.D. dissertation, Yale University, 1974; and Joann Vanek, "Time Spent in Housework," *Scientific American*, November 1974: 116–20, for American case historical materials, and Nona Glazer-Malbin, "Review Essay: Housework," *Signs*, 1: 905–922, for a review of the field.
11. For historical, sociological and political-economic analyses of women's economic position in the labor market, see the special issue of *Signs*, Barbara B. Reagan and Martha Blaxall, eds., "Women and the Workplace," 1976, 1: 3, part 2. See also U.S. Bureau of the Census, *Statistical Abstract of the U.S.*, 1974, for statistical data on demography and workforce participation rates of women.
12. Schneider and Smith, *Class Differences and Sex Roles in American Kinship and Family Structure*, Ch. 5.
13. Rubin, *Worlds of Pain*, Ch. 4.
14. Ibid., 56f.
15. See ibid.; also Shostak, *Blue Collar Life* and Howell, *Hard Living on Clay Street*.
16. See Rubin, *Worlds of Pain*; Shostak, *Blue Collar Life*; Sennett and Cobb, *The Hidden Injuries of Class*; and Terkel, *Working*.
17. Rubin, *Worlds of Pain*.
18. U.S. Bureau of Census, *Statistical Abstract of the U.S.*, 1974, 221f.
19. Sylvia Junko Yanagisako, "Women-Centered Kin Networks in Urban, Bilateral Kinship," *American Ethnologist*, 1977.
20. This literature is reviewed in Yanagisako, op. cit. Further instances are found in the sources listed in note 4. The pattern is given much attention in Peter Wilmott and Michael Young, *Family and Kinship in East London* (London, 1957), and in Elizabeth Bott, *Family and Social Network* (New York, 1971).
21. Batya Weinbaum and Amy Bridges, "The Other Side of the Paycheck: Monopoly Capital and the Structure of Consumption," *Monthly Review*, 1976, 28: 88–103.
22. Seifer, "Absent From the Majority: Working Class Women in America," and Seifer, *Nobody Speaks For Me: Self-Portraits of American Working Class Women*.
23. Howell, *Hard Living on Clay Street*.
24. Throughout her work, Rubin (*Worlds of Pain*) is especially sensitive to this issue, and provides an excellent discussion of individual lifecycles in relation to domestic cycles. She explains why the labeling issue is such a critical one (p. 223, note 5).
25. Howell's study (*Hard Living on Clay Street*) provides important and sensitive insights into the domestic lives of poor and working white families, collected in the style of Oscar Lewis. Composite Black family studies include Ulf Hannerz, *Soulside: Inquiries into Ghetto Culture and Community* (New York, 1969); Joyce Ladner, *Tomorrow's Tomorrow: The Black Woman* (New York, 1971); Elliot Liebow, *Tally's Corner* (Boston, 1967); Lee Rainwater, *Behind Ghetto Walls: Black Families in a Federal Slum* (Chicago, 1970); John Scanzoni, *The Black Family in Modern Society*

(Rockleigh, N.J., 1971); Carol B. Stack, *All Our Kin: Strategies for Survival in a Black Community* (New York, 1974); Charles Valentine, *Culture and Poverty: Critique and Counter-Proposals* (Chicago, 1968); and Valentine, "Black Studies and Anthropology: Scholarly and Political Interests in Afro-American Culture," *McCaleb Module in Anthropology*, No. 15.

26.   Hannerz, *Soulside: Inquiries into Ghetto Culture and Community.*

27.   Liebow, *Tally's Corner.*

28.   Stack, *All Our Kin: Strategies for Survival in a Black Community.*

29.   David Caplowitz, *The Poor Pay More* (New York, 1967).

30.   Meyer Fortes, "Introduction," in *The Development Cycle in Domestic Groups,* Jack Goody, ed. (Cambridge, 1972).

31.   Ladner, *Tomorrow's Tomorrow: The Black Woman,* and Stack, *All Our Kin: Strategies for Survival in a Black Community.*

32.   Stack, *All Our Kin: Strategies for Survival in a Black Community,* Ch. 7.

33.   Ibid., 21.

34.   Ibid., 105–107.

35.   Gans, *The Urban Villagers.*

36.   It is easier to make this point given the consciousness-raising works of Alex Haley, *Roots* (New York, 1976), and Herbert Gutman, *The Black Family in Slavery and Freedom, 1750–1925* (New York, 1976), which point out—in popular and scholarly language respectively—the historical depth and importance of this pattern.

37.   Braverman, *Labor and Monopoly Capital,* Ch. 18.

38.   Vance Packard, "Mobility: Restless America," *Mainliner Magazine,* May 1977.

39.   Schneider and Smith, *Class Differences and Sex Roles in American Kinship and Family Structure,* Ch. 4.

40.   Rubin, *Worlds of Pain.*

41.   I know of no substantial work describing the uses of friendship versus kinship in the middle class. Ingelore Fritsch is currently conducting research on the networks of families in a suburban middle-class East coast community; her results should add to this discussion.

42.   William Hoffman, *David: Report on a Rockefeller* (Secanous, N. J., 1971); E. Digby Baltzell, *Philadelphia Gentlemen: The Making of a National Upper Class* (New York, 1958).

43.   Baltzell, *Philadelphia Gentlemen: The Making of a National Upper Class.*

44.   G. William Domhoff, *The Higher Circles* (New York, 1971).

12

Toward a Unified Theory of Class, Race, and Gender

Karen Brodkin Sacks

RACIAL/ETHNIC AND GENDER DIVERSITY

Capitalism has specifically recruited workers on the basis of race, and of gender and family relations within specific racial-ethnic communities. But this is part of a historical dialectic whose other pole was the age/marital status and gender of those who were "expendable" in a particular culture's division of labor—as for example, the contrast between male-centered farming systems in Euroamerica with "expendable" farm daughters, and female-centered farming in Africa with "expendable" sons. The "value" of such expendable laborers seems to have been set by an inter-action of the social relations and expectations of domestic production with employers' demands for cheap labor, where sons' and daughters' wages were not expected to support them. Recognizing the influence of peasant or agrarian family organization on the age, race, and gender makeup of wage labor forces further highlights continuities among family, community, and workplace for the experience and interpretation of class (Sacks 1984).

The long-term workings out of this dialectic throughout the capitalist world—which began with capitalists' eternal search for cheap labor and nonproletarian communities' turning loose only their less "valuable" laborers—has been a major contributor to racial/ethnic segregation of working-class communities and racial/ethnic and sex segregation. This dialectic operated historically when indus-trialists sought out specifically white, Yankee daughters in nineteenth-century New England textiles and twentieth-century Southeast Asian daughters in apparel (Dublin 1979; Ong 1983); pre-married African boys and men in colonial East and Southern Africa in domestic work as well as mining (Hansen 1989); white mothers in contemporary front office work, and young black women for back offices (Glenn and Feldberg 1977; Machung 1984); black families in pre-World War II agriculture (Jones 1985); white rural daughters in Appalachian textiles before World War II, and black south-erners more recently (Frankel 1984; Hall et al. 1987); European young women as live-in maids and then black women in pre-WWII domestic day work (Katzman 1978; Rollins 1985); teenagers in today's fast food shops; European immigrants in mining and heavy industry, and so on (see Glenn 1985 for a summary of the changing historical patterns of job segregation for black, Latina, and Chinese-American women in the United States).

It is important not to lose sight of women's history of struggles to break through race and gender occupational patterns, but even victories have been eroded through new forms of occupational segregation. Recent work has documented women's gains in the auto industry (Milkman 1987); in the pre-deregulation phone company (Hacker 1982); hospitals (Sacks 1988a); and in heavy industry during World War II (Anderson 1981; Gluck 1987). However, even when women do win battles, they may still face an "up the down escalator" phenomenon—when women and minorities gain access to a job it is redefined as less skilled, becomes intensely supervised, and, at the same time typed as women's/minority's. Thus Carter and Carter (1981) show that women's recent progress in professions like medicine and law are largely into an emergent second-class track characterized by lower pay, less professional autonomy, and fewer opportunities for advancement. The subtitle of their article, "Women Get a Ticket to Ride After the Gravy Train Has Left the Station" is especially apt for the professions, but Hacker (1982) documents a similar down side for women's victory in access to skilled craft jobs in the Bell phone system—except here those jobs were eliminated by more advanced technology shortly after women entered them. Remy (1984) shows the ways in which company and union in meatpacking have manipulated new technologies and job design to eliminate high-seniority women workers. Sacks (1988a), Glenn (1985), and Glenn and Feldberg (1977) deal with minority women's progress in clerical work in the 1960s, but also show these women being simultaneously tracked into an emergent factory-like back office sector.

There has been considerable recent attention devoted to women's work culture in work-places where women predominate, such as department stores, offices, hospitals, and garment factories (Benson 1978, 1986; Feldberg and Glenn 1983; Glenn and Feldberg 1977; Machung 1984; Sacks 1988a; Westwood 1985). It is becoming clear that occupational segregation results in different experiences and consciousness of class for women and men, racial-ethnic and white workers. The concomitant is that "working class-consciousness" has multiple shapes (Eisenstein 1983; Goldberg 1983; Sacks 1988b). It would also appear that women's ways of expressing class consciousness are as often as not drawn from their community- and family-based experiences of being working class. And, because working-class communities in the United States have been segregated, the experience and expressions of class consciousness have also been embedded in ethnically specific forms (Collins 1989; Davis 1981). To some degree, women have used family-based metaphors and values to share these consciousnesses across racial/ethnic lines (see especially Bookman and Morgen 1988; Lamphere 1984; Westwood 1985).

The point of all this is that one should not expect to find any generic worker or essential worker, or for that matter, working-class consciousness; that not only is class experienced in historically specific ways, but it is also experienced in racially specific, gender-specific, and kinship-specific ways.

The big issue is how to go about finding the unities and commonalities of class and class consciousness while being attentive to specificity. Critiques of white feminism by women of color and critiques by socialist feminists of male Marxist views of class offer parallel solutions about how to conceptualize unity in diversity. Both criticize implicit and privileged norms against which "others" are measured, and urge instead taking "the other" as the subject in conceptualizing womanhood, and class.

For example, bell hooks (1984) urges placing women of color at the center of feminist analysis, while Bettina Aptheker (1982) suggests "pivoting the center." Along with Deborah King (1988) they argue for theory that stems directly from the experiences of women of color—in contrast to theory that is generated from comparisons that interpret those experiences with reference to a norm or modal woman, who, in feminist theory, has been white and middle class. As Bonnie Dill (1979) suggested in indicating the importance of understanding the "dialectics of black womanhood," doing so offers the possibility of a more inclusive sisterhood for all American women. Such statements about how to construct theory underlie the concrete analyses cited earlier about racially specific conceptualizations of domestic labor, women's economic dependence, and the sexual stereotypes. In these analyses commonalities emerged from the process of resolving conflicts. I will return to the issue of commonalities underlying racial and class-specific gender stereotypes later.

We have seen parallel socialist feminist critiques of traditional, white, male-centered notions of class, which have asked how women relate to a wage-based class structure. Socialist feminists have answered that women's unwaged domestic labor is a necessary condition for the existence of waged labor. When working-class women are the subjects and narrative voices of case studies, class membership, gender and kinship organization, class-based mobilization, and class consciousness look very different from the way they have been portrayed in nonfeminist Marxist analyses. Feminist theorists, as Martha Acklesberg put it so trenchantly, "talk of the need to unite workplace and community. But women's lives have done that—and do it—on a daily basis, although perhaps without the consciousness that that is what they are about!" (1984:256).

Feminist theory applied to the study of working-class women's lives has birthed questions like: What are the social relations by which the working class sustains and reproduces itself? How do women conceptualize their unwaged labor and community-building activities? How—and where— do working-class women organize to struggle against capital? What are the issues that women find are worth fighting about? What are we learning about the persistence of unwaged labor and the ways it changes forms? What are the experiential sources and metaphors by which working-class women express class consciousness? How do women's constructions of their sexuality relate to issues of class and kinship?

Embedded in these questions, I would suggest, is a definition of the working class in which membership is not determinable on an individual basis, but rather as membership in a community that is dependent upon waged labor, but that is unable to subsist or reproduce by such labor alone. This then is the economic basis of class as a relationship to the means of capitalist production. Following on this, it is not surprising that women of many ethnicities, times, and regions share a broader conception of class struggle than men. In part this results from women's socially assigned responsibility for unwaged domestic labor and their consequent centrality in confrontations with the state over family and community welfare issues (Bookman and Morgen 1988; Hall et al. 1987; Susser 1982; Zavella 1987a). This has led to suggestions that working-class women in general, and women of color in particular, are likely to develop the most radical demands for social change (Giddings 1984; hooks 1984; Kaplan 1982; Kessler-Harris and Sacks 1987).

Many new case studies describe the ways in which women's unwaged work creates community-based and class-based social ties of interdependence that are key to neighborhood and household survival. Many of these build on older understandings that working-class kin networks are important resources for coping with economic adversity (Bott 1957; Young and Willmott 1962). Some show women as central economic and political actors in these kinship networks, and suggest that these networks create and carry parts of what tends to be called working-class culture in European literature (Humphries 1977; Scott and Tilly 1978; Tilly 1981; but see Eisenstein 1983 for an early feminist class analysis in the United States); black culture in Afro-American communities (Day 1982; Gilkes 1980; Jones 1985; Reagon 1986; Stack 1974); Chicana or Latina culture (Zavella 1987a, 1987b); Third World culture (Caulfield 1974); or Southern working-class culture among Southern whites (Hall et al. 1987). Others show the ways in which women use languages and values of kinship to create unity and community in the waged workplace (Lamphere 1984, 1987; Sacks 1988a, 1988b; Westwood 1985).

Although the bulk of these studies focus on the social history of daily life (Westwood 1985; Zavella 1987a), some show the way these ties become the infrastructure of large-scale class protests, whether classic strikes (Cameron 1985; Frankel 1984; Hall et al. 1987; Milkman 1985; Tax 1980) or community-based movements, which make demands on the state for civil rights, housing, health care, education, or welfare (Bookman and Morgen 1988; Kaplan 1982; West 1981). They analyze women's centrality in organizing and sustaining labor unions, civil rights, and community-based movements (Giddings 1984; Gilkes 1980; MacLean 1982; Robinson 1987; Ruiz 1987).

Two "findings" regarding social structure and working-class culture are embedded in this new literature. One is the contributions made by working-class women through household economies and community-based cultures to notions of social justice and entitlement (Acklesberg 1984; Bookman and Morgen 1988). The other is the prevalence of institutions, networks, and cultures that women generate outside family life, in public space in working-class communities (see Zagarell 1988 for an analysis of "novels of community" as a women's literary genre). In short, this literature does more than counter theories of the workplace as the sole source for generating political mobilization around economic issues. It provides the beginnings of a gender-based construction of class that is somewhat attentive to racial/ethnic diversity.

A third set of "findings" about working-class women's conceptions of womanhood is emerging from some very diverse studies that explore long-hidden histories of (mainly) working-class women's challenges to bourgeois ideals of domesticity, femininity, compulsory heterosexuality, motherhood, and reproduction. For example, Emily Martin's (1987) wonderful exploration of how American women understand menstruation, birth, and menopause shows middle-class women tending to accept the dominant, medicalized views of women as ruled by their reproductive organs, while working-class, especially black working-class, women do not see these as ruling events, nor does the medical view of their bodies have much hegemony in their consciousnesses.

In a similar vein, studies of conflicts between Progressive-era reformers' notions of proper domesticity and those of working-class women (Ehrenreich and English 1978; Kessler-Harris 1982) have shown overt and covert resistance to submissive domesticity on the latter's part. They resonate with theoretical suggestions made by Mies (1986) that "house-wifization" is historically a relatively new and middle-class-specific organization of women's unwaged labor. Mies argues that the privatization of women's work, and the cult of domesticity surrounding and sustaining it, were and are resisted by working-class women (though not by working-class men, who benefited from these constructions), who struggle to keep their work "socialized," or collectively organized. Bennholdt-Thomsen (1988) illustrates one such form this struggle takes: in the Isthmus of Tehuantepec, Mexico, women sustain a regional marketing and food preparation system with an elaborate division of labor, interdependence among women, and no subordination to men. Similar arguments are implicit in discussions about women's marketing and subsistence production in Africa (Leis 1974; Mbilinyi 1988), and in the economies of taking in boarders, laundry, and so on— widely described for European-American working-class pre-World War II urban neighborhoods, although the power dynamics of gender need to be explored further (Cott and Pleck 1979; Ewen 1985; Kessler-Harris 1982; see also Kessler-Harris and Sacks 1987; Sacks 1984).

We are also beginning to learn some of the ways in which young working-class women, past and present, white and black, have independently appropriated and refashioned some of the conventional images of sexiness to convey the sense of themselves as autonomous, independent, and assertive adult women, and to challenge—often at high risk to themselves—our culture's insistence on submissive femininity for women (Hall 1986; Ladner 1970; Myerowitz 1988; Peiss 1985; Petchesky 1985; Stansell 1986; Westwood 1985; see also Vance 1984 and Snitow, Stansell, and Thompson 1983). Hall's study, "Disorderly Women," is perhaps the most dramatic discussion of how women used their sexuality as a metaphor of class strength and confrontation, how such use of sexuality was understood in that way by other men and women of their working-class Appalachian community, but how it was seen in conventional "bad women" terms by both employers and outside union representatives.

Just as heterosexuality has been a language of working-class women's resistance to a combined class and gender subordination, so too has lesbian sexual identity and community provided a historically specific tradition of resistance to submissive domesticity. Following Adrienne Rich's (1983) insights on the politics of homophobia and Carol Smith-Rosenberg's work on 19th-century women's worlds of love and ritual (1985), D'Emilio and Freedman (1988), as well as Rapp and Ross (1983), argue that stigmatization of homosexuality (and its complement, celebration of companionate marriages for compulsory heterosexuality), developed about the same time that it became possible for a significant number of women to be able to live on their own earnings, without domestic dependence on men. Davis and Kennedy's (1986) oral history of Buffalo's working-class lesbian community, as well as D'Emilio and Freedman's (1988), Katz's (1976) and D'Emilio's (1983) analyses of the creation of specifically gay and lesbian social identities in the mid-twentieth century show some of these forms of resistance as well as the creation of alternative institutions, roles, and identities.

SUMMARY

As Martha Acklesberg has noted, when "we take seriously the 'relatedness' that seems to characterize the lives of many women," we also challenge "the assumption central to the Marxist paradigm that the development of a truly radical consciousness requires the transcendence, or abandonment, of all sources of community feeling other than class (in particular, those feelings based in racial, ethnic, national, or—we might add—sexual identity). . . . In fact, rather than acting as a 'drag' on radical consciousness, communities—and the network of relationships that they nurture and on which they are based—have been, and can be, important contexts for politicization" (Acklesberg 1988:306).

This essay has reviewed some of the theoretical consequences of socialist feminist critiques of the political economy of "personal life." Its focus has been on efforts to comprehend class, race, and gender oppression as parts of a unitary system, as opposed to analyses that envision capitalism and patriarchy as separate systems. More specifically, I have interpreted analyses of the relations of waged and unwaged labor, work and family in such a way as to expand the meaning of working class to encompass both waged and unwaged workers who are members of a community that is dependent upon waged labor but that is unable to reproduce itself on those wages alone. The implications of such a reading are fairly radical, and each one requires a great deal of further exploration. First and most apparent, it significantly alters conventional Marxist understandings of class and of contemporary social movements. Second, it does so in such a way as to make visible the centrality of people of color and white working-class women to the direction of world history. Third, for feminist theory, it suggests the fruitfulness of recognizing that women's gender identities are not analytically separable from their racial and class identities. Fourth, class emerges as a relation to the means of production that is collective rather than individual, a relation of communities to the capitalist state more than of employees to employers. Fifth, this embeds a critique of the ideology of liberal individualism, and links it to the shapes of post-World War II resistance to capitalism, which have generated the pluralistic visions behind efforts to develop a unified feminist theory that encompasses race and class as well as gender and sexuality.

Acknowledgments: Ancestors and earlier versions of this paper were presented at the Conference on Family and Production at Duke University in 1985, the American Ethnological Society meetings in 1985, and the Center for the Study of Women's Faculty Research Seminar at UCLA and the Los Angeles Chapter of Sociologists for Women in Society in 1988. I have benefited greatly from discussions at each of these forums. In addition, I would like to thank Sharon Bays, Kathleen Gough, Patricia Gumport, Sondra Hale, Nicky Hart, Louise Lamphere, Carol Lasser, Sandra Morgen, Tom Patterson, Rayna Rapp, and "Red Wednesday" for their supportive critiques as this paper evolved.

REFERENCES

Acklesberg, Martha. 1984. "Women's Collaborative Activities and City Life: Politics and Policy." In *Political Women: Current Roles in State and Local Government*, J. Flammang, ed., pp. 242–259. Beverly Hills, CA: Sage.
——. 1988. "Communities, Resistance, and Women's Activism: Some Implications for a Democratic Polity." In *Women and the Politics of Empowerment*, Bookman and Morgen, eds., pp. 297–313. Philadelphia: Temple University Press.
Anderson, Karen. 1981. *Wartime Women*. Westport, CT: Greenwood.
Aptheker, Bettina. 1982. *Women's Legacy: Essays in Race, Sex and Class in American History*. Amherst: University of Massachusetts Press.
Barkley-Brown, Elsa. 1989. "African-American Women's Quilting: A Framework for Conceptualizing and Teaching African-American Women's History." *Signs* 14(4):921–929.
Beneria, Lourdes, ed. 1982. *Women and Development*. New York: Praeger.
Bennholdt-Thomsen, Veronika. 1981. "Subsistence Production and Extended Reproduction." In *Of Marriage and the Market*, K. Young, C. Wolkowitz, and R. McCullagh, eds., pp. 16–29. London: CSE Books.
——. 1984. "Towards a Theory of the Sexual Division of Labor." In *Households and the World Economy*, Joan Smith, I. Wallerstein, and H. D. Evers, eds., pp. 252–271. Beverly Hills, CA: Sage.
——. 1988. "Women's Dignity Is the Wealth of Juchitan" (Oax., Mexico). Paper presented at 12th International Congress of Anthropological and Ethnological Sciences, Zagreb, Yugoslavia, July 24–31.
Benson, Susan Porter. 1978. "The Clerking Sisterhood: Rationalization and the Work Culture of Saleswomen." *Radical America* 12:41–55.
——. 1986. *Counter Cultures: Saleswomen, Managers, and Customers in American Department Stores 1890–1940*. Urbana: University of Illinois Press.
Benston, Margaret. 1969. "The Politic Economy of Women's Liberation." *Monthly Review* 21(4):13–27.
Bookman, Ann, and Sandra Morgen, eds. 1988. *Women and the Politics of Empowerment*. Philadelphia: Temple University Press.
Boris, Eileen, and Peter Bardaglio. 1983. "The Transformation of Patriarchy: The Historic Role of the State." In *Families, Politics and Public Policy: A Feminist Dialogue on Women and the State*, I. Diamond and M. L. Shanley, eds., pp. 70–91. New York: Longman.
Bott, Elizabeth. 1957. *Family and Social Network*. London: Tavistock Publications.
Brecher, Jeremy. 1972. *Strike: The True History of Mass Insurgency from 1877 to the Present*. San Francisco: Straight Arrow.
Brenner, Johanna, and Maria Ramas. 1984. "Rethinking Women's Oppression." *New Left Review* 144:33–71.
Cameron, Ardis. 1985. "Bread and Roses Revisited: Women's Culture and Working-Class Activism in the Lawrence Strike of 1912." In *Women, Work and Protest*, Milkman, ed., pp. 42–61. Boston: Routledge and Kegan Paul.
Cantarow, Ellen, and Sharon O'Malley. 1980. "Ella Baker: Organizing for Civil Rights." In *Moving the Mountain: Women Working for Social Change*, Cantarow, ed., pp. 52–93. Old Westbury, NY: Feminist Press.
Carter, Susan B., and Michael Carter. 1981. "Women's Recent Progress in the Professions, or Women Get a Ticket to Ride After the Gravy Train Has Left the Station." *Feminist Studies* 7:477–504.
Caulfield, Mina Davis. 1974. "Imperialism, the Family and Cultures of Resistance." *Socialist Revolution* 20:76–85.
Collins, Patricia Hill. 1989. "The Social Construction of Black Feminist Thought." *Signs* 14(4):745–773.
Cott, Nancy, and Elizabeth Pleck, eds. 1979. *A Heritage of Her Own: Toward a New Social History of American Women*. New York: Simon and Schuster.
Dalla Costa, Mariarosa, and Selma James. 1972. *The Power of Women and the Subversion of the Community*. Montpelier, England: Falling Wall Press.
Davis, Angela Y. 1981. *Women, Race and Class*. New York: Random House.
Davis, Madeline, and Elizabeth L. Kennedy. 1986. "Oral History and the Study of Sexuality in the Lesbian Community: Buffalo, New York, 1940–1960." *Feminist Studies* 12(Spring):7–26.
Day, Kay. 1982. "Kinship in a Changing Economy: A View from the Sea Islands." In *Holding onto the Land and the Lord*, C. Stack and R. Hall, eds. Athens: University of Georgia Press.
D'Emilio, John. 1983. *Sexual Politics, Sexual Communities: The Making of a Homosexual Minority in the United States, 1940–1970*. Chicago: University of Chicago Press.

D'Emilio, John, and Estelle B. Freedman. 1988. *Intimate Matters: A History of Sexuality in America*. New York: Harper and Row.

Dill, Bonnie Thornton. 1979. "The Dialectics of Black Womanhood." *Signs* 4:543–555.

Dublin, Thomas. 1979. *Women at Work: The Transformation of Class and Community in Lowell, Massachussetts 1826–1860*. New York: Columbia University Press.

Edholm, Felicity, Olivia Harris, and Kate Young. 1977. "Conceptualising Women." *Critique of Anthropology* 3(9–10):101–130.

Ehrenreich, Barbara, and Dierdre English. 1978. *For Her Own Good*. New York: Pantheon.

Eisenstein, Sarah. 1983. *Give Us Bread, but Give Us Roses Too*. Boston: Routledge and Kegan Paul.

Eisenstein, Zillah, ed. 1979. *Capitalist Patriarchy and the Case for Socialist Feminism*. New York: Monthly Review Press.

Evans, Sara. 1980. *Personal Politics: The Roots of Women's Liberation in the Civil Rights Movement*. New York: Random House.

Ewen, Elizabeth. 1985. *Immigrant Women in the Land of Dollars*. New York: Monthly Review Press.

Feldberg, Roslyn, and Evelyn Nakano Glenn. 1983. "Technology and Work Degradation: Effects of Office Automation on Women Clerical Workers." In *Machina ex Dea: Feminist Perspectives on Technology*, J. Rothschild, ed., pp. 59–78. New York: Pergamon.

Frankel, Linda. 1984. "Southern Textile Women: Generations of Struggle and Survival." In *My Troubles Are Going to Have Trouble with Me*. Sacks and Remy, eds., pp. 39–60. New Brunswick, NJ: Rutgers University Press.

Giddings, Paula. 1984. *When and Where I Enter*. New York: Bantam.

Gilkes, Cheryl. 1980. " 'Holding Back the Ocean with a Broom:' Black Women and Community Work." In *The Black Woman*, LaFrances Rodgers-Rose, ed., pp. 217–231. Beverly Hills, CA: Sage.

——. 1988. "Building in Many Places: Multiple Commitments and Ideologies in Black Women's Community Work." In *Women and the Politics of Empowerment*. Bookman and Morgen, eds., pp. 53–76. Philadelphia: Temple University Press.

Glenn, Evelyn Nakano. 1985. "Racial Ethnic Women's Labor: The Intersection of Race, Gender and Class Oppression." *Review of Radical Political Economics* 17(3):86–108.

——. 1986. *Issei, Nissei, War Bride: Three Generations of Japanese American Women in Domestic Service*. Philadelphia: Temple University Press.

Glenn, Evelyn Nakano, and Roslyn Feldberg. 1977. "Degraded and Deskilled: The Proletarianization of Clerical Work." *Social Problems* 25(1):52–64.

Gluck, Sherna B. 1987. *Rosie the Riveter Revisited: Women, the War, and Social Change*. Boston: Twayne Publishers.

Goldberg, Roberta. 1983. *Organizing Women Office Workers: Dissatisfaction, Consciousness and Action*. New York: Praeger.

Hacker, Sally. 1982. "Sex Stratification, Technology and Organizational Change: A Longitudinal Case Study of AT&T." In *Women and Work*, R. Kahn-Hut, A. Daniels, and R. Colvard, eds., pp. 248–266. New York: Oxford University Press.

Hall, Jacquelyn D. 1986. "Disorderly Women: Gender and Labor Militancy in the Appalachian South." *Journal of American History* 73(2):354–382.

Hall, Jacquelyn D., J. Leloudis, R. Korstad, M. Murphy, L. Jones, and C. Daly. 1987. *Like a Family: The Making of a Southern Mill World*. Chapel Hill: University of North Carolina Press.

Hansen, Karen T. 1989. *Distant Companions: Servants and Employers in Zambia, 1900–1985*. Ithaca, NY: Cornell University Press.

Hartmann, Heidi I. 1976. "Capitalism, Patriarchy and Job Segregation by Sex." *Signs* 1(1)pt. 2:137–170.

hooks, bell. 1984. *Feminist Theory from Margin to Center*. Boston: South End Press.

Humphries, Jane. 1977. "Class Struggle and the Persistence of the Working Class Family." *Cambridge Journal of Economics* 1:241–248.

Jaggar, Alison. 1983. *Feminist Politics and Human Nature*. Sussex: Rowman and Allenheld.

Jones, Jacqueline. 1985. *Labor of Love, Labor of Sorrow*. New York: Basic Books.

Kaplan, Temma. 1982. "Female Consciousness and Collective Action: The Case of Barcelona, 1910–1918." *Signs* 7(3):545–567.

Katz, Jonathan, ed. 1976. *Gay American History: Lesbians and Gay Men in the U.S.A.* New York: Thomas Crowell.

Katzman, David. 1978. *Seven Days a Week: Women and Domestic Service in Industrializing America*. New York: Oxford University Press.

Kessler-Harris, Alice, 1982. *Out to Work*. New York: Oxford University Press.

Kessler-Harris, Alice, and Karen Brodkin Sacks. 1987. "The Demise of Domesticity." In *Women, Households and the Economy*, L. Beneria and C. Stimpson, eds., pp. 65–84. New Brunswick, NJ: Rutgers University Press.

King, Deborah. 1988. "Multiple Jeopardy, Multiple Consciousness: The Context of a Black Feminist Ideology." *Signs* 14(1) 42–72.

Ladner, Joyce. 1970. *Tomorrow's Tomorrow*. New York: Doubleday Anchor.

Lamphere, Louise. 1984. "On the Shop Floor: Multi-Ethnic Unity against the Conglomerate." In *My Troubles Are Going to Have Trouble with Me*, K. Sacks and D. Remy, eds., pp. 247–263. New Brunswick, NJ: Rutgers University Press.

——. 1987. *From Working Daughters to Working Mothers: Immigrant Women in a New England Industrial Community*. Ithaca, NY: Cornell University Press.

Leis, Nancy. 1974. "Women in Groups. Ijaw Women's Associations." In *Woman, Culture and Society*, M. Rosaldo and L. Lamphere, eds., pp. 223–242. Stanford, CA: Stanford University Press.

Machung, Anne. 1984. "Word Processing: Forward for Business, Backward for Women." In *My Troubles Are Going to Have Trouble with Me*, K. Sacks and D. Remy, eds., pp. 124–139. New Brunswick, NJ: Rutgers University Press.

MacLean, Nancy. 1982. "The Culture of Resistance: Female Institution-Building in the Ladies Garment Workers' Union 1905–1925." *Occasional Papers in Women's Studies*, University of Michigan.

Mainardi, Pat. 1970. "The Politics of Housework." In *Sisterhood Is Powerful*, R. Morgan, ed., pp. 447–454. New York: Random House.

Martin, Emily. 1987. *The Woman in the Body*. Boston: Beacon.

Mbilinyi, Marjorie. 1988. "Runaway Wives in Colonial Tanganyika: Forced Labour and Forced Marriage in Rungwe District 1919–1961." *International Journal of the Sociology of Law* 16:1–29.

Meillassoux, Claude. 1981. *Maidens, Meal and Money: Capitalism and the Domestic Community*. Cambridge: Cambridge University Press.

Mies, Maria. 1986. *Patriarchy and Accumulation on a World Scale: Women and the International Division of Labour*. London: Zed Books.

Milkman, Ruth, ed. 1985. *Women, Work and Protest*. Boston: Routledge and Kegan Paul.

——. 1987. *Gender at Work: The Dynamics of Job Segregation by Sex During World War II*. Urbana: University of Illinois Press.

Mitchell, Juliet. 1966. "Women—The Longest Revolution." *New Left Review* 40:11–37.

——. 1971. *Woman's Estate*. Baltimore: Penguin Books.

Myerowitz, Joanne J. 1988. *Women Adrift: Independent Wage Earners in Chicago, 1880–1930*. Chicago: Chicago University Press.

Nash, June, and Maria Patricia Fernandez-Kelly, eds. 1983. *Women, Men and the International Division of Labor*. Albany: SUNY Press.

Ong, Aihwa. 1983. "Global Industries and Malay Peasants in Peninsular Malaysia." In *Women, Men and the International Division of Labor*, Nash and Fernandez-Kelly, eds., pp. 426–439. Albany: SUNY Press.

Palmer, Phyllis M. 1983. "White Women/Black Women: The Dualism of Female Identity and Experience in the United States." *Feminist Studies* 9:151–170.

——. 1984. "Housework and Domestic Labor: Racial and Technological Change." In *My Troubles Are Going to Have Trouble with Me*. K. Sacks and D. Remy, eds., pp. 80–94. New Brunswick, NJ: Rutgers University Press.

Peiss, Kathy. 1985. *Cheap Amusements: Working Women and Leisure in Turn-of-the-Century New York*. Philadelphia: Temple University Press.

Petchesky, Rosalind P. 1985. *Abortion and Woman's Choice*. Boston: Northeastern University Press.

Rapp, Rayna. 1978. "Family and Class in Contemporary America: Notes Toward an Understanding of Ideology." *Science and Society* 42(3):278–300.

Rapp, Rayna, and Ellen Ross. 1983. "The Twenties' Backlash: Compulsory Heterosexuality, the Consumer Family and the Waning of Feminism." In *Class, Race and Sex*, A. Swerdlow and H. Lessinger, eds., pp. 93–107. Boston: G. K. Hall.

Reagon, Bernice Johnson. 1986. "African Diaspora Women: The Making of Cultural Workers." *Feminist Studies* 12(1):77–90.

Remy, Dorothy, and Larry Sawers. 1984. "Economic Stagnation and Discrimination." In *My Troubles Are Going to Have Troubles with Me*, K. Sacks and D. Remy, eds., pp. 95–112. New Brunswick, NJ: Rutgers University Press.

Rich, Adrienne. 1983. "Compulsory Heterosexuality and Lesbian Existence." In *Powers of Desire: The Politics of Sexuality*, Snitow, Stansell, and Thompson, eds., pp. 177–205. New York: Monthly Review Press.

Robinson, Jo Ann Gibson. 1987. *The Montgomery Bus Boycott and the Women Who Started It*. David J. Garrow, ed. Knoxville: University of Tennessee Press.

Rollins, Judith. 1985. *Between Women*. Philadelphia: Temple University Press.

Romero, Mary. 1987. "Domestic Service in the Transition from Rural to Urban Life: The Case of La Chicana." *Women's Studies* 13(3):199–222. (Special issue, "As the World Turns," K. B. Sacks and N. Scheper-Hughes, eds.)

Ruiz, Vicki L. 1987. *Cannery Women Cannery Lives: Mexican Women, Unionization and the California Food Processing Industry, 1930–1950*. Albuquerque: University of New Mexico Press.

Sacks, Karen Brodkin. 1974. "Engels Revisited." In *Women, Culture, and Society*, M. Rosaldo and L. Lamphere, eds., pp. 207–222. Stanford, CA: Stanford University Press.

——. 1979. *Sisters and Wives*. Westport, CT: Greenwood Press.

——. 1984. "Generations of Working Class Families." In *My Troubles Are Going to Have Trouble with Me*, K. Sacks and D. Remy, eds., New Brunswick, NJ: Rutgers University Press.

——. 1988a. *Caring by the Hour*. Urbana: University of Illinois Press.

——. 1988b. "Gender and Grassroots Leadership." In *Women and the Politics of Empowerment*, Bookman and Morgen, eds., pp. 77–96. Philadelphia: Temple University Press.

Sargent, Lydia, ed. 1981. *Women and Revolution: A Discussion of the Unhappy Marriage of Marxism and Feminism*. Boston: South End Press.

Scott, Joan W., and Louise Tilly. 1978. *Women, Work and Family*. New York: Holt, Rinehart and Winston.

Smith-Rosenberg, Carol. 1985. "The Female World of Love and Ritual: Relations Between Women in Nineteenth-Century America." Reprinted in *Disorderly Conduct: Visions of Gender in Victorian America*, Carol Smith-Rosenberg. New York: Oxford University Press.

Snitow, Ann, Christine Stansell, and Sharon Thompson, eds. 1983. *Powers of Desire: The Politics of Sexuality*. New York: Monthly Review Press.

Stack, Carol. 1974. *All Our Kin*. New York: Harper Colophon.

Stansell, Christine. 1986. *City of Women: Sex and Class in New York, 1789–1860*. New York: Knopf.

Stolcke, Verena. 1981. "Women's Labours: The Naturalisation of Social Inequality and Women's Subordination." In *Of Marriage and the Market*, K. Young, C. Wolkowitz, and R. McCullagh, eds., pp. 30–48. London: CSE Books.

Susser, Ida. 1982. *Norman Street*. New York: Oxford University Press.

Tax, Meredith. 1980. *The Rising of the Women: Feminist Solidarity and Class Conflict 1880–1917*. New York: Monthly Review Press.

Tilly, Louise A. 1981. "Paths of Proletarianization: Organization of Production, Sexual Division of Labor, and Women's Collective Action." *Signs* 7(2):400–417.

Vance, Carol. 1984. *Pleasure and Danger*. Boston: Routledge and Kegan Paul.

Vogel, Lise. 1983. *Marxism and the Oppression of Women: Toward a Unitary Theory*. New Brunswick, NJ: Rutgers University Press.

West, Guida. 1981. *The National Welfare Rights Movement: The Social Protest of Poor Women*. New York: Praeger.

Westwood, Sallie. 1985. *All Day Every Day*. Urbana: University of Illinois Press.

Wolfe, George C. 1988. *The Colonization of American Culture, or, One playwright(of color)'s not-so-humble opinion*. Performing Arts Westwood Playhouse, Los Angeles.

Young, Michael, and Peter Willmott. 1962. *Family and Kinship in East London*. Baltimore: Penguin Books.

Zagarell, Sandra. 1988. "The Narrative of Community: The Identification of a Genre." *Signs* 13(3):498–527.

Zavella, Patricia. 1987a. " 'Abnormal Intimacy': The Varying Work Networks of Chicana Cannery Workers." *Feminist Studies* 11(3):541–558.

——. 1987b. *Women's Work and Chicano Families: Cannery Workers of the Santa Clara Valley*. Ithaca, NY: Cornell University Press.

13

Immigrant Families in the US

KAREN PYKE

THE STREAM OF IMMIGRANTS to the US since 1965 has contributed to a second great wave of immigration that continues today. Over 28 million foreign-born individuals currently reside in the country (Lollock, 2001). Never before has the US received immigrants from as wide an array of countries and from such differing social, economic, and cultural backgrounds as it does today. And never before have most of the arrivals been from non-European nations (Reimers, 1996).

The new immigration is challenging the racial and cultural hegemony of white, native-born Americans. White Americans now constitute a numeric minority in California, the gateway of the new immigration, and similar patterns will follow in other key immigrant states in the near future (Maharidge, 1996; Nelson and O'Reilly, 2000). Streams of immigrants are also transforming minority America with Latino Americans soon to replace African Americans as the leading racial minority (Zinn and Eitzen, 1996). The study of immigrant families is thus not a marginal concern, but at the very core of our understanding of the demographic and sociocultural dynamics of US society.

[. . .]

Recent decades have witnessed a dramatic shift in the racial composition of immigrants with people of color from Asia, Latin America, and the Caribbean dominating the stream. As recently as the 1950s two-thirds of immigrants to the US came from Europe and Canada. This trend reversed in the 1960s and by the early 1980s, only 11 percent of immigrants to the US hailed from Europe (Mangiafico, 1988; Portes and Zhou, 1993). In 2000, 51 percent of the foreign-born population in the US had arrived from Latin America, 26 percent from Asia, and 15 percent from Europe (Lollock, 2001). Similar trends mark immigration in Canada (Badets and Chui, 1994).

The new immigration has spawned new ethnic groups in the US, including Korean Americans, Hmong Americans, and Vietnamese Americans. New immigrant groups, who do not have the benefit of longstanding ethnic enclaves with firmly established social networks to assist in successful adaptation, must create from scratch the meaning of their ethnicity. Unlike their European predecessors who were gradually incorporated into the stew of white ethnicities, today's immigrant families, most of whom come from countries where they were members of the racial/ethnic majority, must contend for the first time with a racial minority status and the forces of racism. The legal status of immigrants in the US also impacts their ability to adjust. Those who arrive without documents, mostly from Mexico and Central America, are restricted to the most menial types of low wage labor with few opportunities for upward mobility. Their lack of legal access to government supports and protections undermines their health and safety, and makes them easy prey for exploitation. The constant fear of detection and deportation limits their range of movement as they are forced to hide in the shadows (Chavez, 1991).

While earlier waves of immigrants from Europe were mostly manual laborers, there is greater diversity in the skill and educational levels among today's immigrants to North America, which includes manual laborers, the entrepreneurial middle class, and highly educated professionals (the latter arriving particularly from China, India, and the Philippines) (Portes and Rumbaut, 1996). While some professionals are able to apply their skills in the new economy (as is the case with immigrants from India and the Philippines who typically arrive knowing English), others find their credentials and work histories are not recognized by North American employers, thus relegating them to the low-pay service sector and prompting high rates of self-employment in small family-run businesses, most notably among Korean immigrants (Portes and Rumbaut, 1996). Earlier waves of immigrants to the US from Europe were able to find jobs in an expanding manufacturing economy that needed the unskilled labor they could provide. Today's lower skilled immigrants, on the other hand, find an economy reeling from global restructuring, the rapid decline of manufacturing jobs, and a growing gap in the wages and benefits of the professional class and the lower-skilled working class, where immigrants are disproportionately located (Portes and Zhou, 1993). This raises concern that the upward mobility enjoyed previously by children of European immigrants will not be replicated among today's children of immigrants in the US (Gans, 1992).

[. . .]

THEORETICAL DEVELOPMENTS IN THE STUDY OF IMMIGRATION AND IMMIGRANT FAMILIES

Because the post-1965 immigration trends differ tremendously from earlier waves of European immigrants in terms of their cultural diversity, racial composition, and the economic conditions they encounter, immigration scholars have had to revise existing theoretical frameworks that failed to capture the reality of today's immigrant families. Between the 1920s and 1960s assimilation theory and related cultural approaches dominated the immigration research. Based on the experiences of European immigrants at the end of the nineteenth century, the assimilation perspective assumes that, with time, immigrant families shed traditional "outdated" cultural values and structures while adopting patterns of the new "modern" culture. This "straight-line" assimilation model emphasizes a positive process of linear movement into mainstream American society accompanied by upward mobility (Park and Burgess, 1924) The expectation is that succeeding generations will be absorbed into a "melting pot" of mainstream culture.

Scholars initially made few adjustments in the assimilation framework when switching their analytic lens from earlier European immigrants to the new Third World immigrants. A variant of assimilation theory, the culture of poverty approach, gained popularity in the 1960s in the study of immigrant and poor families. Like assimilation theory, the culture of poverty approach centers on mainstream American culture, to which immigrants and their descendants (along with poor whites and African Americans) were expected to assimilate if they were to succeed. As a result, social problems among immigrant groups were attributed to a lack of assimilation, including the maintenance of traditional family patterns that were out of step with the demands of a "modern" society (Zinn, 1994). Problems among Mexican American families, such as poverty, were attributed to a cultural emphasis on familism and traditional patriarchal arrangements or "machismo" (Heller, 1966; Rubel, 1966). The strong family ties and instrumental exchanges with extended kin associated with Mexican American families were believed to contribute to permanent poverty by draining resources and limiting geographic and economic mobility. Implicit in this framework was a model of "normal" family life based on white, middle-class American standards against which immigrant families were judged (Pyke, 2000; Zinn and Wells, 2000). Families that deviated from this model were regarded as problematic. By emphasizing the internal cultural practices and structures of immigrant families, this approach placed blame for many social problems on the victims by ignoring the impact of larger forces, such as racism and the economic order, that limit opportunities for success and present barriers to assimilation.

Scholarly challenges to assimilation and culture of poverty approaches emerged in the late 1960s and 1970s, focusing on the top-down, white-centered approach that marginalized the experiences and perspectives of those studied (Boyd, 1989). Such challenges were bolstered by assimilation theory's inapplicability to the growing waves of immigrants of color to the US. At the same time, mounting evidence suggesting that familism is actually an important survival strategy among immigrants and the poor—a structural response to poverty rather than a cultural antecedent—contributed to a shift toward social structural approaches and away from models of cultural deviance (Alvirez and Bean, 1976; Hoppe and Heller, 1975).

As a result of these forces, in recent decades immigration and family scholars have focused on the effect of political, social, and economic conditions on the adaptation experiences of immigrants. One result is the emergence of segmented assimilation theory as an alternative to straight-line assimilation theory (Portes and Zhou, 1993; Rumbaut, 1994). This approach emphasizes the diversity of adaptation processes and economic outcomes of immigrant groups depending on variations in their place of settlement, regional resources, economic opportunities, community composition, and the human, political, and social capital they bring with them.

Segmented assimilation theory does not completely reject straight-line assimilation into the middle-class mainstream but acknowledges it as only one of many possible pathways. Further, it notes that assimilation into the middle class is a less traveled pathway for today's immigrant families whose non-white racial status marks them as "other" and prevents their complete amalgamation into the white-dominated mainstream. Indeed, recent research suggests some immigrant families face downward mobility in the US, with the second generation experiencing a decline in their economic (Gans, 1992; Portes and Zhou, 1993) and physical well-being (Rumbaut, 1997), which is a reversal of the expectations of assimilation theory. Segmented assimilation theory suggests this pathway of downward mobility occurs predominately among immigrants of color who live in economically deprived communities, far from the resources and opportunities found in white, middle-class communities. For them assimilation into the local underclass community does not increase opportunities for success. A commonly provided example of this pathway is the children of Haitian immigrants living in the black inner city of Miami. Those who assimilate into the native-born community of black, inner-city youth tend to adopt the values of the local youth culture that are reactive to long-standing racism and denigrate academic achievement as "selling out" to the white world. In this scenario assimilation is not associated with educational success and upward mobility but long-term poverty (Portes and Zhou, 1993). Though segmented assimilation is primarily concerned with social structural forces, cultural factors also loom large. For example, in this instance the oppositional culture of poor native-born black youths, rather than the culture of the immigrants themselves, is blamed for negative outcomes in adaptation. Hence remnants of the culture of poverty approach are evident in the application of segmented assimilation theory.

A third pathway described by segmented assimilation stands straight-line assimilation theory on its head. It links positive outcomes among children of immigrants with the maintenance of ethnic practices. This pathway is characterized by the selective assimilation of immigrant families so as to accommodate mainstream society while holding on to ethnic cultural patterns. "Accommodation without assimilation" (Gibson, 1988) appears to provide resources from within the family and ethnic community, such as the support of ethnic organizations and the transmission of cultural values that promote hard work and academic achievement, while ethnic cultural practices are also adjusted to enable the acquisition of educational and economic resources from the mainstream society. Individuals alter their behavior to conform to mainstream expectations, but do not adopt the associated emotions or values. Rather, their maintenance of familism and strong ties to their ethnic community provides social capital that contributes to their success in the mainstream. This acculturative trajectory has been linked to the academic success of children of Vietnamese immigrants growing up in a predominately African American lower-income community (Zhou and Bankston, 1998), and children of Punjabi Sikh immigrants who academically outperform their white, native-born counterparts (Gibson, 1988).

[. . .]

GENDER DYNAMICS

Immigrant research, influenced by the emergence of feminist theory in the 1970s, has provided overdue attention in recent decades to the contributions and experiences of women, which were previously encapsulated under those of men or buried in models of unitary household dynamics (Espiritu, 1997; Hondagneu-Sotelo, 1994; Morokvasic, 1983). Of particular focus in the study of immigrant families has been the impact of US immigration on gender dynamics, centered specifically on the wide-scale entrance of women into the wage labor system upon immigration. Despite the diversity of their cultural origins, contemporary newcomers to the US tend to share established patterns of patriarchal arrangements marked by rigid divisions in the labor of men and women, and the assignment of greater power and authority to male heads of households. Traditional gender arrangements that regard women's paid labor as undesirable are an integral component of the cultural and religious systems of immigrants from Asia, Latin America, the Caribbean, and the Middle East (Grasmuck and Pessar, 1991; Kar et al., 1995–6; Kibria, 1993). By contrast, the US experienced a rapid shift in gender arrangements with the post-1960 stream of middle-class married women into the labor force. Although the empirical record reveals that social relations in the US remain male-dominated, American women are portrayed as enjoying more autonomy, independence, and power than women in Third World countries from which most contemporary immigrants arrive, and having attitudes that are less supportive of patriarchal arrangements (Kim, 1994). Immigrants themselves are acutely aware of these differences and view the continuity of traditional gender arrangements as integral to the maintenance of ethnicity (Das Gupta, 1997). The adoption of more egalitarian gender arrangements is often regarded as a sign of Americanization, a loss of ethnic identity, the failure of men to fulfill their role, and the breakdown of the family unit. Although newcomers to the US are confronted with a mainstream culture that gives a great deal of lip service (if less structural support) to the notion of gender equality, it is the new economic conditions rather than an altered gender consciousness that prompts a reconfiguration of gender relations within immigrant families (Foner, 1986; Kibria, 1993). Immigrant males often face difficulties in finding the kind of jobs that pay a family wage, resulting in unemployment, downward mobility, and an increased dependency on their wives' wage labor. Concurrently, immigrant women find their labor in demand by US employers who specifically target them for low-paying menial jobs (Bonacich, 1994). In fact, the greater demand for immigrant women's labor contributes to a female-dominated flow of immigrants, including married women who immigrate and secure employment prior to their husbands' arrival (Gordon, 1990). The movement of women into the labor force upon immigration is one of the most dramatic changes impacting upon immigrant families. In Korea, for example, only 25 percent of married women in urban areas were in the labor force in 1990 (National Statistical Office, Republic of Korea, 1993: 1), compared with 60 percent of married Korean women in the US (US Bureau of the Census 1993, Table 48). Other immigrant groups exhibit similar patterns of female labor-force participation (Grasmuck and Pessar, 1991).

Much of the immigrant research supports the notion that the greater economic resources, self-esteem, and independence that work provides immigrant wives results in a decline of patriarchal arrangements and male dominance, with husbands more likely to share household tasks, child-care, decision-making, and financial management with wives (Kibria 1993; Grasmuck and Pessar, 1991; Guendelman and Pérez-Itriago, 1987; Lim, 1997; Repack, 1997). In cases of serial migration where husbands arrive before wives—often against the wishes of women—the gender transformation occurs during the years of separation when wives take on the role of head of household in their husband's absence, which frequently involves breadwinning as the earnings husbands send home are typically insufficient (Hondagneu-Sotelo, 1994). Meanwhile, men living independently in the US must manage their own domestic tasks. This leads to different expectations and more egalitarian practices when families are reunited (Hondagneu-Sotelo, 1994). Sometimes women use immigration as an opportunity to reduce their dependence on husbands through employment, to renegotiate gender arrangements, or to insist that husbands who immigrated previously assume their financial obligations (Grasmuck and Pessar, 1991; Hondagneu-Sotelo, 1994; Toro-Morn, 1995). In fact, the act of migrating can be an assertion of power by women when, as is often the case, they do so against the wishes of husbands.

Binary models that locate gender oppression in the family-centered worlds of the homeland and liberation in women's employment in the US have met with challenges (Alicea, 1997; Kibria, 1990). Many families maintain traditional arrangements despite the employment of wives. For example, the concentration of Korean immigrant women in small family-run businesses where they work alongside husbands and do not draw a separate salary seems to undercut the potential positive effects other types of employment have on immigrant women's family power (Min, 1998b). Though research on class differences is scant, some evidence suggests that middle-class, immigrant women have an easier time striking an egalitarian balance (Toro-Morn, 1995). In many immigrant families, men who fear losing their authority and status resist challenges to traditional arrangements, at times relying on abuse to maintain their power (Fernández-Kelly and García, 1990). Some immigrant wives attempt to bolster their husband's threatened self-esteem and the family's sense of tradition by maintaining a submissive stance. Women develop strategies within the patriarchal structure for maximizing their power and resources (Lim, 1997; Kandiyoti, 1988). Indeed, much of the empirical research suggests that immigrant women's economic resources and increase in power vis-à-vis their husbands do not undermine their commitment to a patriarchal structure. Rather, they remain committed to a traditional family structure as a means of preserving their parental authority, long-term economic security, and family networks that assist in the resistance of race and class oppression (Alicea, 1997; Kibria, 1990). In this scenario women's employment and increased independence are viewed as extensions of their traditional position prompted by the conditions of adaptation, and necessary only until the family can establish a firm footing on new soil. Several studies find that immigrant women view their paid employment and increased household power as temporary and aspire toward a middle-class lifestyle that involves their full time housewifery (Fernández-Kelly and García, 1990; Toro-Morn, 1995), though the unintended gains employed women experience in gender relations sometimes promote their commitment to paid labor (Grasmuck and Pessar, 1991). Hence the observed shifts in gender arrangements do not necessarily signal a profound challenge to the gender hierarchy, as some women do not use their power to press for permanently altered gender arrangements, but for the restoration of a traditional family structure.

Gender shifts in immigrant families are neither universal nor without contradictions across domains. Women who lead double lives by enacting independence in the workplace, and a submissive stance at home can experience tremendous emotional conflict and stress in the maintenance of contradictory personalities (Kar et al., 1995–6; Pyke and Johnson, 2003). Further, women's greater status vis-à-vis their husbands does not translate into an increase in their general social status. Indeed, such relative gains are propelled by their husband's loss of status in the class and race configurations of North America, which also constrains their own position in the larger society (Chai, 1987; Espiritu, 1997; Grasmuck and Pessar, 1991). Immigrant women still endure patriarchal arrangements in the workplace, as reflected in the low-wage labor reserved for them. Some suffer downward mobility as they move from higher-status occupations in their homeland to low-paying menial work upon immigration. Similarly, former homemakers whose husbands earned enough to support the family prior to immigration often experience the necessity of their employment, usually in menial jobs, as downward class mobility, and the juggling of both a paid job and domestic obligations as an added burden (Fernández-Kelly and García, 1990). Even if husbands "help out" more than before, the domestic workload is rarely truly shared and immigrant women face the stress of their work overload (Foner, 1986; Min, 1998a). And while immigration can provide women with some distance from controlling elders thereby increasing their autonomy and family power, it also denies them kin-based assistance with child-care and household chores (Chai, 1987). Similarly, immigrant women who relied on maids in the homeland typically find they can ill afford such services in the US (Fernández-Kelly and García, 1990).

The overall increase in power and economic opportunities for women upon immigration while that of men shrinks contributes to a gendered pattern of stated preference for return migration. Immigrant men who experience a marked loss of power both inside and outside of their families are more inclined to want to return than are their wives, who enjoy their new autonomy and power within the family domain (Hondagneu-Sotelo, 1994). Grasmuck and Pessar (1991) found that Dominican immigrant women used their new control of finances to invest family resources in furnishings and the establishment of a home, thereby strategically promoting settlement and draining the funds needed for return migration. Disagreement over return migration contributes to divorce rates in immigrant families.

THE NEW SECOND GENERATION

Scholarly neglect of immigrant children and the US-born children of immigrant parents accounts for a profound gap in our knowledge of the long-term adaptation processes and outcomes among immigrant families. Further, the largest growing segment of the child population in the US since the 1980s—those growing up in immigrant families—has been largely ignored. This began to change in 1994, with the publication of a special issue of the *International Migration Review* devoted to the "new" second generation, launching a massive effort to draw attention to this neglected group.

The growing research on today's second generation tells two distinct though reconcilable tales. On the one hand, strong ties to family and ethnicity have been associated with educational success among second-generation youth. This research, associated with segmented assimilation theory, stresses the role of the family and ethnic culture as an adaptive resource, and presents a somewhat harmonious view of immigrant family life (Caplan, Choy, and Whitmore, 1991; Gibson, 1988; Valenzuela and Dornbusch, 1994). Intensive investigation of the subjective experiences and emotional life of children of immigrants tells yet another tale. Regardless of their level of academic and social success, children in immigrant families tend to feel immense stress and tension in coping with their immigrant parents' expectations in the context of the contradictory pulls of the mainstream culture (Kibria, 1993; Pyke, 2000; Wolf, 1997; Zhou and Bankston, 1998). Glenn (1986) argues that both views of family life are accurate. Families provide a refuge from discrimination and the economic and cultural difficulties of the mainstream society. Families are also a site of conflict, particularly along axes of gender, generation, age, and acculturative differences. As a result the portrait that emerges of immigrant families fluctuates around the opposite poles of harmony and conflict. In this section I discuss the conflictual aspects of intergenerational relations centered around the different acculturative pathways of parents and children.

Immigrant children and children of immigrants tend to acculturate to the mainstream society much more rapidly than do their parents. The second generation gain fluency in English sooner than do parents, and tend to prefer English over the language of their parents (Rumbaut, 1997; Zhou and Bankston, 1998). Hence, parents and children frequently lack fluency in a common tongue (Kibria, 1993). Further restrictions are placed on parent–child interaction by the long work hours of immigrant parents, with some children going for days without seeing one or both of their parents (Sung, 1987). These factors undermine the ability of parents to pass on to children their ethnic language and culture. Parent–child solidarity is also undermined by the limited applicability of parental experiences growing up in the homeland to those of their children in the US.

The gap between faster-changing children and slower-changing parents is further enhanced by the greater acculturative opportunities and pressures that children encounter via school, peers, and the media. Compared to the children of earlier waves of immigrants, today's children spend more time in the educational system and have greater interaction with non-immigrant peers. Adaptation processes have also been transformed by the advent of television. Fully 98 percent of all American households have one or more televisions, making it a tremendous assimilative force (Rumbaut, 1997). The images and values disseminated by a high-tech media, non-immigrant peers, and the school system tend to reflect a narrow Euro-centric view of "normality." Given the weight of the mainstream culture, children of immigrants easily internalize these ideals and draw upon them as an interpretive frame in viewing their own family and ethnic practices as abnormal, deficient, and even pathological. For example, parents who stress instrumental aspects of love, rather than expressive displays, are often criticized as unloving, with children wishing their parents were more like "American" parents (Pyke, 2000). Relatedly, the practice of child fostering in the Caribbean and Mexico assumes new meaning once children immigrate and assimilate a more stigmatized interpretation of such practices (Waters, 1997).

Immigration is linked with a loss of parental authority, and parents tend to blame the permissiveness and individualism of US society (Kibria, 1993; Waters, 1997; Zhou and Bankston, 1998). However, it appears that the dependency of immigrant parents on children's English-speaking skills, often leading to their management of family finances, plays a big role in the transfer of power. The absence of parents who work long days or reside in the homeland further undermines their authority, while the power of older children who assume the supervision and care of younger siblings is enhanced (Pyke, forthcoming).

The divide between faster-changing children and slower-changing parents and the shift in intergenerational power are sources of conflict and tension in immigrant families. Suárez-Orozco and Suárez-Orozco (1995) report, however, that parent–child conflict is no greater among immigrant than native-born Latino families. Due to a lack of empirical research that compares immigrant families with those in the homeland or looks at the longitudinal changes that occur in families as they immigrate, it is difficult to gauge the extent to which immigration increases levels of family conflict. Nonetheless, intergenerational conflicts in immigrant families are shaped by clashes between American and ethnic practices, including issues of arranged marriage, dating, "going out" with friends, choosing a college major, academic performance, and independence versus dependency (Das Gupta, 1997; Kibria, 1993; Pyke, 2000; Wolf, 1997).

Daughters report more parent–child conflict than do sons (Rumbaut, 1994). The discrepancy between mainstream values of egalitarianism and the adherence to traditional gender hierarchies at home is a contributory factor. Daughters frequently complain of a parental double standard with males given more freedom and fewer household chores (Zhou and Bankston, 1998). Not surprisingly, sons are less likely to complain of gender arrangements. Tension also arises from the contradictory messages passed on to daughters who are told to succeed academically and pursue a career but forfeit attendance at distant, high-quality universities so as to stay close to home (Wolf, 1997). Females are often instructed to maintain traditional gender arrangements in the home at the same time as they are pushed to compete with males in school and career. Hence the same gender contradictions that immigrant mothers face in the realms of work and family life are reiterated in the messages and conditions passed on to daughters.

Despite the challenges immigration presents to relations between parents and children, and the tendency of children to challenge ethnic practices, some aspects of ethnic culture are successfully transmitted to children. The most notable is a commitment to familism, including filial care, which is an important means by which children reaffirm their ethnic identity (Pyke, 2000). It is only the more assimilated who show weakened norms of familism (Silverstein and Chen, 1999).

ELDERLY IMMIGRANTS

Most late-life immigrants arrive in order to join family members as permitted by family reunification allowances. Treas (1995) reports that two-thirds of elderly legal immigrants to the US in 1991 were parents of US citizens. The collectivist norms of the sending societies from which most elderly immigrants arrive emphasize the co-residence of elderly parents with adult children, contributing to such living arrangements in North America. However, diversity in living arrangements is related to the length of time that elderly immigrants have resided in the new society. Compared to the elderly who immigrated at younger ages, elderly newcomers are poorer and less likely to speak English (Treas and Mazumdar, 2002). They are thus more dependent upon family members for financial support and assistance in mediating the new culture, and more likely than native-born elders and those who immigrated at younger ages to live with kin in extended households (Boyd, 1991). However, a comparison of co-residence patterns among Asian Americans and white Americans found that Asian Americans, even those born in the US, display stronger patterns of co-residence. And children of Asian immigrants also express a commitment to filial care. Further, a study of Chinese immigrant families found that grown children feel a stronger sense of obligation to the filial care of their parents than their parents believed they should (Lin and Liu, 1993). This suggests that despite the waning of some ethnic practices with acculturation across time and generations, familism and a commitment to parental co-residence tend to persist over time (Kamo and Zhou, 1994). However, the geographic distance that often separates grown immigrant children from their elderly parents means that many are not actively engaged in filial care (Ishii-Kuntz, 1997). So while values of filial piety are important in shaping elder care among immigrants (Kamo and Zhou, 1994), structural factors such as geographical proximity also explain variations in immigrant caregiving.

Although immigrant norms tend to emphasize children's support and care of parents, in actuality immigrant elders provide high levels of assistance to their children through child-care and domestic tasks (Orleck, 1987; Treas and Mazumdar, 2002). Indeed, immigrant children who do not have parents residing nearby complain about the difficulties of raising children without their assistance (Tam and Detzner, 1998).

Even though traditional practices among most immigrant cultures assign greater authority and respect to elders than is the norm in the US, there is evidence that the dependency of immigrant elders on their grown children fosters their submissiveness and deference to the needs of their children and an unwillingness to challenge family arrangements (Treas and Mazumdar, 2002). This suggests that intergenerational dynamics do not conform as closely to immigrant cultural ideals as is often assumed. Departures from cultural expectations can create difficulties for elderly immigrants. Elders who reside in the suburban homes of their employed children, where social contact with coethnics is minimal, report feelings of isolation, loneliness, and depression (ibid.). This is also the case among those elderly immigrants who expected to reside with children but instead live alone and feel cut off from an active role in day-to-day family life, undermining their sense of purpose and identity. These factors contribute to depression (Mui, 1998) and high suicide rates, such as among elderly Asian American female immigrants, who are 65 percent more likely to kill themselves than elderly white American women (Pascual, 2000). However, many immigrant elders who have adapted to life in the US, particularly those who immigrated at younger ages, prefer to live independently (Min, 1998a). Their reasons include an intergenerational cultural gap, and the avoidance of domestic obligations in their children's home.

CONCLUSIONS

Research on today's immigrant families has not yet attracted the sustained and organized attention of a large group of scholars. Hence the picture that emerges of immigrant families is at times fragmentary and contradictory. A lack of comparative research has resulted in the tendency to generalize across ethnic groups inadvertently contributing to the construction of monolithic family types. Much more research is needed that focuses on the differences among as well as within ethnic groups (e.g., comparisons across class, generational status, length of time in the US, and gender). Meanwhile, much of the immigrant research continues to focus on how and why immigrant families differ from the white-dominated mainstream ideal, even studies designed to revise earlier research that found immigrant families deficient. This focus on the white family standard has hindered a richer comparative understanding of differences and similarities among and within immigrant groups.

The ongoing shift in research from the post-1965 first-generation immigrants to their children highlights this group's strategic theoretical importance. The study of the second generation as they grow up, enter the occupational structure, marry, raise children, and respond to the needs of their aging parents can inform scholars about the long-term status and adaptive patterns of immigrant families. Will subsequent generations be incorporated into the higher echelons of the economic structure, or will they form permanently disadvantaged groups? How will assimilation, the maintenance of ethnic ties, racism, the loss of well-paid, blue-collar jobs in the current economy, and other factors, contribute to the economic futures of today's immigrant children? Answering these questions will contribute to the development of current theories of adaptation.

Research on immigrant families also needs to be integrated into the general stream of family studies as well as its subfields. For example, although there has been a growing interest in research on dynamics between gay, lesbian, and bisexual children and their parents, these dynamics have not been examined in immigrant families (Ishii-Kuntz, 2000). Similarly, immigrant families need to be included in studies of the divorced, remarried, and female-headed households. Doing so will expand our theoretical and empirical understanding of the diversity of family types, permit greater comparative analysis, and dramatically transform theoretical paradigms steeped in assumptions about "normal" family life that are derived from a white, middle-class model (Pyke, 2000).

While the current literature emphasizes the affect that contact with mainstream American society has on immigrant families, it is also necessary to examine the ways that mainstream American family practices are impacted by contact with immigrant cultures (Foner, 1997). As norms of familism appear to be maintained among immigrant families and their children, the question arises as to what extent, if any, familism will be incorporated or accommodated in the dominant society. How might immigrant practices of familism be affecting US policies and institutional practices? Or do structures of power and dominance create a hegemonic mainstream culture that is impervious to the influx of immigrant families? Further, to what extent can we attribute long-term patterns of familism among immigrant groups to social structural factors, immigration policies, and institutional practices in the US? These are important theoretical questions that family and immigration scholars have yet to address.

REFERENCES

Alicea, M. (1997) "A chambered nautilus": The contradictory nature of Puerto Rican women's role in the social construction of a transnational community. *Gender and Society*, 11, 597–626.

Alvirez, D., and Bean, F. D. (1976) The Mexican-American family. In C. H. Mindel and R. W. Habenstein (eds.), *Ethnic Families in America*. New York: Elsevier.

Badets, J., and Chui, T. (1994) *Canada's Changing Immigrant Population*. Ottawa: Statistics Canada.

Bonacich, E. (1994) Asians in the Los Angeles garment industry. In P. Ong, E. Bonacich, and L. Cheng (eds.), *The New Asian Immigration in Los Angeles and Global Restructuring*. Philadelphia: Temple University Press.

Boyd, M. (1989) Family and personal networks in international migration: Recent developments and new agendas. *International Migration Review*, 23, 638–70.

Boyd, M. (1991) Immigration and living arrangements: elderly women in Canada. *International Migration Review*, 25, 4–27.

Caplan, N., Choy, M. H., and Whitmore, J. K. (1991) *Children of the Boat People: A Study of Educational Success*. Ann Arbor: University of Michigan Press.

Chai, A. Y. (1987) Freed from the elders but locked into labor: Korean immigrant women in Hawaii. *Women's Studies*, 13, 223–4.

Chavez, L. R. (1991) *Shadowed Lives: Undocumented Immigrants in American Society*. San Diego: Harcourt Brace Jovanovich College Publishers.

Das Gupta, M. (1997) "What is Indian about you?" A gendered, transnational approach to ethnicity. *Gender and Society*, 11, 572–96.

Espiritu, Y. L. (1997) *Asian American Women and Men*. Thousand Oaks, CA: Sage.

Fernández-Kelly, M. P., and García, A. M. (1990) Power surrendered, power restored: The politics of work and family among Hispanic garment workers in California and Florida. In L. A. Tilly and P. Gurin (eds.), *Women, Politics and Change*. New York: Russell Sage Foundation.

Foner, N. (1997) The immigrant family: Cultural legacies and cultural changes. *International Migration Review*, 31, 961–74.

Foner, N. (1986) Sex roles and sensibilities: Jamaican women in New York and London. In R. Simon and C. Brettell (eds.), *International Migration: The Female Experience*. Totowa, NJ: Rowman & Allanheld.

Gans, H. J. (1992) Second-generation decline: Scenarios for the economic and ethnic futures of post-1965 American immigrants. *Ethnic and Racial Studies*, 15, 173–92.

Gibson, M. A. (1988) *Accommodation Without Assimilation: Sikh Immigrants in an American High School*. Ithaca, NY: Cornell University Press.

Glenn, E. N. (1986) *Issei, Nisei, War Bride: Three Generations of Japanese American Women in Domestic Service*. Philadelphia: Temple University Press.

Gordon, M. H. (1990) Dependents or independent workers? The status of Caribbean immigrant women in the United States. In R. W. Palmer (ed,), *In Search of a Better Life: Perspectives on Migration from the Caribbean*. New York: Praeger.

Grasmuck, S., and Pessar, P. R. (1991) *Between Two Islands: Dominican International Migration*. Berkeley: University of California Press.

Guendelman, S., and Pérez-Itriago, A. (1987) Double lives: The changing role of women in seasonal migration. *Women's Studies*, 13, 249–71.

Heller, C. (1966) *Mexican American Youth: Forgotten Youth at the Crossroads*. New York: Random House.

Hondagneu-Sotelo, P. (1994) *Gendered Transitions: Mexican Experiences of Immigration*. Los Angeles: University of California Press.

Hoppe, S. K., and Heller, P. L. (1975) Alienation, familism, and the utilization of health services by Mexican-Americans. *Journal of Health and Social Behavior*, 16, 304–14.

Ishii-Kuntz, M. (1997) Intergenerational relationships among Chinese, Japanese, and Korean Americans. *Family Relations*, 46, 23–32.

Ishii-Kuntz, M. (2000) Diversity within Asian American families. In D. H. Demo, K. R. Allen, and M. A. Fine (eds.), *Handbook of Family Diversity*. New York: Oxford University Press.

Kamo, Y., and Zhou, M. (1994) Living arrangements of elderly Chinese and Japanese in the United States. *Journal of Marriage and the Family*, 56, 544–58.

Kandiyoti, D. (1988) Bargaining with patriarchy. *Gender and Society*, 2, 274–90.

Kar, S. B., Campbell, K., Jimenez, A., and Gupta, S. R. (1995–1996) Invisible Americans: An exploration of Indo-American quality of life. *Amerasia Journal*, 21, 25–52.

Kibria, N. (1990) Power, patriarchy, and gender conflict in the Vietnamese immigrant community. *Gender and Society*, 4, 9–24.

Kibria, N. (1993) *Family Tightrope: The Changing Lives of Vietnamese Americans*. Princeton, NJ: Princeton University Press.

Kim, B. (1994) Value orientations and sex-gender role attitudes on the comparability of Koreans and Americans. In H. Cho and O. Chang (eds.), *Gender Division of Labor in Korea*. Seoul: Ewha Women's University Press.

Lim, I. (1997) Korean immigrant women's challenge to gender inequality at home: the interplay of economic resources, gender, and family. *Gender and Society*, 11, 31–51.

Lin, C., and Liu, W. T. (1993) Intergenerational relationships among Chinese immigrant families from Taiwan. In H. P. McAdoo (ed.), *Family Ethnicity*. Newbury Park, CA: Sage.

Lollock, L. (2001) The foreign-born population in the United States: March 2000, Current Population Reports, 2001, pp. 20–534. Washington, DC: US Census Bureau.

Maharidge, D. (1996) *The Coming White Minority: California Eruptions and American's Future*. New York: New York Times Books.

Mangiafico, L. (1988) *Contemporary American Immigrants*. New York: Praeger.

Min, P. G. (1998a) *Changes and Conflicts: Korean Immigrant Families in New York*. Boston: Allyn & Bacon.

Min, P. G. (1998b) The Korean-American family. In C. H. Mindel, R. W. Habenstein, and R. Wright (eds.), *Ethnic Families in America: Patterns and Variations*. Upper Saddle River, NJ: Prentice Hall.

Morokvasic, M. (1983) Women in migration: beyond the reductionist outlook. In A. Phizacklea (ed.), *One Way Ticket: Migration and Female Labour*. Boston: Routledge & Kegan Paul.

Mui, A. (1998) Living alone and depression among older Chinese immigrants. *Journal of Gerontological Social Work*, 30, 147–8.

National Statistical Office, Republic of Korea (1993) *1990 Population and Housing Census Report, Vol. 6: Economic Activity*. Seoul: National Statistical Office, Republic of Korea.

Nelson, S. S., and O'Reilly, R. (2000) Minorities become majority in state, census officials say. *Los Angeles Times*, August, A1, A16.

Orleck, A. (1987) The Soviet Jews: Life in Brighton Beach, Brooklyn. In N. Foner (ed.), *New Immigrants in New York*. New York: Columbia University Press.

Park, R. E., and Burgess, E. W. (1924) *Introduction to the Science of Sociology*. Chicago: University of Chicago Press.

Pascual, C. (2000) Why more elderly Asian women kill themselves. *Los Angeles Times*, September 14, E1, E4.

Portes, A., and Rumbaut, R. G. (1996) *Immigrant America: A Portrait*. Los Angeles: University of California Press.

Portes, A., and Zhou, M. (1993) The new second generation: segmented assimilation and its variants. *Annals of the American Academy of Political and Social Science*, 530, 74–96.

Pyke, K. (2000) The normal American family as an interpretive structure of family life among grown children of Korean and Vietnamese immigrants. *Journal of Marriage and the Family*, 62, 240–55.

Pyke, K. (2005) "Generational deserters" and "black sheep": Acculturative differences among siblings in Korean and Vietnamese immigrant families. *Journal of Family Issues*, 26, 491–517.

Pyke, K., and Johnson, D. (2003) Asian American women and racialized femininities: "Doing" gender across cultural worlds. *Gender and Society*, 17, 33–53.

Reimers, D. M. (1996) Third World immigration to the United States. In H. O. Duleep and P. V. Wunnava (eds.), *Immigrants and Immigration Policy: Individual Skills, Family Ties, and Group Identities*. Greenwich, CT: JAI Press.

Repack, T. A. (1997) New roles in a new landscape. In M. Romero, P. Hondagneu-Sotelo, and V. Ortiz (eds.), *Challenging Fronteras: Structuring Latina and Latino Lives in the U.S.* New York: Routledge.

Rubel, A. J. (1966) *Across the Tracks: Mexican Americans in a Texas City*. Austin: University of Texas Press.

Rumbaut, R. G. (1994) The crucible within: Ethnic identity, self-esteem, and segmented assimilation among children of immigrants. *International Migration Review*, 28, 748–94.

Rumbaut, R. G. (1997) Assimilation and its discontents. Between rhetoric and reality. *International Migration Review*, 31, 923–60.

Silverstein, M., and Chen, X. (1999) The impact of acculturation in Mexican American families on the quality of adult grandchild-grandparent relationships. *Journal of Marriage and the Family*, 61,188–98.

Suárez-Orozco, C., and Suárez-Orozco, M. (1995) *Transformations: Immigration, Family Life, and Achievement Motivation among Latino Adolescents*. Stanford, CA: Stanford University Press.

Sung, B. L. (1987) *The Adjustment Experience of Chinese Immigrant Children in New York City*. New York: Center for Migration Studies.

Tam, C., and Detzner D. (1998) Grandparents as a family resource in Chinese-American families. In H. I. McCubbin, E. A. Thompson, A. I. Thompson, and J. E. Fromer (eds.), *Resiliency in Native American and Immigrant Families*. Thousand Oaks, CA: Sage.

Toro-Morn, M. I. (1995) Gender, class, family, and migration: Puerto Rican women in Chicago. *Gender and Society*, 9, 712–26.

Treas, J. (1995) Older Americans in the 1990s and beyond. *Population Bulletin*, 50, 8–33.

Treas, J., and Mazumdar, S. (2002) Older people in America's immigrant families: Dilemmas of dependence, integration, and isolation. *Journal of Aging Studies*, 16, 243–58.

US Bureau of the Census (1993) *The 1990 Census of Population, General Population Characteristics, United States*. CP-2–1; Washington, DC: US Government Printing Office.

Valenzuela, A., and Dornbusch, S. M. (1994) Familism and social capital in the academic achievement of Mexican origin and Anglo adolescents. *Social Science Quarterly*, 75, 18–36.

Waters, M. C. (1997) Immigrant families at risk: Factors that undermine chances for success. In A. Booth, A. C. Crouter, and N. Landale (eds.), *Immigration and Family: Research and Policy on U.S. Immigrants*. Mahwah, NJ: Lawrence Erlbaum.

Wolf, D. L. (1997) Family secrets: Transnational struggles among children of Filipino immigrants. *Sociological Perspectives*, 40, 457–82.

Zhou, M., and Bankston, C. (1998) *Growing up American: How Vietnamese Children Adapt to Life in the United States*. New York: Russell Sage Foundation.

Zinn, M. B. (1994) Adaptation and continuity in Mexican-origin families. In R. L. Taylor (ed.), *Minority Families in the United States: A Multicultural Perspective*. Englewood Cliffs, NJ: Prentice Hall.

Zinn, M. B., and Eitzen, D. S. (1996) *Diversity in Families*. New York: HarperCollins.

Zinn, M. B., and Wells, B. (2000) Diversity within Latino families: New lessons for family social science. In D. H. Demo, K. R. Allen, and M. A. Fine (eds.), *Handbook of Family Diversity*. New York: Oxford University Press.

14

Diversity Within Latino Families
New Lessons for Family Social Science

Maxine Baca Zinn and Barbara Wells

Who are Latinos? How will their growing presence in U.S. society affect the family field? These are vital questions for scholars who are seeking to understand the current social and demographic shifts that are reshaping society and its knowledge base. Understanding family diversity is a formidable task, not only because the field is poorly equipped to deal with differences at the theoretical level, but because many decentering efforts are themselves problematic. Even when diverse groups are included, family scholarship can distort and misrepresent by faulty emphasis and false generalizations.

Latinos are a population that can be understood only in terms of increasing heterogeneity. Latino families are unprecedented in terms of their diversity. In this chapter, we examine the ramifications of such diversity on the history, boundaries, and dynamics of family life. We begin with a brief look at the intellectual trends shaping Latino family research. We then place different Latino groups at center stage by providing a framework that situates them in specific and changing political and economic settings. Next, we apply our framework to each national origin group to draw out their different family experiences, especially as they are altered by global restructuring. We turn, then, to examine family structure issues and the interior dynamics of family living as they vary by gender and generation. We conclude with our reflections on studying Latino families and remaking family social science. In this chapter, we use interchangeably terms that are commonly used to describe Latino national-origin groups. For example, the terms Mexican American, Mexican, and Mexican-origin population will be used to refer to the same segment of the Latino population. Mexican-origin people may also be referred to as Chicanos.

INTELLECTUAL TRENDS, CRITIQUES, AND CHALLENGES

Origins

The formal academic study of Latino families originated in the late 19th and early 20th centuries with studies of Mexican immigrant families. As the new social scientists of the times focused their concerns on immigration and social disorganization, Mexican-origin and other ethnic families were the source of great concern. The influential Chicago School of Sociology led scholars to believe that Mexican immigration, settlement, and poverty created problems in developing urban centers. During this period, family study was emerging as a new field that sought to document, as well as ameliorate, social problems in urban settings (Thomas & Wilcox, 1987). Immigrant families became major targets of social reform.

Interwoven themes from race relations and family studies gave rise to the view of Mexicans as particularly disorganized. Furthermore, the family was implicated in their plight. As transplants from traditional societies, the immigrants and their children were thought to be at odds with social requirements in the new settings. Their family arrangements were treated as cultural exceptions to the rule of standard family development. Their slowness to acculturate and take on Western patterns of family development left them behind as other families modernized (Baca Zinn, 1995).

Dominant paradigms of assimilation and modernization guided and shaped research. Notions of "traditional" and "modern" forms of social organization joined the new family social science's preoccupation with a standard family form. Compared to mainstream families, Mexican immigrant families were analyzed as traditional cultural forms. Studies of Mexican immigrants highlighted certain ethnic lifestyles that were said to produce social disorganization. Structural conditions that constrained families in the new society were rarely a concern. Instead, researchers examined (1) the families' foreign patterns and habits, (2) the moral quality of family relationships, and (3) the prospects for their Americanization (Bogardus, 1934).

Cultural Preoccupations

Ideas drawn from early social science produced cultural caricatures of Mexican families that became more exaggerated during the 1950s, when structural functionalist theories took hold in American sociology. Like the previous theories, structural functionalism's strategy for analyzing family life was to posit one family type (by no means the only family form, even then) and define it as "the normal family" (Boss & Thorne, 1989). With an emphasis on fixed family boundaries and a fixed division of roles, structural functionalists focused their attention on the group-specific characteristics that deviated from the normal or standard family and predisposed Mexican-origin families to deficiency. Mexican-origin families were analyzed in isolation from the rest of social life, described in simplistic terms of rigid male dominance and pathological clannishness. Although the earliest works on Mexican immigrant families reflected a concern for their eventual adjustment to American society, the new studies virtually abandoned the social realm. They dealt with families as if they existed in a vacuum of backward Mexican traditionalism. Structural functionalism led scholars along a path of cultural reductionism in which differences became deficiencies.

The Mexican family of social science research (Heller, 1966; Madsen, 1964; Rubel, 1966) presented a stark contrast with the mythical "standard family." Although some studies found that Mexican family traditionalism was fading as Mexicans became acculturated, Mexican families were stereotypically and inaccurately depicted as the chief cause of Mexican subordination in the United States.

New Directions

In the past 25 years, efforts to challenge myths and erroneous assumptions have produced important changes in the view of Mexican-origin families. Beginning with a critique of structural functionalist accounts of Mexican families, new studies have successfully challenged the old notions of family life as deviant, deficient, and disorganized.

The conceptual tools of Latino studies, women's studies, and social history have infused the new scholarship to produce a notable shift away from cultural preoccupations. Like the family field in general, research on Mexican-origin families has begun to devote greater attention to the "social situations and contexts that affect Mexican families" (Vega, 1990, p. 1015). This "revisionist" strategy has moved much Latino family research to a different plane—one in which racial-ethnic families are understood to be constructed by powerful social forces and as settings in which different family members adapt in a variety of ways to changing social conditions.

Current Challenges

Despite important advances, notable problems and limitations remain in the study of Latino families. A significant portion of scholarship includes only Mexican-origin groups (Massey, Zambrana, & Bell, 1995) and claims to generalize the findings to other Latinos. This practice constructs a false social reality because there is no Latino population in the same sense that there is an African American population. However useful the terms *Latino* and *Hispanic* may be as political and census identifiers, they mask extraordinary diversity. The category Hispanic was created by federal statisticians to provide data on people of Mexican, Cuban, Puerto Rican, and other Hispanic origins in the United States. There is no precise definition of group membership, and Latinos do not agree among themselves on an appropriate group label (Massey, 1993). While many prefer the term *Latino*, they may use it interchangeably with *Hispanic* to identify themselves (Romero, 1997). These terms are certainly useful for charting broad demographic changes in the United States, but when used as panethnic terms, they can contribute to misunderstandings about family life.

The labels Hispanic or Latino conceal variation in the family characteristics of Latino groups whose differences are often greater than the overall differences between Latinos and non-Latinos (Solis, 1995). To date, little comparative research has been conducted on Latino subgroups. The systematic disaggregation of family characteristics by national-origin groups remains a challenge, a necessary next step in the development of Latino family research.

We believe that the lack of a comprehensive knowledge base should not stand in the way of building a framework to analyze family life. We can use the burgeoning research on Latinos in U.S. social life to develop an analytical, rather than just a descriptive, account of families. The very complexity of Latino family arrangements begs for a unified (but not unitary) analysis. We believe that we can make good generalizations about Latino family diversity. In the sections that follow, we use a structural perspective grounded in intergroup differences. We make no pretense that this is an exhaustive review of research. Instead, our intent is to examine how Latino family experiences differ in relation to socially constructed conditions.

CONCEPTUAL FRAMEWORK

Conventional family frameworks, which have never applied well to racial-ethnic families, are even less useful in the current world of diversity and change. Incorporating multiplicity into family studies requires new approaches. A fundamental assumption guiding our analysis is that Latino families are not merely an expression of ethnic differences but, like all families, are the products of social forces.

Family diversity is an outgrowth of distinctive patterns in the way families and their members are embedded in environments with varying opportunities, resources, and rewards. Economic conditions and social inequalities associated with race, ethnicity, class, and gender place families in different "social locations." These differences are the key to understanding family variation. They determine labor market status, education, marital relations, and other factors that are crucial to family formation.

Studying Latino family diversity means exposing the structural forces that impinge differently on families in specific social, material, and historical contexts. In other words, it means unpacking the structural arrangements that produce and often require a range of family configurations. It also requires analyzing the cross-cutting forms of difference that permeate society and penetrate families to produce divergent family experiences. Several macrostructural conditions produce widespread family variations across Latino groups: (1) the sociohistorical context; (2) the structure of economic opportunity; and (3) global reorganization, including economic restructuring and immigration.

The Sociohistorical Context

Mexicans, Puerto Ricans, Cubans, and other Latino groups have varied histories that distinguish them from each other. The timing and conditions of their arrival in the United States produced distinctive patterns of settlement that continue to affect their prospects for success. Cubans arrived largely between 1960 and 1980; a group of Mexicans indigenous to the Southwest was forcibly annexed into the United States in 1848, and another has been migrating continually since around 1890; Puerto Ricans came under U.S. control in 1898 and obtained citizenship in 1917; Salvadorans and Guatemalans began to migrate to the United States in substantial numbers during the past two decades.

The Structure of Economic Opportunity

Various forms of labor are needed to sustain family life. Labor status has always been the key factor in distinguishing the experiences of Latinos. Mexicans, Puerto Ricans, Cubans, and others are located in different regions of the country where particular labor markets and a group's placement within them determine the kind of legal, political, and social supports available to families. Different levels of structural supports affect family life, often producing various domestic and household arrangements. Additional complexity stems from gendered labor markets. In a society in which men are still assumed to be the primary breadwinners, jobs generally held by women pay less than jobs usually held by men. Women's and men's differential labor market placement, rewards, and roles create contradictory work and family experiences.

Global Reorganization, Including Economic Restructuring and Immigration

Economic and demographic upheavals are redefining families throughout the world. Four factors are at work here: new technologies based primarily on the computer chip, global economic interdependence, the flight of capital, and the dominance of the information and service sectors over basic manufacturing industries (Baca Zinn & Eitzen, 1998). Latino families are profoundly affected as the environments in which they live are reshaped and they face economic and social marginalization because of underemployment and unemployment. Included in economic globalization are new demands for immigrant labor and the dramatic demographic transformations that are "Hispanicizing" the United States. Family flexibility has long been an important feature of the immigrant saga. Today, "Latino immigration is adding many varieties to family structure" (Moore & Vigil, 1993, p. 36).

The macrostructural conditions described earlier provide the context within which to examine the family experiences of different Latino groups. They set the foundation for comparing family life across Latino groups. These material and economic forces help explain the different family profiles of Mexicans, Puerto Ricans, Cubans, and others. In other words, they enable sociologists to understand how families are bound up with the unequal distribution of social opportunities and how the various national-origin groups develop broad differences in work opportunities, marital patterns, and household structures. However, they do not explain other important differences in family life that cut across national-origin groups. People of the same national origin may experience family differently, depending on their location in the class structure as unemployed, poor, working class or professional; their location in the gender structure as female or male; and their location in the sexual orientation system as heterosexual, gay, lesbian, or bisexual (Baca Zinn & Dill, 1996). In addition to these differences, family life for Latinos is shaped by age, generation living in the United States, citizenship status, and even skin color. All these differences intersect to influence the shape and character of family and household relations.

While our framework emphasizes the social context and social forces that construct families, we do not conclude that families are molded from the "outside in." What happens on a daily basis in family relations and domestic settings also constructs families. Latinos themselves—women, men, and children—have the ability actively to shape their family and household arrangements. Families should be seen as settings in which people are agents and actors, coping with, adapting to, and changing social structures to meet their needs (Baca Zinn & Eitzen, 1996).

Sociohistorical Context for Family Diversity Among Mexicans

Families of Mexican descent have been incorporated into the United States by both conquest and migration. In 1848, at the end of the Mexican War, the United States acquired a large section of Mexico, which is now the southwestern United States. With the signing of the Treaty of Guadalupe Hidalgo, the Mexican population in that region became residents of U.S. territory. Following the U.S. conquest, rapid economic growth in that region resulted in a shortage of labor that was resolved by recruiting workers from Mexico. So began the pattern of Mexican labor migration that continues to the present (Portes & Rumbaut, 1990). Some workers settled permanently in the United States, and others continued in cycles of migration, but migration from Mexico has been continuous since around 1890 (Massey et al., 1995).

Dramatic increases in the Mexican-origin population have been an important part of the trend toward greater racial and ethnic diversity in the United States. The Mexican population tripled in size in 20 years, from an estimated 4.5 million in 1970 to 8.7 million in 1980 to 13.5 million in 1990 (Rumbaut, 1995; Wilkinson, 1993). At present, approximately two thirds of Mexicans are native born, and the remainder are foreign born (Rumbaut, 1995). Important differences are consistently found between the social experiences and economic prospects of the native born and the foreign born (Morales & Ong, 1993; Ortiz, 1996). While some variation exists, the typical Mexican migrant to the United States has low socioeconomic status and rural origins (Ortiz, 1995; Portes & Rumbaut, 1990). Recent immigrants have a distinct disadvantage in the labor market because of a combination of low educational attainment, limited work skills, and limited English language proficiency. Social networks are vital for integrating immigrants into U.S. society and in placing them in the social class system (Fernandez-Kelly & Schauffler, 1994). Mexicans are concentrated in barrios that have social networks in which vital information is shared, contacts are made, and job referrals are given. But the social-class context of these Mexican communities is overwhelmingly poor and working class. Mexicans remain overrepresented in low-wage occupations, especially service, manual labor, and low-end manufacturing. These homogeneous lower-class communities lack the high-quality resources that could facilitate upward mobility for either new immigrants or second- and later-generation Mexicans.

The common assumption that immigrants are assimilated economically by taking entry-level positions and advancing to better jobs has not been supported by the Mexican experience (Morales & Ong, 1993; Ortiz, 1996). Today's Mexican workers are as likely as ever to be trapped in low-wage unstable employment situations (Ortiz, 1996; Sassen, 1993). Studies (Aponte, 1993; Morales & Ong, 1993; Ortiz, 1996) have found that high labor force participation and low wages among Mexicans have created a large group of working poor. Households adapt by holding multiple jobs and pooling wages (Velez-Ibañez & Greenberg, 1992).

Mexicans are the largest Latino group in the United States; 6 of 10 Latinos have Mexican origins. This group has low family incomes, but high labor force participation rates for men and increasing rates for women. Mexicans have the lowest educational attainments and the largest average household size of all Latino groups. (See Table 14.1 and Figure 14.1 for between-group comparisons.)

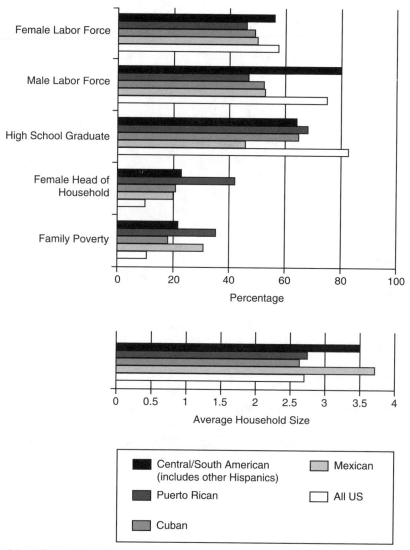

Figure 14.1 Social and Economic Population Characteristics

Table 14.1 Social and Economic Population Characteristics

	Median Income	Poverty	% Female Head of Household	Labor Force Male	Labor Force Female	High School Graduate	Average Household
Mexican	23,609	29.6	19.9	80.9	51.8	46.5	3.86
Puerto Rican	20,929	33.2	41.2	70.6	47.4	61.3	2.91
Cuban	30,584	13.6	21.3	69.9	50.8	64.7	2.56
Central/South American	28,558	23.9	25.4	79.5	57.5	64.2	3.54
Other Hispanic	28,658	21.4	29.5			68.4	
All Hispanic	24,313	27.8	24	79.1	52.6	53.4	2.99
All U.S.	38,782	11.6	12	75	58.9	81.7	2.65
	1994	1994	1995	1995	1995	1995	1995

Sources: US Bureau of the Census, Statistical Abstract of the United States: 1996 (116th ed.) Washington, D.C.: U.S. Government Printing Office, 1996, Tables 53, 68, 241, 615, 622, 723, 738.

Puerto Ricans

The fortunes of Puerto Rico and the United States were joined in 1899 when Puerto Rico became a U.S. possession in the aftermath of Spain's defeat in the Spanish-American War. Puerto Ricans are U.S. citizens and, as such, have the right to migrate to the mainland without regulation. A small stream of migrants increased dramatically after World War II for three primary reasons: high unemployment in Puerto Rico, the availability of inexpensive air travel between Puerto Rico and the United States, and labor recruitment by U.S. companies (Portes & Rumbaut, 1990). Puerto Ricans were concentrated in or near their arrival point—New York City—although migrant laborers were scattered throughout the Northeast and parts of the Midwest. They engaged in a variety of blue-collar occupations; in New York City, they were particularly drawn into the textile and garment industries (Torres & Bonilla, 1993). The unique status of Puerto Rico as a commonwealth of the United States allows Puerto Ricans to engage in a circulating migration between Puerto Rico and the mainland (Feagin & Feagin, 1996).

Puerto Ricans are the most economically disadvantaged of all major Latino groups. The particular context of Puerto Ricans' entry into the U.S. labor market helps explain this group's low economic status. Puerto Ricans with limited education and low occupational skills migrated to the eastern seaboard to fill manufacturing jobs (Ortiz, 1995); their economic well-being was dependent on opportunities for low-skill employment (Aponte, 1993). The region in which Puerto Ricans settled has experienced a major decline in its manufacturing base since the early 1970s. The restructuring of the economy means that, in essence, the jobs that Puerto Ricans came to the mainland to fill have largely disappeared. Latinos who have been displaced from manufacturing have generally been unable to gain access to higher-wage service sector employment (Carnoy, Daley, & Ojeda, 1993).

Compared to Mexicans and Cubans, Puerto Ricans have the lowest median family incomes and the highest unemployment and poverty rates. Puerto Ricans also have a high rate of female-headed households.

Cubans

The primary event that precipitated the migration of hundreds of thousands of Cubans to the United States was the revolution that brought Fidel Castro to power in 1959. This revolution set off several waves of immigration, beginning with the former economic and political elite and working progressively downward through the class structure. Early Cuban immigrants entered the United States in a highly politicized cold-war context as political refugees from communism. The U.S. government sponsored the Cuban Refugee Program, which provided massive supports to Cuban immigrants, including resettlement assistance, job training, small-business loans, welfare payments, and health care (Dominguez, 1992; Perez-Stable & Uriarte, 1993). By the time this program was phased out after the mid-1970s, the United States had invested nearly $1 billion in assistance to Cubans fleeing from communism (Perez-Stable & Uriarte, 1993, p. 155). Between 1960 and 1980, nearly 800,000 Cubans immigrated to the United States (Domiguez, 1992).

The Cuban population is concentrated in south Florida, primarily in the Miami area, where they have established a true ethnic enclave in which they own businesses; provide professional services; and control institutions, such as banks and newspapers (Perez, 1994). The unique circumstances surrounding their immigration help explain the experience of Cubans. U.S. government supports facilitated the economic successes of early Cuban immigrants (Aponte, 1993, Fernandez-Kelly & Schauffler, 1994). High rates of entrepreneurship resulted in the eventual consolidation of an enclave economy (Portes & Truelove, 1987).

Immigrants, women, and minorities have generally supplied the low-wage, flexible labor on which the restructured economy depends (Morales & Bonilla, 1993). However, Cubans "embody a privileged migration" in comparison to other Latino groups (Morales & Bonilla, 1993, p. 17). Their social-class positions, occupational attainments, and public supports have insulated them from the effects of restructuring. Yet Cubans in Miami are not completely protected from the displacements of the new economic order. As Perez-Stable and Uriarte (1993) noted, the Cuban workforce is polarized, with one segment moving into higher-wage work and the other remaining locked in low-wage employment.

Cuban families have higher incomes and far lower poverty rates than do other major Latino groups. Cubans are the most educated major Latino group and have the smallest average household size.

Other Latinos

In each national-origin group discussed earlier, one finds unique socioeconomic, political and historical circumstances. But the diversity of Latinos extends beyond the differences between Mexican Americans, Cuban Americans, and mainland Puerto Ricans. One finds further variation when one considers the experiences of other Latino national-origin groups. Although research on "other Latinos" is less extensive than the literature cited earlier, we consider briefly contexts for diversity in Central American and Dominican families.

Central Americans. Political repression, civil war, and their accompanying economic dislocations have fueled the immigration of a substantial number of Salvadorans, Guatemalans, and Nicaraguans since the mid-1970s (Hamilton & Chinchilla, 1997). The U.S. population of Central Americans more than doubled between the 1980 and 1990 censuses and now outnumbers Cubans (U.S. Bureau of the Census, 1993). These Latinos migrated under difficult circumstances and face a set of serious challenges in the United States (Dorrington, 1995). Three factors render this population highly vulnerable: (1) a high percentage are undocumented (an estimated 49% of Salvadorans and 40% of Guatemalans), (2) they have marginal employment and high poverty rates, and (3) the U.S. government does not recognize them as political refugees (Lopez, Popkin, & Telles, 1996).

The two largest groups of Central Americans are Salvadorans and Guatemalans, the majority of whom live in the Los Angeles area. Lopez et al.'s (1996) study of Central Americans in Los Angeles illumined the social and economic contexts in which these Latinos construct their family lives. In general, the women and men have little formal education and know little English, but have high rates of labor force participation. Salvadorans and Guatemalans are overrepresented in low-paying service and blue-collar occupations. Salvadoran and Guatemalan women occupy a low-wage niche in private service (as domestic workers in private homes). Central Americans, especially the undocumented who fear deportation and usually have no access to public support, are desperate enough to accept the poorest-quality, lowest-paying work that Los Angeles has to offer. These immigrants hold the most disadvantageous position in the regional economy (Scott, 1996). Lopez et al. predicted that in the current restructured economy, Central Americans will continue to do the worst of the "dirty work" necessary to support the lifestyles of the high-wage workforce.

Dominicans. A significant number of Dominicans began migrating to the U.S. in the mid-1960s. What Grasmuck and Pessar (1996) called the "massive displacement" of Dominicans from their homeland began with the end of Trujillo's 30-year dictatorship and the political uncertainties that ensued. Dominican immigrant families did not fit the conventional image of the unskilled, under-employed peasant. They generally had employed breadwinners who were relatively well educated by Dominican standards; the majority described themselves as having urban middle-class origins (Mitchell, 1992).

The Dominican population is heavily concentrated in New York City. They entered a hostile labor market in which their middle-class aspirations were to remain largely unfulfilled because the restructured New York economy offers low-wage, marginal, mostly dead-end employment for individuals without advanced education (Torres & Bonilla, 1993). Dominicans lacked the English language competence and educational credentials that might have facilitated their upward mobility (Grasmuck & Pessar, 1996). More than two thirds of the Dominican-origin population in the United States is Dominican born. As a group, Dominicans have high rates of poverty and female-headed families. Approximately 4 in 10 family households are headed by women.

THE STRUCTURE OF ECONOMIC OPPORTUNITY

Latino families remain outside the economic mainstream of U.S. society. Their median family income stands at less than two thirds the median family income of all U.S. families (U.S. Bureau of the Census, 1996). But the broad designation of "Latino" obscures important differences among national-origin groups. In this section, we explore variations in the structure of economic opportunity and consider how particular economic contexts shape the lives of different groups of Latino families.

Class, Work, and Family Life

A number of studies (see, for example, Cardenas, Chapa, & Burek, 1993; Grasmuck & Pessar, 1996; Lopez et al., 1996; Ortiz, 1995; Perez, 1994) have documented that diverse social and economic contexts produce multiple labor market outcomes for Latino families. The quality, availability, and stability of wage labor create a socioeconomic context in which family life is constructed and maintained. Cuban American families have fared far better socioeconomically than have other Latino families. Scholars consistently cite the role of the Cuban enclave in providing a favorable economic context with advantages that other groups have not enjoyed (Morales & Bonilla, 1993; Perez, 1994; Perez-Stable & Uriarte, 1993). Cuban families have the highest incomes, educational attainments, and levels of upper-white-collar employment. Puerto Rican, Mexican, and Central American families cluster below Cubans on these socioeconomic indicators, with Puerto Ricans the most disadvantaged group.

The structure of Mexican American economic opportunity stands in sharp contrast to that of Cubans. Betancur, Cordova, and Torres (1993) documented the systematic exclusion of Mexicans from upward-mobility ladders, tracing the incorporation of Mexican Americans into the Chicago economy to illustrate the historic roots of the concentration of Mexicans in unstable, poor-quality work. Throughout the 20th century Mexican migrants have constituted a transient workforce that has been continually vulnerable to fluctuations in the labor market and cycles of recruitment and deportation. Betancur et al.'s study highlighted the significance of the bracero program of contract labor migration in institutionalizing a segmented market for labor. The bracero program limited Mexican workers to specific low-status jobs and industries that prohibited promotion to skilled occupational categories. Mexicans were not allowed to compete for higher-status jobs, but were contracted to fill only the most undesirable jobs. Although formal bracero-era regulations have ended, similar occupational concentrations continue to be reproduced among Mexican American workers.

The effects of these diverging social-class and employment contexts on families are well illustrated by Fernandez-Kelly's (1990) study of female garment workers—Cubans in Miami and Mexicans in Los Angeles—both of whom placed a high value on marriage and family; however, contextual factors shaped differently their abilities to sustain marital relationships over time. Fernandez-Kelly contended that the conditions necessary for maintaining long-term stable unions were present in middle-class families but were absent in poor families. That is, the marriages of the poor women were threatened by unemployment and underemployment. Among these Mexican women, there was a high rate of poor female-headed households, and among the Cuban women, many were members of upwardly mobile families.

Women's Work

Several studies (Chavira-Prado, 1992; Grasmuck & Pessar, 1991; Lamphere, Zavella, Gonzales & Evans, 1993; Stier & Tienda, 1992; Zavella, 1987) that have explored the intersection of work and family for Latinas have found that Latinas are increasingly likely to be employed. Labor force participation is the highest among Central American women and the lowest among Puerto Rican women, with Mexican and Cuban women equally likely to be employed. Not only do labor force participation rates differ by national origin, but the meaning of women's work varies as well. For example, Fernandez-Kelly's (1990) study demonstrated that for Cuban women, employment was part of a broad family objective to reestablish middle-class status. Many Cuban immigrants initially experienced downward mobility, and the women took temporary jobs to generate income while their husbands cultivated fledgling businesses. These women often withdrew from the workforce when their families' economic positions had been secured. In contrast, Mexican women in Los Angeles worked because of dire economic necessity. They were drawn into employment to augment the earnings of partners who were confined to secondary-sector work that paid less than subsistence wages or worse, to provide the primary support for their households. Thus, whereas the Cuban women expected to work temporarily until their husbands could resume the role of middle-class breadwinner, the Mexican women worked either because their partners could not earn a family wage or because of the breakdown of family relationships by divorce or abandonment.

GLOBAL REORGANIZATION

Economic Restructuring

The economic challenges that Latinos face are enormous. A workforce that has always been vulnerable to exploitation can anticipate the decline of already limited mobility prospects. A recent body of scholarship (see, for example, Lopez et al., 1996; Morales & Bonilla, 1993; Ortiz, 1996) has demonstrated that the restructuring of the U.S. economy has reshaped economic opportunities for Latinos.

Torres and Bonilla's (1993) study of the restructuring of New York City's economy is particularly illustrative because it focused on Puerto Ricans, the Latino group hit hardest by economic trans-formations. That study found that restructuring in New York City is based on two processes that negatively affect Puerto Ricans. First, stable jobs in both the public and private sectors have eroded since the 1960s because many large corporations that had provided long-term, union jobs for minorities left the New York area and New York City's fiscal difficulties restricted the opportunities for municipal employment. Second, the reorganization of light manufacturing has meant that new jobs offer low wages and poor working conditions; new immigrants who are vulnerable to exploitation by employers generally fill these jobs. The restructuring of the economy has resulted in the exclusion or withdrawal of a substantial proportion of Puerto Ricans from the labor market (Morales & Bonilla, 1993).

Families are not insulated from the effects of social and economic dislocations. Research that has tracked this major social transformation has considered how such changes affect family processes and household composition (Grasmuck & Pessar, 1996; Lopez et al., 1996; Rodriguez & Hagan, 1997). What Sassen (1993) called the "informalization" and "casualization" of urban labor markets will, in the end, shape families in ways that deviate from the nuclear ideal. The marginalization of the Puerto Rican workforce is related not only to high unemployment and poverty rates, but to high rates of nonmarital births and female-headed households (Fernandez-Kelly, 1990; Morrissey, 1987).

Contrasting the experience of Dominicans to that of Puerto Ricans indicates that it is impossible to generalize a unitary "Latino experience" even within a single labor market—New York City. Torres and Bonilla (1993) found that as Puerto Ricans were displaced from manufacturing jobs in the 1970s and 1980s, new Dominican immigrants came into the restructured manufacturing sector to fill low-wage jobs. Dominicans were part of a pool of immigrant labor that entered a depressed economy, was largely ineligible for public assistance, and was willing to accept exploitative employment. Grasmuck and Pessar (1991, 1996) showed how the incorporation of Dominicans into the restructured New York economy has affected families. Although the rate of divorce among early immigrants was high, relationships have become increasingly precarious as employment opportunities have become even more constrained. Currently, rates of poverty and female-headed households for Dominicans approximate those of Puerto Ricans (Rumbaut, 1995).

A Latino Underclass? Rising poverty rates among Latinos, together with the alarmist treatment of female-headed households among "minorities," have led many policy makers and media analysts to conclude that Latinos have joined inner-city African Americans to form part of the "underclass."

According to the underclass model, inner-city men's joblessness has encouraged nonmarital child-bearing and undermined the economic foundations of the African American family (Wilson, 1987, 1996). Researchers have also been debating for some time whether increases in the incidence of female-headed households and poverty among Puerto Ricans are irreversible (Tienda, 1989). Recent thinking, however, suggests that applying the underclass theory to Latinos obscures more than it reveals and that a different analytical model is needed to understand poverty and family issues in each Latino group (Massey et al., 1995). Not only do the causes of poverty differ across Latino communities, but patterns of social organization at the community and family levels produce a wide range of responses to poverty. According to Moore and Pinderhughes (1993), the dynamics of poverty even in the poorest Latino barrios differ in fundamental ways from the conventional portrait of the underclass. Both African Americans and Puerto Ricans have high rates of female-headed households. However, Sullivan's (1993) research in Brooklyn indicated that Puerto Ricans have high rates of cohabitation and that the family formation processes that lead to these household patterns are different from those of African Americans. Other case studies have underscored the importance of family organization. For example, Velez-Ibañez (1993) described a distinctive family form among poor Mexicans of South Tucson—cross-class household clusters surrounded by kinship networks that stretch beyond neighborhood boundaries and provide resources for coping with poverty.

Immigration

Families migrate for economic reasons, political reasons, or some combination of the two. Immigration offers potential and promise, but one of the costs is the need for families to adapt to their receiving community contexts. A growing body of scholarship has focused on two areas of family change: household composition and gender relations.

Household Composition. Immigration contributes to the proliferation of family forms and a variety of household arrangements among Latinos (Vega, 1995). Numerous studies have highlighted the flexibility of Latino family households. Chavez (1990, 1992) identified transnational families, binational families, extended families, multiple-family households, and other arrangements among Mexican and Central American immigrants. Landale and Fennelly (1992) found informal unions that resemble marriage more than cohabitation among mainland Puerto Ricans, and Guarnizo (1997) found binational households among Dominicans who live and work in both the United States and the Dominican Republic. Two processes are at work as families adapt their household structures. First, family change reflects, for many, desperate economic circumstances (Vega, 1995), which bring some families to the breaking point and lead others to expand their household boundaries. Second, the transnationalization of economies and labor has created new opportunities for successful Latino families; for example, Guarnizo noted that Dominican entrepreneurs sometimes live in binational households and have "de facto binational citizenship" (p. 171).

Immigration and Gender. Several important studies have considered the relationship between immigration and gender (Boyd, 1989; Grasmuck & Pessar, 1991; Hondagneu-Sotelo, 1994). In her study of undocumented Mexican immigrants, Hondagneu-Sotelo (1994) demonstrated that gender shapes migration and immigration shapes gender relations. She found that family stage migration, in which husbands migrate first and wives and children follow later, does not fit the household-strategy model. Often implied in this model is the assumption that migration reflects the unanimous and rational collective decision of all household members. However, as Hondagneu-Sotelo observed, gender hierarchies determined when and under what circumstances migration occurred; that is, men often decided spontaneously, independently, and unilaterally to migrate north to seek employment. When Mexican couples were finally reunited in the United States, they generally reconstructed more egalitarian gender relations. Variation in the form of gender relations in the United States is partially explained by the circumstances surrounding migration, such as the type and timing of migration, access to social networks, and U.S. immigration policy.

FAMILY DYNAMICS ACROSS LATINO GROUPS

Familism

Collectivist family arrangements are thought to be a defining feature of the Latino population. Presumably, a strong orientation and obligation to the family produces a kinship structure that is qualitatively different from that of all other groups. Latino familism, which is said to emphasize the family as opposed to the individual, "is linked to many of the pejorative images that have beset discussions of the Hispanic family" (Vega, 1990, p. 1018). Although themes of Latino familism figure prominently in the social science literature, this topic remains problematic owing to empirical limitations and conceptual confusion.

Popular and social science writing contain repeated descriptions of what amounts to a generic Latino kinship form. In reality, a Mexican-origin bias pervades the research on this topic. Not only is there a lack of comparative research on extended kinship structures among different national-origin groups, but there is little empirical evidence for all but Mexican-origin families. For Mexican-origin groups, studies are plentiful (for reviews, see Baca Zinn, 1983; Vega, 1990, 1995), although they have yielded inconsistent evidence about the prevalence of familism, the forms it takes, and the kinds of supportive relationships it serves.

Among the difficulties in assessing the evidence on extended family life are the inconsistent uses of terms like *familism* and *extended family system*. Seeking to clarify the multiple meanings of familism, Ramirez and Arce (1981) treated familism as a multidimensional concept comprised of such distinct aspects as structure, behavior, norms and attitudes, and social identity, each of which requires separate measurement and analysis. They proposed that familism contains four key components: (1) demographic familism, which involves such characteristics as family size; (2) structural familism, which measures the incidence of multigenerational (or extended) households; (3) normative families, which taps the value that Mexican-origin people place on family unity and solidarity; and (4) behavioral familism, which has to do with the level of interaction between family and kin networks.

Changes in regional and local economies and the resulting dislocations of Latinos have prompted questions about the ongoing viability of kinship networks. Analyzing a national sample of minority families, Rochelle (1997) argued that extended kinship networks are declining among Chicanos, Puerto Ricans, and African Americans. On the other hand, a large body of research has documented various forms of network participation by Latinos. For three decades, studies have found that kinship networks are an important survival strategy in poor Mexican communities (Alvirez & Bean, 1976; Hoppe & Heller, 1975; Velez-Ibañez, 1996) and that these networks operate as a system of cultural, emotional, and mental support (Keefe, 1984; Mindel, 1980; Ramirez, 1980), as well as a system for coping with socioeconomic marginality (Angel & Tienda, 1982; Lamphere et al., 1993).

Research has suggested, however, that kinship networks are not maintained for socioeconomic reasons alone (Buriel & De Ment, 1997). Familistic orientation among Mexican-origin adults has been associated with high levels of education and income (Griffith & Villavicienco, 1985). Familism has been viewed as a form of social capital that is linked with academic success among Mexican-heritage adolescents (Valenzuela & Dornbusch, 1994).

The research on the involvement of extended families in the migration and settlement of Mexicans discussed earlier (Chavez, 1992; Hondagneu-Sotelo, 1994; Hondagneu-Sotelo & Avila, 1997) is profoundly important. In contrast to the prevailing view that family extension is an artifact of culture, this research helps one understand that the structural flexibility of families is a social construction. Transnational families and their networks of kin are extended in space, time, and across national borders. They are quintessential adaptations—alternative arrangements for solving problems associated with immigration.

Despite the conceptual and empirical ambiguities surrounding the topic of familism, there is evidence that kinship networks are far from monolithic. Studies have revealed that variations are rooted in distinctive social conditions, such as immigrant versus nonimmigrant status and generational status. Thus, even though immigrants use kin for assistance, they have smaller social networks than do second-generation Mexican Americans who have broader social networks consisting of multigenerational kin (Vega, 1990). Studies have shown that regardless of class, Mexican extended families in the United States become stronger and more extensive with generational advancement, acculturation, and socioeconomic mobility (Velez-Ibañez, 1996). Although an assimilationist perspective suggests that familism fades in succeeding generations, Velez-Ibañez found that highly elaborated second-and third-generation extended family networks are actively maintained through frequent visits, ritual celebrations, and the exchange of goods and services. These networks are differentiated by the functions they perform, depending on the circumstances of the people involved.

Gender

Latino families are commonly viewed as settings of traditional patriarchy and as different from other families because of machismo, the cult of masculinity. In the past two decades, this cultural stereotype has been the impetus for corrective scholarship on Latino families. The flourishing of Latina feminist thought has shifted the focus from the determinism of culture to questions about how gender and power in families are connected with other structures and institutions in society. Although male dominance remains a central theme, it is understood as part of the ubiquitous social ordering of women and men. In the context of other forms of difference, gender exerts a powerful influence on Latino families.

New research is discovering gender dynamics among Latino families that are both similar to and different from those found in other groups. Similarities stem from social changes that are reshaping all families, whereas differences emerge from the varied locations of Latino families and the women and men in them. Like other branches of scholarship on Latino families, most studies have been conducted with Mexican-origin populations. The past two decades of research have shown that family life among all Latino groups is deeply gendered. Yet no simple generalizations sum up the essence of power relations.

Research has examined two interrelated areas: (1) family decision making and (2) the allocation of household labor. Since the first wave of "revisionist works" (Zavella, 1987) conducted in the 1970s and 1980s (Baca Zinn, 1980; Ybarra, 1982), researchers have found variation in these activities, ranging from patriarchal role-segregated patterns to egalitarian patterns, with many combinations in between. Studies have suggested that Latinas' employment patterns, like those of women around the world, provide them with resources and autonomy that alter the balance of family power (Baca Zinn, 1980; Coltrane & Valdez, 1993; Pesquera, 1993; Repack, 1997; Williams, 1990; Ybarra, 1982; Zavella, 1987). But, as we discussed earlier, employment opportunities vary widely, and the variation produces multiple work and family patterns for Latinas. Furthermore, women's employment, by itself, does not eradicate male dominance. This is one of the main lessons of Zavella's (1987) study of Chicana cannery workers in California's Santa Clara Valley. Women's cannery work was circumscribed by inequalities of class, race, and gender. As seasonal, part-time workers, the women gained some leverage in the home, thereby creating temporary shifts in their day-to-day family lives, but this leverage did not alter the balance of family power. Fernandez-Kelly and Garcia's (1990) comparative study of women's work and family patterns among Cubans and Mexican Americans found strikingly different configurations of power. Employed women's newfound rights are often contradictory. As Repack's study (1997) of Central American immigrants revealed, numerous costs and strains accompany women's new roles in a new landscape. Family relations often became contentious when women pressed partners to share domestic responsibilities. Migration produced a situation in which women worked longer and harder than in their countries of origin.

Other conditions associated with varying patterns in the division of domestic labor are women's and men's occupational statuses and relative economic contributions to their families. Studies by Pesquera (1993), Coltrane and Valdez (1993), and Coltrane (1996) found a general "inside/outside" dichotomy (wives doing most housework, husbands doing outside work and sharing some child care), but women in middle-class jobs received more "help" from their husbands than did women with lower earnings.

"Family power" research should not be limited to women's roles, but should study the social relations between women and men. Recent works on Latino men's family lives have made important strides in this regard (Coltrane & Valdez, 1993; Shelton & John, 1993). Still, there is little information about the range and variety of Latino men's family experiences (Mirande, 1997) or of their interplay with larger structural conditions. In a rare study of Mexican immigrant men, Hondagneu-Sotelo and Messner (1994) discussed the diminution of patriarchy that comes with settling in the United States. They showed that the key to gender equality in immigrant families is women's and men's relative positions of power and status in the larger society. Mexican immigrant men's status is low owing to racism, economic marginality, and possible undocumented status. Meanwhile, as immigrant women move into wage labor, they develop autonomy and economic skills. These conditions combine to erode patriarchal authority.

The research discussed earlier suggested some convergences between Latinos and other groups in family power arrangements. But intertwined with the shape of domestic power are strongly held ideals about women's and men's family roles. Ethnic gender identities, values, and beliefs contribute to gender relations and constitute an important but little understood dimension of families. Gender may also be influenced by Latinos' extended family networks. As Lamphere et al. (1993) discovered, Hispanas in Albuquerque were living in a world made up largely of Hispana mothers, sisters, and other relatives. Social scientists have posited a relationship between dense social networks and gender segregation. If this relationship holds, familism could well impede egalitarian relations in Latino families (Coltrane, 1996; Hurtado, 1995).

Compulsory heterosexuality is an important component of both gender and family systems. By enforcing the dichotomy of opposite sexes, it is also a form of inequality in its own right, hence an important marker of social location. A growing literature on lesbian and gay identity among Latinas and Latinos has examined the conflicting challenges involved in negotiating a multiple minority status (Alarcon, Castillo, & Moraga, 1989; Almaguer, 1991; Anzaldua, 1987; Carrier, 1992; Moraga, 1983; Morales, 1990). Unfortunately, family scholarship on Latinos has not pursued the implications of lesbian and gay identities for understanding family diversity. In fact, there have been no studies in the social sciences in the area of sexual orientation and Latino families (Hurtado, 1995). But although the empirical base is virtually nonexistent and making *families* the unit of analysis no doubt introduces new questions (Demo & Allen, 1996), we can glean useful insights from the discourse on sexual identity. Writing about Chicanos, Almaguer (1991) identified the following obstacles to developing a safe space for forming a gay or lesbian identity: racial and class subordination and a context in which ethnicity remains a primary basis of group identity and survival. "Moreover Chicano *family life* [italics added] requires allegiance to patriarchal gender relations and to a system of sexual meanings that directly militate against the emergence of this alternative basis of self identity" (Almaguer, p. 88). Such repeated references to the constraints of ethnicity, gender, and sexual orientation imposed by Chicano families (Almaguer, 1991; Moraga, 1983) raise important questions. How do varied family contexts shape and differentiate the development of gay identities among Latinos? How do they affect the formation of lesbian and gay families among Latinas and Latinos? This area is wide open for research.

Children and Their Parents

Latinos have the highest concentration of children and adolescents of all major racial and ethnic groups. Nearly 40% of Latinos are aged 20 or younger, compared to about 26% of non-Hispanic whites (U.S. Bureau of the Census, 1996). Among Latino subgroups, the highest proportions of children and adolescents are among Mexicans and Puerto Ricans and the lowest among Cubans (Solis, 1995).

Latino socialization patterns have long held the interest of family scholars (Martinez, 1993). Most studies have focused on the child-rearing practices of Mexican families. Researchers have questioned whether Mexican families have permissive or authoritarian styles of child rearing and the relationship of child-rearing styles to social class and cultural factors (Martinez, 1993). Patterns of child rearing were expected to reveal the level of acculturation to U.S. norms and the degree of modernization among traditional immigrant families. The results of research spanning the 1970s and 1980s were mixed and sometimes contradictory.

Buriel's (1993) study brought some clarity to the subject of child-rearing practices by situating it in the broad social context in which such practices occur. This study of Mexican families found that child-rearing practices differ by generation. Parents who were born in Mexico had a "responsibility-oriented" style that was compatible with their own life experience as struggling immigrants. U.S.-born Mexican parents had a "concern-oriented" style of parenting that was associated with the higher levels of education and income found among this group and that may also indicate that parents compensate for their children's disadvantaged standing in U.S. schools.

Mainstream theorizing has generally assumed a middle-class European-American model for the socialization of the next generation (Segura & Pierce, 1993). But the diverse contexts in which Latino children are raised suggest that family studies must take into account multiple models of socialization. Latino children are less likely than Anglo children to live in isolated nuclear units in which parents have almost exclusive responsibility for rearing children and the mothers' role is primary. Segura and Pierce contended that the pattern of nonexclusive mothering found in some Latino families shapes the gender identities of Latinos in ways that conventional thinking does not consider. Velez-Ibañez & Greenberg (1992) discussed how the extensive kinship networks of Mexican families influence child rearing and considered the ramifications for educational outcomes. Mexican children are socialized into a context of "thick" social relations. From infancy onward, these children experience far more social interaction than do children who are raised in more isolated contexts. The institution of education—second only to the family as an agent of socialization—is, in the United States, modeled after the dominant society and characterized by competition and individual achievement. Latino students who have been socialized into a more cooperative model of social relations often experience a disjuncture between their upbringing and the expectations of their schools (Velez-Ibañez & Greenberg, 1992).

Social location shapes the range of choices that parents have as they decide how best to provide for their children. Latino parents, who are disproportionately likely to occupy subordinate social locations in U.S. society, encounter severe obstacles to providing adequate material resources for their children. To date, little research has focused on Latino fathers (Powell, 1995). Hondagneu-Sotelo and Avila's (1997) study documented a broad range of mothering arrangements among Latinas. One such arrangement is transnational mothering, in which mothers work in the United States while their children remain in Mexico or Central America; it is accompanied by tremendous costs and undertaken when options are extremely limited. The researchers found that transnational mothering occurred among domestic workers, many of whom were live-in maids or child care providers who could not live with their children, as well as mothers who could better provide for their children in their countries of origin because U.S. dollars stretched further in Central America than in the United States. Other mothering arrangements chosen by Latinas in the study included migrating with their children, migrating alone and later sending for their children, and migrating alone and returning to their children after a period of work.

Intrafamily Diversity

Family scholars have increasingly recognized that family experience is differentiated along the lines of age and gender (Baca Zinn & Eitzen, 1996; Thorne, 1992). Members of particular families—parents and children, women and men—experience family life differently. Scholarship that considers the internal differentiation of Latino families is focused on the conditions surrounding and adaptations following immigration.

While immigration requires tremendous change of all family members, family adaptation to the new context is not a unitary phenomenon. Research has found patterns of differential adjustment as family members adapt unevenly to an unfamiliar social environment (Gold, 1989). Gil and Vega's (1996) study of acculturative stress in Cuban and Nicaraguan families in the Miami area identified significant differences in the adjustment of parents and their children. For example, Nicaraguan adolescents reported more initial language conflicts than did their parents, but their conflicts diminished over time, whereas their parents' language conflicts increased over time. This difference occurred because the adolescents were immediately confronted with their English language deficiency in school, but their parents could initially manage well in the Miami area without a facility with English. The authors concluded that family members experience "the aversive impacts of culture change at different times and at variable levels of intensity" (p. 451).

Differential adjustment creates new contexts for parent-child relations. Immigrant children who are school-aged generally become competent in English more quickly than do their parents. Dorrington (1995) found that Salvadoran and Guatemalan children often assume adult roles as they help their parents negotiate the bureaucratic structure of their new social environment; for example, a young child may accompany her parents to a local utility company to act as their translator.

Immigration may also create formal legal distinctions among members of Latino families. Frequently, family members do not share the same immigration status. That is, undocumented Mexican and Central American couples are likely, over time, to have children who are born in the United States and hence are U.S. citizens; the presence of these children then renders the "undocumented family" label inaccurate. Chavez (1992, p. 129) used the term *binational family* to refer to a family with both members who are undocumented and those who are citizens or legal residents.

Not only do family members experience family life differently, but age and gender often produce diverging and even conflicting interests among them (Baca Zinn & Eitzen, 1996). Both Hondagneu-Sotelo's (1994) and Grasmuck and Pessar's (1991) studies of family immigration found that Latinas were generally far more interested in settling permanently in the United States than were their husbands. In both studies, the women had enhanced their status by migration, while the men had lost theirs. Hondagneu-Sotelo noted that Mexican women advanced the permanent settlement of their families by taking regular, nonseasonal employment; negotiating the use of public and private assistance; and forging strong community ties. Grasmuck and Pessar observed that Dominican women tried to postpone their families' return to the Dominican Republic by extravagantly spending money that would otherwise be saved for their return and by establishing roots in the United States.

DISCUSSION AND CONCLUSION

The key to understanding diversity in Latino families is the uneven distribution of constraints and opportunities among families, which affects the behaviors of family members and ultimately the forms that family units take (Baca Zinn & Eitzen, 1996). Our goal in this review was to call into question assumptions, beliefs, and false generalizations about the way "Latino families are." We examined Latino families not as if they had some essential characteristics that set them apart from others, but as they are affected by a complex mix of structural features.

Our framework enabled us to see how diverse living arrangements among Latinos are situated and structured in the larger social world. Although this framework embraces the interplay of macro-and microlevels of analysis, we are mindful that this review devoted far too little attention to family experience, resistance, and voice. We do not mean to underestimate the importance of human agency in the social construction of Latino families, but we could not devote as much attention as we would have liked to the various ways in which women, men, and children actively produce their family worlds. Given the sheer size of the literature, the "non-comparability of most contemporary findings" and the lack of a "consistent conceptual groundwork" (Vega, 1990, p. 102), we decided that what is most needed is a coherent framework within which to view and interpret diversity. Therefore, we chose to focus on the impact of social forces on family life.

The basic insights of our perspective are sociological. Yet a paradox of family sociology is that the field has tended to misrepresent Latino families and those of other racial-ethnic groups. Sociology has distorted Latino families by generalizing from the experience of dominant groups and ignoring the differences that make a difference. This is a great irony. Family sociology, the specialty whose task it is to describe and understand social diversity, has marginalized diversity, rather than treated it as a central feature of social life (Baca Zinn & Eitzen, 1993).

As sociologists, we wrote this chapter fully aware of the directions in our discipline that hinder the ability to explain diversity. At the same time, we think the core insight of sociology should be applied to challenge conventional thinking about families. Reviewing the literature for this chapter did not diminish our sociological convictions, but it did present us with some unforeseen challenges. We found a vast gulf between mainstream family sociology and the extraordinary amount of high-quality scholarship on Latino families. Our review took us far beyond the boundaries of our discipline, making us "cross disciplinary migrants" (Stacey, 1995). We found the new literature in diverse and unlikely locations, with important breakthroughs emerging in the "borderlands" between social science disciplines. We also found the project to be infinitely more complex than we anticipated. The extensive scholarship on three national-origin groups and "others" was complicated by widely varying analytic snapshots. We were, in short, confronted with a kaleidoscope of family diversity. Our shared perspective served us well in managing the task at hand. Although we have different family specializations and contrasting family experiences, we both seek to understand multiple family and household forms that emanate from structural arrangements.

What are the most important lessons our sociological analysis holds for the family field? Three themes offer new directions for building a better, more inclusive, family social science. First, understanding Latino family diversity does not mean simply appreciating the ways in which families are different; rather, it means analyzing how the formation of diverse families is based on and reproduces social inequalities. At the heart of many of the differences between Latino families and mainstream families and the different aggregate family patterns among Latino groups are structural forces that place families in different social environments. What is not often acknowledged is that the same social structures—race, class, and other hierarchies—affect *all* families, albeit in different ways. Instead of treating family variation as the property of group difference, recent sociological theorizing (Baca Zinn, 1994; Dill, 1994; Glenn, 1992; Hill Collins, 1990, 1997) has conceptualized diverse family arrangements in *relational* terms, that is, mutually dependent and sustained through interaction across racial and class boundaries. The point is not that family differences based on race, class, and gender simply coexist. Instead, many differences in family life involve relationships of domination and subordination and differential access to material resources. Patterns of privilege and subordination characterize the historical relationships between Anglo families and Mexican families in the Southwest (Dill, 1994). Contemporary diversity among Latino families reveals *new* interdependences and inequalities. Emergent middle-class and professional lifestyles among Anglos and even some Latinos are interconnected with a new Latino servant class whose family arrangements, in turn, must accommodate to the demands of their labor.

Second, family diversity plays a part in different economic orders and the shifts that accompany them. Scholars have suggested that the multiplicity of household types is one of the chief props of the world economy (Smith, Wallerstein, & Evers, 1985). The example of U.S.-Mexican cross-border households brings this point into full view. This household arrangement constitutes an important "part of the emerging and dynamic economic and technological transformations in the region" (Velez-Ibañez, 1996, p. 143). The structural reordering required by such families is central to regional economic change.

Finally, the incredible array of immigrant family forms and their enormous capacity for adaptation offer new departures for the study of postmodern families. "Binational," "transnational," and "multinational" families, together with "border balanced households" and "generational hopscotching," are arrangements that remain invisible even in Stacey's (1996) compelling analysis of U.S. family life at the century's end. And yet the experiences of Latino families—flexible and plastic—as far back as the late 1800s (Griswold del Castillo, 1984), give resonance to the image of long-standing family fluidity and of contemporary families lurching backward and forward into the postmodern age (Stacey, 1990). The shift to a postindustrial economy is not the only social transformation affecting families. Demographic and political changes sweeping the world are engendering family configurations that are yet unimagined in family social science.

These trends offer new angles of vision for thinking about family diversity. They pose new opportunities for us to remake family studies as we uncover the mechanisms that construct multiple household and family arrangements.

REFERENCES

Alarcon, N., Castillo, A., & Moraga, C. (Eds.). (1989). *Third woman: The sexuality of Latinas.* Berkeley, CA: Third Woman.

Almaguer, T. (1991). Chicano men: A cartography of homosexual identity and behavior. *Differences: A Journal of Feminist Cultural Studies, 3*, 75–100.

Alvirez, D., & Bean, F. (1976). The Mexican American family. In C. Mindel & R. Habenstein (Eds.), *Ethnic families in America* (pp. 271–292). New York: Elsevier.

Angel, R., & Tienda, M. (1982). Determinants of extended household structure: Cultural pattern or economic need? *American Journal of Sociology 87*, 1360–1383.

Anzaldua, G. (1987). *Borderlands/La Frontera: The new meztiza.* San Francisco: Spinsters, Aunt Lute Press.

Aponte, R. (1993). Hispanic families in poverty: Diversity, context, and interpretation. *Families in Society: The Journal of Contemporary Human Services, 36*, 527–537.

Baca Zinn, M. (1980). Employment and education of Mexican American women: The interplay of modernity and ethnicity in eight families. *Harvard Educational Review, 50*, 47–62.

Baca Zinn, M. (1983). Familism among Chicanos: A theoretical review. *Humboldt Journal of Social Relations 10*, 224–238.

Baca Zinn, M. (1994). Feminist rethinking from racial-ethnic families. In M. Baca Zinn & B. T. Dill (Eds.), *Women of color in U.S. society* (pp. 303–312). Philadelphia: Temple University Press.

Baca Zinn, M. (1995). Social science theorizing for Latino families in the age of diversity. In R. E. Zambrana (Ed.), *Understanding Latino families* (pp. 177–187). Thousand Oaks, CA: Sage.

Baca Zinn, M., & Dill, B. T. (1996). Theorizing difference from multiracial feminism. *Feminist Studies, 22*, 321–332.

Baca Zinn, M., & Eitzen, D. S. (1993). The demographic transformation and the sociological enterprise. *American Sociologist, 24*, 5–12.

Baca Zinn, M., & Eitzen, D. S. (1996). *Diversity in families* (4th ed.). New York: HarperCollins.

Baca Zinn, M., & Eitzen, D. S. (1998). Economic restructuring and systems in inequality. In M. L. Andersen & P. H. Collins (Eds.), *Race, class and gender* (3rd ed., pp. 233–237). Belmont, CA: Wadsworth.

Betancur, J. J., Cordova, T., & Torres, M. L. A. (1993). Economic restructuring and the process of incorporation of Latinos into the Chicago economy. In R. Morales & F. Bonilla (Eds.), *Latinos in a changing U.S. economy: Comparative perspectives on growing inequality* (pp. 109–132). Newbury Park, CA: Sage.

Bogardus, A. (1934). *The Mexican in the United States.* Los Angeles: University of Southern California Press.

Boss, P., & Thorne, B. (1989). Family sociology and family therapy. In M. McGoldrick, C. M. Anderson, & F. Walsh (Eds.), *Women in families* (pp. 78–96). New York: W. W. Norton.

Boyd, M. (1989). Family and personal networks in international migration: Recent developments and new agendas. *International Migration Review, 23*, 638–670.

Buriel, R. (1993). Childrearing orientations in Mexican American families: The influence of generation and sociocultural factors. *Journal of Marriage and the Family, 55*, 987–1000.

Buriel, R., & De Ment, T. (1997). Immigration and sociocultural change in Mexican, Chinese, and Vietnamese American families. In A. Booth, A. C. Crouter, & N. Landale (Eds.), *Immigration and the family: Research and policy on U.S. immigrants* (pp. 165–200). Mahway, NJ: Lawrence Erlbaum.

Cardenas, G., Chapa, J., & Burek, S. (1993). The changing economic position of Mexican Americans in San Antonio. In R. Morales & F. Bonilla (Eds.), *Latinos in a changing U.S. economy: Comparative perspectives on growing inequality* (pp. 160–183). Newbury Park, CA: Sage.

Carnoy, M., Daley, H. M., & Ojeda, R. H. (1993). The changing economic position of Latinos in the U.S. labor market since 1939. In R. Morales & F. Bonilla (Eds.), *Latinos in a changing U.S. economy: Comparative perspectives on growing inequality* (pp. 28–54). Newbury Park, CA: Sage.

Carrier, J. (1992). Miguel: Sexual life history of a gay Mexican American. In G. Herdt (Ed.), *Gay culture in America* (pp. 202–224). Boston: Beacon Press.

Chavez, L. R. (1990). Coresidence and resistance: Strategies for survival among undocumented Mexicans and Central Americans in the United States. *Urban Anthropology, 19*, 31–61.

Chavez, L. R. (1992). *Shadowed lives: Undocumented immigrants in American society.* Forth Worth, TX: Holt, Rinehart, & Winston.

Chavira-Prado, A. (1992). Work, health, and the family: Gender structure and women's status in an undocumented migrant population. *Human Organization, 51*, 53–64.

Coltrane, S. (1996). *Family man.* New York: Oxford University Press.

Coltrane, S., & Valdez, E. O. (1993). Reluctant compliance: Work-family role allocation in dual earner Chicano families. In J. Hood (Ed.), *Men, work, and family* (pp. 151–175). Newbury Park, CA: Sage.

Demo, D. H., & Allen, K. R. (1996). Diversity within gay and lesbian families: Challenges and implications for family theory and research. *Journal of Social and Personal Relationships, 13,* 415–434.

Dill, B. T. (1994). Fictive kin, paper sons, and compadrazgo: Women of color and the struggle for survival. In M. Baca Zinn & B. T. Dill (Eds.), *Women of color in U.S. society* (pp. 149–169). Philadelphia: Temple University Press.

Dominguez, J. I. (1992). Cooperating with the enemy? U.S. immigration policies toward Cuba. In C. Mitchell (Ed.), *Western hemisphere immigration and United States foreign policy* (pp. 31–88). University Park, PA: Pennsylvania State University Press.

Dorrington, C. (1995). Central American refugees in Los Angeles: Adjustment of children and families. In R. Zambrana (Ed.), *Understanding Latino families: Scholarship, policy, and practice* (pp. 107–129). Thousand Oaks, CA: Sage.

Feagin, J. R., & Feagin, C. B. (1996). *Racial and ethnic relations.* Upper Saddle River, NJ: Prentice Hall.

Fernandez-Kelly, M. P. (1990). Delicate transactions: Gender, home, and employment among Hispanic women. In F. Ginsberg & A. L. Tsing (Eds.), *Uncertain Terms* (pp. 183–195). Boston: Beacon Press.

Fernandez-Kelly, M. P., & Garcia, A. (1990). Power surrendered and power restored: The politics of home and work among Hispanic women in southern California and southern Florida. In L. Tilly & P. Gurin (Eds.), *Women and politics in America* (pp. 130–149). New York: Russell Sage Foundation.

Fernandez-Kelly, M. P., & Schauffler, R. (1994). Divided fates: Immigrant children in a restructured U.S. economy. *International Migration Review, 28,* 662–689.

Gil, A. G., & Vega, W. A. (1996). Two different worlds: Acculturation stress and adaptation among Cuban and Nicaraguan families. *Journal of Social and Personal Relationships, 13,* 435–456.

Glenn, E. N. (1992). From servitude to service work: Historical continuities in the racial division of paid reproductive labor. *Signs: Journal of Women in Culture and Society, 18,* 1–43.

Gold, S. J. (1989). Differential adjustment among new immigrant family members. *Journal of Contemporary Ethnography, 17,* 408–434.

Grasmuck, S., & Pessar, P. R. (1991). *Between two islands: Dominican international migration.* Berkeley: University of California Press.

Grasmuck, S., & Pessar, P. (1996). Dominicans in the United States: First- and second-generation settlement, 1960–1990. In S. Pedraza & R. G. Rumbaut (Eds.), *Origins and destinies: Immigration, race, and ethnicity in America* (pp. 280–292). Belmont, CA: Wadsworth.

Griffith, J., & Villavicienco, S. (1985). Relationships among culturation, sociodemographic characteristics, and social supports in Mexican American adults. *Hispanic Journal of Behavioral Science, 7,* 75–92.

Griswold del Castillo, R. (1984). *La familia.* Notre Dame, IN: University of Notre Dame Press.

Guarnizo, L. E. (1997). Los Dominicanyorks: The making of a binational society. In M. Romero, P. Hondagneu-Sotelo, & V. Ortiz (Eds.), *Challenging fronteras: Structuring Latina and Latino lives in the U.S.* (pp. 161–174). New York: Routledge.

Hamilton, N., & Chinchilla, N. S. (1997). Central American migration: A framework for analysis. In M. Romero, P. Hondagneu-Sotelo, & V. Ortiz (Eds.), *Challenging fronteras: Structuring Latina and Latino lives in the U.S.* (pp. 81–100). New York: Routledge.

Heller, C. (1996). *Mexican American youth: Forgotten youth at the crossroads.* New York: Random House.

Hill Collins, P. (1990). *Black feminist thought: Knowledge, consciousness and the politics of empowerment.* Boston: Unwin Hyman.

Hill Collins, P. (1997). African-American women and economic justice: A preliminary analysis of wealth, family, and black social class. Unpublished manuscript, Department of African American Studies. University of Cincinnati.

Hondagneu-Sotelo, P. (1994). *Gendered transitions: Mexican experiences of migration.* Berkeley: University of California Press.

Hondagneu-Sotelo, P., & Avila, E. (1997). "I'm here, but I'm there": The meanings of transnational motherhood. *Gender and Society, 11,* 548–571.

Hondagneu-Sotelo, P., & Messner, M. A. (1994). Gender displays and men's power: The "new man" and the Mexican immigrant man. In H. Brod & M. Kaufman (Eds.), *Theorizing masculinities* (pp. 200–218). Newbury Park, CA: Sage.

Hoppe, S. K., & Heller, P. L. (1975). Alienation, familism and the utilization of health services by Mexican-Americans. *Journal of Health and Social Behavior 16,* 304–314.

Hurtado, A. (1995). Variations, combinations, and evolutions: Latino families in the United States. In R. E. Zambrana (Ed.), *Understanding Latino families* (pp. 40–61). Thousand Oaks, CA: Sage.

Keefe, S. (1984). Real and ideal extended familism among Mexican Americans and Anglo Americans: On the meaning of "close" family ties. *Human Organization 43,* 65–70.

Lamphere, L., Zavella, P., & Gonzales F., with Evans, P. B. (1993). *Sunbelt working mothers: Reconciling family and factory.* Ithaca, NY: Cornell University Press.

Landale, N. S., & Fennelly, K. (1992). Informal unions among mainland Puerto Ricans: Cohabitation or an alternative to legal marriage? *Journal of Marriage and the Family 54,* 269–280.

Lopez, D. E., Popkin, E., & Telles, E. (1996). Central Americans: At the bottom, struggling to get ahead. In R. Waldinger & M. Bozorgmehr (Eds.), *Ethnic Los Angeles* (pp. 279–304). New York: Russell Sage Foundation.

Madsen, W. (1964). *The Mexican-Americans of South Texas.* New York: Holt, Rinehart & Winston.

Martinez, E. A. (1993). Parenting young children in Mexican American/Chicago families. In H. P. McAdoo (Ed.), *Family ethnicity: Strength in diversity* (pp. 184–194). Newbury Park, CA: Sage.

Massey, D. S. (1993). Latino poverty research: An agenda for the 1990s. Items, *Social Science Research Council Newsletter, 47* (1), 7–11.

Massey, D. S., Zambrana, R. E., & Bell, S. A. (1995). Contemporary issues for Latino families: Future directions for research, policy, and practice. In R. E. Zambrana (Ed.), *Understanding Latino families* (pp. 190–204). Thousand Oaks, CA: Sage.

Mindel, C. H. (1980). Extended familism among urban Mexican-Americans, Anglos and blacks. *Hispanic Journal of Behavioral Sciences 2,* 21–34.

Mirande, A. (1997). *Hombres y machos: Masculinity and Latino culture.* Boulder, CO: Westview Press.

Mitchell, C. (1992). U.S. foreign policy and Dominican migration to the United States. In C. Mitchell (Ed.), *Western hemisphere immigration and United States foreign policy* (pp. 89–123). University Park: Pennsylvania State University Press.

Moore, J. W., & Pinderhughes, R. (Eds.). (1993). *In the barrios: Latinos and the underclass debate.* New York: Russell Sage Foundation.

Moore, J. W., & Vigil, J. D. (1993). Barrios in transition. In J. W. Moore & R. Pinderhughes (Eds.), *In the barrios: Latinos and the underclass debate* (pp. 27–50). New York: Russell Sage Foundation.

Moraga, C. (1983). *Loving in the war years: Lo que nunca paso por sus labios.* Boston: South End Press.

Morales, E. S. (1990). Ethnic minority families and minority gays and lesbians. In F. W. Bozett & M. B. Sussman (Eds.), *Homosexuality and family relations* (pp. 217–239). New York: Harrington Park Press.

Morales, R., & Ong, P. M. (1993). The illusion of progress: Latinos in Los Angeles. In R. Morales & F. Bonilla (Eds.), *Latinos in a changing U.S. economy: Comparative perspectives on growing inequality* (pp. 55–84). Newbury Park, CA: Sage.

Morales, R., & Bonilla, F. (1993). Restructuring and the new inequality. In R. Morales & F. Bonilla (Eds.), *Latinos in a changing U.S. economy: Comparative perspectives on growing inequality* (pp. 1–27). Newbury Park, CA: Sage.

Morrissey, M. (1987). Female-headed families: Poor women and choice. In N. Gerstel & H. Gross (Eds.), *Families and work* (pp. 302–314). Philadelphia: Temple University Press.

Ortiz, V. (1995). The diversity of Latino families. In R. Zambrana (Ed.), *Understanding Latino families: Scholarship, policy, and practice* (pp. 18–30). Thousand Oaks, CA: Sage.

Ortiz, V. (1996). The Mexican-origin population: Permanent working class or emerging middle class? In R. Waldinger & M. Bozorgmehr (Eds.), *Ethnic Los Angeles* (pp. 247–277). New York: Russell Sage Foundation.

Perez, L. (1994). Cuban families in the United States. In R. L. Taylor (Ed.), *Minority families in the United States: A multicultural perspective.* Englewood Cliffs, NJ: Prentice Hall.

Perez-Stable, M., & Uriarte, M. (1993). Cubans and the changing economy of Miami. In R. Morales & F. Bonilla (Eds.), *Latinos in a changing U.S. economy: Comparative perspectives on growing inequality* (pp. 133–159). Newbury Park, CA: Sage.

Pesquera, B. M. (1993). In the beginning he wouldn't lift even a spoon: The division of household labor. In A. de la Torre & B. M. Pesquera (Eds.), *Building with our hands* (pp. 181–198). Berkeley: University of California Press.

Portes, A., & Rumbaut, R. G. (1990). *Immigrant America: A portrait.* Berkeley: University of California Press.

Portes, A., & Truelove, C. (1987). Making sense of diversity: Recent research on Hispanic minorities in the United States. *Annual Review of Sociology, 13,* 357–385.

Powell, D. R. (1995). Including Latino fathers in parent education and support programs: Development of a program model. In R. E. Zambrana (Ed.), *Understanding Latino families* (pp. 85–106). Thousand Oaks, CA: Sage.

Ramirez, O. (1980, March). Extended family support and mental health status among Mexicans in Detroit. *Micro, Onda, LaRed, Monthly Newsletter of the National Chicano Research Network,* p. 2.

Ramirez, O., & Arce, C. H. (1981). The contemporary Chicano family: An empirically based review. In A. Baron, Jr. (Ed.), *Explorations in Chicano Psychology* (pp. 3–28). New York: Praeger.

Repack, T. A. (1997). New rules in a new landscape. In M. Romero, P. Hondagneu-Sotelo, & V. Ortiz (Eds.), *Challenging fronteras: Structuring Latina and Latino lives in the U.S.* (pp. 247–257). New York: Routledge.

Rochelle, A. (1997). *No more kin: Exploring race, class, and gender in family networks.* Thousand Oaks, CA: Sage.

Rodriguez, N. P., & Hagan, J. M. (1997). Apartment restructuring and Latino immigrant tenant struggles: A case study of human agency. In M. Romero, P. Hondagneu-Sotelo, & V. Ortiz (Eds.), *Challenging fronteras: Structuring Latina and Latino lives in the U.S.* (pp. 297–309). New York: Routledge.

Romero, M. (1997). Introduction. In M. Romero, P. Hondagneu-Sotelo, & V. Ortiz (Eds.), *Challenging fronteras: Structuring Latina and Latino lives in the U.S.* (pp. xiii–xix). New York: Routledge.

Rubel, A. J. (1966). *Across the tracks: Mexican Americans in a Texas city.* Austin: University of Texas Press.

Rumbaut, R. G. (1995). *Immigrants from Latin America and the Caribbean: A socioeconomic profile* (Statistical Brief No. 6). East Lansing: Julian Samora Research Institute, Michigan State University.

Sassen, S. (1993). Urban transformation and employment. In R. Morales & F. Bonilla (Eds.), *Latinos in a changing U.S. economy: Comparative perspectives on growing inequality* (pp. 194–206). Newbury Park, CA: Sage.

Scott, A. J. (1996). The manufacturing economy: Ethnic and gender divisions of labor. In R. Waldinger & M. Bozorgmehr (Eds.), *Ethnic Los Angeles.* New York: Russell Sage Foundation.

Segura, D. A., & Pierce, J. L. (1993). Chicana/o family structure and gender personality: Chodorow, familism, and psycho-analytic sociology revisited. *Signs,* 19, 62–91.

Shelton, B. A., & John, D. (1993). Ethnicity, race, and difference: A comparison of white, black, and Hispanic men's household labor time. In J. Hood (Ed.), *Men, work, and family* (pp. 1–22). Newbury Park, CA: Sage.

Smith, J., Wallerstein, I., & Evers, H. D. (1985). *The household and the world economy.* Beverly Hills, CA: Sage.

Solis, J. (1995). The status of Latino children and youth: Challenges and prospects. In R. E. Zambrana (Ed.), *Understanding Latino families* (pp. 62–84). Thousand Oaks, CA: Sage.

Stacey, J. (1990). *Brave new families: Stories of domestic upheaval in late twentieth century America.* New York: Basic Books.

Stacey, J. (1995). Disloyal to the disciplines: A feminist trajectory in the border lands. In D. C. Stanton & A. Stewart (Eds.), *Feminisms in the academy* (pp. 311–330). Ann Arbor: University of Michigan Press.

Stacey, J. (1996). *In the name of the family: Rethinking family values in the postmodern age.* Boston: Beacon Press.

Stier, H., & Tienda, M. (1992). Family, work, and women: The labor supply of Hispanic immigrant wives. *International Migration Review, 26,* 1291–1313.

Sullivan, M. L. (1993). Puerto Ricans in Sunset Park, Brooklyn: Poverty amidst ethnic and economic diversity. In J. W. Moore & R. Pinderhughes (Eds.), *In the barrios: Latinos and the underclass debate* (pp. 1–26). New York: Russell Sage Foundation.

Thomas, D., & Wilcox, J. E. (1987). The rise of family theory. In M. B. Sussman & S. Steinmetz (Eds.), *Handbook of marriage and the family* (pp. 81–102). New York: Plenum.

Thorne, B. (1992). Feminism and the family: Two decades of thought. In B. Thorne & M. Yalom (Eds.), *Rethinking the family: Some feminist questions* (pp. 3–30). Boston: Northeastern University Press.

Tienda, M. (1989). Puerto Ricans and the underclass debate. *Annals of the American Association of Political and Social Sciences, 501,* 105–119.

Torres, A., & Bonilla, F. (1993). Decline within decline: The New York perspective. In R. Morales & F. Bonilla (Eds.), *Latinos in a changing U.S. economy: Comparative perspectives on growing inequality* (pp. 85–108). Newbury Park, CA: Sage.

U.S. Bureau of the Census. (1993). *1990 census of the population: Persons of Hispanic origin in the United States.* Washington, DC: U.S. Government Printing Office.

U.S. Bureau of the Census. (1996). *Statistical abstract of the United States: 1996.* Washington DC: U.S. Government Printing Office.

Valenzuela, A., & Dornbusch, S. (1994). Familism and social capital in the academic achievement of Mexican origin and Anglo adolescents. *Social Science Quarterly, 75,* 18–36.

Vega, W. (1990). Hispanic families in the 1980s: A decade of research. *Journal of Marriage and the Family, 52,* 1015–1024.

Vega, W. A. (1995). The study of Latino families: A point of departure. In R. E. Zambrana (Ed.), *Understanding Latino families* (pp. 3–17). Thousand Oaks, CA: Sage.

Velez-Ibañez, C. (1993). U.S. Mexicans in the borderlands: Being poor without the underclass. In J. Moore & R. Pinderhughes (Eds.), *In the barrios: Latinos and the underclass debate* (pp. 195–220). New York: Russell Sage Foundation.

Velez-Ibañez, C. (1996). *Border visions.* Tucson: University of Arizona Press.

Velez-Ibañez, C. G., & Greenberg, J. B. (1992). Formation and transformation of funds of knowledge among U.S.-Mexican households. *Anthropology and Education Quarterly, 23,* 313–335.

Williams, N. (1990). *The Mexican American family: Tradition and change.* Dix Hills, NY: General Hall.

Wilkinson, D. (1993). Family ethnicity in America. In H. P. McAdoo (Ed.), *Family ethnicity: Strength in diversity* (pp. 15–59). Newbury Park, CA: Sage.

Wilson, W. J. (1987). *The truly disadvantaged: The inner city, the underclass, and public policy.* Chicago: University of Chicago Press.

Wilson, W. J. (1996). *When work disappears: The world of the new urban poor.* New York: Alfred A. Knopf.

Ybarra, L. (1982). When wives work: The impact on the Chicano family. *Journal of Marriage and the Family, 44,* 169–178.

Zavella, P. 1987. *Women's work and Chicano families: Cannery workers of the Santa Clara Valley.* Ithaca, NY: Cornell University Press.

15

Intersectionality and Work–Family Studies

Stephen R. Marks and Leigh A. Leslie

Social categories are often the first thing we notice about people—their race, gender, age, class, sexuality, and that "illimitable et cetera" of other categories through which our visions of others are refracted (Butler, 1990). All people belong to many categories simultaneously, not just one, which raises a number of questions. When do the commonalities established between people who share one category—be it race, gender, or whatever—override differences between them in terms of other categories? What does an average person standing at the intersection of a set of categories feel? What is that point of convergence where race meets class—joined, perhaps, by sexual orientation, age, physical ability, religion, and so forth? What is the phenomenology of being male, Asian-American, wealthy, and elderly? Or white, poor, female, and 15 years old? Or African-American, lesbian, wealthy, physically disabled, and 35 years old? These examples are not merely logical possibilities. Real people embody them, pulling the categories together as they move through their everyday lives.

"Intersectionality"—a concern with how these various categories may converge in different ways and with different consequences—has become a buzzword reaching far beyond the feminists of color who originated the term. An August 2007 Google search on the word "intersectionality" yielded 121,000 pages of URLs. A quick perusal shows a veritable explosion of academic courses, conferences, and journal articles exploring it, while domestic violence workers, lawyers, non-governmental organizations concerned with human rights, and even the United Nations are concerned with it. "One could even say," McCall (2005) boldly suggests, "that intersectionality is the most important theoretical contribution that women's studies . . . has made so far" (p. 1771).

In this article, we trace the evolution of the analysis of intersectionality, survey some of the theoretical approaches to it, and then apply the concept to the study of multiple roles and the work–family interface.

INTERSECTING CATEGORIES: A BRIEF INTELLECTUAL HISTORY

One of the first thinkers to clearly articulate issues of intersecting categories was the great African-American multi-disciplinarian W. E. B. DuBois. "One ever feels his twoness," he wrote (1903/1961): "An American, a Negro; two souls, two thoughts, two unreconciled strivings; two warring ideals in one dark body, whose dogged strength alone keeps it from being torn asunder. . . . [The African-American] wishes neither of the older selves to be lost. . . . He simply wishes to make it possible for a man to be both a Negro and an American, without being cursed and spit upon by his fellows, without having the doors of Opportunity closed roughly in his face" (p. 17). Intersections between race and social class also came under DuBois's scrutiny: "To be a poor man is hard, but to be a poor race in a land of dollars is the very bottom of hardships" (p. 20).

Where DuBois was keenly alert to intersections of race, citizenship, and class, African-American women took the lead in recognizing the intersections of race and gender. As Sojourner Truth warned in 1867, just after the Civil War: "If colored men get their rights, and not colored women theirs, you see the colored men will be masters over the women, and it will be just as bad as it was before" (C. W. White, 1995, p. 531). One hundred years later, Frances Beale (1969) noted the continuing class and race differences between European-American and African-American women, and she chided African-American men for focusing only on racial solidarity without taking account of gender inequities: "Let me state here and now that the black woman in America can justly be described as a 'slave of a slave' " (pp. 342–343).

The concept of intersecting oppressions was further developed in 1977 by a now-celebrated group of African-American lesbian feminists who had been meeting for several years: "We do not have racial, sexual, heterosexual, or class privilege to rely upon, nor do we have even the minimal access to resources and power that groups who possess any one of these types of privilege have" (Combahee River Collective, 1982, p. 18). And in 1980, Lorde (1984) delivered her classic paper on intersections of age, race, class, gender, and sexual orientation—a passionate appeal to enrich oneself through embracing diversity.

By the early 1980s, Adrienne Rich was enjoining heterosexual white feminists to recognize how much their heterosexuality may serve as "a means of assuring male right of physical, economic, and emotional access" to women (1980, p. 647). In return for that access, she argued, some women may get material benefits they would not otherwise have, but it may cost them their self-determination as well as their relationships with other women. Rich also pushed hard against the boundary between gender and sexual orientation, suggesting that all women fall somewhere on a "lesbian continuum" if we broaden the term "lesbian" to include the non-sexual intense female bonding that women so often have.

In the 1980s and 1990s, there emerged a sharper recognition of the complexities that may cluster around any point of intersection. Even at social locations characterized by multiple oppressions, people may still find ways of flourishing and thriving. At the other extreme, intersecting privileges may yield numerous advantages, but they may also narrow non-material opportunities for human growth. As DuBois (1903/1961) observed, along with oppression may come dignity, spiritual connection, strength, and a deep sense of responsibility for other people. And as McIntosh (1988) and Lugones (1990) have shown, privilege may be tarnished at every turn by self-absorption, arrogance, and an inflated sense of entitlement.

To add to the complexity, oppression in a given category may be compounded by more oppression or it may be mixed with privilege coming from other categories. And as Erving Goffman (1963, pp. 137–138) pointed out, people who are victimized by stigmatization are fully capable of dishing it out somewhere else, perhaps in an attempt to salvage an upper hand wherever they think they can get it: "Stigma involves not so much a set of concrete individuals who can be separated into two piles, the stigmatized and the normal, as a pervasive two-role social process in which every individual participates in both roles, at least in some connections and in some phases of life. The normal and the stigmatized are not persons but rather perspectives. . . . In many cases, he who is stigmatized in one regard nicely exhibits all the normal prejudices held toward those who are stigmatized in another regard."

Decades later, Patricia Collins (1990) echoed this sentiment when she wrote that there are "few pure victims or oppressors. Each individual derives varying amounts of penalty and privilege from the multiple systems of oppression which frame everyone's lives" (p. 229). Even as recently as 2005 in that storied gay district known as the Castro in San Francisco, African-American patrons of commercial establishments did not always enjoy the same welcome as white patrons. Investigating complaints about a bar known as SF Badlands, the Human Rights Commission found that the bar "discriminated against African-American customers when they were required to provide multiple forms of identification, discouraged from entering, denied entry for carrying bags, and removed from the bar based on false charges of violating bar policy" (San Francisco Human Rights Commission, April 26, 2005). Clearly, no social category (such as "gay") is so binding that it can spread a supportive umbrella over every presumptive member, overriding the rest of the "et cetera" categories that shape their lives.

In *Zami*, Lorde (1982) wrote of being one of the only African American women in a community of New York lesbian feminists in the 1950s. She agonized about her white friends' lack of reflexivity about their racial privileges and their corresponding ignorance of racial issues encountered routinely by her and by her black friend Felicia. Neither the lesbian umbrella nor the feminist one could fully compensate for these unspoken differences in racialized experience, she argued, noting that even her white lover Muriel "seemed to believe that as lesbians we were all outsiders and all equal in our outsiderhood. 'We're all niggers,' she used to say, and I hated to hear her say it. It was wishful thinking based on little fact: the ways in which it was true languished in the shadow of those many ways in which it would always be false.... I was Black and she was not and that was a difference between us that had nothing to do with better or worse or the outside world's craziness" (pp. 203–204).

In addition to race, social class differences sometimes fractured the potential solidarity among lesbian women. Shane Phelan (1989) noted the split that emerged historically between working-class "bar dykes," whose community was limited to gay bars, and middle-class lesbian feminists, whose community was typically centered in universities and who scorned the butch and femme pattern of relationship that was typical of the bar dykes (see also Faderman, 1991).

Identity complexities mutiply because the potential that one identity will be given precedence over any other is ever present. Coalition-building may sometimes work miracles of bridging (see Reagon, 1983), but coalitions are often fragile. Bonding with others on the basis of a categorical connection may be easier when we simply forget, temporarily, about those of our identities that might easily divide us. But that "illimitable et cetera" of other categories may at any time clamor again for attention. And once we shift our focus to privilege some forgotten category, the bridges we had built can easily come down. Butler (1990, 1993) pointed out that "woman" itself is a shifty category because particular women are always not just women in the abstract; they are wealthy women or poor women, African-American, white, Muslim, Asian, or Hispanic women and so on, and there is too little left for the category "woman" alone to provide a meaningful basis for uniting women in feminist projects.

Queer theory, that unruly child of postmodernism, added still another twist to the critical scrutiny of categories in the 1990s. Along with its in-your-face celebration of the term "queer," it launched an assault on all binary oppositions such as straight versus gay and men versus women. Drawing on postmodern concepts such as Butler's "performativity," queer theorists promote resistance to all "regimes of the normal" (Warner, 1993). Outcasts become heralded as vanguards of change. For example, every time drag queens turn female gender into a performance challenge, they remind us that away from the stage, gender is *always* maintained through performance.

Conventional masculinity and femininity are both hard work. Our gender and our sexuality are far more something we do, put on, or act out than something we essentially are.

APPROACHES TO THE STUDY OF INTERSECTIONALITY

Much of the impetus for intersectionality studies has come from the personal narratives of individuals facing unique difficulties at understudied intersections. An exemplar is Herb Green (1996), who yearned to retain the supportive resources of his local black community while recognizing that there was no room for gay men under this nurturing umbrella, even within his own family.

Other studies have focused on intersecting categories as they play out in particular social settings. Freeman's (2000) ethnography explores gender and social class among Afro-Caribbean informatics workers, who perform high tech service sector jobs dressed in high heels and fashionable attire. Their work is highly disciplined and almost indistinguishable from assembly-line production, but their professionalized demeanor and their carefully cultivated attention to fashion distinguish them from traditional industrial laborers. They identify more as professionals than as members of a working-class community, and it is doubtful that they would be seen as potential allies by other industrial and service workers.

Acker (2006) locates the study of intersectionality within organizations. She discusses "inequality regimes," the "practices, processes, actions, and meanings" that produce and maintain inequalities along the lines of social class, gender, and race/ethnicity in most organizations (p. 443). The focus is on unequal control of organizational goals and resources. How does work get organized and promotions get determined? How are job security, benefits, pay, respect, and work enjoyment distributed? Organizations vary in their degree of inequality, even office by office within the same organization. Although hierarchy is not inevitable, usually "work is organized on the image of a white man who is totally dedicated to the work and who has no responsibilities for children or family demands other than earning a living . . . Thus, gender, race, and class inequalities are simultaneously created in the fundamental construction of the working day and of work obligations" (p. 448).

Large national quantitative data sets sometimes yield statistics that provide a clear window on the hierarchies of intersectionality. We know from Department of Justice statistics, for example, that in 1994 and again in 2005, African-Americans at every level of family income were more likely than whites to be victimized by robbery. The 2005 data show that even among people with annual family incomes of upwards of $75,000, African-Americans had a rate of victimization by robbery that was two-and-a-half times greater than that for whites, and the rate for these highest-income African-Americans was almost as high as the rate for the lowest income category of whites (Bureau of Justice Statistics, 2005 and 1997). In other words, the social class "protection" from victimization that wealthy black people might have enjoyed was more than neutralized by their racial disadvantage in a racialized society.

And within each racial group, there are differences by gender. A national survey question about fear of walking alone in your neighborhood at night found that in both 1996 and 2004 African-American women were the most afraid, followed by white women, African-American men, and finally, white men (Davis & Smith, 2004, 1996).

A study of family practice physicians' income by gender and race in the 1990s yielded a slightly different pattern of racial and gender advantage. White and black male physicians had the highest incomes (not significantly different from each other). White female physicians had incomes 9 percent lower than white males, but black female physicians' incomes were 22 percent lower than white males, even after controlling for work effort, practice characteristics, and provider characteristics (Weeks & Wallace, 2006).

Findings such as these are instructive because they demonstrate unmistakably that the relative advantage of membership in a particular category varies according to the specific location and nature of the intersection, and those variations have real consequences for people at particular intersections. But beyond these comparative demographics, can there be a phenomenology—an experiential *feeling*—of intersectionality? Perhaps such a feeling is most likely in the area of sexuality. Whittier and Simon (2001) suggest that the experience of sexual attraction on the part of the men they interviewed was an intersectional experience: It was not purely gender characteristics that triggered these men's desire. Elements of race or ethnicity, class, and age were also simultaneously involved (see Nemoto, this volume, on similar intersections in some Asian-American women's attraction to white men).

Outside of sexual desire, however, awareness of intersection may remain elusive, and removed from conscious awareness. Those whose intersecting categories increase their risk of victimization may feel a heightened sense of the world being an unsafe place, accompanied by an inchoate sense of defeat, while those in the dominating position may have little more than the vaguest sense of how particular intersections protect and privilege them. In both cases, people may have little or no sense of what they are perceiving and responding to.

The recent focus on metaphors of intersection (such as border person; see Rockquemore and Brunsma, this volume) may be an attempt to crystallize the "feeling" of intersectionality. Theorists also use additive or "multiplicative metaphors" (such as "interlocking categories" or "distinct axes"), while "intersectionality" is itself a spatial metaphor. West and Fenstermaker (1995) prefer a temporal metaphor—"simultaneity"—as the way to call attention to how people actually experience multiple categories. They also offer the term "doing difference." The process of rendering someone into an "other" by invoking their social categories is something we actively "do," or produce. There is a metaphor of work here, of something getting fabricated.

Experiences, words, analysis, and action are usually intertwined. Linguistic changes in a culture could help drive a more expansive phenomenology of intersection. New categories may of course create new stereotypes, but they might also add some layers of complexity to what people can name and feel. The word "lesbian" was simply a new name for the intersecting categories of "woman" and "homosexual," but it made a difference for the generation of women who were inspired to build communities based on this particular intersection (Stein, 1997).

The Queer Theory Approach to Intersectionality

The contemporary incarnation of the category "queer" has sometimes been greeted as precisely this kind of transformative linguistic tool. "Queer identity is intersectional," argued Rosenblum (1994), "since most queers face multiple aspects of discrimination, as women, as people of color, as poor people, as cross-gendered people, and as sexual subversives. The multiplicity of the discrimination that queers face is thus greater than anti-lesbian and anti-gay discrimination. Queer identity implicates opposition to these discriminations" (p. 89).

However, Walters (1996, p. 842) is doubtful about the "opening up of queerness to articulations of 'otherness,' " pointing out that "queer can 'de-race' the homosexual of color . . ., effectively erasing the specificity of 'raced' gay existence under a queer rubric in which whiteness is not problematized."

Butler (1990, 1993) is likewise doubtful that any identity category can adequately capture the intersectionality of race, class, gender, and sexuality. She recognizes that people often form communities on the basis of their shared identifications, but she also worries that when people's bonds are rooted merely in categorical similarities, they also often form convictions about what "true" representation of the category really means, and then they start policing and regulating one another about the extent to which they display the identity correctly. We believe that Butler's position is a bit too extreme. Not all categories are regulatory or exclusionary, history will never stop creating them, and it remains a worthy project to promote those categories that help broaden rather than narrow down people's imaginations of who they are.

Patricia Hill Collins and Oppression Theory

At a considerable remove from postmodernism and queer theory, Collins (1990, p. 222) issued a celebrated call for "reconceptualizing race, class, and gender as interlocking systems of oppression," and for recognizing how "each [of these systems] needs the others in order to function." She added that although race, class, and gender oppressions have been especially salient for African-American women, other combinations of social categories may become the flashpoints of oppression for other subordinated groups, and researchers must therefore uncover the particular "matrix of domination" that is present in any specific situation. Similarly, Bordo (1990, p. 139) warns that there is often a "coercive, mechanical requirement that all enlightened feminist projects attend to 'the intersection of race, class and gender.' " This trilogy leaves out ethnicity, age, and sexual orientation. But Bordo also signals the impossibility of paying attention to everything at once: "No matter . . . how attentive the scholar is to the axes that constitute social identity, some of these axes will be ignored and others selected. . . . We always 'see' from points of view that are invested with our social, political, and personal interests, inescapably 'centric' in one way or another . . ." (p. 140).

Andersen and Collins's (1998) "matrix of domination" is essentially a framework that focuses us squarely on issues of oppression and steers us to become "centric" about issues created by domination and subordination. They begin their analysis with a macrolevel focus and then follow identified patterns of oppression into various microlevel outcomes, challenging these patterns wherever they appear. They see the matrix of domination as a "structural pattern [that] affects individual consciousness, group interaction, and group access to institutional power and privileges" (p. 3; see also Few, 2007).

A Theory of Intercategorical Complexity: McCall

A final intersectional approach, recently identified by McCall (2005), springs from strategic use of large, quantitative survey data sets, many of which were created outside the specific sensibilities of a feminist or critical race theory perspective. She seeks to explore "the complexity of relationships among multiple social groups within and across analytical categories," not simply the complexities *within* single social groups, single categories, or both. "The subject is multigroup, and the method is systematically comparative" (p. 1786). In her research on wage inequality, for example, she showed how the intersectionality of race, class, and gender may work differently from one region to another. In blue-collar cities with strong unions (e.g., recently de-industrializing Detroit), employed men have only modest social-class and racial wage inequality while employed women have elevated levels. "In contrast, a postindustrial city such as Dallas exhibits the opposite structure of [wage] inequality—it is marked more by class and racial inequality than gender inequality" (p. 1789).

Then McCall turned to a slightly more fine-grained analysis by looking at class variations only among the women. She found that in Dallas, wage inequality (relative to comparable men) is higher for college educated than for non-college educated women, whereas in Detroit it is higher for non-college educated than for college educated women. "This indicates that the same economic environment creates advantage for some groups of women and disadvantage for other groups of women . . ." (p. 1790).

Having looked at hundreds of cities, McCall's conclusion is that "no single dimension of overall inequality can adequately describe the full structure of multiple, intersecting, and conflicting dimensions of inequality." Indeed, "some forms of inequality seem to arise from the same conditions that might reduce other forms, including, potentially, a conflict between reducing gender inequality and reducing inequality among women" (p. 1791). The watchword here is complexity. The notion of any overall oppressed category or intersection (e.g., African-American women) becomes qualified: It all depends upon what subgroup comparisons you are making, and where, regionally, the comparisons are being made.

INTERSECTING CATEGORIES AND WORK–FAMILY RESEARCH

We turn now to the study of social categories and intersections within multiple-roles research and work–family studies. Like workplaces, families are social organizations that may be governed either by "inequality regimes" or in a more egalitarian manner. Families may contain "good jobs" and "bad jobs," and their members may struggle to maximize their rewards and benefits while minimizing their disadvantages. A focus on intersectionality within the work–family nexus is especially challenging, because we must deal with at least two different organizational domains (work and family), each, perhaps, with different entrenched inequality regimes to be uncovered. Consider, too, that changes within one of these regimes may alter what is happening in the other regime through "spillover effects." When a family contains two or more earners, the analytical challenges of course multiply, as there are typically at least two different workplaces potentially creating and receiving spillover effects for the couple and from the couple.

Empirical work–family studies began to accelerate in tandem with middle-class white women's increasing presence in the labor force in the 1960s and 1970s. Researchers became increasingly curious about how these mothers, fathers, husbands, and wives would mange to juggle the sometimes competing roles of work and family. Early models of this juggling act were often rooted in a scarcity model: individuals' resources of time and energy were seen to be naturally limited, and therefore this "new" problem of multiple role management would generate role overload, role conflict, and role strain (Goode, 1960). Contesting this scarcity model was an "enhancement" model (Marks, 1977; Sieber, 1974), which suggested that multiple roles often elevate people's well-being rather than detract from it. In the ensuing thirty or more years, research exploring these competing perspectives, along with the companion research focus on the division of household labor, has flourished.

Ironically, however, this empirical focus on multiple roles both highlighted and ignored diversity. While gender received extensive attention, variations by race or social class were hardly acknowledged. The changes that were accelerating within white middle-class marriages were old news to women and men of color and to working-class and poor couples, none of whom had ever had the opportunity for sharp gender divisions in who does paid labor and who does domestic labor (see Raley, Mattingly, & Bianchi, 2006). This unevenness in attention has attenuated somewhat over the past decade, with more attention directed to variations by race, social class, household structure, and sexual orientation.

Gender as the Focal Category

While the research lens has widened, gender still remains a primary organizing concept in questions concerning the relationship between multiple roles and individual and couple well-being. The major emphasis has been on how the roles of spouse, parent, and employee affect marriage, health, and the division of household labor. Initially, researchers assumed a primacy of employment roles for men and family roles for women (Barnett & Baruch, 1987), and they therefore had to reorient their thinking when they discovered that employment roles matter for women's well-being (particularly mothers'), just as family roles matter for men's well-being (Barnett & Baruch, 1987; Coleman, Antonucci, Adelmann, & Crohan, 1987; Voydanoff, 1988).

In addition to well-being questions, another area of empirical research has been the impact of multiple roles on changes in the household division of labor. Since 1965, employed women have cut back their time doing domestic labor by about a half, while husbands have approximately doubled their own domestic labor. But since wives had previously been doing almost all of it and husbands hardly any, the net result of this change is that far less housework is actually getting done (Bianchi, Milkie, Sayer, & Robinson, 2000; Leslie & Anderson, 1988). Recent studies show that among all married parents, if you add paid work time to unpaid work time (including housework and childcare), husbands and wives both put in about 65 hours per week, with husbands averaging about two-thirds of the paid work and wives averaging about two-thirds of the unpaid work (Bianchi, Robinson, & Milkie, 2006).

But again, attention to variations of couple's domestic labor based on racial or structural family differences has been lacking. In general, multiple-roles research has remained an outgrowth of increasing career opportunities for white, middle-class women and the white feminist agenda that promoted them. If these women were to compete effectively for exciting careers, they needed their husbands to more equitably share the burdens of domestic responsibilities and child care.

This agenda, however, did not resonate with women and men of color, people living in poverty, or lesbians and gays. A more comprehensive approach would recognize, at minimum, a five-dimensional space of gender, race, social class, household structure (e.g., married/single), and sexual orientation, even if attention to all these dimensions is impossible for every study.

Current Intersectional Approaches to Multiple Roles

Fortunately, more recent authors do recognize how racism has structured racial minority men and women's involvement in the labor force. Given that economic survival depended on the contributions of both men and women, gendered patterns of participation in family roles have historically been less rigid, particularly in African-American families where men engage in more child care than do their white counterparts (Billingsley, 1992; Taylor, 2000).

Dillaway and Broman (2001) present what is arguably the most explicit intersectional approach to multiple roles and family issues currently in the literature. Drawing on a national sample and focusing on marital satisfaction and the division of household labor among dual-earner couples, these authors call for the study of variations "across unique race-class-gender groups" (p. 314). They found that although husbands as a group report higher marital satisfaction than wives, black husbands report still higher levels than white husbands, at least when they do not do a lot of domestic labor. At high levels of housework, black husbands' marital satisfaction falls below white husbands. And although wives report lower levels of marital satisfaction than husbands, black wives report still lower levels than white wives, regardless of how domestic labor is divided.

Although Dillaway and Broman's analytical strategy is nicely tailored to the exploration of race, class, and gender intersectionality in marriage, and they do offer some speculations about what their findings mean, there is an unfortunate ad hoc quality to these speculations. In fairness, they did not design the data set, and the interests that they bring to it were not necessarily anticipated by the people who did design it.

An examination of two other studies illustrates the need for research on work–family intersectionality to explore how different social locations may actually mediate the work and family connection. In other words, it may not be enough to look at differences between groups such as African-Americans and whites. Instead, research may need to examine how being the member of a particular group structures one's experience. A case in point is the work of Frone, Russell, and Cooper (1992), who found that their models of the work–family interface apply equally well to both African-Americans and whites. Specifically, three types of work stress (work pressure, lack of autonomy, role ambiguity) did not vary by race, nor was there race variation in the impact of these stressors on depression or work and family conflict. But because the questions in this study focused only on racial category and were not tailored to uncover the specifics of racialized experiences at the workplace, the significance of race may have unintentionally been neutralized. For example, white employees' colleagues and coworkers rarely suspect that they got their job because of racial preferences or use this suspicion as a basis for questioning their white colleagues' competence or ability. Likewise, when white employees air grievances at work, their issues are rarely if ever minimized as racial discontent. Unique sources of "racialized work stress" such as these may lead African-American employees to work longer hours, not air their complaints, isolate themselves from coworkers, or not share their workday experience with their spouse or partner, any of which could contribute to personal stress or family conflicts.

A second example is a recent study by Roehling, Jarvis and Swope (2005). Drawing on the 1997 National Study of the Changing Workforce (NSCW), the authors make a valiant effort to consider intersectionality issues among black, white, and Hispanic male and female workers who were married or partnered. Once again, the data set was not designed to tease out differences in racialized experience. There are good measures of negative work-to-family spillover and negative family-to-work spillover, along with measures of job flexibility, work autonomy, and pressures at work. There is also a measure of traditionalism in gender attitudes. The findings are interesting. Concerning gender attitudes, Hispanics are the most traditional, followed by whites and finally blacks. Negative spillover from work to family was greatest among Hispanic women, "for whom the work role was inconsistent with their traditional role" (p. 859). It was least for Hispanic men, "who have strong cultural support for the primacy of their role as a breadwinner" (p. 859). White men and women without children in the home had similar levels of work-to-family negative spillover, but white women had higher levels than white men when children were present. As for negative spillover from family to work, again Hispanics had the greatest disparity between men and women. Without children in the home, white and black men and women report similar levels of family-to-work spillover, but when children are present, gender disparities once again surface, with women experiencing more spillover than men.

Yet in order to interpret their spillover findings, the authors invoke assumptions about respondents' life-experiences without having any data to support these assumptions. They assume that Hispanics have a more traditional background ruled by machismo and marianismo. They also assume that their African-American respondents inherit a legacy of greater acceptance for both men and women being workers, dating back to the days of slavery, and therefore these respondents have a "cultural template" (p. 860) for working out the stresses of how to manage dual-earner involvements in the work and family domains. And finally, they assume that among white couples, the large-scale entrance of women into the labor force since the 1960s has provided couples with at least two decades worth of experience to develop the same kind of template. These are a lot of assumptions! Without them, however, there is no explanation of the findings because the data set provides no information about racialization and how it works among the people in the sample. "It is inaccurate," the authors concede in their limitations section, "to characterize an entire group as fitting these stereotypes. Within each group studied there is broad diversity of thought and attitude. In the current study, we ignored these differences and combined people from divergent regions and socioeconomic backgrounds based solely on their ethnic identification" (p. 861). A more thorough-going approach to intersectional studies of family life will require more fine-grained variables to be built into the study.

Intersectionality Studies with Fine-Grained Data

Two recent work/family studies come closer to exploring intersectionality as a lived experience. Both draw on the 1997 National Study of the Changing Workforce (NSCW). Foley, Linnehan, Greenhaus, and Weer (2006), and Winfield and Rushing (2005) explored supervisor–subordinate relationships, hoping to find out if gender similarity and/or racial similarity result in more family-supportive supervision as perceived by the subordinate. Family supportiveness is framed in two ways. "Interactional support" has to do with conversational responsiveness when the topic of the subordinate's family life comes up, and "instrumental support" is more about actual accommodations the supervisor makes in response to the subordinate's family needs.

Both studies found that working in a more family-supportive organizational culture is ultimately more important than the gender or racial "match" between supervisor and subordinate. That is, when the organization itself is perceived to be family-friendly, the supervisor is perceived to be likewise. But even in family-friendly workplaces, a gender and racial match between supervisor and subordinate adds still further to the perception that the supervisor is family-friendly, at least regarding interactional support (there is no effect for instrumental support).

Beyond these similar findings, the two studies diverge somewhat. Foley et al. (2006) found that racial similarity and gender similarity, each separately, result in perceptions of greater family supportive interaction between supervisor and subordinate, but when there is a match in both race and in gender, the perception of family-supportiveness is still greater. In other words, they found a cumulative effect of demographic similarity: the more similar the supervisor and subordinate are, the more family-supportive the supervision is.

Winfield and Rushing (2005) found no such cumulative effect. They did find, like Foley et al., that gender similarity and racial similarity separately make for perceptions of more family-supportive supervision, but the story they uncover is more complex: "Women supervised by women perceived greater interactional support for bridging the boundaries between work and family; this was true regardless of race/ethnicity. . . . Perhaps women supervisors are thought to understand and sympathize more with women employees relative to family-related problems. Importantly, both White and Black women perceived White men supervisors as least supportive. However, Hispanic women reported that Hispanic men supervisors were least supportive of their family-related concerns. Thus, the one finding in support of the cumulative effects question appears for Hispanic women who perceive women Hispanic supervisors as the most supportive" (Winfield & Rushing, p. 75).

For men, on the other hand, racial/ethnic similarity figured more importantly than gender similarity. "Men of all race/ethnic groups perceived more support from a supervisor of their own race/ethnicity than from a supervisor of a different race/ethnic group. White men preferred a White woman supervisor to a minority man," but they saw more support coming from a male minority supervisor than from a female minority supervisor. "Gender matters in a different way to Black and Hispanic men. If they do not have a same-race-ethnic supervisor, they perceived that a woman of any race/ethnicity provided more interactional support than a man of a different race/ethnicity did" (Winfield & Rushing, p. 75).

These findings must be put in the context of the differing chances that different categories of people have of being supervised by a person who is a race or gender match to themselves. Most white men have supervisors who are also white men, and white women have almost a fifty-fifty chance of being supervised by another white woman. In sharp contrast, minority workers have a much smaller likelihood of being supervised by someone who is a race and gender match to themselves. Foley et al. (2006) neatly summarize some implications of the disparity: "Because minority and women subordinates are more likely to be in cross-race and cross-gender situations, respectively, they may not get the support they need. In our increasingly diverse U.S. workplaces, it is not realistic to expect that demographically similar supervisor–subordinate dyads will be the norm and that the provision of family support can be assumed. What may be needed is diversity training that includes sensitivity to work–family issues. Supervisors should be made aware that when their subordinates are dissimilar in race and gender, the tendency is to provide less family support than if they were similar . . ." (p. 436). Winfield and Rushing (2005) summarize the situation more pointedly: "One of the invisible privileges of being in the dominant group is that members do not have to think about any other experience besides their own" (p. 77).

The foregoing two studies probably represent the current state of the art, as both explore the work and family interface in a way that is mindful of race and gender intersectionality. What is missing is more detail. We find out whether or not the subordinate is "comfortable" bringing up personal or family issues in conversations with the supervisor. We learn what the gender and racial match is between supervisor and subordinate, and following that, we see if the comfort level is greater or lesser, depending on the particular racial and gender match. What we do not learn is how respondents actually see race and gender (and other categories) manifesting in their work relationships with supervisors and co-workers, and how these experiences may be affecting their family lives.

Marks (2006) recently suggested a program for this kind of fine-grained exploration. Put simply, if dominant groups are over-rewarding people similar to themselves and under-rewarding people they perceive to be different, then we need to include specific information about prejudice and discrimination in our work/family studies. Sociologists of health have recently been developing this strategy in epidemiological studies. For example, Kessler, Mickelson, and Williams (1999) developed a survey instrument to measure "major events" of perceived discrimination (e.g., not being hired for a job, or not being given a promotion), and "day to day discrimination" (e.g., people treating you "as if you are inferior," or acting "as if you are not smart"). The authors found that people of color report far more frequently than whites that they have been victimized by discriminatory treatment (both "major events" and "day to day"), and they also are more likely than whites to indicate that their race was the reason for the discrimination (for other examples of this kind of survey strategy, see Marks, 2006).

Other researchers have developed useful strategies for including identity measures in their studies. The interest here is to explore whether strong, proud identification with a category that has been historically denigrated may buffer people from some of the distress caused by others' mistreatment. For example, among young African-Americans, the psychological distress stemming from perceived discrimination was less when the person's race was a highly central identity (Sellers, Caldwell, Schmeelk-Cone, & Zimmerman, 2003). Similarly, American Indians who reported instances of prejudice or discrimination had lower levels of depressive symptoms if they had been involved in traditional Indian identity-strengthening practices such as the use of tribal language or participation in a powwow (Whitbeck, McMorris, Hoyt, Stubben, & LaFromboise, 2002).

Work/family researchers might follow these creative leads, only we would be more interested in work-to-family conflicts, or marital distress, than in outcome variables such as depressive symptoms. We have often studied outcomes such as "overload" or "role strain," and we have often called attention to family "stressors." We need to recognize that prejudice and discrimination at work may be powerful contributors to stress and strain. Racial, gender, social-class, sexual, and ageist oppressions on the job may generate enormous spillover effects at home, even while a strong, central identity in one's race or other denigrated category may buffer a person from the impact of these stressors.

The challenge for work/family scholars is to devise strategies for explicitly researching categorical oppressions and privileges at work and at home. Once we accomplish that first step, the more difficult one will be to create research designs that are complex enough to uncover the intersectionality of those categories that produce oppression and advantage.

REFERENCES

Acker, J., Inequality regimes: Gender, class, and race in organizations. *Gender & Society* 20 (2006), 441–464.

Andersen, M. & Collins, P. H. (Eds.), *Race, class, and gender: An anthology* (3rd ed.). (Belmont, CA: Wadsworth, 1998).

Barnett, R. C., & Baruch, G. K., Social roles, gender, and psychological distress. In R. C. Barnett, L. Biener, & G. K. Barnett (Eds.), *Gender and stress* (New York: Free Press, 1987), pp. 122–143.

Beale, F., Double jeopardy: To be black and female. In R. Morgan, *Sisterhood is powerful*. (New York: Vintage, 1969), pp. 340–353.

Bianchi, S. M., Milkie, M. A., Sayer, L. C., & Robinson, J. P., Is anyone doing the housework? Trends in the gender division of household labor. *Social Forces, 79* (2000), 191–228.

Bianchi, S. M., Robinson, J. P., & Milkie, M. A., *Changing rhythms of American family life*. (New York: Russell Sage, 2006).

Billingsley, A., *Climbing Jacob's ladder: The enduring legacy of African-American families*. (New York: Simon & Schuster, 1992).

Bordo, S., Feminism, postmodernism, and gender-scepticism. In L. J. Nicholson (Ed.), *Feminism/postmodernism* (New York: Routledge, 1990), pp. 133–156.

Bureau of Justice Statistics. *Criminal victimization in the United States, 1994: A national crime victimization survey report*. (Washington, DC: U.S. Department of Justice, 1997).

Bureau of Justice Statistics. www.ojp.usdoj.gov/bjs/pub/pdf/cvus/current/cv0515.pdf (2005) (retrieved September 12, 2007).

Butler, J., *Gender trouble: Feminism and the subversion of identity*. (New York: Routledge, 1990).

Butler, J., *Bodies that matter: On the discursive limits of "sex."* (New York: Routledge, 1993).

Coleman, L. M., Antonucci, T. C., Adelmann, P. K., & Crohan, S. E., Social roles in the lives of middle-aged and older black women. *Journal of Marriage and the Family* 49 (1987), 761–771.

Collins, P. H., *Black feminist thought: Knowledge, consciousness, and the politics of empowerment*. (New York: Routledge, 1990).

Combahee River Collective. A black feminist statement. In G. T. Hull, P. B. Scott, & B. Smith (Eds.), *All the women are white, all the blacks are men, but some of us are brave*. (New York: Feminist Press, 1982), pp. 13–22.

Davis, J. A., & Smith, T. W., *General Social Surveys, 2004, 1996*. Principal investigator, J. A. Davis; Director and Co-principal investigator, T. W. Smith; Co-principal investigator, P. V. Marsden, NORC ed. Chicago: National Opinion Research Center, producer, 2002, Storrs, CT. The Roper Center for Public Opinion Research, University of Connecticut, distributor, (2004, 1996).

Dillaway, H., & Broman, C., Race, class, and gender differences in marital satisfaction and divisions of household labor among dual-earner couples: A case for intersectional analysis. *Journal of Family Issues* 22 (2001), 309–327.

DuBois, W. E. B., *The souls of black folk*. (New York: Crest, 1961). (Original work published 1903.)

Faderman, L., *Odd girls and twilight lovers: A history of lesbian life in twentieth-century America*. (New York: Penguin, 1991).

Few, A., Integrating black consciousness and critical race feminism into family studies research. *Journal of Family Issues* 28 (2007) 452–473.

Foley, S., Linnehan, F., Greenhaus, J. H., & Weer, C. H., The impact of gender similarity, racial similarity, and work culture on family-supportive supervision. *Group & Organization Management* 31 (2006), 420–441.

Freeman, C., *High tech and high heels in the global economy: Women, work, and pink-collar identities in the Caribbean.* (Durham, NC: Duke University Press, 2000).

Frone, M. R., Russell, M., & Cooper, M. L., Antecedents and outcomes of work–family conflict: Testing a model of work–family interface. *Journal of Applied Psychology* 77 (1992), 65–78.

Goffman, E., *Stigma: Notes on the management of spoiled identity.* (Englewood Cliffs, New Jersey: Prentice Hall, 1963).

Goode, W. J., A theory of role strain. *American Sociological Review* 25 (1960), 483–496.

Green, H., Turning the myths of black masculinity inside out. In B. Thompson & S. Tyagi (Eds.), *Names we call home: Autobiography on racial identity.* (New York: Routledge, 1996), pp. 253–264.

Kessler, R. C., Mickelson, K. D., & Williams, The prevalence, distribution, and mental health correlates of perceived discrimination in the United States. *Journal of Health and Social Behavior* 40 (1999), 208–230.

Leslie, L. A., & Anderson, E. A., Men's and women's participation in domestic roles: Impact on quality of life and marital adjustment. *Journal of Family Psychology* 2 (1988), 212–226.

Lorde, A., Age, race, class and sex: Women redefining difference. In *Sister outsider.* (Freedom, CA: The Crossing Press, 1984), pp. 114–123.

Lorde, A., *Zami: A new spelling of my name.* (Freedom, CA.: The Crossing Press, 1982).

Lugones, M., Hablando cara a cara/Speaking face to face: An exploration of ethnocentric racism. In L. Richardson & V. Taylor (Eds.), *Feminist frontiers III.* (New York: McGraw-Hill, 1990), pp. 51–56.

Marks, S. R., Multiple roles and role strain: Some notes on human energy, time, and commitment. *American Sociological Review* 42 (1977), 921–936.

Marks, S. R., Understanding diversity of families in the 21st Century and its impact on the work–family area of study. In M. Pitt-Catsouphes, E. E. Kossek, & S. Sweet (Eds.), *The work and family handbook: Multi-disciplinary perspectives and approaches.* (Mahwah, NJ: Lawrence Erlbaum Associates, 2006), pp. 41–65.

McCall, L., The complexity of intersectionality. *Signs* 30 (2005), 1171–1800.

McIntosh, P., White privilege and male privilege: A personal account of coming to see correspondences through work in women's studies. In M. L. Andersen & P. H. Collins (Eds.), *Race, class, and gender: An anthology* (3rd ed.). (Belmont, CA: Wadsworth, 1988), pp. 94–105.

Phelan, S., *Identity politics: Lesbian feminism and the limits of community.* (Philadelphia: Temple University, 1989).

Raley, S. B., Mattingly, M. J., & Bianchi, S. M., How dual are dual-income couples? Documenting change from 1970 to 2001. *Journal of Marriage and the Family* 68 (2006), 11–28.

Reagon, B. J., Coalition politics: Turning the century. In B. Smith (Ed.), *Home girls: A black feminist anthology.* (New York: Kitchen Table Press, 1983), pp. 356–358.

Rich, A., Compulsory heterosexuality and lesbian existence. *Signs* 5 (1980), 631–660.

Roehling, P. V., Jarvis, L. H., & and Swope, H. E., Variations in negative work–family spillover among white, black, and Hispanic American men and women: Does ethnicity matter? *Journal of Family Issues* 26 (2005), 840–865.

Rosenblum, D., Queer intersectionality and the failure of lesbian and gay "victories." *Law and Sexuality* 4 (1994), 83–122.

San Francisco Human Rights Commission. Director's finding. http://www.sflnc.com/binary.php/528/Badlands%20Finding%20.pdf (April 26, 2005) (retrieved August 23, 2007).

Sellers, R. M., Caldwell, C. H., Schmeelk-Cone, K. H., & Zimmerman, M. A., Racial identity, racial discrimination, perceived stress, and psychological distress among African American young adults. *Journal of Health and Social Behavior* 43 (2003), 302–317.

Sieber, S., Toward a theory of role accumulation. *American Sociological Review* 39 (1974), 567–578.

Stein, A., *Sex and sensibility: Stories of a lesbian generation.* (Berkeley, CA: University of California, 1997).

Taylor, R., Diversity within African American families. In D. H. Demo, K. R. Allen, & M. A. Fine (Eds.), *Handbook of family diversity.* (New York: Oxford, 2000), pp. 232–251.

U.S. Bureau of the Census. *Statistical abstracts of the U.S.: The national data book.* (Washington, DC: U.S. Department of Commerce: Economics and Statistics Administration, 1995).

Voydanoff, P., Work role characteristics, family structure demands, and work/family conflict. *Journal of Marriage and the Family* 50 (1988), 749–761.

Walters, S. D., From here to queer: Radical feminism, postmodernism, and the lesbian menace (Or, why can't a woman be more like a fag?). *Signs* 21 (1996), 830–869.

Warner, M., Introduction. *Fear of a queer planet: Queer politics and social theory.* (Minneapolis: University of Minnesota Press, 1993).

Weeks, W. B., & Wallace, A., The influence of race and gender on family physicians' annual incomes. *Journal of the American Board of Family Medicine* 19 (2006), 548–556.

Welter, B., The cult of true womanhood. *American Quarterly* 18 (1966), 151–174.

West, C., & Fenstermaker, S., Doing difference. *Gender & Society* 9 (1995), 8–37.

Whitbeck, L. B., McMorris, B. J., Hoyt, D. R., Stubben, J. D., & LaFromboise, T., Perceived discrimination, traditional practices, and depressive symptoms among American Indians in the upper Midwest. *Journal of Health and Social Behavior* 43 (2002), 400–418.

White, C. W., Toward an Afra-American feminism. In J. Freeman (Ed.), *Women: A feminist perspective* (5th ed.), (Mountain View, CA: Mayfield, 1995), pp. 529–546.

Whittier, D., & Simon, W., The fuzzy matrix of 'my type' in intrapsychic sexual scripting. *Sexualities* 4 (2001), 139–165.

Winfield, I., & Rushing, B., Bridging the border between work and family: The effects of supervisor-employee similarity. *Sociological Inquiry* 75 (2005), 55–80.

III

GLOBAL HOUSEHOLDS: GLOBALIZATION, IMMIGRATION, AND FAMILY LIFE

16

"Management by Stress"—The Reorganization of Work Hits Home

Sarah Ryan

An almost constant sense of insecurity haunts American families in the first decade of the twenty-first century. Fear of job loss and benefit cuts is pervasive. Almost half the population worries that someone in their household will be out of work in the next year. Forty percent of parents no longer expect their children to have a higher standard of living than themselves. Most believe large-scale layoffs and pension cuts are a permanent feature of the modern economy. Meanwhile, families are contributing more and more hours to the job and experiencing more stressful working conditions.[1]

These changes are consequences of a fundamental reorganization of work in the last two decades. Comparable in scope to the changes that took place with the industrial revolution, this restructuring represents a revolutionary break with the post-World War II social contract, in which employers accommodated themselves to unions and granted workers a high degree of job security in return for access to a stable workforce.

Reorganization of work is often seen as the natural result of global competition and techno-logical change. But as the *Wall Street Journal* recognizes in labeling it "the re-engineering move-ment,"[2] the re-engineering of work is not an accidental product of "globalization," but the achievement of a concerted *movement*—a corporate political and economic effort to intensify work and to abandon the older tactic of ensuring social peace by guaranteeing special privileges and security to some groups of workers.

This movement, spearheaded by American corporations, has dramatically increased productivity and raised stock indexes to record highs. But it has also produced deepening inequality of wealth and mounting stress for many workers. According to a 2006 global public health conference on worklife and stress, people around the world are experiencing chronic fatigue, job insecurity, longer hours, physical and mental health problems, and spillover of work stress to family life as the workforce has become more "Americanized."[3]

WHAT ARE THE MAJOR ASPECTS OF THIS REORGANIZATION OF WORK AS THE TWENTY-FIRST CENTURY BEGINS?

1. Stagnant Wages in the Midst of Astounding Productivity Gains and Increases in Work Time

In 2005, the real (adjusted for inflation) weekly earnings for non-supervisory workers were no higher, on average, than in 1979, while wages for the lowest-paid workers were actually 2.3 percent lower.[4] Two other forms of compensation traditionally associated with "good" jobs—health insurance and private pensions—have been drastically reduced, increasing the fear and insecurity of families. From 1979 to 2004, the percentage of private sector workers with employer-provided health insurance fell from 69 percent to 55.9 percent. Less than a quarter of lower wage workers have any health coverage. Pension coverage has declined as well, falling 5 percent overall, and by 10 percent for men.[5]

Stagnant wages and compensation are not due to low worker productivity. Indeed, during the decade from 1995–2005, productivity grew at an unprecedented rate. In the years from 1973 to 1995, the annual productivity growth rate was 1.4 percent. Since 1995, it has expanded at 2.9 percent. Productivity growth could have provided some real growth in wages and family incomes, but instead it has boosted profits.[6]

The grinding down of compensation levels represents a successful campaign by businesses to avoid wage increases, hire new workers at lower pay levels, roll back previous gains and defeat or restrain labor unions. In fact, the aggressive employer stance toward unions, endorsed by federal policy, has played a major role in reducing unionization from just over 20 percent in 1983 to a mere 12 percent in 2006.[7]

In an unusually frank admission, Stephen Roach of Morgan Stanley, a Wall Street brokerage firm, wrote in *The New York Times* that corporations "have gone too far in squeezing the worker to boost corporate profitability and competitiveness . . . pay rates have now been squeezed so that they are running below the productivity curve."[8]

Stagnant wages require families to send more of their members to the work force, spend more hours working, or get second jobs. Individual work hours increased by 199 hours per year, or nearly five full-time weeks, from 1973–2000.[9] This increase in individual work hours takes a toll on family life even when only one member of the family is employed, but the rise in total family work hours has been even more dramatic. Low-income couples added almost 6 weeks from 1975 to 2000, middle-income couples added over 13 weeks, and prime age (25–54 years old) couples added an astounding 22 weeks.[10]

Combined with speed-up in employers' work demands, these hours raise workers' stress. The Families and Work Institute conducted a survey of 2,800 wage and salary workers in 2002 and found that 35 percent often, or very often, felt overwhelmed by the amount of work they had to do, while 57 percent felt they had to work "very fast" on their jobs. "The changes [made by some employers] in the workplace don't appear to offset the conflicts employees face—longer work hours, more demanding jobs, and technology that blurs the lines between work and family," remarked James T. Bond, lead author of the study.[11]

2. Automation of Production, Information and Service Work

Technologies of the information age and automation of production have eliminated millions of jobs. The steel industry is a prime example of the dramatic effect of technology on production and employment. U.S. Steel (now called USX), the nation's largest steel company, employed 120,000 in 1980. By 1990, it produced roughly the same output with 20,000 workers.[12] Employment in the telephone industry, the economy's automation pacesetter, declined by 179,800 from 1981–1988.[13] AT&T alone laid off an estimated 40,000 workers in the mid-1990s and 13,500 more in the first three years of the new century. In early 2006, Intel reported record-breaking profits of $12.1 billion, yet a few months later, its CEO announced plans to eliminate 10,500 jobs—10 percent of its labor force—in order to become a "more agile" company.[14]

The insecurity triggered by these trends has colored the lives of all workers. In 2006, almost a third of Americans told Gallup pollsters that they worried their benefits would be reduced; one in five feared their wages would be cut, and one in six feared being laid off.[15]

3. Internationalization of Production, with Manufacturing Exported to Low Wage Areas

Trade agreements such as the North American Free Trade Agreement (NAFTA) and the Global Agreement on Tariffs and Trade (GATT) have loosened government restrictions and sped up the rate at which industries are moving production to countries like Mexico and China, where wages are about one-tenth of U.S. averages. The "maquiladora" program—the establishment of production factories along the U.S./Mexican border—allows U.S. industrial corporations to take advantage of the drastically lower wages they can pay just across the border. Maquiladora employment grew especially rapidly in the 1980s and 1990s, increasing eleven-fold from 1980 to peak in 2000 at 1.3 million workers. In 2004, over 2,800 plants were in operation, producing for the biggest name U.S. industrial corporations.[16] Labor economist Harley Shaiken estimated that these programs can save U.S. auto manufacturers $100 million annually in wages per plant, as Mexican automobile workers' total compensation averages $2 per hour, compared with U.S. auto workers' $30.[17]

Whether their collars are white or blue, Americans face increased stress over the very real threat of having their jobs outsourced, across the border or across the globe. Looking at data from the Census and Department of Labor, the Economic Policy Institute estimates that between 1993 and 2002, more than 879,000 Americans lost jobs due to NAFTA alone.[18] Hundreds of thousands of jobs, from call-center work to software engineering, have been moved to India, as corporations take advantage of that country's vigorous investment in education and the availability of English-speakers. The job market in the U.S. lost 154,000 software jobs between 2000 and 2002. By 2010, the IBM corporation alone is expected to employ 100,000 in India.[19]

4. Corporate Mergers and Reorganization, with Workforce "Downsizing"

Nearly three-quarters of all households have had a close encounter with layoffs since 1980. The *New York Times'* 1996 feature series and book, *The Downsizing of America,* examined the chaos, insecurity and destruction in people's lives resulting from corporate downsizing. Workers who had staked their futures on the idea that their loyalty to the company would be returned told of their sense of loss and betrayal. One in ten adults said a lost job had precipitated a major crisis in their lives. Yet since the 1990s it has become commonplace for corporate CEOs to find their bonuses soar after announcement of mass layoffs.[20]

Between 1979 and 1996, 43 million jobs were downsized. While manufacturing jobs are typically thought of as most vulnerable to layoffs, the *Times* researchers found that white collar work was equally threatened. In the banking and financial sector alone, 447,000 jobs were lost due to mergers and acquisitions in the 1990s.[21]

"Extended mass layoffs" are defined by the Department of Labor as those separating more than 50 workers for more than 30 days. Such layoffs, usually attributed to company reorganization, claimed over 10 million jobs over the years 1996–2003, or an average of 1.3 million per year.[22]

The most troubling news about mergers, reorganizations and mass layoffs is that they often result in permanent downward mobility. Workers typically find it difficult or impossible to replace their lost jobs with anything that pays a similar salary or benefits.

5. Newly Created Jobs are Part-Time and Temporary as Companies Shift to a Contingent Workforce

"It's really a revolution," said Gary Burtless, a labor economist with the Brookings Institution. Temporary employment tripled in only one decade, from 1985 to 1995. By 2005, 2 million workers labored for agencies and contract firms, and another 2.5 million were on-call to their employers.[23] Even government agencies have increased temporary employment. The U.S. Postal Service alone has tens of thousands of contingent workers who have no job security, no health care insurance, and receive lower wages. Some state governments actually require a minimum ratio of temporaries in their agencies.

Corporations face no additional cost or penalty for downsizing their permanent workforce and replacing long-term employees with temporaries, and they can hire and fire rapidly when business demands change. Temporary workers earn lower wages, usually have no benefits, and never know from one day to the next if they will be working. A Bureau of Labor Statistics survey found that "most firms reported that less than 10% of their temporary workers participated in a company-sponsored health insurance program."

High levels of skill and education do not guarantee stable or secure work. More than 40 percent of college faculty now work part-time, and only 4.5 percent of part-time faculty have any job security.[24] Computer professionals often find themselves working as "permatemps" with no security and few benefits.

As Jacobs and Gerson explain later in this volume, the flip side of long work weeks for some workers is shortened work weeks, insufficient funds, and no health benefits for others.

6. Increased Use of Overtime and Rotating Shifts, Particularly in Manufacturing

While economic pressures sometimes compel workers to seek overtime, there is nothing voluntary about longer work weeks for many employees who retain full-time jobs in down-sized occupations. Workers often face firings or other disciplinary actions for refusing overtime because of family needs. Bell Atlantic telephone, for example, after cutting thousands of jobs, suspended workers who refused overtime. Joe Bryant, a single father of two children, had worked overtime on week-ends but was unable to put in extra hours during the week due to child care problems. He was given a suspension for refusing overtime so that he could pick up his children at school. Another Bell Atlantic technician, who had already worked 69 of the previous 73 days, was suspended for 3 days for refusing more overtime. "Families have been literally torn apart by workers forced to work up to 70 hours a week for months and years at a time," said Sue Pisha, CWA's chief negotiator at U.S. West.[25]

Night shifts, rotating shifts, and weekend work, all considered "nonstandard," are the reality for two-fifths of U.S. workers, according to Harriet Presser, author of *Working in a 24/7 Economy*. She found that the stress on bodies and family lives was profound and often most damaging to the most vulnerable people.[26]

In Decatur, Illinois, a corn products plant, a tire factory and a tractor manufacturer all demanded 12-hour rotating schedules from their workers. In manufacturing operations like the A.E. Staley plant, 12-hour days, with three days on and three days off, were imposed, and workers were switched from days to nights every 30 days. Staley workers Dick and Sandy Schable explained how their family life was severely disrupted by these schedules: "After the first day on 12 hours you were pretty much shot. The other problem was each week you'd have a different day off. And you could be called in during your time off at any shift at any time they deemed it necessary."

Low-income Americans are the most likely to have to work night shifts or rotating shifts, with no flexibility granted to them for their families. While the nation has debated reasons for the educational failures of low income children, the subject of their parents' jobs hardly ever comes up. Yet researcher Jody Heymann found that "poor parental working conditions disastrously limited the extent to which parents could be available to help children whose education was in trouble." She discovered that the more hours parents worked in the evenings, the more likely their children were to be in the bottom quarter on achievement tests. Their kids were also almost three times more likely to be suspended from school.[27]

7. "Lean Production" Practices, Including Work Teams and "Total Quality" Management Systems

Worker/management cooperation plans swept the corporate world in the 1980s and 1990s. A 1992 survey of Fortune 1000 corporations found that 80 percent used management techniques such as Quality of Work Life, Quality Circles or Employee Involvement.[28] While these programs were initially presented as signs of a new respect for the worker, they were accompanied by wage cutting, downsizing, and a new, intense pressure for more production, often applied by one's peers in addition to management. The Nissan Corporation was an early team concept "lean production" leader. Company literature claimed the system was built on teamwork, cooperation and trust, declaring that "people are our most valued resource," but workers described the job as "eight hour aerobics. You feel like you've done three days' work at the end of the shift."

A former Nissan manager described the long-range results of such aerobics: "We hired exceptionally good people, people we thought we could keep for the rest of their working lives. I ran into one of them at the pharmacy the other day. He looked like he was dead . . . He said to me, 'I think they've got us on a four or five year cycle. They'll wear us out and then hire new blood.' I think he may be right."[29]

Today, lean production practices, originally designed for the auto industry, are being used widely across the economy, including in the health care industry. Some for-profit hospitals report dramatically increased revenues; but nurses report higher injury rates.[30]

While seemingly contradictory, team concept and high pressure cost-cutting strategies are two sides of the same coin, according to labor journalists Jane Slaughter and Mike Parker, who say that the function of participation programs is to introduce "management by stress."[31]

A good example of management by stress is found in United Parcel Service, which has called itself "the tightest ship in the shipping business" and is well known for a demanding and injurious work atmosphere. The company's lost time accident rate has long exceeded twice the national average, yet in the late 1990s, it increased the weight limit of parcels from 70 pounds to 150 pounds.[32] At the parcel sorting hubs, the system is designed to push the individual workers beyond normal capacity, as mechanized belt and box lines are operated at speeds with which virtually no worker can keep pace. When workers loading trucks inevitably fall behind, packages pile up, and extra "floaters" make rounds helping them catch up.[33]

WHAT CAN BE DONE?

Trying to revive the male-breadwinner, female-homemaker family is no solution to today's work–family stresses. Even comparatively high-earning workers often need two incomes to help pay the rising cost of college tuition and of housing. And most women do not want to be forced to choose between work and family. Men also resent being forced into choosing between being breadwinners and parents. As a male postal worker told me, "men wish they could work fewer hours too. For men, it seems there's only a choice between full-time or overtime."

A shorter work week with no pay cut is among the most promising ideas for addressing the new realities of the work world and the family needs of both men and women. Proponents argue that since fewer workers are now needed to produce needed goods and services, the available work, income, and leisure should be shared by reducing the number of hours in a "full-time" job. Europe has an active shorter hours movement, and European countries have reduced work time through lengthened paid vacations and holidays. European unions and political bodies have adopted the goal of shortening work time and have negotiated 27 to 34 hour work weeks with corporations like Volkswagen, Hewlett-Packard, and Digital Equipment.[34] In consequence, Europeans work about 200 hours less each year than Americans do.[35]

In the United States, oddly, it is in the course of fighting forced overtime, massive layoffs, and speedup that workers have won shorter hours with no cuts in pay. Steel workers at National Steel's Granite City, Illinois mill, for example, had worked five eight-hour shifts for years. When the company demanded "alternative work schedules" involving up to 16 hours per day with rotating shifts, the workers struck and shut down the mill. Their "Cold Mill Committee for a Decent Schedule" held public rallies involving spouses and children who denounced the company's alternative schedule as "a family wrecker." The union proposed its own four-crew schedule and won a 36 hour work week with 40 hours pay and no forced overtime.[36]

Recently, unions with a majority female membership have taken the lead in fighting mandatory overtime. They have found that organizing for state legislation is the most effective strategy. By 2007, nurses in eleven states had succeeded in getting legislation passed to limit mandatory overtime, and more efforts were underway. They've tied the issue of their own working conditions to the health of patients. As a New York nurses' union leader explained, "The practice of mandatory overtime for nurses is risky as it places both nurses and the patients they care for in a perpetually dangerous situation."[37]

In California, women's organizations and unions worked together to support a new paid family leave program that allows most workers to receive six weeks of leave, paid at about 55 percent of their salary, to care for a new child or sick relative. In 2007, Washington became the second state to pass a paid family leave bill, which will take effect in 2009. Under the bill, parents of newborn and newly adopted children will be able to take up to five weeks off, though with a benefit of only $250 per week, pro-rated for part-time workers.

Paid vacation time is being put on the agenda by Take Back Your Time, an organization promoting shorter work time. They launched a national effort in 2007 to pass legislation requiring every American worker be offered three weeks of paid vacation. The United States, they point out, is the only industrial country that fails to legally protect workers' vacation time. And they warn that even current meager vacations should be considered endangered, as many companies are reducing or eliminating paid time off. Activists are seeking support from unions, environmentalists and health providers for state and local efforts to require paid vacation.

The emerging shorter hours movement and the new energy evident in the coalition between unions and women's organizations make it possible to envision a future where families control their work, not the other way around. The very technologies that allow us to produce so much should allow us to have a richer life, not just a higher Dow Jones average. Our quality of life in the future depends not on our ability to adapt our lives to work, but to adapt work to our individual, family, and community needs.

NOTES

1. *New York Times* poll, "Class Project," March 3–14, 2005.
2. Al Ehrbahr, " 'Re-Engineering' Gives Firms New Efficiency, Workers the Pink Slip," *Wall Street Journal*, March 16, 1993, p. 1.
3. Cary L. Cooper, "The Changing Nature of Work: The New Psychological Contract and Associated Stressors," in *Stress and Quality of Working Life: Current Perspectives in Occupational Health* (Greenwich, CT: Information Age Publishing, 2006), p. 1.
4. Lawrence Mishel et al., *The State of Working America.* (Washington, DC: Economic Policy Institute, 2006), 119, 121.
5. Ibid, pp. 135–138.
6. Lawrence Mishel et al., *The State of Working America.* (Washington, DC: Economic Policy Institute, 2006), 41; Mark Whitehouse, "Fear of Inflation Lurks in U.S. Recovery," *Wall Street Journal*, July 2, 2007, p. 12.
7. "Union Members Summary" Washington, DC: Bureau of Labor Statistics Pub USDL 07–0113, January 25, 2007.
8. "Three Views, No Agreement," by Floyd Norris, *New York Times* 2/4/96, p. F5.
9. Juliet Schor, "The (Even More) Overworked American," in *Take Back Your Time*, John DeGraaf, ed. (San Francisco, CA: Berrett-Koehler, 2003), p. 7.
10. Lawrence Mishel, et al., *The State of Working America 2006/2007* (Washington, DC: Economic Policy Institute), pp. 89–90.
11. "Highlights of the 2002 National Study of the Changing Workforce" (New York: Families and Work Institute, 2003).
12. Drucker, Peter, *Post Capitalist Society* (HarperCollins, 1993), p. 72.
13. *Outlook for Technology and Labor in Telephone Communications*, U.S. Department of Labor, Bureau of Labor Statistics, July 1990, Bulletin 2357, pp. 1, 11–12.
14. Uchitelle, Louis and Kleinfield, N.R., "The Downsizing of America: A National Heartache," *New York Times*, March 3, 1996, p. 15. Seth Schleisel, "TECHNOLOGY: AT&T to Cut About 5% of Work Force," *New York Times*, January 7, 2003; James Lardner, "The Specter Haunting Your Office," *New York Review of Books*, June 14, 2007.
15. "Work and Workplace," Gallup Poll, August, 2006. Available at: http://www.gallup.com/
16. Cañas, J., Coronado, R., and Gilmer, R.W., "Texas Border Employment and Maquiladora Growth," Federal Reserve Bank of Dallas, October 2005, http://www.dallasfed.org
17. LaBotz, Dan, "The Team in Mexico," Working Smart, Labor Education and Research Project, 1994, pp. 239–240.
18. Robert E. Scott, "The High Price of 'Free' Trade" (Washington, DC: Economic Policy Institute, 2003).
19. Price, Lee, and Bivens, Josh, "Economic Snapshots," Economic Policy Institute, March 24, 2004 and Hira, Ron, EPI Briefing Paper #187, Economic Policy Institute, March 28, 2007.
20. *New York Times*, "The Downsizing of America," March 3, 1996, p. 1.
21. "The employment impact of mergers and acquisitions in the banking and financial services sector" (International Labour Office, Geneva: International Labour Organization, 2001).
22. U.S. Bureau of Labor Statistics, "Extended Mass Layoffs Separations, 1996–2003."
23. "Contingent and Alternative Employment Arrangements," February 2005, USDL 05–1433 (Washington, DC: Bureau of Labor Statistics).
24. "2004 National Study of Postsecondary Faculty (NSOPF:04) Report on Faculty and Instructional Staff in Fall 2003" (National Center for Educational Statistics, Washington, DC 2004).
25. "Overtime Tyrant Gets Tough," CWA News, Communications Workers of America, Washington, DC Vol. 55 #9, October 1995, p. 7; "CWA Settles Strike at U.S. West with Pact Guaranteeing Health and Income Security, Limits on Forced Overtime Hours," Communications Workers of America, http://www.cwa-union.org/news/page.jsp?itemID=27350838, August 31, 1998.
26. Presser, Harriet B., *Working in a 24/7 Economy* (New York: Russell Sage, 2003).
27. Jody Heymann, "Inequalities at Work and at Home: Social Class and Gender Divides," in Heymann and Beem, eds., *Unfinished Work: Building Equality and Democracy in an Era of Working Families* (New York: New Press, 2004), p. 97.
28. Adrienne Eaton, "New Production Techniques, Employee Involvement and Unions," *Labor Studies Journal*, Vol. 20, No. 3, Fall 1995.
29. John Junkerman, "Nissan, Tennessee: It ain't what it's cracked up to be," *The Progressive*, June, 1987, pp. 16–20.
30. Rebecca A. Clay, " 'Lean production' may also be a lean toward injuries," APA Monitor Online, May 1999. Washington, D.C.: American Psychological Association.
31. Mike Parker and Jane Slaughter, "Working Smart: Guide to Participation Programs and Reengineering" (Labor Education and Research Project, Detroit, MI, 1994), Chapter 1, p. 1.
32. "In the Productivity Push, How Much is Too Much?" *New York Times*, 12/17/95, sec. 3 p. 1; "UPS facilities cited for injuries, illness," *Atlanta Business Chronicle*, March 21, 2003.
33. Interview with Tom Bernard, Business Agent, Teamsters local 174, Seattle, 5/1/96.
34. Jeremy Rifkin, *The End of Work* (GB Putnam, NY, 1995), pp. 224–226.
35. Fact-Finding Report p. 19.
36. Kim Moody and Simone Sagovac, "Time Out!" Labor Education and Research Project, Detroit, MI, 1995, pp. 40–42.
37. "Assembly passes mandatory nurse overtime bill" NYSUT News Wire—June 12, 2007, http://www.nysut.org

17

excerpts from

Families on the Fault Line

America's Working Class Speaks about the Family, the Economy, Race, and Ethnicity

Lillian B. Rubin

"They're letting all these colored come in and soon there won't be any place left for white people," broods Tim Walsh, a thirty-three-year-old white construction worker. "It makes you wonder: Is this a white country, or what?"

It's a question that nags at white America, one perhaps that's articulated most often and most clearly by the men and women of the working class. For it's they who feel most vulnerable, who have suffered the economic contractions of recent decades most keenly, who see the new immigrants most clearly as direct competitors for their jobs.

It's not whites alone who stew about immigrants. Native-born blacks, too, fear the newcomers nearly as much as whites do—and for the same economic reasons. But for whites the issue is compounded by race, by the fact that the newcomers are primarily people of color. For them, therefore, their economic anxieties have combined with the changing face of America to create a profound uneasiness about immigration.

While there's little doubt that racial anxieties are at the center of white concerns, our historic nativism also plays a part in escalating white alarm. The new immigrants bring with them languages and ethnic cultures that are vividly expressed wherever they congregate. And it's this also, the constant reminder of an alien presence from which whites are excluded, that's so troublesome to them.

The nativist impulse isn't, of course, given to the white working class alone. But for those in the upper reaches of the class and status hierarchy—those whose children go to private schools, whose closest contact with public transportation is the taxicab—the immigrant population supplies a source of cheap labor, whether as nannies for their children, maids in their households, or workers in their businesses. They may grouse and complain that "nobody speaks English anymore," just as working-class people do. But for the people who use immigrant labor, legal or illegal, there's a payoff for the inconvenience. For while it may be true that American workers aren't eager for many of the jobs immigrants are willing to take, it's also true that the presence of a large immigrant population—especially of those who come from developing countries where living standards are far below our own—helps to make these jobs undesirable by keeping wages depressed well below what most American workers are willing to accept.

Indeed, the economic basis of our immigration policies too often gets lost in the lore that we are a land that says to the world, "Give me your tired, your poor, your huddled masses, yearning to breathe free." I don't mean to suggest that our humane impulses are a fiction, only that the reality is far more complex than Emma Lazarus's poem suggests. The massive immigration of the nineteenth and early twentieth centuries didn't just happen spontaneously. America may have been known as the land of opportunity to the Europeans who dreamed of coming here—a country where, as my parents once believed, the streets were lined with gold. But they believed these things because that's how America was sold by the agents who spread out across the face of Europe to recruit workers— men and women who were needed to keep the machines of our developing industrial society running and who, at the same time, gave the new industries a steady supply of hungry workers willing to work for wages well below those of native-born Americans.

The enormous number of immigrants who arrived during that period accomplished both those ends. In doing so, they set the stage for a long history of antipathy to foreign workers. For today, also, one function of the new immigrants is to keep our industries competitive in a global economy. Which is simply another way of saying that they serve to depress the wages of native-born American workers.

It's not surprising, therefore, that working-class women and men speak so angrily about the recent influx of immigrants. They not only see their jobs and their way of life threatened, they feel bruised and assaulted by an environment that seems suddenly to have turned color and in which they feel like strangers in their own land. So they chafe and complain: "They come here to take advantage of us, but they don't really want to learn our ways," Beverly Sowell, a thirty-three-year-old white electronics assembler, grumbles irritably. "They live different than us; it's like another world how they live. And they're so clannish. They keep to themselves, and they don't even *try* to learn English. You go on the bus these days and you might as well be in a foreign country; everybody's talking some other language, you know, Chinese or Spanish or something. Lots of them have been here a long time, too, but they don't care; they just want to take what they can get."

But these complaints reveal an interesting paradox, an illuminating glimpse into the contradictions that beset native-born Americans in their relations with those who seek refuge here. On the one hand, they scorn the immigrants; on the other, they protest because they "keep to themselves." It's the same contradiction that dominates black-white relations. Whites refuse to integrate blacks but are outraged when they stop knocking at the door, when they move to sustain the separation on their own terms—in black theme houses on campuses, for example, or in the newly developing black middle-class suburbs.

I wondered, as I listened to Beverly Sowell and others like her, why the same people who find the lifeways and languages of our foreign-born population offensive also care whether they "keep to themselves."

"Because like I said, they just shouldn't, that's all," Beverly says stubbornly. "If they're going to come here, they should be willing to learn our ways—you know what I mean, be real Americans. That's what my grandparents did, and that's what they should do."

"But your grandparents probably lived in an immigrant neighborhood when they first came here, too," I remind her.

"It was different," she insists. "I don't know why; it was. They wanted to be Americans; these here people now, I don't think they do. They just want to take advantage of this country."

She stops, thinks for a moment, then continues, "Right now it's awful in this country. Their kids come into the schools, and it's a big mess. There's not enough money for our kids to get a decent education, and we have to spend money to teach their kids English. It makes me mad. I went to public school, but I have to send my kids to Catholic school because now on top of the black kids, there's all these foreign kids who don't speak English. What kind of an education can kids get in a school like that? Something's wrong when plain old American kids can't go to their own schools.

"Everything's changed, and it doesn't make sense. Maybe you get it, but I don't. We can't take care of our own people and we keep bringing more and more foreigners in. Look at all the homeless. Why do we need more people here when our own people haven't got a place to sleep?"

"Why do we need more people here?"—a question Americans have asked for two centuries now. Historically, efforts to curb immigration have come during economic downturns, which suggests that when times are good, when American workers feel confident about their future, they're likely to be more generous in sharing their good fortune with foreigners. But when the economy falters, as it did in the [early] 1990s, and workers worry about having to compete for jobs with people whose standard of living is well below their own, resistance to immigration rises. "Don't get me wrong; I've got nothing against these people," Tim Walsh demurs. "But they don't talk English, and they're used to a lot less, so they can work for less money than guys like me can. I see it all the time; they get hired and some white guy gets left out."

It's this confluence of forces—the racial and cultural diversity of our new immigrant population; the claims on the resources of the nation now being made by those minorities who, for generations, have called America their home; the failure of some of our basic institutions to serve the needs of our people; the contracting economy, which threatens the mobility aspirations of working-class families—all these have come together to leave white workers feeling as if everyone else is getting a piece of the action while they get nothing. "I feel like white people are left out in the cold," protests Diane Johnson, a twenty-eight-year-old white single mother who believes she lost a job as a bus driver to a black woman. "First it's the blacks; now it's all those other colored people, and it's like everything always goes their way. It seems like a white person doesn't have a chance anymore. It's like the squeaky wheel gets the grease, and they've been squeaking and we haven't," she concludes angrily.

Until recently, whites didn't need to think about having to "squeak"—at least not specifically as whites. They have, of course, organized and squeaked at various times in the past—sometimes as ethnic groups, sometimes as workers. But not as whites. As whites they have been the dominant group, the favored ones, the ones who could count on getting the job when people of color could not. Now suddenly there are others—not just individual others but identifiable groups, people who share a history, a language, a culture, even a color—who lay claim to some of the rights and privileges that formerly had been labeled "for whites only." And whites react as if they've been betrayed, as if a sacred promise has been broken. They're white, aren't they? They're *real* Americans, aren't they? This is their country, isn't it?

The answers to these questions used to be relatively unambiguous. But not anymore. Being white no longer automatically assures dominance in the politics of a multiracial society. Ethnic group politics, however, has a long and fruitful history. As whites sought a social and political base on which to stand, therefore, it was natural and logical to reach back to their ethnic past. Then they, too, could be "something"; they also would belong to a group; they would have a name, a history, a culture, and a voice. "Why is it only the blacks or Mexicans or Jews that are 'something'?" asks Tim Walsh. "I'm Irish, isn't that something, too? Why doesn't that count?"

In reclaiming their ethnic roots, whites can recount with pride the tribulations and transcendence of their ancestors and insist that others take their place in the line from which they have only recently come. "My people had a rough time, too. But nobody gave us anything, so why do we owe them something? Let them pull their share like the rest of us had to do," says Al Riccardi, a twenty-nine-year-old white taxi driver.

From there it's only a short step to the conviction that those who don't progress up that line are hampered by nothing more than their own inadequacies or, worse yet, by their unwillingness to take advantage of the opportunities offered them. "Those people, they're hollering all the time about discrimination," Al continues, without defining who "those people" are. "Maybe once a long time ago that was true, but not now. The problem is that a lot of those people are lazy. There's plenty of opportunities, but you've got to be willing to work hard."

He stops a moment, as if listening to his own words, then continues, "Yeah, yeah, I know there's a recession on and lots of people don't have jobs. But it's different with some of those people. They don't really want to work, because if they did, there wouldn't be so many of them selling drugs and getting in all kinds of trouble."

"You keep talking about 'those people' without saying who you mean," I remark.

"Aw c'mon, you know who I'm talking about," he says, shifting uneasily in his chair. "It's mostly the black people, but the Spanish ones, too."

In reality, however, it's a no-win situation for America's people of color, whether immigrant or native born. For the industriousness of the Asians comes in for nearly as much criticism as the alleged laziness of other groups. When blacks don't make it, it's because, whites like Al Riccardi insist, their culture doesn't teach respect for family; because they're hedonistic, lazy, stupid, and/or criminally inclined. But when Asians demonstrate their ability to overcome the obstacles of an alien language and culture, when the Asian family seems to be the repository of our most highly regarded traditional values, white hostility doesn't disappear. It just changes its form. Then the accomplishments of Asians, the speed with which they move up the economic ladder, aren't credited to their superior culture, diligence, or intelligence—even when these are granted—but to the fact that they're "single-minded," "untrustworthy," "clannish drones," "narrow people" who raise children who are insufficiently "well-rounded."

True, the remarkable successes of members of the Asian immigrant community have engendered grudging, if ambivalent, respect. "If our people were as hard working and disciplined as the Asians, we'd be a lot better off," says Doug Craigen, a thirty-two-year-old white truck driver.

But the words are barely out of his mouth before the other side surfaces and he reaches for the stereotypes that are so widely accepted. "I'm not a racist, but sometimes they give me the creeps. You've got to watch out for them because they'll do anything for a buck, anything. I guess the thing that bothers me most is you can't get away from them," he explains, as if their very presence is somehow menacing. "They're all over the place, like pushy little yellow drones. You go to the bank, they're working there. You go to a store, they're behind the counter. It's like they're gobbling up all the jobs in town."

The job market isn't the only place where Asians are competing successfully with whites. From grade school to college, Asian students are taking a large share of the top honors, leaving white parents in a state of anxious concern. "I don't know if our kids can compete with those Chinese kids," worries Linda Hammer, a thirty-year-old white beautician who hopes to see her children in college one day. "My kids aren't bad students, but those Asian kids, that's all they live for. I don't think it's good to push kids so hard, do you? I mean, I hear some of those people beat their kids if they don't get A's. They turn them into little nerds who don't do anything but study. How can American kids compete with that?"

Whites aren't alone in greeting Asian successes so ambivalently. Like Doug Craigen. Lurine Washington, a black thirty-year-old nurse's aide, speaks admiringly of the accomplishments of her

Asian neighbors. "I could get killed for saying this, but I don't care. The Asians are a lot more disciplined than blacks as a whole. That's not a racist statement; it's a fact because of their culture. Saying that doesn't mean I don't like my people, but I'm not blind either. All I know is if our kids worked as hard in school as theirs do, they could make something of themselves, too. And those families, all of them working together like that. You've got to respect that, don't you?"

Moments later, however, Lurine complains, "If we don't watch out, they'll take over everything. I mean, they already own half the country, even Rockefeller Center. You know what I mean. They're like ants; there's so many of them, and they're so sneaky and everything. And they think they're better than other people; that's what really makes me mad."

Not surprisingly, as competition increases, the various minority groups often are at war among themselves as they press their own particular claims, fight over turf, and compete for an ever shrinking piece of the pie. In several African-American communities, where Korean shopkeepers have taken the place once held by Jews, the confrontations have been both wrenching and tragic. A Korean grocer in Los Angeles shoots and kills a fifteen-year-old black girl for allegedly trying to steal some trivial item from the store. From New York City to Berkeley, California, African-Americans boycott Korean shop owners who, they charge, invade their neighborhoods, take their money, and treat them disrespectfully. But painful as these incidents are for those involved, they are only symptoms of a deeper malaise in both communities—the contempt and distrust in which the Koreans hold their African-American neighbors, and the rage of blacks as they watch these new immigrants surpass them.

Latino-black conflict also makes headlines when, in the aftermath of the riots in South Central Los Angeles, the two groups fight over who will get the lion's share of the jobs to rebuild the neighborhood. Blacks, insisting that they're being discriminated against, shut down building projects that don't include them in satisfactory numbers. And indeed, many of the jobs that formerly went to African-Americans are now being taken by Latino workers. In an article entitled, "Black vs. Brown," Jack Miles, an editorial writer for the *Los Angeles Times*, reports that "janitorial firms serving downtown Los Angeles have almost entirely replaced their unionized black work force with non-unionized immigrants."

On their side of the escalating divide, the Latino community complains bitterly that they always take second place to black demands. "Nobody pays attention to us like they do to the blacks," protests Julio Martinez, a thirty-year-old Latino warehouseman. "There's a saying in Spanish: You scratch where it itches. There's plenty of problems all around us here," he explains, his sweeping gesture encompassing the Latino neighborhood where he lives, "but they don't pay attention because we don't make so much trouble. But people are getting mad. That's what happened in L.A.; they got mad because nobody paid attention."

But the disagreements among America's racial minorities are of little interest or concern to most white working-class families. Instead of conflicting groups, they see one large mass of people of color, all of them making claims that endanger working-class whites' own precarious place in the world. It's this perception that has led some white ethnics to believe that reclaiming their ethnicity alone is not enough, that so long as they remain in their separate and distinct groups, their power will be limited. United, however, they can become a formidable countervailing force, one that can stand fast against the threat posed by minority demands. But to come together solely as whites would diminish their impact and leave them open to the charge that their real purpose is simply to retain the privileges of whiteness. A dilemma that has been resolved, at least for some, by the birth of a new entity in the history of American ethnic groups—the "European-Americans."

At the University of California at Berkeley, for example, white students and their faculty supporters insisted that the recently adopted multicultural curriculum include a unit of study on European-Americans. At Queens College in New York City, where white ethnic groups retain a more distinct presence, Italian-American students launched a successful suit to win recognition as a disadvantaged minority and gain the entitlements accompanying that status, including special units of Italian-American studies.

White high school students, too, talk of feeling isolated and, being less sophisticated and wary than their older sisters and brothers, complain quite openly that there's no acceptable and legitimate way for them to acknowledge a white identity. "There's all these things for all the different ethnicities, you know, like clubs for black kids and Hispanic kids, but there's nothing for me and my friends to join," Lisa Marshall, a sixteen-year-old white high school student explains with exasperation. "They won't let us have a white club because that's supposed to be racist. So we figured we'd just have to call it something else, you know, some ethnic thing, like Euro-Americans. Why not? They have African-American clubs."

Ethnicity, then, often becomes a cover for "white," not necessarily because these students are racist but because racial identity is now such a prominent feature of the discourse in our social world. In a society where racial consciousness is so high, how else can whites define themselves in ways that connect them to a community and, at the same time, allow them to deny their racial antagonisms?

Ethnicity and race—separate phenomena that are now inextricably entwined. Incorporating newcomers has never been easy, as our history of controversy and violence over immigration tell us. But for the first time, the new immigrants are also people of color, which means that they tap both the nativist and racist impulses that are so deeply a part of American life. As in the past, however, the fear of foreigners, the revulsion against their strange customs and seemingly unruly ways, is only part of the reason for the anti-immigrant attitudes that are increasingly being expressed today. For whatever xenophobic suspicions may arise in modern America, economic issues play a critical role in stirring them up.

"THIS COUNTRY DON'T OWE NOBODY NOTHING!"

Two decades ago, when I began the research for *Worlds of Pain*, we were living in the immediate aftermath of the civil rights revolution that had convulsed the nation since the mid-1950s. Significant gains had been won. And despite the tenacity with which this headway had been resisted by some, most white Americans were feeling good about themselves. No one expected the nation's racial problems and conflicts to dissolve easily or quickly. But there was also a sense that we were moving in the right direction, that there was a national commitment to redressing at least some of the worst aspects of black-white inequality.

In the intervening years, however, the national economy buckled under the weight of three recessions, while the nation's industrial base was undergoing a massive restructuring. At the same time, government policies requiring preferential treatment were enabling African-Americans and other minorities to make small but visible inroads into what had been, until then, largely white terrain. The sense of scarcity, always a part of American life but intensified sharply by the history of these economic upheavals, made minority gains seem particularly threatening to white working-class families.

It isn't, of course, just working-class whites who feel threatened by minority progress. Wherever racial minorities make inroads into formerly all-white territory, tensions increase. But it's working-class families who feel the fluctuations in the economy most quickly and most keenly. For them, these last decades have been like a bumpy roller coaster ride. "Every time we think we might be able to get ahead, it seems like we get knocked down again," declares Tom Ahmundsen, a forty-two-year-old white construction worker. "Things look a little better; there's a little more work; then all of a sudden, boom, the economy falls apart and it's gone. You can't count on anything; it really gets you down."

This is the story I heard repeatedly: Each small climb was followed by a fall, each glimmer of hope replaced by despair. As the economic vise tightened, despair turned to anger. But partly because we have so little concept of class resentment and conflict in America, this anger isn't directed so much at those above as at those below. And when whites at or near the bottom of the ladder look down in this nation, they generally see blacks and other minorities.

True, during all of the 1980s and into the 1990s, white ire was fostered by national administrations that fanned racial discord as a way of fending off white discontent—of diverting anger about the state of the economy and the declining quality of urban life toward the foreigners and racial others in our midst. But our history of racial animosity coupled with our lack of class consciousness made this easier to accomplish than it might otherwise have been.

The difficult realities of white working-class life notwithstanding, however, their whiteness has accorded them significant advantages—both materially and psychologically—over people of color. Racial discrimination and segregation in the workplace have kept competition for the best jobs at a minimum. Obviously, working-class whites have to compete with each other for the resources available. But that's different. It's a competition among equals; they're all white. They don't think such things consciously, of course; they don't have to. It's understood, rooted in the culture and supported by the social contract that says they are the superior ones, the worthy ones. Indeed, this is precisely why, when the courts or the legislatures act in ways that seem to contravene that belief, whites see themselves as victims.

From the earliest days of the republic, whiteness has been the ideal, and freedom and independence have been linked to being white. "Republicanism," writes labor historian David Roediger, "had long emphasized that the strength, virtue and resolve of a people guarded them from enslavement." And it was whites who had these qualities in abundance, as was evident, in the peculiarly circuitous reasoning of the time, in the fact that they were not slaves.

By this logic, the enslavement of blacks could be seen as stemming from their "slavishness" rather than from the institution of slavery. Slavery is gone now, but the reasoning lingers on in white America, which still insists that the lowly estate of people of color is due to their deficits, whether personal or cultural, rather than to the prejudice, discrimination, and institutionalized racism that has barred them from full participation in the society.

This is not to say that culture is irrelevant, whether among black Americans or any other group in our society. The lifeways of a people develop out of their experiences—out of the daily events, large and small, that define their lives; out of the resources that are available to them to meet both individual and group needs; out of the place in the social, cultural, and political systems within which group life is embedded. In the case of a significant proportion of blacks in America's inner cities, centuries of racism and economic discrimination have produced a subculture that is both personally and socially destructive. But to fault culture or the failure of individual responsibility without understanding the larger context within which such behaviors occur is to miss a vital piece of the picture. Nor does acknowledging the existence of certain destructive subcultural forms among some African-Americans disavow or diminish the causal connections between the structural inequalities at the social, political, and economic levels and the serious social problems at the community level.

In his study of "working-class lads" in Birmingham, England, for example, Paul Willis observes that their very acts of resistance to middle-class norms—the defiance with which these young men express their anger at class inequalities—help to reinforce the class structure by further entrenching them in their working-class status. The same can be said for some of the young men in the African-American community, whose active rejection of white norms and "in your face" behavior consigns them to the bottom of the American economic order.

To understand this doesn't make such behavior, whether in England or the United States, any more palatable. But it helps to explain the structural sources of cultural forms and to apprehend the social processes that undergird them. Like Willis's white "working-class lads," the hip-hoppers and rappers in the black community who are so determinedly "not white" are not just making a statement about black culture. They're also expressing their rage at white society for offering a promise of equality, then refusing to fulfill it. In the process, they're finding their own way to some accommodation and to a place in the world they can call their own, albeit one that ultimately reinforces their outsider status.

But, some might argue, white immigrants also suffered prejudice and discrimination in the years after they first arrived, but they found more socially acceptable ways to accommodate. It's true—and so do most of today's people of color, both immigrant and native-born. Nevertheless, there's another truth as well. For wrenching as their early experiences were for white ethnics, they had an out. Writing about the Irish, for example, Roediger shows how they were able to insist upon their whiteness and to prove it by adopting the racist attitudes and behaviors of other whites, in the process often becoming leaders in the assault against blacks. With time and their growing political power, they won the prize they sought—recognition as whites. "The imperative to define themselves as white," writes Roediger, "came from the particular 'public and psychological wages' whiteness offered to a desperate rural and often preindustrial Irish population coming to labor in industrializing American cities."

Thus does whiteness bestow its psychological as well as material blessings on even the most demeaned. For no matter how far down the socioeconomic ladder whites may fall, the one thing they can't lose is their whiteness. No small matter because, as W. E. B. DuBois observed decades ago, the compensation of white workers includes a psychological wage, a bonus that enables them to believe in their inherent superiority over nonwhites.

It's also true, however, that this same psychological bonus that white workers prize so highly has cost them dearly. For along with the importation of an immigrant population, the separation of black and white workers has given American capital a reserve labor force to call upon whenever white workers seemed to them to get too "uppity." Thus, while racist ideology enables white workers to maintain the belief in their superiority, they have paid for that conviction by becoming far more vulnerable in the struggle for decent wages and working conditions than they might otherwise have been.

Politically and economically, the ideology of white supremacy strips from white workers the ability to make the kind of interracial alliances that would benefit all of the working class. Psychologically, it leaves them exposed to the double-edged sword of which I spoke earlier. On one side, their belief in the superiority of whiteness helps to reassure them that they're not at the bottom of the social hierarchy. But their insistence that their achievements are based on their special capacities and virtues, that it's only incompetence that keeps others from grabbing a piece of the American dream, threatens their precarious sense of self-esteem. For if they're the superior ones, the deserving ones, the ones who earned their place solely through hard work and merit, there's nothing left but to blame themselves for their inadequacies when hard times strike.

In the opening sentences of *Worlds of Pain* I wrote that America was choking on its differences. If we were choking then, we're being asphyxiated now. As the economy falters, and local, state, and federal governments keep cutting services, there are more and more acrimonious debates about who will share in the shrinking pie. Racial and ethnic groups, each in their own corners, square off as they ready themselves for what seems to be the fight of their lives. Meanwhile, the quality of life for all but the wealthiest Americans is spiraling downward—a plunge that's felt most deeply by those at the lower end of the class spectrum, regardless of color.

As more and more mothers of young children work full-time outside the home, the question of who will raise the children comes center stage. Decent, affordable child care is scandalously scarce, with no government intervention in sight for this crucial need. In poor and working-class families, therefore, child care often is uncertain and inadequate, leaving parents apprehensive and children at risk. To deal with their fears, substantial numbers of couples now work different shifts, a solution to the child-care problem that puts its own particular strains on family life.

In families with two working parents, time has become their most precious commodity—time to attend to the necessary tasks of family life; time to nurture the relationships between wife and husband, between parents and children; time for oneself, time for others; time for solitude, time for a social life. Today more than ever before, family life has become impoverished for want of time, adding another threat to the already fragile bonds that hold families together.

While women's presence in the labor force has given them a measure of independence unknown before, most also are stuck with doing two days' work in one—one on the job, the other when they get home at night. Unlike their counterparts in the earlier era, today's women are openly resentful about the burdens they carry, which makes for another dimension of conflict between wives and husbands.

Although the men generally say they've never heard of Robert Bly or any of the other modern-day gurus of manhood, the idea of men as victims has captured their imagination. Given the enormous amount of publicity these men's advocates have garnered in the last few years, it's likely that some of their ideas have filtered into the awareness of the men in this study, even if they don't know how they got there. But their belief in their victimization is also a response to the politics of our time, when so many different groups—women, gays, racial minorities, the handicapped—have demanded special privileges and entitlements on the basis of past victimization. And once the language of victimization enters the political discourse, it becomes a useful tool for anyone wanting to resist the claims of others or to stake one of their own.

As the men see it, then, if their wives are victims because of the special burdens of womanhood, the husbands, who bear their own particular hardships, can make the claim as well. If African-American men are victims because of past discrimination, then the effort to redress their grievances turns white men into victims of present discrimination.

To those who have been victimized by centuries of racism, sexism, homophobia, and the like, the idea that straight white men are victims, too, seems ludicrous. Yet it's not wholly unreal, at least not for the men in this study who have so little control over their fate and who so often feel unheard and invisible, like little more than shadows shouting into the wind.

Whether inside the family or in the larger world outside, white men keep hearing that they're the privileged ones, words that seem to them like a bad joke. How can they be advantaged when their inner experience is that they're perched precariously on the edge of a chasm that seems to have opened up in the earth around them? It's this sense of vulnerability, coupled with the conviction that their hardships go unseen and their pain unattended, that nourishes their claim to victimhood.

Some analysts of family and social life undoubtedly will argue that the picture I've presented here is too grim, that it gives insufficient weight to both the positive changes in family life and the gains in race relations over these past decades. It's true that the social and cultural changes we've witnessed have created families that, in some ways at least, are more responsive to the needs of their members, more democratic than any we have known before. But it's also true that without the economic stability they need, even the most positive changes will not be enough to hold families together.

Certainly, too, alongside the racial and ethnic divisions that are so prominent a part of American life today is the reality that many more members of these warring groups than ever before are living peaceably together in our schools, our factories, our shops, our corporations, and our neighborhoods. And, except for black-white marriages, many more are marrying and raising children together than would have seemed possible a few decades ago.

At the same time, there's reason to fear. The rise of ethnicity and the growing racial separation also means an escalating level of conflict that sometimes seems to threaten to fragment the nation. In this situation, ethnic entrepreneurs like Al Sharpton in New York and David Duke in Louisiana rise to power and prominence by fanning ethnic and racial discord. A tactic that works so well precisely because the economic pressures are felt so keenly on all sides of the racial fissures, because both whites and people of color now feel so deeply that "it's not fair."

As I reflect on the differences in family and social life in the last two decades, it seems to me that we were living then in a more innocent age—a time, difficult though it was for the working-class families of our nation, when we could believe that anything was possible. Whether about the economy, race relations, or life inside the family, most Americans believed that the future promised progress, that the solution to the social problems and inequities of the age were within our grasp, that sacrifice today would pay off tomorrow. This is perhaps the biggest change in the last twenty years: The innocence is gone.

But is this a cause for mourning? Perhaps only when innocence is gone and our eyes are unveiled will we be able to grasp fully the depth of our conflicts and the sources from which they spring.

We live in difficult and dangerous times, in a country deeply divided by class, race, and social philosophy. The pain with which so many American families are living today, and the anger they feel, won't be alleviated by a retreat to false optimism and easy assurances. Only when we are willing to see and reckon with the magnitude of our nation's problems and our people's suffering, only when we take in the full measure of that reality, will we be able to find the path to change. Until then, all our attempts at solutions will fail. And this, ultimately, will be the real cause for mourning. For without substantial change in both our public and our private worlds, it is not just the future of the family that is imperiled but the very life of the nation itself.

18

Migrant Filipina Domestic Workers and the International Division of Reproductive Labor

RHACEL SALAZAR PARREÑAS

MIGRANT FILIPINA WOMEN ARE employed as domestic workers in more than 130 countries (Tyner 1999). They comprise a substantial proportion of labor migrants in various nations in Europe and Asia as well as Canada (Bakan and Stasiulis 1997; Catholic Institute for International Relations [CIIR] 1987; Constable 1997). To a lesser extent, they are also employed as domestic workers in the United States (Hogeland and Rosen 1990). Even though Filipina migration is often assumed to be a middle-class professional stream (e.g., of nurses), two-thirds of female labor migrants from the Philippines are, in fact, domestic workers (Tolentino 1996). Only in the United States do Filipina migrant nurses outnumber domestic workers (Tyner 1999).[1]

Looking at the migration and entrance of Filipina women into domestic work, this article documents the creation of a division of reproductive labor in the global economy. This particular division of labor occurs among working women and arises out of the demand for low-wage service workers in postindustrial nations. By reproductive labor, I refer to the labor needed to sustain the productive labor force. Such work includes household chores; the care of elderly, adults, and youth; the socialization of children; and the maintenance of social ties in the family (Brenner and Laslett 1991). Relegated to women more so than men, reproductive labor has long been a commodity purchased by class-privileged women. As Evelyn Nakano Glenn (1992) has observed, white class-privileged women in the United States have historically freed themselves of reproductive labor by purchasing the low-wage services of women of color. In doing so, they maintain a "racial division of reproductive labor," which establishes a two-tier hierarchy among women (Nakano Glenn 1992).

Two analytical goals motivate my query into the structural relationship between the politics of reproductive labor and the flow of Filipina domestic worker migration. First, I return to the discussion of the commodification of reproductive labor initiated by Nakano Glenn (1992) to extend her discussion to an international terrain. In this way, my analysis of the division of reproductive labor considers issues of globalization and the feminization of wage labor (Sassen 1984, 1988). Second, I extend discussions of the international division of labor in globalization from a sole consideration of productive labor to include analyses of reproductive labor. By analyzing the structural relationship between reproductive labor and the feminization of the migrant labor force, I show another dimension by which gender shapes the economic divisions of labor in migration.

The globalization of the market economy has extended the politics of reproductive labor into an international level. As I show in this article, the migration and entrance into domestic work of Filipino women constitutes an international division of reproductive labor. This division of labor, which I name the *international transfer of caretaking*, refers to the three-tier transfer of reproductive labor among women in sending and receiving countries of migration. While class-privileged women purchase the low-wage services of migrant Filipina domestic workers, migrant Filipina domestic workers simultaneously purchase the even lower-wage services of poorer women left behind in the Philippines. In other words, migrant Filipina domestic workers hire poorer women in the Philippines to perform the reproductive labor that they are performing for wealthier women in receiving nations.

The international transfer of caretaking links two important but separate discourses on the status of women—Nakano Glenn's (1992) discussion of the "racial division of reproductive labor" and Sassen's discussion of the "international division of labor." It demonstrates that these important formulations need to be expanded to take into account transnational issues of reproduction. To develop my argument, I begin by reviewing the two relevant bodies of literature—one on domestic work and reproductive labor and the second on female migration. Then, I describe my research methodology and the characteristics of my sample. To build my conceptual case, I first analyze the situation of Filipina domestic workers in the Philippines and the "receiving nations" of the United States and Italy. Then, I build on this by adding the migration links that illustrate the international transfer of care-taking. This three-tier process is not merely a conceptual idea but has consequences for migrant Filipina domestic workers, which I give voice to in the final section. These consequences are particularly important to consider because they define the migratory experiences of the increasing number of migrant domestic workers from the Philippines.

REPRODUCTIVE LABOR AND PAID DOMESTIC WORK

My discussion of reproductive labor builds from research on domestic work and female migration. As I have noted, it is grounded in Nakano Glenn's (1992) important formulation of the "racial division of reproductive labor." Although reproductive labor has historically been relegated to women, Nakano Glenn argues that there is a hierarchical and interdependent relationship, one that interlocks the race and class status of women, in its distribution in the formal and informal labor market. According to Nakano Glenn (1992, 30), class-privileged women free themselves of the "mental, emotional, and manual labor" needed for "the creation and recreation of people as cultural and social, as well as physical beings" by hiring low-paid women of color. This form of low-wage labor encompasses a wide array of jobs including food-service production, hotel house-keeping, and nursing aide. In the commodification of reproductive labor, women are linked by gender and differentiated by race and class. Moreover, in its commodification, the worth of reproductive labor declines in society. As Katz Rothman (1989, 43) poignantly states, "When performed by mothers, we call this mothering . . . when performed by hired hands, we call it unskilled."

Various case studies on domestic work establish that women often use their class privilege to buy themselves out of their gender subordination (Palmer 1989; Romero 1992; Thornton Dill 1994). As Mary Romero (1992, 129–30) puts it: "The never-ending job described by housewives is transferred to workers employed by women who treat domestic service as an opportunity to 'hire a wife.' " From discussions of the spatial segregation of paid domestic workers to the documentation of the script of "deference and maternalism" (Rollins 1985) in the workplace, numerous studies have also shown that the race and class inequalities that structure this division of labor are aggravated in the daily practices of paid household work (Romero 1992; Thornton Dill 1994). Documenting the hierarchy of womanhood in the United States during the pre-World War II period, Phyllis Palmer (1989), for example, describes the reflection of race and class hierarchies in the division of labor between "clean mistresses" and "dirty servants." According to Palmer, the more physically strenuous labor of the servant enabled the mistress to attain the markers of ideal femininity—fragility and cleanliness. This hierarchy continues today as the most demanding physical labor in the household is still relegated to the paid domestic worker.

While scholarship on domestic work establishes the unequal relations between domestics and their employers, it has yet to interrogate substantially the consequences of paid domestic work on the families of domestic workers themselves. An exception to this is Romero's (1997) research on the children of domestic workers. One of the questions that needs to be addressed further is, "Who cares for the domestics' family?" Elaine Bell Kaplan (1987) notes that the oldest daughters of domestics usually take over their familial duties. David Katzman (1978) similarly observed that African American domestics in the South turned to their families, specifically grandparents, for the care of children. In their article on transnational mothering, Pierrette Hondagneu-Sotelo and Ernistine Avila (1997) ask a similar question: "Who is taking care of the nanny's children?" They found that transnational Latina mothers, many of whom are domestic workers, frequently rely on other female relatives as well as paid domestic workers for the care of their children left in the sending country. The observation of Hondagneu-Sotelo and Avila raises questions about the new forms of structural inequalities and social consequences that are engendered by the extension of commodified reproductive labor to an international terrain. To address international relations of inequality in reproductive labor, I now situate my discussion of the politics of reproductive labor in literature of female migration and the globalization of the market economy.

WOMEN AND MIGRATION

Contemporary labor migration is situated in the globalization of the market economy. As Saskia Sassen has further indicated, globalization has sparked the feminization of migrant labor. Contributing an insightful theoretical framework on the position of women in the global economy, Sassen (1984, 1988) establishes that globalization simultaneously demands the low-wage labor of Third World women in export processing zones of developing countries and in secondary tiers of manufacturing and service sectors in advanced, capitalist countries. The case of women in the Philippines provides an exemplary illustration. While Filipina women comprised 74 percent of the labor force in export processing zones by the early 1980s (Rosca 1995), they constituted more than half of international migrants (55 percent) by the early 1990s (Asis 1992).

In globalization, the penetration of manufacturing production in developing countries creates a demand for women to migrate to advanced, capitalist countries. First of all, the manufacturing production (e.g., garment, electronics, and furniture) that remains in the latter set of countries must compete with low production costs in developing countries. This results in the decentralization and deregulation of manufacturing production (i.e., subcontracting or homework). Second, multinational corporations with production facilities across the globe, by and large, maintain central operations in new economic centers, or what Sassen (1994) refers to as "global cities," where specialized professional services (e.g., legal, financial, accounting, and consulting tasks) are concentrated. For the most part, global cities require low-wage service labor such as domestic work to maintain the lifestyles of their professional inhabitants. Notably, many of the low-paying jobs created in advanced, capitalist countries are considered traditional "women's work." As a result, many of the immigrants who respond to the increasing demand for low-wage workers in advanced, capitalist countries are women.

The movement of manufacturing production to newly industrialized countries of Asia also generates a demand for female migrant workers. The increase in production activities in these economies has subsumed the traditional proletariat female workforce who would otherwise perform low-paying service jobs such as domestic work. This shift in labor market concentration has consequently generated a need for the lower-wage labor of women from neighboring countries such as Indonesia and the Philippines to fill the void created in the Asian service sector (Chin 1998).

Independent female migration has correspondingly increased with the feminization of wage labor in the global economy. For example, in a study of Central American refugees in Washington, D.C., Repak (1995) establishes that gender is a structural determinant of migration by showing that the greater demand for low-wage female workers in this particular receiving community initiated the primary migration of women. In the case of the Philippines, the independent nature of female migration is shown by the different destinations of male and female labor migrants in the diaspora. As male and female migrants fill different niches in the global economy, migration from the Philippines results in two gendered flows with women initiating migration to countries with a greater demand for female workers and men migrating to countries with a greater demand for male workers (Tyner 1994). In fact, the gender composition of many Filipino migrant communities is skewed. Women compose more than 70 percent of migrant Filipinos in Asian and European cities (Constable 1997; Salazar Parreñas 1998), where labor markets have a greater demand for low-wage service workers. In contrast, men compose the majority of Filipino labor migrants in the Middle East (Tyner 1994), where there are more jobs available in construction and oil industries.

On one hand, the case of Filipina domestic workers fits Sassen's theoretical formulation. As low-wage service workers, they meet the rising demand for cheap labor in the global cities of Asia and Europe and, to a lesser extent, the United States. On the other hand, this theoretical formulation only concentrates on relations of production in globalization. The structural relationship between work and family is not examined in macro-level accounts of the demand for migrant laborers. In contrast, literature on female migration has turned to the institutional-level perspective to pay closer attention to the analytical principle of gender in the family. By analyzing social relations of men and women in the family, feminist scholars of migration have shown that gender organizes, shapes, and distinguishes the immigration patterns and experiences of men and women (Grasmuck and Pessar 1991; Hondagneu-Sotelo 1994). In my study of the politics of reproductive labor under globalization, I take note of this rich discussion in feminist migration studies.

Situating migrant Filipina domestic workers in the transnational politics of reproductive labor extends Sassen's formulation by stressing the fact that participants in the new international division of labor, from the low-wage migrant worker to the professionals whom they serve, have families. Accounting for these families allows us to give greater consideration to gender in discussions of divisions of labor in globalization and enables us to more fully describe the labor processes of migration.

METHOD

This article is based primarily on open-ended interviews that I collected with 46 female domestic workers in Rome and 26 in Los Angeles. I tape-recorded and fully transcribed each of my interviews, which were mostly conducted in Tagalog and then translated into English.

[. . .]

My sample of domestic workers in Rome and Los Angeles reveals women who are mostly mothers with a fairly high level of educational attainment. Contrary to the popular belief that Filipina domestic workers are usually young and single (CIIR 1987), my study shows a larger number of married women. Women with children living in the Philippines constitute the majority of my sample in both Rome and Los Angeles: 25 of 46 in Rome and 14 of 26 in Los Angeles.

Because they perform jobs that are considered unskilled, domestic workers are often assumed to lack the training needed for higher status jobs in the labor market. In the case of Filipina domestics in Italy and the United States, the prestige level of their current work does not in any way reveal their level of educational training. Most of my interviewees had acquired some years of postsecondary training in the Philippines. In Rome, my interviewees include 23 women with college degrees, 12 with some years of college or postsecondary vocational training, and 7 who completed high school. In Los Angeles, my interviewees include 11 women with college diplomas, 8 with some years of college or postsecondary vocational training, and 5 with high school degrees.

Even with a high level of educational attainment, Filipina women migrate and enter domestic work because they still earn higher wages as domestic workers in postindustrial nations than as professional workers in the Philippines. [. . .]

REPRODUCTIVE LABOR IN SENDING AND RECEIVING NATIONS

Migrant Filipina domestic workers depart from a system of gender stratification in the Philippines only to enter another one in the advanced capitalist and industrialized countries of the United States and Italy. In both sending and receiving nations, they confront societies with similar gender ideologies concerning the division of labor in the family; that is, reproductive labor is relegated to women. Yet, in the receiving nation of either Italy or the United States, racial, class, and citizenship inequalities aggravate the position of migrant Filipinas as women (Andall 1992; Nakano Glenn 1992). In this section, I discuss the politics of reproductive labor at both ends of the migration spectrum. My discussion gives greater consideration to those in the receiving nations, because of their greater relevance for our understanding of the labor market incorporation of migrant Filipina domestic workers in globalization.

In the Philippines, men are expected to sustain the family and women to reproduce family life. In fact, ideological constructs of feminine identity are molded from "mothering and caring roles in the domestic arena" (Israel-Sobritchea 1990). The ideology of women as caretakers constrains the productive labor activities of women in many ways, including sex segregating them into jobs resembling "wife-and-mother roles" (Chant and McIlwaine 1995; Uy Eviota 1992), such as household work on plantations and professional work in nursing and teaching. Because women are expected only to subsidize the primary income of men, women's jobs are often less valued and far less lucrative than comparable men's work (e.g., fieldwork as opposed to household work in plantations) (Uy Eviota 1992). Despite these constraints, women do participate in the productive labor force (Aguilar 1988) and in 1992, the female share of total employment in the Philippines reached 37.7 percent (Chant 1997): Considering that only 2 percent of all households in the Philippines can afford to hire domestic help, these working women are plagued by the double day (Aguilar 1988).

For the remainder of this section, I situate the migration of Filipina domestic workers in the politics of reproductive labor in the receiving countries of the United States and Italy. I do so to place their labor market incorporation in the context of the racial division of reproductive labor. In the United States, women represented 46.5 percent of gainfully employed workers in 1992, a considerable increase over 32.1 percent in 1960 (Reskin and Padavic 1994, 24–25). In Italy, the downward trend in the labor force participation of women from 1959 to 1972 has since reversed (Meyer 1987). In fact, Italy has witnessed an increasing number of married women in the labor force, but a surprising decline among younger single women (Goddard 1996). It has been argued that Italian women are turning away from reproducing families and concentrating on their advancement in the labor market (Specter 1998). Italy, although known to be "the traditional 'bambini' country," has the lowest birthrate in the world at only 9.6 per 1,000 inhabitants (Beck and Beck-Gernsheim 1995, 102).

According to Arlie Hochschild (1989), at least in the United States, the majority of men do less housework than do their gainfully employed partners, and men who earned less than their wives were even less likely to share housework. And so today, a significantly larger number of women have to cope with the double day. Similarly in Italy, *doppio lavoro* (literally meaning double work) has been a recurring theme in the Italian feminist movement since the early 1970s (Chiavola Birnbaum 1986). Notably, the amount of household work expected of women has increased with advances in technology (Glazer 1993).

While a higher income does not guarantee a more gender egalitarian distribution of house-work, it does give families the flexibility to afford the services of other women. To ease the double day, many overwhelmed women in the United States have turned to day care centers and family day care providers, nursing homes, after-school baby-sitters, and also privately hired domestic workers (Glazer 1993; Katz Rothman 1989; Nakano Glenn 1992; Nelson 1990; Reskin and Padavic 1994). In Italy, this same trend is reflected in the concentration of women from the Philippines, Cape Verde, and Peru in domestic services as well as the estimated 36.4 percent of illegal workers who are doing domestic work (Calavita 1994). Notably, Italian women have turned to new tactics to minimize their reproductive labor. While Italian feminists demanded "wages for housework" in the 1970s (Chiavola Birnbaum 1986, 135), it can be said that Italian women have since taken to refusing to reproduce the family altogether. Without doubt, this is a unique means by which many Italian women minimize their reproductive labor directly.

The labor market incorporation of migrant Filipina domestic workers into the United States and Italy fits into Nakano Glenn's schema. In both countries, they join the ranks of other groups of subordinated women who have historically performed the reproductive labor of more privileged women. In making this assertion, I do not claim that Filipinas in the United States are defined racially as domestic workers like Latina migrants. They are more so categorized and identified as nurses, because of their concentration in health care services. Yet, in the Filipino migrant community, it is known that recent migrants frequently turn to domestic work.[2]

Reflecting the observations of Nakano Glenn, Andall (1992, 43) associates the entrance of migrant women into Italy—as they are concentrated in domestic work—with the entrance of Italian women into the labor force:

> The migration of women into Italy began at the same time as a number of changes were taking place in the role and position of Italian women within society . . . in the 1970s, an increased number of Italian women began to assert themselves outside the domestic sphere. . . . This change in Italian women's activity became a pull factor in the migration of women from developing countries.

Nakano Glenn's (1992) formulation of the racial division of reproductive labor suggests that the demand for low-wage service workers, particularly domestic workers, arises not solely from the concentration of highly specialized professional services in global cities, as Sassen has argued correctly, but also from persisting gender inequalities in the families of these professionals. To fully consider the politics of reproductive labor in the migration of Filipina domestic workers, I now expand and reformulate the concept of the racial division of reproductive labor by placing it in a transnational setting. In doing so, I situate the increasing demand for paid reproductive labor in receiving nations in the context of the globalization of the market economy.

THE INTERNATIONAL DIVISION OF REPRODUCTIVE LABOR

Globalization has triggered the formation of a singular market economy. As such, production activities in one area can no longer be understood solely from a local perspective. Likewise, I argue that reproduction activities, especially as they have been increasingly commodified, have to be situated in the context of this singular market economy. In this sense, I insist that reproduction activities in one area have concrete ties to reproduction activities in another area. With the feminization of wage labor, global capitalism is forging the creation of links among distinct systems of gender inequality. Moreover, the migration of women connects systems of gender inequality in both sending and receiving nations to global capitalism. All of these processes occur in the formation of the international division of reproductive labor.

This division of labor places Nakano Glenn's (1992) "racial division of reproductive labor" in an international context under the auspices of Saskia Sassen's discussion of the incorporation of women from developing countries into the global economy. It is a transnational division of labor that is shaped simultaneously by global capitalism, gender inequality in the sending country, and gender inequality in the receiving country. This division of labor determines the migration and entrance into domestic service of women from the Philippines.

The international transfer of caretaking is a distinct form of the international division of labor in which Filipina domestic workers perform the reproductive labor or the "private sphere" responsibilities of class-privileged women in industrialized countries as they leave other women in the Philippines to perform their own. This international division of labor refers to a three-tier transfer of reproductive labor among women in two nation-states. These groups of women are (1) middle-class women in receiving countries, (2) migrant Filipina domestic workers, and (3) Filipina domestic workers in the Philippines who are too poor to migrate.

Under the international transfer of caretaking, women's migration from the Philippines is embedded in the process of global capitalism. At the same time, gender is also a central factor of their migration. The process of migration for women involves escaping their gender roles in the Philippines, easing the gender constraints of the women who employ them in industrialized countries, and finally relegating their gender roles to women left in the Philippines.[3]

The international transfer of caretaking refers to a social, political, and economic relationship between women in the global labor market. This division of labor is a structural relationship based on the class, race, gender, and (nation-based) citizenship of women. In the international transfer of caretaking, Filipina domestic workers do not just ease the entrance of other women into the paid labor force but also assist in the economic growth of receiving countries. Patricia Licuanan (1994, 109), in reference to households in Hong Kong and Singapore, explains,

> Households are said to have benefited greatly by the import of domestic workers. Family income has increased because the wife and other women members of working age are freed from domestic chores and are able to join the labour force. This higher income would normally result in the enlargement of the consumer market and greater demand on production and consequently a growth in the economy.

In the article "Economy Menders," Linda Layosa (1995, 7), the editor of the transnational monthly magazine *Tinig Filipino*, describes the international transfer of caretaking:

> Indeed, our women have partially been liberated from the anguish of their day-to-day existence with their families and from economic problems, only to be enslaved again in the confines of another home, most of the time trampling their rights as human beings . . . we have to face the reality that many of our women will be compelled to leave the confines of their own tidy bedrooms and their spotless kitchens only to clean another household, to mend other's torn clothes at the same time as they mend our tattered economy.

In her description, she falls short of mentioning who takes up the household work that migrant Filipina domestic workers abandon upon migration. Most likely, they are other female relatives, but also less privileged Filipina women, women unable to afford the high costs of seeking employment outside of the Philippines. Thus, migrant Filipina domestic workers are in the middle of the three-tier hierarchy of the international transfer of caretaking.

The case of Carmen Ronquillo provides a good illustration of the international transfer of caretaking.[4] Carmen is simultaneously a domestic worker of a professional woman in Rome and an employer of a domestic worker in the Philippines. Carmen describes her relationship to each of these two women:

> When coming here, I mentally surrendered myself and forced my pride away from me to prepare myself. But I lost a lot of weight. I was not used to the work. You see, I had maids in the Philippines. I have a maid in the Philippines that has worked for me since my daughter was born twenty-four years ago. She is still with me. I paid her three hundred pesos before and now I pay her one thousand pesos.[5]
>
> I am a little bit luckier than other because I run the entire household. My employer is a divorced woman who is an architect. She does not have time to run her household so I do all the shopping. I am the one budgeting. I am the one cooking. [Laughs.] And I am the one cleaning too. She has a 24 and 26 year old. The older one graduated already and is an electrical engineer. The other one is taking up philosophy. They still live with her. . . . She has been my only employer. I stayed with her because I feel at home with her. She never commands. She never orders me to do this and to do that.

The hierarchical and interdependent relationship between Carmen, her employer in Italy, and her domestic worker in the Philippines forms from the unequal development of industrialized and developing countries in transnational capitalism, class differences in the Philippines, and the relegation of reproductive labor to women. The case of Carmen Ronquillo clearly exemplifies how three distinct groups of women participate in the international transfer of caretaking. While Carmen frees her employer (the architect) of domestic responsibilities, a lower paid domestic worker does the household work for Carmen and her family.

Wage differences of domestic workers illuminate the economic disparity among nations in transnational capitalism. A domestic worker in Italy such as Carmen could receive U.S.$1,000 per month for her labor:

> I earn 1,500,000 lira (U.S.$1,000) and she pays for my benefits (e.g., medical coverage). On Sundays, I have a part-time (job), I clean her office in the morning and she pays me 300,000 lira (U.S.$200). I am very fortunate because she always gives me my holiday pay (August) and my thirteenth month pay in December. Plus, she gives me my liquidation pay at the end of the year. Employers here are required to give you a liquidation pay—equivalent to your monthly salary for every year you worked for them, but they usually give it to you when you leave but she insists on paying me at the end of the year. So, on December, I always receive 5,400,000 lira (U.S.$3,600).

The wages of Carmen easily afford her a domestic worker in the Philippines, who, on average, only earns the below-poverty wage of U.S.\$40 per month. Moreover, the domestic worker in the Philippines, in exchange for her labor, does not receive the additional work benefits Carmen receives for the same labor, for example, medical coverage. Not surprisingly, migrant Filipina domestic workers, as shown by their high level of educational attainment, tend to have more resources and belong in a more comfortable class strata than do domestic workers in the Philippines. Such resources often enable Carmen and other migrant Filipina women to afford the option of working outside of the country.

THE OVERLOOKED PARTICIPANTS: CHILDREN AND WOMEN IN THE PHILIPPINES

> The private world remains devalued, as poor people become the wives and mothers of the world, cleaning the toilets and raising the children. The devaluing of certain work, of nurturance, of private "domestic" work, remains: rearing children is roughly on a par—certainly in terms of salary—with cleaning the toilet. (Katz Rothman 1989, 252)

While the devaluation of "rearing children" could be lamented as a tragedy for children, the experiences of the different groups of children (and elderly) in the international transfer of care-taking should be distinguished between those who remain cared for and those who are not and those who regularly see their parents/children and those who cannot. The fact that "rearing children is roughly on a par . . . with cleaning the toilet" means that migrant Filipina domestic workers usually cannot afford the higher costs of maintaining a family in industrialized countries due to their meager wages. In the United States, where people of color have traditionally been caregivers and domestic workers for white families, mothering is diverted away from people of color families. Sau-ling Wong (1994, 69) defines *diverted mothering* to be the process in which the "time and energy available for mothering are diverted from those who, by kinship or communal ties, are their more rightful recipients." Historically, a married Black domestic worker in the United States "typically saw her children once every two weeks, leaving them in the care of the husband or older siblings, while remaining on call around the clock for the employer's children" (Wong 1994, 71). Now, in an international context, the same pattern of diverted mothering could be described for Filipina, Latina, and Caribbean domestic workers as many are forced to leave their children behind in the country of origin (Colen 1995; Hondagneu-Sotelo and Avila 1997).[6] The question then is, Who cares for these "other" children?

In the Philippines, it is unusual for fathers to nurture and care for their children, but, considering that not all migrant Filipina domestic workers hire domestic workers, some are forced to give in to the renegotiations of household division of labor led by the migration of their wives. Other female relatives often take over the household work of migrant Filipinas. In these cases, nonegalitarian relations among family members should be acknowledged considering that for female family members left in the Philippines, "the mobility they might achieve through migration is severely curtailed" (Basch, Glick Schiller, and Szanton Blanc 1994, 241). However, hired domestic workers—a live-in housekeeper or *labandera* (laundry woman who hand washes clothes)—also free migrant Filipina domestics of their household labor. Almost all of my interviewees in both Rome and Los Angeles hire domestic workers in the Philippines. This should not be surprising considering that the average wage of domestics in the Philippines is considerably less than the average wage of migrant domestics.

In discussions of the international division of (productive) labor, women who cannot afford to work as domestic workers in other countries are equated with those who do so. For example, migrant Filipina domestic workers and female low-wage workers in the Philippines are considered to be equally displaced in global capitalism. Maya Areza, who dreams of retiring in the Philippines after a few more years in the United States, reminds us of the structural inequalities characterizing relations among women in developing countries when she states,

> When I retire I plan to go home for good. I plan to stay at my parents' house . . . I would just lounge and smoke. I will get a domestic helper who I can ask to get my cigarettes for me. . . . My children and my cousins all have domestic workers. You can hire one if you have money. It's cheap, only one thousand pesos ($40). Here, you earn $1,000 doing the same kind of work you would do for one thousand pesos there! I won't have a problem with hiring one.

Because migrant Filipina domestic workers are usually in the middle of the hierarchical chain of caretaking, they maintain unequal relations with less privileged women in the Philippines. Under the international transfer of caretaking, the unequal economic standing of nation-states and discrepancies in monetary currencies are prominent factors that distinguish the position of female low-wage workers in advanced, capitalist, and developing countries. They differentiate, for example, the position of domestic workers in the United States and Italy from domestic workers in the Philippines. Migrant Filipina domestic workers surely take advantage of these differences in wages and maintain a direct hierarchical relationship with the domestic workers whom they hire in the Philippines. In the international transfer of caretaking, domestic workers (e.g., housekeepers and laundry women) hired by families of domestic workers abroad are the truly subaltern women.

THE SOCIAL CONSEQUENCES OF "BEING IN THE MIDDLE"

So far, I have established the formation of the international division of reproductive labor. As a structural process that determines the migration of Filipina domestic workers, this division of labor also results in particular social consequences that are embodied in the lived experience of its participants. In this section, I illuminate the social consequences of "being in the middle" of this division of labor. The process in which reproductive labor is transferred to migrant Filipinas is not as smooth as it sounds. For many, the process involves multiple contradictions in their positions in the family and the labor market.

To illuminate the consequences of "being in the middle," I return to the story of Carmen Ronquillo. Before migrating to Rome, Carmen, who is in her mid-40s, had worked for 15 years as a project manager of the military food services at Clark Air Force Base. With the closure of this U.S. military base in 1992, Carmen thought that she could not find a job that offered a comparably lucrative income in the Philippines. Therefore, Carmen decided to follow her sister to Rome, where she could earn much more as a domestic worker than as a professional in the Philippines. Seeking employment in Italy was a huge investment for her family. Carmen paid an agency U.S.$5,000 to enter Italy without a visa. The high costs of migration from the Philippines suggest that this option is usually limited to those with financial means. Consequently, labor migration for Carmen and the many other middle-class women who can afford to leave the Philippines usually entails the emotional strains brought by their downward mobility to the lower status job of domestic work. As Carmen describes.

> My life is difficult here. Would you believe that here I am a "physical laborer"? When I was working in the Philippines, I was the one supervising the supervisors. [Laughs.] So, when I came here, especially

when I cleaned the bathrooms, I would talk to myself. [Laughs hysterically.] I would commend and praise myself, telling myself, "Oh, you clean the corners very well." [Laughs.] You see, in my old job, I would always check the corners first, that was how I checked if my workers had cleaned the place well. So, sometimes I would just cry. I felt like I was slapped in the face. I resent the fact that we cannot use our skills especially because most of us Filipinos here are professionals. We should be able to do other kinds of work because if you only do housework, your brain deteriorates. Your knowledge deteriorates. Your whole being is that of a maid.

As reflected in the bitter attitude of Carmen toward domestic work, a central contradiction of being in the middle of the international transfer of caretaking is the experience of *conflicting class mobility*. For migrant Filipinas, domestic work simultaneously involves an increase and decrease in class status. They earn more than they ever would have if they had stayed as professional women in the Philippines. Yet, at the same time, they experience a sharp decline in occupational status and face a discrepancy between their current occupation and actual training. For the women "in the middle," this discrepancy highlights the low status of domestic work.

Vanessa Dulang, an office worker in the Philippines and domestic worker in Rome since 1990, describes the gains and losses that migrant women such as herself incur from the limited labor market option of either staying in the Philippines or working as a domestic outside of the country:

> Life is hard in the Philippines. You don't earn enough. Nothing will happen to you if you stay there. Even though you are a maid here, at least you are earning money. What I couldn't buy in the Philippines, I could buy here. . . . But work is difficult. You bend your back scrubbing. You experience what you would never experience in the Philippines. In the Philippines, your work is light but you don't have any money. Here you make money, but your body is exhausted.

In the spatial politics of globalization—unequal development of regions—the achievement of material security in the Philippines entails the experience of downward mobility in other countries. According to Basch, Glick Schiller, and Szanton Blanc (1994, 234), this decline in social status in migration generally pushes migrants to build "deterritorialized national identities." They cope with their marginal status in the receiving country by basing their identities on the increase in their class status in the country of origin. In the same vein, migrant Filipina domestic workers resolve their conflicting class mobility by stressing their higher social and class status in the Philippines.

They do just that by hiring their very own domestic workers or perceiving themselves as rightful beneficiaries of servitude. In this way, they are able to mitigate their loss of status in migration. As Joy Manlapit of Los Angeles tells me,

> When I go back, I want to experience being able to be my own boss in the house. I want to be able to order someone to make me coffee, to serve me food. That is good. That is how you can take back all the hardships you experienced before. That is something you struggled for.

Gloria Yogore, her counterpart in Rome, finds similar comfort in the knowledge of the higher social status she occupies and will occupy once she returns to the Philippines:

> In the Philippines, I have maids. When I came here, I kept on thinking that in the Philippines, I have maids and here I am one. I thought to myself that once I go back to the Philippines, I will not lift my finger and I will be the *signora*. [Laughs.] My hands will be rested and manicured and I will wake up at 12 o'clock noon.

Ironically, migrant Filipina domestic workers find comfort from the contradiction of the simultaneous decline and increase in their class background by stressing the greater privilege that they have and will have in relation to poorer women in the Philippines.

Another consequence of being in the middle is the experience of the *pain of family separation.* Being in the middle is contingent on being part of a transnational household, meaning a household whose members are located in two or more nation-states. Among my interviewees, 41 of 46 women in Rome and 20 of 26 women in Los Angeles maintain such households. I placed my interviewees categorically under this type of household structure on the basis that their remittances sustain the day-to-day living expenses of their immediate and extended families in the Philippines. Almost all of the never-married single women without children in my sample (14 in Rome and 6 in Los Angeles) are, in fact, part of transnational households. Notably, only one single woman does not send remittances to the Philippines regularly.

Emotional strains of transnational family life include feelings of loss, guilt, and loneliness for the mothers and daughters working as domestics in other countries. Plagued by the *pain of family separation,* women like Carmen struggle with the emotional strains of family separation in their daily lives:

> My son, whenever he writes me, he always draws the head of Fido the dog with tears on the eyes. Whenever he goes to mass on Sundays, he tells me that he misses me more because he sees his friends with their mothers. Then, he comes home and cries. He says that he does not want his father to see him crying so he locks himself in his room. When I think of them [her children] is when I feel worst about being here. I was very very close to my two children. . . . Whenever I think of my children, I am struck with this terrible loneliness.

Being in the middle of the international division of reproductive labor entails geographical distance in families and consequently emotional strains for "lonely" mothers and "miserable" children in the Philippines.

Another contradiction of being in the middle of the international division of reproductive labor or the international transfer of caretaking is the fact that women in the middle must care for someone else's grandchildren, children, or parents while being unable to care for their own. In contrast to the two other social consequences that I have previously described, this is not unique to the transnational situation of migrant domestic workers. It has been observed in the United States with nonmigrant domestics (Katzman 1978). However, it does reflect one of the structural constraints faced by Filipina domestic workers in the process of globalization: The choice of maximizing their earnings as transnational low-wage workers denies them the intimacy of the family. Thus, caregiving is made a more painful experience. As Christina Manansala, a domestic worker in Rome since 1990, states, "Of course it is hard to take care of other children. Why should I be taking care of other children when I cannot take care of my own child myself?" Another domestic worker in Rome adds,

> Sometimes when I look at the children that I care for, I feel like crying. I always think about how if we did not need the money, we would all be together and I would be raising my children myself. (Analin Mahusay, children are three and five years old)

The pain of caregiving leads to another contradiction and that is the experience of *displaced mothering* or more generally, *displaced caretaking,* which is also a social consequence that is not unique to the international division of reproductive labor.

Unable to take care of their own families, migrant Filipina domestic workers, like the nonmigrant domestics forced into "diverted mothering" in the United States, find themselves needing to "pour [their] love" to their wards. As Vicky Diaz, a mother in Los Angeles who left five children between the ages of 2 and 10 years old in the Philippines 10 years ago, describes her relationship to her ward, "The only thing you can do is give all your love to the child. In my absence from my children, the most I could do with my situation is give all my love to that child." Trinidad Borromeo of Rome finds similar comfort from "pouring her love" to her elderly ward: "When I take care of an elderly, I treat her like she is my own mother." Notably, some women develop an aversion to caregiving, like Ruby Mercado of Rome, who states, "I do not like taking care of children when I could not take care of my own children. It hurt too much." However, most of my interviewees do indeed feel less guilt for leaving behind their families in the Philippines when caring for and "pouring [their] love" to another family. Ironically, as mothering is transferred to domestic workers, those without children, such as Jerrisa Lim of Los Angeles, begin to feel that they know what it is like to mother: "After doing child care, I feel like I experienced what it is like to be a mother. It is hard to have children. There are pleasures that go with it. That is true. But it is hard." The idea that domestic work involves the act of "pouring love" suggests that a certain degree of emotional bonds to dependents in the family, including children and elderly persons, are passed down in the transfer of caretaking. By operating in the realm of emotion, the commodification of caretaking is further heightened in globalization.

CONCLUSION

The hierarchy of womanhood—based on race, class, and nation—establishes a work transfer system of reproductive labor among women—the international transfer of caretaking. It is a distinct form of transnational division of labor that links women in an interdependent relationship. Filipina domestic workers perform the reproductive labor of more privileged women in industrialized countries as they relegate their reproductive labor to poorer women left in the Philippines. The international division of reproductive labor shows us that production is not the sole means by which international divisions of labor operate in the global economy. Local economies are not solely linked by the manufacturing production of goods. In globalization, the transfer of reproductive labor moves beyond territorial borders to connect separate nation-states. The extension of reproductive labor to a transnational terrain is embedded in the operation of transnational families and the constant flow of resources from migrant domestic workers to the families that they continue to support in the Philippines. While acting as the primary income earners of their families, migrant Filipina domestic workers hire poorer domestic workers to perform the household duties that are traditionally relegated to them as women. In this way, they continue to remain responsible for the reproductive labor in their families but at the same time, as migrant workers, take on the responsibility of productive labor.

The formulation of the international division of reproductive labor treats gender as a central analytical lens for understanding the migration of Filipina domestic workers. It shows that the movement of Filipina domestic workers is embedded in a gendered system of transnational capitalism. While forces of global capitalism spur the labor migration of Filipina domestic workers, the demand for their labor also results from gender inequities in receiving nations, specifically the relegation of reproductive labor to women. This transfer of labor strongly suggests that despite their increasing rate of labor market participation, women continue to remain responsible for reproductive labor in both sending and receiving countries. At both ends of the migratory stream, they have not been able to negotiate directly with male counterparts for a fairer division of household work but instead have had to rely on their race and/or class privilege by participating in the transnational transfer of gender constraints to less-privileged women.

Ironically, women in industrialized (Western) countries are often assumed to be more liberated than women are in developing countries. Yet, many women are able to pursue careers as their male counterparts do because disadvantaged migrant women and other women of color are stepping into their old shoes and doing their household work for them. As women transfer their reproductive labor to less and less privileged women, we can see that the traditional division of labor in the patriarchal nuclear household has not been significantly renegotiated in various countries in the world. This is one of the central reasons why there is a need for Filipina domestic workers in more than 100 countries today.

NOTES

AUTHOR'S NOTE: *I wish to thank Evelyn Nakano Glenn, Arlie Hochschild, Raka Ray, Michael Omi, Pietrette Hondagneu-Sotelo, Jennifer Lee, and an anonymous reviewer for their helpful comments on earlier versions of this article and Christine Bose for her editorial suggestions. The University of California Office of the President and Babilonia Wilner Foundation provided support during the writing of this article.*

1. Responding to the shortage of medical personnel in the U.S. labor market, Filipina nurses entered the United States through the third preference category of the 1965 *Immigration and Nationality Act* with the assistance of recruitment agencies in both the Philippines and the United States. See Ong and Azores (1994) for an extensive discussion of the migration of Filipina nurses.
2. This is caused by a combination of their undocumented status, inability to use their training and work experience from the Philippines, and/or the ethnic niche in caregiving that has developed in the Filipino migrant community. In a study of undocumented women in the United States, Hogeland and Rosen (1990, 43) found that 64 percent of 57 survey participants from the Philippines are employed as domestic workers.
3. Notably, in the Philippines, older (female) children, not fathers, are more likely to look after younger siblings while their mothers work (Chant and McIlwaine 1995). In addition, daughters are traditionally expected to care for aging parents.
4. I use pseudonyms to protect the anonymity of my informants.
5. One thousand pesos amount to approximately U.S.$40.
6. In most other receiving nations, migrant Filipinos are deterred from family migration by their relegation to the status of temporary migrants or their ineligibility for family reunification (Constable 1997).

REFERENCES

Aguilar, Delia, 1988. *The feminist challenge: Initial working principles toward reconceptualizing the feminist movement in the Philippines.* Metro Manila, Philippines: Asian Social Institute.

Andall, Jaqueline. 1992. Women migrant workers in Italy. *Women's Studies International Forum* 15 (1): 41–48.

Asis, Maruja M. B. 1992. The overseas employment program policy. In *Philippine labor migration: Impact and policy*, edited by G. Battistella and A. Paganoni. Quezon City, Philippines: Scalabrini Migration Center.

Bakan, Abigail, and Daiva Stasiulis. 1997. Foreign domestic worker policy in Canada and the social boundaries of modern citizenship. In *Not one of the family: Foreign domestic workers in Canada*, edited by A. Bakan and D. Stasiulis. Toronto: University of Toronto Press.

Basch, Linda, Nina Glick Schiller, and Christina Szanton Blanc. 1994. *Nations unbound: Transnational projects, postcolonial predicaments, and deterritorialized nation-states.* Langhome, PA: Gordon and Breach.

Beck, Ulrich, and Elisabeth Beck-Gernsheim. 1995. *The normal chaos of love.* Cambridge, MA: Polity.

Bell Kaplan, Elaine. 1987. "I don't do no windows": Competition between the domestic worker and the housewife. In *Competition: A feminist taboo?*, edited by V. Miner and H. E. Longino. New York: The Feminist Press.

Brenner, Johanna, and Barbara Laslett. 1991. Gender, social reproduction and women's self-organization: Considering the U.S. welfare state. *Gender & Society* 5 (3): 311–33.

Calavita, Kitty. 1994. Italy and the new immigration. In *Controlling immigration: A global perspective*, edited by W. Cornelius, P. Martin, and J. Hollifield. Stanford, CA: Stanford University Press.

Catholic Institute for International Relations. 1987. *The labour trade: Filipino migrant workers around the globe.* London: Catholic Institute for International Relations.

Chant, Sylvia. 1997. *Women-headed households: Diversity and dynamics in the developing world.* New York: St. Martin's.

Chant, Sylvia, and Cathy McIlwaine. 1995. *Women of a lesser cost: Female labour, foreign exchange and Philippine development.* London: Pluto.

Chiavola Birnbaum, Lucia. 1986. *Liberazione della donne.* Middletown, CT: Wesleyan University Press.

Chin, Christine. 1998. In *Service and servitude: Foreign female domestic workers and the Malaysian "modernity" project.* New York: Columbia University Press.

Colen, Shellee. 1995. "Like a mother to them": Stratified reproduction and West Indian childcare workers and employers in New York. In *Conceiving the new world order: The global politics of reproduction,* edited by F. D. Ginsburg and R. Rapp. Berkeley: University of California Press.

Constable, Nicole. 1997. *Maid to order in Hong Kong: Stories of Filipina workers.* Ithaca, NY: Cornell University Press.

Glazer, Nona. 1993. *Women's paid and unpaid labor: The work transfer in health care and retailing.* Philadelphia: Temple University Press.

Goddard, V. A. 1996. *Gender, family and work in Naples.* Oxford, UK: Berg.

Grasmuck, Sherri, and Patricia Pessar. 1991. *Between two islands: Dominican international migration.* Berkeley: University of California Press.

Hochschild, Arlie. 1989. *The second shift.* New York: Avon.

Hogeland, Chris, and Karen Rosen. 1990. *Dreams lost dreams found: Undocumented women in the land of opportunity.* San Francisco; Coalition for Immigrant Rights and Services.

Hondagneu-Sotelo, Pierrette. 1994. *Gendered transitions: Mexican experiences of migration.* Berkeley: University of California Press.

Hondagneu-Sotelo, Pierrette, and Ernistine Avila. 1997. "I'm here, but I'm there": The meanings of Latina transnational motherhood. *Gender & Society* 11 (5): 548–71.

Israel-Sobritchea, Carolyn. 1990. The ideology of female domesticity: Its impact on the status of Filipino women. *Review of Women's Studies* 1 (1): 26–41.

Katz Rothman, Barbara. 1989. *Recreating motherhood: Ideology and technology in a patriarchal society.* New York: Norton.

Katzman, David M. 1978. *Seven days a week: Women and domestic service in industrializing America.* New York: Oxford University Press.

Layosa, Linda. 1995. Economy menders. *Tinig Filipino,* June, 7.

Licuanan, Patricia. 1994. The socio-economic impact of domestic worker migration: Individual, family, community, country. In *The trade in domestic workers: Causes, mechanisms, and consequences of international migration,* edited by N. Heyzer, G. Lycklama á Nijeholt, and N. Weerakoon. London: Zed.

Meyer, Donald, 1987. *The rise of women in America, Russia, Sweden, and Italy.* Middletown, CT: Wesleyan University Press.

Nakano Glenn, Evelyn. 1992. From servitude to service work: The historical continuities of women's paid and unpaid reproductive labor. *Signs: Journal of Women in Culture and Society* 18 (1): 1–44.

Nelson, Margaret K. 1990. Mothering other's children: The experiences of family day care providers. In *Circles of care: Work and identity in women's lives,* edited by E. K. Abel and M. K. Nelson. Albany: State University of New York Press.

Ong, Paul, and Tania Azores. 1994. The migration and incorporation of Filipino nurses. In *The new Asian immigration in Los Angeles and global restructuring,* edited by P. Ong, E. Bonacich, and L. Cheng. Philadelphia: Temple University Press.

Palmer, Phyllis. 1989. *Domesticity and dirt: Housewives and domestic servants in the United States, 1920–1945.* Philadelphia: Temple University Press.

Repak, Terry. 1995. *Waiting on Washington: Central American workers in the nation's capital.* Philadelphia; Temple University Press.

Reskin, Barbara, and Irene Padavic. 1994. *Women and men at work.* Thousand Oaks, CA: Pine Forge Press.

Rollins, Judith. 1985. *Between women: Domestics and their employers.* Philadelphia; Temple University Press.

Romero, Mary. 1992. *Maid in the U.S.A.* New York: Routledge.

——— . 1997. Life as the maid's daughter: An exploration of the everyday boundaries of race, class, and gender. In *Challenging fronteras: Structuring Latina and Latino lives in the U.S.,* edited by M. Romero, P. Hondagneu-Sotelo, and V. Ortiz. New York: Routledge.

Rosca, Ninotchka. 1995. The Philippines' shameful export. *The Nation* 260 (15): 522–27.

Salazar Parreñas, Rhacel. 1998. The global servants: Migrant Filipina domestic workers in Rome and Los Angeles, Ph.D. diss., University of California, Berkeley.

Sassen, Saskia. 1984. Notes on the incorporation of Third World women into wage labor through immigration and offshore production. *International Migration Review* 18 (4): 1144–67.

——— . 1988. *The mobility of labor and capital: A study in international investment and labor.* New York: Cambridge University Press.

——— . 1994. *Cities in a world economy.* Thousand Oaks, CA: Pine Forge Press.

Specter, Michael. 1998. The baby bust. *New York Times,* 10 July.

Thornton Dill, Bonnie. 1994. *Across the boundaries of race and class: An exploration of work and family among Black domestic servants.* New York: Garland.

Tolentino, Roland. 1996. Bodies, letters, catalogs: Filipinas in transnational spaces. *Social Text* 48 (3): 49–76.

Tyner, James. 1994. The social construction of gendered migration from the Philippines. *Asian and Pacific Migration Journal* 3 (4): 589–615.

——— . 1999. The global context of gendered labor migration from the Philippines to the United States. *American Behavioral Scientist* 42 (4): 671–89.

Uy Eviota, Elizabeth. 1992. *The political economy of gender: Women and the sexual division of labour in the Philippines*. London: Zed.

Wong, Sau-ling. 1994. Diverted mothering: Representations of caregivers of color in the age of "multiculturalism." In *Mothering: Ideology, experience, and agency*, edited by E. Glenn, G. Chang, and L. Forcey. New York: Routledge.

19

excerpt from

Asian American Youth: Culture, Identity, and Ethnicity

"The Making of Culture, Identity, and Ethnicity among Asian American Youth"

Min Zhou and Jennifer Lee

Asian American youth as a group have been almost entirely omitted from research on youth and youth culture in the United States. This omission has not been accidental, but rather, deeply rooted in the legacies of racism and legal exclusion. From the first significant wave of Chinese immigrants reaching America's shores in the late 1840s to the outbreak of World War II, Asian Americans were made up mostly of Chinese and Japanese, with significantly smaller numbers of Filipinos, Koreans, and Indians. Because of various anti-Asian immigration laws, the earlier Asian immigrant groups were small in size and, with the exception of the Japanese, dominated by foreign-born men, with few traditional families. Not only isolated by national-origin groups, Asian Americans were also segregated from other Americans at work, in school, and at their place of residence, essentially ensuring that they would be excluded from fully participating in American life.

During the exclusionary era, people of Asian descent were viewed as clannish, unassimilable aliens, and their cultures backward, corrupt, or simply negligible. The only images that most Americans held of Asians were those promoted in the media: the yellow peril personified in the evil of Fu Manchu; feminized and asexual Chinese men such as Charlie Chan (and later kung-fu masters and fighting machines); exotic geishas, China dolls, and seductresses; or the dragon ladies. These distorted images carried and perpetuated the Eurocentric perception of Americans of Asian ancestry as the exotic Oriental—"foreign" and non-American (Hong, 1993). Asian American youth of the time were all too aware of such misrepresentation, and as a result, they attempted to combat the negative stereotypes by redefining the meaning of being American and expressing their experiences through various forms of cultural practices, such as forums, dances, and ethnic presses. However, exclusion, segregation, and the disrupted community life constrained their cultural practices and limited their voices to the margins of their own ethnic communities.

Even when the racial stereotypes were challenged during the ethnic consciousness movements, including the civil rights movement of the 1960s, new stereotypes of Asian Americans emerged, most prominently that of the "model minority." The new stereotype—the model worker, the overachiever, the math maniac, or the science/computer nerd—carried with it a new set of distorted images of Asian-origin Americans and characterized them as anything but "normal."

This time, however, Asian Americans took their struggles beyond their ethnic communities into mainstream America. For instance, since the late 1960s, Asian American literary work, mostly by U.S.-born or U.S.-raised young Asian American writers and critics, aimed to counteract the misrepresentation of Asian-ancestry Americans and reclaim their place in America. Spearheaded by Jeffrey Paul Chan and his associates in their groundbreaking collection *Aiiieeeee!: An Anthology of Asian American Writers* (1974) and Maxine Hong Kingston in her autobiography *The Woman Warrior* (1976), Asian American cultural works—first in literature and then in film, theater, and the English-language press—have not only flourished but also have become visible in mainstream America. Most of the work recounts the personal and communal histories and experiences of growing up American in immigrant households, in ethnic communities, as well as in mainstream America—all from the perspective of youth.

[. . .]

"ASIAN AMERICAN" AS A MEANINGFUL SOCIAL CATEGORY FOR ANALYSIS

Before developing a framework for studying Asian American youth and youth culture, we must first ask whether "Asian American" is a meaningful analytical category. Our answer is affirmative. In the United States, race often overrides many major socioeconomic and cultural factors—including education, occupation, language, and religion—to affect the everyday lives of all Americans. While social scientists generally agree that race is a social and cultural rather than biological category, there is often a tendency to racialize others into a limited and discrete set of racial categories such as white, black, Hispanic, American Indian, and Asian. Furthermore, those who do not neatly fit into one of the readily available categories are either overlooked, ignored, or may even cause anxiety for those who do the labeling (Kibria, 1996; Omi and Winant, 1994). Hence, while race is a social construct, the lived experiences of race are real and consequential (Lee, 2002).

Coined by the late historian and activist Yuji Ichioka, "Asian American" was a term initially used to describe a politically charged group identity in the ethnic consciousness movements of the late 1960s. This self-proclaimed category emerged to reject the Western-imposed category "Oriental" and to fight invisibility. Today, "Asian American" is widely considered an umbrella term that includes native- and foreign-born U.S. citizens and permanent residents from Asia (east of Pakistan) or who have ancestors from this region. Asian-origin Americans, especially those of East Asian origins who have long been dubbed Oriental, adopt the pan-ethnic label because of convenience and because other Americans cannot and often do not even try to make ethnic distinctions, despite vast differences in national origin, religion, language, and culture. Moreover, the pan-ethnic label has become instrumental for political mobilization and activism (Zhou, 2004).

Although the category "Asian" is both convenient and instrumental, behind closed doors, few Americans of Asian ancestry actually identify themselves as Asian, and even fewer as Asian American. Instead, they identify with their specific countries of origin such as Chinese, Japanese, Korean, Filipino, Indian, Vietnamese, and so on. For example, in a study of Vietnamese youth in San Diego in the mid-1900s, 53 percent identified themselves as Vietnamese, 32 percent as Vietnamese American, and only 14 percent as Asian American. Moreover, nearly 60 percent of these youth considered their chosen identity as very important to them (Zhou, 2001).

Not only do Americans of Asian ancestry not identify themselves as Asian or Asian American, in private they often contest the imposed pan-ethnic identity for a myriad of reasons. First, Asian Americans are a group predominated by the first generation (or foreign born) from diverse national origins. While some have family histories in the United States that date back further than those of Eastern or Southern European origins, most Asians arrived in the United States after the liberalization of immigration laws in the late 1960s. To put this growth into perspective, in 1970, there were only 1.4 million Asians, and in 2000, this figure soared to 11.9 million, now accounting for 4 percent of the total U.S. population.

Before 1970, the Asian-ancestry population was largely composed of Japanese, Chinese, and Filipinos. Now, Americans of Chinese and Filipino ancestries are the largest subgroups (at 2.8 million and 2.4 million, respectively), followed by Indians, Koreans, Vietnamese, and Japanese (at more than one million each). Some 20 other national-origin groups, such as Cambodians, Pakistanis, Lao, Thai, Indonesians, and Bangladeshis were officially counted in government statistics only after 1980 and together amounted to more than two million residents in 2000. Except for the Japanese who are proceeding into the fourth generation, all other Asian-origin groups (including the Chinese and Filipinos) are disproportionately made up of the first generation.

Diverse national origins lead to differences in language, religion, food-ways, customs, histories of international relations, contexts of emigration, reception in the host society, and patterns of adaptation. Moreover, for some national-origin groups, such as Chinese and Indians, internal differences in language, dialect, and religion are substantial. While such differences persist most prominently in the private domain and mainly affect the immigrant generation, they also have a significant impact on the second and succeeding generations. Even though the ethnic distinctiveness associated with homeland traditions and cultures blurs with each succeeding generation (due to acculturation and rapid and high rates of intermarriage), the experiences of growing up among Asian American youth are intrinsically linked with immigration. Today's Asian American youth balance their time and attention between the larger society and their immigrant families and ethnic communities as well as their parents' ancestral homelands, making this balancing act uniquely Asian American.

In addition to the diverse national origins among the Asian immigrant population, Asian Americans also hail from diverse socioeconomic backgrounds (unlike earlier immigrants from Asia and Europe who were mostly low-skilled laborers who came to the United States in search of work). Today's immigrants from Asia migrate for a number of reasons: to join their families; to invest their money in the U.S. economy; to fulfill the demand for highly skilled labor; or to escape war, political or religious persecution, and economic hardship. The diverse socioeconomic backgrounds give rise to varied settlement and mobility patterns. Whereas middle-class immigrants are able to start their American lives with high-paying professional careers and reside in comfortable suburbs, low-skilled immigrants and refugees often have to endure low-paying, menial jobs and settle in urban ghettos, creating a bifurcated distribution of the Asian American population along class lines. The sharp divergence along class lines is likely to lead to fragmentation within the larger Asian American community, making the rise of a pan-Asian identification ambiguous and questionable.

Class bifurcation has direct implications for the identity formation of today's second generation. Unlike the second generation of the 1960s and 1970s—most of whom grew up in segregated urban enclaves—a visible proportion of today's second generation grows up in affluent middle-class suburban neighborhoods, making their experiences distinct not only from yesterday's second generation but also from their contemporary working-class counterparts. Members of the suburban middle class maintain little contact with their working-class co-ethnics in urban enclaves, and show limited interest in working-class issues. In short, socioeconomic diversity marks yet another unique characteristic of today's Asian American youth.

Last but not least, intergenerational differences among Asians complicate intragroup dynamics and family relations. Most notably, native-born children and grandchildren of Asian ancestry feel a sense of ambivalence toward newer arrivals. Because about two-thirds of the Asian American population is first generation, native-born Asians must now confront renewed images of Asians as "foreigners." Resembling the new immigrants in phenotype, but not necessarily in behavior, language, and culture, the more "assimilated" native born find that they must actively and constantly distinguish themselves from the newer arrivals. The "immigrant shadow" looms large for Asian American youth and can weigh heavily on the identity formation of native-born youth. However, native- and foreign-born youth react differently to the "immigrant shadow." For instance, comments about one's "good English" or inquiries about where one comes from are often taken as insensitive at best, and offensive or even insulting at worst, to native-born Asian Americans. By stark contrast, similar encounters tend to be interpreted or felt more positively among foreign-born Asians. Different lived experiences between the native and foreign-born are thus not only generational but also cultural.

Similar to other Americans in speech, thought, and behavior, native-born Asian Americans and their foreign-born counterparts often hold contradictory values and standards about fundamental issues such as individualism, civil liberties, labor rights, and ultimately, the ideology of assimilation. While they are infuriated by their unfair treatment as foreigners, native-born Asian Americans find themselves caught between two vastly different social worlds and at ease with neither. The ambiguity caused by the contradictory perception of "forever foreigner" and "honorary white" further pushes native-born Asian Americans into a dilemma of whether to include or exclude immigrants in their struggle for racial equality (Zhou and Gatewood, 2000). The uncertainty of their status, along with bicultural and intergenerational conflicts, marks a third unique feature of today's Asian American youth.

While recognizing the vast diversity among Asian Americans, we argue that intragroup dynamics and their consequences render the Asian American experience unique, and the imposed pan-ethnic category meaningful for analysis. However, we do not lose sight of the fact that "Asian American" is an imposed identity and most often, not adopted by either the first or second generation, who are much more likely to identify with their national origins than other Americans.

For the second generation, ethnicities based on national origins will recede under the pressure of assimilation, but assimilation does not necessarily lead to diminishing ethnic distinctiveness as predicted by the classic model of acculturation and assimilation conceived by Milton Gordon (1964) decades ago. Instead, the process of assimilation may give rise to a heightened sense of nonwhiteness or a "pan-minority identity" that may be expressed in a variety of ethnic identities rather than a single one. Thus, as members of the second and later generations become more fully incorporated into America's racialized social system, a pan-ethnic identity may become more salient, more inclusive, and more quintessentially American in everyday practices. It is precisely from this point of departure that we study Asian American youth culture and its effect on identity and ethnicity.

UNDERSTANDING ASIAN AMERICAN YOUTH: OPPORTUNITIES AND CONSTRAINTS

Given the complexity of Asian American experiences, we argue that research on Asian American youth and youth culture should be located first and foremost within the dual processes of international migration and American racialization. These dual processes unfold two distinct yet intertwined social worlds that every Asian American child must confront, and present the dialectics of opportunities and constraints for the younger generation who continue to create a culture of their own.

Immigration

Immigration is the most immediate process that shapes the cultural formation of Asian American youth. As noted earlier, Asian Americans are a predominantly immigrant group, which in turn has an enormous impact on the experiences of Asian American youth. As they grow up, they are intimately influenced and often intensely constrained by the immigrant family, the ethnic community, and their parents' ancestral homeland. Research has illustrated how the immigrant family and ethnic community have been the primary sources of support as well as the primary sites of conflict (Zhou and Bankston, 1998).

Asian American children, despite their diverse origins, share certain common family experiences—most prominently the strong familial obligation to obey their elders and repay parental sacrifices, along with the extraordinarily high parental expectations for educational and occupational achievement. Many Asian immigrant parents (especially those who had already secured middle-class status in their home countries) migrated to provide better opportunities for their children. As new immigrants, the first generation often endure difficulties associated with migration such as lack of English-language proficiency, American cultural literacy, and familiarity with the host society. Moreover, those who gave up their middle-class occupations often endure downward occupational mobility, relative deprivation, and discrimination from the host society (Lee, 2000). In their directed quest to achieve socioeconomic mobility, the first generation appears to their children as little more than one-dimensional hard workers who focus too much on material achievement and too little on leisure.

Although their children may feel that their immigrant parents have a narrow vision of success, first generation parents are all too aware of their own limits in ensuring socioeconomic mobility for their children, and hence, turn to education as the surest path to move ahead. Thus, not only do they place an enormous amount of pressure on their children to excel in school, but they also provide the material means to assure success. For example, they move to neighborhoods with strong public schools, send their children to private after-school programs (including language programs, academic tutoring, and enrichment institutions in the ethnic community), spend time to seek out detailed academic information, and make decisions about schools and majors for their children (Zhou and Li, 2003).

Although the parents feel that they are doing what is best for their children, the children—whose frame of reference is "American"—see things differently. From their point of view, their parents appear rigid and "abnormal," that is, unacculturated, old-fashioned, and traditional disciplinarians who are incapable of having fun with them and unwilling to show respect for their individuality. The children view the immigrant family and ethnic community as symbols of the old world— strictly authoritarian, severely demanding, and overwhelmingly stifling.

At the same time, however, the children witness at first hand their parents' daily struggles as new immigrants trying to make it in America, and consequently, develop a unique respect and sensitivity toward them. One of the most prominent ways that they demonstrate their respect and sensitivity is through a subtle blend of conformity to and rebellion against their parents. Asian American youth are less likely to talk back or blatantly defy their parents than other American youth. For example, in her study of Nisei daughters during the years of Asian exclusion, Valerie Matsumoto depicts the tension between native-born daughters and their immigrant parents in the way they defined womanhood. However, rather than challenging their parents head-on, running away from the family, or leaving the ethnic community, the native-born daughters judiciously negotiated the roles assigned to them by their parents and the tightly knit community by creating various cultural forms—dances, dating, and courtship romances—to assert a gender identity that was simultaneously feminine, "Americanized," and "Japanese." Although this delicate balancing act may take a heavy emotional toll on Asian American youth, it is precisely their ambivalence toward their immigrant families that makes the youth culturally sensitive, which, in turn, expands their repertoire for cultural expression.

Racial Exclusion

Along with the experiences associated with immigration, racialization is a second important process that shapes the cultural formation of Asian American youth. The youth confront the consequences of racialization in a number of ways, the first of which is their encounter with racial exclusion. During the period of Asian exclusion, Asian Americans—who were considered an "inferior race"— were confined to ethnic enclaves. The youth who grew up in this era had few social, educational, or occupational options beyond the walls of the ethnic enclave and were barred from full participation in American life. Consequently, some Asian American youth turned their attention overseas to their parents' ancestral homeland for opportunities that were denied to them in the United States. For example, frustrated by their limited mobility options in America, native-born Chinese youth in the 1930s promoted the "Go West to China" movement to seek better opportunities in their ancestral homeland. As Gloria Chun illustrates, second-generation Chinese youth strongly advocated for and disseminated the information regarding the move back to China through public forums and ethnic presses.

Cultural forms and expressions such as ethnic presses, dances, and beauty pageant contests not only affirmed ethnic identities but also inadvertently reinforced Asian Americans as the foreign "Other." While the days of racial segregation in ethnic enclaves have long since disappeared, the effects of racialization still remain a part of growing up in the United States for Asian American youth. For instance, today's Asian American youth develop an awareness of their nonwhite racial identity that functions as a marker of exclusion in some facets of American society, as Nazli Kibria (2002) describes in her study of second-generation Chinese and Korean Americans.

Racial Stereotyping

Another way in which Asian American youth face the consequences of racialization is through racial stereotyping. Excluded from fair representation in mainstream American media, most portrayals of Asian Americans have been either insidious stereotypes of the "foreign" *other* or celebrated images of the "super" *other*, setting Asian Americans apart from other Americans. So pervasive are racial stereotypes of Asian Americans that Asian American youth culture is, in part, produced within the context of counteracting these narrowly circumscribed, one-dimensional images, most prominently that of the model minority.

The celebrated "model minority" image of Asian Americans was born in the mid-1960s, at the peak of the civil rights and ethnic consciousness movements, but *before* the rising waves of immigration and refugee influx from Asia. Two articles published in 1966—"Success Story, Japanese-American Style," by William Petersen in the *New York Times Magazine* and "Success of

One Minority Group in U.S.," by the *U.S. News and World Report* staff—marked a significant departure from the portrayal of Asian Americans as aliens and foreigners, and changed the way that the media depicted Asian immigrants and their descendants. Both articles extolled Japanese and Chinese Americans for their persistence in overcoming extreme hardship and discrimination in order to achieve success (unmatched even by U.S.-born whites) with "their own almost totally unaided effort" and "no help from anyone else." The press attributed their winning wealth and ability to get ahead in American society to hard work, family solidarity, discipline, delayed gratification, nonconfrontation, and disdain for welfare.

Although the image of the model minority may seem laudatory, it has far-reaching consequences that extend beyond Asian Americans. First, the model minority stereotype serves to buttress the myth that the United States is a country devoid of racism, and one that accords equal opportunity for all who take the initiative to work hard to get ahead. The image functions to blame those who lag behind and are not making it for their failure to work hard, their inability to delay gratification, and their inferior culture. Not only does the image thwart other racial/ethnic minorities' demands for social justice, it also pits minority groups against each other.

REFERENCES

For the list of works cited in this chapter, please see the original book by Jennifer Lee and Min Zhou, *Asian American You: Culture, Identity, and Ethnicity* (New York: Routledge, 2004).

20

Gender Displays and Men's Power
The "New Man" and the Mexican Immigrant Man

Pierrette Hondagneu-Sotelo and Michael A. Messner

In our discussions about masculinity with our students (most of whom are white and upper-middle class), talk invariably turns to critical descriptions of the "macho" behavior of "traditional men." Consistently, these men are portrayed as "out there," not in the classroom with us. Although it usually remains an unspoken subtext, at times a student will actually speak it: Those men who are still stuck in "traditional, sexist, and macho" styles of masculinity are black men, Latino men, immigrant men, and working-class men. They are not us; we are the New Men, the Modern, Educated, and Enlightened Men. The belief that poor, working-class, and ethnic minority men are stuck in an atavistic, sexist "traditional male role," while white, educated middle-class men are forging a more sensitive egalitarian "New," or "Modern male role," is not uncommon. Social scientific theory and research on men and masculinity, as well as the "men's movement," too often collude with this belief by defining masculinity almost entirely in terms of gender display (i.e., styles of talk, dress, and bodily comportment), while ignoring men's structural positions of power and privilege over women and the subordination of certain groups of men to other men (Brod, 1983–1984). Our task in this chapter is to explore and explicate some links between contemporary men's gender displays and men's various positions in a social structure of power. Scott Coltrane's (1992) comparative analysis of gender display and power in ninety-three non-industrial societies provides us with an important starting point. Coltrane found that men's "fierce public displays and denigration of women . . . competitive physical contests, vociferous oratory, ceremonies related to warfare, exclusive men's houses and rituals, and sexual violence against women" are common features in societies where men control property and have distant relations with young children (Coltrane, 1992, p. 87). By contrast, "in societies in which women exercise significant control over property and men have close relationships with children, men infrequently affirm their manliness through boastful demonstrations of strength, aggressiveness, and sexual potency" (p. 86). This research suggests that men's public gender displays are not grounded in some essential "need" men have to dominate others but, instead, tend to vary according to the extent of power and privilege that men hold vis-à-vis women. Put another way, the micropolitics of men's and women's daily gender displays and interactions both reflect and reconstruct the macropolitical relations between the sexes (Henley, 1977).

But in modern industrial societies, the politics of gender are far more complex than in non-industrial societies. Some men publicly display verbal and physical aggression, misogyny, and violence. There are public institutions such as sports, the military, fraternities, and the street where these forms of gender display are valorized (Connell, 1991a, 1992b; Lyman, 1987; Martin & Hummer, 1989; Messner, 1992; Sabo, 1985). Other men, though, display more "softness" and "sensitivity," and this form of gender display has been recently lauded as an emergent "New Masculinity."

In this chapter, we will contrast the gender display and structural positions of power (in both public and domestic spheres of life) of two groups of men: class-privileged white men and Mexican immigrant men. We will argue that utilizing the concepts of Modern (or New) and Traditional men to describe these two groups oversimplifies a complex reality, smuggles in racist and classist biases about Mexican immigrant men, and obscures the real class, race, and gender privileges that New Men still enjoy. We will argue that the theoretical concepts of hegemonic, marginalized, and subordinated masculinities best capture the dynamic and shifting constellation of contemporary men's gender displays and power (Brod, 1987; Connell, 1987; Kaufman, 1987; Segal, 1990). We will conclude by arguing that a critical/feminist sociology of men and masculinity should decenter and problematize hegemonic masculinity by proceeding from the standpoint of marginalized and subordinated masculinities.

THE "NEW MAN" AS IDEOLOGICAL CLASS ICON

Today there is a shared cultural image of what the New Man looks like: He is a white, college-educated professional who is a highly involved and nurturing father, "in touch with" and expressive of his feelings, and egalitarian in his dealings with women. We will briefly examine two fragments of the emergent cultural image of the contemporary New Man: the participant in the mythopoetic men's movement and the New Father.[1] We will discuss these contemporary images of men both in terms of their larger cultural meanings and in terms of the extent to which they represent any real shift in the ways men live their lives vis-à-vis women and other men. Most important, we will ask if apparent shifts in the gender displays of some white, middle-class men represent any real transformations in their structural positions of power and privilege.

Zeus Power and the Mythopoetic Men's Movement

A recently emergent fragment of the cultural image of the New Man is the man who attends the weekend "gatherings of men" that are at the heart of Robert Bly's mythopoetic men's movement. Bly's curious interpretations of mythology and his highly selective use of history, psychology, and anthropology have been soundly criticized as "bad social science" (e.g., Connell, 1992a; Kimmel, 1992; Pelka, 1991). But perhaps more important than a critique of Bly's ideas is a sociological interpretation of why the mythopoetic men's movement has been so attractive to so many predominantly white, college-educated, middle-class, middle-aged men in the United States over the past decade. (Thousands of men have attended Bly's gatherings, and his book was a national bestseller.) We speculate that Bly's movement attracts these men not because it represents any sort of radical break from "traditional masculinity" but precisely because it is so congruent with shifts that are already taking place within current constructions of hegemonic masculinity. Many of the men who attend Bly's gatherings are already aware of some of the problems and limits of narrow conceptions of masculinity. A major preoccupation of the gatherings is the poverty of these men's relationships with their fathers and with other men in workplaces. These concerns are based on very real and often very painful experiences. Indeed, industrial capitalism undermined much of the structural basis of middle-class men's emotional bonds with each other as wage labor, market competition, and instrumental rationality largely supplanted primogeniture, craft brotherhood, and intergenerational mentorhood (Clawson, 1989; Tolson, 1977). Bly's "male initiation" rituals are intended to heal and reconstruct these masculine bonds, and they are thus, at least on the surface, probably experienced as largely irrelevant to men's relationships with women.

But in focusing on how myth and ritual can reconnect men with each other and ultimately with their own "deep masculine" essences, Bly manages to sidestep the central point of the feminist critique—that men, as a group, benefit from a structure of power that oppresses women as a group. In ignoring the social structure of power, Bly manages to convey a false symmetry between the feminist women's movement and his men's movement. He assumes a natural dichotomization of "male values" and "female values" and states that feminism has been good for women in allowing them to reassert "the feminine voice" that had been suppressed. But, Bly states (and he carefully avoids directly blaming feminism for this): "the masculine voice" has now been muted—men have become "passive ... tamed ... domesticated." Men thus need a movement to reconnect with the "Zeus energy" that they have lost. "Zeus energy is male authority accepted for the good of the community" (Bly, 1990, p. 61).

The notion that men need to be empowered *as men* echoes the naïveté of some 1970s men's liberation activists who saw men and women as "equally oppressed" by sexism (e.g., Farrell, 1975). The view that everyone is oppressed by sexism strips the concept of oppression of its political meaning and thus obscures the social relations of domination and subordination. Oppression is a concept that describes a relationship between social groups; for one group to be oppressed, there must be an oppressor group (Freire, 1970). This is not to imply that an oppressive relationship between groups is absolute or static. To the contrary, oppression is characterized by a constant and complex state of play: Oppressed groups both actively participate in their own domination and actively resist that domination. The state of play of the contemporary gender order is characterized by men's individual and collective oppression of women (Connell, 1987). Men continue to benefit from this oppression of women, but, significantly, in the past twenty years, women's compliance with masculine hegemony has been counterbalanced by active feminist resistance.

Men do tend to pay a price for their power: They are often emotionally limited and commonly suffer poor health and a life expectancy lower than that of women. But these problems are best viewed not as "gender oppression," but rather as the "costs of being on top" (Kann, 1986). In fact, the shifts in masculine styles that we see among some relatively privileged men may be interpreted as a sign that these men would like to stop paying these costs, but they do not necessarily signal a desire to cease being "on top." For example, it has become commonplace to see powerful and successful men weeping in public—Ronald Reagan shedding a tear at the funeral of slain U.S. soldiers, basketball player Michael Jordan openly crying after winning the NBA championship. Most recently, the easy manner in which the media lauded U.S. General Schwartzkopf as a New Man for shedding a public tear for the U.S. casualties in the Gulf War is indicative of the importance placed on *styles of masculine gender display* rather than the institutional *position of power* that men such as Schwartzkopf still enjoy.

This emphasis on the significance of public displays of crying indicates, in part, a naïve belief that if boys and men can learn to "express their feelings," they will no longer feel a need to dominate others. In fact, there is no necessary link between men's "emotional inexpressivity" and their tendency to dominate others (Sattel, 1976). The idea that men's "need" to dominate others is the result of an emotional deficit overly psychologizes a reality that is largely structural. It does seem that the specific type of masculinity that was ascendant (hegemonic) during the rise of entrepreneurial capitalism was extremely instrumental, stoic, and emotionally inexpressive (Winter & Robert, 1980). But there is growing evidence (e.g., Schwartzkopf) that today there is no longer a neat link between class-privileged men's emotional inexpressivity and their willingness and ability to dominate others (Connell, 1991b). We speculate that a situationally appropriate public display of sensitivity such as crying, rather than signaling weakness, has instead become a legitimizing sign of the New Man's power.[2]

Thus relatively privileged men may be attracted to the mythopoetic men's movement because, on the one hand, it acknowledges and validates their painful "wounds," while guiding them to connect with other men in ways that are both nurturing and mutually empowering.[3] On the other hand, and unlike feminism, it does not confront men with the reality of how their own privileges are based on the continued subordination of women and other men. In short, the mythopoetic men's movement may be seen as facilitating the reconstruction of a new form of hegemonic masculinity— a masculinity that is less self-destructive, that has revalued and reconstructed men's emotional bonds with each other, and that has learned to feel good about its own Zeus power.

The New Father

In recent years Western culture has been bombarded with another fragment of the popular image of the New Man: the involved, nurturant father. Research has indicated that many young heterosexual men do appear to be more inclined than were their fathers to "help out" with housework and child care, but most of them still see these tasks as belonging to their wives or their future wives (Machung, 1989; Sidel, 1990). Despite the cultural image of the "new fatherhood" and some modest increases in participation by men, the vast majority of child care, especially of infants, is still performed by women (Hochschild, 1989; La Rossa, 1988; Lewis, 1986; Russell, 1983).

Why does men's stated desire to participate in parenting so rarely translate into substantially increased involvement? Lynn Segal (1990) argues that the fact that men's apparent attitudinal changes have not translated into widespread behavioral changes may be largely due to the fact that men may (correctly) fear that increased parental involvement will translate into a loss of their power over women. But she also argues that increased paternal involvement in child care will not become a widespread reality unless and until the structural preconditions—especially economic equality for women—exist. Indeed, Rosanna Hertz (1986) found in her study of upper-middle class "dual career families" that a more egalitarian division of family labor sometimes developed as a rational (and constantly negotiated) response to a need to maintain his career, her career, and the family. In other words, career and pay equality for women was a structural precondition for the development of equality between husbands and wives in the family.

However, Hertz notes two reasons why this is a very limited and flawed equality. First, Hertz's sample of dual-career families in which the women and the men made roughly the same amount of money is still extremely atypical. In two-income families, the husband is far more likely to have the higher income. Women are far more likely than men to work part-time jobs, and among full-time workers, women still earn about sixty-five cents to the male dollar and are commonly segregated in lower paid, lower status, dead-end jobs (Blum, 1991; Reskin & Roos, 1990). As a result, most women are not in the structural position to be able to bargain with their husbands for more egalitarian divisions of labor in the home. As Hochschild's (1989) research demonstrates, middle-class women's struggles for equity in the home are often met by their husbands' "quiet resistance," which sometimes lasts for years. A woman is left with the choice of either leaving the relationship (and suffering not only the emotional upheaval, but also the downward mobility, often into poverty, that commonly follows divorce) or capitulating to the man and quietly working her "second shift" of family labor.

Second, Hertz observes that the roughly egalitarian family division of labor among some upper-middle-class dual-career couples is severely shaken when a child is born into the family. Initially, new mothers are more likely than fathers to put their careers on hold. But eventually many resume their careers, as the child care and much of the home labor is performed by low-paid employees, almost always women, and often immigrant women and/or women of color. The construction of the dual-career couple's "gender equality" is thus premised on the family's privileged position within a larger structure of social inequality. In other words, some of the upper-middle-class woman's gender oppression is, in effect, bought off with her class privilege, while the man is let off the hook from his obligation to fully participate in child care and housework. The upper-middle-class father is likely to be more involved with his children today than his father was with him, and this will likely enrich his life. But given the fact that the day-to-day and moment-to-moment care and nurturance of his children is still likely to be performed by women (either his wife and/or a hired, lower-class woman), "the contemporary revalorisation of fatherhood has enabled many men to have the best of both worlds" (Segal, 1990, p. 58). The cultural image of the New Father has given the middle-class father license to choose to enjoy the emotional fruits of parenting, but his position of class and gender privilege allows him the resources with which he can buy or negotiate his way out of the majority of second shift labor.

In sum, as a widespread empirical reality, the emotionally expressive, nurturant, egalitarian New Man does not actually exist; he is an ideological construct, made up of disparate popular images that are saturated with meanings that express the anxieties, fears, and interests of relatively privileged men. But this is not to say that some changes are not occurring among certain groups of privileged men (Segal, 1990). Some men are expressing certain feelings that were, in the past, considered outside the definition of hegemonic masculinity. Some men are reexamining and changing their relationships with other men. Some men are participating more—very equitably in some cases, but marginally in many others—in the care and nurturance of children. But the key point is that when examined within the context of these men's positions in the overall structure of power in society, these changes do not appear to challenge or undermine men's power. On the contrary, the cultural image of the New Man and the partial and fragmentary empirical changes that this image represents serve to file off some of the rough edges of hegemonic masculinity in such a way that the possibility of a happier and healthier life for men is created, while deflecting or resisting feminist challenges to men's institutional power and privilege. But because at least verbal acceptance of the "New Woman" is an important aspect of this reconstructed hegemonic masculinity, the ideological image of the New Man requires a counterimage against which to stand in opposition. Those aspects of traditional hegemonic masculinity that the New Man has rejected— overt physical and verbal displays of domination, stoicism and emotional inexpressivity, overt misogyny in the workplace and at home—are now increasingly projected onto less privileged groups of men: working-class men, gay body-builders, black athletes, Latinos, and immigrant men.

MEXICAN IMMIGRANT MEN

According to the dominant cultural stereotype, Latino men's "machismo" is supposedly characterized by extreme verbal and bodily expressions of aggression toward other men, frequent drunkenness, and sexual aggression and dominance expressed toward normally "submissive" Latinas. Manuel Peña's (1991) research on the workplace culture of male undocumented Mexican immigrant agricultural workers suggests that there is a great deal of truth to this stereotype. Peña examined the Mexican immigrant male's participation in the *charritas coloradas* (red jokes) that characterize the basis of his workplace culture. The most common basis of humor in the *charritas* is sexualized "sadism toward women and symbolic threats of sodomy toward other males" (Paredes, 1966, p. 121).

On the surface, Peña argues, the constant "half-serious, half-playful duels" among the men, as well as the images of sexually debased "perverted wenches" and "treacherous women" in the *charritas*, appear to support the stereotype of the Mexican immigrant male group as being characterized by a high level of aggressive masculine posturing with shared antagonisms and hatred directed toward women. But rather than signifying a fundamental hatred of women, Peña argues that these men's public displays of machismo should be viewed as a defensive reaction to their oppressed class status:

> As an expression of working-class culture, the folklore of machismo can be considered a realized signifying system [that] points to, but simultaneously displaces, a class relationship and its attendant conflict. At the same time, it introduces a third element, the gender relationship, which acts as a mediator between the signifier (the folklore) and the signified (the class relationship). (Peña, 1991, p. 40)

Undocumented Mexican immigrant men are unable to directly confront their class oppressors, so instead, Peña argues, they symbolically displace their class antagonism into the arena of gender relations. Similar arguments have been made about other groups of men. For instance, David Collinson (1988) argues that Australian male blue-collar workers commonly engage in sexually aggressive and misogynist humor as an (ultimately flawed) means of bonding together to resist the control of management males (who are viewed, disparagingly, as feminized). Majors and Billson (1992) argue that young black males tend to embody and publicly display a "cool pose," an expressive and often sexually aggressive style of masculinity that acts as a form of resistance to racism. These studies make important strides toward building an understanding of how subordinated and marginalized groups of men tend to embody and publicly display styles of masculinity that at least symbolically resist the various forms of oppression that they face within hierarchies of intermale dominance. These studies all share the insight that the public faces of subordinated groups of men are *personally and collectively constructed performances of masculine gender display*. By contrast, the public face of the New Man (his "sensitivity," etc.) is often assumed to be one-and-the-same as who he "is," rather than being seen as a situationally constructed public gender display.

Yet in foregrounding the oppression of men by men, these studies risk portraying aggressive, even misogynist, gender displays primarily as liberatory forms of resistance against class and racial oppression (e.g., Mirandé, 1982). Though these studies view microlevel gender display as constructed within a context of structured power relations, macrolevel gender relations are rarely viewed as a constituting dynamic within this structure. Rather gender is commonly viewed as an epiphenomenon, an effect of the dominant class and/or race relations. What is obscured, or even drops out of sight, is the feminist observation that masculinity itself is a form of domination over women. As a result, women's actual experiences of oppression and victimization by men's violence are conspicuously absent from these analyses, thus leaving the impression that misogyny is merely a symbolic displacement of class (or race) antagonism. What is needed, then, is an examination of masculine gender display and power within the context of intersecting systems of class, race, and gender relations (Baca Zinn, Cannon, Higginbotham, & Dill, 1986; Collins, 1990). In the following section we will consider recent ethnographic research on Mexican immigrant communities that suggests that gender dynamics help to constitute the immigration process and, in turn, are reconstituted during and following the immigrant settlement process.

The Rhetoric of Return Migration as Gender Display

Mexican immigrant men who have lived in the United States for long periods of time frequently engage in the rhetoric of return migration. These stated preferences are not necessarily indicative of what they will do, but they provide some telling clues to these men's feelings and perceptions about their lives as marginalized men in the United States. Consider the following statements:[4]

> I've passed more of my life here than in Mexico. I've been here for thirty-one years. I'm not putting down or rejecting this country, but my intentions have always been to return to Mexico . . . I'd like to retire there, perhaps open a little business. Maybe I could buy and sell animals, or open a restaurant. Here I work for a big company, like a slave, always watching the clock. Well I'm bored with that.

> I don't want to stay in the U.S. anymore. [Why not?] Because here I can no longer find a good job. Here, even if one is sick, you must report for work. They don't care. I'm fed up with it. I'm tired of working here too. Here one must work daily, and over there with my mother, I'll work for four, maybe five months, and then I'll have a four- or five-month break without working. My mother is old and I want to be with the family. I need to take care of the rancho. Here I have nothing. I don't have my own house, I even share the rent! What am I doing here?

> I would like to return, but as my sons are born here, well that is what detains me here. Otherwise, I would go back to Mexico . . . Mexico is now in a very inflationary situation. People come here not because they like it, but because the situation causes them to do so, and it makes them stay here for years and years. As the song says, this is a cage made of gold, but it is still a cage.

These statements point to disappointments with migration. In recent years, U.S.-bound migration has become institutionalized in many areas of Mexico, representing a rite of passage for many young, single men (Davis, 1990; Escobar, Gonzalez de la Rocha, & Roberts, 1987). But once in the United States the accomplishment of masculinity and maturity hinges on living up to the image of a financially successful migrant. If a man returns homes penniless, he risks being seen as a failure or a fool. As one man explained: "One cannot go back without anything, because people will talk. They'll say 'oh look at this guy, he sacrificed and suffered to go north and he has nothing to show for it.' "

Although most of these men enjoyed a higher standard of living in the United States than in Mexico, working and settling in the United States significantly diminished their patriarchal privileges. Although the men compensated by verbally demonstrating their lack of commitment to staying in the United States, most of these men realized that their lives remained firmly anchored in the United States and that they lacked the ability to return. They could not acquire sufficient savings in the public sphere to fund return migration, and in the domestic sphere, they did not command enough authority over their wives or children, who generally wished to remain in the United States, to coerce the return migration of their families. Although Mexican immigrant men blamed the terms of U.S. production as their reason for wanting to return to Mexico, we believe that their diminished patriarchal privileges significantly fueled this desire to return.[5] Here, we examine the diminution of patriarchy in three arenas: spatial mobility, authority in family decision-making processes, and household labor.

Mexican immigrant men, especially those who were undocumented and lacked legal status privileges, experienced limited spatial mobility in their daily lives and this compromised their sense of masculinity (Rouse, 1990). As undocumented immigrants, these men remained fearful of apprehension by the Immigration Naturalization Service and by the police.[6] In informal conversations, the men often shared experiences with police harassment and racial discrimination. Merely "looking Mexican," the men agreed, was often cause for suspicion. The jobs Mexican immigrant men commonly took also restricted their spatial mobility. As poor men who worked long hours at jobs as gardeners, dishwashers, or day laborers, they had very little discretionary income to afford leisure activities. As one man offered, "Here my life is just from work to the home, from work to the home."

Although the men, together with their families, visited parks, shops, and church, the public spaces open to the men alone were typically limited to street corners and to a few neighborhood bars, pool halls, and doughnut shops. As Rouse (1990) has argued, Mexican immigrant men, especially those from rural areas, resent these constrictions on their public space and mobility and attempt to reproduce public spaces that they knew in Mexico in the context of U.S. bars and pool halls. In a California immigrant community Rouse observed that "men do not come to drink alone or to meet with a couple of friends . . . they move from table to table, broadening the circuits of information in which they participate and modulating social relationships across the widest possible range." Although these men tried to create new spaces where they might recapture a public sense of self, the goal was not so readily achieved. For many men, the loss of free and easy mobility signified their loss of publicly accorded status and recognition. One man, a junkyard assembler who had worked in Mexico as a rural *campesino* (peasant), recalled that in his Mexican village he enjoyed a modicum of public recognition: "I would enter the bars, the dances, and when I entered everyone would stand to shake my hand as though I were somebody—not a rich man, true, but I was famous. Wherever you like, I was always mentioned. Wherever you like, everyone knew me back there." In metropolitan areas of California, anonymity replaced public status and recognition.

In Mexico many of these men had acted as the undisputed patriarchs in major family decision-making processes, but in the United States they no longer retained their monopoly on these processes. When families were faced with major decisions—such as whom to seek for legal help, whether or not to move to another town, or the decision to lend money or make a major purchase—spousal negotiation replaced patriarchal exertions of authority. These processes did not go uncontested, and some of the decision-making discussions were more conflictual than harmonious, but collaboration, not domination, characterized them.

This trend toward more egalitarian patterns of shared authority often began with migration. In some families, men initially migrated north alone, and during their absences, the women acted decisively and autonomously as they performed a range of tasks necessary to secure family sustenance. Commentators have referred to this situation as one in which "thousands of wives in the absence of their husbands must 'take the reigns' " (Mummert, 1988, p. 283) and as one in which the wives of veteran migrants experience "a freedom where women command (*una libertad donde mujeres mandan*)" (Baca & Bryan, 1985). This trend toward more shared decision making continued after the women's migration and was also promoted by migration experiences as well as the relative increase in women's and the decrease in men's economic contributions to the family (Hondagneu-Sotelo, 1992). As the balance of relative resources and contributions shifted, the women assumed more active roles in key decision-making processes. Similar shifts occurred with the older children, who were now often reluctant to subordinate their earnings and their autonomy to a patriarchal family hierarchy. As one man somewhat reluctantly, but resignedly, acknowledged:

"Well, each person orders one's self here, something like that . . . Back there [Mexico], no. It was still whatever I said. I decided matters."

The household division of labor is another arena that in some cases reflected the renegotiation of patriarchal relations. Although most families continued to organize their daily household chores along fairly orthodox, patriarchal norms, in some families—notably those in which the men had lived for many years in "bachelor communities" where they learned to cook, iron, and make tortillas—men took responsibility for some of the housework. In these cases, men did part of the cooking and housework, they unselfconsciously assumed the role of hosts in offering guests food and beverages, and in some instances, the men continued to make tortillas on weekends and special occasions. These changes, of course, are modest if judged by ideal standards of feminist egalitarianism, but they are significant when compared to patriarchal family organization that was normative before immigration.

This movement toward more egalitarian divisions of labor in some Mexican immigrant households cannot be fully explained by the men's acquisition of household skills in bachelor communities. (We are reminded, for instance, of several middle-class male friends of ours who lived in "bachelor" apartments during college, and after later marrying, conveniently "forgot" how to cook, wash clothes, and do other household chores.) The acquisition of skills appears to be a necessary, but not a sufficient, condition for men's greater household labor participation in reunited families.

A key to the movement toward greater equality within immigrant families was the change in the women's and men's relative positions of power and status in the larger social structure of power. Mexican immigrant men's public status in the United States is very low, due to racism, insecure and low-paying jobs, and (often) illegal status. For those families that underwent long periods of spousal separation, women often engaged in formal- or informal-sector paid labor for the first time, developed more economic skills and autonomy, and assumed control over household affairs. In the United States nearly all of the women sought employment, so women made significant economic contributions to the family. All of these factors tend to erode men's patriarchal authority in the family and empower women to either directly challenge that authority or at least renegotiate "patriarchal bargains" (Kandiyoti, 1988) that are more palatable to themselves and their children.

Although it is too soon to proclaim that gender egalitarianism prevails in interpersonal relations among undocumented Mexican immigrants, there is a significant trend in that direction. This is indicated by the emergence of a more egalitarian household division of labor, by shared decision-making processes, and by the constraints on men's and expansion of women's spatial mobility. Women still have less power than men, but they generally enjoy more than they previously did in Mexico. The stereotypical image of dominant macho males and submissive females in Mexican immigrant families is thus contradicted by actual research with these families.

MASCULINE DISPLAYS AND RELATIVE POWER

We have suggested that men's overt public displays of masculine bravado, interpersonal dominance, misogyny, embodied strength, and so forth are often a sign of a lack of institutional power and privilege, vis-à-vis other men. Though it would be a mistake to conclude that Mexican immigrant men are not misogynist (or, following Peña, that their misogyny is merely a response to class oppression), there is considerable evidence that their actual relations with women in families—at least when measured by family divisions of labor and decision-making processes—are becoming more egalitarian than they were in Mexico. We have also argued that for more privileged men, public displays of sensitivity might be read as signs of class/race/gender privilege and power over

Table 20.1 Comparison of Public and Domestic Gender Displays of White, Class-Privileged Men and Mexican Immigrant Men

	Public		Domestic	
	Power/Status	*Gender Display*	*Power/Status*	*Gender Display*
White, class-privileged men	High, built into position	"Sensitive," little overt misogyny	High, based on public status/high income	"Quiet control"
Mexican immigrant men	Low (job status, pay, control of work, legal rights, public status)	"Hombre": verbal misogyny, embodied toughness in work/ peer culture	Contested, becoming more egalitarian	Exaggerated symbols of power and authority in family

women and (especially) over other men (see Table 20.1 for a summary comparison of these two groups).

Coltrane (1992) argues that in nonindustrial societies, "men's displays of dominance confirm and reinforce existing property relations rather than compensate for a lack of control over valued resources" (pp. 102–103). His claim that men's *control* (rather than lack of control) of resources is correlated with more extreme microdisplays of masculinity seems, at first, to contradict findings by Peña, Collinson, and Billson and Majors, who claim that in industrial societies, *lack* of access to property and other material resources by Mexican immigrant, working-class, and black males correlates with more overt outward displays of aggressive, misogynist masculinity. The key to understanding this apparent contradiction is that Coltrane is discussing societies where women enjoy high social status, where men are highly involved in child care, and where women have a great deal of control over property and other material resources. In these types of societies, men do not "need" to display dominance and masculine bravado. But in complex, stratified societies where the standards of hegemonic masculinity are that a man should control resources (and other people), men who do not have access to these standards of masculinity thus tend to react with displays of toughness, bravado, "cool pose," or "hombre" (Baca Zinn, 1982).

Marginalized and subordinated men, then, tend to overtly display exaggerated embodiments and verbalizations of masculinity that can be read as a desire to express power over others within a context of relative powerlessness. By contrast, many of the contemporary New Man's highly celebrated public displays of sensitivity can be read as a desire to project an image of egalitarianism within a context where he actually enjoys considerable power and privilege over women and other men. Both groups of men are "displaying gender," but the specific forms that their masculine displays take tend to vary according to their relative positions in (a) the social structure of men's overall power relationship to women and (b) the social structure of some men's power relationships with other men.

CONCLUSION

We have argued for the importance of viewing microlevel gender displays of different groups of men within the context of their positions in a larger social structure of power. Too often critical discussions of masculinity tend to project atavistic, hypermasculine, aggressive, misogynist masculinity onto relatively powerless men. By comparison, the masculine gender displays of educated, privileged New Men are too often uncritically applauded, rather than skeptically and critically examined. We have suggested that when analyzed within a structure of power, the gender displays of the New Man might best be seen as strategies to reconstruct hegemonic masculinity by projecting aggression, domination, and misogyny onto subordinate groups of men. Does this mean that all of men's changes today are merely symbolic and ultimately do not contribute to the types of changes in gender relations that feminists have called for? It may appear so, especially if social scientists continue to collude with this reality by theoretically framing shifts in styles of hegemonic masculinity as indicative of the arrival of a New Man, while framing marginalized men as Other— as atavistic, traditional men. Instead, a critical/feminist analysis of changing masculinities in the United States might begin with a focus on the ways that marginalized and subordinated masculinities are changing.

This shift in focus would likely accomplish three things: First, it would remove hegemonic masculinity from center stage, thus taking the standpoints of oppressed groups of men as central points of departure. Second, it would require the deployment of theoretical frameworks that examine the ways in which the politics of social class, race, ethnicity, and sexuality interact with those of gender (Baca Zinn, Cannon, Higginbotham, & Dill, 1986; Collins, 1990; Harding, 1986; Hondagneu-Sotelo, 1992; Messner, 1990). Third, a sociology of masculinities that starts from the experience of marginalized and subordinated men would be far more likely to have power and politics—rather than personal styles or lifestyles—at its center. This is because men of color, poor and working-class men, immigrant men, and gay men are often in very contradictory positions at the nexus of intersecting systems of domination and subordination. In short, although they are oppressed by class, race, and/or sexual systems of power, they also commonly construct and display forms of masculinity as ways of resisting other men's power over them, as well as asserting power and privilege over women. Thus, to avoid reverting to the tendency to view masculinity simply as a defensive reaction to other forms of oppression, it is crucial in such studies to keep women's experience of gender oppression as close to the center of analysis as possible. This sort of analysis might inform the type of progressive coalition building that is necessary if today's changing masculinities are to contribute to the building of a more egalitarian and democratic world.

NOTES

The authors thank Harry Brod, Scott Coltrane, and Michael Kaufman for helpful comments on earlier versions of this chapter.

1. This section of the chapter is adapted from Messner (1993).
2. It is significant, we suspect, that the examples cited of Reagan, Jordan, and Schwartzkopf publicly weeping occurred at moments of *victory* over other men in war and sport.
3. Our speculation on the class and racial bias of the mythopoetic men's movement and on the appeal of the movement to participants is supported, in part, by ongoing (but as yet unpublished) research by sociologist Michael Schwalbe. Schwalbe observes that the "wounds" of these men are very real, because a very high proportion of them are children of alcoholic parents and/or were victims of childhood sexual abuse or other forms of violence. Many are involved in recovery programs.
4. Material in this section is drawn from Hondagneu-Sotelo's study of long-term undocumented immigrant settlers, based on 18 months of field research in a Mexican undocumented immigrant community. See Hondagneu-Sotelo (1994). *Gendered Transitions: Mexican Experiences of Immigrants.* Berkeley: University of California Press.
5. For a similar finding and analysis in the context of Dominican immigrants in New York City, see Pessar (1986).
6. This constraint was exacerbated by passage of the Immigration Reform and Control Act of 1986, which imposed employer sanctions and doubly criminalized undocumented immigrants' presence at the workplace.

REFERENCES

Baca, R., & Bryan, D. (1985). Mexican women, migration and sex roles. *Migration Today, 13*, 14–18.

Baca Zinn, M. (1982). Chicano men and masculinity. *Journal of Ethnic Studies, 10*, 29–44.

Baca Zinn, M., Cannon, L. W., Higginbotham, E., & Dill, B. T. (1986). The costs of exclusionary practices in women's studies. *Signs: Journal of Women in Culture and Society, 11*, 290–303.

Blum, L. M. (1991). *Between feminism and labor: The significance of the comparable worth movement.* Berkeley: University of California Press.

Bly, R. (1990). *Iron John: A book about men.* Reading, MA: Addison-Wesley.

Brod, H. (1983–1984). Work clothes and leisure suits: The class basis and bias of the men's movement. *Changing Men, 11* (Winter), 10–12, 38–40.

Brod, H. (Ed.) (1987). *The making of masculinities: The new men's studies.* Boston: Allen & Unwin.

Clawson, M. A. (1989). *Constructing brotherhood: Class, gender, and fraternalism.* Princeton, NJ: Princeton University Press.

Collins, P. H. (1990). *Black feminist thought: Knowledge, consciousness, and the politics of empowerment.* Boston: Unwin Hyman.

Collinson, D. L. (1988). "Engineering humor": Masculinity, joking and conflict in shop-floor relations. *Organization Studies, 9*, 181–199.

Coltrane, S. (1992). The micropolitics of gender in nonindustrial societies. *Gender & Society, 6*, 86–107.

Connell, R. W. (1987). *Gender and power.* Stanford, CA: Stanford University Press.

Connell, R. W. (1991a). Live fast and die young: The construction of masculinity among young working-class men on the margin of the labor market. *Australian & New Zealand Journal of Sociology, 27*, 141–171.

Connell, R. W. (1991b). *Men of reason: Themes of rationality and change in the lives of men in the new professions.* Unpublished paper.

Connell, R. W. (1992a). Drumming up the wrong tree. *Tikkun, 7*, 517–530.

Connell, R. W. (1992b). Masculinity, violence, and war. In M. S. Kimmel & M. A. Messner (Eds.), *Men's lives* (2nd ed., pp. 176–182). New York: Macmillan.

Davis, M. (1990). *Mexican voices, American dreams: An oral history of Mexican immigration to the United States.* New York: Henry Holt.

Escobar, A. L., Gonzales de la Rocha, M., & Roberts, B. (1987). Migration, labor markets, and the international economy: Jalisco, Mexico and the United States. In J. Eades (Ed.), *Migrants, workers, and the social order* (pp. 42–64). London: Tavistock.

Farrell, W. (1975). *The liberated man.* New York: Bantam.

Freire, P. (1970). *Pedagogy of the oppressed.* New York: Herder & Herder.

Harding, S. (1986). *The science question in feminism.* Ithaca, NY: Cornell University Press.

Henley, N. M. (1977). *Body politics: Power, sex, and nonverbal communication.* Englewood Cliffs, NJ: Prentice Hall.

Hertz, R. (1986). *More equal than others: Women and men in dual career marriages.* Berkeley: University of California Press.

Hochschild, A. (1989). *The second shift: Working parents and the revolution at home.* New York: Viking.

Hondagneu-Sotelo, P. (1992). Overcoming patriarchal constraints: The reconstruction of gender relations among Mexican immigrant women and men. *Gender & Society, 6*, 393–415.

Kandiyoti, D. (1988). Bargaining with patriarchy. *Gender & Society, 2*, 274–290.

Kann, M. E. (1986). The costs of being on top. *Journal of the National Association for Women Deans, Administrators, & Counselors, 49*, 29–37.

Kaufman, M. (Ed.) (1987). *Beyond patriarchy: Essays by men on pleasure, power, and change.* Toronto: Oxford University Press.

Kimmel, M. S. (1992). Reading men: Men, masculinity, and publishing. *Contemporary Sociology, 21*, 162–171.

La Rossa, R. (1988). Fatherhood and social change. *Family Relations, 37*, 451–457.

Lewis, C. (1986). *Becoming a father.* Milton Keynes, UK: Open University Press.

Lyman, P. (1987). The fraternal bond as a joking relation: A case study of the role of sexist jokes in male group bonding. In M. Kimmel (Ed.), *Changing men: New directions in research on men and masculinities* (pp. 148–163). Newbury Park, CA: Sage.

Machung, A. (1989). Talking career, thinking job: Gender differences in career and family expectations of Berkeley seniors. *Feminist Studies, 15.*

Majors, R., & Billson, J. M. (1992). *Cool pose: The dilemmas of black manhood in America.* New York: Lexington.

Martin, P. Y., & Hummer, R. A. (1989). Fraternities and rape on campus. *Gender & Society, 3*, 457–473.

Messner, M. A. (1990). Men studying masculinity: Some epistemological questions in sport sociology. *Sociology of Sport Journal, 7*, 136–153.

Messner, M. A. (1992). *Power at play: Sports and the problem of masculinity.* Boston: Beacon.

Messner, M. A. (1993). "Changing men" and feminist politics in the U.S. *Theory & Society, 22*, 723–737.

Mirandé, A. (1982). Machismo: Rucas, chingasos y chagaderas. *De Colores: Journal of Chicano Expression and Thought, 6*(1/2), 17–31.

Mummert, G. (1988). Mujeres de migrantes y mujeres migrantes de Michoacán: Nuevos papeles para las que se quedan y para las que se van. In T. Calvo & G. Lopez (Eds.), *Movimientos de población en el occidente de Mexico* (pp. 281–295). Mexico, DF: Centre de'etudes mexicaines et centroamericaines and El colegio de Mexico.

Paredes, A. (1966). The Anglo-American in Mexican folklore. In R. B. Browne & D. H. Wenkelman (Eds.), *New voices in American studies.* Lafayette, IN: Purdue University Press.

Pelka, F. (1991). Robert Bly and Iron John: Bly romanticizes history, trivializes sexist oppression and lays the blame for men's "grief" on women. *On the Issues, 19,* 17–19, 39.

Peña, M. (1991). Class, gender and machismo: The "treacherous women" folklore of Mexican male workers. *Gender & Society, 5,* 30–46.

Pessar, P. (1986). The role of gender in Dominican settlement in the United States. In J. Nash & H. Safa (Eds.), *Women and change in Latin America* (pp. 273–294). South Hadley, MA: Bergin & Garvey.

Reskin, B. F., & Roos, P. A. (1990). *Job queues, gender queues: Explaining women's inroads into male occupations.* Philadelphia: Temple University Press.

Rouse, R. (1990). *Men in space: Power and the appropriation of urban form among Mexican migrants in the United States.* Paper presented March 14 at the Residential College, University of Michigan, Ann Arbor.

Russell, G. (1983). *The changing role of fathers.* London: University of Queensland Press.

Sabo, D. F. (1985). Sport, patriarchy, and male identity: New questions about men and sport. *Arena Review, 9,* 1–30.

Sattel, J. W. (1976). The inexpressive male: Tragedy or sexual politics? *Social Problems, 23,* 469–477.

Segal, L. (1990). *Slow motion: Changing masculinities, changing men.* New Brunswick, NJ: Rutgers University Press.

Sidel, R. (1990). *On her own: Growing up in the shadow of the American dream.* New York: Penguin.

Tolson, A. (1977). *The limits of masculinity: Male identity and women's liberation.* New York: Harper & Row.

Winter, M. F., & Robert, E. R. (1980). Male dominance, late capitalism, and the growth of instrumental reason. *Berkeley Journal of Sociology, 25,* 249–280.

21

Migration and Vietnamese American Women

Remaking Ethnicity

Nazli Kibria

One of the most important and dominant frameworks on immigrant adaptation in the United States is the assimilationist perspective (Gordon 1964; Hirschman 1983; Park and Burgess 1969).[1] A central assumption of this perspective is that immigrant groups gradually become Americanized, that is, they shed their loyalties and connections with the traditional immigrant culture and community and become assimilated into the "melting pot" of America. In this process, women have been seen in two capacities. On the one hand, immigrant women, viewed as staunch supporters of immigrant traditions and culture, have been viewed as barriers to assimilation. Alternatively, they have been seen as important intermediaries or vehicles of integration into the dominant society (see Deutsch 1987:719–720). But regardless of the particular role into which immigrant women are cast, assimilation is viewed as synonymous with greater gender equality. Since immigrant ties are seen as a source of patriarchal oppression—as the group assimilates into American culture, immigrant women are expected to be freed from the shackles of tradition and male authority.

The assimilation model has been subject to a series of sharp and wide-ranging attacks in recent decades (Hirschman 1983; Morawska 1985). One of the fundamental criticisms has been that the characterization of the immigrant assimilation process as one of unilineal, progressive development from the "traditional" to the "modern" is far too simplistic. Instead, scholars have argued for a perspective that recognizes the uneven quality of modernization processes, and the ability of traditional values and institutions to coexist with modern ones. But perhaps the most serious criticism of the assimilation model is that it fails to take into account the distinct situation and experience of people of color within American society. The assimilation model was formulated with reference to the experiences of White European immigrants in the United States. As a result, it neglects the ways in which race shapes the adaptation of minority groups to the dominant society.

Feminist scholarship has both shared and contributed to the critique of the assimilation model. For example, the model's dichotomous characterization of migration as a movement from the "traditional" to the "modern" has been brought under question by studies which show that migration may be detrimental rather than favorable to women's status. In fact, rather than leading to greater gender equality, migration, like economic development, may result in losses for women, in terms of traditional sources of support and power in the domestic sphere as well as access to production processes and thus economic resources (Beneria and Sen 1981; Deutsch 1987). Feminist scholars have also been sensitive to the assimilation model's neglect of racial oppression and its role in shaping the experience of minority groups.

In fact, much recent scholarship on immigrant women has focused not on assimilation processes but on the disadvantaged status of immigrant women within the dominant society. Terms such as "multiple jeopardy" and "triple oppression," signifying the complex intertwining of class, racial-ethnic, and gender oppression, increasingly dominate discussions of racial-ethnic women's experience (Brettell and Simon 1986:10; King 1988). As women, as racial-ethnics, and as inhabitants of the lower rungs of the social class ladder, racial-ethnic women experience multiple disadvantages in the dominant society. This emphasis on the marginal location of racial-ethnic women within dominant society structures has been accompanied by a shift in how scholars view the relationship of racial-ethnic women to their families and communities. These "traditional" institutions are not simply sources of patriarchal oppression. Rather, family and community represent modes of resistance to dominant society constraints, or vehicles by which the minority group struggles to survive (Caulfield 1974; Glenn 1986; Dill 1988). While immigrant women may struggle against the oppression they experience as women within the immigrant family and community, the oppression they experience from the dominant society as members of a racial-ethnic group generates needs and loyalties of a more immediate and pressing nature. Thus, immigrant women may remain attached to, and indeed support, traditional patriarchal family and community structures. This is due not simply to the entrenched cultural beliefs or cultural conservatism of the women, but also to the benefits that they gain from retaining these structures, given the multiple disadvantages they face in the dominant society. In short, for immigrant women, the traditional family and community are ways of surviving and maintaining cultural autonomy in the "new" society. The need to sustain family and community may take priority over the internal struggles against male dominance in the immigrant family and community.

In general, this view of ethnic affiliation—that it is a resource for coping with the dominant society—has become increasingly important in the scholarship on immigration, including studies that are not explicitly concerned with the gendered dimensions of the racial-ethnic experience. Thus many contemporary studies of ethnicity focus on the persistence and adaptive relevance of "traditional" immigrant affiliations (see, for example, Kim 1981; Morawska 1985; Portes and Bach 1985). These studies suggest that immigrant ties may actually be a vehicle for or a product of individual and collective modernization, rather than an impediment or barrier to modernity (Morawska 1985; See and Wilson 1988). Ethnic boundaries are seen as dynamic and situational, and there is an emphasis on the active part played by the immigrant group in generating and shaping group membership. To summarize, from varied and diverse currents in social science scholarship on immigrants, there has emerged a theoretical consensus of sorts about immigrant institutions, one that is critical of the assimilation model. For immigrant women and men, the immigrant family and community are sources of economic, political, and cultural resistance, vehicles for adaptation to the dominant society.

The emphasis on the notion of adaptation that has come to dominate much of the literature on the immigrant experience does, however, raise some critical questions. For one thing, the focus on the adaptive quality of the immigrant family and community has led to a neglect of the divisions and conflicts within these institutions. To see ethnic institutions only as vehicles of resistance to dominant society oppression implies a uniformity and consensuality of experience within the ethnic group. But to what extent is this true—do all participants benefit in the same way from ethnic solidarities? In recent years feminist scholarship has become increasingly critical of the concept of the family or household economy, which assumes that families act in unison and agreement on their economic strategies (Beneria and Roldan 1987). This emphasis on consensus serves to whitewash the conflictual aspects of family life (Beneria and Roldan 1987). However, this critique of familial consensus has not been fully and adequately extended to the study of ethnic ties and institutions. This is so, despite the existence of many studies that document the conflicts and tensions between men and women that have been a part of the political struggles and social movements of racial-ethnic groups (Chow 1987; King 1988; Baca Zinn 1975). In general, it seems essential to acknowledge that women and men may gain vastly different kinds of benefits and rewards from ethnic resources, given the different statuses and powers of women and men in the immigrant family and community. There is evidence, for example, that the ethnic enclave economy, which has been celebrated by scholars as an example of how ethnic ties may function as a resource, confers quite different economic rewards on men and women (Zhou and Logan 1989).

Both sources of oppression—those within and those without—are important in an understanding of immigrant women's experience. But a perspective that acknowledges both the oppressive and the supportive dimensions of the family and community leaves certain questions unanswered. How do immigrant women respond to this division, the "double-edged" quality and meaning of ethnic family and community in their lives? I suggest that it is important to see the immigrant family and community as contested and negotiated arenas. Immigrants play an important part in actively shaping and constructing their ethnic institutions. But these institutions are also gender-contested, that is, arenas of conflict and struggle between men and women. The processes by which the ethnic family and community are shaped and negotiated thus ultimately reflect gender divisions, as men and women clash over the question of how to define and construct family and community. In their struggles, they attempt to gain control of and shape the resources of family and ethnicity, in ways that enhance their interests both as members of the family and community, and as men or women.

The struggle between men and women to shape immigrant institutions will vary in its strength and visibility, depending on the balance of power between women and men in the group. This balance of power is deeply shaped by the comparative access of the immigrant men and women to economic, political, and social resources in the dominant society. Particularly when migration is concurrent with a drastic shift in the resources of women and men relative to each other, the gender-based struggle to control family and community may become especially visible. While men and women jockey to control family and community, to redefine it on their terms, they are also, of course, engaged in a conflict over gender relations—the place and power of men and women within the family and community. As family and community life are reorganized by men and women, their roles and relations also undergo change. Thus the study of change in immigrant family life, gender relations, and ethnic organizations must approach these spheres as deeply intertwined rather than as separate aspects of immigrant life. In my research on Vietnamese Americans, I found the impact of migration on family life and the status of women to be issues of major debate in the ethnic community. For Vietnamese Americans, the future of their family and gender relations has been tied to cultural identity—what it means "to be Vietnamese in America." In other words, the importance and fervor of the debate about family and gender stems in part from the implications of these debates for the core of ethnic identity and meaning itself.

VIETNAMESE AMERICANS AND THE RISE IN WOMEN'S POWER

My research on the adaptive strategies of a community of Vietnamese refugees in Philadelphia revealed some of the ways in which women and men struggled and clashed with each other in efforts to shape the social organization of family and community life. From 1983 to 1985, I gathered information on family life and gender relations through participant observation in household and community settings, as well as in-depth interviews with women and men in the ethnic community.

The Vietnamese of the study were recent immigrants who had arrived in the United States during the late 1970s and early 1980s. Most were from urban, middle-class backgrounds in southern Vietnam. At the time of the study, over 30 percent of the adult men in the households of study were unemployed. Of the men who were employed, over half worked in low-paying, unskilled jobs in the urban service sector or in factories located in the outlying areas of the city. Women tended to work periodically, occupying jobs in the informal economic sector as well as in the urban service economy. Eight of the twelve households had members who collected public assistance. Both the family economy and informal community exchange networks were important means by which the households dealt with economic scarcities. Family and community were of tremendous economic salience to the group, as they were important resources for survival in the face of a rather inhospitable economic and social environment.

As suggested by the high rate of the men's unemployment, settlement in the United States had generated some shifts in power in favor of the women in the group. Traditional Vietnamese family and gender relations were modeled on Confucian principals, which placed women in subordination to men in every aspect of life. A key aspect of the social and economic oppression of women in traditional Vietnamese life was the patrilineal extended household. Its organization dictated that women married at a young age, following which they entered the household of their husband's father. This structure ensured the concentration of economic resources in the hands of men and men's control of women through the isolation of women from their families of origin.[2]

It is important to note the deep-seated changes in traditional family and gender structures in Vietnam during this century. War and urbanization eroded the structure of the patrilineal extended household. While unemployment was high in the cities, men from middle-class backgrounds were able to take advantage of the expansion of middle-level positions in the government bureaucracy and army. Such occupational opportunities were more limited for women: the women study participants indicated that they engaged in seasonal and informal income-generating activities or worked in low-level jobs in the growing war-generated service sector in the cities. The transition from rural to urban life had generated a shift in the basis of men's control over economic and social resources. However, families relied on men's income to maintain a middle-class standard of living. Thus women remained in a position of economic subordination to men, a situation that served to sustain the ideals of the traditional family system and men's authority in the family. Restrictions on women's sexuality were important for middle-class families seeking to distinguish themselves from the lower social strata. My data suggest that families were especially conscious of the need to distance themselves from poorer "fallen" women who had become associated with the prostitution generated by the American military presence.

Within the Vietnamese American community of study, I found several conditions that were working to undermine the bases on which male authority had rested in Vietnam. Most important, for the Vietnamese men, the move to the United States had involved a profound loss of social and economic status. Whereas in pre-1975 Vietnam the men held middle-class occupations, in the United States they had access to largely unskilled, low-status, and low-paying jobs. Also, because of their difficulties with English and their racial-ethnic status, the men found themselves disadvantaged within social arenas of the dominant society. Compounding these problems was the dearth of strong formal ethnic organizations in the community that could have served as a vehicle for the men's political assertion into the dominant society.

As a result of these losses, the comparative access of men and women to the resources of the dominant society had to some extent become equalized. In contrast to the experiences of the men, migration had not significantly altered the position of the women in the economy. As in Vietnam, the women tended to work sporadically, sometimes in family businesses or, more commonly, in temporary jobs in the informal and service-sector economies of the city. However, the economic contributions of women to the family budget had risen in proportion to those of the men. I have suggested that in modern, urban South Vietnam the force and legitimacy of male authority had rested heavily on the ability of men to ensure a middle-class status and standard of living for their families. In the United States, the ability of men to fulfill this expectation had been eroded. Among the men, there was widespread concern about the consequences of this situation for their status in the family, as is revealed by the words of a former lieutenant of the South Vietnamese army: "In Vietnam, the man earns and everyone depends on him. In most families, one or two men could provide for the whole family. Here the man finds he can never make enough money to take care of the family. His wife has to work, his children have to work, and so they look at him in a different way. The man isn't strong anymore, like he was in Vietnam."

Such changes had opened up the possibilities for a renegotiation of gender relations, and were the cause of considerable conflict between men and women in the family and community. The shifts in power had also enhanced the ability of women to construct and channel familial and ethnic resources in ways that they chose. Previously I suggested that the changes in the balance of power between men and women generated by migration are crucial to understanding the manner and degree to which immigrant family and community reveal themselves to be gender contested. How, then, did the fairly drastic shift in the gender balance of power among the Vietnamese Americans reflect itself in the ability of the men and women in this group to influence family and community life? In the following section, I describe some of the ways in which gender interests and conflict shaped family and community life for the Vietnamese Americans.

FAMILY AND ETHNICITY AS GENDER-CONTESTED

One of the most intriguing and important strategies of Vietnamese American adaptation that I observed was the rebuilding of kinship networks. Family ties had undergone tremendous disruption in the process of escape from Vietnam and resettlement in the United States. Despite this, the households of the group tended to be large and extended. The process by which household growth occurred was one in which the study participants actively worked to reconstruct family networks by building kin relationships. In order for this to take place, the criteria for inclusion in the family had become extremely flexible. Thus close friends were often incorporated into family groups as fictive kin. Also, relationships with relatives who were distant or vaguely known in Vietnam were elevated in importance. Perhaps most important for women, the somewhat greater significance traditionally accorded to the husband's kin receded in importance.[3] Given the scarcity of relatives in the United States, such distinctions were considered a luxury, and the demands of life made the rebuilding of family a valuable, if not a necessary, step in the process of adaptation to the dominant society.

While important for the group as a whole, the reconstruction of kinship as it took place had some special advantages for women. One consequence of the more varied and inclusive nature of the kinship network was that women were rarely surrounded exclusively by the husband's relatives and/or friends. As a result, they were often able to turn to close fictive kin and perhaps members of their families of origin for support during conflicts with men in the family. Another condition that enhanced the power of married women in the family was that few had to deal with a mother-in-law's competing authority in the household, because elderly women have not been among those likely to leave Vietnam.

The reconstruction of kinship thus had important advantages for women, particularly as it moved the Vietnamese perhaps even further from the ideal model of the patrilineal extended household than they had been in the past. But women were not simply passive beneficiaries of the family rebuilding process. Rather, they played an active part in family reconstruction, attempting to shape family boundaries in ways that were to their advantage. I found women playing a vital part in creating fictive kin by forging close ties. And women were often important, if not central, "gatekeepers" to the family group and household. Thus the women helped to decide such matters as whether the marriage of a particular family member was a positive event and could be taken as an opportunity to expand kinship networks. At other times the women passed judgment on current or potential family members, as to whether they had demonstrated enough commitment to such important familial obligations as the sharing of economic and social resources with kin.

Although women undoubtedly played an important part in family reconstruction, their control over decisions about family membership was by no means exclusive or absolute. In fact, the question of who was legitimately included in the family group was often a source of tension within families, particularly between men and women. The frequency of disputes over this issue stemmed in part from the fluidity and subsequent uncertainty about family boundaries, as well as the great pressures often placed on individuals to subordinate their needs to those of the family collective. Beyond this, I also suggest that disputes over boundaries arose from the fundamental underlying gender divisions in the family. That is, the different interests of women and men in the family spurred efforts to shape the family in ways that were of particular advantage to them. For the reasons I have previously discussed, the Vietnamese American women had greater influence and opportunity in the shaping of family in the United States than they had in the past. The women tended to use this influence to construct family groups that extended their power in the family.

In one case that I observed, considerable tension developed between a couple named Nguyet and Phong concerning the sponsorship[4] of Nguyet's nephew and his family from a refugee camp in Southeast Asia. Nguyet and Phong had been together with their three children (two from Nguyet's previous marriage) for about seven years, since they had met in a refugee camp in Thailand. Phong remained married to a woman who was still living in Vietnam with his children, a fact that was the source of some stress for Nguyet and Phong. The issue of the nephew's sponsorship seemed to exacerbate tensions in the relationship. Phong did not want to undertake the sponsorship because of the potentially heavy financial obligations it entailed. He also confessed that he was worried that Nguyet would leave him after the nephew's arrival, a threat often made by Nguyet during their quarrels. Finally, he talked of how Nguyet's relationship with the nephew was too distant to justify the sponsorship. Nguyet had never even met the nephew, who was the son of a first cousin rather than of a sibling.

Confirming some of Phong's fears, Nguyet saw the presence of the nephew and his family as a potentially important source of support for herself. She spoke of how she had none of "my family" in the country, in comparison with Phong, whose sister lived in the city. She agreed that she did not know much about her nephew, but nonetheless felt that his presence would ease her sense of isolation and also would provide a source of aid if her relationship with Phong deteriorated. Eventually she proceeded with the sponsorship, but only after a lengthy dispute with Phong.

While the issue of sponsorship posed questions about kinship in an especially sharp manner, there were other circumstances in which women and men clashed over family boundaries. When kin connections could not be questioned (for example, in the case of a sibling), what came under dispute was the commitment of the particular person involved to familial norms and obligations. One of my woman respondents fought bitterly with her older brother about whether their male cousin should live with them. Her brother objected to the cousin's presence in the household on the grounds that he had not responded to their request for a loan of money two years ago. The woman respondent wanted to overlook this breach of conduct because of her extremely close relationship with the cousin, who had been her "best friend" in Vietnam.

Regardless of the particular circumstances, gender conflict seemed an important part of the family reconstruction process. Women and men shared an interest in creating and maintaining a family group that was large and cohesive enough to provide economic and social support. However, their responses to the family reconstruction process were framed by their differing interests, as men and women, within the family. Men and women attempted to channel family membership in ways that were to their advantage, such that their control over the resources of the family group was enhanced.

Gender divisions and conflicts also entered into the community life of the group. The social networks of the Vietnamese American women were central to the dynamics and organization of the ethnic community. They served to organize and regulate exchange between households. While "hanging out" at informal social gatherings, I observed women exchanging information, money, goods, food, and tasks such as child care and cooking. Given the precarious economic situation of the group, these exchanges played an important role in ensuring the economic survival and stability of the households. The women's centrality to these social networks gave them the power not only to regulate household exchange but also to act as agents of social control in the community in a more general sense. I found that women, through the censure of gossip and the threat of ostracism, played an important part in defining community norms. In short, the relative rise in power that had accrued to the Vietnamese American women as a result of migration expressed itself in their considerable influence over the organization and dynamics of the ethnic community. Like kinship, community life was a negotiated arena, one over which women and men struggled to gain control.

The gender-contested quality of ethnic forms was also apparent in the efforts of women to reinterpret traditional Vietnamese familial ideologies on their own terms. In general, the Vietnamese American women continued to espouse and support traditional ideologies of gender relations as important ideals. For example, when asked during interviews to describe the "best" or ideal roles of men and women in the family, most of my respondents talked of a clear division of roles in which women assumed primary responsibility for maintaining the home and taking care of the children, and men for the economic support of the family. Most felt that household decisions should be made jointly, although the opinion of the man was seen to carry more weight. About half of those interviewed felt that a wife should almost always obey her husband. Even more widespread were beliefs in the importance of restrictions on female (but not male) sexuality before marriage.

While women often professed such beliefs, their relationship to traditional ideologies was active rather than passive and inflexible. In other words, the women tended to emphasize certain aspects of the traditional familial ideology over others. In particular, they emphasized parental authority and the obligation of men to sacrifice individual needs and concerns in order to fulfill the needs of the family, traditional precepts they valued and hoped to preserve in the United States. The women's selective approach to Vietnamese "tradition" emerged most clearly in situations of conflict between men and women in the family. In such disputes, women selectively used the traditional ideologies to protect themselves and to legitimate their actions and demands (Kibria 1990). Thus, husbands who beat their wives were attacked by other women in the community on the grounds that they (the husbands) were inadequate breadwinners. The women focused not on the husband's treatment of his wife but on his failure to fulfill his family caretaker role. Through this selective emphasis, the women managed to condemn the delinquent husband without appearing to depart from "tradition." In short, for the Vietnamese American women, migration had resulted in a greater ability to shape family and community life.

CONCLUSION

For immigrant women, ethnic ties and institutions may be both a source of resistance and support, and of patriarchal oppression. Through an acknowledgment of this duality we can arrive at a fuller understanding of immigrant women's lives: one that captures the multifaceted constraints as well as the resistances that are offered by immigrant women to the oppressive forces in their lives. In patterns similar to those noted in studies of other racial-ethnic groups (Stack 1976; Baca Zinn 1975), the Vietnamese Americans presented here relied on family and community for survival and resistance. Their marginal status made the preservation of these institutions an important priority.

Like other racial-ethnic women, the ability of the Vietnamese American women to shape ethnicity was constrained by their social-structural location in the dominant society. These women saw the traditional family system as key to their cultural autonomy and economic security in American society. Migration may have equalized the economic resources of the men and women, but it had not expanded the economic opportunities of the women enough to make independence from men an attractive economic reality. The Vietnamese American women, as is true for other women of color, were especially constrained in their efforts to "negotiate" family and community in that they faced triple disadvantages (the combination of social class, racial-ethnic, and gender statuses) in their dealings with the dominant society.

Recognition of the role of ethnic institutions in facilitating immigrant adaptation and resistance is essential. However, it is equally important not to lose sight of gender divisions and conflicts, and the ways in which these influence the construction of ethnic institutions. Feminist scholars have begun to explore the diverse ways in which immigrant women manipulate family and community to enhance their own power, albeit in ways that are deeply constrained by the web of multiple oppressions that surround them (Andezian 1986; Bhachu 1986; Kibria 1990). Such work begins to suggest the complexity of immigrant women's relationship to ethnic structures, which is informed by both strength and oppression.

NOTES

1. My definition of the assimilationist model includes its subvariations, such as "cultural pluralism" and "Anglo conformity."
2. Some scholars stress the fact that the reality of women's lives was far different from that suggested by these Confucian ideals. Women in traditional Vietnam also had a relatively favorable economic position in comparison with Chinese women due to Vietnamese women's rights of inheritance as well as their involvement in commercial activities (see Hickey 1964; Keyes 1977). Despite these qualifications, there is little to suggest that the economic and social subordination of women was not a fundamental reality in Vietnam.
3. Hy Van Luong (1984) has noted the importance of two models of kinship in Vietnamese life, one that is patrilineal in orientation and another in which bilateral kin are of significance. Thus the flexible, encompassing conceptions of family that I found among the study group were not entirely new, but had their roots in Vietnamese life; however, they had acquired greater significance in the context of the United States.
4. Refugee resettlement in the United States involves a system of sponsorship by family members or other interested parties who agree to assume part of the responsibility for taking care of those sponsored for a period of time after their arrival.

REFERENCES

Andezian, Sossie. 1986. "Women's Roles in Organizing Symbolic Life: Algerian Female Immigrants in France." Pp. 254–266 in *International Migration: The Female Experience*, edited by R. J. Simon and C. B. Brettell. Totowa, N.J.: Rowman and Allenheld.

Baca Zinn, Maxine. 1975. "Political Familism: Toward Sex Role Equality in Chicano Families." *Aztlan* 6, no. 1: 13–26.

Beneria, Lourdes, and Martha Roldan. 1987. *The Crossroads of Class and Gender*. Chicago: University of Chicago Press.

Beneria, Lourdes, and Gita Sen. 1981. "Accumulation, Reproduction and Women's Role in Economic Development: Boserup Revisited." *Signs* 7, no. 2 (Winter): 279–298.

Bhachu, Parminder K. 1986. "Work, Dowry and Marriage Among East African Sikh Women in the U.K." Pp. 241–254 in *International Migration: The Female Experience*, edited by R. J. Simon and C. B. Brettell. Totowa, N.J.: Rowman and Allenheld.

Brettell, Caroline B., and Rita J. Simon. 1986. "Immigrant Women: An Introduction." Pp. 3–21 in *International Migration: The Female Experience*, edited by Rita J. Simon and Caroline B. Brettell. Totowa, N.J.: Rowman and Allenheld.

Caulfield, Mina D. 1974. "Imperialism, the Family, and Cultures of Resistance." *Socialist Review* 4, no. 2: 67–85.

Chow, Esther Ngan-Ling. 1987. "The Development of Feminist Consciousness Among Asian American Women." *Gender and Society* 1, no. 3: 284–299.

Deutsch, Sarah. 1987. "Women and Intercultural Relations: The Case of Hispanic New Mexico and Colorado." *Signs* 12: 719–740.

Dill, Bonnie Thornton. 1988. "Our Mothers' Grief: Racial-Ethnic Women and the Maintenance of Families." *Journal of Family History* 13, no. 4: 415–431.

Glenn, Evelyn Nakano. 1986. *Issei, Nissei, War Bride*. Philadelphia: Temple University Press.

——— . 1987. "Gender and the Family." Pp. 348–381 in *Analyzing Gender: A Handbook of Social Science Research*, edited by Beth B. Hess and Myra M. Ferree. Newbury Park, Calif.: Sage.

Gordon, Milton. 1964. *Assimilation in American Life*. New York: Oxford University Press.

Hickey, Gerald C. 1964. *Village in Vietnam*. New Haven: Yale University Press.

Hirschman, Charles. 1983. "America's Melting Pot Reconsidered." *Annual Review of Sociology* 9: 397–423.

Keyes, Charles F. 1977. *The Golden Peninsula*. New York: Macmillan.

Kibria, Nazli. 1990. "Power, Patriarchy and Gender Conflict in the Vietnamese Immigrant Community." *Gender and Society* 4, no. 1 (March): 9–24.

Kim, Ill Soo. 1981. *New Urban Immigrants: The Korean Community in New York*. Princeton: Princeton University Press.

King, Deborah H. 1988. "Multiple Jeopardy, Multiple Consciousness: The Context of a Black Feminist Ideology." *Signs* 14, no. 1: 42–72.

Luong, Hy Van. 1984. " 'Brother' and 'Uncle': An Analysis of Rules, Structural Contradictions and Meaning in Vietnamese Kinship." *American Anthropologist* 86, no. 2: 290–313.

Morawska, Ewa. 1985. *For Bread with Butter*. Cambridge: Cambridge University Press.

Park, Robert, and Ernest Burgess. 1969. *Introduction to the Science of Society*. Student ed. abridged by Morris Janowitz. Chicago: University of Chicago Press.

Portes, Alejandro, and Robert L. Bach. 1985. *Latin Journey: Cubans and Mexican Immigrants in the U.S.* Berkeley: University of California Press.

See, Katherine O'Sullivan, and William J. Wilson. 1988. "Race and Ethnicity." Pp. 223–243 in *Handbook of Sociology*, edited by Neil J. Smelser. Newbury Park, Calif.: Sage.

Stack, Carol. 1974. *All Our Kin*. New York: Harper & Row.

Zhou, Min, and John R. Logan. 1989. "Returns on Human Capital in Ethnic Enclaves: New York City's Chinatown." *American Sociological Review* 54 (October): 809–820.

IV

LIFE AT THE MARGINS: FAMILIES IN EXTREME POVERTY

22

Poverty in the Era of Welfare Reform
The "Underclass" Family in Myth and Reality

Thomas J. Sugrue

In 1996, after pledging to "end welfare as we know it," President Clinton signed into effect a new welfare program that was a radical departure from the past. Certainly, the existing welfare system had major problems. Applicants faced long lines, hostile administrators, probing and personal questions, and arbitrary cutoffs. Furthermore, welfare reached only a portion of the poor. The vast majority of welfare recipients were women with children. Very few men received AFDC monies. Many of the changes that replaced Aid to Families with Dependent Children by the TANF program—Temporary Assistance to Needy Families—grew from a desire to provide poor people with stable, secure, and well-paying jobs (to "make work pay").[1]

To understand why that has not occurred, and cannot occur under existing policies, we need to trace the changes in poverty during the 1970s and 1980s that were the background to the discussion of welfare in the 1990s, and to analyze the growing influence of an ideologically-driven, ahistorical analysis of the causes of poverty. This article describes the obstacles that poor urban families have faced over the last several decades and explains how the causes of poverty were misrepresented by an influential group of social scientists—with consequences that still deform the public understanding of poverty and the political response to it.

By the early 1990s, increasingly isolated by class and race, the families of the urban poor were scraping together a meager existence in areas left behind by investors and denounced or ignored by politicians. One such place was North Philadelphia's Badlands. Home to thousands of black and Hispanic poor people, by the 1990s it was one of hundreds of neighborhoods around the country identified as "high poverty areas"—places where poverty rates exceeded 40 percent and where a majority of the adult population was unemployed. Ringing the once-bustling neighborhood were the shells of abandoned factories, grim reminders of the economic depredations that had reshaped the city. The ghost of a prosperous industrial past hovered over debris-strewn vacant lots, haunting the lives of area residents who remembered the days when union-wage industrial jobs were plentiful. Abandoned houses marred virtually every block, graffiti scarred the ubiquitous red-brick building facades, and crack vials and hypodermic needles lay scattered among broken bottles and shattered car glass along the streets. On the horizon, only a few miles away, Philadelphia's glimmering downtown was more closely connected to New York's stock exchanges, to the money markets of London and Paris, to the courtrooms of Chicago and Washington, than to the gritty postindustrial neighborhoods in its shadow.[2]

Prevailing explanations of the decline of places like the Badlands focus on the behavior and culture of poor people. American social policy is driven by assumptions that urban poverty is the consequence of dysfunctional families, parents who lack the motivation to work, and children who engage in crime and sexual libertinism. Anti-poverty policy rests on the assumption that jobs are plentiful but that poor people need to be inculcated in the values of thrift, deferred gratification, and work discipline. But the plight of families in the Badlands and other urban centers cannot be understood outside of the context of several generations of economic dislocation, political marginalization, and massive capital disinvestment. Residents of America's countless badlands have found themselves increasingly superfluous to the high-tech global labor market. In a suburban-dominated political order, their needs (from infrastructure to human services) have become peripheral to the national political agenda.[3]

The tangled roots of today's urban poverty and family stress can be traced to the interaction of profound economic and demographic changes that began in the seemingly prosperous 1940s and 1950s. American cities lost millions of entry-level jobs, largely in manufacturing, over the next fifty years. Between 1947 and 1977 alone, twelve of the largest Northeastern and Midwestern cities lost 2.1 million manufacturing, wholesale, and retail jobs, while gaining only 316,000 service jobs. The hemorrhage began at the very same time that millions of Southern blacks were pushed out of the South by disruptions in the agricultural economy.[4]

The postwar boom and the emerging civil rights movement led many Southern blacks to hope that they could find steady, secure, and relatively well-paid employment in the Northern cities. But that promise proved to be short-lived. Even as blacks gained new opportunities to join unions and break the color barrier in entering industrial jobs, major employers increasingly relocated production to suburban areas, small towns, and even to sites outside the United States, benefiting whites at the expense of young African-Americans who continued to flock to the cities seeking work.

In the ensuing decades, most new jobs that opened up in major cities were in the service sector. These jobs fell into two distinct categories: high-tech and information-dependent firms like finance, real estate, and the law, attracting highly educated professionals, and menial employment where wages remained low and benefits virtually nonexistent. The leading area of job growth since 1980 has been temporary work, often part-time and usually without benefits. In Philadelphia, like many old industrial cities retooling as entertainment and convention centers, tourist-related employment has boomed. That growth, however, has been concentrated in insecure, difficult, and mostly poorly paying jobs like kitchen help, room cleaning, and janitorial services. An expansion in retail employment, driven by the growth of big box retailers like Wal-Mart, has depended on a supply of low-wage workers.[5]

Meanwhile, persistent income inequality has ravaged American cities. Between 1975 and 1990, the gap between rich and poor widened steadily. The urban real estate boom of the 1990s and early twenty-first century—evidenced by the construction of downtown lofts, condominiums, and apartments—led observers to proclaim that "the city is back," but the benefits of rising property values seldom trickled down into poor neighborhoods. The growing prosperity of gentrified urban neighborhoods was, to a great extent, a manifestation of deepening urban inequalities in wealth and income. As we shall see, welfare reform has done nothing to slow this down. For the poorest segment of the American population, incomes have continued to stagnate. Between 1979 and 2004, using inflation-adjusted dollars, household income for the poorest fifth increased only 6 percent, or $800, compared to a 69 percent or $63,100 increase, for the top fifth. Since 1979, America has had two economic realities: staggering economic advances for the wealthy and bare subsistence for the poorest. By 2004, the average yearly income for the poorest fifth of households in the country was a mere $14,700, in contrast to a remarkable and rising $155,200 for the richest fifth.[6]

Over all these decades, workplace discrimination, despite civil rights legislation and litigation, remained a pressing problem. Weakened by the Supreme Court (but never wholly gutted), affirmative action improved opportunities for many blacks and women, but it was least effective in helping those with low levels of education and few marketable skills. The result was a growing concentration of poorly-educated, low-income residents in cities where jobs were extremely scarce. Anthropologist Katherine Newman found that when a McDonald's in Harlem opened in the mid-1990s, an average of fourteen people applied for every job opening.[7] Interviews with Detroit, Boston, Atlanta, and Los Angeles-area employers show that inner-city blacks have consistently faced, and still face, much suspicion in the hiring office and are regularly turned away by employers who are skeptical about their work skills, motivation, and intellectual ability.[8]

Exacerbating the plight of urban minorities has been the persistence of residential racial segregation. Since World War II, urban blacks (and in many cities the growing Latin American immigrant population) have found themselves trapped in expanding yet increasingly isolated urban ghettos. In the 1960s, 1970s, and 1980s, the real estate market, combined with the legal and extralegal activities of white neighborhood associations, subdivided cities by race and magnified racial tensions. Zoning restrictions kept minorities and the poor out of most suburban communities.[9] Federal and local governments further perpetuated racial divisions in major metropolitan areas by placing public housing in older, predominantly poor sections of cities and bankrolling white suburbanization through racially discriminatory housing subsidies. Despite incremental declines in segregation rates in most major metropolitan areas between 1990 and 2000 most minorities—especially African-Americans—continued to live in racially isolated neighborhoods and attend racially segregated, usually inferior, schools.[10]

By the early 1990s, the interaction of economic restructuring and racial discrimination had devastated the lives of the urban poor. A growing number of poor families were—and remain—entrapped in neighborhoods bereft of economic and social institutions that could help to mitigate poverty. In addition, residence in the inner city steadily became a self-perpetuating stigma, with employers often using place of residence as a means of screening potential workers. Further exacerbating the situation was the uneven economic growth of metropolitan areas. The lion's share of new jobs was created in outlying suburban communities. But most poor people cannot commute to distant suburbs: they often do not have access to reliable automobile transportation. And public transportation has seldom penetrated the suburbs with any degree of effectiveness. It also became increasingly difficult for the urban poor to gain access to information about jobs in suburban locales. More recently, many low-wage employers began to accept only on-line applications, a further barrier to poor people who do not have access to reliable computers.[11]

As one might expect, decades of economic insecurity, underemployment, and joblessness, on top of years of defeats and dashed hopes, proved devastating to poor families. Young men found it more and more difficult to find steady, well paying jobs, particularly at the entry level. Between 1950 and 1985, the proportion of black men aged sixteen to twenty-four who were employed fell from about 70 percent to under 45 percent. Reviewing the evidence on black youth unemployment, labor economists Richard Freeman and Harry Holzer have noted that black youth "are out of work for very long periods of time and that, once non-employed, they have great difficulty securing another job." Since 1985, black male labor force participation has remained low.[12]

Even more destabilizing for urban families—especially African-Americans—was the staggering increase in the number of incarcerated black men that began in the 1970s and accelerated over the next three decades with the dramatic expansion of the prison-industrial complex. In the last decades of the twentieth century, incarceration became the single most important tactic in the "war against crime," but it also had a devastating impact on the health, economic status, and well-being of ex-convicts and their families. At the turn of the twenty-first century, social scientists Michael Katz and Mark Stern found that one-third of black men in their twenties were in jail or on probation or parole. With employers reluctant to hire ex-criminals and many professions forbidden by law from hiring people with criminal records, ex-cons often had no choice but to work off the books or drift back into the underground economy, the only place where they could find work. Both criminals and unemployed ex-cons with children have found it nearly impossible to provide reliable child support, further hindering their families' opportunities for self-sufficiency.[13]

Whatever their values or original intentions, and no matter how strong their love, it is difficult for families with few resources to cope with the emotional costs of long-term joblessness, irregular employment, and financial uncertainty. In poor, inner-city communities, devoid of supportive communal institutions to help families cope and move forward, the strains of dislocation are all the greater. As dozens of ethnographic studies have noted, many inner-city residents have found themselves part of an informal economy over the past 30 years—one that includes under-the-table employment, scavenging of recyclable materials, and often illicit activities including gambling, drug sales, prostitution, and theft. In the Badlands, men tinker with broken-down cars on vacant lots, trading parts and labor, to save expenses. Some women operate unlicensed day care out of their homes, to remain with their children, to assist family members or friends who cannot afford commercial childcare, and to make enough money to survive. Others rely on the unreported income of lovers, sons, and brothers who work the drug trade, one of the neighborhood's few well-paying, if horrifically dangerous, employment opportunities.[14]

Had observers of Philadelphia's Badlands over all these years bothered to look at the historical background of economic disinvestment, racial segregation, and community decline, they would have seen street corners and porch stoops filled not with "lazy bums" and "welfare queens," but men and women who had lost access to the security and relatively stable wages and benefits that their neighborhood's industries once provided. Since then, poor families have been failed by weak schools, and further hobbled by crime and incarceration. Those who have been lucky enough to find work in a still-shrinking labor market are usually trapped in mediocre service-sector jobs, cleaning up attorneys' offices, making hotel beds, staffing the counters in fast-food restaurants, busing tables, doing food preparation work, or working the floors at megastores. In the hostile environment of the inner city and a shrinking labor market dominated by mediocre jobs, maintaining enough income for mere subsistence became far more difficult. The wages of a single breadwinner are often insufficient to pay for adequate housing, food, childcare, and health insurance—especially if that breadwinner is a woman. But since 1979, the wages of two underemployed workers have also been barely enough to pull a family above the poverty line. In 2005, food prep workers in Pennsylvania made only $14,828 per year; retail salespeople earned only $18,783 per year, and janitors garnered a little over $20,000 per year (in part because some janitorial jobs have been unionized). Vulnerable to layoffs and firing, usually without day-care or health benefits, their lives are drained by the nearly impossible struggle to pay monthly rents, utility bills, childcare, and basic food, clothing, and healthcare expenses out of poor wages or meager public assistance payments.[15]

For most of the last two-thirds of the twentieth century, poor families could rely on some support—however meager—from the government to help cushion the effects of poverty. Between 1935 and 1996—when President Clinton signed the law creating TANF, which ended the federal entitlement to income support for impoverished parents—poor people, especially single women with small children, depended on a bundle of federal and local aid programs, most notably Aid to Families with Dependent Children (AFDC) and the General Assistance Program (GA). As noted above, this system had major problems. AFDC and GA payments were extremely low. Indeed, the value of AFDC checks actually fell during most of the 1970s and 1980s. Many welfare recipients held minimum-wage jobs surreptitiously (making them "welfare cheaters"), to avoid losing their benefits and falling even further into poverty. Pennsylvania, like many other penurious states, virtually eliminated its General Assistance program, cutting off all single adults deemed to be "able-bodied" in the early 1980s. Nevertheless, as part of a combination of income sources—legal or under-the-table—welfare and other benefits provided a safety net for poor families.[16]

All that changed in 1996, when decades of clamor for "welfare reform" came to fruition in the TANF legislation. The intentions of many of the architects of this plan were laudable. Most wanted to reduce poverty and encourage work. Yet ending poverty was not even listed as one of the program's primary goals. Instead, the legislation that created TANF talked about fostering personal responsibility and increasing the incidence of marriage. These goals reflected the failure of policy makers to grapple with the wrenching structural changes that had created persistent, concentrated urban poverty. Instead, as the political spectrum in the United States drifted rightward in the 1980s and 1990s, individualistic and moralistic behavioral and cultural explanations of poverty had gradually moved into the mainstream. These explanatory frameworks blamed poverty on the supposed individual irresponsibility and cultural deficits of the poor, and were eventually incorporated into contemporary welfare debate and policymaking.[17] The rest of this article traces the emergence and arguments of the social scientists who popularized these views of poverty.

Welfare reform was a response to decades of political opposition to programs that targeted poor people's needs. But in the 1980s and 1990s a new breed of social scientists provided scholarly legitimation for the effort to reshape the welfare state. They argued that the emergence of the new urban "underclass" had nothing to do with the structural changes described above. Instead, they claimed, "underclass" poverty was rooted in antisocial attitudes and actions. The causes of contemporary poverty could be found in family breakdown, out-of-wedlock childbearing (the old-fashioned term illegitimacy moved back into popular currency in the 1990s), welfare dependence, and a new, violent youth culture. At the root of arguments about the "underclass" was an assumption that female-headed households in the inner city were the primary source of poverty and related social ills. In the hands of these scholars and pundits, the term "underclass" became a powerfully evocative metaphor. Allowing commentators to ignore a reality far more diverse than they care to admit, the term has since become a shorthand way of bundling together America's poor under a label that conjures up images of racial inferiority, violence, family breakdown, and uncontrolled sexuality. In a single word, the term "underclass" encapsulates middle-class Americans' most intimate fears and reaffirms their sense of social and moral superiority.[18]

The emphasis on culture and behavior that emerged in the 1980s in American poverty scholarship and public policy was both a reprise of old themes of morality, virtue, and vice, and a new agenda at the cutting edge of scholarly research. Profound skepticism about the moral capacity of the poor has a long history in Anglo-American political discourse, which is informed by an ethic of self-help and a theory of citizenship that emphasizes personal virtue and responsibility. Reagan-era conservatives advocated a sort of scholarly Calvinism, which presumed the inherent moral depravity of the poor and their susceptibility to the sins of sloth (not working), lust (promiscuous sex and out-of-wedlock pregnancy), and greed (grasping for government handouts).[19] In the early 1980s, Charles Murray and George Gilder—arguably the two most influential right-wing policy theorists even today—argued that "the perverse incentives of welfare" created laziness, dependency, and promiscuity among the poor, all subsidized by taxpayers' money.[20]

Conservative arguments about poverty integrated old racial and ethnic biases into a new narrative about a fearsome underclass created by welfare policy during the New Deal and War on Poverty, from the 1930s through the 1960s. In his widely-read study of poverty and public policy, conservative political scientist Lawrence Mead argued that blacks have a "deep conviction that they have to 'get things from white people' if they are to live a decent life." In Mead's view, residential segregation was the fault of blacks: "If poor blacks functioned better, whites would show less resistance to living among them." Mead also claimed that blacks have abandoned the work ethic of their grandparents' generation. "In that era, working hard and going to church were much of what black culture meant. Today, tragically, it is more likely to mean rock music or the rapping of drug dealers on ghetto street corners. That change rather than any change in the surrounding society seems to lie at the origin of the underclass." New Latin American immigrants are, according to Mead, equally at fault for their impoverishment: they are "less interested in economic progress, suspicious of individual striving, and slower to change."[21]

Somewhat contradictorily, Richard Herrnstein and Charles Murray, authors of the 1994 best-seller, *The Bell Curve*, attributed family breakdown and impoverishment not to abandonment of ancestral values but to the inheritance of intellectual deficiencies. The poor, they asserted—particularly blacks and Hispanics—are simply less intelligent and thus more likely to be at the bottom of the economic ladder.[22]

The right, then, cast its arguments in terms of moral defects and innate deficiencies: poor people are poor because of their lack of motivation, their unwillingness to work, and their propensity to sexual libertinism. Conservative academics and policymakers offered a romantic evocation of the two-parent nuclear family as the exemplar of hard work, sexual restraint, and responsibility. This idealized past stood in sharp contrast to their dire picture of the current single-parent family as the breeder of crime, promiscuity, and laziness. Ignoring the two-parent families that still exist in the inner cities and suffer from many of the same problems that plague single-parent households, they downplayed the practical difficulties of forming or maintaining families under conditions of high unemployment. They overlooked the actual diversity (including the success stories) among many single-parent families. And they argued, with scant evidence, that government policies had actively encouraged the destruction of the "traditional family" by rewarding women for bearing children outside of marriage (see Raley, this volume). In their final analysis, poverty is not rooted in economic and historical forces, but instead is a manifestation of family breakdown. If only we had strong, independent, male-headed families, they argue, these parents would instill in children the values of hard work and self-motivation, breaking the cycle of poverty. The free market, with its abundant jobs, would then readily absorb poor people.[23]

But the political right was not the only group to revive a moral and behavioral analysis of poverty in the years leading up to the creation of TANF. Joining the conservatives were prominent liberal social scientists, most notably William Julius Wilson, Paul Peterson, David Ellwood, Mary Jo Bane, and Christopher Jencks, and journalists such as Ken Auletta and Nicholas Lemann. These liberals offered some qualifications to the dominant conservative framework. They conceded, at least in principle, that poverty is rooted in a changing labor market and that poor people, especially minorities, face barriers to equal opportunity. But as conservatives began to dominate the debate over poverty, liberals also put increasing emphasis on the behavior of the poor. Wilson, for example, combined a thorough analysis of urban industrial decline and joblessness with a discussion of the "pathologies" of the black urban poor such as out-of-wedlock childbearing.[24] Auletta and Lemann wrote moving pseudo-ethnographic accounts of poor families that included alarming depictions of family dysfunctionality, violence, and substance abuse—reinforcing popular beliefs that antisocial

behaviors generated poverty.[25] Peterson acknowledged the impact of discrimination and technological change on the poor, but also focused increasingly on the "perverse incentives" of
welfare.[26]

The work of influential sociologist Christopher Jencks is representative of the generation of
liberal poverty scholars who imported conservative ideas into mainstream policy debates and, in the
process, gained a hearing among policymakers during the Clinton administration. Jencks's work
combined rigorous statistical analysis of economic causes of poverty with a self-described "cultural
conservatism" condemning poor people who do not "follow norms of behavior that most of society
endorses."[27] Ignoring the fact that most children of unwed mothers in the inner cities would be
poor even if their parents were married, Jencks suggests that permissive sexuality, rather than
unemployment for men and discriminatory wages paid to women, is the ultimate problem. "Poor
children," he claims, "have suffered most from our newly permissive approach to reproduction.
Shotgun weddings and lifetime marriages caused adults a lot of misery, but they ensured that every
child had a claim on some adult male's earnings unless his father died. That is no longer the case.
This change is, I think, a byproduct of growing individualism and commitment to personal
freedom."[28]

Similarly, David Ellwood and Mary Jo Bane, prominent liberal academics who worked in the
Clinton administration as the key architects of the welfare reform, based their vision of welfare
reform on a contrast between "long-term dependency" that they believe has characterized the
American poor and the "independence and self-support" that they see as the proper goal of
government policy.[29]

Thus right and left alike refocused the debate over poverty onto values and culture, shunting
aside rigorous analyses of inequality and laying blame instead on individual characteristics. The
new liberal emphasis on the behavioral origins of poverty came to fruition in the bipartisan
consensus to abolish AFDC—and remains the prevailing framework shaping anti-poverty policy
today.

Both the conservative and the liberal frameworks shared a number of fundamental assumptions.
The most important include an emphasis on personal responsibility, the belief that family structure
is a cause rather than a symptom of poverty, and a preoccupation with dependence, which they
believe destroys personal responsibility. They also shared the commonsensical—but fundamentally
mistaken—belief that everyone has equal access to decent jobs, if only they would try hard enough
to find and retain them. In the end, both liberals and conservatives agreed that policies needed to
be reformulated "to reinforce our values of work, family, independence, and responsibility."
The desired goal of liberal welfare reform, like that of its conservative kin, is moral rather than
economic, resting on an ideological celebration of "self-reliance" and "independence."

But as Nancy Fraser and Linda Gordon have persuasively argued, the dichotomy between
dependency and independence is false, resting on the erroneous assumption that "the normal
human condition is independence and that dependence is deviant." It ignores abundant evidence—
from history and ethnography—that the ability to depend on others for a helping hand has often
been the route to independence for both individuals and groups. The World War II vets who
established stable lives due to government funding of their education and massive subsidies for their
homeownership are a case in point.[30]

The new bipartisan orthodoxy on poverty assumes that in the past, most poor people were self-
reliant, ignoring the countless ways that families in the past have survived only through a bundle
of government support, charitable assistance, and mutual support.[31] In fact, other groups in
American society are far more dependent on the state than the poor, yet manage to escape moral

condemnation. Middle-class homeowners benefit from government-backed loans, mortgage guarantees, and tax deductions; they travel to malls (built with the assistance of tax abatements) on government-subsidized highways. Government insurance programs protect people from the consequences of building homes on flood plains or eroding sea cliffs. Returning veterans have been beneficiaries of a form of affirmative action through the GI Bill and through the VA housing program. Scientists, defense contractors, agribusinesses, lumber and mining firms, and savings and loan associations survive because of government handouts. Yet few people label white suburbanites, the elderly, veterans, the military industrial complex, or bankers as pathological victims of a culture of dependency. Seldom do cries about "perverse incentives" fill the air. The largest group to benefit from federal largesse in the last half century has been the elderly because of Social Security and Medicare, yet they face no stigma for their reliance on government programs.[32]

Despite these widely accepted and highly effective government subsidies for the nonpoor, the new conventional wisdom is that government assistance to the poor has created or at least exacerbated poverty. One of the most influential right-wing critics of welfare, Charles Murray, has made a now-widely accepted argument that Johnson's Great Society programs of the 1960s sapped the initiative of poor people by discouraging them from working and by subsidizing family breakup. The result, Murray contended, was the emergence of a new, pernicious form of poverty bankrolled by the state. Murray and other conservatives argue that more people are poor now than in the 1960s, not because of changes in the job market, a restructuring of the global economy, or the persistence of racial discrimination, but because generous government programs have permitted poor people to live indolently. Welfare payments, in this view, set into motion a dangerous cycle of intergenerational dependency that saps individual initiative, discourages responsible parenting, and contributes to rising rates of crime, adolescent pregnancy, and school dropouts.[33]

This damning interpretation of the Great Society is based on ignorance or misrepresentation of the history of welfare and of recent trends among the poor. First, it overlooks the fact the War on Poverty was a short-lived and incomplete attempt to expand the safety net. Given the meager funding of Johnson's domestic programs in comparison to expenditures such as those for the military, it was quite effective when it was in place: rates of child poverty reached their lowest point in 1969–1970, when the Great Society programs were at their height. But a systematic war on welfare began under Richard Nixon and gathered momentum in the 1980s and 1990s.[34] It was a war of attrition: welfare shrank as conservatives continued to denounce its supposed excesses. The proportion of female household heads with children receiving AFDC declined from 63 percent in 1972 to 45 percent in 1988, at the same time that the mean payment of AFDC diminished from $435 per month in 1970 to $350 a month in 1980. States also cut back welfare payments sharply. In 1993, the average AFDC benefit in Connecticut, the third-highest-paying state, was a meager $2,400 per year; in Mississippi, the stingiest state, it was only $504 per year. The real value of welfare benefits fell dramatically in the twenty-five years before TANF because AFDC payments, unlike Social Security installments, were not indexed to inflation. Thus median AFDC payments in 1992 were 43 percent lower than they were in 1970. By 1990, AFDC payments for a family of four were lower, in constant dollars, than they were in 1960. If there was any crisis in welfare, it was one of meager funds—not of over-generosity.[35]

The attack on welfare policy was accompanied and fueled by growing moral outrage directed against the poor. Media accounts depicted the majority of poor people as people of color (when in reality most poor people were—and are—white). Visual images of the black urban poor, in particular, reinforced age-old stereotypes of blacks as lazy, dependent, and undeserving of public assistance.[36] Fanning the fires of outrage, politicians evoked the specter of an "epidemic" of teenage pregnancy, supposedly made possible by the easy access that unmarried mothers had to AFDC benefits. (For a detailed refutation of this myth, see Raley, this volume.)

But these media-inflamed myths and flawed assumptions shaped the direction and implementation of TANF. The new system of assistance to needy families varied in its specifics from state to state (one of the major contributions of the new law was to give increased power to state and local officials to modify assistance programs and their requirements). But across the country, TANF established stringent eligibility rules, enacted job training and work requirements for aid recipients, and set short time limits for the receipt of aid. The effects were often harsh. The new, daunting eligibility rules discouraged many needy parents from applying for TANF, even though they were eligible for support. The emphasis on "work first" under TANF prevented many welfare recipients from getting the education and training necessary to find stable, remunerative jobs. Some states created programs to support TANF recipients in the workplace—including childcare or transportation subsidies—but these programs were never well-funded and often badly run. Time limits also had a significant effect. In the past, most families who were on welfare used it as a stop-gap measure during periods of unemployment or family crisis. Under the new limits, families in extreme financial crisis who have exhausted their benefits are out of luck. They have to fend for themselves, left to the vagaries of the urban job market or the informal economy.[37]

Along with TANF, anti-poverty policy took another direction, especially in the administration of George W. Bush. If, as conservatives argued, family breakdown was the cause of poverty, the solution was programs to encourage traditional marriage. If the poor married, the argument went, the family dysfunctionality that was at the root of poverty would be eliminated. The emphasis on marriage promotion was closely linked to another Bush administration initiative: the encouragement of "faith-based" social service provision. Blurring the distinction between church and state, Bush administration officials channeled hundreds of millions of dollars to religious organizations that provided all sorts of aid to the poor. Among the most visible and controversial were Christian-based programs that made biblical arguments in favor of heterosexuality, sexual abstinence, and marriage.[38]

Conservatives and liberals alike have celebrated TANF for dramatically reducing "welfare dependency." In the 1990s, and during the first several years of TANF, poverty rates fell nationwide—largely as a result of the country's near full-employment economy. But the economic improvements had begun before TANF was implemented, and when the economy turned sour after 2000, poverty rates began to rise again. Even as the country moved out of recession beginning in 2004, the percentage of families in poverty failed to fall.[39]

So TANF had little effect on poverty. But ultimately, it was not an anti-poverty program. It was, instead, an anti-welfare program. In this respect, it met the expectations of conservative policymakers and represented an ideological victory for those who oppose government programs to reduce inequality. The rate of welfare receipt fell to record lows. In the decade following the enactment of TANF, welfare rolls nationwide dropped by nearly 60 percent.[40]

One unintended consequence of the dramatic reduction of welfare benefits is that a rising number of poor people must rely on outside, unreported sources of income to make ends meet. As in previous periods in American history, the poor have ingeniously cobbled together resources—working, borrowing, and bartering—to survive. Such statistics testify both to the resilience and interdependence of poor families and to the absurdity of abstract notions of "dependency" (see Gerstel and Sarkisian, this volume). Welfare reform also forced poor people—especially poor women—into the types of menial work that seldom made ends meet, that made caring for children and family members difficult, and that arguably weakened rather than strengthened families.[41]

While public policies encourage abstinence among poor teenage girls, fund church groups to promote Christian marriage, and attempt to reinvigorate a work ethic among the poor by stiffening mandatory training and work requirements under TANF, structural changes in the economy continue to wreak havoc on poor people's lives. The deficiency of the last decade of welfare reform is that it rests on grand theories about human behavior rather than on an understanding of the real experience of the poor themselves. The obsession with personal morality, values, and behavior has blinded observers to the bleak reality that most poor people face, as well as to the lack of options they have in coping with this reality. Few scholars and fewer policymakers have any sense of the day-to-day struggles of poor families. The run-down apartments, boarded-up houses and vacant lots, crumbling schools, pothole-ridden streets, and abandoned factories that stand in virtually every inner city offer a powerful explanation for the persistence of poverty. They also explain why some people find themselves in situations where behaviors that might seem pathological in a middle-class suburb may be a necessary, if risky, way to get by—a temporary survival mechanism, not a deep-seated cultural value.

The current debate over family policy and welfare compresses the complex lives and strategies of poor people into a few simple buzzwords: "underclass," "dependence," "laziness," "family breakdown," "crime," "drugs." The precarious existence of poor people is forgotten inside the Beltway, in the corridors of state capitals, and on the green lawns of suburbia, as policymakers shape programs that are firmly rooted in unreality. While Democrats and Republicans quibble over the merits of two- or five-year cutoffs for welfare beneficiaries, poor mothers lose their minimum-wage jobs because they have to spend time at home with sick children. Poor families struggle to survive in a hostile environment in which political leaders ignore their plight or blame it on the poor themselves, in an economy from which textile jobs have fled to Mexico and Haiti, from which electronics and toy manufacturing jobs have vanished to China, and from which machinery jobs have been lost to a new generation of exploited third-world laborers.

Any serious discussion of today's urban crisis must confront the awful reality of the profound transformation of American cities over the past half-century. Instead, the emphasis on race, culture, behavior, and values allows elected officials to avoid grappling with the difficult, seemingly intractable structural problems at the root of contemporary urban poverty while demagogues earn easy political points by denouncing the poor for their deviance.

Poverty is ultimately an economic problem, not a cultural problem. Until public policy contends with the consequences of massive job loss, persistent racial segregation and discrimination, and growing income inequality, poverty will remain a pressing social problem, families will continue to suffer, and young people will only grow increasingly alienated and desperate. Devising effective policies to combat poverty and create remunerative work may be expensive, but the alternatives—joblessness, mass incarceration, chronic health problems, household instability, and crime—will prove far more costly in the long run.

NOTES

Thanks to Dana Barron and Stephanie Coontz for assistance on this essay and to Alice O'Connor for advice on a previous version.

1. Public Law 104–193, 22 August 1996, 110 *Stat.* 2105.
2. For context, see Carolyn Adams, David Bartelt, David Elesh, Ira Goldstein, Nancy Kleniewski, and William Yancey, *Philadelphia: Neighborhoods, Division, and Conflict in a Postindustrial City* (Philadelphia: Temple University Press, 1991). On the growth of high poverty areas in Philadelphia and elsewhere, see Paul Jargowsky and Mary Jo Bane,

"Neighborhood Poverty: Basic Questions," in Laurence E. Lynn, Jr. and Michael G.H. McGeary, eds., *Inner City Poverty in the United States* (Washington, DC: National Academy Press, 1990), pp. 16–67.

3. Kenneth T. Jackson, *Crabgrass Frontier: The Suburbanization of the United States* (New York: Oxford University Press, 1985); Margaret Weir, "Urban Poverty and Defensive Localism," *Dissent* (Summer 1994), 337–342; Kevin M. Kruse and Thomas J. Sugrue, eds., *The New Suburban History* (Chicago: University of Chicago Press, 2006).

4. For a historical overview of the process of economic change, see Thomas J. Sugrue, "The Structures of Urban Poverty: The Reorganization of Space and Work in Three Periods of American History," in Michael B. Katz, ed., *The "Underclass" Debate: Views From History* (Princeton: Princeton University Press, 1993), pp. 85–117. See also William Julius Wilson and Loic J.D. Wacquant, "The Cost of Racial and Class Exclusion in the Inner City," *Annals of the American Academy of Political and Social Science* 501 (January 1989), 26–47; Barry Bluestone and Bennett Harrison, *The Deindustrialization of America: Plant Closings, Community Abandonment, and the Dismantling of Basic Industry* (New York: Basic Books, 1982). For statistical overviews of urban labor market restructuring, see John D. Kasarda, "Urban Change and Minority Opportunities," in Paul E. Peterson, ed., *The New Urban Reality* (Washington, DC: The Brookings Institution, 1985), pp. 33–67, figures on job loss from Table 1. See also John D. Kasarda, "Structural Factors Affecting the Location and Timing of Urban Underclass Growth," *Urban Geography* 11 (1990), esp. 242. Most recently, see William Julius Wilson, *When Work Disappears: The World of the New Urban Poor* (New York: Knopf, 1996).

5. On temporary work, see Chris Tilly, *Short Hours, Short Shrift: Causes and Consequences of Part-Time Work* (Washington, DC.: Economic Policy Institute, 1990); Polly Callaghan and Heidi Hartmann, *Contingent Work: A Chart Book on Part Time and Temporary Employment* (Washington, DC: Economic Policy Institute, 1991); Nelson Lichtenstein, *Wal-Mart: A Field Guide to America's Largest Company and the World's Largest Employer* (New York: New Press, 2006).

6. Arloc Sherman and Aviva Aron-Dine, "New CBO Data Show Income Inequality Continues to Widen," Center for Budget and Policy Priorities, January 23, 2007, available at http://www.cbpp.org/1-23-07inc.htm. For a historical overview, see Sheldon H. Danziger and Daniel H. Weinberg, "The Historical Record: Trends in Family Income, Inequality, and Poverty," in Danziger, et al., *Confronting Poverty*, 22–24.

7. "Take this Job: Up From Welfare, It's Harder and Harder," *New York Times* (April 16, 1995), Section 4, p. 1; "A Long Line for Fast Food Jobs," *Business Week* (July 31, 1995), 30; Katherine S. Newman, *No Shame in My Game: The Working Poor in the Inner City* (New York: Knopf and Russell Sage Foundation, 1999).

8. Particularly valuable are reports from the Multi-City Study of Urban Inequality, sponsored by the Ford and Russell Sage Foundations, which integrate household and employer survey data from Detroit, Los Angeles, Boston, and Atlanta. See especially Philip Moss and Chris Tilly, *Stories Employers Tell: Race, Skill, and Hiring in America* (New York: Russell Sage Foundation, 2003); Alice M. O'Connor, et al., eds., *Urban Inequality: Evidence from Four Cities* (New York: Russell Sage Foundation, 2001); Harry Holzer, *What Employers Want: Job Prospects for the Less Educated* (New York: Russell Sage Foundation, 1996).

9. Arnold Hirsch, *Making the Second Ghetto: Race and Housing in Chicago, 1940–1960* (Cambridge: Cambridge University Press, 1983); Thomas J. Sugrue, *The Origins of the Urban Crisis: Race and Inequality in Postwar Detroit*, Princeton Classic Edition (Princeton: Princeton University Press, 2005), chapters 2, 8, 9; Michael Danielson, *The Politics of Exclusion* (New York: Columbia University Press, 1976).

10. Kenneth T. Jackson, "Race, Ethnicity, and Real Estate Appraisal: The Home Owners Loan Corporation and the Federal Housing Administration," *Journal of Urban History* 6 (1980), 419–452; John Bauman, *Public Housing, Race, and Renewal: Urban Planning in Philadelphia, 1920–1974* (Philadelphia: Temple University Press, 1987); Hirsch, *Making the Second Ghetto*, 212–275; for an overview of recent trends, see John Iceland, Daniel H. Weinberg, and Erika Steinmetz, U.S. Census Bureau, Series CENSR-3, *Racial and Ethnic Segregation in the United States, 1980–2000, Census 2000 Special Reports* (Washington, DC: U.S. Government Printing Office, 2002), available online at http://www.census.gov/prod/2002pubs/censr-3.pdf, accessed January 26, 2007; Jonathan Kozol, *The Shame of the Nation: The Restoration of Apartheid Schooling in America* (New York: Crown Publishers, 2005).

11. John F. Kain, "Housing Segregation, Negro Employment, and Metropolitan Decentralization," *Quarterly Journal of Economics* 82 (May 1968), 175–197; Rabin, "Highways as a Barrier," 69; Keith R. Ihlanfeldt and David L. Sjoquist, "Job Accessibility and Racial Differences in Youth Employment Rates," *American Economic Review* 80 (1990), 267–276; see also Margaret Pugh, "Barriers to Work: The Spatial Divide Between Jobs and Welfare Recipients in Metropolitan Areas," Brookings Institution, Center for Metropolitan and Urban Policy Working Paper, September 1998; John Pucher and John L. Penne, "Socioeconomics of Urban Travel: Evidence from the 2001 NHTS," *Transportation Quarterly* 57:3 (Summer 2003), 49–77.

12. The most prominent discussion of the phenomenon is in Charles Murray, *Losing Ground: American Social Policy 1950–1980* (New York: Basic Books, 1984), pp. 69–82. Murray, however, does not consider the relationship of youth unemployment to the decline in entry-level manufacturing jobs in the center cities. An important scholarly examination of the problem is John Cogan, "The Decline in Black Teenage Employment, 1950–1970," *American Economic Review* 72 (1982), 621–638, but Cogan emphasizes the decline in agricultural employment, an issue not relevant to the labor force participation of black youth in major cities. The best overview is Richard B. Freeman and Harry J. Holzer, eds., *The Black Youth Employment Crisis* (Chicago: University of Chicago Press, 1986), quote from 9. See also Troy Duster, "Postindustrialism and Youth Employment: African Americans as Harbingers," in Katherine McFate, Roger Lawson, and William Julius Wilson, eds., *Poverty, Inequality, and the Future of Social Policy: Western States in the New World Order* (New York: Russell Sage Foundation, 1995), pp. 466–473. On the changing fortunes of women,

see Lourdes Benaria and Catherine Stimpson, eds., *Women, Households, and the Economy* (New Brunswick: Rutgers University Press, 1988). Figures from Gerald David Jaynes and Robin M. Williams, Jr., eds., *A Common Destiny: Blacks and American Society* (Washington, DC: National Academy Press, 1989), pp. 301–302.

13.   Michael B. Katz and Mark J. Stern, *One Nation Divisible: What America Was and What It Is Becoming* (New York: Russell Sage Foundation, 2006), pp. 88–90; Bruce Western, Jeffrey R. Kling, and David F. Weiman, "The Labor Market Consequences of Incarceration," *Crime and Delinquency* 47 (2001), 410–427.

14.   For a few examples of studies of the impact of economic dislocation, see E.W. Bakke, *The Unemployed Worker* (New Haven: Yale University Press, 1940); Gregory Pappas, *The Magic City: Unemployment in a Working-Class Community* (Ithaca: Cornell University Press, 1989); Katherine Newman, *Falling From Grace: The Experience of Downward Mobility in the American Middle Class* (New York: Free Press, 1988). Sudhir Alladi Venkatesh, *Off the Books: The Underground Economy of the Urban Poor* (Cambridge, MA: Harvard University Press, 2006).

15.   Diana Pearce, *The Self-Sufficiency Standard for Pennsylvania, Fifth Edition 2006*, Tables 6, 8 and 17, available at http://pathwayspa.org/policy/FINAL_PA-2006_full%20report5-15-06.pdf

16.   Michael B. Katz, *In The Shadow of the Poorhouse: A Social History of Welfare in America*, Tenth Anniversary Edition (New York: Basic Books, 1996), pp. 293–294.

17.   One of the best analyses of welfare "reform" is R. Kent Weaver, "Ending Welfare as We Know It," in Margaret Weir, ed., *The Social Divide: Political Parties and the Future of Activist Government* (Washington, DC: The Brookings Institution, 1998), pp. 361–416.

18.   A particularly perceptive discussion of the relationship of social science and poverty policy is Alice M. O'Connor, *Poverty Knowledge* (Princeton: Princeton University Press, 2000). Prominent critiques of the term "underclass" include Michael B. Katz, "The 'Underclass' as a Metaphor of Social Transformation," chapter 1 in Katz, ed., *The "Underclass" Debate: Views From History*, 3–23; Herbert Gans, *The War Against the Poor* (New York: Basic Books, 1995); Adolph Reed, "The Underclass as Myth and Symbol," *Radical America* 24 (1992), 21–40.

19.   Katz, *Shadow of the Poorhouse*; on Britain, see Gertrude Himmelfarb, *The Idea of Poverty: England in the Early Industrial Age* (New York: Knopf, 1983). On attitudes toward work, see Daniel Rodgers, *The Work Ethic in Industrial America, 1850–1920* (Chicago: University of Chicago Press, 1978). On notions of virtue and responsibility in republican thought, see Drew R. McCoy, *The Elusive Republic: The Political Economy of Jeffersonian America* (Chapel Hill: University of North Carolina Press, 1980).

20.   George Gilder, *Wealth and Poverty* (New York: Basic Books, 1981). Gilder is a prominent advocate of "supply-side economics" who enjoyed great influence in the early Reagan years. Charles Murray, *Losing Ground: American Social Policy, 1950–1980* (New York: Basic Books, 1984). Murray, affiliated with conservative think tanks such as the Manhattan Institute and the American Enterprise Institute, set the anti-welfare state agenda with his widely cited *Losing Ground*; he has also played a major role reinvigorating scientific racism. See Charles Murray and Richard Herrnstein, *The Bell Curve: Intelligence and Class Structure in American Life* (New York: The Free Press, 1994).

21.   Lawrence Mead, *The New Politics of Poverty: The Nonworking Poor in America* (New York: Basic Books, 1992), pp. 57, 151 (emphasis added); see also Mead's earlier book, *Beyond Entitlement: The Social Obligations of Citizenship* (New York: The Free Press, 1985). For a critique of Mead, see Thomas J. Sugrue, "The Impoverished Politics of Poverty," *Yale Journal of Law and the Humanities* 6 (1994), esp. 169–179. For a wide-ranging discussion of poverty politics in the twentieth century, see James T. Patterson, *America's Struggle Against Poverty in the Twentieth Century* (Cambridge, MA: Harvard University Press, 2000).

22.   Murray and Herrnstein, *The Bell Curve*.

23.   Mead, *The New Politics of Poverty*, 12.

24.   William Julius Wilson, *The Truly Disadvantaged: The Inner City, the Underclass, and Public Policy* (Chicago: University of Chicago Press, 1987). Wilson, a University of Chicago sociologist and director of the multiyear Chicago Poverty and Family Life project, has influenced a whole generation of recent scholarship on urban poverty.

25.   Ken Auletta, *The Underclass* (New York: Random House, 1982); Nicholas Lemann, "The Origins of the Underclass," *Atlantic* 257 (June 1986); Lemann, *The Promised Land: The Great Black Migration and How It Changed America* (New York: Knopf, 1991). Auletta and Lemann, liberal journalists, played a key role in bringing the issue of the urban "underclass," the fear of ominous changes in American urban life, and the findings of poverty scholars into the public agenda.

26.   Paul Peterson, ed., *The New Urban Reality* (Washington, DC: The Brookings Institution, 1985); Paul Peterson and Mark Rom, *Welfare Magnets: A New Case for a National Standard* (Washington, DC: The Brookings Institution, 1990). Peterson, former head of governmental studies at the Brookings Institution, and professor of government at Harvard, has shaped the poverty research agenda through his books and his role as leader of the Social Science Research Council's Committee on the Urban Underclass.

27.   Christopher Jencks, *Rethinking Social Policy: Race, Poverty, and the Underclass* (Cambridge, MA: Harvard University Press, 1992).

28.   Jencks, *Rethinking Social Policy*, 135.

29.   David T. Ellwood and Mary Jo Bane, *Welfare Realities: From Rhetoric to Reform* (Cambridge, MA: Harvard University Press, 1994), esp. pp. 67–123, quote from 161. Compare with David T. Ellwood, *Poor Support: Poverty in the American Family* (New York: Basic Books, 1987); David T. Ellwood, "The Spatial Mismatch Hypothesis: Are There Teenage Jobs Missing in the Ghetto," in Richard Freeman and Harry Holzer, eds., *The Black Youth Unemployment Problem* (Chicago: University of Chicago Press, 1986).

30. The most prominent liberal evocation of "dependency" is Bane and Ellwood, *Welfare Realities*, a powerful critique of the politics of dependency is Nancy Fraser and Linda Gordon, " 'Dependency' Demystified: Inscriptions of Power in a Keyword of the Welfare State," *Social Politics* 1 (Spring 1994), 4–31, quote from 24.

31. Stephanie Coontz, *The Way We Never Were: American Families and the Nostalgia Trap* (New York: Basic Books, 1992); Kathryn M. Neckerman, "The Emergence of 'Underclass' Family Patterns, 1900–1940," in Katz, ed., *The "Underclass" Debate*, 194–219; Jacqueline Jones, *Labor of Love, Labor of Sorrow: Black Women, Work, and the Family from Slavery to the Present* (New York: Basic Books, 1985).

32. See especially Ira Katznelson, *When Affirmative Action Was White* (New York: W.W. Norton, 2005).

33. Murray, *Losing Ground*. For an especially forceful version of this argument, see Myron Magnet, *The Nightmare and the Dream: The Sixties Legacy to the Underclass* (New York: William Morrow, 1993). For a popularization of it, see "Personal Responsibility Act," in Ed Gillespie and Bob Schellhas, eds., *Contract With America* (New York: Times Books, 1994), pp. 65–77.

34. See especially Felicia Kornluh, *The Battle for Welfare Rights* (Philadelphia: University of Pennsylvania Press, 2007) and Annelise Orleck, *Storming Caesar's Palace: How Black Mothers Fought Their Own War on Poverty* (Boston: Beacon Press, 2005).

35. On the limitations of the Great Society, see Hugh Heclo, "Poverty Politics," in Sheldon H. Danziger, Gary D. Sandefur, and Daniel H. Weinberg, eds., *Confronting Poverty: Prescriptions for Change* (Cambridge, MA: Harvard University Press, 1994), pp. 407–412; Thomas F. Jackson, "The State, the Movement, and the Urban Poor: The War on Poverty and Political Mobilization in the 1960s," in Katz, ed., *The "Underclass" Debate*, 403–439; Jill Quadagno, *The Color of Welfare: How Racism Undermined the War on Poverty* (New York: Oxford University Press, 1994). For a comprehensive overview, see Michael B. Katz, *The Undeserving Poor: From the War on Poverty to the War on Welfare* (New York: Pantheon, 1989). Figures from Jencks, *Rethinking Social Policy*, 77. See also Rebecca M. Blank, "The Employment Strategy: Public Policies to Increase Work and Earnings," in Danziger et al., *Confronting Poverty*, 179–180. For figures on statewide payments, see R. Kent Weaver and William T. Dickens, eds., *Looking Before We Leap: Social Science and Welfare Reform* (Washington, DC: The Brookings Institution, 1995), table 3-6.

36. Martin Gilens, *Why Americans Hate Welfare: Race, Media, and the Politics of Anti-Poverty Policy* (Chicago: University of Chicago Press, 1999).

37. Ellen Reese, *Backlash Against Welfare Mothers: Past and Present* (Berkeley and Los Angeles: University of California Press, 2005).

38. See Michael B. Katz, *The Price of Citizenship: Redefining the American Welfare State* (New York: Metropolitan Books, 2003), pp. 155–162; Lew Daly, *God and the Welfare State* (Cambridge, MA: MIT Press, 2006).

39. Carmen deNavas Walt, Bernadette D. Proctor, and Jessica Smith, U.S. Census Bureau, Current Population Reports P60–233, *Income, Poverty, and Health Insurance Coverage in the United States: 2006* (Washington, DC: U.S. Government Printing Office, 2007), figure 3.

40. The most prominent defense of welfare reform, by one of its leading Republican architects, is Ron Haskins, *Work Over Welfare: The Inside Story of the 1996 Welfare Reform Law* (Washington, DC: The Brookings Institution, 2006).

41. For powerful depictions of welfare reform and its effects on poor women and their families, see Sharon Hays, *Flat Broke With Children: Women in the Age of Welfare Reform* (New York: Oxford University Press, 2002) and Jason DeParle, *American Dream: Three Women, Ten Kids, and a Nation's Drive to End Welfare* (New York: Viking, 2004).

23

Avenue to Adulthood
Teenage Pregnancy and the Meaning of Motherhood in Poor Communities

Gabrielle Raley

First the good news: the rate of teenage childbearing in the United States has been falling since the 1950s, and it has taken a nosedive in the last decade, plunging by 35 percent between 1991 and 2005. Rates of adolescent childbearing are now at historic lows for *all* racial-ethnic groups. And this isn't because more pregnant teens are opting for abortions. In fact, the teenage abortion rate has been falling steadily since the 1980s, a trend that continues today. By 2002, the Guttmacher Institute reports, the teen abortion rate was 50 percent lower than its peak in 1988.[1]

But now the bad news: the United States still has the highest occurrence of teenage childbearing in the industrialized world at just over 40 births per 1000 teenage girls aged 15 to 19. To put that in perspective, the comparable rate is 22 births in Canada, 13 births in Germany, and 4 births per 1000 girls in Japan. Our rates parallel those in many developing countries. And in 2006, for the first time in 15 years, there was a new uptick in teen births. These figures are disturbing because teen childbearing is much more of a problem today than it was in the past, when it was less necessary for girls to postpone motherhood to invest in their education and prepare to make their own living in a competitive labor market.[2]

The birth rates of all American teens except Asian-Americans (17.3 births per 1000 Asian-American girls) outpace teen birth rates in industrialized countries. But there are substantial racial-ethnic differences in teenage childbearing within the United States. In 2005, the U.S. teen birth rate was 81.5 per thousand girls for Latinas, 60.9 for African-Americans, 52.5 for Native Americans and 26.0 for whites.[3]

These figures lead many people to wonder why American teens are so irresponsible.[4] The issue came up recently in a sociology course I teach. We had been discussing how an increasing number of families are feeling the crunch of falling real wages and job out-sourcing, especially in areas of concentrated poverty. "I get that these things make life harder if you're an adult and already have a family," one student interrupted. "But if you're a teenager, why would you *start* a family before you've gotten out of poverty? You're just going to trap yourself and your kid forever. Why don't you just *wait* to have a baby?" Many heads nodded in agreement as she concluded, "It seems so selfish!"

At first glance, the causal relationship between teen childbearing and poverty seems self-evident. Teen mothers are more likely to be poor and to receive welfare, and are less likely to finish high school, than women who delay childbearing. Their children are more likely to be born at low birth weights, have behavioral problems, do poorly in school, and drop out before graduation. Female children of teen mothers are also more likely to end up as teen mothers themselves, while male children have a greater chance of going to prison. One advocacy group estimates that all this costs U.S. taxpayers around $9.1 billion per year in social services.[5]

But if we are further to reduce the rate of teenage childbearing, we need to understand it more thoroughly, looking more closely at its complicated causes and consequences. The first step in this effort is to see teenage pregnancy *in social context*. When we look at the problem in context, we see a very different picture than the stereotype of promiscuous girls popping out babies to collect a welfare check. Instead, we see adolescents growing up in neighborhoods with a long history of limited access to adequate schools and secure jobs—teens whose parents or grandparents paid their dues by holding down menial jobs, only to watch their neighborhoods fall deeper into decay and job prospects for their children dwindle. We see that, in the poorest areas of our country, motherhood may be the only way that an impoverished girl can envision having a future, or a measure of control in her life. Looking at the issue in context, it is not that teenage childbearing represents a *good* choice, but that it is an often *understandable* one, given the lack of better options.

Rather than being the fundamental cause of poverty, adolescent childbearing is often more a result of pre-existing impoverishment, most especially of growing up in concentrated poverty. Experts estimate that 83 percent of teenage mothers come from disadvantaged backgrounds. In fact, teenage childbearing and poverty are so intertwined that taking the 15 states with the highest rates of poverty in the country and comparing them with the 15 states with the highest rates of teenage pregnancy, we find that 11 states appear on both lists.[6]

Looking at teenage childbearing in context suggests the need for social policies much different than the ones pursued in the last two decades. Offering poor unwed mothers "incentives" for marriage or providing teens with better abstinence-only sex education is unlikely to lower our current rates of teenage childbearing because such programs do not address the simple fact that poor teens often do not have much reason to put off childbearing. If we want to help teenagers make different choices about parenthood, we need to give urgent attention to the appalling quality of education offered in poor—usually segregated—schools, the social isolation and lack of decent jobs in areas of concentrated poverty, and the tenacious racism that blames the desperate poverty of many urban populations of color on flawed moral values. If we want teenagers to wait to have kids, we need to give them other options for the future, real incentives to wait.

In historical perspective, the concern over the birth rates of impoverished girls is nothing new. Pundits have always worried about the wrong sort of people—especially the poor and immigrants—having too many children. What sets contemporary teenage parents apart from their historical counterparts is that most births to teenagers today occur outside of marriage. But teenagers are hardly unique in this regard. Nonmarital childbearing has doubled in the last 25 years, and currently 37 percent of all births in the U.S. are to unmarried mothers.[7]

Nevertheless, the rise in unmarried childbearing, its high visibility in many African-American communities, and the socioeconomic consequences attributed to teenage pregnancy fueled the 1996 Personal Responsibility and Work Opportunity Reconciliation Act (PRWORA), which famously ended "welfare as we know it." At the time, public concern over unmarried teenage childbearing was at its peak. In 1995, a year before he signed PRWORA into law, President Clinton called teenage pregnancy "our most serious social problem." Welfare was seen as spawning the rise in female-headed families and encouraging a "culture of poverty" that promoted unwed childbearing, especially among African-Americans. Unmarried teenage pregnancy was singled out for special consideration under PRWORA and its state-controlled block assistance program, Temporary

Assistance to Needy Families (TANF). Specifically, TANF mandated that teen mothers live with their parents and stay in school to receive benefits. It also limited them, along with other welfare recipients, to a maximum of five years during which they could receive assistance. Proponents hoped that "getting tough" on welfare recipients would end teen childbearing and reduce poverty.[8]

The fact is, however, that prior to the passage of PRWORA, scholars had been in "widespread agreement" that welfare did *not* cause unmarried childbearing, teenage or otherwise. It is true that there was a rise in unmarried female-headed families from the 1960s to the 1980s. But the real value of welfare payments declined significantly during this same period. If mothers could buy increasingly less with their monthly welfare checks, it's hard to imagine that this was an incentive to create *more* mouths to feed. Sociologist Mark Robert Rank studied 3,000 welfare recipients over eight years; they simply laughed at the suggestion that they would have additional children in order to collect an extra $60–90 a month in benefits. Although such research did not receive much attention in the popular press, the government was well aware of it. As early as the Reagan administration, the White House Working Group on the Family acknowledged that when it came to claims that welfare encouraged women to bear more children, the "statistical evidence does not prove those suppositions."[9]

When we look at the United States in global perspective, the welfare incentive argument makes even less sense. If welfare encourages teens to bear children out of wedlock, many European countries offering more generous welfare benefits should be overrun with the children of unmarried teen parents by now. Instead the opposite is true: the rates of teenage childbearing are so low in France, Germany, and Sweden that public health officials in these countries neglect to see teenage childbearing as much of a problem at all.[10]

The rate of U.S. teen childbearing has fallen markedly since 1991, prompting some to proclaim the welfare reform of 1996 a success. It's a politically convenient coincidence, but research does not support the conclusion that welfare reform is responsible for the recent decline in teen fertility. To study the relationship between welfare reform and adolescent childbearing, social demographers compared the fertility of teenage girls before and after welfare reform, using several methods to control for subtle differences in family background and socioeconomic disadvantage. When they compared rates of teenage fertility in the pre- and post-reform eras, they found that "welfare policy has little effect on the decisions of teenage girls to have births."[11]

In another study, researchers compared teenage pregnancy and birth before and after PRWORA and found no statistically significant differences between the two time periods. They concluded that none of their data "suggests that welfare reform had its intended effect of reducing teenage fertility."[12]

Arguments that welfare is the cause of teenage pregnancy generally fail to consider teen mothers' socioeconomic backgrounds *prior* to getting pregnant. Study after study has shown that when background characteristics such as poverty, neighborhood, and social isolation from job networks are controlled for, welfare and race-ethnicity cease to explain variations in teenage pregnancy at all. For example, Christopher Jencks and Susan Mayer found that, controlling for race and family background, sixteen- to eighteen-year-old girls were considerably more likely to bear children while unmarried if they lived in poor neighborhoods than if they lived in economically average neighborhoods.[13]

Casting further doubt on the notion of a racialized "culture of poverty," Jonathan Crane found that the white teens living in the poorest areas of the largest cities demonstrated patterns of teenage childbearing that were "more like [those of] black teens than other whites in terms of childbearing."

In another study of the effect of neighborhood on teenage sexual activity, researchers found "the frequency with which youth engage in sexual intercourse, the number of partners they have sex with, and the likelihood of engaging in unprotected intercourse all increase with the level of socioeconomic disadvantage of their communities."[14]

Other researchers found that what had first seemed to be a strong racial-ethnic difference in teenage attitudes about childbearing—with African-American teens far more approving of it than whites—evaporated when they controlled for neighborhood economic disadvantage. Based on their results, they concluded that in fact, "neighborhood economic disadvantage accounts for a substantial proportion of the racial difference in sexual attitude[s]. . . . In short, race is not the explanation for the observed racial differences" in attitudes about adolescent sexuality and childbearing.[15]

So concentrated poverty is a better explanation for teenage childbearing than race-ethnicity or welfare receipt.[16] And scholars have also found that socioeconomic disadvantage explains most of the problems that the children of teen parents are assumed to inherit. Recall that the children of teenage mothers are more likely to do poorly in school and on standardized tests, to drop out of school, and to have more behavioral and health problems than kids born to adult mothers. Some of that variation remains after controlling for socioeconomic background: kids of teen moms are more likely repeat a grade in school, for instance, even after controlling for poverty. But on the whole, kids of teen parents are less disadvantaged by their mother's age at birth than first assumed. In a 2007 study of the well-being of kids born to teen mothers, researchers found that once socioeconomic background was controlled for, teenage pregnancy itself had little or no effect on children's standardized test scores or a variety of negative behavioral outcomes. In another study, sociologists Judith Levin, Harold Pollack and Maureen Comfort come to similar conclusions. They state, "we find that early motherhood's strong negative correlation with children's test scores and positive correlation with children's grade repetition is almost entirely explained by the individual and family background factors of teen mothers themselves."[17]

While advances in statistical methods have allowed scholars to control for more subtle background variance, and neighborhood disadvantage is a reasonable control for class background, it is worth noting that there is no perfect way to separate racial-ethnic factors from those associated with economic disadvantage in the U.S. Structural and economic forces have consigned people of color to economically disadvantaged and socially isolated neighborhoods over long periods of time, subjecting them to the material consequences of racial-ethnic discrimination.

Class is not just defined by a person's income or educational status at a particular point in time. It is a *social* relationship that places one group of people in a certain pattern of interaction with other groups and gives group members a set of shared experiences, expectations, problem-solving habits, vulnerabilities, and privileges. It is one's long-term options, not just a particular income or job, that determines class status. This is why a college student who is broke is in a higher and more secure class, with completely different dynamics, than a resident of an inner city, even one who is currently flush. In our country, class has been constructed not just by economic processes but also by racial exclusion and ethnic stratification over a long period of time.[18]

The idea of class as a social relationship must inform our understanding of why teenage childbearing occurs disproportionately among some segments of the population. It is true, for instance, that Latina and African-American teens experience higher rates of childbearing than their white counterparts. But this fact demonstrates first of all the embedded relationship of race, ethnicity, and class in our country, not that racially or ethnically derived values cause disadvantage, as "culture of poverty" proponents maintain.

Contrary to the history most people are raised on, the historical oppression of African-Americans did not end with slavery. In the late nineteenth century, they were driven out of skilled trades, exploited in Southern agriculture, confined to the oldest, most dilapidated sections of Northern cities, and excluded from industrial jobs and union work. After World War II, thousands of African Americans moved North to seek work. As late as the 1950s, African Americans were the frequent target of organized mob actions and riots. Nevertheless, despite facing continuing violence and segregation, many managed to gain footholds in manufacturing, especially in the then-heavily-unionized automobile, rubber, and steel industries. These occupational improvements, combined with the struggle for civil rights, opened up new employment and educational opportunities in the 1960s.[19]

For many African Americans, however, these victories were offset by losses in "foothold industries" and the simultaneous transition of goods-based to service-based industries. As technological advances led to a constriction of blue-collar jobs and the labor market began to divide into low-wage and high-wage sectors, the "window of opportunity" that had opened in the 1960s slammed shut.

African-Americans were particularly hard hit in the 1970s and 1980s by the relocation of many industries from central-city locations to more remote suburban sites. Sociologist William Julius Wilson reports that the relocation of over 2,300 companies from Illinois cities to suburbs in the 1970s resulted in a 24.3 percent drop in that African-American employment, while the white employment rate declined by just 9.8 percent. Furthermore, the manufacturing industries in which blacks were heavily concentrated have gone through tremendous restructuring and consolidation since the 1970s. The movement of jobs to the suburbs in the 1970s combined with racially biased housing patterns to leave working-class blacks clustered in poor, segregated neighborhoods in which there were few connections to job networks. Most middle- and working-class families relocated during this time period, leaving the remaining inner-city residents all the more isolated, and with few tangible examples of neighbors experiencing successful employment or economic security.[20]

In recent decades, the percentage of Latinos in our country's poor has risen sharply. Although Latinos face many of the same factors that have historically constrained job opportunities for African-Americans, their situation is also significantly shaped by immigration. Undocumented Latinos are overrepresented in the low-wage, unregulated service sector of our economy and have few legal routes to pursue workplace and social equity.[21]

Due to a mutually reinforcing cycle of discrimination and economic inequality, people of color are not only more likely to be more poor than whites, but are also more likely to reside in areas of concentrated poverty. While only 7 percent of all poor whites live in what are termed "extreme poverty areas," 32 percent of all poor Latinos and 39 percent of all poor African-Americans reside in such areas. Here residents face substandard housing, ill-funded schools, and social isolation, although they do get more than their fair share of liquor stores and landfills.[22]

Despite historical differences in the occupational patterns and cultural adaptations of various racial-ethnic groups, socioeconomic disadvantage is more important than race-ethnicity in explaining rates of teenage pregnancy. Cultural explanations of teenage childbearing are, all too often, thinly disguised appeals to racial and ethnic prejudices. As Thomas J. Sugrue argues (this volume), the emphasis on an independent causal role of values ignores the matrix of economic isolation and discrimination in which people absorb and modify generally held social values on the basis of practical experience. Politically, the culture-of-poverty thesis systematically ignores social class, appealing to racial-ethnic prejudice to justify meager social spending, reasoning that funding will be worthless until inner-city residents acquire the right values. But values can't explain why there are fewer decent jobs in inner-city areas, even though the link between employment and teenage pregnancy is clear. Lopoo and DeLeire found in a 2006 study that state unemployment rates were positively and statistically significantly related to teen birth rates, while sociologists Mignon Moore and Lindsay Chase-Lansdale found that "the risk of pregnancy is reduced when adolescents report more working adults in their social networks."[23]

The tendency to explain teen pregnancy through the lens of "culture" or "values" is itself a hard cycle to break. For instance, researchers often explain Latino teens' lower contraceptive use as a result of cultural patterns or religious beliefs. For example, a qualitative study of teenage-pregnancy practitioners working with Latino youth reported that counseling teens to avoid pregnancy so they could pursue education seemed to be "at odds with traditional Hispanic cultural values," especially with regard to female self-sufficiency.[24]

But while all teens make choices about sex and childbearing in a cultural context, that context is often more complicated than such statements imply. Gloria González-López interviewed immigrant men in Los Angeles about their daughters' sexual activity. She found that while most fathers wanted their daughters to wait to have sex until they were married, "protecting their daughters from a sexually dangerous society and improving their socioeconomic future is of greater concern to these men than preserving virginity per se."[25]

Buttressing an economic rather than cultural reading of Latina teen childbearing, a recent study found that many Latino immigrant youth experience significant structural hurdles to obtaining contraceptives: language barriers make finding and using family planning services difficult, and undocumented teens, in particular, worry that seeking such services will alert the authorities to their illegal status in the country and put their families at risk of deportation. While many non-Latino sexually active teens worry that their parents will disapprove of their actions, most don't have to consider their family's legal and residential security when they seek contraception.[26]

Class, culture, and family background interact in complicated ways. In many studies, poor academic skills and low prospects for educational attainment rank as high as poverty in predicting the incidence of adolescent childbearing. One study finds that the likelihood that a teen will have a child while unmarried is significantly reduced if she has high grades, high standardized test scores, and plans to graduate from college. Linda Waite and her colleagues at the Rand Corporation found that teen birth rates were highest among girls who had the greatest economic disadvantage and the lowest academic ability. Again however, educational attainment is difficult to disentangle from class and from the long and continuing history of racial segregation in public schools. Although terms such as "academic ability" and "educational aspirations" have a neutral ring, they are factors highly tempered by social privilege.[27]

Most people believe that able and committed children will automatically stay in school, and that their efforts will pay off in an economically stable future. But the social isolation of the poorest of the poor creates neighborhoods with few connections to the job market and few opportunities to get a decent education. To be sure, a gifted student can occasionally, with a little luck, get a good education. But many equally intelligent students run into dead ends, while average students, or less-able students who might have succeeded with the extra help available in more affluent communities, fall further behind.

The correlation between educational discouragement and bearing a child in one's teens is striking: high school dropouts are six times more likely than their contemporaries who remain in school to become unmarried parents. In a state-by-state study of school segregation, researchers at Harvard University's Civil Rights Project found that in 2001, only 50 percent of African-American students, 51 percent of Native American students, and 53 percent of Latino students graduated from high school (the comparable rates for whites and Asian-Americans are 75 percent and 77 percent, respectively).[28] A high school teacher in a poor school in East St. Louis explains the connection between poverty, dropping out of school, and bearing a child as a teenager:

> I have four girls right now in my senior home room who are pregnant or have just had babies. When I ask they why this happens, I am told, "Well, there's no reason not to have a baby. There's nothing for me in public school." The truth is, that's a pretty honest answer. A diploma from a ghetto high school doesn't count for much in the United States today. So, if this is really the last education that a person's going to get, she's probably perceptive in that statement.[29]

Just how little does a diploma from a poor high school count? Designs for Change, a Chicago-based research center, found in a survey of the eighteen poorest schools in the country that only 3.5 percent of the students both graduate and can read at the national level. In other words, if 6,700 students enter the ninth grade in these eighteen schools each year, only 300 will make it out with both a diploma and adequate reading skills.[30]

Due to inequitable and antiquated systems of school funding, most schools in impoverished minority communities do not possess the funds to offer college preparatory or advanced classes, even though residents of such communities often tax themselves at higher rates than more affluent areas. Residents of New York's underprivileged Roosevelt school district have one of the highest property tax rates in the state, for example.[31]

Because educational opportunities are so unequal in the U.S., some experts have argued that schools do much more than prepare kids for future jobs or education, but in fact sort children by their probable class destinations. In schools, both rich and poor, children are instilled with a sense of the opportunities available to them, of their place in the social order. Children who attend poor, segregated schools soon learn to doubt their capabilities as well as their opportunities, giving them little incentive to engage in what middle-class Americans would consider rational planning for the future. Jonathan Kozol, author of some of the most incisive work on public school inequity, found many "industry-embedded schools" in the poor and segregated districts he studies. For example, one inner-city school in Chicago offers a comprehensive "culinary arts" educational track to its high school students to prepare them to work in restaurant kitchens (the program is co-sponsored by Hyatt Hotels, which offers jobs to students upon completion of their training). Sociologist William Julius Wilson argues that most inner-city schools "train minority youth so that they feel and appear capable of only performing jobs in the low-wage sectors."[32]

Such training starts young. One kindergarten Kozol visited had a retail corner in its classroom, complete with a "poster that displayed the names of several retail stores: JCPenney, Wal-Mart, Kmart, Sears, and a few others. 'It's like working in a store,' a classroom aide explained. 'The children are learning to pretend that they're cashiers.' "[33]

Children in inner-city schools are well aware of the inequity of their situation. Students in suburban schools, they realize, don't have to put up with rat infestations, sewage and heating problems, or chronic shortages of books and supplies. They get the message quite quickly about society's assessment of their relative worth.[34] As this Puerto Rican student at a poor high school in New York points out:

> If you threw us into some different place . . . and put white children in this building in our place, this school would start to shine . . . They'd fix it fast, no question. People on the outside may think that we don't know what it is like for other students, but we *visit* other schools, and we have eyes and we have brains. You cannot hide the differences. You see it and compare . . .[35]

The differences are glaring. For instance, in 2002–2003, the wealthy (and 90 percent white) district of Highland Park, Illinois, spent $17,291 per pupil, while the Chicago school district (87 percent black and Latino) spent just $8,482 per pupil. Similar disparities were reported in the cities and suburbs of Philadelphia, New York, Detroit, and other U.S. metropolitan areas. While economically disadvantaged students should be getting high-quality and amply-funded schooling to help assuage the deficits of growing up in poverty, in reality they get less than half the resources that affluent suburban kids receive.[36]

The public may be more willing to change public school financing than politicians believe. A 1998 Gallup poll found that only 21 percent of people think that public schools should be financed by local property taxes; 60 percent said they would be willing to pay *more* taxes to provide funds to improve the quality of the nation's inner-city public schools. But despite such polls, few politicians have shown willingness to tackle school finance reform.[37]

Poverty, racial-ethnic discrimination, and unfair school funding are great enough burdens for any child or adolescent to shoulder. But teens must also make decisions about sex in a culture that inundates them with sexual commodification at every turn, yet allows them few socially acceptable ways to engage in responsible sex while unmarried.

All adolescents face conflicting messages about sex, responsibility, and future goals. Laurence Steinberg argues that contemporary adolescents have gained access to adult consumption patterns but have lost access to responsible adult roles, a condition he terms "adolescent rolelessness." Furthermore, teens become sexually mature earlier than in the past (currently, menarche occurs at 12 years of age), while the average age at first marriage has risen to almost 26 for women and 28 for men. This presents adolescents with a simple time-management problem. Most will face a decade or more in which they are both sexually mature and unmarried.[38]

Expecting teens to remain abstinent for a decade, or until they are married, is naïve at best.[39] Nevertheless, from 1996 until 2007, this was the form of "sex education" singled out for special government promotion and funding (as this book goes to press, a new bill—the Responsible Education About Life Act—is being debated in Congress and may change funding streams for sex education). According to the Washington, DC-based Advocates for Youth, under the abstinence-only sex education of the past decade, Congress funneled more than $1.4 billion to abstinence-only-until-marriage programs and *zero* dollars to comprehensive sex education. States had to agree to promote abstinence as the major component of their sex instruction in order to receive federal funding for sex education (some states refused funding in protest).[40]

The results of abstinence-only education have not been encouraging for proponents. According to sociologists Hannah Brückner and Peter Bearman, the majority of teens in grades 7 to 12 who vowed to remain virgins until marriage had nonmarital sex before their follow-up survey six years later. Furthermore, "vow breakers" were less likely than other teens to use condoms when they did have sex. In another study, researchers at Mathematica Policy Research followed middle-school students enrolled in four abstinence programs for five years and found that they had sex at roughly the same age as peers who had not had abstinence education. The two groups initiated sex at the same mean age and had similar numbers of sexual partners. While researchers allow that a small percentage in the recent drop in teenage pregnancy may be explained by fewer teens having sex overall, studies show that approximately 85 percent of the decline in teen pregnancy rates is due to more consistent and effective contraceptive use among teens, not abstinence education.[41]

Yet despite the availability of contraceptive information, impoverished teens continue to have children at much higher rates than other adolescents. A 2005 ethnographic study by Kathryn Edin and Maria Kefalas provides a compelling possible explanation for this variation. Over a five-year period, Edin and Kefalas interviewed 162 low-income black, Latino, and white mothers, most of whom had children as teens. Edin and Kefalas lived in the poor Philadelphia neighborhoods they studied and followed their respondents (and their partners) through the early days of their relationship, through pregnancy, and after the birth of their child(ren).

Only a small number of the women Edin and Kefalas studied *planned* to get pregnant in their teens (nationally about 82 percent of teenage pregnancies are not planned). But neither were their pregnancies entirely unplanned. Most women Edin and Kefalas interviewed described their pregnancies as somewhere in between: "not exactly planned" and "not exactly avoided" (only a few of their respondents were using contraception when they conceived their child).[42]

The explanation for this lack of consistent effort to avoid pregnancy lies in understanding how the social location of these young women shapes their sense of current and future options. With seriously limited opportunities for continued education and future employment, carrying a baby to term is often the one avenue through which low-income girls can assert their grown-up status. Many mothers Edin and Kefalas studied said they wanted someone to love and take care of, while others reported wanting to seal a romance by having a child. For many of these young women, moreover, raising children is the one job for which they've had ample training—most poor kids have had to care for younger siblings. As one eighteen-year-old white mother of two toddlers explained: "When we was living with my mom, I was taking care of my little sister and my little brother anyway. She was working two jobs, so I was taking care of them mostly."[43]

The women interviewed by Edin and Kefalas reported having reasonable access to contraception, but many stopped using it when their romantic relationship became serious. Although they got pregnant earlier than they wanted, many mothers say their timing was off by only a year or two. Most now claim there are advantages to being young and energetic mothers and, in the absence of plans or possibilities for higher schooling, they see few costs to having had a baby in their teens.

Indeed, the "cost" of motherhood for poor teens in terms of later outcomes in life is much less than is often assumed. Arline Geronimus and Sanders Korenman did a study comparing a large group of sisters in which one had a child in their teens and the other waited, reasoning that because sisters come from the same socioeconomic and family background, many "unobserved" characteristics that might affect their life chances are effectively "controlled" for. They found no significant differences in economic outcomes later in life for the women who had a child in their teens and those who did not. Another study compared the later life outcomes of teen mothers with teens who got pregnant but miscarried, reasoning again that this controls for background factors that may differentiate teen mothers from their childless peers. They found that ten years later, teen mothers were doing as well as, or better than, teens who had miscarried. Put another way, the women who had not had a child as a teen had not managed to achieve any greater social and economic mobility than those who had. For individuals already living in poverty, the researchers concluded, "delaying childbirth until the end of the teenage years seemed not to produce better adult outcomes than having a child as a teenager."[44]

It is not that the teens Edin and Kefalas studied do not see pregnancy and motherhood as a challenge. But it is one of the few challenges they believe they can meet. Most residents of the neighborhoods Edin and Kefalas studied said that learning one is pregnant is the first "test" of one's capacity for motherhood. Having an abortion is seen as taking the "easy way" out or as punishing the baby for the mother's mistake. Carrying the pregnancy to term signals that the mother is taking responsibility for her actions and is ready to "grow up." Pregnancy thus symbolizes the beginning of the transition to adulthood for many poor women. Since children are not seen as a roadblock to future success, there is often no reason not to rise to the challenge.[45]

While it is important to acknowledge the complex motivations and personal agency of teens who have babies, we also need to recognize the constrained and deprived situations in which they make their choices. These constraints are not only economic but often sexual. In two out of three births to unmarried teen mothers, the father is not a teen at all but twenty years of age or older, often much older than the mother. It is highly probable that many of these relationships involved some measure of sexual coercion for young teen mothers. One research team estimates that "more than a quarter of teens who had intercourse before age fourteen said they didn't want their first sexual experience to happen." In other cases, much younger women may simply not feel able to negotiate the terms of their sexual relationship, including contraceptive use.[46]

But even for couples whose relationships are truly consensual, there are fewer obstacles to getting pregnant than there are to getting married. Experts estimate that over 50 percent of babies born officially to "single mothers" are actually born to cohabiting couples. Mirroring these findings, Edin and Kefalas report that most of the women in their study lived with their child's father at the time of the birth. And most intended to marry their baby's father . . . later. Indeed, one of the most surprising findings of this study is the high regard for marriage that the women Edin and Kefalas interviewed expressed, and this attitude holds across all racial-ethnic groups they studied. Respondents see marriage as a serious, lifelong commitment that should only be entered into if one plans on staying the course permanently. Given the uncertain and often desperate economic conditions in which they live, this permanence is hard to come by, and many women reported that they did not intend to marry until they had enough economic security with their partners to improve their chance of making it in the long run.[47]

Thus, while motherhood is, as Edin and Kefalas put it, the "primary vocation for young women" in inner-city neighborhoods, marriage is something that should only be entered into if a couple can do it right, and this means attaining a certain level of financial stability and social respectability. Said one young mother of two children, currently living with—though not married to—the father of one of her children, "I want my kids to be stable before I do anything to alter their lives . . . I wanna have an established environment for my kids so that my kids are happy, my kids are healthy, they're safe, they have their own house, their own toys, their own couch, their own television."[48]

In a later study of unmarried couples, Paula England and Edin asked women what their minimum economic standards were for marriage. Few were unrealistic about what was needed to achieve a measure of stability. Most couples defined such stability as one or both of them having a good enough job so that they could pay their bills each month without asking for assistance from family, friends, charity, or the government. Many also said they'd like to be able to afford to rent or buy a house. But the majority of England's and Edin's respondents were not able to meet these modest hopes even four years after their child's birth.[49]

In the earlier study by Edin and Kefalas, the women reported that most fathers try to stay employed at the low-wage semi-stable jobs available in nearby neighborhoods. But if they lose them or are laid off, even short-term, "the continuing pressure to bring in money makes the street corner [drug dealing] hard to resist." With spotty employment records and intermittent involvement in the underground economy of drugs and crime, such fathers can become an economic liability to their child's mother. While teen mothers are often mature enough to care and provide for their children, it appears that teen fathers have a harder time achieving adulthood through similar actions. Staying home and caring for her baby "brings [the mother] social recognition for behaving the way a good mother should." But a teen father "wins no points with friends for staying home in the evening and on weekends, no matter how good a father he desires to be."[50]

Clearly, such a difference in socially valued avenues of attaining adult status in poor communities puts a strain on teenage relationships. And this strain reinforces the obstacles that women see to getting married, even as it increases the emotional meaning of motherhood in their lives. Contrary to the "culture of poverty" argument, however, this disconnect between marriage and motherhood in impoverished communities reflects the socioeconomic dilemmas facing these young men and women more than it reflects deviant or irresponsible values. Indeed, it is precisely because impoverished young women share so many mainstream values about the importance of marriage and the centrality of breadwinning to a man's "marriageability" that they are reluctant to marry. And it is their lack of access to other fulfilling and rewarding social roles that reinforces their attraction to motherhood and their ambivalence about avoiding pregnancy.

At the end of the class where we discussed teen motherhood, I turned the question around and asked my students when they thought poor women *should* have children. "When they're stable," several answered, "when they can provide for their kids." "If they can wait for marriage until they can afford it, why can't they wait for kids until they marry?" asked another.

But recall that England and Edin found that only a minority of the couples they studied were able to subsist without handouts four years after their initial interviews, and that other studies have shown that little if any economic advantage accrues to poor women who delay motherhood. With financial stability so difficult to attain and so precarious in neighborhoods of concentrated poverty, it is understandable that putting off having children until they achieve that elusive goal is a risk many poor women are not willing to take. And any public policy based on the idea that the way to end poverty is to convince impoverished Americans to not have children is unrealistic and inhumane.

NOTES

Thanks to Todd Smith, Benjamin Smithraley, Stephanie Coontz, Kurtuluş Gemici, Herman Raley, and Susan Raley for their generous support of this project, and to Stephanie Coontz and Will Reissner for an especially astute edit of the chapter.

1. For statistics on rates of teenage childbearing, including racial-ethnic variation, see "Facts at a Glance," *Child Trends*, June 2007 #2007-12 and "Teen Birth Rates in the United States, 1940–2005," National Campaign to Prevent Teen Pregnancy, Washington, DC, n.d. On teenage abortion rates, see "U.S. Teenage Pregnancy Statistics: National and State Trends and Trends by Race and Ethnicity," Guttmacher Institute, New York, 2006.
2. U.S. teen pregnancy rate: "Facts at a Glance," *Child Trends*, June 2007. Statistics on international teenage childbearing rates in Andrew L. Cherry, Mary E. Dillon, and Douglas Rugh, eds., *Teenage Pregnancy: A Global View* (Westport, CT: Greenwood Publishing Group, 2001). Comparison of U.S. rate to developing countries: ibid., p. 187; Gardiner Harris, "Teen Birth Rate Rises for First Time Since '91," *New York Times*, December 6, 2007.
3. Data on Asian-American and Native American teenage birth rates are from 2004. "Fact Sheet: Teen Sexual Activity, Pregnancy, and Childbearing Among Asians and Pacific Islanders in the United States," National Campaign to Prevent Teen Pregnancy, Washington, DC, 2006, p. 2. "Fact Sheet: Teen Sexual Activity, Pregnancy, and Childbearing Among Native Americans," National Campaign to Prevent Teen Pregnancy, Washington, DC, 1996, p. 2. Statistics on white, black, and Latina teen childbearing from "Facts at a Glance," *Child Trends*, June 2007.
4. It's worth noting that this irresponsible teen is, in the minds of most Americans, usually African-American. See Patricia Hill Collins on the "controlling image" of the black teenage welfare mother: *Black Feminist Thought: Knowledge, Consciousness, and the Politics of Empowerment* (Boston: Unwin Hyman, 1990).
5. On the negative consequences of teenage childbearing, see Saul D. Hoffman, "By the Numbers: The Public Costs of Teen Childbearing," Washington, DC: National Campaign to Prevent Teen Pregnancy, 2006. See also Kelleen Kaye, "Differences in Nonmarital Childbearing Across States," in Lawrence L. Wu and Barbara Wolfe, eds., *Out of Wedlock: The Causes and Consequences of Nonmarital Fertility* (New York: Russell Sage Foundation, 2001), p. 49.
6. "Teenage Pregnancy and the Welfare Reform Debate," Guttmacher Institute, New York, 1998. State-level teenage fertility data: "Facts at a Glance: State-by-State Comparison," *Child Trends*, June 2007. State poverty data from U.S. Census 2005.
7. "Facts at a Glance," *Child Trends*, June 2007. On recent trends in unmarried childbearing in the U.S. see Cynthia Osborne, "Is Marriage Protective for all Children? Cumulative Risks at Birth and Subsequent Child Behavior among Urban Families," Center for Research on Child Wellbeing, Working Paper #2007-09-FF, March 2007.

8. Clinton quote cited in Saul D. Hoffman, "Teenage Childbearing Is Not So Bad After All . . . Or Is It? A Review of the New Literature," *Family Planning Perspectives*, Vol 30., No. 5, 1998, p. 236. On PRWORA stipulations for teen mothers Lingxin Hao, Nan M. Astone, and Andrew J. Cherlin, "Effects of Child Support and Welfare Policies on Nonmarital Teenage Childbearing and Motherhood," *Population Research and Policy Review*, Vol. 26, No. 3, 2007, p. 236.

9. For details of the "widespread agreement" and real value of welfare payments 1960s–1980s, see Robert A. Moffitt, "Welfare Benefits and Female Headship in U.S. Time Series" in Lawrence L. Wu and Barbara Wolfe, eds., *Out of Wedlock: The Causes and Consequences of Nonmarital Fertility*, p. 145. Richard Morin, "The Tooth Fairy, the Easter Bunny, and the Welfare Mom," *Washington Post National Weekly Edition*, 25 April–1 May 1994. White House Working Group on the Family quote cited in Jerry Watts, "The End of Work and the End of Welfare" *Contemporary Sociology*, Vol. 26, No. 4, 1997, p. 412.

10. Andrew L. Cherry, Mary E. Dillon, and Douglas Rugh, eds., *Teenage Pregnancy: A Global View*.

11. Lingxin Hao, Nan M. Astone, and Andrew J. Cherlin, "Effects of Child Support and Welfare Policies on Nonmarital Teenage Childbearing and Motherhood," p. 253.

12. Lingxin Hao and Andrew Cherlin. "Welfare Reform and Teenage Pregnancy, Childbirth, and School Dropout," *Journal of Marriage and Family*, Vol. 66, February 2004. Other researchers have found that welfare reform had a small negative effect on teenage childbearing in poor families. For this perspective, see Robert Kaestner, Sanders Korenman, and June O'Neill, "Has Welfare Reform Changed Teenage Behaviors?," *Journal of Policy Analysis and Management*, Vol. 22, No. 2, 2003, P. Offner "Teenagers and Welfare Reform," Washington, DC: Urban Institute, 2003.

13. Christopher Jencks and Susan E. Mayer, "The Social Consequences of Growing Up in a Poor Neighborhood," in Laurence E. Lynn Jr. and Michael G.H. McGeary, eds., *Inner-City Poverty in the United States* (Washington, DC: National Academy Press, 1990), p. 167.

14. Jonathan Crane, "Effects of Neighborhoods on Dropping Out of School and Teenage Childbearing," in Christopher Jencks and Paul E. Peterson, eds., *The Urban Underclass* (Washington, DC: Brookings Institution, 1991), p. 311. Eric P. Baumer and Scott J. South, "Community Effects on Youth Sexual Activity," *Journal of Marriage and Family*, Vol. 63, May 2001, p. 552.

15. Christopher R. Browning and Lori A. Burrington, "Racial Differences in Sexual and Fertility Attitudes in an Urban Setting," *Journal of Marriage and Family*, Vol. 68, February 2006, p. 248.

16. Ibid., p. 248.

17. Sanders Korenman, Robert Kaestner, and Theodore J. Joyce, "Unintended Pregnancy and the Consequences of Nonmarital Childbearing," in Lawrence L. Wu and Barbara Wolfe, eds., *Out of Wedlock: The Causes and Consequences of Nonmarital Fertility*, p. 280. Kathryn Edin and Maria Kefalas, *Promises I Can Keep: Why Poor Women Put Motherhood Before Marriage* (Berkeley: University of California Press, 2005). Eric P. Baumer and Scott J. South, "Community Effects on Youth Sexual Activity." Arline Geronimus and Sanders Korenman, "The Socioeconomic Consequences of Teen Childbearing Reconsidered," *Quarterly Journal of Economics* CVII, 1992. Jeff Grogger and Stephen Bronars, "The Socioeconomic Consequences of Teenage Childbearing: Findings from a Natural Experiment," *Family Planning Perspectives*, Vol. 25, No. 4, 1993. V. Joseph Hotz, Seth G. Sanders, and Susan Williams McElroy, "Teenage Childbearing and Its Life Cycle Consequences: Exploiting a Natural Experiment," National Bureau of Economic Research Working Paper No. 7397, New York, 1999. Constance Willard Williams, *Black Teenage Mothers: Pregnancy and Child Rearing from Their Perspective* (Lexington, MA: Lexington Books, 1991). On the disadvantage teen mothers' kids may inherit, see Saul D. Hoffman, "By the Numbers: The Public Costs of Teen Childbearing," 2006, Judith A. Levine, Clifton R. Emery, and Harold Pollack, "The Well-Being of Children Born to Teen Mothers," *Journal of Marriage and Family*, Vol. 69, February 2007; and Judith A. Levine, Harold Pollack, and Maureen E. Comfort, "Academic and Behavioral Outcomes Among the Children of Young Mothers," *Journal of Marriage and Family*, Vol. 63, No. 2, 2001, p. 355.

18. On the relational nature of class in the U.S. see William G. Roy, *Making Societies: The Historical Construction of Our World* (Thousand Oaks, CA: Pine Forge Press, 2001).

19. William Julius Wilson, *The Truly Disadvantaged* (Chicago: University of Chicago Press, 1987).

20. Wilson, *The Truly Disadvantaged*, pp. 50–56, 135. Douglas A. Massey and Nancy A. Denton, *American Apartheid: Segregation and the Making of the Underclass* (Cambridge, MA: Harvard University Press, 1993). Robert A. Moffitt, "Welfare Benefits and Female Headship in U.S. Time Series," in Lawrence L. Wu and Barbara Wolfe, eds., *Out of Wedlock: The Causes and Consequences of Nonmarital Fertility*, p. 153.

21. However, such workers have been a key factor in swelling unionization rates in service occupations. See Roger D. Waldinger, Chris Erickson, Ruth Milkman, Daniel Mitchell, Abel Valenzuela, Kent Wong, and Maurice Zeitlin, "Helots No More: A Case Study of the Justice for Janitors Campaign in Los Angeles," The Ralph and Goldy Lewis Center for Regional Policy Studies. Working Paper Series. Paper 15, 1996.

22. Wilson, *The Truly Disadvantaged*, p. 58.

23. Thomas J. Sugrue, chapter 22 in this volume. Leonard M. Lopoo and Thomas DeLeire, "Did Welfare Reform Influence the Fertility of Young Teens?," *Journal of Policy Analysis and Management*, Vol. 25, No. 2, 2006, p. 285. Mignon R. Moore and P. Lindsay Chase-Lansdale, "Sexual Intercourse and Pregnancy Among African American Girls in High-Poverty Neighborhoods: The Role of Family and Perceived Community Environment," *Journal of Marriage and Family*, Vol. 63, No. 4, 2001, p. 1146.

24. Stephen T. Russell, Faye C. H. Lee and the Latina/o Teen Pregnancy Prevention Workshop, "Practitioners'

Perspectives on Effective Practices for Hispanic Teenage Pregnancy Prevention," *Perspectives on Sexual and Reproductive Health*, Vol. 36, No. 4, 2004, p. 142.

25. Gloria González-López, "Fathering Latina Sexualities: Mexican Men and the Virginity of Their Daughters," *Journal of Marriage and Family*, Vol. 66, No. 5, p. 1118.

26. Maxine Baca Zinn and Melissa Riba, "Childbearing Among Latina Youth," *Sage Race Relations Abstracts*, Vol. 24, No. 1, 1991, p. 12.

27. M.L. O'Connor, "Academically Oriented Teenage Women Have Reduced Pregnancy Risk," *Family Planning Perspectives*, Vol. 31, No. 2, 1999. Kristin Luker, *Dubious Conceptions: The Controversy Over Teen Pregnancy*, p. 169.

28. Lisbeth Schorr, *Within Our Reach: Breaking the Cycle of Disadvantage* (New York: Anchor Press/Doubleday, 1988), p. 9. G. Orfield, D. Losen, J. Wald, and C. Swanson. *Losing Our Future: How Minority Youth are Being Left Behind by the Graduation Rate Crisis.* Cambridge, MA: The Civil Rights Project at Harvard University. Contributors: Advocates for Children of New York, The Civil Society Institute, 2001, p. 2.

29. Jonathan Kozol, *Savage Inequalities: Children in America's Schools* (New York: Crown Publishers, 1991), p. 29.

30. Ibid., pp. 58–59.

31. Jonathan Kozol, *The Shame of the Nation: The Restoration of Apartheid Schooling in America* (New York: Crown Publishers, 2005).

32. Ibid., pp. 101–103. Wilson, *The Truly Disadvantaged*, p. 103.

33. Kozol, *The Shame of the Nation*, p. 90.

34. Ibid., pp. 172, 177. Kozol, *Savage Inequalities*.

35. Ibid., p. 104.

36. Kozol, *The Shame of the Nation*, Appendix.

37. Gallup Poll, June, 1998.

38. William Cameron Chumlea, Christine M. Schubert, Alex F. Roche, Howard E. Kulin, Peter A. Lee, John H. Himes, and Shumei S. Sun, "Age at Menarche and Racial Comparisons in US Girls," *Pediatrics*, Vol. 111, No. 1, 2003. Stephanie Coontz, *Marriage, A History: From Obedience to Intimacy or How Love Conquered Marriage* (New York: Viking, 2005).

39. For an excellent discussion of the history and effectiveness of abstinence-only sex education, see AnneMarie Murdock, "Reversing Course: The Impact of 'Faith-Based' Sexual Health and Family Planning Policies At Home and Abroad," Briefing Paper, Council on Contemporary Families, January 17, 2006.

40. Ibid. GovTrack.us. H.R. 1653–110th Congress (2007): Responsible Education About Life Act, GovTrack.us, www.govtrack.us/congress/bill.xpd?bill=h110–1653, accessed September 17, 2007. "Responsible Education About Life (REAL) Act," Advocates for Youth, Washington, DC, 2007, www.advocatesforyouth.org, accessed September 17, 2007.

41. Hannah Brückner and Peter Bearman, "The Limits of Abstinence-Only in Preventing Sexually Transmitted Infections," *Journal of Adolescent Health*, Vol. 36, No. 4, 2005. Christopher Trenholm, Barbara Devancy, Ken Fortson, Lisa Quay, Justin Wheeler, Melissa Clark, "Impacts of Four Title V, Section 510 Abstinence Education Programs," Mathematica Policy Research, April 2007. John S. Santelli, Laura Duberstein Lindberg, Lawrence B. Finer, and Susheela Singh, "Explaining Recent Declines In Adolescent Pregnancy in the United States: The Contribution of Abstinence and Improved Contraceptive Use," *American Journal of Public Health*, Vol. 97, No. 1, 2007.

42. L.B. Finer and S.K. Henshaw, "Disparities in Rates of Unintended Pregnancy in the United States, 1994 and 2001," *Perspectives on Sexual and Reproductive Health*, Vol. 38, No. 2, 2006. Edin and Kefalas, *Promises I Can Keep*, p. 37.

43. Ibid., p. 33.

44. Arline Geronimus and Sanders Korenman, "The Socioeconomic Consequences of Teen Childbearing Reconsidered," 1992. V. Joseph Hotz, Seth G. Sanders, and Susan Williams McElroy, "Teenage Childbearing and Its Life Cycle Consequences: Exploiting a Natural Experiment," 1999.

45. Edin and Kefalas, *Promises I Can Keep*, p. 45.

46. Mireya Navarro, "Teen-Age Mothers Viewed as Abused Prey of Older Men," *New York Times*, May 19, 1996. Elizabeth Terry-Humen, Jennifer Manlove, and Sarah Cottingham, "Trends and Recent Estimates: Sexual Activity Among U.S. Teens," Child Trends Research Brief, 2006, p. 5.

47. Sara McLanahan, Irwin Garfinkel, Nancy Reichman, Julien Teitler, Marcia Carlson, and Christina Norland Audigier, "The Fragile Families and Child Wellbeing Study: Baseline National Report," March 2003. Lisa Mincieli, Jennifer Manlove, Molly McGarrett, Kristin Moore, and Suzanne Ryan, "The Relationship Context of Births Outside of Marriage: The Rise of Cohabitation," Child Trends, May 2007 #2007-13.

48. Edin and Kefalas, *Promises I Can Keep*, pp. 107, 179–180.

49. Paula England and Kathryn Edin, *Unmarried Couples with Children* (New York: Russell Sage, 2007).

50. Edin and Kefalas, *Promises I Can Keep*, pp. 83, 100.

24

Mothering Through Recruitment
Kinscription of Nonresidential Fathers and Father Figures in Low-Income Families[*]

Kevin Roy and Linda Burton

How low-income single mothers and nonresidential fathers sort out responsibilities for taking care of their children remains a keen policy interest in American society. Social demographers have noted the separation of marriage from childbearing in recent decades (Ventura & Bachrach, 2000), leading current scholarly and political discourse to focus on variations in formal partner (e.g., marital) statuses in poor families and paternal involvement. However, few studies have explored the implications of the separation of intimate relations from childrearing, and we have limited insight into the processes underlying whether and how nonresidential fathers maintain involvement with unmarried mothers and their children (Carlson, McLanahan, & England, 2004; Waller & McLanahan, 2005). Paternal involvement is particularly relevant in low-income families, in which men's providing and caregiving can help pull children out of poverty.

As single mothers, many low-income women seek out resources to support their children's well-being. Often, they turn to nonresidential fathers and related male role models to secure contributions. From this perspective, recruitment and maintenance of paternal involvement can be considered to be a strategy for unmarried women in economically disadvantaged families to be "good mothers." Unfortunately, few researchers have explored paternal involvement from the perspective of what low-income single mothers do to acquire resources for their families (Dominguez & Watkins, 2003). Survey research in particular can obscure subtle variations of men's behaviors and mothers' paternal recruitment strategies.

Following basic assumptions from a grounded theory approach (LaRossa, 2005), our goal in this analysis was to discover new theoretical perspectives on coparenting and partnering in low-income families. We modified this approach by drawing on a kinscription framework (Stack & Burton, 1993), which describes the recruitment of individuals to do family labor. We defined paternal recruitment as the negotiation of connections with a range of men (biological fathers, boyfriends, nonintimate friends, paternal and maternal kin) in order to improve children's life chances in economically disadvantaged communities. By contextualizing a critical dimension of kinscription, we examined how mothers recruited specific men to fulfill essential parenting needs. The processes of recruitment, we assert, were the first steps in mothers' negotiation of fathers' contribution to children's development.

MOTHERS' INFLUENCE ON PATERNAL INVOLVEMENT IN LOW-INCOME FAMILIES

Although researchers have recognized that mothers influence the roles of fathers, and more point-edly, paternal involvement with children, the nature and degree of this influence is a matter of considerable debate (Doherty, Kouneski, & Erikson, 1998; Walker & McGraw, 2000). The concept of maternal gatekeeping has been used to describe primarily exclusionary measures, such as mothers' motivations to monitor, discourage, or deflect men's interaction with children (Allen & Hawkins, 1999). Gatekeeping has emerged from studies with a primary focus on residential, married couples, most of whom have been middle-class and European American (Allen & Hawkins, 1999; DeLuccie, 2001; see Fagan & Barnett, 2003 for exception). Pleck and Masciadrelli (2004) noted that many gatekeeping studies have linked discouragement of paternal involvement to mothers' attitudes but rarely to actual family processes.

Studies of unmarried parents in economically disadvantaged families, in contrast, have often relied on rational choice models to account for mothers' efforts to secure resources from fathers. Wilson (1987) described mothers' attempts to secure potential marital partners (and contributors to children's well-being) with the concept of the limited marriageability pool for low-income African American women. Edin and Lein (1997) noted women's packaging of resources by requiring fathers to "pay to stay," to contribute to a household in exchange for an intimate relation-ship. Like gatekeeping studies, these studies on low-income families did not broadly capture the range of processes of mothers' encouragement and discouragement of male involvement across a wide array of family configurations.

As an alternative approach, studies of women's kinwork have conceptualized how mothers ensure their children's well-being and influence men's family involvement. DiLeonardo (1987) identified "keeping families together" as the core of women's work activities (including household labor, child/elder care, and market labor) that require the women to embody a mix of altruism and self-interest. Others have described being a kinkeeper as encompassing emotional work, communication activities, physical labor, and financial obligations (Gerstel & Gallagher, 1993; Rosenthal, 1985). Previous research also revealed that mothers have identified, created, maintained, and even dissolved a range of supportive kin networks for daily survival and social mobility of their families (Nelson, 2000; Stack, 1974). Further, these mothers worked to advocate and improve their children's life chances by personalizing connections with significant kinworkers, usually grandmothers, sisters, aunts and friends (Glenn, Chang, & Forcey, 1994).

Focused recruitment of men into kinwork roles is a distinct advocacy strategy that could potentially enhance families, although we recognize the ambivalence of such involvement. Stack (1974) demonstrated how even the establishment of paternity itself could bring resources to mothers and their children through the contributions of paternal kin. However, family members also felt that poor men drained valuable resources that help sustain family systems (Stack, 1974), and they held tight to time-proven mental representations of low-income fathers as "renegade relatives" (Stack & Burton, 1993, p. 164) who do more harm than good.

Indeed, there is some evidence that low-income men's transitions in residences, relationships, and employment put low-income families at risk for loss of resources, conflict, and potential abuse (Sano, 2004; Waller & Swisher, 2006). Specifically, fathers often are obligated to more than one set of nonresident and/or resident children (Manning, Stewart, & Smock, 2003; Roy, 1999). According to researchers (Edin, 2000; Edin & Kefalas, 2005), some single mothers believe that low wages combined with inconsistent employment render poor men unprepared for family relationships. Despite these risks, mothers have been found to tailor flexible paternal roles in multigenerational

African American families to expand the range of men who can contribute to children's well-being (Jarrett, Roy, & Burton, 2002).

THE PRESENT STUDY

This analysis draws from the kinscripts framework (Stack & Burton, 1993), which situates kinwork within complex family relationships over time. This framework shifts the focus of study from mother/father relationships to extrafamilial relationships constructed to enhance children's well-being (Crosbie-Burnett & Lewis, 1999). Based on the experiences of multigenerational African American families, a kinwork perspective acknowledges family members' ongoing actions to "regenerate families, maintain lifetime continuities, sustain intergenerational responsibilities, and reinforce shared values" (Stack & Burton, 1993, p. 160). Family scripts guide social expectations and lead to efficiency and consistency in taking care of family responsibilities (Byng-Hall, 1985, 1988). We theorized that paternal recruitment is a critical dimension of mothers' kinscription efforts and has relevance for both their own and their children's well-being.

Previous studies have limited their focus to the need for men's instrumental contributions, typically financial resources for themselves and their children (Gibson, Edin, & McLanahan, 2005; Kotchick, Dorsey, & Heller, 2005; Mincy, Garfinkel, & Nepomnyaschy, 2005; Roy, 1999). However, other studies have indicated that mothers also need a contribution of time to provide care from trustworthy kinworkers. Roy, Tubbs, and Burton (2004) identified how low-income mothers in Chicago sought relief from the demands of food preparation, transportation, and grooming activities in 24-hr child care. Low-income single mothers also sought out the guidance that fathers provided for their children and the emotional support that they offered to them as mothers who parented alone (Jarrett et al., 2002).

To summarize, this study explored low-income single mothers' recruitment of men as an open-ended and contested process, inclusive of multiple family needs and multiple actors. We defined recruitment as the negotiation of connections with a range of men (biological fathers, boyfriends, nonintimate friends, paternal and maternal kin) in order to improve children's life chances in economically disadvantaged communities. To explore the processes of recruitment, we asked how did low-income mothers involve nonresidential fathers and other men to fulfill family needs? Specifically, we examined three processes that emerged in analyses of interview data:

Single mothers' negotiated legitimacy of normative expectations for men;
Mothers' reconciliation of the overlap of maternal advocacy with the demands of intimate
    relationships;
Mothers' minimization of risks to their children during recruitment.
        [. . .]

Search for Conventional Fathers and Partners

Low-income mothers aspired to conventional parenthood like other families in American society (Anderson, 1990; Edin, 2000). Given limited economic opportunities, however, parenthood not only preceded marriage but often occurred in the absence of a committed relationship altogether (Jarrett et al., 2002). In these circumstances, mothers in this study sought to recruit men who could fulfill some of the most basic expectations of fatherhood (see Figure 24.1).

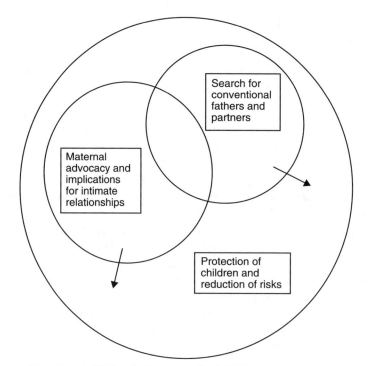

Figure 24.1 Processes of Recruitment of Fathers by Low-Income Single Mothers.

Legitimacy through "that gold standard." Mothers referred to being brought up with traditional family values, with gendered divisions of work in their families. Normative father roles fit easily into this vision. For example, Sonya, a 24-year-old African American mother of three children in Boston, was raised to aspire to "that gold standard, you know—that there should be a mother in the home, a father at work. She should cook, clean, and nurture the kids, while the man provided for his family and provided discipline." If fathers were recruited and maintained some level of involvement with their children, mothers believed that they could be "strong influences" who could emerge as role models for their children.

For poor mothers without partners, just the presence of a father in the household conveyed a strong sense of social legitimacy for themselves and their children. Yolanda, a 40-year-old mother in Chicago, tried repeatedly to involve the biological father of her infant son, through appeals to join her and become "a real family . . . I want to have a normal family." For Yolanda, "it had to be him, there is no one else that could fit, I can't imagine anyone else playing [his] father." Even after the father moved to New York, she intended to ask him to move back in with her and her son. She firmly believed that her son knew his estranged father by his smell, insisting "la sangre llama" ("blood calls") to children.

Mothers responded to their children's sense of legitimacy as well. Children wanted to identify who their fathers were, and this line of questioning led mothers to reflect on the impact of recruiting men as fathers. Tanya, an African American mother in Boston, grew increasingly ambivalent about remaining a single parent. "[My daughter Cara] asks me questions about where her father is . . . What would it be like if there was someone in the house for her?" Tanya also recognized that a father could ease the "emotional burden" of being a single parent. She said, "I blame myself at times for a father not being there, but I try not to think about it, because I've got to do everything I can for my daughter."

Mothers often framed recruitment as the responsibility that biological fathers had to their children. For men with resources, this appeal for legitimacy was persuasive and could lead to their consistent interaction in families. Carla, a young Latina mother in Chicago with a 4-year-old daughter and 18-month-old twin sons, was able to maintain a supportive relationship with her ex-husband. In addition to paying $100 in weekly child support, he remained integrally involved as a caregiver for his children. He stopped by at the family's apartment after work every day at 4 pm, ate dinner with the family frequently, and took his daughter to stay with him at his parents' house on weekends. Carla had emphasized that he needed to take care of his children who "he had brought into this world."

Monitoring and accountability. However, such arrangements were typically short lived, and mothers needed to monitor men and hold them accountable for their involvement. For example, it was a common discussion among mothers in the study that "[the biological father] has no right to see his children unless he's contributing." Since material support was usually the most urgent family need, it was also the breaking point for many recruitment strategies. Samora, a young Latina mother in San Antonio, regretted that she had to monitor the work activities of the biological father of her 3-year-old son. She could not believe that "he's working [in a car lot] and he's 6, 7 months behind in payment. He doesn't act like a daddy." When recruitment of men grew volatile and/or too complicated, mothers could find that their roles as coordinators were "too much hassle" for too little material support.

Paternal involvement also required a level of maturity and commitment that went beyond simple material support. Gisella, a Puerto Rican mother in Chicago, held onto her high expectations and grew frustrated at the lack of responsibility of her baby's father. He moved back and forth to Puerto Rico repeatedly, without direction and with little ambition. Eventually, he served 5 months in jail, and he did not seem intent on maintaining his relationship with his infant daughter. Gisella adamantly refused to let him sign the birth certificate or to give the baby his last name, saying "When he shows me that he can be a father, then he can sign."

Barriers to recruitment and lowered expectations. The common experience of incarceration was one of the most critical barriers to achieving conventional roles through recruitment. Almost 20% of the families in the study reported that at least one nonresidential father or intimate partner was incarcerated. As with Gisella, it was difficult for mothers to maintain recruitment efforts when men were incarcerated; despite their best intentions, men could not confer legitimacy as conventional parents when they were in jail, prison, or work release.

The dynamic context of immigration presented another disruption to mothers' efforts to link fathers with children. The ambiguity of residency status, the search for jobs, and return home to visit or care for family members across international borders shaped recruitment strategies for Mexican and Puerto Rican families. Even though Clarissa moved into an apartment in Boston with Alex, the biological father of their young son, she never felt comfortable as a "conventional" family.

> He has done very little for our son. He told me never to leave him alone with the baby. But I don't want to take the baby's father away from him. Family is very important to me—maybe this is why I let it continue. Latino men learned American values when they [came to the States], so that [they believe] "nobody can depend on me, what's mine is mine and what's yours is yours." If he leaves us, I will continue living.

Clarissa believed that most men had partners in the States and at home, in Puerto Rico. Alex, in fact, had an older son from a previous relationship, and he continued to send money to his sisters and to his son. A year later, he returned from a visit to Puerto Rico with his older son, who "had no one to care for him." Clarissa confronted him about the differences in how he treated his two sons, but he misinterpreted her comments, assuming that she did not want his older son to stay with them. Eventually, Alex returned to Puerto Rico with his older son, built a house, and cut off ties with Clarissa and her child.

A third barrier to recruitment for legitimacy was men's commitments to multiple kin networks. Many men continued to live with their aging parents and were partially responsible for their parents' well-being. Mothers often felt that this commitment was wrongly placed when men had their own children. Mothers also feared that support from successfully recruited fathers would grow tenuous if these men had children with a new partner. For example, one mother described her ex-partner as a "good father" who contributed diapers, clothes, and other important resources, and cared for his children nightly and during weekends. However, she was concerned that he would "wash his hands of us" when his current partner gave birth.

The expectations for conventional fatherhood could be set too high for most men in low-income families, and some mothers lowered expectations for involvement. Consistent contributions were a challenge for low-income men who did not have access to good jobs. Sabine, a 23-year-old African American mother of two daughters, focused on the efforts, not the contributions, of their biological father. She described Earl as "a good man" when he took them shopping for clothes, shoes, and food or "put money in a savings account for their future." Earl abused drugs on and off for 7 years, but she gave him credit for doing "the right thing" and giving what he could when he was "clean." Similarly, Juanita, a young mother of two preschoolers in San Antonio, settled for the efforts of her baby's father, despite his commitment to three other children. "Just as long as he sees his daughter," she said, "That's what's important. He's part of her life. I'd rather have him part of her life than giving me money and not coming around at all."

For both these mothers, some involvement was better than none. They took advantage of what one mother described as "what was offered, when it was offered." Men who even tried to achieve conventional success as fathers put their families a step closer to "that gold standard" of legitimacy. As one mother argued, "Any help is welcome, from any of these men. I need to bring them all along." In effect, many mothers felt that they had little choice but to encourage a complicated configuration of men to become involved, even if accepting inconsistent contributions led to ambiguity and conflict in their lives.

Maternal Advocacy and Implications for Intimate Relationships

If "bringing [men] along" as involved *parents* proved problematic, mothers' advocacy had even more complicated implications for men as potential intimate *partners*. As DiLeonardo (1987) suggested, the early stages of kinwork (in this case, recruitment of fathers) unfolded in fits and starts, competition and cooperation, and guilt and gratification. Negotiation over men's involvement left open the question of how participation in children's lives would lead, or not lead, to intimacy, companionship, and long-term commitment. For mothers, advocacy for children's well-being was infused with self-interest, as the promise of a conventional father folded into the promise of a conventional partner.

In the next section, we examine implications for relationships with biological fathers and intimate partners separately. Mothers' recruitment appeals were tailored to biological imperatives (with biological fathers) or social opportunities (with intimate partners).

Investments and "settling" for biological fathers. When mothers pursued the involvement of their children's biological fathers, they recognized the significant investment of work and emotion, often over many years, that shaped their recruitment. Due to this "history," most mothers gave priority to the recruitment of biological fathers. However, reinvolvement of biological fathers opened negotiation over intimate relations, and mothers struggled to redefine their relationships. Clarissa (above) found that her relationship with her son's father could not be defined with conventional descriptions of marital partner or coparent.

> Marriage is what women dream about, society asks that of a woman, or the economic situation, or love, but more than anything, to get married by God's law is a serious compromise. But [Alex] is my *marido*—like a companion or a boyfriend . . . In Latino countries, the man gets a house for the woman, but things are different here—a man moves into a woman's house. The relationship has changed now—it's like a schedule, I get up, clean, he goes to work, I cook, take care of Justin . . . I'm trying to hold the relationship together for Justin. I'm not confident we'll remain together.

When mothers appealed to recruit biological fathers for involvement with their children, as Clarissa did, they often explicitly communicated the imperative that biological fathers must support their children. These appeals could imply that intimate relationships were "back on track." The implications were often unintended, and few mothers accepted them without question. Karen, a 45-year-old European American mother of two young children, relied solely on her own father for child care while she worked. Upon his death, she regrettably appealed for her ex-husband's involvement "for the kids."

> I work at night, and I needed to find someone new. It's easier for him to move back in. I'm not entirely happy with the situation—it's more economical, more for the kids than for me. Our relationship has not really improved but Beth and Brian are happy to have him around. Unless he makes changes—stop drinking, his swearing, his work ethic—I don't actually see myself with him. But I don't have time to meet anyone new. I really just need his help. I'm tired of worrying about having enough money and resources for my kids. I tried living on my own, went on welfare for a few months, but I can't make ends meet. I went into credit debt and thought about filing bankruptcy. I just don't know how single mothers are supposed to work full-time and take care of children.

Mothers could make their relationships contingent on men fulfilling expectations as good providers and caregivers. One mother in Chicago asked her baby's father to move in, even after he cheated on her. But she insisted, "We're not really 'together' together. I told him, 'The only way you're going to stay here is if you pay all the bills, do everything.' " If the potential for financial contribution faded, mothers then dampened recruitment strategies and ended relationships. After her children's father lost his job at the tail end of 4 years of engagement, Katherine, a European American mother in Boston, ultimately rejected his marriage proposal.

Although these mothers described recruitment through clear-cut offers to "pay to stay" (Edin & Lein, 1997), the daily process of recruitment was actually quite open ended. Most mothers had few alternatives to their heavy investments with biological fathers, and they could not readily anticipate the consequences of their appeal for paternal involvement. Rejection of biological fathers meant letting go of the chance of legitimacy with fathers as well as the promise of marriage with a partner. Yesenia was a young Chicago mother with five children, and she secured a restraining order for 18 months against the children's biological father, after he served 3 months in jail for a domestic violence offense. However, she still needed someone to watch her children when she was at work during the day.

I'm trying to give him a second chance. We've been doing well since he came back, we're much happier. He's promised not to drink. But that makes his temper short, and I don't want him to lash out, so we don't talk very much. He's helping more around the house, doing things that needed to be done for some time now. I want this to work out, for the kids' sake. He's a great father and the kids love him. I don't mind him being back, and they really missed him.

Looking for "more" with intimate partners. Men who were not the biological fathers of children did not carry a history of disappointments. They represented the chance to start again, with the promise of legitimacy. Mothers downplayed the message of recruitment for paternal involvement and explicitly communicated the social opportunity of a promising relationship with a good man. However, the often unspoken implications were, as one mother said, that "A relationship with me is not an option if [the guy] doesn't support my kids—they come first." For example, Valerie had completed an alcoholic anonymous (AA) course after splitting up with the father of her sons. She had begun to develop a relationship with another AA member who lived in sober housing. "He's divorced, with two kids, a good job," she said, "And I like spending time with him—he's intelligent, he's a good conversationalist." Valerie backed up her assessment by noting that "he supports his children too, he hasn't run out on them. That's good for my kids. He's a good catch."

For some mothers, material support from intimate partners led to the end of reliance on inconsistent contributions or conflict with biological fathers. New partners gave mothers renewed confidence, as well as scarce resources needed to nurture children. Eva, a young Latina mother of three preschool-age children in San Antonio, left her abusive former partner, who threatened to pursue custody. Her new fiancé's consistent financial contributions and offers to help with child care allowed Eva to avoid contacting her former partner for financial support or child care. Her ability to move past a threatening relationship was contingent on the involvement of her fiancé with her children.

On the other hand, renewed support from biological fathers could lead mothers to look more critically at the limits of relationships with intimate partners. Kate, a European American mother of a 2-year-old son, began to receive formal child support and regular child care from the father of her child, while her live-in partner contributed little. She tolerated her partner's lack of commitment for a few months before ending their relationship, "for not offering anything to me and my kids." Kim, an African American mother in Boston, reflected on the necessity of companionship, in the context of limitations of both biological fathers and potential partners.

I'm lonely. I know with that touch, I can stop working on myself . . . But I've learned that no man can destroy me. Men don't see my heart—they're just looking to take from me. With all my kids' fathers, what got me first was they'd give me money and take me out. But then that ended, and it was more as if they were another one of my children. I'm not having it, I can't grow with someone like that. It's not my responsibility to believe in my kids' fathers and make them constantly accountable to their children. Men can get away with it—they do me like that.

As Clarissa noted, "what society/economics/love/God asks of" women—to find involved fathers and partners—propelled some mothers to continue to seek men for support of children and themselves. The conflation of intimate relations and parenting often led them to accept the risks of some men's involvement. Kris, a mother of five children, knew that "when my kids needed a father figure, I tried to find one . . . I tried to make sure that there is a man in my life that loved me and respected me and loved my kids." She was consumed with finding legitimacy and stability with a father and partner and in turn entered into relationships with three men who abused her and her children. Kris held onto her ideals and blamed herself, in spite of the damage that these men had brought into her family's lives: "It was my fault maybe, and I'm sorry for ruining my kids' lives."

Protection of Children and Reduction of Risks

Recruitment of father figures as alternatives. Negotiations to recruit biological fathers and intimate partners proved to be exhausting for mothers in low-income families, and they often put women and children at risk for abuse or gaps in material or caregiving supports. The recruitment of men in nonintimate relationships offered alternative choices. Although only 6% of all the men identified in the sample were nonintimate relations, they offered critical short-term and "bridge" care options for mothers. Mothers explored web chat rooms, workplaces, parties, and neighborhood gathering places to elicit the support of male acquaintances and close friends. Once involved, the loss of these father figures could be "devastating." Lucy, a pregnant Mexican American mother of four children, lost her home and moved into a family shelter. At the shelter, a new friend, Sean, convinced her to not put her baby up for adoption, and 3 years later had assumed the title of "father" for her daughter. Lucy insisted that Sean was "the only constant person in my life."

By recruiting a network of fathers and father figures, mothers secured a consistent web of support that would not put their children at risk for lack of resources. Emma, a 50-year-old European American grandmother in Boston, agreed that "Daddy" was a complicated term for Sunny, her 4-year-old custodial granddaughter. Sunny did not live or interact regularly with her biological father or her mother's new boyfriend, but her uncle and her stepgrandfather were both "Daddy" because they shared a household with her. At a picnic on Father's Day, Emma celebrated the efforts of fathers in the extended family, including these four men as well as seven other men with children (her father-in-law, her husband's brother and his son, a son by her first husband, her brother, her nephew, and her next-door neighbor). Paternal involvement with Sunny was shared among a number of men, most of whom were non-kin related father figures. Expectations for their involvement were kept vague and fluid, based on who was there and which needs arose. With a complex array of father figures, Emma flexibly tailored parenting needs to the demands of shifting residence, employment, and care arrangements.

In the aftermath of dissolved relationships with biological fathers and intimate partners, many mothers could only trust "the men of my family." Mothers and their male siblings set up regular swaps of child care in reciprocal care arrangements. Like some women, Crystal, a 45-year-old African American mother in Chicago, turned to her older sons to care for her younger children, whose biological fathers were incarcerated. In Boston, Jamilla recruited her godfather to care for and play with her child. After a few months, her boyfriend and the child's biological father returned to the neighborhood, and her godfather's obligations faded out. Again, the commitments of father figures typically were limited in focus and short-term in duration.

Recruitment and legacies of paternal kin. Stack (1974) found that paternal kin were activated in the lives of mothers and children through the basic act of paternity establishment. For mothers in this study, explicit recruitment of paternal kin ensured the continuation of this support. The involvement of paternal kin did not reintroduce unwanted intimacies and was often more trustworthy, in part due to the commitment of "women who are mothers in *his* family." Paternal grandmothers were central figures in an "as-needed" optional daycare network for many mothers, as well as purchasers of clothing and sole custodians for children during emergency situations. Men's brothers and sisters were confidantes for both parents on parenting, jobs, and money matters, as well as caregivers who could offer weekend visits to households filled with cousins. If direct paternal involvement was problematic, mothers made direct appeals for housing or financial assistance to paternal kin who felt obligated to children through biological ties. Young mothers also lived with paternal grandparents to remain in school during the early years after birth.

When biological fathers completely fell out of their children's lives, paternal kin often felt compelled to take up responsibility for care and support of their youngest family members. Billie, an African American mother of 3- and 6-year-old daughters in Chicago, encouraged one of her children's fathers to contribute whatever financial support he could, but due to his incarceration, she had to rely more heavily on another of her children's fathers. He and his mother cared for all of her children regularly, bought her and the children clothes, and, in a crisis, supported the family with money when Billie's welfare benefits were terminated.

However, recruitment of paternal kin could become problematic and even unproductive for some mothers. Many mothers grew critical when the involvement of paternal kin enabled biological fathers to be seen as "involved parents" despite not being involved. Cassandra, a young European American mother in Chicago, was separated from the Puerto Rican father of her two children, and she minimized her former partner's contributions, saying, "He's a chicken daddy—his family watches my baby, and he gets the credit."

A few mothers went beyond ordinary measures to secure a paternal family legacy for their children's sense of identity and development. Francesca, a 22-year-old European American mother in Boston, maintained a strong relationship with the family of Roberto, her daughter's father. She communicated regularly by phone with them in the Dominican Republic and eventually saved enough money to visit with her daughter. Francesca wanted her daughter to know her 5-year-old half brother and agreed to have him come visit her and her daughter for periods of time as he grew up. Some mothers stopped trying to recruit men for support and opted to recruit paternal kin directly. For example, Javier denied his biological ties to his son, but after positive DNA identification, Yolanda photocopied the test results and mailed them to his mother and sisters in Mexico. She explained that "esto es por si todavia dudan . . . this is in case they still doubt [who the father is]."

Through recruitment of biological fathers, intimate partners, nonintimate male friends, and paternal kin, mothers were engaged in a process of minimizing risks for their children. Mothers usually gave priority to pursuing recruitment in this order as well. For example, Lorena, a 29-year-old Puerto Rican mother of three children, moved to Boston after a string of abusive relationships with the biological fathers of her children. She chose not to rely on her new partner for financial support, however, and found that friends and her children's paternal kin offered inconsistent support at best. After a few years, Lorena moved South to look for better jobs. The exhausting and often risky process of recruitment of fathers and father figures was no longer an option. Instead, she relied solely on her own employment and personal resources for her children. For 30% of the *Three-City Study* families who were not involved in this analysis, mothers may have opted out of recruitment of fathers and father figures for similar reasons.

DISCUSSION

In Figure 24.1, we outline a model for three related processes in the recruitment of fathers by low-income single mothers in our sample. First, mothers seek legitimacy through recruiting men to fulfill conventional roles as good fathers and good partners/husbands. For single mothers in nontraditional family structures, involved fathers offer a chance for social legitimacy. Second, mothers negotiate how the needs for maternal advocacy shape potential intimate relationships. As single parents, negotiation of intimate relationship is particularly contested. As in the cases of Yesenia, Karen, and Gisella in our analysis, mothers struggle to understand how the search for ideal fathers is linked to the status of these men as partners. In this area of overlap of these two processes, recruitment is marked by men who could not live up to conventional expectations as fathers, and who are often risks as partners as well. Finally, mothers try to minimize risks to their children at every step of recruitment. If they are unable to secure conventional fathers or to find intimate partners who contribute to their families, they often turn to nonintimate friends and acquaintances, men in their own families, or paternal kin as options for involvement.

In effect, recruitment of fathers is a way of mothering for single, economically disadvantaged women. In spite of "hassles" from men in their lives, women advocate for their children and often themselves. In the model (see Figure 24.1), the first two processes are placed "inside" the third and the arrows suggest a preferred sequence: first, mothers begin recruitment efforts with biological fathers, using the explicit message of conventional involvement; second, they struggle to define how their family needs are shaped by potential intimate relationships. As mothers move away from these strategies, they continue to minimize risks through involvement of nonintimate family members and friends.

This model of recruitment contributes to new theory development about parenting and partnering. First, it offers insight into family processes in low-income communities. A sole focus on men's financial support in previous studies has limited understanding of mothers' strategies to enhance their children's well-being. We found, in contrast to the rather clear-cut process of "no pay, no stay" (Edin & Lein, 1997), that mothers are often unsure of the consequences of asking potential partners to contribute financially to their children or to care for their children. Moreover, it proved difficult to transform a relationship based on men's financial contributions into a parental commitment to emotional support, child care, or role modeling.

Often, it is assumed that mothers are at fault when gaps emerge in caregiving practices for children (Garey, 1999). Recruitment strategies aim to fill gaps in resources and care but also to reallocate and dissolve "blame." In this study, mothers' encouraged men's efforts, symbolic and otherwise, to ensure that children feel wanted and that mothers are "not the only one" who is responsible for family well-being. The processes of mothers' recruitment also challenge us to reconsider the limited concept of maternal gatekeeping. Low-income mothers recognized real barriers that men faced as providers and caregivers. Despite frustration in not being able to count on men's support, women often did not "give up" on fathers and returned to encourage their efforts. Similar to studies of emotion work in father/child relationships (Seery & Crowley, 2000), mothers praised men's involvement and crafted positive images for fathers.

However, these previous conceptualizations do not entirely account for the necessity for disadvantaged mothers to solicit and cultivate support. To reconceptualize caregiving in contemporary families, Garey, Hansen, Hertz, and MacDonald (2002) directed attention to patterns of interdependence within families. In this study, mothers created scripts for men's kinwork roles, informed by different family needs. They also crafted bonds of reciprocity that were flexible enough to allow for inconsistent support as well as minimal "efforts" at support.

Second, low-income single mothers had to negotiate men's involvement, and these negotiations led to complex family configurations. There are clear patterns of which family needs are most important across racial/ethnic groups (material support being the most common need), but the pathways to secure these needs are diverse. A structured discovery approach allows us to consider a full range of relationships without making assumptions about who performed paternal roles. For example, recruitment, unlike gatekeeping, is not confined to marital relationships; if mothers exclude nonresidential biological fathers from involvement, they recruit other men or paternal kin to support children's well-being. By identifying conditions in which biological fathers, intimate partners, male friends and family members, and paternal kin participate as kin-workers, this study extends theory development on men's fulfillment of normative roles (Townsend, 2002) for a single biological child.

Recruitment is also shaped by life circumstances for low-income fathers. In particular, men's immigration patterns (Portes & Sensenbrenner, 1993) force mothers to shift and supplement their strategies to secure material support across international borders and multiple family systems. In addition, incarceration removes many potential fathers and father figures from children's lives (Arditti, Lambert-Shute, & Joest, 2003; Nurse, 2002). Paternal kin step up often during incarceration, as do other biological fathers, for children within the same family; however, men's job instability, physical abuse, and substance use increasingly lead mothers to assess how the risks may outstrip the benefits of often inconsistent paternal involvement (Sano, 2004).

Finally, our findings show that mothers recruit men to secure support in specific times and places. This model is attuned to specific historical and developmental contexts in the first stages of kinscription. These are not long-standing relationships between mothers and biological fathers, and these men and women were often unfamiliar with what would be demanded of them during the first few years of coparenting with young children. Further, these fragile relationships unfolded at the height of pressure to identify paternity under new provisions of welfare reform in the late 1990s.

[. . .]

IMPLICATIONS FOR POLICY AND PRACTICE

This study has important policy and program implications for unmarried mothers, nonresidential fathers, and economically disadvantaged children. Many mothers cope with lack of adequate support for their families by recruiting fathers for their contributions. Through child support regulations, state and federal agencies attempt to secure finances as well, but policies and programs aimed at poor nonresidential fathers are usually punitive in nature and force mothers to identify fathers in order to qualify for welfare assistance (Edelman, Holzer, & Offner, 2006). Consequently, children and their mothers see little money from child support, as poor fathers are unmotivated to divert scarce resources to reimburse state outlays of welfare benefits (Johnson, Levine, & Doolittle, 1999). Recent tax initiatives in New York, in which nonresidential fathers can receive earned income tax credits for their children, may motivate some fathers to contribute financial support (Kaufman, 2005). However, social policy has failed to offer job training and placement services by which recruited fathers can support both mothers and their children. In effect, formal programs and policies may divert or even harm mothers' informal strategies to secure consistent and supportive fathers.

As this analysis indicates, mothers cannot secure support simply through identification and recruitment of biological fathers. For example, with the increasingly common experience of incarceration of both biological fathers and intimate partners, mothers must consider a wider array of men to contribute supports for children. However, policies and related program services are typically driven by guidelines to identify only biological fathers. Program staff who work with low-income mothers should note the array of fathers and father figures who are active in children's lives and who can provide them with material and social support. Paternal involvement in low-income families also requires a disproportional investment of kinwork from mothers. As the study shows, mothers who pursue resources for daily subsistence must package together the social support of a variety of fathers, just as they package together different kinds of material resources (Edin & Lein, 1997).

Mothers in this study indicated that contributions of guidance, time, and attention became vital sources of social support for children's development. However, these contributions did not translate as dollars, and few programs since 1990 have recognized and encouraged alternatives to financial provision, such as in-kind contributions (Pirog-Good, 1993). The study suggests that a sense of belonging through family and family-like relationships drives some aspects of mothers' recruitment of fathers. It also suggests that families expect different commitments from different men, and that involvement of nonbiological fathers is significant. Although nonbiological fathers may not compensate for financial support of biological fathers (McLanahan & Sandefur, 1994), they may compensate for other aspects of paternal involvement, such as caregiving. We need to explore systematically the contexts in which compensation may occur, and how to promote such compensation, to maximize resources and supports for children and their families.

Finally, social policy should acknowledge that care responsibilities, particularly in low-income and minority families, extend beyond the relationship of biological parents to obligate both maternal and paternal kin. Current policy initiatives encourage paternal involvement through funding for marriage promotion among low-income couples. Although marriage is one option to secure men's support, it focuses exclusively on partnering processes. In contrast, this study finds that paternal involvement also calls for a child-centered parenting process embedded in extended kin systems. In many families, the interdependence of extended family members' kinwork can be at odds with policy goals of locating biological fathers or enforcing work requirements for low-income mothers under welfare reform. Often, program eligibility is defined by one's status as mother or biological father, and involved kin are not considered for services. Stabilization and strengthening of adults' lives through good jobs, child care, health care, and housing will cultivate more parental figures to support children in low-income families.

NOTE

* This study was conducted with support from the National Institute for Child Health and Human Development under Project No. 5 R03 HD 42074-2 and the Purdue Research Foundation at Purdue University. We gratefully acknowledge the funders of the ethnographic component of *Welfare, Children, and Families: A Three-City Study* including the National Institute of Child Health and Human Development; Assistant Secretary for Planning and Evaluation, U.S. Department of Health and Human Services; Social Security Administration; the Henry J. Kaiser Family Foundation; the Robert Wood Johnson Foundation; the W. K. Kellogg Foundation; and the John D. and Catherine T. MacArthur Foundation. We extend special thanks to our 210-member ethnographic team (http://www.jhu.edu/-welfare), particularly the Penn State team, who provided the infrastructure, organization, and data management for the multisite ethnography. Most importantly, we thank the families who have graciously participated in the project and have given us access to their lives.

REFERENCES

Allen, S., & Hawkins, A. (1999). Maternal gatekeeping: Mothers' beliefs and behaviors that inhibit greater father involvement in family work. *Journal of Marriage and Family, 61*, 199–212.
Anderson, E. (1990). *Streetwise: Race, class, and change in an urban community*. Chicago: University of Chicago Press.
Arditti, J., Lambert-Shute, J., & Joest, K. (2003). Saturday morning at the jail: Implications of incarceration for families and children. *Family Relations, 52*, 195–204.
Byng-Hall, J. (1985). The family script: A useful bridge between theory and practice. *Journal of Family Therapy, 7*, 301–305.

Byng-Hall, J. (1988). Scripts and legends in families and family therapy, *Family Process*, 27, 167–179.

Carlson, M., McLanahan, S., & England, P. (2004). Union formation in fragile families. *Demography*, 41, 237–261.

Crosbie-Burnett, M., & Lewis, E. (1999). Use of African American family structures and functioning to address the challenges of European American postdivorce families. In S. Coontz (Ed.), *American families: A multicultural reader* (pp. 455–468). New York: Routledge.

DeLuccie, M. (2001). Mothers as gatekeepers: A model of maternal mediators of father involvement. *Journal of Genetic Psychology*, 156, 115–131.

DiLeonardo, M. (1987). The female world of cards and holidays: Women, families, and the work of kinship. *Signs: Journal of Women in Culture and Society*, 12, 440–453.

Doherty, W., Kouneski, E., & Erikson, M. (1998). Responsible fathering: An overview and conceptual framework. *Journal of Marriage and the Family*, 60, 277–292.

Dominguez, S., & Watkins, C. (2003). Creating networks for survival and mobility: Social capital among African Americans and Latin American low-income mothers. *Social Problems*, 50, 111–135.

Edelman, P., Holzer, H., & Offner, P. (2006). *Reconnecting disadvantaged young men*. Washington, DC: The Urban Institute Press.

Edin, K. (2000). What do low-income single mothers say about marriage? *Social Problems*, 47, 112–133.

Edin, K., & Kefalas, M. (2005). *Promises I can keep: Why poor women put motherhood before marriage*. Berkeley: University of California Press.

Edin, K., & Lein, L. (1997). *Making ends meet: How single mothers survive welfare and low-wage work*. New York: Russell Sage Foundation.

Fagan, J., & Barnett, M. (2003). The relationship between maternal gatekeeping, paternal competence, mothers' attitudes about the father role, and father involvement. *Journal of Family Issues*, 24, 1020–1043.

Garey, A. (1999). *Weaving work and motherhood*. Philadelphia: Temple University Press.

Garey, A., Hansen, K., Hertz, R., & MacDonald, C. (2002). Care and kinship: An introduction. *Journal of Family Issues*, 23, 703–715.

Gerstel, N., & Gallagher, S. (1993). Kinkeeping and distress: Gender, recipients of care, and work-family conflict. *Journal of Marriage and the Family*, 55, 598–607.

Gibson, C., Edin, K., & McLanahan, S. (2005). High hopes but even higher expectations: The retreat from marriage among low-income couples. *Journal of Marriage and Family*, 67, 1301–1312.

Glenn, E. N., Chang, G., & Forcey, L. R. (1994). *Mothering: Ideology, experience, and agency*. New York: Routledge.

Jarrett, R., Roy, K., & Burton, L. (2002). Fathers in the 'hood': Qualitative research on low-income African-American men. In C. Tamis-LeMonda & N. Cabrera (Eds.), *Handbook of father involvement: Multidisciplinary perspectives* (pp. 211–248). New York: Erlbaum.

Johnson, E., Levine, A., & Doolittle, F. (1999). *Fathers' fair share: Helping poor men manage child support and fatherhood*. New York: Russell Sage Foundation.

Kaufman, L. (2005, January 17). Unmarried fathers gain tax incentive in Pataki proposal. *New York Times*, p. A1.

Kotchick, B., Dorsey, S., & Heller, L. (2005). Predictors of parenting among African American single mothers: Personal and contextual factors. *Journal of Marriage and Family*, 67, 448–460.

LaRossa, R. (2005). Grounded theory methods and qualitative family research. *Journal of Marriage and Family*, 67, 837–857.

Manning, W., Stewart, S., & Smock, P. (2003). The complexity of fathers' parenting responsibilities and involvement with nonresident children. *Journal of Family Issues*, 24, 645–667.

McLanahan, S., & Sandefur, G. (1994). *Growing up with a single parent: What hurts, what helps*. Cambridge, MA: Harvard University Press.

Mincy, R., Garfinkel, I., & Nepomnyaschy, L. (2005). In-hospital paternity establishment and father involvement in fragile families. *Journal of Marriage and Family*, 67, 611–625.

Nelson, M. (2000). Single mothers and social support: The commitment to, and retreat from, reciprocity. *Qualitative Sociology*, 23, 291–317.

Nurse, A. (2002). *Fatherhood arrested: Parenting from within the juvenile justice system*. Nashville, TN: Vanderbilt University Press.

Pirog-Good, M. (1993). In-kind contributions as child support: The teen alternative parenting program. In R. Lerman & T. Ooms (Eds.), *Young unwed fathers: Changing roles and emerging policies* (pp. 251–266). Philadelphia: Temple University Press.

Pleck, J., & Masciadrelli, B. (2004). Paternal involvement in US resident fathers: Levels, sources, and consequences. In M. Lamb (Ed.), *The role of fathers in child development* (4th ed.). Hoboken, NJ: Wiley.

Portes, A., & Sensenbrenner, J. (1993). Embeddedness and immigration: Notes on the social determinants of economic action. *American Journal of Sociology*, 98, 1320–1350.

Rosenthal, C. (1985). Kinkeeping in the familial division of labor. *Journal of Marriage and the Family*, 47, 965–974.

Roy, K. (1999). Low-income fathers in an African-American community and the requirements of welfare reform. *Journal of Family Issues*, 20, 432–457.

Roy, K., Tubbs, C., & Burton, L. (2004). Don't have no time: Daily rhythms and the organization of time for low-income families. *Family Relations*, 53, 168–178.

Sano, Y. (2004). The unanticipated consequences of promoting father involvement: A feminist perspective. In V. Bengston, A. Acock, K. Allen, P. Dilworth Anderson, & D. Klein (Eds.), *Sourcebook of family theory and research* (pp. 355–356). Thousand Oaks, CA: Sage.

Seery, B., & Crowley, M. S. (2000). Women's emotion work in the family: Relationship management and the process of building father-child relationships. *Journal of Family Issues, 21*: 100–127.

Stack, C. (1974). *All our kin: Strategies for survival in a Black community.* New York: Random House.

Stack, C., & Burton, L. (1993). Kinscripts. *Journal of Comparative Family Studies, 24*, 157–170.

Townsend, N. (2002). *The package deal: Marriage, work and fatherhood in men's lives.* Philadelphia: Temple University Press.

Ventura, S., & Bachrach, C. (2000). *Nonmarital childbearing in the United States, 1949–99.* National Vital Statistics Report, 48 (16). Hyattsville, MD: National Center for Health Statistics.

Walker, A., & McGraw, L. (2000). Who is responsible for responsible fathering? *Journal of Marriage and the Family, 62*, 563–569.

Waller, M., & McLanahan, S. (2005). "His" and "her" marriage expectations: Determinants and consequences. *Journal of Marriage and Family, 67*, 53–67.

Waller, M., & Swisher, R. (2006). Fathers' risk factors in fragile families: Implications for "healthy" relationships and father involvement. *Social Problems, 53*, 392–420.

Wilson, W. J. (1987). *The truly disadvantaged: The inner-city, the underclass, and public policy.* Chicago: University of Chicago Press.

25

Windfall Child Rearing
Low-Income Care and Consumption

Allison J. Pugh

INTRODUCTION

Consumption practices factor strongly in shaping children's daily lives, from the food that kids eat to the shows they watch to the things they desire. Consumption, Daniel Miller (1998) points out, is also part of what constitutes relationships between parents and children. In the USA, some $215 billion are spent by, on or for children (McNeal, 1999). Yet families vary considerably in their ability to participate fully in consumer culture. How do income constraints configure family consumption practices? Amid the marketization of childhoods, how do low-income families construct a 'good enough' childhood (Cross, 2000; Winnicott, 1971)?

I investigated these questions as part of an ongoing ethnography in Oakland, California. Based on interviews and fieldwork with mostly low- and middle-income families in this city, I found that *income instability* was as important as *income scarcity* in determining the ways in which families consumed on behalf of children. For low-income families, the unpredictability of resources gives rise to a set of behaviors and outcomes that I term 'windfall child rearing', with particular origins and implications for children's lives.

THE IMPACT OF RESOURCES ON CHILD-REARING CONSUMPTION

How do resources influence child-rearing consumption or the consumption that is undertaken on behalf of a child's nurture, needs and pleasure? How do families construct a 'good enough' childhood for their children in contexts of affluence and constraint? Modifying a term from the psychoanalyst D.W. Winnicott (1971), I intend a 'good enough childhood' to signify one in which a child is relatively safe and nurtured, in accordance with standards set and shared by the community of which the child's family is a part. In addition, I hope the phrase allows for some rhetorical distance from the project of judging what would make a perfect childhood, as if such an entity could exist. Instead, definitions of childhood are constructed in particular social contexts, and just what makes one 'good enough' depends on local definitions as well as the availability of resources to carry them out (Ruddick, 1998).

Some scholars have noted that definitions of an adequate childhood vary considerably depending on family socioeconomic status. In her exhaustive ethnography of family life, Annette Lareau found that working-class and middle-class children's lives differed dramatically (Lareau,

2003). Middle-class families worked to provide their children with 'concerted cultivation', involving the development of skills and talents through teams, lessons and tutors, while families of more limited means pursued a strategy that Lareau dubbed 'the accomplishment of natural growth'. Influenced by Bourdieu, Lareau investigated how class-inflected child rearing laid down certain *dispositions* with implications for future class mobility. While the childhoods she examined differed in other ways as well, it was in the organization of daily life that family consumption practices were most implicated. Middle-class children's lives were scheduled around practices and performances while working-class and poor children had more free time and spent far more of it in front of the television (Lareau, 2003). Good enough working-class and poor childhoods, according to this picture, were also less expensive to provide.

However, other studies have found that childhoods look remarkably similar when we compare their material goods. Patricia Berhau (2000), a student of Lareau's working with the same fertile data, found that while both poor and affluent families may have bought the same sneakers for their child, families diverged in the processes of acquisition leading up to the purchase. Affluent families would make

> a last-minute decision to stop off at a sporting goods shop on the way home from an afternoon at the movies . . . likely place the sneakers on a credit card, paying all or most of the balance off at the end of the month. Failing to do so may require an occasional stock liquidation to relieve the debt, but would not significantly alter the family's buying habits. (Berhau, 2000: 334)

In contrast, in working-class or poor families, parents would scan sale papers and store prices, put away a little each week towards the purchase, take on extra hours of work to pay for it or solicit contributions from the child. Because of their income constraints, Berhau argued, poor and working-class consumers shared a particular time orientation in which 'small and (near) immediate intervals of time [were] meaningful and relevant' (2000: 337), as well as a cognitive clarity, brought about by pointed thinking and planning about near-term issues of acquisition. In each family, however, she points out, 'the children in question may very well wind up with identical sneakers' (2000: 334).

When we consider Lareau and Berhau together, we might surmise that while the organization of time in childhoods varies widely according to class, the distribution of stuff is more similar; in other words, parents of varying socioeconomic backgrounds seem to largely agree on the material basis of a 'good enough' childhood. However, for the poorest of families, the cost of that agreement is high: in a highly unequal society like the USA, families differ widely in their capacity to meet these perceived needs (Center on Budget and Policy Priorities/Economic Policy Institute, 2002). While the provision of all that goes into 'concerted cultivation' is expensive – the lessons, instruments, uniforms and travel – buying even the basics of childhood, from balls to backpacks to back-to-school clothes, also requires significant outlays. Thus, quantitative researchers have found that poor families spend disproportionately *more* on children than their rich counterparts, suggesting that children's needs are perceived to be more fixed than adults' in a context of severe income constraints (Lazear and Michael, 1988; Mayer, 1997).

Daniel Miller's work provides an explanation for this prioritization of children's needs. In *A Theory of Shopping* (1998), Miller portrays shopping as a ritual of sacrifice, transforming 'mere expenditure' into relationships of love and care. Shopping is the way in which consumers (primarily mothers) make the relationships within the family through the 'daily conscientiousness' of thinking about the individual preferences of those for whom they buy. In this sense, consumption is objectified love (Miller, 1998).

Miller's treatise is important, as it recognizes consumption as an act that makes connections, contrary to popular notions of it as an individual solipsistic act 'devoted largely to indulging itself' (1998: 68). But, perhaps surprisingly given his thesis about how it constitutes relationships, shopping is ultimately portrayed as a one-way activity, a 'gift' or 'sacrifice', without regard for its reception. A crucial feature of the experience of provisioning is, of course, the interactive element: members of the household (including children, as I have written about elsewhere; see Pugh [2003a]) reflect, reject or rework the terms of intimacy embodied in the consumption done on their behalf.

Children are central to Elizabeth Chin's (2001) ethnography on consumption in a primarily African American low-income community in New Haven. Chin's nine- and 10-year-old informants are active agents in producing their own childhoods, moving their birthday parties to protect their cakes from marauding brothers, participating in elaborate exchange rituals in the school lunchroom and considering the needs of their household others when making purchases. Chin powerfully evokes the creative ways in which the children handle the symbolic and material oppressions implicated in their social contexts of bleak urban settings and, at the nearby mall, luxurious consumer 'possibilities'. Her focus on the children stands out for its unusual reckoning of their roles in constructing their lives. Nonetheless, caregivers are given only the most shadowy treatment in the book, thus eliding much of the extensive child-rearing consumption that goes into providing a good enough childhood, even in low-income settings.

From the perspective of low-income caregivers, the equation of care and consumption puts them in a precarious position. On the one hand, they want to participate fully in a consumer culture that uses consumption to make and shape relationships of love and care; on the other hand, their resource constraints severely curtail their ability to provide for all household needs without interruption. They are, as Zygmunt Bauman (1998) writes, 'flawed consumers'. As Power (2003) argues, the desire to avoid being considered flawed consumers and, thus, flawed mothers shapes the consumption practices of low-income women caregivers. Indeed, Power's welfare-reliant informants asserted that 'one of their highest priorities was to try to ensure that their children fit in with their peers, even if household items, food or personal items for themselves had to be sacrificed to do so' (2003: 4). The low-income women in Edin and Lein's landmark study *Making Ends Meet* agreed: 'You gotta do what you gotta do to make your kids feel normal', one mother said flatly (1997: 30).

The drive to 'do what you gotta do' conflicts with the reality of available resources in many low-income households in the US, where more than one in every six children lives in poverty (Madrick, 2002). How do income constraints shape and alter the child-rearing consumption of low-income parents? How do these practices influence the family relationships thus constituted?

I investigated these questions through interviews and ethnographic fieldwork in three sites in Oakland. In brief, I found that the *instability* of income was as influential as the *scarcity* of income for my low-income respondents, as they tried to construct their versions of a good enough child-hood, with important implications for parent–child relationships. [. . .]

MONEY IN THE AIR . . . BUT NOT IN THE POCKET

A few blocks from the highway, amid the small houses, iron fences and busy stoops of West Oakland and across the street from the Wilson Elementary School, a long low cement building housing the Sojourner Truth after-school center is flanked by two asphalt playgrounds. The gate to the left playground stands ajar, and parents, older siblings and babysitters leave cars curbside, sometimes idling, to go through it unchallenged, re-emerging with a child in tow. In the playground, kids sometimes play basketball, with the space between two of the monkey bars acting as a hoop, or swing an old telephone wire for a double-dutch jump rope or kick dead balls from one end of the yard to the other, running to retrieve them as they land and stay put.

One afternoon, the head teacher Ms Plum and I sit on a bench in the playground, and Alvin, a small African American kindergartener, comes over. 'I got $25', he announces. 'You have $25? That's more money than I have', says Ms Plum. 'How'd you get that money? Is it in your bank?', she asks. Alvin nods. 'You save that money. It's better to save money than to spend it.' He jumps onto the climbing structure as a man arrives to pick up his daughter and stops to chat with Ms Plum. He is half Mexican, half Puerto Rican, about 35 years old, and he is going fishing that weekend. They talk about the kind of fish they like. She asks about his boat and he mentions that he received a $600 ticket for doing 80mph on a lake. His daughter, a first grader with pigtails, comes over with her backpack on, ready to go, and Ms Plum tells her: 'Show him your tongue and then you can remember what you owe me.' Her tongue is bright blue, the telltale blue of the 'icys' that Ms Plum sells for 25 cents each to raise money for summer field trips. 'You can get that out of your money, girl', the father tells her, grinning.

Money is everywhere at the Sojourner Truth Center, at least in people's talk. Adults talk about how much things cost them, about cars and TVs and swim classes and birthday cakes. Kids and adults negotiate for candy and snacks from Ms Plum. Kids trade stories about the tooth fairy, about birthday presents, about the money they get from adults for treats.

Nonetheless, evidence abounds of the tight budgets into which these families squeeze themselves. One little girl wears sandals with the back strap cut through so that her feet can still fit in them, even as her heels hang over the back. Patricia and her sister Linda have little sausage bodies that hang out over and through their old tight clothes, pants that are too short and shirts several sizes too small. For several weeks, Delisha carries a cheap blue bag that she explains she got on a giveaway day at a local store. Ms Plum makes sure that parents know that this or that service or class is free and hands parents some of the extra food that the center receives for holidays – bags of chips, pickles – which the parents gladly carry away, their kids dragging their book bags alongside them.

My preliminary findings suggest that, just as important as resource *constraints* in shaping the construction of child rearing for low-income families, however, is *what those resources are like* when they do arrive. Among the low-income families in my sample, central to the experience of money in this world is its seeming unpredictability. From the kids' perspective, sometimes their parents had money and sometimes they didn't, and little that the child did had any effect on the matter. The very instability of money had broad implications for the daily lives of low-income children, a phenomenon that I term windfall child rearing and that I discuss further below.

WINDFALLS AND BAD LUCK

For the most part, the flow of money and goods was unpredictable for low-income families because it depended on four unstable sources: variable access to government assistance; the ebb and flow of the availability of low-paid service work; the sporadic largess of friends and relatives; and the winds of good and bad fortune, to which these families of limited means remained particularly susceptible in an environment of structured racism and concentrated poverty.

Government Assistance

The most significant public assistance offered to these families is in affordable housing programs, particularly the Section 8 voucher program, by which renters pay a subsidized rate to landlords, who receive the balance of a fair market rate from federal authorities. A tight rental market, such as exists in the San Francisco Bay area, makes landlords less inclined to go through the added hassle of the extra paperwork to be a Section 8 participant and, thus, there is a finite number of apartment owners who take the vouchers. The program's biggest flaw, however, is its limited scope; it has received far more eligible applicants than it can provide for at its current funding levels. The program is currently closed to new applicants and last accepted new applications in December 2001, when it received more than 12,700. 'We do not anticipate opening our Section 8 waiting list until 2005', the website stated drily in the fall of 2003. Section 8 vouchers can be passed down from parent to child and can also be awarded under special circumstances, such as in cases of 'family reunification', when parents are able to retrieve children from foster care.

One of my low-income informants, Mary, had been stuck in an abusive relationship when she realized that, in order to get out, she would have to find a place to live for her and her kids:

Mary: So I applied first for Section 8, not knowing, not ever thinking, that I was going to get it as soon as I did. Because it usually takes people five, six years. I got it in a year.

The enormous waiting list makes the day you find out that you are entitled to Section 8 feel like winning the lottery; indeed, in a market where a two-bedroom apartment in a dangerous neighborhood can cost $1000 monthly, the savings are considerable.

Availability of Work

Some of the families at the Sojourner Truth Center had regular service jobs and long-term employment histories as security guards, nurse's aides or transportation workers. Others had more intermittent records, particularly those who worked in retail. The closing of a Kmart superstore in the area had hit several families hard. During the winter holiday season, Labor Day and other peak shopping periods, parents took on extra jobs or worked overtime to bring in extra money. This kind of employment – sporadic and temporary – often gave families a small momentary infusion of funds before the jobs melted away with the customers.

Friends and Family

My low-income informants offered stories that suggested that they would not be able to get by without a particular friend or family member, while, in the same breath, telling of the friend who stole from them or the partner who was only a drain on their resources. Jackie reported making $882 per month in food stamps and aid from CalWORKS, the state program that replaced welfare. However, her rent for a tiny two-bedroom apartment to house her five-person family, located next to a crack house, was $975 per month and she was not eligible for Section 8, she said, because of a previous felony conviction. How does she get by? Her first son's 73-year-old grandfather gives her money for rent and other items: 'He's been dishing out a lot. Like he comes up with part of the rent and $375 for each month's bills, too. Plus gas for the car. [Her son's] haircut money.' She knows that the arrangement is not reliable in the long term, however, and her husband is working two jobs to be ready for the change:

Grandpa already told us – he loves us, but he's bold, too – he goes, 'You got a man who needs to go out and provide because I'm really old and I need to save my money for retirement'. That's what he said. Which is understandable. That's true.

On the other hand, Lashona, who has two kids and is training to be a nurse's aide, describes her boyfriend as a drain on her resources and also invokes traditional gender ideologies to underscore her outrage: 'This isn't the way it's supposed to be, where the man is living off of the woman and her kids, living off of her Section 8 and her food stamps.' Yet, she's reluctant to kick him out because he saved her when she was homeless, apart from her children and living in a motel with no way to pay for another week:

Lashona: So then that week was up. And it was a Friday. And I met him. So he let me come and stay with him. He didn't even know me.

AJP: Wow.

Lashona: It was so weird. I said, 'wait a minute, something is wrong with this picture'. This man, something is wrong with him, you don't just let people come to your house. I don't know.

AJP: He must have had a good feeling that you wouldn't . . .

Lashona: But it was just me. And that's what he said, he said he didn't feel like he had to worry about anything. And he had to go to work that night. He let me stay there by myself. And the next day I had the key and everything just started going. And then he went to court every time I had to go to court. He went to every meeting, every visit – everything until I got the kids back. I got the kids back. We got the kids back the day before Thanksgiving. And we cooked a big Thanksgiving dinner.

Carol Stack (1974) and others have documented the ways in which social networks simultaneously buoy up the poor – at times enabling them to survive – *and* hold them back from individual mobility projects. My informants corroborate this finding. Yet, these arrangements are not at all stable, relying, as they do, on the shifting fortunes of others in this community on the edge. The aid often seems to require some level of desperation to present itself before it comes forth, diverted from other less immediately pressing needs. Then, and only then, and only for the fortunate who have them, do friends and family come up with something to meet the emergency. While it seems that they can often count on friends and family to step in, therefore, low-income families cannot budget for such help as if it were income, but rather only welcome it as parched earth greets rain.

The Caprice of Fortune

Weather is an apt analogy for the forces of luck buffeting low-income families in my sample, luck that Berhau (2000) termed 'normal accidents'. My informants mostly used a passive language, often of luck or fortune rather than personal efficacy or religion, to describe their evolving situations, for example, 'we came into money' as opposed to 'I earned more money' or 'thanks to God's grace, we . . .'.

As we learn from recent scholarship on natural disasters, however, social forces like poverty and racism affect the way luck is experienced (Klinenberg, 2002). Families had cars that broke down or were stolen, requiring significant outlays to retrieve them from city lots. At the same time, the cars they drove were older and they parked them in areas of higher crime, given that these were the neighborhoods they lived in. Parents suffered from depression and anxiety that impeded their ability to function, to get ahead at work or to reliably transport their kids to school. Low-income people are more prone to psychological distress as well as other health problems (Williams and Collins, 1995), as the daily grind of poverty and the difficulties of maintaining a household in such strained circumstances surely make depression and anxiety more likely. Many of my low-income informants talked about moving out of their dangerous and poverty-stricken neighborhoods, but most had been dissuaded by the daunting search for apartments that owners would be prepared to rent to them. Lashona told a story in which one owner confirmed that he took Section 8 over the phone, so she and her boyfriend, both African American, went over there to meet him, dressed carefully in clean and tidy clothes. However, when they got there, he informed her that it had been rented since they got off the phone, an incident certainly suggestive of discrimination. The prevalence of such racialized practices, particularly around housing, contributing in part to the extensive residential segregation in US cities, makes the 'luck' of finding a good apartment more structured than just happenstance.

Is money more unpredictable for low-income families than for more affluent groups? Do only low-income families get windfalls or hit bad luck? In my sample, middle-income families did not talk about unreliable money, but this silence perhaps stemmed from the fact that their predictable base incomes were high enough to make the extras flowing in and out less noticeable. While people in middle-income families also got depressed or found their cars had been stolen or received a higher than expected tax refund, it did not make or break their budget for living.

WINDFALL CHILD REARING

For parents and children, the implications of experiencing money like the rain – capricious, unpredictable and yet necessary for life – are great. With the windfall child rearing that ensues, parents are limited as to how much their consumption for their children can be linked to behavior goals, they lose a critical source of parent–child connectedness during periods of high conflict, such as adolescence, and they cannot escape an image of parental helplessness before their watchful children. In addition, when money is available, my low-income informants told me that they would buy their kids small items, like letting them buy a lip gloss at the corner store. Thus, in what is often a compensatory move, parents pass down to their children the experience of money as windfall, in that they cannot grant more stable regular access to resources they don't have (Pugh, 2002). Finally, windfall child rearing teaches children that money does not reflect moral worth, but rather just someone's good luck.

No Behavior Modification

If money is not predictably there, parents cannot use it to reward their children's good behavior, such as completing homework or chores. Even if they do reward their kids later, the time and distance between the good behavior and the reward will often erode the message that parents might be intending to send. Therefore, without links to behavior, buying signifies love, social networks and obligations to care – more like 'I appreciate you' than 'I appreciate what you did'. These messages are more like that which contemporary parenting advice books, often aimed at middle-class readers, suggest will make a child feel valued, but they are not the messages my low-income informants necessarily preferred sending. I asked Carol, a nurse's aide with three kids living with her, when she gave her children money. She answered: 'When they're good. When I have extra money to give them. When they do what they're told. Most of the time that's never!'

No Material Ties that Bind

In a related vein, when children and their caregivers are experiencing conflict, sometimes material ties may be among the only strands connecting them. Particularly in adolescence, control over a car or movie money can be the one thing linking the teenager to the adult. Without the ability to command that kind of material power, low-income parents face the challenge of relying solely on their emotional ties with their children to exert their influence.

Impotence before an Audience

Low-income parents cannot escape leaving the impression with their children of parental helplessness. All children go through a stage of denouement when they realize that their parents are not omnipotent. My data suggest that low-income parents convey that message earlier and to a more profound degree than more affluent parents. Adults demonstrate their inability to secure funds from government sources or employers when needed and this powerlessness can also seed a certain impotence in interpersonal relationships. Brenda noticed that her older brother had developed strategies for keeping his own money, even when her mother needed it for groceries or other family necessities:

Brenda: He hides the money where my mom can't get it. And he hides it where she can't even find it.

AJP: And how come he doesn't have to, you know, 'look, Nicholas, we need food and you've got to help us?'. How come that . . .

Brenda: My mom does ask him.

AJP: How come it doesn't work?

Brenda: He says no.

At the same time, this powerlessness must be juxtaposed with the particular savvy I witnessed among several of my low-income informants when they handled creditors and cashiers. They may not have been able to secure long-term or well-paid employment or do much about when a government check would arrive, but they knew which companies' bills to pay first and how to conduct themselves with other low-wage workers so that they would get refunds they were due or overcharging corrected.

Windfall Childhood

None of my low-income families administered any sort of regular allowance, as there just wasn't enough extra money around on a regular basis to dole out to the kids predictably. That said, the kids often had money. They got it when their father dropped by on a morning visit or from their neighbor who let them work in the backyard every once in a while or from their mother when she returned from the mailbox, check in hand. Sometimes parents even took their children's money, such as when Brenda's mother used part of $60 that Brenda received from her non-custodial father in order to buy groceries for the home. 'She only took a little bit', Brenda said carefully.

One day at the Sojourner Truth Center, Vivian asked her mom Lashona for a quarter for an 'icy'. 'No, you can't', her mother said shortly and without elaborating. Jackie, another mother and a neighbor, pulled out a quarter and handed it to Vivian without fanfare, presuming (correctly, as it turned out) that her mother's 'no' came from money woes and not as an edict against sweets. For comparison's sake, we can see that it could have been a shocking thing to do in a middle-income environment, as such an act would be perceived as intervening in a private family issue.

The kids' experience with money mirrored that of the adults in their lives. As such, they came to understand it as a random but powerful entity, with the ability to confer autonomy and re-establish social connections, but only as an unexpected pleasure.

Lady Luck, not Horatio Alger

The seemingly random quality of money, disconnected as it was from how much their parents worked or whether or not they had been good children, belied the ideology of the American dream and its promise of getting ahead through assiduous and honest labor. Disassociated from moral worth and purity, money became something you got when you were lucky, not because you were good. For all sorts of American families, the tooth fairy and Santa Claus are conduits of money and objects to children, conduits that use myth and ritual to obscure the true parental origins of this largess. In a very low-income urban environment such as Sojourner Truth, it all feels like the tooth fairy.

WINDFALL 'CHILDING'

Windfall child rearing has equally important ramifications for what I term 'childing' or the project of growing up in interaction with one's caregiving adults. If most money is a windfall, then negotiating or using logical arguments is not the way to get more of it. Rather, children at Sojourner Truth seemed engaged in short bursts of emotional tactics of wheedling, cajoling and pleading that subsided relatively quickly if rejected. Sometimes, mainly in interactions with each other, the children grabbed, stole or 'borrowed' money and/or possessions. Most often, I saw a culture of restraint, corroborating the findings of other researchers (Chin, 2001; Lareau, 2003).

In contrast, middle- to upper-income kids negotiated, whined, staged emotional episodes and, in general, were more persistent in communicating their desires. When Chloe, the elder daughter in an upper-income family, wanted to raise her allowance from $2 per week, she made a yearly budget that included items like 'notebooks', 'pens' and 'gifts for family' which, when averaged out over the year, came to $6 per week. Her parents, a university professor and a stay-at-home mother, reviewed the list and conceded her arguments had merit and, thus, her negotiations were successful.

While Chloe's tactics were unusual, even for one in her social milieu, they were unheard of among the low-income sample. One could argue that this was due to parenting differences, including varying degrees of comfort with linguistic tactics or familiarity with budgets and presentations. Undoubtedly, these factors are components that contribute to shaping these children's behavior. However, the hard fact that, in low-income families, there was no money to vie for most of the time made such maneuvering as Chloe's entirely inappropriate.

DISCUSSION AND CONCLUSION

I have argued that families' differential access to steady income and expenses leads, for low-income caregivers, to a phenomenon that I have dubbed windfall child rearing. Unstable resources serve to disassociate the time when parents buy for children from the time when the children ask for something, when they need it or when they exhibit good behavior. This separation in time has ramifications for children's daily lives, for how they behave and how they interpret consumption practices. Thus, beyond the short-term time orientation that Berhau discerned among her working-class and poor informants, I found that low-income families shared an experience of *time fragmentation* that affected their children rearing.

Previous research into the impact of resources on child rearing has contended that low-income families are fighting off images of the 'flawed consumer' and the 'flawed mother' and that the conflation of these two ideas may comprise a sort of symbolic oppression, to use Chin's (2001) words (see also Power 2003). The specter of these images could be what is leading such families to render children's expenses more fixed and less reducible than those of adults in an environment of severe income constraints. As families 'do what they gotta do', the price of normalcy grows ever higher (Cross, 1997). In addition, it is possible that windfall child rearing also leads parents to spend more, since the delay in buying the item might erode parents' ability to replace it with something smaller or bargain with the child, as they attempt to constitute their relationship with the child, but do so (in both the child's and the parents' eyes) late.

This research, while suggestive, is preliminary; planned comparisons with upper-income families and with mixed-income settings will enable us to ascertain with confidence how much windfall child rearing is limited to lower-income populations. I have also written elsewhere about the effect of windfall child rearing in the income-homogeneous classroom, finding an absence of teasing that I argue is related in part to the instability of honor-through-possessions in this setting (Pugh, 2003b). In addition, further research could establish the extent to which windfall child rearing exists in other racial/ethnic groups, including poor whites. Such work would illuminate the degree to which friends and families contribute to the waxing and waning of personal wherewithal among other social groups less well known for their reciprocal networks.

With this research on caregivers and their relationship to children around consumption, I have tried to center the experience of low-income people. How households spend their money is one route to understanding present day inequality and the ways it is experienced in families making tradeoffs between one choice and another. In addition, how and when parents spend their money on children provide a glimpse of inequality's future as part and parcel of constructing the different childhoods that are the pathways leading to different adult lives (Bourdieu, 1984). Through the prism of consumption, we can view the construction of good enough childhoods in different social contexts to understand how children and adults across the income ladder make meaning out of the experience of inequality.

REFERENCES

Bauman, Zygmunt (1998) *Work, Consumerism and the New Poor*. Buckingham and Philadelphia, PA: Open University Press.

Berhau, Patricia (2000) 'Class and the Experience of Consumers: A Study of Practices of Acquisition', unpublished dissertation, Temple University.

Bourdieu, Pierre (1984) *Distinction: A Social Critique of the Judgement of Taste* (trans. Richard Nice). Cambridge, MA: Harvard University Press.

Center on Budget and Policy Priorities/Economic Policy Institute (2002) 'Pulling Apart: A State-by-state Analysis of Income Trends'. URL: http://www.cbpp.org/4-23/-2sfp.htm

Chin, Elizabeth (2001) *Purchasing Power: Black Kids and American Consumer Culture*. Minneapolis: University of Minnesota Press.

Cross, Gary (1997) *Kids' Stuff: Toys and the Changing World of American Childhood*. Cambridge, MA and London: Harvard University Press.

Cross, Gary (2000) *An All-consuming Century: Why Commercialism Won in Modern America*. New York: Columbia University Press.

Edin, Kathryn and Lein, Laura (1997) *Making Ends Meet: How Single Mothers Survive Welfare and Low-wage Work*. New York: Russell Sage Foundation.

Klinenberg, Eric (2002) *Heat Wave: A Social Autopsy of Disaster in Chicago*. Chicago, IL: University of Chicago Press.

Lareau, Annette (2003) *Unequal Childhoods: Class, Race, and Family Life.* Berkeley: University of California Press.

Lazear, Edward P. and Michael, Robert T. (1988) *Allocation of Income within the Household.* Chicago, IL: University of Chicago Press.

McNeal, James U. (1999) *The Kids Market: Myths and Realities.* Ithaca, NY: Paramount Market.

Madrick, Jeff (2002) 'A Rise in Child Poverty Rates Is at Risk in US', *New York Times* (6 June): 13.

Mayer, Susan E. (1997) *What Money Can't Buy: Family Income and Children's Life Chances.* Cambridge, MA: Harvard University Press.

Miller, Daniel (1998) *A Theory of Shopping.* Ithaca, NY: Cornell University Press.

Power, Elaine (2003) 'Freedom and Belonging through Consumption: The Disciplining of Desire in Single Mothers on Welfare', paper presented to the British Sociological Association annual conference, University of York.

Pugh, Allison J. (2002) *From Compensation to Childhood Wonder: Why Parents Buy* (Working Paper No. 39). Center for Working Families, University of California, Berkeley.

Pugh, Allison J. (2003a) 'The Terms of Intimacy: Children and Caregivers' Interactions around Consumption', paper submitted to the Pluridisciplinary Perspectives on Child and Teen Consumption conference, France, March 2004.

Pugh, Allison J. (2003b) 'Money, Inequality and Teasing in Children's Social Worlds', paper submitted to the annual meetings of the American Sociological Association, San Francisco, August 2004.

Ruddick, Sara (1998) 'Care as Labor and Relationship', in *Norms and Values: Essays on the Work of Virginia Reed*, pp. 3–25. Lanham, MD: Rowman & Littlefield.

Stack, Carol (1974) *All Our Kin.* New York: Harper & Row.

Williams, David R. and Collins, Chiquita (1995) 'US Socioeconomic and Racial Differences in Health: Patterns and Explanations', *Annual Review of Sociology* 21: 349–86.

Winnicott, D.W. (1971) *Playing and Reality.* London: Tavistock Press.

V

REVISIONING CONTEMPORARY FAMILY ISSUES THROUGH THE LENS OF RACE, ETHNICITY, AND CLASS

26

Moms and Jobs
Trends in Mothers' Employment and Which Mothers Stay Home

DAVID COTTER, PAULA ENGLAND, AND JOAN HERMSEN[1]

Overview of the Findings

THE EMPLOYMENT OF WIVES and mothers rose dramatically from 1960 to about 1990, and thereafter has leveled off. There was a small dip from 2000 to 2004, but employment rates had inched back to 2000 levels by 2006, the latest figures available. Contrary to recent press accounts, there has not been an "opt-out" revolution. Rather than a strong downward trend, there has been a flattening out of the trend line, so that mothers' employment has stabilized, with a majority employed. This strong upward thrust followed by a flattening of the trend holds for most groups of women, but there are significant variations in employment trends by race and class.

Well-educated women are especially likely to be employed, despite the fact that they generally have well-educated, and thus high earning, husbands. Surprisingly, the percentage of married moms staying home doesn't go up consistently as husbands' earnings go up. In fact, it is women with the poorest husbands (in the bottom quarter of male earnings) who are most likely to stay home, followed by women with the very richest husbands (those in the top 5 percent of male earners). The effect of husbands' income on the odds of employment is about the same for both black and white married mothers, but there are significant racial differences in the effects of marital status on mothers' employment. While married white moms are significantly less likely to be employed than single white moms, married black moms are equally likely to be employed as unmarried ones.

WHAT'S THE TREND IN MOTHERS' EMPLOYMENT?

Recent media reports have talked about an "opt-out revolution," reporting on a real but very small downturn in women's employment rates since 2000.[2] These media reports have been misleading in two ways, as Figure 26.1 shows.

1. They ignore the dramatic upsurge in mothers' employment in the 1960s, 1970s, and 1980s.
2. They focus on a small downturn since 2000, but a fairer characterization of the years since 1990 is a plateau.

Figure 26.1 shows trends in employment for all women and men aged 25–54. All figures in this article refer to whether individuals were in the labor force (which means employed or actively

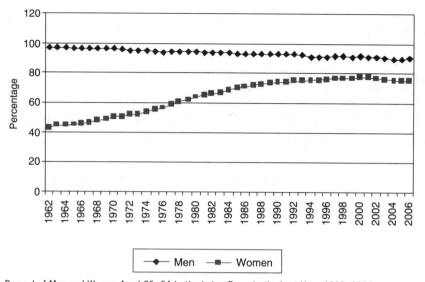

Figure 26.1 Percent of Men and Women Aged 25–54 in the Labor Force in the Last Year, 1962–2006
(Source: Current Population Survey)

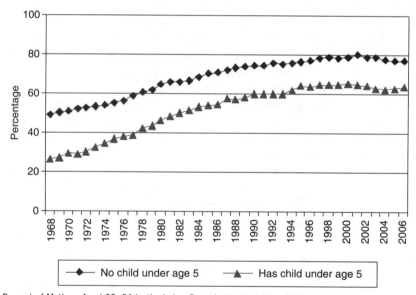

Figure 26.2 Percent of Mothers Aged 25–54 in the Labor Force in the Last Year, 1968–2006, by Age of their Children
(Source: Current Population Survey)

looking for work) any time in the last year, and refer exclusively to individuals between 25 and 54 in age. The data come from the U.S. Government's Current Population Survey for each year.

What's the trend for women with children? This is shown in Figure 26.2. Moms with children under age 5 are most likely to stay home, but they are much less likely to do so than in the past.

There was a tiny dip in their employment between 2000 and 2004, but it then inched back up to the 2000 level in 2006 (Figure 26.2).

In 1970, only 30 percent of mothers of children under 5 had been employed in the last year. But then huge increases ensued—from 30 percent in 1970 to 46 percent in 1980, and to 60 percent in 1990. The next decade saw just a small increase—from 60 percent to 65 percent between 1990 and 2000, a much slower rate of increase than previously. Moms' participation in paid labor then dropped a bit to 64 percent by 2004, but inched back to 65 percent by 2006. Up or down, the changes since 2000 are tiny. As with women overall, the big picture is dramatic increase followed by a leveling off in the rate of change—a plateau.

Moms with no preschoolers are more likely to be working for pay than are those with preschoolers (Figure 26.2). But their workforce participation rates also leveled off in the past 6 years, after a substantial increase over the last several decades. The percent of these mothers employed was 56 percent in 1970, 67 percent in 1980, and 77 percent in 1990. After these big increases, the rate has hovered right around 79 or 80 percent from 2000 to 2006. Again, the picture is of dramatic increase in employment rates to 1990, followed by a leveling off.

This is hardly an "opt-out revolution." Sixty-five percent of mothers with preschoolers and 79 percent of mothers of older children were employed at least part of the time in 2006.

RACIAL-ETHNIC DIFFERENCES IN MOTHERS' EMPLOYMENT

The patterns of maternal employment noted above generally hold for women of color as well as white women. However, black mothers have particularly high rates of labor force participation relative to other mothers. For example, in 2006, 73 percent of black mothers with preschoolers were in the labor force as compared to 63 percent of white mothers with preschoolers (see Figure 26.3). Interestingly, in the mid-1990s the labor force participation rate of black mothers and other

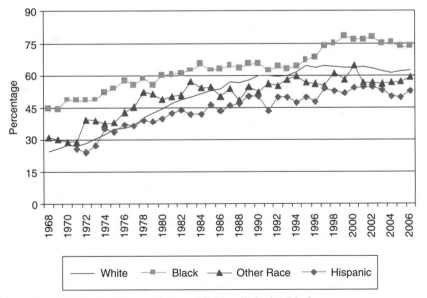

Figure 26.3 Labor Force Participation Rates for Mothers of Children Under Age 5 by Race
(Source: Current Population Survey)

mothers diverged. While rates had already started plateauing for other groups by the early 1990s, black mothers experienced a steep increase in the early 1990s and only started plateauing at the end of the decade. The steep increase likely reflected changes that disproportionately affected poor, single mothers: welfare reform added more stringent employment mandates, and increases in the earned income tax credit (EITC) made employment more lucrative for low earners with kids.[3] In addition a strong economy drew more women into the labor force, especially black women who often suffer the greatest employment setbacks in economic downturns.

Since the late 1990s, marital status has had less of an impact on the employment of black mothers than white mothers (see Figure 26.4). Both married and single black mothers work at high rates—about 75 percent in 2006. In contrast, while nearly 75 percent of single white mothers were in the labor force in 2006, only 60 percent of married white mothers were in the labor force.

WHY DID THE TREND IN WOMEN'S EMPLOYMENT RATES GO UP THEN LEVEL OFF?

What caused the big increase in women's employment in the 60s, 70s, and 80s? Many factors contributed. Women began having smaller families. The increase in single mothers made more women absolutely need a job. The fall in men's real wages since 1980 increased the need for two earners even in married couple families. Probably even more important were increases in women's education, better job opportunities for women, and the "equal opportunity" ideology of the women's movement. All these things increased women's access to interesting and good paying jobs, raising the cost of having a woman quit work and give up that extra income. All this contributed to the dramatic upsurge of women's employment.[4]

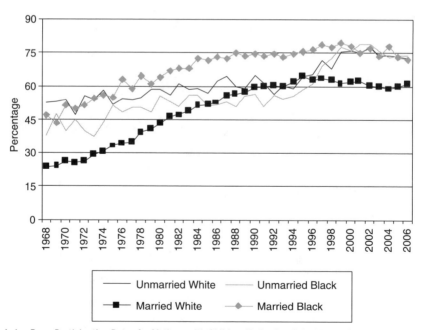

Figure 26.4 Labor Force Participation Rates for Mothers with Children Under Age 5, by Marital Status, for Whites and Blacks, 1968–2006
(Source: Current Population Survey)

Why did the trend level off? Social scientists really aren't sure. One possibility is that women's employment, which has gotten much closer to men's, can't move all the way to parity with men's unless men take on a more equal share of child rearing, and unless employers or the state adopt policies making it easier for parents to combine work and family. Men have increased the time they spend caring for children and doing housework, but nowhere near enough to offset women's increased employment.[5] And the U.S. lags way behind other countries in family leave, childcare provision and other policies that make it easier for people to be parents and workers.[6] Perhaps a cultural backlash to the women's movement is a factor as well.[7]

What does the future hold? We do not know if the trend in moms' employment will turn up again, go down a bit more, or stay stable. It is too early to tell. But it seems extremely unlikely that it will go down significantly. What is clear is that, as in many affluent nations, women's employment in the U.S. is at high levels, with about 80 percent of all mothers without a preschooler and 64 percent of even women with preschoolers in the workforce last year.

EDUCATION ENCOURAGES WOMEN'S EMPLOYMENT

Which moms are working for pay and which are working as full-time homemakers? Moms are much more likely to be working for pay if they have more education, as Figures 26.5 and 26.6 show, separately for those with pre-schoolers and for those with only older kids.

In 2006, among mothers with no pre-schoolers at home, Figure 26.6 shows that 82 percent of mothers with a college degree were employed, 76 percent of those who had just finished high school, but only 56 percent of those who hadn't finished high school. The figures are lower for moms with kids under 5, but they show an even stronger relationship between education and

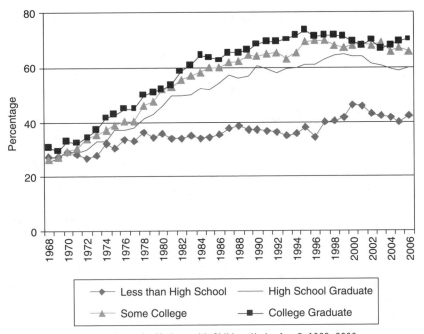

Figure 26.5 Labor Force Participation Rates for Mothers with Children Under Age 5, 1968–2006
(Source: Current Population Survey)

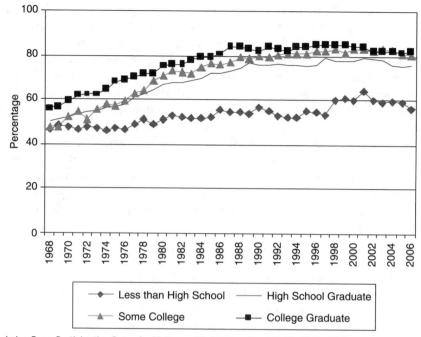

Figure 26.6 Labor Force Participation Rates for Mothers with Children Aged 5–18, 1968–2006
(Source: Current Population Survey)

employment. The employment gap between the most and least educated moms was smaller in the 1970s than it has been since 1980.

Why do more educated moms work for pay more? In one sense it isn't surprising that well educated moms have jobs; after all, many of them got that education to pursue the career they are in. Education improves access to well-paying and interesting jobs that make employment more worthwhile. Women with low education may not be able to make enough to pay for the child care required when they go to work. But what makes the higher employment of well-educated women a challenge to conventional wisdom is that they tend to be married to well-educated and high-earning men.[8]

HUSBANDS' EARNINGS AND MARRIED MOTHERS' EMPLOYMENT

The conventional wisdom is that married women with kids stay home when the family can afford for them to, and work for pay mainly when the family needs the money. If this were the main factor, we'd expect that the higher their husbands' income, the lower women's employment. But Figure 26.7 shows that the conventional wisdom is wrong.

As Figure 26.7 shows, over the last 10 years, the largest group of stay-at-home mothers is found among wives whose husbands are in the *lowest* 25 percent of the male earnings distribution. (Cutting points for each quartile and the top 5 percent were established separately for each year, using the annual earnings distribution of married men for that year.) The next largest group of stay-at-home mothers is found among women married to men who are in the highest 5 percent of the

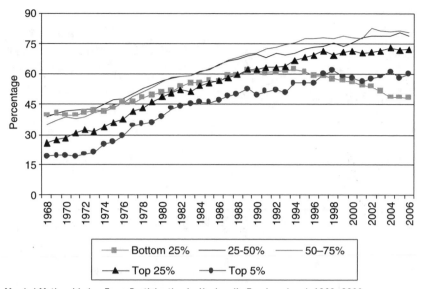

Figure 26.7 Married Mothers' Labor Force Participation by Husband's Earnings Level, 1968–2006
(Source: Current Population Survey)

income distribution. Oddly enough, then, the two groups of married moms with the lowest employment rates are those with both the poorest and the richest husbands!

Figure 26.7 shows that in the most recent year, 2006, less than half (48 percent) of mothers with husbands in the bottom quarter of the male earnings distribution were employed. Among married moms whose husbands were in the very highest 5 percent of earnings, 60 percent were employed. These two groups probably have different reasons for their relatively low employment rates. Moms with the highest earning husbands have little economic need to be employed and are often heavily involved in volunteer work outside the home. Moms with the poorest husbands have great economic need for a job, but they often have low education and earning potential themselves, so they may not be able to earn enough above childcare costs to make a job pay.

The highest employment rates were among mothers whose husbands had earnings toward the middle of the pack—between the 25th percentile and the 75th percentile. Approximately 80 percent of mothers married to husbands in these groups were employed in 2006.

These patterns are similar comparing white and black married mothers. As shown in Figure 26.8, white and black mothers with low earning husbands are the least likely to be in the labor force (42 and 51 percent respectively in 2006). For both white and black mothers married to low earning men, rates of labor force participation increased from the 1960s until the mid-1990s after which the rates fell off dramatically. Although the labor force participation rates of both black and white mothers married to high earning men has plateaued in more recent years, approximately three-quarters of both groups were employed in the latest data.[9]

So contrary to the idea that men's earnings predict whether their wives will stay home, the poorest men are most likely to have stay-at-home wives, the very richest men are the next most likely, and the men earning middle-range earnings are the least likely. These findings complicate our analysis of why families make the decisions they do and what social support systems they need.

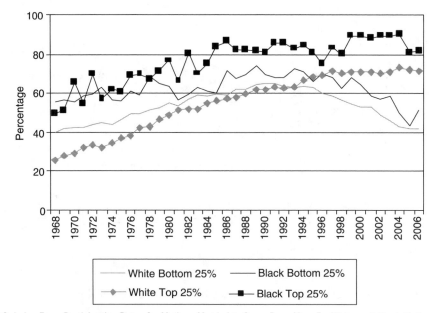

Figure 26.8 Labor Force Participation Rates for Mothers Married to Same Race Men, For White and Black Mothers Married to Men Earning in Top or Bottom Earnings Quartile, 1968–2006
(Source: Current Population Surveys)

NOTES

1. The authors are David Cotter, Department of Sociology, Union College, Schenectady, New York 12308, cotterd@union.edu; Paula England, Department of Sociology, Stanford University, Stanford, CA 94305-2047, pengland@stanford.edu, 650-723-4912 or 650-815-9308; Joan Hermsen, Department of Sociology, University of Missouri, Columbia, MO 65211, HermsenJ@missouri.edu. An earlier version of this paper appeared as a Council on Contemporary Families Fact Sheet at www.contemporaryfamilies.org.
2. See Joan Williams, " 'Opt Out' or Pushed Out?: How the Press Covers Work/Family Conflict." Center on Work Life Law, University of California Hastings School of the Law, available at http://www.uchastings.edu/site_files/WLL/OptOutPushedOut.pdf.
3. See Blank, Rebecca M., 2002, "Evaluating Welfare Reform in the United States," *Journal of Economic Literature* 40: 62.
4. See Chinhui Juhn and Kevin M. Murphy, 1997, "Wage Inequality and Family Labor Supply," *Journal of Labor Economics* 15: 72–79; Barbara Bergmann, 2005, *The Economic Emergence of Women*, Second Edition, New York: Basic Books.
5. See Suzanne Bianchi, John P. Robinson, and Melissa A. Milkie, 2006, *Changing Rhythms of American Family Life*. New York: Russell Sage Foundation.
6. See Joan Williams, " 'Opt Out' or Pushed Out?: How the Press Covers Work/Family Conflict." Center on Work Life Law, University of California Hastings School of the Law, available at http://www.uchastings.edu/site_files/WLL/OptOutPushedOut.pdf; Janet Gornick and Marcia K. Meyers, 2005, *Families That Work: Policies for Reconciling Parenthood and Employment*. New York, Russell Sage Foundation.
7. For trends in attitudes to gender issues, see David A. Cotter, Joan M. Hermsen, and Reeve Vanneman, 2004, *Gender Inequality at Work*. New York: Russell Sage Foundation and Population Reference Bureau.
8. See Mare, Robert D, 1991, "Five Decades of Educational Assortative Mating," *American Sociological Review* 56: 15–32.
9. The percentiles of black and white married men are not race-specific—that is, all married men are compared against all other married men of all races for the given year to assess their percentile.

27

A War Against Boys?

Michael Kimmel

HERE'S A NEW TWIST on the question of preferential treatment or affirmative action for people who have experienced discrimination. In 2004, Doug Anglin, a 17-year-old senior at Milton High School outside Boston, sued the school district to retroactively raise his B-grade point average. Anglin's lawsuit, brought with the aid of his father, a Boston lawyer, argued that schools routinely discriminate against males. "From the elementary level, they establish a philosophy that if you sit down, follow orders, and listen to what they say, you'll do well and get good grades," Anglin told a journalist. "Men naturally rebel against this."

Laughable though it may be, this ploy is simply the logical extension of a cultural campaign to convince us that feminism has gone too far and that males are now the disadvantaged sex. Feminist-inspired programs enabled a whole generation of girls to enter the sciences, medicine, law, and the professions, to continue their education, to imagine careers outside the home. But now, we're told, those same feminists have pathologized boyhood. Elementary schools, we read, "feminize" boys, forcing active, healthy and naturally rambunctious boys to conform to a regime of obedience—"pathologizing what is simply normal," as one psychologist put it. By the time they get to college, they've been steeped in anti-male propaganda. "Why would any self-respecting boy want to attend one of America's increasingly feminized universities?" asks George Gilder in *The National Review*. The American university is now a "fluffly pink playpen of feminist studies and agitprop 'herstory,' taught amid a green goo of eco-motherism . . ."[1]

ARE BOYS IN TROUBLE?

There is no doubt that boys are not faring particularly well in school. From elementary school to high school they have lower grades, lower class rank and fewer honors than girls. They are 50 percent more likely to repeat a grade in elementary school, one third more likely to drop out of high school, and six times more likely to be diagnosed with Attention Deficit and Hyperactivity Disorder.[2]

By the time they get to college—if they get there at all—they get lower grades and honors as well. Women now constitute the majority of students on college campuses. They outnumber men in the social and behavioral sciences by about 3 to 1, and have invaded such traditionally male bastions as engineering (where they now make up 20 percent) and biology and business (virtually par). One expert, Tom Mortensen, warns that if present trends continue, "the graduation line in 2068 will be all females."[3] (For the less statistically-minded, that's like predicting, forty years ago, that if the enrollment of black students at Ol' Miss was 1 in 1964, and, say, 200 in 1968 and 1000 in 1976, that "if present trends continue" there would be no white students on campus by 1982.)

These three issues—lower achievement, problematic behavior, and declining percentages in higher education—form the empirical basis of the current debate. But the idea that males are now the disadvantaged sex, and that the solution is to re-value "traditional" male values such as competition and aggression, rests on a misunderstanding of the challenges facing boys.

WHAT'S WRONG WITH THE "WHAT ABOUT THE BOYS" DEBATE?

For one thing, it creates a false opposition between girls and boys, implying that educational reforms undertaken to enable girls to perform better have actually hindered boys' educational development. But these reforms—new initiatives, classroom arrangements, teacher training, increased attentiveness to students' individual learning styles—actually enable larger numbers of boys to get a better education. Though the current boy advocates claim that schools used to be more "boy friendly" before all these feminist reforms, they obviously didn't go to school in those halcyon older days, when the classroom was far more regimented and teachers far more authoritarian; they even gave grades for "deportment." Rambunctious boys were simply not tolerated in the 1950s; they dropped out—or were expelled.

Some educational changes over the past ten years *have* hurt boys, but these changes were initiated by Congress, not by feminists. The net effect of the No Child Left Behind Act has been a zero-sum competition, as school districts scramble to stretch inadequate funding, leaving them little choice but to cut all non-curricular programs to ensure that their curricular mandates are followed. This disadvantages boys, since many of these programs were after-school athletics, gym and recess. Cutting "unnecessary" school counselors and other remedial programs also disadvantages boys, who compose the majority of children in behavioral and remedial educational programs.

THE NUMBERS GAME

Another problem is that the numbers themselves don't add up. More *people*—that is males and females—are going to college than ever before. In 1960, 54 percent of boys and 38 percent of girls went directly to college; today the numbers are 64 percent of boys and 70 percent of girls. It is true that the *rate of increase* among girls is higher than the rate of increase among boys, but the numbers are increasing for both.

Most critically, the imbalance between girls and boys is not uniform across class and race. The numerical imbalance between "problem" boys and "problem" girls turns out to be more of a problem of race and class than of gender per se. It is what Cynthia Fuchs Epstein calls a "deceptive distinction"—a difference that appears to be about gender, but is actually about something else—in this case race and class.[4]

Middle-class boys continue to complete high school and go on to college in similar proportions to girls. Among middle-class white high school graduates going to college this year, half are male and half are female. But working-class men—of all races—are less likely to go to college than working-class women. The racial disparities are even more stark. Only 37 percent of black college students are male, compared to 63 percent female, and only 45 percent of Hispanic students are male, compared with 55 percent female.

Why don't we "see" race and class, but are so drawn to gender? Perhaps because we are encouraged to see some parts of the picture but not to see others. Consider this front-page article in *The New York Times* from March 25, 2001: "Troubling Label for Hispanics: 'Girls Most Likely to Drop Out' " reads the headline. The fifth paragraph of the article describes a "troubling trend"—

Table 27.1 Distribution of Undergraduate Enrollment Among Students Aged 24 or Younger, by Race/Ethnicity, Gender, and Income: 1995–96

	Low Income (less than $30,000)		Middle Income ($30,000 to $69,999)		Upper Income ($70,000 or more)	
	Men	Women	Men	Women	Men	Women
White	46	54	50	50	52	48
African American	32	68	48	52	41	59
Hispanic	43	57	46	54	50	50
Asian American	53	47	57	43	52	48
American Indian	23	77	53	47	N/A	N/A
All Students	44	56	50	50	51	49

Source: U.S. Department of Education, National Postsecondary Student Aid Study: 1995–96.
N/A: The sample size is too small to generate a reliable estimate.

"Hispanic girls are dropping out at a far greater rate than any other group of girls in the United States." According to government data, 26 percent of Hispanic girls leave high school before receiving a diploma, compared with 13 percent of black girls and 6.9 percent of white girls.

"Hmm," you might say to yourself, "what is up with these Hispanic girls?" That is, until you read the very next paragraph (here quoted in full):

> The only group that has a higher dropout rate among all students is Hispanic boys. Thirty-one percent of Hispanic boys drop out, compared with 12.1 percent of black boys and 7.7 percent of white boys.

So the dropout rates among Hispanics—both boys and girls—are exceptionally high. This isn't about gender at all: it's entirely a problem of race and ethnicity. (And, since race and ethnicity are so indelibly linked to class, it's a problem of class as well.) The article should have been titled "Hispanics—Boys *and* Girls—Most Likely to Drop Out."

Local studies also reveal the race- and class-based underpinnings of the trends usually attributed to gender. A study of high school students in the Boston area by the Rennie Center for Education Research & Policy found substantial gender differences in dropout rates. For 2005, the study found an attrition rate of 21 percent between 9th and 12th grade. The male dropout rate was 4 percent higher than the girls' rate, but most of the enrollment decline overall was accounted for by Hispanic and black males. The number of Hispanic males enrolled in Massachusetts by grade 12 was just barely half of the number that had entered in 9th grade.[5]

Why don't the pundits acknowledge these race and class differences? To many who would now propose to "rescue" boys from feminist "political correctness," such differences are incidental because, in their eyes, all boys are the same and they need special treatment that takes into account their naturally aggressive, competitive natures.

Men need to be tough, the theory goes, to see themselves as leaders who can take charge of others. They can then channel their natural urges into responsible social roles such as becoming the family breadwinner or serving in the military. Michael Gurian, for example, celebrates such masculine rites of passage as "military boot camp" and "fraternity hazings" as "essential parts of every boy's life."

But encouraging this definition of masculinity is part of the problem, not the solution, to the issues facing boys. Countless surveys suggest that young boys today still subscribe to a traditional notion of masculinity, stressing the suppression of emotion, stoic resolve, aggression, power, success, and other stereotypic features. I believe that an over-reliance on these norms of masculinity—and the suppression of a wider range of emotional expressions, behaviors and psychological traits in the name of masculinity—is the underlying cause of the current boy crisis.

ACHIEVING MANHOOD—AT THE EXPENSE OF ACADEMIC ACHIEVEMENT

How does a focus on the ideology of masculinity explain why boys are more likely to have problems with school? Carol Gilligan's work on adolescent girls describes how these assertive, confident, and proud young girls "lose their voices" when they hit adolescence and gender norms come down on them more harshly. They become more diffident, less sure of themselves, more "feminine." At that same moment, William Pollack notes in his book *Real Boys*, the boys become *more* confident, even beyond their abilities. You might even say that boys *find* their voice, but it is the inauthentic voice of bravado, of constant posturing, of foolish risk-taking and gratuitous violence. He calls it "the boy code." The Boy Code teaches them that they are supposed to be in power, and thus they begin to act like it.[6]

In adolescence, both boys and girls begin to conform to the traditional norms of gender inequality: girls suppress ambition, boys inflate it. Recent research on the gender gap in school achievement bears this out. Girls are more likely to undervalue their abilities, especially in the more traditionally "masculine" educational arenas such as math and science. Boys, however, possessed of this false voice of bravado (and many facing strong family pressure) are likely to *over-value* their abilities, to remain in programs even though they are less qualified and capable of succeeding.

This difference, and not some putative discrimination against boys, is the reason that girls' mean test scores in math and science are now, on average, approaching that of boys. Too many boys who over-value their abilities remain in difficult math and science courses longer than they should; they pull the boys' mean scores down. By contrast, the few girls whose abilities and self-esteem are sufficient to enable them to "trespass" into a male domain skew female data upwards.

A parallel process is at work in the humanities and social sciences, where girls' test scores actually outpace those of boys. This is not the result of "reverse discrimination," but because the boys bump up against the norms of masculinity. Boys regard English as a "feminine" subject. Pioneering research in Australia and Britain found that boys are uninterested in English because of how it might challenge their (inauthentic) masculine pose. "Reading is lame, sitting down and looking at words is pathetic," commented one boy. "Most guys who like English are faggots." The traditional liberal arts curriculum is seen as feminizing; as Catharine Stimpson recently put it sarcastically, "real men don't speak French."[7]

Boys tend to hate English and foreign languages for the same reasons that girls love them. In English, they observe, there are no hard and fast rules, but rather one expresses one's opinion about the topic and everyone's opinion is equally valued. "The answer can be a variety of things, you're never really wrong," observed one boy. "It's not like maths and science where there is one set answer to everything." Another boy noted:

> I find English hard. It's because there are no set rules for reading texts . . . In English you have to write down how you feel and that's what I don't like.

Compare this to the comments of girls in the same study:

> I feel motivated to study English because . . . your view isn't necessarily wrong. There is no definite right or wrong answer and you have the freedom to say what you feel is right without it being rejected as a wrong answer.

It is not the "feminized" school experience that prevents boys from succeeding in school, but rather the ideology of traditional masculinity that keeps boys from *wanting* to succeed. "The work you do here is girls' work," one boy commented to a researcher. "It's not real work."[8]

The gender gap in achievement has almost everything to do with ideologies of gender—what people believe makes them masculine and feminine—and much less to do with biology. And these problems are exacerbated by race and class.

BAD BOYS?

It has been nearly three decades since Paul Willis first documented the ways that working-class British lads created their own masculinity codes in schools, and how their lack of achievement, their disinterest and disruptions were based on a class-based opposition to middle-class norms. And nearly two decades ago, John Ogbu first noticed that same oppositional culture among black students whose relentless criticism of higher achieving black students for "acting white" constrained black achievement.[9]

Several important ethnographies of inner city schools have built on Ogbu's and Willis's original insights, among them Signithia Fordham's *Blacked Out* and Ann Ferguson's *Bad Boys*.[10] Fordham's study echoed Ogbu's: when black students worked hard in school or achieve academic success, their peers accused them of "acting white." But when black *boys* worked hard or achieved, they were also accused of "acting like girls."

The origins of this oppositional subculture are hotly debated. As Sugrue and Raley point out (this volume), job loss in the central cities, declining real wages for blue-collar workers, cutbacks in affordable housing subsidies, and chronic underfunding of inner-city schools, often combined with self-fulfilling prophecies on the part of educators, have left many impoverished youth with no sense that that they have a shot at upward mobility. And when people do not expect to succeed at something, and others also expect them to fail, they may try to ward off defining themselves as failures by deciding that they wouldn't *want* to succeed at it anyway.

Individual psychological remedies rarely get through to these youths. In fact, Pedro Noguera has found that adolescent black males are the only group—race or class or gender—for which there is no relationship whatever between self-esteem and academic achievement. For all other groups, raising self-esteem is a psychological way to raise achievement. But many young black males are so disaffected, so alienated from the system, that they are immune to its effects.[11]

Self-fulfilling prophecies, chronic underfunding, and oppositional gendered racial subcultures also combine to affect behavior in schools. Young black males are expected to be behavioral problems—and given the material circumstances and cultural milieu in which they go to school, they often are. According to research at Indiana University, African-Americans are four times as likely to be suspended from school and about two-and-a-half times as likely to be expelled as white students. Hispanics are about twice as likely to be suspended or expelled as white students. And in the era of "zero tolerance," a part of the No Child Left Behind approach, this releases a significant number of boys of color onto the streets—which almost serves as an incentive, since you get to skip school.[12] (Incidentally, the study also found absolutely no effect of "zero tolerance" on achievement or even school behavior.)

CONCLUSION

Whether one focuses on numbers, achievement or behavior, the current boy crisis is unevenly distributed among boys by race and class. Focusing our attention on the psychological anxieties of upper-middle-class white boys, who are and will continue to be college bound, will not address the structural crisis—a crisis of political and economic urgency—that simmers below the surface. That requires that we ask "which boys?" and that our remedies take into account both race and class. And those boys' voices will be essential in our conversation.

For much of American history, poor men and men of color have endured a constant questioning of their manhood—indeed, that they are not "real men" has often been used as an "explanation" of their condition. They are either lazy, irresponsible, and dependent, on the one hand, or hyper-masculine sexualized violent thugs on the other. Or both. As a result, proving manhood among poor men and minorities has often led to a sort of hyper-masculine over-compensation, as though to demonstrate masculinity one must exaggerate all the man-making qualities offered by the society.[13]

Note that I wrote "often." There is another side to the problematization of minority and working-class masculinities besides compensatory hypermasculinity. And that other side is constructive resistance. It invariably surprises my students, for example, when they learn that black husbands do more housework and childcare than white husbands, or that working-class men do more than middle-class men (although middle-class men are more ideologically egalitarian).

Questioning someone's "manliness" has been, for decades, a way to start a fight. But for some courageous young men, questioning "manliness" might also offer an alternative path, a path away from racialized and class-based demonstrations of manhood, and toward a definition of masculinity that embraces connections with friends, intimacy with one's family, academic success, and solidarity instead of competition with others.

NOTES

An earlier version of this article was published in *Dissent*, Fall, 2006.

1.   George Gilder, "The Idea of the (Feminized) University," in *National Review*, December 31, 2005.
2.   See for example Brad Knickerbocker, "Young and Male in America: It's Hard being a Boy," in *Christian Science Monitor*, April 29, 1999.
3.   Tamar Lewin, "American Colleges Begin to Ask, Where Have All the Men Gone?," in *The New York Times*, December 6, 1998; Brendan Koerner, "Where the Boys Aren't," in *U.S. News and World Report*, February 8, 1999.
4.   Cynthia Fuchs Epstein, *Deceptive Distinctions* (New Haven: Yale University Press, 1988).
5.   Rennie Center for Education Research & Policy, "Are Boys Making the Grade? Gender Gaps in Achievement and Attainment," October 2006; available at www.renniecenter.org
6.   See Carol Gilligan, *In a Different Voice* (Cambridge, MA: Harvard University Press, 1982); Carol Gilligan and Lyn Mikel Brown, *Meeting at the Crossroads: Women's Psychology and Girls' Development* (New York: Ballantine, 1993); William Pollack, *Real Boys* (New York: Henry Holt, 1999).
7.   Stimpson quoted in Tamar Lewin, "American Colleges begin to Ask, Where Have all the Men Gone?," in *The New York Times*, December 6, 1998, A-20.
8.   All quotes are from Wayne Martino, "Gendered Learning Practices: Exploring the Costs of Hegemonic Masculinity for Girls and Boys in Schools," in *Gender Equity: A Framework for Australian Schools* (Canberra, 1997); " 'Cool Boys,' 'Party Animals', 'Squids,' and 'Poofters': Interrogating the Dynamics and Politics of Adolescent Masculinities in School," in *British Journal of Sociology of Education*, 20(2), 1999; Mairtin Mac an Ghaill, *The Making of Men: Masculinities, Sexualities and Schooling* (London: Open University Press, 1994); "What About the Boys?: Schooling, Class and Crisis Masculinity," in *Sociological Review*, 44(3), 1996.

9. See, for example, Paul Willis, *Learning to Labor* (New York: Columbia University Press, 1981); John Ogbu, *Black American Students in An Affluent Suburb: A Study of Academic Disengagement* (New York: TF-LEA Press, 2003). See also R. Patrick Soloman, *Black Resistance in High School: Forging a Separatist Culture* (Albany: SUNY Press, 1992). Of course, James Coleman noticed this oppositional anti-intellectual adolescent subculture two decades earlier—including its gendered component. See *The Adolescent Society* (New York: The Free Press, 1961).

10. Signithia Fordham, *Blacked Out: Dilemmas of Race, Identity, and Success at Capital High* (Chicago: University of Chicago Press, 1996); Ann Ferguson, *Bad Boys: Public Schools in the Making of Black Masculinity* (Ann Arbor: University of Michigan Press, 2001).

11. Pedro Noguera, Professor of Education, New York University, personal communication.

12. http://ceep.indiana.edu/ChildrenLeftBehind/printsummary.html

13. See, for example, my *Manhood in America: A Cultural History* (10th anniversary edition) (New York: Oxford University Press, 2006).

28

Diversity Among Same-Sex Couples and Their Children

GARY GATES

CURRENT CONTROVERSIES ABOUT MARRIAGE and parenting rights for lesbians and gay men provide a good example of why it is essential to take account of race and class in discussions of sexuality and family life, and why it is also necessary to integrate race and class into our discussion of issues such as marriage for same-sex couples. The success of television shows such as *Will and Grace* and *Queer Eye for the Straight Guy* contribute to an increasingly visible role for lesbians and gay men in American news media and in popular culture. Unfortunately, popular images rarely display the diversity of the lesbian and gay community in the United States, focusing disproportionately on relatively wealthy, white, and urban gay men. A recent analysis of American television broadcast media by the Gay and Lesbian Alliance Against Defamation (2007) found that the gay community was commonly portrayed as both white and male. But the real life world of the lesbian and gay community, especially those who are raising children, is often far removed from trendy lofts, expensive cocktails, and designer labels. To cite a few examples:

- Mississippi, not California, is the state where same-sex couples are most likely to be raising children.
- The median household income of same-sex couples with children is substantially lower than that of different-sex married couples with children.
- More than half of the children being raised by same-sex couples are non-white.

This essay explores the diversity of same-sex couples and their families, focusing primarily on analyses of data from the 2000 United States Census. In doing so, I offer a demographic portrait of lesbian and gay couples and their families that challenges stereotypes and myths about this under-studied population.

CHILD REARING AMONG LESBIANS AND GAY MEN

Perhaps the most intriguing finding from Census 2000 was that more than one in five same-sex couples were raising children—which translates into more than 250,000 children being raised by openly gay and lesbian couples (Gates and Ost, 2004).[1] Evidence from the 2002 National Survey of Family Growth (NSFG) demonstrates that these couples represent only the tip of the lesbian and gay child-rearing iceberg. Not only does the Census understate the actual number of same-sex couples currently raising children, but it also does not take into account the growing desire and

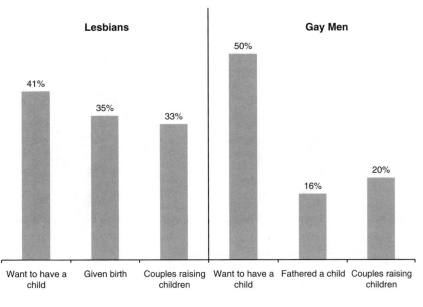

Figure 28.1

ability of gays and lesbians to have children in the future (Figure 28.1).[2] Among childless lesbians and gay men, four in ten lesbians and fully half of gay men want to have a child. Furthermore, a third of lesbians and one in six gay men already have children, even if they are not presently raising them as part of a couple (Macomber, Badgett, Gates, and Chambers, 2007).

So where are all of these children coming from? Among children under age 18 living with same-sex couples, only 7 percent are adopted and 1.5 percent are foster children.[3] The vast majority, more than 70 percent, are either the "natural born" child or a "step-child" of the householder. An additional 5 percent are grandchildren, with another 5 percent other relatives such as siblings and cousins, and 10 percent are "non-relatives" (at least in relation to the householder). Clearly, a portion of the 70 percent of children who are "natural born" or "step-children" are likely the product of reproductive technologies like artificial insemination or surrogacy. Unfortunately, we have no way of estimating how common this practice is among same-sex couples or lesbian and gay people in general. However, given the expenses associated with these procedures and evidence regarding the economic disadvantage of many of these couples discussed below, it seems likely that a large portion of these children are the product of a prior heterosexual relationship. Not surprisingly, men and women in same-sex couples who were previously married are nearly twice as likely as their never-married counterparts to have a child under 18 in the home (Figure 28.2).

Contrary to most television images of same-sex couples raising children, diversity by race and ethnicity is one of the more striking demographic characteristics of such couples. African-American and Latina women in same-sex couples are more than twice as likely as their white counterparts to be raising a child. And gay African-American men and Latinos are three times as likely to be raising children as are gay white men. Consistent with this finding, 40 percent of individuals in same-sex couples raising children are non-white. And more than half of the children of same-sex couples are non-white.

Same-sex couples raising children defy the stereotype of lesbian and gay people as wealthy, urban, sophisticates perhaps more than any segment of the lesbian and gay community. Across all

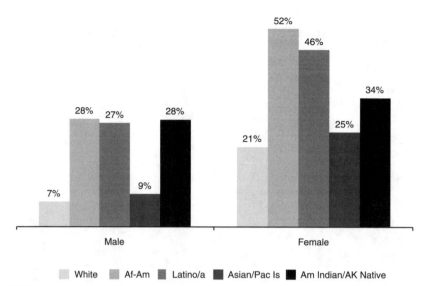

Figure 28.2 Child under age 18 in the home

racial and ethnic groups, same-sex couples raising children have lower median household incomes than do married couples raising children. The median household income of African-Americans in a same-sex couple raising children is more than 20 percent lower than that of their married counterparts. For Whites and Asian/Pacific Islanders, the comparable difference is about 10 percent (Sears and Gates, 2005). Clearly, same-sex couples raising children are not particularly wealthy (Figure 28.3).

They also do not tend to live in areas known as gay enclaves. More than four in ten same-sex couples in Mississippi are raising children, making it the state where same-sex couples are most likely to have a child. Mississippi is followed by South Dakota, Alaska, South Carolina, and

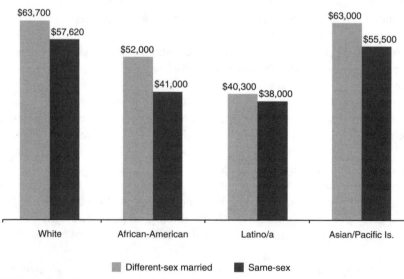

Figure 28.3 Median Household Income: Families raising children under age 18

Louisiana. Among similarly ranking metropolitan areas, San Antonio, Texas, where more than 36 percent of same-sex couples are raising children, tops the list. The top five include Bergen-Passaic (New Jersey), Memphis, Houston, and Fort Worth (Gates and Ost, 2004).

CHANGES IN THE FUTURE

As more gay men and lesbians feel free to come out about their identity and relationships, we are likely to see the similarities between gay and lesbian and heterosexual families become even greater. Polling from the last few decades demonstrates a marked change in American attitudes toward gay and lesbian people. In 1988, a Gallup poll found that only 33 percent of Americans thought that homosexual relations between consenting adults should be legal. By 2007, that figure had increased to 59 percent.[4] As the social stigma surrounding lesbians and gay men declines, more of them appear willing to "come out" on surveys and provide information about their sexual orientation and the nature of their relationships, and that process is now spreading beyond the urban areas where gays and lesbians historically felt freer to reveal their sexual orientation. In 1990, the first year that the Census used the "unmarried partner" category, there were more than 290,000 individuals who identified themselves as part of a same-sex couple in the United States (Smith and Gates, 2001). In 2000, the Census recorded nearly 1.2 million individuals in same-sex couples. By 2005, the figure had risen to more than 1.5 million (Gates, 2007). Analyses of the 2005 American Community Survey show that states throughout the Midwest have experienced the largest increases in same-sex couples since the Census 2000 (Gates, 2007). This offers further evidence that we need to alter our perception that lesbians and gay men are concentrated in the coastal regions of the country (Gates and Ost, 2004). As the proverbial closet doors open wider in areas such as the Midwest and the South, more gay men and lesbians will feel free to move to these regions and more long-term gay and lesbian residents in those regions will feel free to come out.

Changes in the location preferences of same-sex couples demonstrate this pattern. In 1990, 93 percent of self-identified same-sex couples were located in a metropolitan area, compared to just 80 percent of all American households. By 2000, this demographic gap had narrowed. While the rate at which all American households were located in a metropolitan area had not changed much (rising to 81 percent), the comparable figure for same-sex couples had dropped to 86 percent.[5] The U.S. Census Bureau defines "urban clusters" as areas with population densities that exceed 1,000 people per square mile. In 1990, about 75 percent of all American households lived in these urban areas compared to 90 percent same-sex couples. By 2000, that gap too had narrowed, with 80 percent of all American households living in urban clusters compared to 84 percent of same-sex couples.

Child-rearing rates among same-sex couples are also on the rise, creating more convergence among heterosexual and same-sex couples. In 1990, only about 5 percent of same-sex male couples and 20 percent of same-sex female couples were raising children. By 2000, child-rearing rates had increased to nearly 20 percent of male couples and a third of female couples.

The racial and ethnic composition of same-sex couples provides a third example of the increasing similarity between the characteristics of same-sex and heterosexual couples. In 1990, 20 percent of Americans identified as non-white.[6] In that same year, only 13 percent of men and women who identified themselves as being in a same-sex couple were non-white. By Census 2000, the percentage of Americans who were non-white had risen to 30 percent. Among those in same-sex couples, the figure rose more dramatically to nearly a quarter who were non-white. The data suggest a demographic convergence of sorts. As lesbians and gay men in minority communities feel more comfortable in coming out, the "visible" gay community looks increasingly like the broader American population. Analyses of Census data provide clear evidence of a gay and lesbian community reflecting the diversity of America in family form, socio-economic status, and race and ethnicity.

WHY DOES THIS MATTER?

Census data offer a portrait of lesbian and gay families that challenges monolithic and stereotyped images of them as wealthy, white, childless, and urban—an image that likely never reflected the truth about this diverse population. The demographic diversity of the lesbian and gay community has bearing on policy debates regarding marriage and adoption rights. Among other things, marriage provides legal and economic protections that cannot be completely replicated through non-marital legal contracts. For example, federal social security survival benefits are not awarded to same-sex partners nor can these partners file wrongful death lawsuits in states that do not recognize their relationships. These rights, so important to economic security in times of crisis like the death of a spouse, would certainly be even more important to lower-income same-sex couples.

Census analyses showing economic disadvantages among same-sex couples raising children are also cogent to these debates. Marriage and legal adoption provide myriad legal and economic protections specifically for parents and their children. In the absence of marriage or adoption, some partners in same-sex couples have no legal standing in relation to their children. Among other problems, this lack of standing could impact their ability to cover their children on employee healthcare plans and create difficulties in an emergency medical situation where the legal parent is not available to authorize appropriate care. Again, among lower-income lesbian and gay families, the rights and protections afforded by marriage and legal adoption can be even more critical.

Marriage and adoption rights for lesbians and gay men may be seen as luxuries by some members of the public, something that an affluent community wants as a whim or an abstract statement of principle. But these rights can be absolutely vital to lower-income people and their families, who, Census data confirm, comprise a large portion of the lesbian and gay community. The struggle for equal rights for sexual minorities should not be understood as merely a struggle among elites; it should be a key part of larger efforts promoting racial and social justice.

NOTES

1. Identification of same-sex couples in the 2000 U.S. Decennial Census relies on information provided about the nature of the relationship between the person who filled out the Census form and his or her relationship to other members of the household. If this person describes another adult of the same sex as his or her "unmarried partner" or "husband/wife," the couple counts as a same-sex unmarried partner household (see Gates and Ost, 2004 for a detailed explanation of counting same-sex couples). Because only couples are counted, the Census data do not capture single gay men, lesbians, or bisexuals nor do they offer a way to separately identify bisexuals or transgender individuals.
2. The Census most likely undercounts the population of same-sex couples. Concerns about revealing the nature of their relationships to the federal government may lead many same-sex couples not to use categories like "unmarried partner" or "husband/wife" to describe their partnerships. In addition, some couples may believe that "unmarried partner" or "husband/wife" does not accurately describe their relationship.
3. An estimated 65,500 adopted children and 14,000 foster children are living with a lesbian and gay parent, both single and partnered (Macomber, Badgett, Gates, and Chambers, 2007).
4. See http://www.galluppoll.com/content/?ci=27694 (accessed 5 July 2007).
5. Some caution should be noted in comparing same-sex couples identified in the 1990 and 2000 Census enumerations. The 2000 Census includes couples where one same-sex partner was identified as the "husband," "wife," or "unmarried partner" of the other partner. The 1990 counts only include couples where a same-sex partner is identified as an "unmarried partner." Same-sex spouses were not included in the 1990 counts.

6.   Census Bureau figures report race and Hispanic/Latino(a) ethnicity separately. These figures for the percent of the non-white population are based only on reported race and therefore do not take ethnicity into account. Americans of any racial category may also be Hispanic or Latino/a.

REFERENCES

Gates, G.J., and Ost., *The Gay and Lesbian Atlas* (Washington: Urban Institute Press, 2004).

Gates, G.J., Same-sex Couples and the Gay, Lesbian, and Bisexual Population: New Estimates from the American Community Survey. (Los Angeles: Williams Institute, University of California, 2007).

Gay and Lesbian Alliance Against Defamation. Network Responsibility Index, Primetime Programming 2006–2007, a special report. (2007).

Macomber, J.E., Badgett, M.V.L., Gates, G., and Chambers, K., *Adoption and Foster Care by Lesbian and Gay Parents in the United States.* (Washington, DC: The Urban Institute, The Williams Institute, UCLA School of Law, 2007).

Sears, R.B., and Gates, G.J., Same-Sex Couples and Same-Sex Couples Raising Children in The United States: Data from Census 2000. (Los Angeles: Williams Institute, University of California, 2005).

Smith, D. and Gates, G.J., Gay and Lesbian Families in the United States: Same-sex unmarried partner households. (Human Rights Campaign Report (Washington DC, 2001).

29

excerpts from
Unequal Childhoods
Class, Race, and Family Life

ANNETTE LAREAU

LAUGHING AND YELLING, a white fourth-grader named Garrett Tallinger splashes around in the swimming pool in the backyard of his four-bedroom home in the suburbs on a late spring afternoon. As on most evenings, after a quick dinner his father drives him to soccer practice. This is only one of Garrett's many activities. His brother has a baseball game at a different location. There are evenings when the boys' parents relax, sipping a glass of wine. Tonight is not one of them. As they rush to change out of their work clothes and get the children ready for practice, Mr. and Mrs. Tallinger are harried.

Only ten minutes away, a Black fourth-grader, Alexander Williams, is riding home from a school open house.[1] His mother is driving their beige, leather-upholstered Lexus. It is 9:00 P.M. on a Wednesday evening. Ms. Williams is tired from work and has a long Thursday ahead of her. She will get up at 4:45 A.M. to go out of town on business and will not return before 9:00 P.M. On Saturday morning, she will chauffeur Alexander to a private piano lesson at 8:15 A.M., which will be followed by a choir rehearsal and then a soccer game. As they ride in the dark, Alexander's mother, in a quiet voice, talks with her son, asking him questions and eliciting his opinions.

Discussions between parents and children are a hallmark of middle-class child rearing. Like many middle-class parents, Ms. Williams and her husband see themselves as "developing" Alexander to cultivate his talents in a concerted fashion. Organized activities, established and controlled by mothers and fathers, dominate the lives of middle-class children such as Garrett and Alexander. By making certain their children have these and other experiences, middle-class parents engage in a process of *concerted cultivation*. From this, a robust sense of entitlement takes root in the children. This sense of entitlement plays an especially important role in institutional settings, where middle-class children learn to question adults and address them as relative equals.

Only twenty minutes away, in blue-collar neighborhoods, and slightly farther away, in public housing projects, childhood looks different. Mr. Yanelli, a white working-class father, picks up his son Little Billy, a fourth-grader, from an after-school program. They come home and Mr. Yanelli drinks a beer while Little Billy first watches television, then rides his bike and plays in the street. Other nights, he and his Dad sit on the sidewalk outside their house and play cards. At about 5:30 P.M. Billy's mother gets home from her job as a house cleaner. She fixes dinner and the entire family sits down to eat together. Extended family are a prominent part of their lives. Ms. Yanelli touches base with her "entire family every day" by phone. Many nights Little Billy's uncle stops by, sometimes bringing Little Billy's youngest cousin. In the spring, Little Billy plays baseball on a local team. Unlike for Garrett and Alexander, who have at least four activities a week, for Little Billy, baseball is his only organized activity outside of school during the entire year. Down the road, a white working-class girl, Wendy Driver, also spends the evening with her girl cousins, as they watch a video and eat popcorn, crowded together on the living room floor.

Farther away, a Black fourth-grade boy, Harold McAllister, plays outside on a summer evening in the public housing project in which he lives. His two male cousins are there that night, as they often are. After an afternoon spent unsuccessfully searching for a ball so they could play basketball, the boys had resorted to watching sports on television. Now they head outdoors for a twilight water balloon fight. Harold tries to get his neighbor, Miss Latifa, wet. People sit in white plastic lawn chairs outside the row of apartments. Music and television sounds waft through the open windows and doors.

The adults in the lives of Billy, Wendy, and Harold want the best for them. Formidable economic constraints make it a major life task for these parents to put food on the table, arrange for housing, negotiate unsafe neighborhoods, take children to the doctor (often waiting for city buses that do not come), clean children's clothes, and get children to bed and have them ready for school the next morning. But unlike middle-class parents, these adults do not consider the concerted development of children, particularly through organized leisure activities, an essential aspect of good parenting. Unlike the Tallingers and Williamses, these mothers and fathers do not focus on concerted cultivation. For them, the crucial responsibilities of parenthood do not lie in eliciting their children's feelings, opinions, and thoughts. Rather, they see a clear boundary between adults and children. Parents tend to use directives: they tell their children what to do rather than persuading them with reasoning. Unlike their middle-class counterparts, who have a steady diet of adult organized activities, the working-class and poor children have more control over the character of their leisure activities. Most children are free to go out and play with friends and relatives who typically live close by. Their parents and guardians facilitate the *accomplishment of natural growth.*[2] Yet these children and their parents interact with central institutions in the society, such as schools, which firmly and decisively promote strategies of concerted cultivation in child rearing. For working-class and poor families, the cultural logic of child rearing at home is out of synch with the standards of institutions. As a result, while children whose parents adopt strategies of concerted cultivation appear to gain a sense of entitlement, children such as Billy Yanelli, Wendy Driver, and Harold McAllister appear to gain an emerging sense of distance, distrust, and constraint in their institutional experiences.

America may be the land of opportunity, but it is also a land of inequality. This book identifies the largely invisible but powerful ways that parents' social class impacts children's life experiences. [. . .] I argue that key elements of family life cohere to form a cultural logic of child rearing.[3] In other words, the differences among families seem to cluster together in meaningful patterns. In this historical moment, middle-class parents tend to adopt a cultural logic of child rearing that stresses the concerted cultivation of children. Working-class and poor parents, by contrast, tend to undertake the accomplishment of natural growth. In the accomplishment of natural growth, children experience long stretches of leisure time, child-initiated play, clear boundaries between adults and children, and daily interactions with kin. Working-class and poor children, despite tremendous economic strain, often have more "childlike" lives, with autonomy from adults and control over their extended leisure time. Although middle-class children miss out on kin relationships and leisure time, they appear to (at least potentially) gain important institutional advantages. From the experience of concerted cultivation, they acquire skills that could be valuable in the future when they enter the world of work. Middle-class white and Black children in my study did exhibit some key differences; yet the biggest gaps were not within social classes but, as I show, across them. It is these class differences and how they are enacted in family life and child rearing that shape the ways children view themselves in relation to the rest of the world.

CULTURAL REPERTOIRES

Professionals who work with children, such as teachers, doctors, and counselors, generally agree about how children should be raised. Of course, from time to time they may disagree on the ways standards should be enacted for an individual child or family. For example, teachers may disagree about whether or not parents should stop and correct a child who mispronounces a word while reading. Counselors may disagree over whether a mother is being too protective of her child. Still, there is little dispute among professionals on the broad principles for promoting educational development in children through proper parenting.[4] These standards include the importance of talking with children, developing their educational interests, and playing an active role in their schooling. Similarly, parenting guidelines typically stress the importance of reasoning with children and teaching them to solve problems through negotiation rather than with physical force. Because these guidelines are so generally accepted, and because they focus on a set of practices concerning how parents should raise children, they form a *dominant set of cultural repertoires* about how children should be raised. This widespread agreement among professionals about the broad principles for child rearing permeates our society. A small number of experts thus potentially shape the behavior of a large number of parents.

Professionals' advice regarding the best way to raise children has changed regularly over the last two centuries. From strong opinions about the merits of bottle feeding, being stern with children, and utilizing physical punishment (with dire warnings of problematic outcomes should parents indulge children), there have been shifts to equally strongly worded recommendations about the benefits of breast feeding, displaying emotional warmth toward children, and using reasoning and negotiation as mechanisms of parental control. Middle-class parents appear to shift their behaviors in a variety of spheres more rapidly and more thoroughly than do working-class or poor parents.[5] As professionals have shifted their recommendations from bottle feeding to breast feeding, from stern approaches to warmth and empathy, and from spanking to time-outs, it is middle-class parents who have responded most promptly.[6] Moreover, in recent decades, middle-class children in the United States have had to face the prospect of "declining fortunes."[7] Worried about how their children will get ahead, middle-class parents are increasingly determined to make sure that their children are not excluded from any opportunity that might eventually contribute to their advancement.

Middle-class parents who comply with current professional standards and engage in a pattern of concerted cultivation deliberately try to stimulate their children's development and foster their cognitive and social skills. The commitment among working-class and poor families to provide comfort, food, shelter, and other basic support requires ongoing effort, given economic challenges and the formidable demands of child rearing. But it stops short of the deliberate cultivation of children and their leisure activities that occurs in middle-class families. For working-class and poor families, sustaining children's natural growth is viewed as an accomplishment.[8]

What is the outcome of these different philosophies and approaches to child rearing? Quite simply, they appear to lead to the *transmission of differential advantages* to children. In this study, there was quite a bit more talking in middle-class homes than in working-class and poor homes, leading to the development of greater verbal agility, larger vocabularies, more comfort with authority figures, and more familiarity with abstract concepts. Importantly, children also developed skill differences in interacting with authority figures in institutions and at home. Middle-class children such as Garrett Tallinger and Alexander Williams learn, as young boys, to shake the hands of adults and look them in the eye. In studies of job interviews, investigators have found that potential employees have less than one minute to make a good impression. Researchers stress the importance of eye contact, firm handshakes, and displaying comfort with bosses during the interview. In poor families like Harold McAllister's, however, family members usually do not look each other in the eye when conversing. In addition, as Elijah Anderson points out, they live in neighborhoods where it can be dangerous to look people in the eye too long.[9] The types of social competence transmitted in the McAllister family are valuable, but they are potentially less valuable (in employment interviews, for example) than those learned by Garrett Tallinger and Alexander Williams.

The white and Black middle-class children in this study also exhibited an emergent version of the *sense of entitlement* characteristic of the middle-class. They acted as though they had a right to pursue their own individual preferences and to actively manage interactions in institutional settings. They appeared comfortable in these settings; they were open to sharing information and asking for attention. Although some children were more outgoing than others, it was common practice among middle-class children to shift interactions to suit *their* preferences. Alexander Williams knew how to get the doctor to listen to his concerns (about the bumps under his arm from his new deodorant). His mother explicitly trained and encouraged him to speak up with the doctor. Similarly, a Black middle-class girl, Stacey Marshall, was taught by her mother to expect the gymnastics teacher to accommodate her individual learning style. Thus, middle-class children were trained in "the rules of the game" that govern interactions with institutional representatives. They were not conversant in other important social skills, however, such as organizing their time for hours on end during weekends and summers, spending long periods of time away from adults, or hanging out with adults in a nonobtrusive, subordinate fashion. Middle-class children also learned (by imitation and by direct training) how to make the rules work in their favor. Here, the enormous stress on reasoning and negotiation in the home also has a potential advantage for future institutional negotiations. Additionally, those in authority responded positively to such interactions. Even in fourth grade, middle-class children appeared to be acting on their own behalf to gain advantages. They made special requests of teachers and doctors to adjust procedures to accommodate their desires.

The working-class and poor children, by contrast, showed an emerging *sense of constraint* in their interactions in institutional settings. They were less likely to try to customize interactions to suit their own preferences. Like their parents, the children accepted the actions of persons in authority (although at times they also covertly resisted them). Working-class and poor parents sometimes were not as aware of their children's school situation (as when their children were not doing homework). Other times, they dismissed the school rules as unreasonable. For example, Wendy Driver's mother told her to "punch" a boy who was pestering her in class; Billy Yanelli's parents were proud of him when he "beat up" another boy on the playground, even though Billy was then suspended from school. Parents also had trouble getting "the school" to respond to their concerns. When Ms. Yanelli complained that she "hates" the school, she gave her son a lesson in powerlessness and frustration in the face of an important institution. Middle-class children such as Stacey Marshall learned to make demands on professionals, and when they succeeded in making the rules work in their favor they augmented their "cultural capital" (i.e., skills individuals inherit that can then be translated into different forms of value as they move through various institutions) for the future.[10] When working-class and poor children confronted institutions, however, they generally were unable to make the rules work in their favor nor did they obtain capital for adulthood. Because of these patterns of legitimization, children raised according to the logic of concerted cultivation can gain advantages, in the form of an emerging sense of entitlement, while children raised according to the logic of natural growth tend to develop an emerging sense of constraint.[11]

[...]

In terms of income and wealth, the richest 10 percent of families in our society own almost 80 percent of all real estate (other than family homes), more than 90 percent of all securities (stocks and bonds) and about 60 percent of all the money in bank accounts.[12] One widely used indicator of inequality in income is the child poverty rate, a rate that is heavily dependent on social policy. (There are many more poor children in the United States than in most Western European countries.)[13] In the United States, one-fifth of all children live below the poverty level, and the figure is approximately twice as high for Black children.[14] The distribution of income and wealth became even more heavily concentrated in the hands of a few during the last decades of the twentieth century.[15] Still, during the study period, one-seventh of Black Americans were making over fifty thousand dollars annually.[16]

Educational accomplishments are also lopsided. In the United States, just under one-quarter of all adults have completed a bachelor's degree; the figure is a bit higher for individuals in their twenties. More than 10 percent of high school students drop out.[17] Even among younger people, for whom college education is becoming increasingly common, a clear majority (from two-thirds to three-quarters) do not graduate.[18] Although some studies show that, after taking into account parents' social position, Black youth are *more* likely to pursue higher education than whites, overall levels of educational attainment are far lower for Black children.[19] Substantial stratification also exists within higher education, ranging from community colleges to elite universities. The more elite the school, the more richly graduates are rewarded.[20]

Moreover, there has been a profound shift in the U.S. and world economies, with a decline in "good jobs" with high wages, pensions, health benefits, and stability, and a rise in "bad jobs" with relatively low wages, no benefits, little opportunity for career promotion, and lack of stability.[21] In the lives of most people, these separate threads – their educational attainment, what kind of job they get, and how much money they earn – are all tightly interwoven. Together, these factors constitute parents' social position or social structural location.

Many studies have demonstrated that parents' social structural location has profound implications for their children's life chances. Before kindergarten, for example, children of highly educated parents are much more likely to exhibit "educational readiness" skills, such as knowing their letters, identifying colors, counting up to twenty, and being able to write their first names.[22] Schooling helps, and during the school year the gap in children's performance narrows quite a bit (but widens again during the summer). Children of highly educated mothers continue to outperform children of less educated mothers throughout their school careers. By the time young people take the SAT examinations for admission to college, the gap is dramatic, averaging 150 points (relative to an average score of 500 points) between children of parents who are high school dropouts and those with parents who have a graduate degree.[23] There are also differences in other aspects of children's school performance according to their parents' social structural location.[24] Many studies demonstrate the crucial role of educational success in determining occupational success. Parents' social class position predicts children's school success and thus their ultimate life chances.[25]

[...]

Class position influences critical aspects of family life: time use, language use, and kin ties. Working-class and middle-class mothers may express beliefs that reflect a similar notion of "intensive mothering," but their behavior is quite different.[26] For that reason, I have described sets of paired beliefs and actions as a "cultural logic" of child rearing. When children and parents move outside the home into the world of social institutions, they find that these cultural practices are not given equal value. There are signs that middle-class children benefit, in ways that are invisible to them and to their parents, from the degree of similarity between the cultural repertoires in the home and those standards adopted by institutions. In the next section, I acknowledge areas of family life that did not appear to be heavily influenced by social class. Then I turn to highlighting the ways that social class membership matters and to discussing why these differences exist and what can be done to lessen or eliminate them.

THE LIMITS OF SOCIAL CLASS

Among the families we observed, some aspects of daily life did not vary systematically by social class. There were episodes of laughter, emotional connection, and happiness as well as quiet comfort in every family.[27] Harold McAllister and his mother laughed together as he almost dropped his hot dog but then, in an awkward grab, caught it. After a baseball game, Mr. Williams rubbed Alexander's head affectionately and called him "handsome." Ms. Handlon gave her daughter a big squeeze around her shoulders after the Christmas Eve pageant, and Melanie beamed. One summer afternoon, Mr. Yanelli and Billy played cards together, sitting cross-legged on the sidewalk. These moments of connection seemed deeply meaningful to both children and parents in all social classes, even as they take different shape by social class, in terms of language, activity, and character.

All the families we observed also had rituals: favorite meals they often ate, television programs they watched, toys or games that were very important, family outings they looked forward to, and other common experiences. The content of their rituals varied (especially by social class); what did not vary was that the children enjoyed these experiences and they provided a sense of membership in a family. Also, in all social classes, a substantial part of the children's days was spent in repetitive rituals: getting up, making the bed, taking a shower, getting dressed, brushing hair and teeth, eating breakfast, finding school books and papers, and waiting for adults to get ready. These moments were interspersed with hours, days, and weeks of household work, tedious demands, mundane tasks, and tension. This was true for all families, regardless of social class. Nor were any families immune to life tragedies: across all social classes there were premature deaths due to car accidents or suicides. Across all social classes children and parents had different temperaments: some were shy and quiet; some were outgoing and talkative. Some had a sense of humor and some did not. The degree of organization and orderliness in daily life also did not vary systematically by social class. Some houses were clean and some were a disaster. Some of the messiest ones were middle-class homes in which the entryway was a paragon of order but the living spaces, particularly the upstairs, were in a tumble. Despite the formidable differences among the families detailed previously, in each home, after a few visits, the research assistants and I found that the surroundings felt normal, comfortable, and safe. Put differently, they all felt like home.

CONCERTED CULTIVATION AND THE ACCOMPLISHMENT OF NATURAL GROWTH

Despite these important areas of shared practices, social class made a significant difference in the routines of children's daily lives. The white and Black middle-class parents engaged in practices of *concerted cultivation.* In these families, parents actively fostered and assessed their children's talents, opinions, and skills. They scheduled their children for activities. They reasoned with them. They hovered over them and outside the home they did not hesitate to intervene on the children's behalf. They made a deliberate and sustained effort to stimulate children's development and to cultivate their cognitive and social skills. The working-class and poor parents viewed children's development as unfolding spontaneously, as long as they were provided with comfort, food, shelter, and other basic support. I have called this cultural logic of child rearing the *accomplishment of natural growth.* As with concerted cultivation, this commitment, too, required ongoing effort; sustaining children's natural growth despite formidable life challenges is properly viewed as accomplishment. Parents who relied on natural growth generally organized their children's lives so they spent time in and around home, in informal play with peers, siblings, and cousins. As a result, the children had more autonomy regarding leisure time and more opportunities for child-initiated play. They also were more responsible for their lives outside the home. Unlike in middle-class families, adult-organized activities were uncommon. Instead of the relentless focus on reasoning and negotiation that took place in middle-class families, there was less speech (including less whining and badgering) in working-class and poor homes. Boundaries between adults and children were clearly marked; parents generally used language not as an aim in itself but more as a conduit for social life. Directives were common. In their institutional encounters, working-class and poor parents turned over responsibility to professionals; when parents did try to intervene, they felt that they were less capable and less efficacious than they would have liked. While working-class and poor children differed in important ways, particularly in the stability of their lives, surprisingly there was not a major difference between them in their cultural logic of child rearing. Instead, in this study the cultural divide appeared to be between the middle class and everyone else.

Across all social classes, child-rearing practices often appeared to be natural. Like breathing, child rearing usually seemed automatic and unconscious. Parents were scarcely aware that they were orienting their children in specific ways.[28] For example, the Handlon and the Tallinger children had cousins their own ages who lived within a twenty-minute drive. They saw their cousins, however, only on special occasions, not several times per week as did children in the Driver and McAllister families. While firmly committed to the strategy of concerted cultivation, Mr. and Ms. Williams did not seem especially conscious of their approach. Although both parents mentioned the pleasure they experienced from knowing that Alexander was curious, they did not appear to link that trait to their own extensive use of reasoning with him. Nor did they analyze their failure to use directives. The fact that most of Alexander's time was spent with other children his own age, rather than with his cousins (in part because they lived so far away), also was not a subject of reflection or discussion. Parts of their lives, of course, did reflect conscious choices and deliberate actions, including Ms. Williams's vehement objections to television and both parents' commitment to furthering Alexander's musical talents. The scarcity of time was also a subject of discussion. Even here, however, the focus was on the details of life (e.g., missing a baseball game to take part in a school play) rather than on the overall approach to child rearing.

Similarly, in families using the accomplishment of natural growth, there was tremendous economic constraint and almost constant talk about money. But there was a "taken for granted" character to daily life that presumed a focus on natural growth rather than concerted cultivation. Ms. McAllister stressed her strengths as a mother. As she fed, clothed, and cared for her children, took them on picnics, and watched out for them, she compared her actions favorably to the behavior of mothers living nearby, including those who took drugs. She did not compare herself to the Ms. Tallingers or Ms. Williamses of the world.

THE INTERSECTION OF RACE AND CLASS

In *Race Matters*, Professor Cornell West reports his frustration in trying to hail a cab to get to a photo shoot for the cover of his latest book. As he waited and waited, ten taxis without passengers passed him by, stopping (often within his vision) instead to pick up people whose skin color was not black. Furious, he gave up, took the subway, and was late for the appointment.[29] Professor West and other middle-class African Americans report feeling enraged over this inability to signal their class position in social interactions with strangers. In these situations, race trumps social class.[30]

The middle-class Black fathers in this study told similar tales. One father reported white women clutching their purses and looking terrified as he walked briskly one evening to use the cash machine in an upscale shopping district. Also, as I have shown, the mothers and fathers of middle-class African American children kept a keen eye out for signs of racial problems. Their worries were confirmed, as when a first-grade boy told Alexander Williams (son of a lawyer) that he could only be a garbage man when he grew up, or when Fern Marshall, the only Black girl in a camp of a hundred white girls, had fun during the morning basketball activities but at lunchtime found it more difficult (than if she had been white) to blend into the groups of girls chattering away. Although they moved heavily within white worlds, parents sought to avoid having their children be the only Black child at an event. In addition, parents sought to have their children develop a positive self-image that specifically included their racial identity. Thus, for example, they attended all-Black middle-class Baptist churches every Sunday.

Given this evidence, it would be a mistake to suggest that race did not matter in children's lives. It did. Nevertheless, the role of race was less powerful than I had expected. In terms of the areas this book has focused on – how children spend their time, the way parents use language and discipline in the home, the nature of the families' social connections, and the strategies used for intervening in institutions – white and Black parents engaged in very similar, often identical, practices with their children.[31] As the children age, the relative importance of race in their daily lives is likely to increase.[32] Most African Americans do not date or marry outside their own racial and ethnic groups. Housing markets are heavily segregated for Black homeowners, regardless of their income.[33] African Americans also are likely to encounter racism in their interpersonal contact with whites, particularly in employment settings. In fourth grade, however, in very central ways, race mattered less in children's daily lives than did their social class.[34] Black and white middle-class children were given enormous amounts of individualized attention, with their parents organizing their own time around their children's leisure activities. This prioritizing profoundly affected parents' leisure time. In these situations, race made little to no difference. Mr. Williams, after a week of working until midnight preparing for a trial, spent Sunday driving Alexander to baseball practice, home for a quick shower and change, and then off to a school play. Mr. Tallinger flew across the country on a red-eye, had a short nap, went to work, and then was out late at a soccer practice on a chilly spring evening, yearning for the event to be over so that he could get home and sleep.

Similarly, it was the middle-class children, Black and white, who squabbled and fought with their siblings and talked back to their parents. These behaviors were simply not tolerated in working-class and poor families, Black or white.[35] Still, the biggest differences in the cultural logic of child rearing in the day-to-day behavior of children in this study were between middle-class children on the one hand (including wealthy members of the middle class) and working-class and poor children on the other. As a middle-class Black boy, Alexander Williams had much more in common with *white* middle-class Garrett Tallinger than he did with less-privileged Black boys, such as Tyrec Taylor or Harold McAllister.

HOW DOES IT MATTER?

Both concerted cultivation and the accomplishment of natural growth offer intrinsic benefits (and burdens) for parents and their children. Nevertheless, these practices are accorded different social values by important social institutions. There are signs that some family cultural practices, notably those associated with concerted cultivation, give children advantages that other cultural practices do not.

In terms of the rhythms of daily life, both concerted cultivation and the accomplishment of natural growth have advantages and disadvantages. Middle-class children learn to develop and value an individualized sense of self. Middle-class children are allowed to participate in a variety of coveted activities: gymnastics, soccer, summer camps, and so on. These activities improve their skills and teach them, as Mr. Tallinger noted, to be better athletes than their parents were at comparable ages. They learn to handle moments of humiliation on the field as well as moments of glory. Middle-class children learn, as Mr. Williams noted, the difference between baroque and classical music. They learn to perform. They learn to present themselves. But this cultivation has a cost. Family schedules are disrupted. Dinner hours are very hard to arrange. Siblings such as Spencer and Sam Tallinger spend dreary hours waiting at athletic fields and riding in the car going from one event to another. Family life, despite quiet interludes, is frequently frenetic. Parents, especially mothers, must reconcile conflicting priorities, juggling events whose deadlines are much tighter than the deadlines connected to serving meals or getting children ready for bed. The domination of children's activities can take a toll on families. At times, everyone in the middle-class families – including ten-year-old children – seemed exhausted. Thus, there are formidable costs, as well as benefits to this child-rearing approach.

Working-class and poor children also had advantages, as well as costs, from the cultural logic of child rearing they experienced. Working-class and poor children learned to entertain themselves. They played outside, creating their own games, as Tyrec Taylor did with his friends. They did not complain of being bored. Working-class and poor children also appeared to have boundless energy. They did not have the exhaustion that we saw in middle-class children the same age. Some working-class and poor children longed to be in organized activities – Katie Brindle wanted to take ballet and Harold McAllister wanted to play football. When finances, a lack of transportation, and limited availability of programs conspired to prevent or limit their participation, they were disappointed. Many were also deeply aware of the economic constraints and the limited consumption permitted by their family's budget. Living spaces were small, and often there was not much privacy. The television was almost always on and, like many middle-class children growing up in the 1950s, working-class and poor children watched unrestricted amounts of television. As a result, family members spent more time together in shared space than occurred in middle-class homes. Indeed, family ties were very strong, particularly among siblings. Working-class and poor children also developed very close ties with their cousins and other extended family members.

Within the home, these two approaches to child rearing each have identifiable strengths and weaknesses. When we turn to examining institutional dynamics outside the home, however, the unequal benefits of middle-class children's lives compared to working-class and poor children's lives become clearer. In crucial ways, middle-class family members appeared reasonably comfortable and entitled, while working-class and poor family members appeared uncomfortable and constrained. For example, neither Harold nor his mother seemed as comfortable as Alexander and his mother had been as they interacted with their physician. Alexander was used to extensive conversation at home; with the doctor, he was at ease initiating questions. Harold, who was used to responding to directives at home, primarily answered questions from the doctor, rather than posing his own. Unlike Ms. Williams, Ms. McAllister did not see the enthusiastic efforts of her daughter Alexis to share information about her birthmark as appropriate behavior. Ms. Williams not only permitted Alexander to hop up and down on the stool to express his enthusiasm; she explicitly trained him to be assertive and well prepared for his encounter with the doctor. Harold was reserved. He did not show an emerging sense of entitlement, as Alexander and other middle-class children did. Absorbing his mother's apparent need to conceal the truth about the range of foods in his diet, Harold appeared cautious, displaying an emerging sense of constraint.

This pattern occurred in school interactions, as well. Some working-class and poor parents had warm and friendly relations with educators. Overall, however, working-class and poor parents in this study had much more distance or separation from the school than did middle-class mothers. At home, Ms. McAllister could be quite assertive, but at school she was subdued. The parent-teacher conference yielded Ms. McAllister few insights into her son's educational experience.[36]

Other working-class and poor parents also appeared baffled, intimidated, and subdued in parent-teacher conferences. Ms. Driver, frantically worried because Wendy, a fourth-grader, was not yet able to read, resisted intervening, saying, "I don't want to jump into anything and find it is the wrong thing." When working-class and poor parents did try to intervene in their children's educational experiences, they often felt ineffectual. Billy Yanelli's mother appeared relaxed and chatty when she interacted with service personnel, such as the person who sold her lottery tickets on Saturday morning. With "the school," however, she was very apprehensive. She distrusted school personnel. She felt bullied and powerless.

There were also moments in which parents encouraged children to outwardly comply with school officials but, at the same time, urged them to resist school authority. Although well aware of school rules prohibiting fighting, the Yanellis directly trained their son to "beat up" a boy who was bothering him. Similarly, when Wendy Driver complained about a boy who pestered her and pulled her ponytail, and the teacher did not respond, her mother advised her to "punch him." Ms. Driver's boyfriend added, "Hit him when the teacher isn't looking."[37]

The unequal level of trust, as well as differences in the amount and quality of information divulged, can yield unequal *profits* during a historical period such as ours, when professionals applaud assertiveness and reject passivity as an inappropriate parenting strategy.[38] Middle-class children and parents often (but not always) accrued advantages or profits from their efforts. Alexander Williams succeeded in having the doctor take his medical concerns seriously. The Marshall children ended up in the gifted program, even though they did not qualify.

Overall, the routine rituals of family life are not equally legitimized in the broader society. Parents' efforts to reason with children (even two-year-olds) are seen as more educationally valuable than parents' use of directives. Spending time playing soccer or baseball is deemed by professionals as more valuable than time spent watching television. Moreover, differences in the cultural logic of child rearing are attached to unequal currency in the broader society. The middle-class strategy of concerted cultivation appears to have greater promise of being capitalized into social profits than does the strategy of the accomplishment of natural growth found in working-class and poor homes. Alexander Williams's vocabulary grew at home, in the evenings, as he bantered with his parents about plagiarism and copyright as well as about the X-Men. Harold McAllister, Billy Yanelli, and Wendy Driver learned how to manage their own time, play without the direction of adults, and occupy themselves for long periods of time without being bored. Although these are important life skills, they do not have the same payoff on standardized achievement tests as the experiences of Alexander Williams.

These potential benefits for middle-class children, and costs for working-class and poor children, are necessarily speculative, since at the end of the study, the children were still in elementary school. Still, there are important signs of hidden advantages being sown at early ages. The middle-class children have extensive experience with adults in their lives with whom they have a relatively contained, bureaucratically regulated, and somewhat superficial relationship. As children spend eight weeks playing soccer, baseball, basketball, and other activities, they meet and interact with adults acting as coaches, assistant coaches, car pool drivers, and so on. This contact with relative strangers, although of a different quality than contact with cousins, aunts, and uncles, provides work-related skills. For instance, as Garrett shakes the hand of a stranger and looks him or her in the eye, he is being groomed, in an effortless fashion, for job interviews he will have as an adult (employment experts stress the importance of good eye contact). In the McAllister home, family members have great affection and warmth toward one another, but they do not generally look each other in the eye when they speak; this training is likely to be a liability in job interviews. In settings as varied as health care and gymnastics, middle-class children learn at a young age to be assertive and demanding. They expect, as did Stacey Marshall, for institutions to be responsive to *them* and to accommodate their individual needs. By contrast, when Wendy Driver is told to hit the boy who is pestering her (when the teacher isn't looking) or Billy Yanelli is told to physically defend himself, despite school rules, they are not learning how to make bureaucratic institutions work to their advantage. Instead, they are being given lessons in frustration and powerlessness.

WHY? THE SEARCH FOR EXPLANATIONS[39]

As I discuss shortly, some commentators today decry the "overscheduled" lives of children; they long for the days when most children had unstructured lives, filled with informal play. But this is a romanticized view of the family in the past. Although there have always been important social class differences in childhood, for much of U.S. history, children played an important economic role in family life. For example, in colonial America, a boy of six or seven was expected to move out of his parents' home to live with a skilled craftsman as an apprentice. As the country gradually industrialized, children's small, "nimble fingers" were useful in factory work.[40] Children also were economic assets on family farms. According to a 1920 study in North Dakota children helped herd cattle and dig holes for fence posts. They also had daily responsibilities, as this description of a nine-year-old boy's chores shows: "Built the fires in the morning, swept the floor of a two-room house, and brought in fuel and water; in addition, before he made a two-mile trip to school, he helped feed stock (five horses and twelve cows) and chopped wood; in the evening he did the chores and washed dishes."[41] Children, especially working-class and poor children, also helped with the informal paid labor their mothers did, such as laundry and "sewing, embroidering, flower making, and tag tying"; most older siblings looked after younger siblings, as well. Children did have some time for unstructured leisure, but it was limited.

Viviana Zelizer shows that through the end of the nineteenth century and into the early decades of the twentieth century, these practices were accompanied by beliefs supporting the importance of children working hard. If anything, the concern was that without specific training in "useful work," children might grow up to be "paupers and thieves."[42] In children's books and magazines, in which stories stressed "the virtues of work, duty, and discipline," Zelizer notes, "The standard villain . . . was an idle child."[43] The period after 1920 saw a dramatic decline in children's economic contributions, however, as child labor laws were put into place and a new vision of the "economically useless but sentimentally priceless child" took hold.[44]

Thus, although a definitive account of historical changes in children's leisure practices remains to be written, it appears that it was for only a relatively brief historical period that children were granted long stretches of leisure time with unstructured play. In the period after World War II, white and Black children were permitted to play for hours on end with other neighborhood children, after school, during evenings, and on weekends. Other than going to church, the few organized activities children participated in (e.g., music lessons or Scouts) began at a later age than is typical today. The "institutionalization of children's leisure" and the rise of concerted cultivation more generally are recent developments.[45] Today's parents are not transmitting practices they learned in their families of origin. Parents of the eighty-eight children in our study were born in the 1950s and 1960s. *None* reported having had a very active schedule of organized activities as a child. Rather, the middle-class parents in this study and, possibly throughout the country, appear to have been raised according to the logic of the accomplishment of natural growth.

In attempting to understand this historical shift, particularly the institutionalization of children's leisure and the emphasis on "intensive mothering," commentators often point to the impact of modern life, especially the impact of increasing "rationalization."[46] This view, termed the "McDonaldization of society" by George Ritzer, finds an increasing standardization of daily life, with an emphasis on efficiency, predictability, control, and calculability.[47] Ritzer notes that these principles from the world of fast food have been adapted to other parts of social life, including Kidsports Fun and Fitness Club, Kinder Care, Kampgrounds of America, Toys 'R' Us, and other stores.[48] Family life, too, is becoming increasingly rationalized, being

> invaded by not only public schools, the courts, social service workers, gardeners, housekeepers, day-care providers, lawyers, doctors, televisions, frozen dinners, pizza delivery, manufactured clothing, and disposable diapers, but also, and more critically, by the *ideology* behind such institutions, persons, and products. They bring with them . . . the logic of . . . impersonal, competitive, contractual, commodified, efficient, profit-maximizing, self-interested relations.[49]

Busy affluent parents can hire chauffeurs to take children to their organized activities, hire educators at "Learning Centers" in shopping malls to help children do homework and improve in school, and hire personal shoppers to help buy and wrap holiday gifts. The services available for birthday parties (e.g., a special room at McDonald's, an overnight at a science museum, or a professional party coordinator) are signs of the increasing rationalization of family life.

The rationalization of children's leisure is evident in the proliferation of organized activities with a predictable schedule, delivering a particular quantity of experience within a specific time period, under the control of adults. That children's time use has shifted from unstructured play to organized activities does not mean that families no longer have fun during their leisure hours. Many find the time spent together during soccer and baseball games, for example, to be very enjoyable. The point is that areas of family life are growing more systematic, predictable, and regulated than they have been in the recent past. Forces that have converged to bring about this change include increasing concerns about the safety of children who play unsupervised on local streets, rises in employment (resulting in adults being at home less), and a decline in the availability of neighborhood playmates due to a dropping birth rate and the effects of suburbanization, especially the increased size of homes and decreased density of housing.[50]

Greater emphasis on the use of reasoning in the home, particularly as a form of discipline, as well as interventions in institutions, can also be seen as a form of rationalization, particularly the well-documented trend of "scientific motherhood." Still, any analysis of the rise of concerted cultivation must also, I believe, grapple with the changing position of the United States in the world economy, and the accompanying decline in highly paid manufacturing jobs and increase in less desirable service-sector jobs. This restructuring makes it very likely that when today's children are adults, their standard of living will be lower than that of their parents. It means that there will be fewer "good jobs" and more "bad jobs," and that the competition for them will be intense. Moreover, since children must be successful in school to gain access to desirable positions, many middle-class parents are anxious to make sure their children perform well academically. Institutional gate-keepers, such as college admissions officers, applaud extracurricular activities. Thus, many parents see children's activities as more than interesting and enjoyable pastimes. They also provide potential advantages for children in the sorting process.

[. . .]

WHAT IS TO BE DONE?

In his thoughtful book *The Price of Citizenship*, historian Michael Katz shows that in recent years Americans' conception of welfare has grown excessively narrow.[51] A preoccupation with public assistance to the poor has led Americans to overlook two other important forms of social distribution: social insurance programs and taxation policies. Yet in size and scope, social insurance programs, particularly Social Security and Medicare, dwarf the cost of payments to poor families. Moreover, these programs have been effective in reducing the percentage of poor among the elderly. It is very likely that the state could take similar steps to reduce inequality among American families. State intervention would probably be the most direct and effective way to reduce the kinds of social inequality described in this book. For example, a child allowance, similar to what Sweden and other Western European nations provide, would likely be very effective in eliminating child poverty and reducing the gap in economic and social resources.[52] As David Karen points out, increasing the "safety net" for poor and working-class families would be helpful:

> Anything that can be done to provide a safety net for the poor (and working class) will increase the resources of . . . children and therefore make it possible for them to engage in some of the activities that they're currently excluded from. This exclusion takes place not only because they don't have the money to participate but also because parental time is so limited. If parental time (say, thanks to fewer hours at work) were more available, there might be more access to participation. Under this rubric, I'd put things like universal health care, state-supported daycare, (and) a guaranteed minimum income.[53]

In addition, an increase in federal and state recreation monies would be useful since, in interviews I conducted with directors of recreation programs in the regions surrounding Swan and Lower Richmond schools, it was clear that as the township became more affluent, more elaborate recreational programs were available. Vouchers for extracurricular activities *and* transportation to activities (e.g., music lessons, art lessons, sports programs, and specialized summer camps) are another possibility. A problem is that neighborhoods are often relatively homogenous by social class. Consolidating neighborhoods so that working-class and poor children become part of more affluent neighborhoods would be likely to increase access to desirable facilities. What is far less likely, however, is the existence of the political will to support this redistribution of wealth. Instead, Americans, as is their wont, are likely to remain preoccupied with more individual solutions. Since, however, the problems differ by social class, the solutions do as well. Below, I review some of the possibilities.

Slowing It Down: Policy Implications for Middle-Class Families

The frenetic schedule of some middle-class families is a topic that increasingly bubbles up in media reports. As a result, there is an emerging social movement of professionals and middle-class parents to resist the scheduling of children's lives. Books, including *The Over-Scheduled Child*, insist that children's schedules are out of control:

> It is Tuesday at 6:45 A.M. Belinda, age seven, is still asleep. School doesn't start until 9.00 A.M. and her mother usually lets her sleep until 7:30 A.M. But not on Tuesdays. That's the day Belinda has a 7:30 A.M. piano lesson. From it she goes directly to school, which lasts until three. Then the babysitter drives Belinda to gymnastics for the 4:00–6:30 P.M. class. While Tuesday is the busiest day, the rest of the week is filled up too, with religious school and choir practice, ballet, and (Belinda's favorite) horseback riding. "She's pretty worn out by the end of the day," her mother laments . . . "I'm not really sure it is a good thing [to be so busy]. But I want to give her the advantages I didn't have."[54]

The authors are outraged by this kind of schedule:

> We sense that our family lives are out of whack, but we aren't sure why. We know we are doing too much for our kids, but we don't know where it might be okay to cut back – . . . every time we . . . turn [around] . . . someone else is adding something new to the list of things we are supposed to be doing for our children to make sure they turn out right.[55]

Resistance is spreading. At the collective level, grassroots organizations such as "Family Life First," based in Wayzata, Minnesota, are pressuring coaches and adult leaders of other organized activities to make family time a priority (by, for example, not scheduling events on Sundays or not penalizing children who miss games while on family vacations). Ridgewood, New Jersey, gained national attention when citizens declared a community-wide (voluntary) "Family Night" and arranged for children's organized activities (and homework) to be canceled for the evening. These incipient movements have in common an explicit recognition that children's schedules are absurd, that family life is in thrall to a frenzy of "hyper-scheduling."[56] Decrying the development of children's appointment books, professionals call for children to have more opportunities for unstructured play.[57] At the individual level, parents are encouraged to set strict limits on children's activities. Some parents proudly announce on websites that they require their children to limit themselves to only one activity at a time.

A systematic critique of parents' role in supervising and intervening in institutions has not yet emerged. Indeed, many professionals actively recruit and encourage parental involvement in schooling. Doubts about the value of extensive reasoning with children, on the other hand, are mounting. Problems stemming from the blurring of boundaries between parents and children are especially well covered by professionals and the media. With titles such as *Parents in Charge: Setting Healthy, Loving Boundaries for You and Your Child* and *I'll Be the Parent, You Be the Child*, professionals are signaling the need for parents to provide directives to children. The books provide cautionary tales of rude, obnoxious, and ungrateful children who refuse to be polite to guests, who feel that they, as children, may decide when they will or will not join the family for dinner, and who are unable to convey appreciation for the gifts they receive. Describing these children as out of control and craving adult intervention, the authors call for parents to "set limits and make decisions." The solution the experts offer calls mainly for individual action: each parent is encouraged to look within her or himself to find the necessary strength to take charge, to give clear directives to children, and to resist the temptation to seek their children's approval.

Ironically, the new agenda for middle-class parents, whether expressed collectively or individually, amounts to a reinstatement of many of the elements of the strategy of the accomplishment of natural growth. For overburdened and exhausted parents, the policy recommendations center on setting limits: reducing the number of children's activities, scheduling family time, making family events a higher priority than children's events, and generally putting the needs of the group ahead of the needs of the individual.

Gaining Compliance with Dominant Standards: Implications for Working-Class and Poor Families

For working-class and poor families, the policy recommendations center on trying to gain advantages for children in institutional settings. Some programs stress the importance of reading to children, bolstering vocabulary, and addressing "summer setback" (a reference to working-class and poor children's tendency to lose academic ground when they are out of school while middle-class children's academic growth spurts ahead).[58] Here, it is important to bear in mind the ever-changing nature of institutional standards (phonics is "in" one year, whole language the next; computers are promoted and then challenged). Providing children with the resources needed to comply with institutional standards may be helpful, but it leaves unexamined the problematic nature of class-based childrearing methods themselves. It is possible that policies could be developed to help professionals learn how to be more sensitive to differences in cultural practices and how to "code switch"; they, in turn, might be able to teach children to "code switch" as they move between home and encounters with institutions. One promising development is the success of programs that offer to working-class and poor children the kinds of concerted cultivation middle-class children get at home. Examples include intensive interventions in high schools and in "I Had a Dream" philanthropic ventures through which schools and private tutors take on the roles often carried out by middle-class parents (and the tutors they hire). These programs have improved children's school performance; reduced suspensions, behavior problems, and teen pregnancies; and increased college admittance rates. Many have been shown to double the high school graduation rates of students.[59] Other interventions have produced similarly positive results.[60] In some, for example, high school teachers provide low-income students with tours of college campuses, remind them about key deadlines, and help them fill out college applications. Programs such as these, as well as more traditional programs, such as "Big Brother/Big Sister," have improved school experiences.[61] In sum, policy recommendations for working-class and poor children do not address hectic schedules or the need for greater parental control, as those for middle-class children do. Rather, they focus on gaining institutional advantages for children by encouraging parents to use reasoning to bolster their children's vocabulary and to play a more active role in their children's schooling.

NOTES

1. Choosing words to describe social groups also becomes a source of worry, especially over the possibility of reinforcing negative stereotypes. I found the available terms to describe members of racial and ethnic groups to be problematic in one way or another. The families I visited uniformly described themselves as "Black." Recognizing that some readers have strong views that Black should be capitalized, I have followed that convention, despite the lack of symmetry with the term white. In sum, this book alternates among the terms "Black," "Black American," "African American," and "white," with the understanding that "white" here refers to the subgroup of non-Hispanic whites.

2. Some readers have expressed concern that this phrase, "the accomplishment of natural growth," underemphasizes all the labor that mothers and fathers do to take care of children. They correctly note that working-class and poor parents themselves would be unlikely to use such a term to describe the process of caring for children. These

concerns are important. As I stress in the text it does take an enormous amount of work for parents, especially mothers, of all classes to take care of children. But poor and working-class mothers have fewer resources with which to negotiate these demands. Those whose lives the research assistants and I studied approached the task somewhat differently than did middle-class parents. They did not seem to view children's leisure time as their responsibility; nor did they see themselves as responsible for assertively intervening in their children's school experiences. Rather, the working-class and poor parents carried out their chores, drew boundaries and restrictions around their children, and then, within these limits, allowed their children to carry out their lives. It is in this sense that I use the term "the accomplishment of natural growth."

3. I define a child-rearing context to include the routines of daily life, the dispositions of daily life, or the "habitus" of daily life. I focus on two contexts: concerted cultivation and the accomplishment of natural growth. In this book, I primarily use the concept of child rearing, but at times I also use the term *socialization*. Many sociologists have vigorously criticized this concept, noting that it suggests (inaccurately) that children are passive rather than active agents and that the relationship between parents and their children is unidirectional rather than reciprocal and dynamic. See, for example, William Corsaro, *Sociology of Childhood*; Barrie Thorne, *Gender Play*; and Glen Elder, "The Life Course as Development Theory." Nonetheless, existing terms can, ideally, be revitalized to offer more sophisticated understandings of social processes. Child rearing and socialization have the virtue of being relatively succinct and less jargon laden than other alternatives. As a result, I use them.

4. For discussions of the role of professionals, see Eliot Freidson, *Professional Powers*; Magali Sarfatti Larson, *The Rise of Professionalism*; and, although quite old, the still valuable collection by Amitai Etzioni, *The Semi-Professionals and Their Organizations*. Of course, professional standards are always contested and are subject to change over time. I do not mean to suggest there are not pockets of resistance and contestation. At the most general level, however, there is virtually uniform support for the idea that parents should talk to children at length, read to children, and take a proactive, assertive role in medical care.

5. Sharon Hays, in her 1996 book *The Cultural Contradictions of Motherhood*, studies the attitudes of middle-class and working-class mothers toward child rearing. She finds a shared commitment to "intensive mothering," although there are some differences among the women in her study in their views of punishment (with middle-class mothers leaning toward reasoning and working-class women toward physical punishment). My study focused much more on behavior than attitudes. If I looked at attitudes, I saw fewer differences; for example, all exhibited the desire to be a good mother and to have their children grow and thrive. The differences I found, however, were significant in how parents *enacted* their visions of what it meant to be a good parent.

6. See Urie Bronfenbrenner's article, "Socialization and Social Class through Time and Space."

7. Katherine Newman, *Declining Fortunes*, as well as Donald Barlett and James B. Steele, *America: What Went Wrong?* See also Michael Hout and Claude Fischer, "A Century of Inequality."

8. Some readers expressed the concern that the contrast to natural would be "unnatural," but this is not the sense in which the term *natural growth* is used here. Rather, the contrast is with words such as cultivated, artificial, artifice, or manufactured. This contrast in the logic of child rearing is a heuristic device that should not be pushed too far since, as sociologists have shown, all social life is constructed in specific social contexts. Indeed, family life has varied dramatically over time. See Philippe Aries, *Centuries of Childhood*, Herbert Gutman, *The Black Family in Slavery and Freedom, 1750–1925*, and Nancy Scheper-Hughes, *Death without Weeping*.

9. Elijah Anderson, *Code of the Street*; see especially Chapter 2.

10. For a more extensive discussion of the work of Pierre Bourdieu see the theoretical appendix; see also David Swartz's excellent book *Culture and Power*.

11. I did not study the full range of families in American society, including elite families of tremendous wealth, nor, at the other end of the spectrum, homeless families. In addition, I have a purposively drawn sample. Thus, I cannot state whether there are other forms of child rearing corresponding to other cultural logics. Still, data from quantitative studies based on nationally representative data support the patterns I observed. For differences by parents' social class position and children's time use, see especially Sandra Hofferth and John Sandberg, "Changes in American Children's Time, 1981–1997." Patterns of language use with children are harder to capture in national surveys, but the work of Melvin Kohn and Carmi Schooler, especially *Work and Personality*, shows differences in parents' child-rearing values. Duane Alwin's studies of parents' desires are generally consistent with the results reported here. See Duane Alwin, "Trends in Parental Socialization Values." For differences in interventions in institutions, there is extensive work showing social class differences in parent involvement in education. See the U.S. Department of Education, *The Condition of Education, 2001*, p.175.

12. In this book, all statistics, unless otherwise noted, are targeted to 1993–1995 (usually 1995), which was the time of data collection. William Kornblum, *Sociology: The Central Questions*, p. 159.

13. Childhood poverty has been demonstrated to predict a host of negative life outcomes, including lower levels of health, scores on standardized tests, school grades, and emotional well-being. See Greg J. Duncan and Jeanne Brooks-Gunn, eds., *Consequences of Growing Up Poor*. For a comparative view of poverty rates in the United States and other industrialized countries, see Rainwater and Smeeding, "Doing Poorly."

14. See Greg J. Duncan and Jeanne Brooks-Gunn, eds., *Consequences of Growing Up Poor*. In 1997, 20% of all children were officially poor, but for white children the figure was 16% and for Black children it was 37%; for Black children under the age of six, 40% were poor. Lawrence Mishel, Jared Bernstein, and John Schmitt, *The State of Working America 1998–1999*, p. 281.

15. For example between 1989 and 1997 the wealth of the top fifth of the country grew by 9% while it declined by 6% for

the bottom tenth of the population. Mishel et al., *The State of Working America*, p, 264. See also Michael Hout and Claude S. Fischer, "A Century of Inequality."

16. See Dalton Conley, *Being Black, Living in the Red*, and Melvin Oliver and Thomas Shapiro, *Black Wealth/White Wealth*.

17. The high school dropout rate in 1995 was 9% for whites and 12% for Black youth; by the end of the decade it had dropped slightly for white youth and increased slightly for Black youth. See U. S. Department of Education, *The Condition of Education, 2001*, p. 142.

18. In 1995, 28% of young people 25–29 had completed a bachelor's degree; by 2000 it had risen to 33%. There is a significant difference between the proportion of white high school graduates who eventually earn college degrees (31% in 1995, 36% in 2001) and Black high school graduates who eventually earn degrees (18% in 1995, and 21% in 2001). For the adult population as a whole, (ages 25–64) the proportion of college graduates is 24%. See U. S. Department of Education, *Condition of Education 1995*, pp. 245–249, and U. S. Department of Education, *Condition of Education 2001*, pp. 142, 150–151.

19. See Dalton Conley, *Being Black, Living in the Red*, as well as U. S. Department of Education, *The Condition of Education, 2001*.

20. See Derek Bok and William G. Bowen, *The Shape of the River*.

21. See Donald Barlett and James B. Steele, *America: What Went Wrong?* and Arne Kalleberg, Barbara F. Reskin, and Ken Hudson, "Bad Jobs in America."

22. For example, only 51% of children of high school dropouts can recognize the colors red, yellow, blue, and green by name, but the figure for high school graduates is 78%, for parents with some college it is 92%, and for college graduates it is 95%. For knowing all of the letters of the alphabet, the respective figures are 9%, 19%, 29%, and 42%. U. S. Department of Education, *Condition of Education 1995*, p. 182.

23. See U. S. Department of Education, *Condition of Education, 1995* and Entwhistle et al., *Children, Schools, and Inequality*. At the same level of parental education, white students generally receive higher scores than do Black students. See also Christopher Jencks and Meredith Phillips, eds., *The Black-White Test Score Gap*.

24. In 1995, 61% of high school graduates enrolled in college; for children of high school dropouts, the rate was 27%, for children of high school graduates 47%, and for children of college graduates, 88%. U. S. Department of Education, *Condition of Education, 2001*, p. 147.

25. As Paul Kingston has noted (personal communication) the relationship between parents' educational level and occupational level is far from automatic. There is a considerable amount of downward mobility. Also, there is variation among brothers and sisters in the same family. Still, parents' social class position remains one of the most powerful predictors of children's educational success and life outcomes. See Paul Kingston's book *The Classless Society* for an elaboration of this position as well as Christopher Jencks et al., *Inequality*, and *Who Gets Ahead?*

26. See Sharon Hays, *The Cultural Contradictions of Motherhood*.

27. Some researchers claim that happiness is not particularly connected to age, gender, race, or affluence. See David G. Meyers and Ed Diener, "Who Is Happy?"

28. Middle-class parents were self-aware of how hectic their lives were; they often talked about the lack of time. Some parents also mentioned how their own childhoods had been so different from those of their own children in terms of organized activities. But middle-class parents did not seem to be particularly aware of their emphasis on reasoning and, especially, their interventions in institutions. Nor were they, or working-class and poor parents, particularly aware that radically different approaches to child rearing were being carried out. Instead, parents viewed their approaches to child rearing as natural.

29. Cornell West, *Race Matters*.

30. See Jennifer Hochschild, *Facing Up to the American Dream*; Ellis Cose, *The Rage of a Privileged Class*; Beverly Daniel Tatum, *Why Are the Black Kids Sitting Together in the Cafeteria?*; and Elizabeth Higginbotham, *Too Much to Ask*.

31. In this study there were also, in some contexts, differences in sociolinguistic terms (including special words for white people). For a more general discussion of this issue see Mary Patillo-McCoy, *Black Picket Fences*, and Douglas Massey and Nancy Denton, *American Apartheid*. I also did not study a racially isolated school. See, among others, Eric A. Hanushek et. al., "New Evidence about Brown v. Board of Education."

32. See Ellis Cose, *The Rage of a Privileged Class*, and Mary Waters, *Black Identities*.

33. Douglas Massey and Nancy Denton, *American Apartheid*.

34. This study's findings are compatible with others that have shown children to be aware of race at relatively early ages. Indeed, girls often played in racially segregated groups on the playground. (Boys were likely to be in racially integrated groups.) Thus, this study suggests that racial dynamics certainly exist in children's lives, but they are not (yet) an organizing feature in the same way that social class membership is. For a piece that stresses the salience of race in the lives of preschoolers, see Debra Van Ausdale and Joe R. Feagin, "Using Racial and Ethnic Concepts."

35. A majority of middle-class and working-class parents self-report the use of reasoning in child rearing. Since there is an emphasis in broader cultural repertoires of the importance of using reasoning, it is not surprising that parents of all social classes might report that they use reasoning. Indeed, for many of the working-class and poor parents, physical discipline was a "last resort." Studies do consistently show that more educated mothers, however, are more likely to stress reasoning. See, among others, Cheryl Blueston and Catherine S. Tamis-LeMonda, "Correlates of Parenting Styles in Predominantly Working- and Middle-Class African American Mothers."

36. Of course, some middle-class parents also appeared slightly anxious during parent-teacher meetings. But overall,

middle-class parents spoke more, and they asked educators more questions, including more critical and penetrating ones, than did working-class and poor parents.

37. Working-class and poor children often resisted and tested school rules, but they did not seem to be engaged in the same process of seeking an accommodation by educators to their own *individual* preferences that I witnessed among middle-class children. Working-class and poor children tended to react to adults' offers or, at times, plead with educators to repeat previous experiences, such as reading a particular story, watching a movie, or going to the computer room. In these interactions, the boundaries between adults and children were firmer and clearer than those with middle-class children.

38. Carol Heimer and Lisa Staffen, *For the Sake of the Children*.

39. My discussion here is necessarily speculative. Parents of all social classes took for granted key aspects of their child rearing and thus had difficulty articulating the rationale behind their actions.

40. In the South, children between the ages of ten and thirteen comprised one-third of the workers in textile mills between 1870 and 1900. Viviana Zelizer, *Pricing the Priceless Child*. See especially chapter 2.

41. Quoted in Zelizer, *Pricing the Priceless Child*, p. 78.

42. Zelizer, *Pricing the Priceless Child*, p. 67.

43. Zelizer, *Pricing the Priceless Child*, p. 59.

44. Zelizer, *Pricing the Priceless Child*, p. 97.

45. See William Corsaro, *Sociology of Childhood*.

46. As Randall Collins notes, Max Weber assigns multiple meanings to the term *rationalization*. Here I am referring to the meaning that "emerges when Weber compares different types of institutions. Bureaucracy is described as a rational form of administrative organization as opposed to the irrational elements found in patrimonialism. . . . The key [conditions] here seem to be predictability and regularity. . . . There is a strong implication that rationality is based on written rules, and hence on paperwork." Randall Collins, *Max Weber: A Skeleton Key*, pp. 63, 78.

47. Ritzer also discusses the importance of efficiency. See George Ritzer, *The McDonaldization of Society*.

48. Ritzer, *The McDonaldization of Society*, p. 3.

49. Hays, *The Cultural Contradictions of Motherhood*, p. 11.

50. On safety see Mark Warr and Christopher G. Ellison, "Rethinking Social Reactions to Crime," as well as Joel Best, *Threatened Children*. On changes in work-family relationships see Rosanna Hertz and Nancy L. Marshall, *Working Families*, as well as demographic research. On time spent with children, see Suzanne Bianchi, "Maternal Employment and Time with Children." On suburbanization see Kenneth T. Jackson, *Crabgrass Frontier*.

51. Michael Katz, *The Price of Citizenship*.

52. See Lawrence Mishel et al., *The State of Working America*, p. 289.

53. David Karen, letter to author, 7 June 2002. See Jody Heymann, *The Widening Gap*.

54. Alvin Rosenfeld and Nicole Wise, *The Over-Scheduled Child*, pp. 1–2.

55. Rosenfeld and Wise, *The Over-Scheduled Child*, pp. 1–2.

56. See Maria Newman, "Time Out! (for Overextended Families): A Town Takes a Rare Break from the Frenzy of Hyperscheduling."

57. For example: "Like wild animals raised in captivity who never develop their inborn potential to hunt for themselves, children who are robbed of the opportunity to come up with their own games and entertain themselves at those times in their lives when these capacities are developing may very well become dependent upon others to determine their good times." Dana Chidekel, *Parents in Charge*, pp. 94–95.

58. See work by Doris Entwistle and Karl Alexander on this topic, including Entwistle, Alexander, and Olsen, *Children, Schools, and Inequality*.

59. For details of one program, see a series of articles by Dale Mezzacappa in the *Philadelphia Inquirer*, including, "Ten Years of Learning, Living, Loving." Overall, the program was most successful for students in the regular educational track (as opposed to those in special education) and for young men rather than women.

60. For example, in the Chicago-based "I Had a Dream" program, 72% of the cohort graduated from high school, compared to 35% of the control group. For Paterson, New Jersey, 60% of the 1993 cohort graduated compared to 33% of the control group. These interventions begin in third grade (as opposed to sixth in the Say Yes program). See the "I Had a Dream Foundation" Web site for a summary of in-house statistics as well as research evaluations conducted by independent researchers <http://www.ihad.org> (accessed 12 December 2002).

61. Among others, see Hugh Mehan et al., *Constructing School Success*, and an evaluation by Public/Private Ventures of the Big Brother/Big Sister Program, Joseph Tierney et al., "Making a Difference."

30

A Black Feminist Reflection on the Antiviolence Movement

BETH E. RICHIE

FOR THE FEMINIST-BASED antiviolence movement in the United States, the new millennium marks the beginning of an interesting third decade that poses particular challenges and concerns for Black feminist activists and our work to end violence against women. The mainstream social movement, organized over twenty years ago in response to an emerging consciousness that regarded gender violence as the most extreme point along the continuum of women's oppression, can claim numerous victories, such as legal reforms that protect the rights of battered women and sexual assault survivors, the criminalization of sexual harassment, and legislative moves to call attention to the needs of children who witness domestic violence. In addition, an elaborate apparatus of social services has been developed to provide emergency shelter, crisis intervention counseling, medical and legal advocacy, and ongoing assistance with housing, employment, and custody issues that women who experience violence need. African-American and other women of color have been at the forefront of the most radical dimensions of this work.

Services and support at the individual level have been matched with an array of academic and public policy initiatives designed to address violence against women. There are several journals dedicated to presenting new research and intervention discussions related to gender violence, and at least four university-based research centers focus on violence against women. Each year witnesses a growing number of national conferences on issues related to gender violence, which attract a range of audiences, some with more activist goals and others with more professional and bureaucratic interests. The National Institute for Justice, the Centers for Disease Control, the Departments of Housing and Urban Development and Health and Human Services, and – paradoxically – even the Department of Defense have established federal initiatives that attempt to reduce or respond to violence against women in this country. The feminist campaign at the grassroots level has influenced government and public policy to a considerable extent, which has resulted in a significant influx of public funding for victim services, law enforcement training, and prevention services. This growth, due in no small part to the grassroots activism of survivors and other women, has deeply influenced the mainstream consciousness. Evidence of this influence appears in several recent public awareness campaigns and opinion polls that suggest that tolerance for gender-based violence has decreased significantly in the past ten years. Feminist activism has paid off; we have witnessed a considerable shift in public consciousness with regard to the problem of violence against women.

Arguably, a critical dimension of the public awareness campaign that has led to this expansion in resources for, and the credibility of, the antiviolence movement in this country is the assertion that violence against women is a common experience, that any woman or child can be the victim of gender violence. In fact, many of us who do training, public speaking, teaching, and writing on violence against women traditionally begin our presentations by saying, "It can happen to anyone." This notion has become a powerful emblem of our rhetoric and, some would argue, the basis of our mainstream success. Indeed, many people in this country finally understand that they and their children, mothers, sisters, coworkers, and neighbors can be victimized by gender violence – that it really can happen to anyone.

The ideas that any woman can be a battered woman and that rape is every woman's problem were part of a strategic attempt by early activists to avoid individualizing the problem of domestic and sexual violence, to focus on the social dimensions of the problem of gender violence, and to resist the stigmatization of race and class commonly associated with mainstream responses to social problems. This approach was based not only on the empirical data available at the time but also on the lived experiences of most women who – at many points in our lives – change our behavior to minimize our risk of assault. This generalized construction helped to foster an analysis of women's vulnerability as both profound and persistent, rather than as particular to any racial/ethnic community, socioeconomic position, religious group, or station in life. As a result, from college campuses to private corporations, from public housing complexes to elite suburban communities, and in all manner of religious institutions progress has been made in increasing awareness that violence against women is an important social problem that requires a broad-based social response.

And yet, to a Black feminist activist committed to ending violence against women, something seems terribly wrong with this construction at this point in time, something that leaves many African-American women and other women of color still unsafe and renders our communities for the most part disconnected from the mainstream antiviolence movement. I would even argue that the notion that every woman is at risk – one of the hallmarks of our movement's rhetorical paradigm – is in fact a dangerous one in that it has structured a national advocacy response based on a false sense of unity around the experience of gender oppression. For, as the epistemological foundation of the antiviolence movement was institutionalized, the assumption of "everywoman" fell into the vacuum created by a white feminist analysis that did not very successfully incorporate an analysis of race and class.

In the end, the assumed race and class neutrality of gender violence led to the erasure of low-income women and women of color from the dominant view. I contend that this erasure, in turn, seriously compromised the transgressive and transformative potential of the antiviolence move-ment's potentially radical critique of various forms of social domination. It divorced racism from sexism, for example, and invited a discourse regarding gender violence without attention to the class dimensions of patriarchy and white domination in this country.

Put another way, when the national dialogue on violence against women became legitimized and institutionalized, the notion that "It could happen to anyone" meant that "It could happen to those in power." Subsequently, the ones who mattered most in society got the most visibility and the most public sympathy; those with power are the ones whose needs are taken most seriously. When mainstream attention to the needs of victims and survivors was gradually integrated into the public realm of social service and legal protection and became visible in research studies, "every-woman" became a white middle-class woman who could turn to a private therapist, a doctor, a police officer, or a law to protect her from abuse. She consumed the greater proportion of attention in the literature, intervention strategies were based on her needs, she was featured in public aware-ness campaigns, and she was represented by national leaders on the issue of violence against women.

So what began as an attempt to avoid stereotyping and stigma has resulted in exactly that which was seen early in the antiviolence movement as a threat to the essential values of inclusion, equality, and antioppression work. The consequence of this paradigmatic problem is that victimization of women of color of low-income communities is invisible to the mainstream public, at best. Worse yet, when poor African-American, Latina, Native American women and other women of color are victimized, the problem is cast as something other than a case of gender violence.

Similarly, scholarship and activism around racial/ethnic and class oppression often ignores gender as an essential variable. This argument is supported by the growing body of research on women who use drugs, women in prison, women who live in dangerous low-income neighborhoods, lesbians of color, or young women who are involved with street gangs. Where women and girls are included in these studies or activist campaigns, they are seen as "special cases" within those populations rather than as women per se. Gender is not considered a central, defining part of their identity, and their experiences are subsumed by other master categories, typically race and class. They are essentially de-gendered, which renders them without access to claims of gender oppression and outside the category of individuals at risk of gender violence.

It is here, at a critical crossroads, that I ponder my work in the antiviolence movement as a Black feminist activist and academic. From here I offer critical observations and make recommendations for the future. First, it seems that to continue to ignore the race and class dimensions of gender oppression will seriously jeopardize the viability and legitimacy of the antiviolence movement in this country, a dangerous development for women of color in low-income communities, who are most likely to be in both dangerous intimate relationships and dangerous social positions. The overreliance on simplistic analyses (as in the case of "everywoman") has significant consequences for the potential for radical social change. I suggest that we revisit our analytic frame and develop a much more complex and contextualized analysis of gender violence, one rooted in an understanding of the historical and contemporary social processes that have differentially affected women of color.

I argue for a reassessment of the responses that have been central to antiviolence work – in particular, the reliance on law enforcement as the principal provider of women's safety. For over a decade, women of color in the antiviolence movement have warned against investing too heavily in arrest, detention, and prosecution as responses to violence against women. Our warnings have been ignored, and the consequences have been serious: serious for the credibility of the antiviolence movement, serious for feminist organizing by women of color, and, most important, serious for women experiencing gender violence who fall outside of the mainstream.

The concern with overreliance on law enforcement parallels a broader apprehension about the expansion of state power in the lives of poor women of color in this country. Just as the antiviolence movement is relying on legal and legislative strategies to criminalize gender violence, women in communities of color are experiencing the negative effects of conservative legislation regarding public assistance, affirmative action, and immigration. And, while the antiviolence movement is working to improve arrest policies, everyday safety in communities of color is being threatened by more aggressive policing, which has resulted in increased use of force, mass incarceration, and brutality. The conflict between the antiviolence movement's strategy and the experiences of low-income communities of color has seriously undermined our work as feminists of color fighting violence against women.

Obviously, leadership emerges as central to this dilemma. While there is a renewed call for unity and diversity from some corners of our movement, others (women of color who have dedicated years to this work) are appalled at the persistent whiteness of the nationally recognized leadership.

As the bureaucratic and institutional apparatus of the antiviolence movement grows – bringing more funding, more recognition, and also more collaborations with partners who do not share our radical goals – there is little evidence of increasing racial/ethnic and class diversity. Despite some notable exceptions, the lack of women of color in leadership roles in antiviolence programs is startling and contrasts sharply with the rhetoric of inclusion, diversity, and commitment to antioppression work. While there may be structural excuses for this, the fact that so few national organizations (even feminist ones) have successfully promoted the leadership of women of color is almost a mockery of the values on which the movement was built. Given the similar invisibility of women of color as leaders in struggles for racial justice (again, with some exceptions), the situation can seem dire as we face the new millennium.

Yet, for better or worse, the solutions are not enigmatic; they exist within our core values and the principles on which the antiviolence movement was organized. Feminist women of color need to step forward as never before, reclaiming our place as leaders both in the antiviolence movement and in struggles for gender equality in our communities. The antiviolence movement needs only to acknowledge the contradictions between its rhetoric and practice and to deal honestly with the hypocrisy in its work. As members of a social justice movement committed to ending oppression, we must reconsider the complexity of rendering justice by paying attention to specific vulnerabilities of race and class. As we claim victories on some very important fronts, our understanding of gender oppression must be broadened to include state-sanctioned abuse and mistreatment of women. If we are prepared to go there, we can begin the millennium ready to face the really hard, radical work of ending violence against women – for each and any woman.

31

Intimacy, Desire, and the Construction of Self in Relationships between Asian American Women and White American Men

Kumiko Nemoto

INTRODUCTION

This study examines interracial relationships between Asian Americans and white Americans. The goal is to understand how the social construction of sexual desire is shaped by race and gender. [...]

Several previous studies have found that Asian American women are almost twice as likely to outmarry as are Asian American men.[1] This gender gap is unique to Asian Americans' intermarital pattern, since in other racial groups men outmarry more than women.[2] [...]

FINDINGS

I found that the formation of relationships between Asian American women and white American men relies on a range of desires among Asian American women for four aspects of white hegemonic masculinity: narcissistic gaze; middle-class status; material security; and egalitarian knighthood. While similar desires and attractions for white hegemonic masculinity were expressed by other Asian American women whom I interviewed, the following four cases vividly illustrate the complex relationship between power and sexual desires as experienced by Asian American women. The story of "Grace," an unmarried, second-generation Chinese American woman, illustrates how her choice of a white man stems from her aversion to ethnic patriarchy and desire for an egalitarian relationship, common feelings among the second-generation Asian American women whom I interviewed. The story of Irene, also an unmarried, second-generation Chinese American woman, addresses racialized alienation as it is linked to the narcissistic male gaze and to commodified images of Asian women, a theme that emerged in interviews with other women as well. The stories of two married, first-generation Filipina American women, here called Angelina and Linda, illustrate the importance of financial resources and socioeconomic status in structuring desire for white men. Angelina's story represents the desire for middle-class status, while Linda's story evinces a pronounced desire for material security. Angelina's and Linda's stories demonstrate how their desire for upward mobility is related to their reaction to U.S. military dominance and globalization in the Philippines. They are striking examples of how Asian American women's personal relationship choices are bound up with the social and economic conditions that shape their lives.

NARCISSISTIC GAZE AND DESIRE IN WHITE AMERICAN MASCULINITY

When white men fetishize "Asian" women as their love objects, their objectification of the race and culture of the "other" can cause a sense of emotional tension and racial alienation for Asian American women. Some of these women strongly resist this fetishization, while others try to compromise with it. Women who find themselves in such self-alienating experiences sometimes react with a form of denial, blaming themselves for overreacting rather than expressing their discomfort or resentment toward their white partners. Some of the women whom I interviewed felt that the notion of "Asian woman" was imposed upon them by white men, and some had experienced an explicitly sexualized gaze on their body as "Asian." One woman described her experience in Brooklyn, New York, saying, "Being Asian there [in New York] is very hot right now. Guys really like it. There's a porn industry for that, too. Like escort services and stuff like that. So, you get a lot of whistling and catcalls."[3]

The following story illustrates the reaction of a Chinese American woman to her white boyfriend's preference for and fetishization of Asian women. Irene Huan, a 25-year-old Chinese American and a film major, was born and grew up in the United States. Her parents divorced when she was sixteen. Irene explained why her mother, isolated from the Chinese community and having blamed herself for being a bad wife, went back to Taiwan: "A lot of times, in the Asian family, when there is a divorce, they kind of blame the woman. You know, she isn't a good enough wife. She should've kept the family together, that sort of thing. . . . I think she wanted to get away from that."[4] Irene used to go to Taiwan to see her mother once a year, but now she only talks with her by phone once a month. She described herself as "not very close to my family."[5]

Irene's father, an engineer in the computer industry whom she described as "very unconventional and very liberal," had lived with a white woman for several years at the time of Irene's interview. Irene's father once told her not to date or marry Asian American men, and he himself dates only white women: "I remember him telling me, 'I never want you to ever marry an Asian guy.' And, I was like, 'Why?' He goes, 'Well, I know how they are, and I don't want you to marry an Asian.' "[6] Irene speculated that her father was "rebelling against Chinese culture," since he had never gotten along with his traditional family in Taiwan.

Irene always had felt foreign and missed a sense of racial and cultural belonging. She said, "When I go back to Taiwan, I don't really feel like I fit in there. But when I'm here, I don't feel like I'm fitting in here. . . . I'm not one hundred percent. . . . I'm American but . . . I was born here, but I'm still a minority."[7] Irene felt that she was always a foreigner and that she would never be the same as white people in this country. She remembered how the families of her past boyfriends would react to her:

> They always treat you the same way. They treat you as someone Asian first before they treat you as American. I remember so many times going to my boyfriends' houses for Thanksgiving. You know, my ex-boyfriend's mother has a place setting for everyone; in my place, there were chopsticks. I felt uncomfortable with that. Of course, they always ask you questions like—you know, my name is Irene—"How do you get that name? It's just unusual for a Chinese girl to have that name, you know. How long have you been in the States?" Stuff like that. You have to react politely.[8]

Irene's sense of not belonging and of being foreign led her to date both white men and Asian American men, despite her father's advice. Irene said that she had tried to find the most comfortable place and person with whom to be: "There was a while when I wanted to marry someone Asian if I was going to get married. I think, growing up in America as an Asian person, every Asian kind of goes through that phase." She also had found among young generations of Asians a strong racial animosity that she had never before encountered, to which she alluded in speaking of her ex-boyfriend:

> He was the kind of person, he is like, 'I just don't like white people.' He didn't like to talk to white people. He's kind of very closed-minded about that. So, he knew he wanted to date, he wanted to marry, an Asian woman. I think he's kind of a traditional Asian guy.[9]

Rather than viewing this racial hostility as historical or social, Irene saw it as simple closed-mindedness. She also interpreted Asian American men's racial tension toward white men as a "traditional" defensiveness of Asian American masculinity. After a year of dating him, Irene was still hesitant to call him a boyfriend: "I never considered him really as my boyfriend. I knew that he wasn't the one for me."

Irene met her boyfriend, Brian Thompson, a 26-year-old law school student, at a club: "I remember the first thing he said was, like, he asked about my tattoo, and he thought it was Kanji. It's just insects. But from far away, it looks like a Chinese character."[10] Brian had asked Irene if it was a Chinese character and had told her that he was considering getting a tattoo on his back that said, "Shiao-Guei," little ghost. "In Chinese, we call white people ghosts because they are white," laughed Irene. Shiao-Guei was the nickname that Brian's Chinese ex-girlfriend had given him. Irene had reacted strongly and turned him down at first when he asked for her phone number. She initially thought, "Oh, no, he likes Asian girls. I didn't like dating guys like that. No, not at all. Growing up Asian, you inevitably meet guys like, 'Oh, I love Asian culture'. . . . I hate that." From a very young age, Irene had been aware that the white men around her exoticized and sexualized Asian and Asian American women just because they were Asian. Until she began dating Brian, she had avoided going out with those white men who simply fetishized her Asian-ness. Irene emphasized, "I had made this conscious decision not to date a guy that was interested in Asian women."

Eventually, Irene called Brian, and they had been in a relationship for three months at the time of the interview. "He is very smart. I like intelligent people," Irene said. On the other hand, Irene still was trying to make sense of the fact that Brian had dated only Asian girls and was primarily attracted to Asians. Irene speculated that he liked the physical appearance of Asian and Asian American women and not necessarily Asian cultures or languages: "That's what his idea of beauty is. So, that's acceptable. I mean it is. He finds a certain type of person attractive. . . . There's nothing you can do about it logically."[11]

However, Irene suspected that Brian liked all Asian girls:

> That's another one of the weird suspicions when you date a guy that likes Asian girls a lot because you think he is indiscriminate about it. And, he's always making these comments. There would be some girls at a club. He would be like, 'Oh, she is really cute,' some Asian girl. She is totally not attractive. I would be like, 'Okay, you know, . . . she is cute because she is Asian.'[12]

Brian had many female Asian friends and knew a lot about Chinese, Korean, and Japanese cultures, in part because those were the cultures of his former girlfriends. When Brian proudly expressed his knowledge of Asian cultures, Irene felt ambivalent about his attraction to her. She said, "Sometimes

I ask myself if it is because I'm Asian that he's attracted to me because I know that initially, of course, that's what it was. But sometimes, I kind of ask myself, like, if that is the only reason why. I know it is not. But in the back of your head. . . ."[13]

Irene noticed how white men lump "Asian" cultures and people together as one, and how they are sometimes oblivious to her Chinese origin. Every time Brian pointed out certain Asian characters in a movie or talked excitedly about a Japanese film he had seen, Irene remembered a man she had dated several years before who always told her how fascinated he was by Japanese culture and girls. "Chinese culture and Japanese culture are different," said Irene. "People basically think all the groups are similar, and they all think the same way." Irene questioned whether Brian cared about what she thought when he said, "We should really go and see this Japanese film." She sighed, "I was sort of like, 'Okay, but not because it's my culture, and I need to see it, because it's not my culture.' "[14]

Irene felt that she was "othered" and "exoticized" as an Asian woman in her relationship with Brian. Irene, having failed in an effort to erase her foreign-ness in a relationship with an Asian man, went on to struggle with her sense of "other-ness" and "foreign-ness" in her relationship with a white man. She complained about the difficulty of "being made to feel that you are different."[15] This difference, she meant, stemmed from Brian's constant re-imposition of "foreign-ness," or "Asian-ness," on her.

Women like Irene seem to serve as pleasurable objects, similar to the characters in Asian stories and films, for men like Brian, who exoticize and are fascinated by Asian media and culture. Irene, in her interaction with Brian, felt pressured to be exotic and different as an Asian woman. She said that she felt that men like Brian want a girlfriend who is different, that this is what attracts them. She characterized Brian as not wanting "just a white girl," and yet she felt she wanted to be just a regular person in a relationship.

[. . .]

DESIRE FOR WHITE MASCULINITY AS MIDDLE CLASS STATUS

Asian American women sometimes regard white men as the possessors of superior socioeconomic capital. Frankenberg writes, "[W]hiteness is made out of materials that include socioeconomic status, cultural practice, peer group acceptance, parental teaching and community participation."[16] The next two stories demonstrate how Asian and Asian American women often view marriage with white men as one of the few available ways through which they can gain upward mobility and assimilate as "honorary whites."

Angelina Brown, a petite 39-year-old Filipina American with a very warm smile and a quiet demeanor, showed me pictures of her and her mother at a younger age and told me that she had always wanted to be beautiful like her mother. Her husband, Thomas Brown, a 38-year-old computer engineer, was, by contrast, big and talkative. Thomas, while often expressing his affection towards Angelina with comments such as, "I'm true to her," and, "I can't really imagine myself without Angelina," did not hesitate to take over the entire couple interview by interrupting Angelina often and presenting his own view as the couple's view.

Angelina had come to Mississippi at the age of 18, when her mother married an American serviceman who was stationed in the Philippines. This was her mother's second marriage. Angelina's mother had run away from her first, Filipino, husband, Angelina's father, because of his serious physical abuse of her. When Angelina was about two, her father, who already had abandoned his wife and nine children, had completely stopped contact with the family. To raise nine children,

Angelina's mother had worked at an American military base as a waitress "all day and night," and Angelina had grown up mainly with her grandparents.

Angelina had started working as a waitress at the military base in the Philippines at the age of 16, to help her mother. Soon after, her mother had told her that she would be leaving Angelina and the family again. This time, she was moving to the United States because she had married an American serviceman, who then also had started abusing her after marriage. Angelina had moved to Mississippi, where her mother and her American stepfather lived, to study as a college student. At the age of 21, she had met Thomas, a serviceman at the military base there, in one of the classes that she was taking, and they had married two years later.

Angelina's willingness to take on the traditional feminine role complemented Thomas, who believed in playing the traditional male role and in keeping Angelina as a mother and a wife. Thomas said, ". . . as a white guy, my culture would have me keep my wife at home. . . . It's recommended that the woman stays home and raises the kids."[17] Thomas viewed traditional gender roles as racialized status and said, somewhat defensively, "We are supposed to be the dominant male, protecting women and providing for the family. If we are equal partners, then what are we?"

In her individual interview, Angelina said that she had chosen to marry Thomas because she thought the marriage would provide financial and emotional security: "I think I did that for security reasons, to be honest. Because I felt like this person really cares for me. I really enjoyed being with him, and he wants to marry me. Should I turn down or should I look for further opportunity?"[18] Angelina confessed that she saw marriage as a material and psychological opportunity: "He's like an investment. I was like, you buy this mutual fund in the beginning, and it gets bigger and bigger, and at the end, you know, you got all of this and you get to enjoy it."

For Angelina, marrying a white American had meant marrying into American society and transforming herself into an American. She said that she already had decided to "be an American" by the age of 10, when she first saw the high standard of living on the U.S. military base in the Philippines. After that, images from the media filled her with prosperous visions of "being an American," as she explained in her individual interview:

> If you marry American, you get to go to America. You enjoy your life. America is great. So, I get this American mentality all of the sudden. I'm nothing in this country. My goal is to go to America. And, I didn't want to have Filipino boyfriend. I didn't care for them . . . because if I married them, I didn't get to go to America. . . . My first boyfriend was American. . . . I never dated Filipino, never. . . . I like tall men. I like speaking English.[19]

Angelina's sexual desire was subsumed by her desire to gain power via the racial, gender, and class privileges of white middle-class America. In her imagination, marrying an American was an opportunity not only to go to America but also to "be" an American who enjoyed a prosperous lifestyle and spoke English. A Filipino man, as a marital partner, was coded as inferior and lacking in resources. Angelina continued, "I guess, to me, the white American was the highest standard, and I chose somebody who's higher standard. I'm sorry; it's a shame, but that's how I thought. That's how I was formed."[20] Her desire to gain the same resources as white middle-class Americans was to be realized, for her, through heterosexual romantic love with a white man: "I like tall guys and I like the American standards, the way the white people live. I could show them what a good woman I can be for them. I like to serve that person." The American standard was naturally assumed to be a white standard, possibly that of the middle class, and tall guys were regarded as the normative masculine figure, which Asian American men did not embody.

[. . .]

This desire to gain a higher, assimilated status through the relationship was not unique to Angelina, or even to first-generation Asian American women. The second-generation Korean American women whom I interviewed also spoke of similar desire. One 20-year-old Korean American student said her desire to assimilate and her lack of confidence as a racial minority had driven her to find an upper-class white boyfriend whom she described as "so white," "popular," and a "typical suburban kid."[21]

Stoler, citing Fanon, writes that in colonialism the man "uses sex as a vehicle to master a practical world."[22] Marrying the colonizer gives the colonized access to privileged schooling, well-paying jobs, and certain residential quarters.[23] Fanon's insight on colonial desire, that "to marry white culture" is "to grasp white civilization and dignity and make them mine,"[24] well explains Angelina's imaginary transformation towards the "highest standard" of marrying the powerful other. Feminist psychoanalysis argues that women's alienated desire takes the form of submission to and envy of men.[25] Women often seek to fulfill their desire by identifying with the ideal lover's power. Benjamin perceives women's submission to and sacrifice for male heroes as the quest for paternal recognition and glory, which she argues is the necessary effect of society's privileging of masculinity. Angelina desired to gain approval by "serving" a white man, and stated, "My purpose in coming to this world is to marry someone who is white."[26]

But, we also must look at Angelina's desire for a white American man in the context of her history in the Philippines. Engaging as a good mother and wife in the middle-class white family represented Angelina's resistance to and will to overturn what she and her mother had endured: poverty, abuse, abandonment, and excessive labor. Motherhood for Angelina, as for many of the first-generation Asian American women whom I interviewed, was the space of resistance against the gender and economic inequality that she and her mother had experienced in the Philippines. Her desires were deeply racialized in the sense that she regarded whiteness as a significant marker of ascension and privileges, a measure by which she had found herself lacking. White masculinity and Asian American femininity, in Angelina and Thomas's relationship, conformed to the ideal of white middle-class ideology and family values. The majority of the first-generation Asian American women whom I interviewed similarly engaged with their white male partners in traditional, racialized gender roles.

DESIRE FOR WHITE MASCULINITY AS MATERIAL SECURITY

For Asian women who enter into marriage as "mail-order brides," sexual desire takes the form of desire for a white man, who will embody the social, cultural, and economic privileges that enable one to attain one's future potential and ideal-self.[27] For these women, global inequality becomes another factor, along with traditional gender roles and racial stereotypes, that influences their choice of marriage. The story of one Filipina American woman's deliberate choice of marriage as a mail-order bride illustrates the complex interworkings of these economic, social, and cultural factors on a global scale.

Linda Miller, a petite, 34-year-old Filipina American woman with straight black hair and round brown eyes, informed me in a quiet but serious tone that her husband was not interested in participating in this interview. She had been married to her husband, Jack, a 41-year-old computer engineer, for ten years at the time of our interview, and the couple had two children whom Linda described as "white." Linda had first contacted Jack through what she called a "pen-pal relationship," while she was working in Hong Kong as a domestic worker. In the living room of the couple's apartment, Jack was working intensely on his laptop. He glanced at me without stopping his fingers and said, "Hi," very curtly. We decided to go to the children's bedroom for the interview.

Linda had started working as a maid for an American serviceman's family when she was 12 years old. Her father had worked at an American military base as a maintenance man, and her family had run a small store. She always had given half of her income to her family. As with most people in the Philippines, work had been a part of her life since she was a child. Linda said, "We just work because work is there."[28] At twenty-one, Linda had discovered few choices available to her. She faced either going to Hong Kong to work as a domestic worker or going to Japan to work as a waitress or a singer. She had chosen to go to Hong Kong. "All I did was just to clean the house and cook," said Linda. At that time, she had been earning the equivalent of 250 U.S. dollars a month. The family for whom she had worked owned a small house, but they did not give her a private room and fired her when she expressed her displeasure: "I said, 'I need space even though I am a domestic.' But in Hong Kong, you don't have that choice unless your employer is really rich."[29]

At that time, her Filipino friends had been circulating lists of American men who were looking for Filipina brides. Linda had chosen her current husband because he was the youngest of all the Americans on the list, which included men in their sixties and seventies. She had gone back to the Philippines, and her husband had come over to meet her and marry her. Although Linda had not experienced any romantic feelings toward him, she nonetheless accepted his offer of marriage, which had taken place four days after his arrival in the Philippines. "He was a quiet, simple person. That's it. I can't think of any other words . . . but I thought he was okay, a macho man, a big guy,"[30] Linda replied without any smile. Asked about any concerns she might have had about marriage, Linda expressed a combination of disassociation and irritation. Her attitude toward her husband was distant and mechanical. "It's just, this is my man. I am going to be with him. . . . I didn't feel anything about him," Linda said, "Not excitement. Not fear."

[. . .]

For legal reasons, it had taken Linda about two years before she could start her new life in America. During the two years of waiting for legal permission to immigrate, her husband, Jack, supported her financially by giving her a credit card as well as supplying enough cash so that she did not have to work. "When he came to the Philippines, he told me I didn't have to go back to Hong Kong," said Linda. Once Linda and Jack were together in the United States, Jack continued to send $150 a month to her family in the Philippines. She sighed, "That's not enough for them. It's not enough to support them. . . . It's still a poor economy."[31] Linda appreciated her husband's financial support of her and her family, but her words could not conceal the emotional distance underneath, especially when she talked about Jack showing no interest in her family and culture:

> He doesn't ask how my brothers and sisters are doing. I'm getting used to it. It doesn't matter any more. I don't care. . . . I talk to his family. But, he doesn't talk to my family. I just accept it. I can't do anything. You are not expecting him to talk more or be happy about what he hears from you. I wish he were. I wish he could commit more to my family and my background. Yeah . . . it bothers me. But, I can't make him do that.[32]

Her husband apparently expected her to serve him in the traditional sense as a docile, good wife in exchange for financial security. Describing her marriage and housework, Linda repeated many times in the interview, "I expected more," and, "You just have to live with it, just do it." Linda said she cooked every day but had never heard him say anything about her cooking: "He doesn't show any, you cannot hear any, you just cook and put them on the table. He puts them in the sink. It's like your kid. You don't want to wait for a kid to say, 'Thank you.' "[33] Linda barely finished her sentence and seemed about to cry. She did not move or speak for a while.

[. . .]

Having resisted her material deprivation in the Philippines and Hong Kong, Linda finally acquired upward mobility by crossing the border to the United States. However, she had little power to transform her husband's perceptions or the dynamics of the marital relationship. Linda's hope, and strategy of resistance, was to live one day with her parents, who had been waiting in the Philippines for ten years for legal permission to immigrate to the United States: "Here in the U.S., when they get old, you just throw your parents into the nursing home. But me, my kids, we don't do that. You take care of your parents when they get old."[34] Being an assimilated middle-class American appealed much less to Linda than it did to Angelina. The main desire driving Linda's decision was the desire for material security.

DESIRE FOR WHITE MASCULINITY AS EGALITARIAN KNIGHTHOOD

Common among many of the Asian American women whom I interviewed was an aversion toward Asian and Asian American men, due to their small physical size and attitude of ethnic patriarchy. For these Asian American women, the white man's body, in contrast to the Asian body, symbolized not only physical strength but also Western civility and the ideal of gender equality—"white knighthood." The following story illustrates one Chinese American woman's desire for an egalitarian white knight, with whom she could resist ethnic patriarchy and realize ideal independent womanhood.

Grace Wong, a 24-year-old computer engineer, welcomed me into the brand-new condominium she had recently purchased. Grace had been born in Taiwan but had come to the U.S. soon afterward. When her family first moved to the U.S., they had suffered a hard time economically. Her father had helped his family's business for a while, then had been "a day trader" and "lived by stocks." Grace's mother had worked at a jewelry store full-time since they arrived in the United States. Grace, after a moment's pause, started to talk about her mother in a bitter tone. "I think the reason why my sisters and I, we date outside of our race, is because my mother herself is pretty unhappy with her marriage."[35] Grace's mother had worked all her life and taken care of the children. Grace described her father as "very quiet and withdrawn." She went on to say, "He thinks that our personal lives are my mom's responsibility." He "controls the money my mother makes," does not allow her mother to spend money, and "bullies her around." Grace resented the fact that her father neglected her mother and controlled all the family members: "He never gave her anything as a present, not for her birthday and not for Christmas, nothing . . . I hate my dad." Grace's father went out with his friends, often until past midnight. If these were the standard Chinese cultural privileges of men, her mother's "privilege" was being alone all the time.

[. . .]

For Grace, her father's negative characteristics and her mother's anger were easily transferred onto the gender characteristics of the Asian American men around her. Grace remembered what her mother used to say to her: "Once in a while, she would say, like, American guys are, they are just a lot more polite, and they are so much nicer. They treat women so much more fairly." The unfulfilled desire of Grace's mother was thus transferred onto Grace, and she unconsciously retained her mother's anger and directed it towards Asian men in general.

This intergenerational transference became a gender strategy through which to resist Asian male dominance. Grace armed herself with a higher racial and gender power: white masculinity. Race was the significant weapon by which she could attack the male dominance that haunted her. Kelsky, in her ethnographic studies of Japanese women, has demonstrated that it is not only Western Orientalist discourse that creates fetishized stereotypes of Asian women, but also Japanese women themselves.[36] Kelsky has observed that these women appropriate such racialized images "for an act of revenge against the patriarchal Japanese nation-state,"[37] even though this appropriation might arguably perpetuate "self-colonization" and feed the value of white supremacy.

[. . .]

Grace perceived Asian American men as being incapable of dealing with her independence and assertiveness. As she put it, "I feel Asian guys are intimidated by me. So, they would never approach me."[38] Grace understood Asian American men to date only quiet and submissive Asian American women. She thus effeminized both Asian American men and Asian American women, while presenting herself as clearly different from the feminine stereotype. She was not alone in this view; another Chinese American woman whom I interviewed said she had never dated Asian or Asian American men because "Asian guys like quiet girls" and would not like a woman like her, who is "so vocal, talkative, and kind of opinionated."[39] [. . .]

Grace's rejection of Asian American men represented a combination of her aversion to repeating her parents' unequal relationship and her desire to identify with the image of independent womanhood, an image that she felt Asian American men could not accept. Grace saw her mother as a powerless feminine figure and avoided identifying with her powerlessness by rejecting Asian American women in general as "quiet" and "submissive." Grace's contemptuous view of Asian American women as submissive and dainty, shared by other Asian American women whom I interviewed, thus reinforced mainstream stereotypes. Similarly, Asian American women's aversion to Asian American men, even though it appears to have originated in a resistance to Chinese patriarchy, was complicit with Western stereotypes of Asian American men.

DISCUSSION AND SUMMARY

Social institutions and cultural discourses have perpetuated and legitimized white male authority and privileges, even in the fields of desire and imagination. As Moore comments, "It is not that the material world, as a form of cultural discourse, reflects the natural division of the world into women and men, but rather that cultural discourses, including the organization of the material world, actually produce gender difference in and through their workings."[40]

Intimacy is a major technology of modernity for achieving self-realization and forming identity.[41] The Asian American women whom I interviewed understood intimacy as a "potential avenue for controlling the future as well as a form of psychological security,"[42] and strategically deployed their desires toward white men. The feminine strategy of the two Filipina American women whose stories I examine in this paper has strong links to the economic deprivation in their country of origin as well as to the Philippines' neo-colonial/colonial relationship to the United States. Angelina's childhood dream of being an American and attaining middle-class prosperity was realized in her marriage to an American serviceman. Linda's husband, through a U.S. bride importation service, appeared as a savior figure who took her from Asia, where she was a domestic worker, to the United States. Linda's relationship with her husband reflected the neo-colonial structure of the relationship of the United States to third-world Asian countries, in which "women with dependent immigration status are often more economically, psychologically and linguistically dependent on their spouse."[43]

It is critical to note that Angelina's and Linda's gender strategy was a strategy of survival, and of escape from economic deprivation and ethnic patriarchy in their home country. Furthermore, their desire for white men corresponded to their desire for status as an ideal white American citizen, who possesses access to the global and local privileges in a place where whites constitute "a 'nation' with whiteness,"[44] and where non-European immigrants "encounter the challenges of being treated as second-class citizens" and "can at best become 'honorary whites.' "[45] [. . .]

Conversely, the two Chinese American women sought white men not because of their desire for the American dream but because of their aversion to racialized images of "Asian" men and women, and, in Irene's case only, out of a desire to resolve a racialized sense of "non-belongingness." [. . .] In my interviews, the majority of the first-generation married Asian American women engaged in traditional gender roles, while the second-generation non-married Asian American women tended to express their aversion to submissive images of Asian women and their desire to have relationships based on gender equality.

[. . .] In all four cases, Asian American women's sexual desire for white men is grounded in their aspiration for upward mobility and discovery of true-self. The feminine positions in which Asian American women engage are highly regulated by the local and global discourses of romantic love, and by neo-colonial hierarchies of race. I emphasize again here, however, that what has led these women to engage in feminine subjugation is not their subservient nature in a stereotypical sense, but rather the culturally embedded imaginary discourses that promise their upward mobility and realization of self.

The four desires for white masculinity that I discuss through the stories of Angelina, Linda, Irene, and Grace reflect common perceptions of and subordination to whiteness among the Asian American women whom I interviewed. Irene's story illustrates the racial and gendered tension deriving from white men's fetishization of Asian women. Many Asian American women silently negotiate with racialized images of themselves in their daily lives and intimate relationships. In my interviews, those who explicitly addressed or were aware of the damaging consequences of commodified and objectifying images of Asian and Asian American women usually had high familiarity with American culture due to their native-born or high socioeconomic status. Yet, as in Irene's case, they seemed to be torn between their resistance to these images and their reluctance to acknowledge them in their own relationships. Grace's case shows us how Asian American women's preference of white men, while deriving from an aversion to ethnic patriarchy and submissive images of Asian women, ironically may reinforce negative images of Asians and Asian Americans.[46] Projecting visions of equality onto white men is common among both first- and second-generation Asian American women. Six of the ten Asian American women with whom I conducted interviews as part of a couple stated such a belief directly or indirectly. For many of them, a desire for white male egalitarian knighthood corresponded to the belief that egalitarian relationships were not possible with Asian American men.

The desire for white masculinity as a gateway to middle-class American status and for white masculinity as material security, as represented by Angelina's and Linda's stories, are deeply mediated by economic and immigration status. Choices of white men for their socioeconomic and cultural privileges derive from women's strategic resistance to powerless positions, but such choices also inevitably increase Asian American women's vulnerability to white power over them.

The combination of cultural stereotypes of Asian and Asian American women and the actual desires that Asian American women have for white hegemonic masculinity has created a "mutual attraction"[47] between Asian American women and white men. This attraction, grounded as it is in profound inequalities and controlling images, also "promotes Asian American women's availability to white men and makes them particularly vulnerable to mistreatment."[48] Much discussion in academic and popular culture in the United States has addressed the nature of white men's attraction to Asian and Asian American women. In contrast, the four kinds of desire I discuss here are ways to understand the attraction of Asian American women to white men. This discussion begins to reveal the complexity and paradox of the racial and gender inequalities that emerge within intimate relationships.

[. . .]

Regarding the question of whether Asian American women's feminine strategy can be one of self-liberation or is mere complicity with the dominant ideology, I do not reduce my findings to a dichotomized discourse of either liberation or self-colonization. Rather, the importance of this work lies in showing how, contrary to popular utopian celebration of mixed-race marriage as a sign of multiracialization,[49] interracial intimacy is still regulated by racial, gender, class, and national hierarchies.

NOTES

1. Sharon Lee and Keiko Yamanaka, "Patterns of Asian American Intermarriage and Marital Assimilation," *Journal of Comparative Family Studies* 21 (1990): 287–305; Sharon Lee and Marilyn Fernandez, "Trends in Asian American Racial/Ethnic Intermarriage: A Comparison of 1980 and 1990 Census Data," *Sociological Perspectives* 41 (1998): 323–342; Larry Shinagawa and Gin Yong Pang, "Intraethnic, interethnic, and interracial marriages among Asian Americans in California, 1980," *Berkeley Journal of Sociology* 33 (1988): 95–114; Larry Shinagawa and Gin Yong Pang, "Asian American Panethnicity and Intermarriage," *Amerasia Journal* 22 (1996): 127–152.
2. Lee and Yamanaka, "Patterns," 294.
3. Vivian Kwan, individual interview by author, Austin, Texas, May 13, 2001.
4. Irene Huan, individual interview by author, Austin, Texas, December 8, 2000.
5. Ibid.
6. Ibid.
7. Ibid.
8. Ibid.
9. Ibid.
10. Ibid.
11. Ibid.
12. Ibid.
13. Ibid.
14. Ibid.
15. Ibid.
16. Ruth Frankenberg, *Displacing Whiteness: Essays in Social and Cultural Criticism* (Durham: Duke University Press, 1997), 28.
17. Thomas Brown, individual interview by author, Austin, Texas, October 22, 2000.
18. Angelina Brown, individual interview by author, Austin, Texas, October 20, 2000.
19. Ibid.
20. Ibid.
21. Lisa Kim, individual interview by author, Austin, Texas, August 2, 2001.
22. Ann Stoler, *Race and the Education of Desire: Foucault's History of Sexuality and the Colonial Order of Things* (Durham: Duke University Press, 1995), 190.
23. Ibid.
24. Franz Fanon, *Black Skin, White Masks* (New York: Grove Press, 1967), 63.
25. Jessica Benjamin, *The Bonds of Love* (New York: Pantheon, 1988); Nancy Chodorow, *The Reproduction of Mothering: Psychoanalysis and the Sociology of Gender* (Berkeley: University of California Press, 1978).
26. Angelina Brown, October 20, 2000.
27. Fanon, *Black Skin*; Stoler, *Race*.
28. Linda Miller, individual interview by author, Austin, Texas, March 22, 2001.
29. Ibid.
30. Ibid.
31. Ibid.
32. Ibid.
33. Ibid.

34. Ibid.
35. Grace Wong, individual interview by author, Austin, Texas, April 23, 2001.
36. Karen Kelsky, *Women on the Verge: Japanese Women, Western Dreams* (Durham: Duke University Press, 2001).
37. Ibid, 186.
38. Grace Wong, April 23, 2001.
39. Rebecca Chu, individual interview by author, Austin, Texas, December 1, 2001.
40. Henrietta Moore, *A Passion for Difference: Essays in Anthropology and Gender* (Oxford: Polity Press, 1995), 85.
41. Anthony Giddens, *Modernity and Self-Identity: Self and Society in the Late Modern Age* (Stanford: Stanford University Press, 1991); *The Transformation of Intimacy: Sexuality, Love and Eroticism in Modern Societies* (Cambridge: Polity Press, 1993).
42. Giddens, *Transformation*, 41.
43. Uma Narayan, " 'Male-Order' Brides: Immigrant Women, Domestic Violence and Immigration Law," *Hypatia* 10 (1995): 109.
44. Patricia Collins, "Like One of the Family: Race, Ethnicity, and the Paradox of US National Identity," *Ethnic and Racial Studies* 24 (2001): 3–28.
45. Ibid., 20.
46. In "Asian American Women and Racialized Femininities: 'Doing' Gender across Cultural Worlds," *Gender & Society* 17 (2003): 43–44, Karen Pyke and Denise Johnson argue that "the perception that whites are more egalitarian than Asian-origin individuals and thus preferred partners in social interaction further reinforces anti-Asian racism and white superiority."
47. Kelsky, *Women*.
48. Pyke and Johnson, "Asian American Women," 46.
49. Nicholas Kristof, "Love and Race," *New York Times*, December 6, 2002, A33.

32

excerpts from

Beyond Black

Biracial Identity in America

KERRY ANN ROCKQUEMORE AND DAVID L. BRUNSMA

WHO IS BLACK?

EARLY IN THE 1990s, a coalition of mixed-race individuals and advocacy groups from across the nation lobbied the Office of Management and Budget (OMB) for the addition of a multiracial category to the 2000 census. The request was not denied outright. Instead, a lengthy period of public debate ensued over the proposed adjustment to existing racial classifications. After a three-year study, a multiagency governmental task force recommended that the OMB reject the proposed multiracial category. While the need for reliable data on racial groups is ongoing, the addition of more categories was deemed both unnecessary and divisive. As a compromise, the 2000 census enabled individuals to check more than one racial category if they desired. The compromise plan, which was adopted for the collection of all government data on race, received unanimous support from thirty federal agencies including the U.S. Bureau of the Census, the Department of Justice, and the National Center for Health Statistics.[1]

Support for the multiracial initiative was led by grassroots organizations such as Project RACE and the Association of MultiEthnic Americans. These advocacy groups argued for the creation of a new racial category for both demographic and cultural reasons. Their demographic justification cited the trend toward increasing interracial marriages and births of mixed-race children in the United States. In the past three decades, the number of interracial marriages in the United States has increased from 300,000 to 1.4 million, and these households (in addition to cohabiting interracial households) have spawned a boom in the mixed-race population.[2] Their other argument was that mixed-race individuals view themselves as multiracial rather than as belonging exclusively to the racial group of one of their parents. The addition of a multiracial category, its advocates argued, was essential to accurately represent existing demographic shifts in the population *and* to provide a true reflection of biracial people's understanding of their racial identity. For some multiracial advocates, increasing numbers of mixed-race people represent the need for a new social consciousness that permits greater fluidity in the way individuals racially identify themselves.[3]

Leading the opposition to the mixed-race initiative were well-known civil rights leaders, such as Jesse Jackson, Kweisi Mfume (representing the Congressional Black Caucus), and representatives of the NAACP. They argued that the underlying purpose of legislative directives mandating the collection of data on racial groups was to enable the enforcement of civil rights legislation and to document the existence of racial inequalities. Adding a multiracial category, they argued, would increase the difficulty of collecting accurate data on the effects of discrimination and, therefore, deviated from the legal directive given to the Census Bureau.[4]

[. . .]

It seems worthwhile to quote at length Molefi Kete Asante, an ardent Afrocentrist, as he distinctly articulates his opposition, not to the addition of a multiracial category to the census but to the *idea* of mixed-race identity:

> One cannot read magazines like *New People* and *Interrace* without getting the idea that self-hatred among some African Americans is at an all-time high. Both of these magazines, founded by interracial couples and appealing most to interracial families, see themselves as the vanguard to explode racial identity by claiming to be a third race in addition to African and European. Of course, in the context of a racist society the white parent wishes for his/her offspring the same privileges that he/she has enjoyed often at the expense of Africans. However, the offspring is considered by tradition, custom, appearance, and history to be black. In a white racist society blackness is considered a negative attribute which carries with it the burden of history and discrimination. Thus, the *New People* and the *Interrace* group attempt to minimize the effects of blackness by claiming that they are neither white nor black, but colored. The nonsense in this position is seen when we consider the fact that nearly 70 percent of all African Americans are genetically mixed with either Native Americans or whites. The post-Du Bois, and perhaps more accurately, the post-Martin Luther King, Jr., phenomenon of seeking to explode racial identity has two prongs: one is white guilt and the other is black self-hatred. In the case of interracial families one often sees the urgent need to provide the offspring with a race other than that defined by custom, tradition, appearance, and history.[5]

This statement articulates the underlying frustration of some opponents of the multiracial category. Asante's comments force a questioning of where race relations stand in post-civil rights America. He suggests that a negative consequence of the discourse on race is the emergence of the myth that, at the turn of the millennium, race no longer matters. However, the mere desire of white parents for their children to be identified as mixed-race (as opposed to black) signifies an implied acknowledgment that racial groups exist, that they exist in a hierarchy, and that separation from the subordinate group brings an individual closer to the dominant group. Opponents view the demand of advocates for a new racial category, in combination with their middle-class economic status, as a movement with an assimilationist ideological underpinning.

What is critical to this tension between multiracial advocates and leaders of the black community is the racial self-understanding of biracial people. In other words, it is less important whether or not biracial people appear black "on the outside"; it's how they understand themselves "on the inside" that counts. Black identity is not characterized by physical traits because members of the black community have an enormous variety of physical appearance, including those who physically appear white. Instead, black identity is conceptualized as developing out of the common experience of being black in America. Black leaders point to the numerous people who may have one black and one white parent, yet experience the world as black people and are understood by others in society as members of the black community.[6] As Asante stated, biracial children are "considered by tradition, custom, appearance, and history to be black."

In contrast, leaders of the multiracial movement point to the push for self-determination by individuals who understand their racial identity not as black in accordance with the one-drop rule, but as "biracial." They argue that being biracial is a unique experience that is different from being black. According to activists, individuals, regardless of physical appearance, experience the world from the unique perspective of being mixed-race; have common experiences with blacks, whites, and other biracial people; and are understood by others as biracial (not exclusively as black). To have a biracial self-understanding, this identity must be validated by others in their social environment. It is precisely this claim of validation that leads individuals to believe that the category has meaning and is a necessary addition to the existing racial landscape.

Understanding the tension between interest groups and, at the broadest level, the competing visions of the future of black-white race relations is critical to grasping the profound importance of a potentially new answer to the very old question, Who is black? For both parties in the census debate, understanding biracial identity is critical. Each perspective holds a differing and singular view of how mixed-race people understand their place in America's racial system. Their positions are fundamentally dependent on how people within the emerging mixed-race population understand their racial identity.

This book is an examination of the dynamic meaning of racial identity for black/white biracial people in the United States and asks the question, What does biracial identity mean to individuals within this population? [. . .]

Our data suggest some tentative descriptive categories for the ways that black/white multiracial people understand their biracialism: (a) a border identity, (b) a singular identity, (c) a protean identity, and/or (d) a transcendent identity. These categories of self-understanding are not necessarily mutually exclusive; rather, they should be viewed as ideal types. Each of these different interpretations of biracial identity is explored and discussed in the context of the data collected.

A Border Identity

Anthony was a six-foot tall, 18-year-old college football player.[7] His appearance can be best described as ambiguous; it would be difficult for anyone to guess his racial background, although he does not appear white. Anthony was raised in a small rural community in northern Ohio. His father (black) left his mother (white) when Anthony and his brother were young; therefore, they were raised exclusively by their mother and her extended family. There was a deep sense of tangible resentment when Anthony spoke about his father and a self-satisfied revenge that he and his brother had become successful, despite their abandonment.

Anthony was popular in his high school and reported attending a school with several other self-identified biracial students. His hometown was predominately white; however, half of the non-white students in his high school were mixed-race. This accessible group of peers and their location in a predominately white setting helped account for the fact that Anthony had a very strong identity as biracial. When asked, he told me, "I'm *not* black, I'm biracial," with such a forceful expression that I could not doubt the seriousness of his conviction. Anthony told numerous stories about incidents in high school where biracial students boldly differentiated themselves from black students by teasing them about the darkness of their skin. They affectionately referred to themselves as the "high yelluhs."

Gloria Anzaldua conceptualizes biracial identity as a border identity, one that lies between predefined social categories.[8] In essence, the border identity highlights an individual's existence between two socially distinct races as defining one's biracialism. Meaning lies in their location of in-betweenness, and this unique status serves to ground their racial identity. Mixed-race people who understand being biracial as a border identity don't consider themselves to be either black or white but, instead, incorporate both blackness and whiteness into a unique hybrid category of self-reference. One respondent explained that it was not only being on the border of socially defined categories but also experiencing the border status itself that brought with it an additional dimension:

> It's not that just being biracial is like you're two parts [white and black], you know, you have two parts but then there is also the one part of being biracial where you sit on the fence. There's a third thing, a unique thing.

The idea of a border identity has been the focus of numerous studies over the past 20 years.[9] In addition, a significant line of research has focused on developmental models of racial identity formation among biracials, where the border identity is the underlying ideal.[10] Christine Hall, studying black-Asian biracials, states that her adult respondents had all achieved a "multicultural existence," and they identified exclusively as biracial.[11] Barbara Tizard and Ann Phoenix found that 49 percent of their biracial British sample identified themselves as mixed-race and used terms such as *half-and-half, mixed,* or *brown.*[12] G. Reginald Daniel calls this identity a "blended identity" and describes it as one that "resists both the dichotomization and hierarchical valuation of African American and European American cultural and racial differences."[13]

A border identity is the most common way of conceptualizing biracialism among contemporary researchers focusing on the biracial population.[14] It can be inferred from most recent work that focuses on biracial people that when the term *biracial identity* is used it is being understood as a border identity. In addition, this conceptualization of biracial was most privileged by multiracial advocates in their quest for the addition of a multiracial category to the 2000 census.

In our sample, the border interpretation was the most common category of self-understanding. About 58 percent of those surveyed defined their racial identity as neither exclusively black nor white but, instead, as a third and separate category that draws from both of these group characteristics and has some additional uniqueness in its combination. It is important to note that these individuals fell into two distinguishable kinds of border identities: (a) those that are validated by others through social interactions (the validated border identity) and (b) those that are not (the unvalidated border identity). The importance of this distinction cannot be understated.

The Validated Versus Unvalidated Border Identity (the Real Tragic Mulattos?)

Chris was a calm woman who displayed a level of maturity beyond her years. Most people would assume that she is African American based on her appearance; however, she described her identity as "biracial, but I experience the world as a black woman." She talked freely about both her black and white extended families, recalling fond memories of the uniqueness of growing up in a loving family that was a patchwork of traditional black and Irish influences. However, she was acutely cognizant of how others viewed her, both strangers and those in her intimate social network.

Chris told me that because of her appearance race functioned as the first thing that many people saw about her and that many of the other roles that she played at school and in society were differentiated by her race. She was seen by others as the "*black* intern," a "*black* feminist," "a *black* student," and "a *black* friend." She expressed a close affiliation to other African Americans based on a common life experience of negotiating interactions as a person of color within a predominantly white culture. She felt that those close to her appreciated and understood her as biracial, but when she had to interact with people outside of her immediate social network, they categorized her as black, attributing to her all the assumptions and preconceived ideas that go along with that particular racial group membership. This made her feel both sad and somewhat resigned to the fact that there would always be a chasm between her self-identification (as biracial) and society's identification of her (as black).

For about 20 percent of the total respondents, their racial identity was exclusively biracial and that identity was validated by others. They described their racial identity in the following way: "I consider myself exclusively as biracial (neither black nor white)." However, more than 38 percent of respondents answered, "I consider myself biracial, but I experience the world as a black person." This is of interest because whereas 58 percent of *all* our respondents identified themselves as biracial (as opposed to exclusively black or white), more than half of that group expressed a disjuncture between their self-understanding and the way in which they socially experienced race. The difference between these two sets of responses seems to suggest the importance of interactional validation, which can best be understood by unpacking this second, unvalidated response.

Interviews with people like Chris offer additional insight into the unvalidated border identity. Although she views herself as biracial, the social world fails to validate her chosen category of self-understanding. Given both the consistency and frequency of this nonvalidation, she lives in a gray area between her own self-understanding and the differential view that others have of her. She may consider herself biracial, being neither black nor white but something that lies uniquely in between. She qualifies this, however, with the honest recognition that she "experiences the world as a black person," meaning that within her social context her self-understanding of being biracial is not always validated by others. Consistent with this self-understanding/validation split is the fact that when asked about different arenas of identity expression, respondents in the unvalidated border group were more likely to report their cultural, political, physical, and bureaucratic identity (i.e., the identity they select on forms) as black than as biracial.

If these unvalidated border individuals, as social actors, appropriate an identity for themselves as biracial, then why do others fail to place them as a social object into the same category? There seem to be two logical possibilities to answer that question. First, others may not understand biracial as an existing category of racial classification, so they may be operating with only the dichotomous, mutually exclusive categories black and white. This is the very situation that the multiracial movement is attempting to address. The second possible explanation for this classification failure is that even if others possess cognitive categories for black, white, and biracial, the individual's appearance may be composed of characteristics that would lead others to nonetheless classify them as black. Although the first explanation is certainly a viable possibility, we are unable to explore it with the existing data. The second explanation, however, led us to examine the differences between the self-reported appearance of the validated and unvalidated border identities.

Finally, it may be asked how individuals could develop a racial identity that is unvalidated if identity itself has been conceptually defined as an interactionally validated self-understanding. In other words, how can the unvalidated border identity be developed and maintained if others do not recognize its existence? We need only return to Chris to see that, in reality, her identity as biracial is validated by her significant others, such as her parents and friends. At the primary level of social intimacy, she feels that her authentic self is validated and realized. It is in the more everyday, nonintimate social meetings with strangers and acquaintances that she is unvalidated and routinely misidentified. We have parenthetically referred to the unvalidated border identity as the real "tragic mulattos" because it is precisely this group that experiences an internalized social dislocation because of its continual oscillation between having its self-understanding validated by some and unvalidated by others. The clinical and therapeutic literature focusing on biracial identity has primarily dealt with the group of black/white biracials whom we refer to as unvalidated borders.[15]

A Singular Identity

John looked white. When he first walked into my classroom, I unconsciously had him categorized as a "typical white fraternity guy."[16] He was medium height, in his early twenties, and quiet. The fact that he was biracial didn't surface until much later in the course when another student was presenting a project. He volunteered the fact that his mother (white) had been raped by a black man and had twins, a sibling who died in the hospital and himself. John was raised in an affluent, exclusively white community. He had a highly strained relationship with his stepfather, who had not revealed the circumstances of his conception and birth to John until he was 18 years old.

John had lived his entire life assuming that he was white, that he came from a white family, and that his stepfather was his biological father, despite the fact that they had no physical similarities. When John was a teenager, he was told that his lips and nose were a bit wide for the modeling career he envisioned, so he had plastic surgery to thin his lips and trim his nose. His identity as white was entirely unaffected by the sudden revelation that his biological father was black. It didn't cause him to rethink his identity nor to question his whiteness. He was simply a white man who happened to have a black father.

John illustrates the racial identity option of individuals with one black and one white parent, an option that we term the *singular identity*. In the singular understanding, the individual's racial identity is exclusively either black or white. Being biracial means merely acknowledging the racial categorization of a person's birth parents. At the extreme, respondents did not deny the existence of their opposite race parent, but it was not salient in defining their self-understanding and may not have been offered as identifying information unless specifically requested.

Researchers, past and present, have unquestionably considered this identity option, given that the singular black identity has been the historical norm. Maria Root suggested the singular identity as one (of several) resolutions of "Other Status," proposing that biracial individuals may choose to identify with a single racial group.[17] This identity option encompasses both the singular black and singular white options. However, Root narrowed the parameters for the singular white option by asserting geographic specificity (i.e., this option is not available in the South), thus emphasizing the importance of sociocultural context and the racial composition of a biracial individual's socialization networks. The singular black identity is characterized by Root as the biracial person "accepting the identity that society assigns."[18] This identity option has been heavily studied and is still assumed to be the primary option for black/white biracial individuals. Interestingly, the singular identity was highly contested in the census debate. Whereas African Americans emphasized this identity option as the identity choice of black/white biracials, many multiracial activists doubted the very existence of the singular black identity. Both sides in the census debate, however, fell silent on the possibility of a singular white identity.

About 13 percent of our sample considered themselves "exclusively black (or African American)," and almost 4 percent of the sample considered themselves "exclusively white (not black or biracial)." Given the centrality of the assumption that the one-drop rule would dictate most directly how biracial individuals would racially self-identity, some may find it surprising that such a small number of the respondents chose the singular black identity. This finding illustrates the complex nature of racial identity among biracial people in the United States.

A Protean Identity

Mike was a gregarious and enjoyable individual. He was a popular student at the university and seemed to know almost everyone who walked into the coffee shop on the evening of our interview.

Mike had finished college when we interviewed and was completing a semester of student teaching at a local public high school. Mike was raised in a small town in the Midwest. His parents were the only interracial couple in the area. In fact, they were such an anomaly that he had a newspaper clipping in which his parents were featured on the front page. Mike's father was a minister in the local church, which afforded his family a uniquely high and visible status in their community.

Although Mike was the only non-white person in his neighborhood, school, and friendship circle, he had close ties with his black extended family, whom he saw on a regular basis. Mike thought that it was his particular upbringing that led him to view his racial identity as he now understands it, which he describes as changing and shifting according to the group of people that he is with and the social context. The lesson he has learned from being around homogeneous groups of blacks and whites his entire life is that there are different ways of being in a group of blacks versus a group of whites.

Although many people might agree with this idea, regardless of their race, Mike's version is a bit different from most. Not only does he realize that these situations require different social behaviors, but he has the unique experience of feeling more than knowledgeable about these different behaviors, sensing that when he is in these groups, he is accepted by members of the group as an insider. Although most people might adjust their *behavior* to differing circumstances, Mike adjusts his *identity* to these different circumstances. He feels that he has the capacity to understand himself as black when he is with blacks and that his self-understanding is fully validated. He feels that he is able to understand himself as white when he is with whites and that this self-understanding is fully validated.

Furthermore, he feels that he is able to understand himself as biracial when he is in a hetero-geneous group, and that self-understanding is also validated. For Mike, any social situation must be assessed for what identity will "work," and then that particular identity is presented. Is this shape shifting viewed as problematic for him? On the contrary, he views his ability effectively to possess, present, and have different identities accepted as authentic by different groups of people as the "gift of being biracial."

Respondents like Mike understand biracial identity as their protean capacity to move among cultural contexts.[19] Their self-understanding of biracialism is directly tied to their ability to cross boundaries between black, white, and biracial, which is possible because they possess black, white, and biracial identities. These individuals feel endowed with a degree of cultural savvy in several social worlds and understand biracialism as the way in which they are accepted, however condition-ally, in varied interactional settings. They believe their dual experiences with both whites and blacks have given them the ability to shift their identity according to the context of any particular interaction. This contextual shifting leads individuals to form a belief that their multiple racial backgrounds are but one piece of a complex self composed of assorted identifications that are not culturally integrated. When the topic of racial identification was initially broached with Mike, he said, "Well, shit, it depends on what day it is and where I'm goin'."

The understanding of biracialism as the ability to be black, white, and/or biracial in different contexts has been discussed by several multiracial researchers.[20] Root, although not using the term *protean*, briefly discussed this option as one where individuals have "fluidity"; however, she says no more and does not separate these individuals out as any different from the border/biracial option.[21] In her later work, Root describes these individuals as having "both feet in both groups."[22] Both Root and Cookie Stephan have depicted this shifting as practicing "situational race."[23] Daniel alluded to the protean option when he discussed those who had an "Integrative Identity," individuals who reference themselves *simultaneously* in black and white communities.[24] This is different from the border identity, in that those individuals typically seek biracial communities and networks. Daniel makes a further distinction into two subtypes: (a) a synthesized integrative identity, where individuals feel equally comfortable in both black and white cultural settings; and (b) a functional integrative identity, where individuals are able to identify and function in both communities but feel a stronger orientation to, acceptance in, and comfort with either blacks or whites. Empirically, Tizard and Phoenix's study of mixed-race individuals in Great Britain found that 10 percent of respondents said they were black "in some situations," whereas another 10 percent felt they were white "in some situations."[25] Robin Miller also briefly mentions that it is probable that many biracials have fluid identities that adjust to their surroundings and social contexts.[26]

Understanding biracialism as a protean identity was the least frequent choice made by the mixed-race people we surveyed. Only 4 percent of the respondents selected this option when asked about their identity. Despite the small number of our respondents who chose this identity option, it is one that is of great theoretical interest, given the persistent self-monitoring of the actors' presentation of self and their purposive manipulation of appearance.

A Transcendent Identity

Rob was in his senior year of college when we arranged to meet in a coffee shop on campus. Typically, when I arrived, I could pick out my interviewee immediately. When I went to meet Rob, however, I couldn't tell who I was supposed to meet, because everyone in the coffee shop looked white. Finally, a tall young man came up to my table and asked if we were supposed to meet for an interview; he had been watching me look around for him all along. I told him immediately that he didn't look mixed, and he responded, "Neither do you. I just saw you looking around the room and figured you were the person I was supposed to meet." This first incident in our meeting is illustrative of our conversation about race and identity because it reveals both Rob's and my own construction of reality. Throughout our interview, I stayed locked in a social world that is perceived through the lens of race, and Rob consistently and repeatedly questioned my "fixation."

Rob was born and raised in a medium-size midwestern city. His parents were both teachers, and he had several brothers and sisters. He recalled growing up in an intellectually stimulating household, where parents and siblings were encouraged to read, write, and discuss political and social matters openly. Rob attended an integrated public school and found friendship within diverse circles. Rob was adamant that race was a false categorization of humanity and did not want to be thought of as a member of any racial category whatsoever. Rob's greatest desire was to be understood by others as the unique individual he was, to be appreciated for his particular gifts and talents, and not to be "pigeon-holed" into a preformulated category that carried with it a multitude of assumptions about the content of his character. Rob was not black, white, or biracial. He was a musician, a thinker, a kind-hearted individual, a good friend, a Catholic, and a hard-working student with dreams and ambitions. For Rob, race had interfered with others perceiving his authentic self, and he could see that it would continue to color how others viewed him, his work, and his personal talents in the future.

After conducting the first round of interviews, Rob was given a transcript of our interview and a draft of a conference paper that was in progress based on our data analysis. He contacted us shortly thereafter to ask if we could meet again. At that time, we had only conceptualized three of the identity options we ultimately determined (the border, singular, and protean identities). He confronted us with the fact that he didn't see himself in any of these categories and that he resented being either falsely stuffed into a rigid and unrepresentative typology or being excluded as an "outlying case." After a lengthy discussion, we were forced to rethink the initial grouping and added this additional type of understanding that race has for biracial individuals. We call this nonracial self-understanding the transcendent identity.

The literature on biracial identity has been remarkably silent on this option for black/white biracial individuals. The transcendent identity, as described here, is noteworthy because these individuals claim to opt out of the categorization game altogether. Only Daniel recognizes that being biracial could produce a transcendent understanding of the self when he argues that individuals who possess both "pluralistic" (neither black, white, nor necessarily biracial) and "integrative" (a blending of black and white) identities can display transcendent characteristics.[27] He suggests that the transcendent phenomenon is more likely to be found among biracial people who identify with and reference themselves in both white and black communities in roughly equal amounts than among those who feel more comfortable in the company of other mixed-race people.

After examining the survey data, it became clear that some individuals understood their biracialism as transcendent and similar to Robert Park's classic conception of the "marginal man."[28] In other words, their status as biracial provided them with the perspective of the stranger. They perceived their detached, outsiders' perspective as enabling them to objectively articulate the social meaning placed on race and discount it as a "master status" altogether. These individuals responded to questions about their identity with answers that were unrelated to their racial status, as in the following example:

> I'm just John, you know. I never thought this was such a big deal to be identified, I just figured I'm a good guy, just like me for that, you know. But, when I came here [to college], it was like I was almost forced to look at people as being white, black, Asian, or Hispanic. And so now, I'm still trying to go "I'm just John," but uh, you gotta be something.

This respondent later talked about "using" race (to benefit others as a mentor or role model) in a way that suggested it was not only a pliable category that a person could fit into at will but, more important, that its reality was highly questionable. Slightly less than 13 percent of our total sample understood being biracial as a transcendent identity.[29]

The transcendent identity seems, at first glance, to negate the theoretical framework of identity construction that we have proposed. How can an individual exist in a racially stratified society and have a nonracial identity validated? However, a closer look at the social psychological processes involved in the construction of these individuals' racial identities (or lack thereof) actually underscores the importance of validation as an indispensable mechanism of identity maintenance. If, in fact, individuals who have this self-understanding truly possess the perspective of the stranger, then validation is meaningless. In other words, if individuals perceive themselves to have no racial identity and consciously view the existing system of racial classification as biologically baseless, yet symbolically meaningful to other members of society, then their participation in that system is equally meaningless to their individual self-understanding. To be explicit, if there is no racial identity to be validated, then the lack of validation for that identity is meaningless. For our respondents, claiming an identity on a form is simply filling out a box, devoid of any reflection of their personal self-understanding. Experiences of discrimination, perceived from the standpoint of the stranger, neither reinforce nor negate their existing sense of self. Respondents who chose the transcendent identity seemed content to be at the periphery of a racially divided America, annoyed by the inconveniences yet playing their role when necessary.

DISCUSSION

Many researchers and multiracial advocates have assumed that mixed-race people share a singular understanding of what biracial identity means. Specifically, contemporary researchers have assumed that biracial identity is equivalent to the border identity, treating it as an idea for which a conceptual definition is unnecessary. A common assumption is that members of this population hold a clear and unified understanding of what biracial identity means and how that term translates into a racial self-understanding and/or group affiliation.[30] Both the in-depth interviews and survey data suggest that this is a misguided assumption because what it means to be biracial is conceptually complex and varies among biracial respondents. In other words, an analysis of the data suggests there is no singular understanding among black/white mixed-race people as to what biracial identity means or how it translates into an individual self-understanding.

NOTES

1. Although a compromise was adopted allowing respondents to check all racial categories that apply, for civil rights monitoring and enforcement, the data are collapsed back into the previously established five-category system with the addition of the four most common double-race combinations. See Jacob Lew, "Guidance on Aggregation and Allocation of Data on Race for Use in Civil Rights Monitoring and Enforcement," *OMB Bulletin* No. 00–02, 2000.

2. For statistical data on interracial marriages, see Bureau of the Census, *Statistical Abstract of the United States* (Washington, D.C.: Government Printing Office, 1998), Table 67. See also David Harris and Hiromi Ono, "Estimating the Extent of Intimate Contact Between the Races: The Role of Metropolitan Area Factors and Union Type in Mate Selection" (paper presented at the Meetings of the Population Association of America, Los Angeles, 2000), and Susan Kalish, "Interracial Baby Boomlet in Progress?" *Population Today* 20 (1992): 1–2, 9.

3. This description of the multiracial movement is meant to provide an overview of the main arguments presented in favor of adding a multiracial category to the 2000 census. It is admittedly general, and readers interested in a thorough analysis of the multiracial movement should see Heather Dalmage, *The Politics of Multiracialism* (Albany: State University of New York Press, forthcoming).

4. Joel Perlmann, " 'Multiracials', Racial Classification, and American Intermarriage: The Public's Interest" (Working Paper No. 195, The Jerome Levy Economics Institute of Bard College, 1997).

5. Molefi Kete Asante, "Racing to Leave the Race: Black Postmodernists Off-Track," *Black Scholar* 23 (Spring/Fall 1993), 50–51. Reprinted with permission.

6 See, for example, Lisa Jones, *Bulletproof Diva: Tales of Race, Sex, and Hair* (New York: Doubleday, 1994); James McBride, *The Color of Water: A Black Man's Tribute to His White Mother* (New York: Riverhead Books, 1996); Judy Scales-Trent, *Notes of a White Black Woman* (University Park: Pennsylvania State University Press, 1995); and Gregory Williams, *Life on the Color Line: The True Story of a White Boy Who Discovered He Was Black* (New York: Dutton, 1995).

7. All names are pseudonyms.

8. Gloria Anzaldua, *Borderlands/La Frontera: The New Mestiza* (San Francisco: Spinsters/Aunt Lute Foundation, 1987).

9. Bowles, "Bi-racial Identity"; Philip Brown, "Biracial Identity and Social Marginality," *Child and Adolescent Social Work Journal 7* (1990): 319–37; G. Reginald Daniel, "Black and White Identity in the New Millennium: Unsevering the Ties That Bind," in *The Multiracial Experience: Racial Borders as the New Frontier*, ed. Maria Root (Thousand Oaks, Calif.: Sage, 1996); Field, "Piecing Together the Puzzle"; Christine Hall, "The Ethnic Identity of Racially Mixed People: A Study of Black-Japanese" (Ph.D. diss., University of California, Los Angeles, 1980); Herring, "Developing Biracial Ethnic Identity"; Poston, "The Biracial Identity Development Model"; and Gibbs, "Biracial Adolescents."

10. Herring, "Developing Biracial Ethnic Identity"; Deborah Johnson, "Developmental Pathways: Toward an Ecological Theoretical Formulation of Race Identity in Black-White Biracial Children," in *Racially Mixed People in America*, ed. Maria Root (Newbury Park, Calif.: Sage, 1992); Kerwin et al., "Racial Identity in Biracial Children"; George Kich, "The Developmental Process of Asserting a Biracial, Bicultural Identity," in *Racially Mixed People in America*, ed. Maria Root (Newbury Park, Calif.: Sage, 1992); Poston, "The Biracial Identity Development Model"; Francis Wardle, "Are We Sensitive to Interracial Children's Special Identity Needs?" *Young Children* 43 (1987): 53–59; and Francis Wardle, *Biracial Identity: An Ecological and Developmental Model* (Denver, CO: Center for the Study of Biracial Children, 1992).

11. Hall, *The Ethnic Identity of Racially Mixed People.*

12. Barbara Tizard and Ann Phoenix, "The Identity of Mixed Parentage Adolescents," *Journal of Child Psychology and Psychiatry* 36 (1995): 1399–1410.

13. Daniel, "Black and White Identity," 133.

14. Carla Bradshaw, "Beauty and the Beast: On Racial Ambiguity," in *Racially Mixed People in America*, ed. Maria Root (Newbury Park, Calif.: Sage, 1992); Field, "Piecing Together the Puzzle"; Rebecca King and Kimberly DaCosta, "Changing Face, Changing Race: The Remaking of Race in the Japanese American and African American Communities," in *The Multiracial Experience*, ed. Maria Root (Thousand Oaks, Calif.: Sage, 1996); Williams, "Race as Process."

15. Herring, "Developing Biracial Ethnic Identity"; Johnson, "Developmental Pathways"; Kerwin et al., "Racial Identity in Biracial Children"; Kich, "The Developmental Process"; Poston, "The Biracial Identity Development Model"; Wardle, "Are We Sensitive?"; Wardle, *Biracial Identity*.

16. All interviews presented in this chapter were conducted by Kerry Ann Rockquemore. The vignettes are taken from interviewer notes, hence the use of *I* as opposed to *we*.

17. Maria Root, "Resolving 'Other' Status: Identity Development of Biracial Individuals," *Women and Therapy* 9 (1990): 185–205; Root, "The Multiracial Experience."

18. Root, "Resolving 'Other' Status," 588.

19. Robert Lifton, *The Protean Self: Human Resilience in an Age of Fragmentation* (New York: Basic Books, 1993).

20. Daniel, "Black and White Identity"; Robin Miller, "The Human Ecology of Multiracial Identity," in *Racially Mixed People in America*, ed. Maria Root (Newbury Park, Calif.: Sage, 1992); Root, "Resolving 'Other' Status"; Tizard and Phoenix, "The Identity of Mixed Parentage Adolescents."

21. Root, "Resolving 'Other' Status."

22. Ibid., xxi.

23. Cookie Stephan, "Mixed-Heritage Individuals: Ethnic Identity and Trait Characteristics," in *Racially Mixed People in America*, ed. Maria Root (Newbury Park, Calif.: Sage, 1992); Root, "Resolving 'Other' Status."

24. Daniel, "Black and White Identity."

25. Tizard and Phoenix, "The Identity of Mixed Parentage Adolescents."

26. Miller, "The Human Ecology of Multiracial Identity."

27. Daniel, "Black and White Identity."

28. Park, *Race and Culture*.

29. The total percentage of our respondents falling into each of the four identity types does not total 100 percent because we provided individuals with the option of writing in their own response to our survey question on racial identity. Only 8 percent of respondents chose to write in something other than what was provided. Many of the write-in responses were subtle variations of the options we provided and could have been collapsed back into the categories presented in this chapter. However, we chose not to do this and treated these cases as missing data. The fact that 92 percent of our sample found the range of responses we provided accurately described their racial identity lends support to the authenticity of our multidimensional model of racial identity among biracial people.

30. Bradshaw, "Beauty and the Beast"; Field, "Piecing Together the Puzzle"; King and DaCosta, "Changing Face, Changing Race"; and Williams, "Race as Process."

VI

RECOGNIZING DIVERSITY,
BUILDING SOLIDARITY:
INTEGRATING RACE AND
CLASS ISSUES INTO
PUBLIC POLICY

33

The Color of Family Ties
Race, Class, Gender, and Extended Family Involvement

Naomi Gerstel and Natalia Sarkisian

When talking about family obligations and solidarities, politicians and social commentators typically focus on the ties between married couples and their children. We often hear that Black and Latino/a, especially Puerto Rican, families are more disorganized than White families, and that their family ties are weaker, because rates of non-marriage and single parenthood are higher among these minority groups. But this focus on the nuclear family ignores extended family solidarities and caregiving activities. Here we examine these often overlooked extended kinship ties.[1]

Taking this broader perspective on family relations refutes the myth that Blacks and Latinos/as lack strong families. Minority individuals are more likely to live in extended family homes than Whites and in many ways more likely to help out their aging parents, grandparents, adult children, brothers, sisters, cousins, aunts, uncles, and other kin.

According to our research using the second wave of the National Survey of Families and Households, as Figures 33.1 and 33.2 show, Blacks and Latinos/as, both women and men, are much more likely than Whites to share a home with extended kin: 42 percent of Blacks and 37 percent of Latinos/as, but only 20 percent of Whites, live with relatives. Similar patterns exist for living near relatives: 54 percent of Blacks and 51 percent of Latinos/as, but only 37 percent of Whites, live within two miles of kin. Blacks and Latinos/as are also more likely than Whites to frequently visit kin. For example, 76 percent of Blacks, 71 percent of Latinos/as, but just 63 percent of Whites see their relatives once a week or more.

Even if they don't live together, Blacks and Latinos/as are as likely as Whites—and in some ways more likely—to be supportive family members. But there are important racial and ethnic differences in the type of support family members give each other. Whites are more likely than ethnic minorities to give and receive large sums of money, and White women are more likely than minority women to give and receive emotional support, such as discussing personal problems and giving each other advice. When it comes to help with practical tasks, however, we find that Black and Latino/a relatives are more likely than Whites to be supportive: they are more likely to give each other help with household work and childcare, as well as with providing rides and running errands. These differences are especially pronounced among women.

This is not to say that Black and Latino men are not involved with kin, as is implied in popular images of minority men hanging out on street corners rather than attending to family ties. In fact,

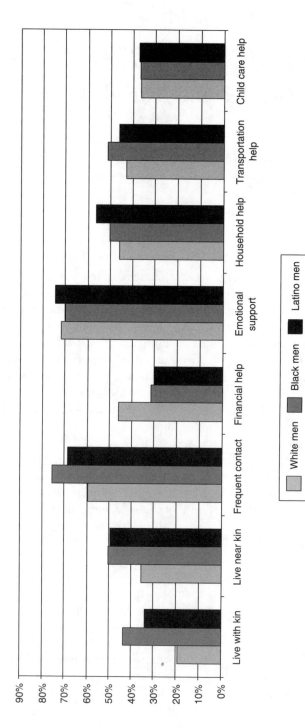

Figure 33.1 Ethnicity and extended kin involvement among men
Source: National Survey of Families and Households, 1992–94.

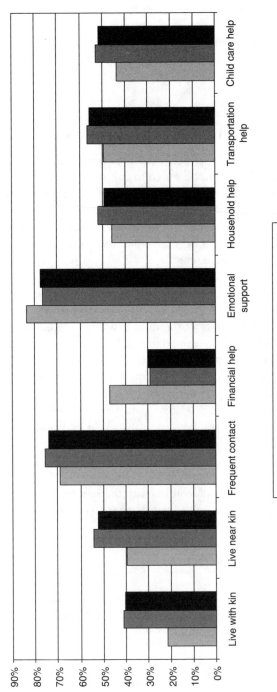

Figure 33.2 Ethnicity and extended kin involvement among women
Source: National Survey of Families and Households, 1992–94.

Black and Latino men are more likely than White men to live near relatives and to stay in touch with them. White men, however, are more likely to give and receive large-scale financial help. Moreover, the three groups of men are very similar when it comes to giving and getting practical help and emotional support.

These data suggest that if we only consider married couples or parents and their young children, we are missing much of what families in general and families of color in particular do for each other. A focus on nuclear families in discussions of race differences in family life creates a biased portrait of families of color.

EXPLAINING RACE DIFFERENCES: IS IT CULTURE OR CLASS?

When discussing differences in family experiences of various racial and ethnic groups, commentators often assume that these differences can be traced to cultural differences or competing "family values." Sometimes these are expressed in a positive way, as in the stereotype that Latino families have more extended ties because of their historical traditions and religious values. Other times these are expressed in a negative way, as when Blacks are said to lack family values because of the cultural legacy of slavery and subsequent years of oppression. Either way, differences in family behaviors are often explained by differences in cultural heritage.

In contrast, in our research, we find that social class rather than culture is the key to understanding the differences in extended family ties and behaviors between Whites and ethnic minorities. To be sure, differences in cultural values do exist. Blacks and Latinos/as are more likely than Whites to say they believe that extended family is important; both groups are also more likely to attend religious services. Blacks tend to hold more egalitarian beliefs about gender than Whites, while Latinos/as, especially Mexican Americans, tend to hold more "traditional" views. But these differences in values do not explain racial differences in actual involvement with relatives. It is, instead, social class that matters most in explaining these differences.

It is widely known (and confirmed by U.S. Census data presented in Table 33.1) that Blacks and Latinos/as tend to have far less income and education than Whites. Families of color are also are much more likely than White families to be below the official poverty line. In our research, we find that the differences in extended family ties and behaviors between Whites and ethnic minorities are primarily the result of these social class disparities.

Simply put, White, Black, and Latino/a individuals with the same amount of income and education have similar patterns of involvement with their extended families. Just like poor minorities,

Table 33.1 Education, Income, and Poverty Rates by Race.

	Whites	Blacks	Latinos/as
Median household income	$50,784	$30,858	$35,967
Percentage below poverty line	8.4%	24.7%	22.0%
Education:			
Less than high school	14.5%	27.6%	47.6%
High school graduate	58.5%	58.1%	42.0%
Bachelor's degree or higher	27.0%	14.3%	10.4%

Source: U.S. Census Bureau, 2005.

impoverished Whites are more likely to exchange practical aid and visit with extended kin than are their wealthier counterparts. Just like middle-class Whites, middle-class Blacks and Latinos/as are more likely to talk about their personal concerns or share money with relatives than are their poorer counterparts.

More specifically, it is because Whites tend to have more income than Blacks and Latinos/as that they are more likely to give money to their relatives or get it from them. And the higher levels of emotional support among White women can be at least in part traced to their higher levels of education, perhaps because schooling encourages women to talk out their problems and makes them more likely to give (and get) advice.

Conversely, we find that the relative economic deprivation of racial/ethnic minorities leads in many ways to higher levels of extended family involvement. Individuals' lack of economic resources increases their need for help from kin and boosts their willingness to give help in return. Because Blacks and Latinos/as typically have less income and education than Whites, they come to rely more on their relatives for daily needs such as child care, household tasks, or rides. The tendency of Blacks and Latinos/as to live with or near kin may also reflect their greater need for kin cooperation, as well as their decreased opportunities and pressures to move away, including moving for college.

SOCIAL CLASS AND FAMILIAL TRADE OFFS

How do our findings on race, social class, and familial involvement challenge common under-standings of minority families? They show that poor minority families do not necessarily lead lives of social isolation or lack strong family solidarities. The lower rates of marriage among impoverished groups may reflect not a rejection of family values but a realistic assessment of how little a woman (and her children) may be able to depend upon marriage. Sociologists Kathryn Edin and Maria Kefalas (2007) recently found that because disadvantaged men are often unable to offer women the kind of economic security that advantaged men provide, poor women are less likely to marry. Instead, these women create support networks beyond the nuclear family, regularly turning to extended kin for practical support.

Reliance on extended kin and lack of marital ties are linked. In another analysis of the National Survey of Families and Households, we found that, contrary to much rhetoric about marriage as a key source of adult social ties, marriage actually diminishes ties to kin. Married people—women as well as men—are less involved with their parents and siblings than those never married or previously married. These findings indicate a trade off between commitments to nuclear and extended family ties. Marriage, we have found, is a "greedy" institution: it has a tendency to consume the bulk of people's energies and emotions and to dilute their commitments beyond the nuclear family.

On the one hand, then, support given to spouses and intimate partners sometimes comes at the expense of broader kin and community ties. Indeed, married adult children take care of elderly parents less often than their unmarried siblings. Marriage can also cut people off from networks of mutual aid. Married mothers, for example, whether Black, Latina, or White, are often unable to obtain help from kin in the way that their single counterparts can. Although the "greedy" nature of marriage may pose a problem across social class, it is especially problematic for those less well off economically, as these individuals most need to cultivate wider circles of obligation, mutual aid, and reciprocity.

On the other hand, support to relatives sometimes comes at the expense of care for partners, and can interfere with nuclear family formation or stability. Indeed, individuals who are deeply immersed in relationships with extended families may be less likely to get married or, if they marry, may be less likely to put the marital ties first in their loyalties. Several decades ago in her observations of a poor Black community, anthropologist Carol Stack (1974) found that the reciprocal patterns of sharing with kin and "fictive kin" forged in order to survive hardship often made it difficult for poor Blacks either to move up economically or to marry. To prevent the dilution of their social support networks, some extended families may even discourage their members from getting married, or unconsciously sabotage relationships that threaten to pull someone out of the family orbit. As sociologists Domínguez and Watkins (2003) argue, the ties of mutual aid that help impoverished individuals survive on a day-to-day basis may also prevent them from saying "no" to requests that sap their ability to get ahead or pursue individual opportunities.

Overall, we should avoid either denigrating or glorifying the survival strategies of the poor. Although social class disparities are key to understanding racial and ethnic variation in familial involvement, it is too simple to say that class differences create "more" involvement with relatives in one group and "less" in another. In some ways economic deprivation increases ties to kin (e.g., in terms of living nearby or exchanging practical help) and in other ways it reduces them (e.g., in terms of financial help or emotional support). These findings remind us that love and family connections are expressed both through talk and action. Equally important, focusing solely on the positive or on the negative aspects of either minority or White families is problematic. Instead, we need to think in terms of trade offs—among different kinds of care and between the bonds of kinship and the bonds of marriage. Both trade offs are linked to social class.

WHY DO THESE DIFFERENCES IN FAMILY LIFE MATTER?

Commentators often emphasize the disorganization and dysfunction of Black and Latino/a family life. They suggest that if we could "fix" family values in minority communities and get them to form married-couple households, all their problems would be solved. This argument misunderstands causal connections by focusing on the family as the source of problems. Specifically, it ignores the link between race and class and attributes racial or ethnic differences to cultural values. Instead, we argue, it is important to understand that family strategies and behaviors often emerge in response to the challenges of living in economic deprivation or constant economic insecurity. Therefore, social policies should not focus on changing family behaviors, but rather aim to support a range of existing family arrangements and improve economic conditions for the poor.

Social policies that overlook extended family obligations may introduce, reproduce, or even increase ethnic inequalities. For example, the relatives of Blacks and Latinos/as are more likely than those of Whites to provide various kinds of support that policymakers tend to assume is only provided by husbands and wives. Such relatives may need the rights and support systems that we usually reserve for spouses. For instance, the Family and Medical Leave Act is an important social policy, but it only guarantees unpaid leave from jobs to provide care to spouses, children or elderly parents requiring medical attention. Our findings suggest that, if we really want to support families, such policies must be broadened to include adult children, needy grown-up brothers and sisters, cousins, aunts and uncles. Similarly, Medicaid regulations that only pay for non-familial care of ill, injured, or disabled individuals implicitly discriminate against Blacks and Latinos/as who provide significant amounts of care to extended kin. "Pro-marriage" policies that give special incentives to impoverished women for getting married may penalize other women who turn down marriage to a risky mate and rely instead on grandparents or other relatives to help raise their children.

Extended family obligations should be recognized and accommodated where possible. But they should not be counted on as a substitute for anti-poverty measures, nor should marriage promotion be used in this way. Policymakers must recognize that support from family—whether extended or nuclear—cannot fully compensate for the disadvantages of being poor, or minority, or both. Neither marital ties nor extended family ties can substitute for educational opportunities, jobs with decent wages, health insurance, and affordable child care. Instead of hoping that poor families pull themselves out of poverty by their own bootstraps, social policy should explicitly aim to rectify economic disadvantages. In turn, improvements in economic opportunities and resources will likely shape families.

NOTE

1. For the extensive analysis underlying this discussion, see: (1) Natalia Sarkisian, Mariana Gerena, and Naomi Gerstel, "Extended Family Integration among Mexican and Euro Americans: Ethnicity, Gender, and Class," *Journal of Marriage and Family*, 69 (2007), 1 (February), 40–54. (2) Natalia Sarkisian, Mariana Gerena, and Naomi Gerstel, "Extended Family Ties among Mexicans, Puerto Ricans and Whites: Superintegration or Disintegration?," *Family Relations*, 55 (2006), 3 (July), 331–344. (3) Natalia Sarkisian and Naomi Gerstel, "Kin Support Among Blacks and Whites: Race and Family Organization," *American Sociological Review*, 69 (2004), 4 (December), 812–837. (4) Amy Armenia and Naomi Gerstel, "Family Leaves, The FMLA, and Gender Neutrality: The Intersection of Race and Gender," *Social Science Research*, 35 (2006), 871–891. (5) Naomi Gerstel and Natalia Sarkisian, "A Sociological Perspective on Families and Work: The Import of Gender, Class, and Race," in Marcie Pitt Catsouphes, Ellen Kossek, and Steven Sweet (eds.), *The Work and Family Handbook: Multi-disciplinary Perspectives, Methods, and Approaches* (Mahwah, NJ: Lawrence Erlbaum, 2006), pp. 237–266. (6) Naomi Gerstel and Natalia Sarkisian, "Marriage: The Good, the Bad, and the Greedy," *Contexts*, 5 (2006) 4 (November), 16–21. (7) Naomi Gerstel and Natalia Sarkisian, "Intergenerational Care and the Greediness of Adult Children's Marriages," in J. Suitor and T. Owens (eds.), *Interpersonal Relations across the Life Course. Advances in the Life Course Research, Volume 12.* (Greenwich, CT: Elsevier/JAI Press, 2007).

REFERENCES

Domínguez, Silvia, and Celeste Watkins "Creating Networks for Survival and Mobility: Examining Social Capital Amongst Low-Income African-American and Latin-American Mothers." *Social Problems*, 50 (2003), 1(February), 111–135.

Edin, Kathryn, and Kefalas, Maria *Promises I Can Keep: Why Poor Women Put Motherhood Before Marriage.* (Berkeley, CA: University of California Press, 2007).

Stack, Carol B. *All Our Kin: Strategies for Survival in a Black Community.* (New York: Harper and Row, 1974).

34

Work and American Families
Diverse Needs, Common Solutions

JERRY A. JACOBS AND KATHLEEN GERSON

MANY AMERICAN FAMILIES FIND their lives increasingly rushed. The tempo may vary from steady to hectic to frantic, but a large and growing group perceives that life moves at a faster pace than it did for previous generations. Are these perceptions accurate? And, if they are, what has caused this speed up in the pace of life? In this chapter, we address the thicket of competing claims about whether or not daily life has become more hurried and less leisurely, and, if so, whether "overwork" is the main culprit creating this dilemma. Is the shortage of "time for life" real, or is it yet another example of an ambiguous and isolated social trend that has become exaggerated by anecdotal reporting and a lack of historical perspective?

In important ways, these questions—and the prevailing answers—are too simple. No one trend can adequately portray the complicated changes taking place in the American labor force and among American households. A more accurate account must recognize the diversity among workers and their families. In our study of how American working time has changed and how these changes have created new work–family conflicts for women and men, we drew on information from the *Current Population Survey* to compare the weekly working hours of U.S. workers in 2000 with those of workers in 1970.[1] These comparisons show that while one large segment of the labor force *is* working longer and harder than ever, another group of workers confronts the challenge of finding enough work. There are thus two aspects of the growing time divide. In its most obvious form, Americans are increasingly torn between commitments to work and to family life. Less apparent, however, are the ways in which the American labor force is diverging as some workers face increasing demands on their time and others struggle to find enough work to meet their own and their families' needs. Once this divergence is acknowledged, the discrepant claims about whether Americans are working more or enjoying more leisure can be resolved.

For a growing group of American families, feelings of overwork are real and well founded. Workers in these households are putting in very long hours at work. And even those not working especially long hours are facing new time squeezes as they cope with the challenges of managing a two-earner or a single-parent household. The lack of time for family life is not simply a matter of questionable choices made by some individuals, but instead reflects the way people's choices are constrained and deformed by our economy and the structure of our work organizations. The experience of feeling squeezed for time reflects fundamental and enduring changes in the nature and composition of American society. From this perspective, the scarcity of time for the tasks of daily life is not just a personal problem, but a public issue of great importance.

OUR OVERLAPPING TIME DIVIDES

Contrary to widespread belief, the average American work week has not changed dramatically over the last several decades. This does not mean that people's perception of not having enough time for family life is not real, but it does suggest that focusing only on the problem of long work weeks is not the only policy response required to meet the needs of today's diverse families.

A growing group of Americans are clearly and strongly pressed for time. These workers include employees who are putting in especially long hours, often against their own desires, and people in dual-earner and single-parent families who cannot rely on a support system anchored by a "stay-at-home" member. Women and men alike increasingly face challenging work without the "wives" once taken for granted by husbands in upwardly mobile careers and highly demanding jobs. Yet employers have not responded to these changed realities, assuming that devoted workers have—or should have—unpaid partners able to devote full-time to the myriad of domestic tasks on which not only family life but successful careers and secure communities depend. In the context of these dramatic social shifts in Americans' private lives, it is no surprise that many Americans *feel* that they are squeezed for time and working more than ever. The rise of highly demanding jobs, especially at the upper levels of the occupational hierarchy, and the lack of change in the structure of work pose dilemmas for many workers.

A "time bind" has clearly emerged in the contemporary United States. However, it has two different sources. For many workers, the time bind is rooted as much in the changing nature of family life and women's commitments as in the expansion of working time for individuals. Working parents in dual-earner and single-parent households have always faced a time bind, and the principal change over the last 30 years has been a marked growth in the number of people living in these family situations.

Other workers do face a time squeeze created by spending longer hours at paid work. This problem, however, is not universal, but rather concentrated among the professionals and managers who are especially likely to shape the terms of public discussion and debate. Although there are also blue-collar workers who put in substantial overtime or who work at two (or more) jobs (see Ryan, this volume), the highest proportion of extended-hour workers is found among professionals and managers. In addressing the new challenges and insecurities facing American workers and their families, we should be careful to move beyond generalizations about the "average" worker to focus on the variety of dilemmas workers are facing.

The Occupational Divide and the Bifurcation of the Labor Market

Even though the average working time of individuals has increased only slightly, important changes have nevertheless occurred in the American labor force. The continuity of the "average" work week obscures a new divergence between extremes at both ends of the spectrum. We have found a growing divide between those who are putting in very long hours at the workplace and those who are not able to work as many hours as they need. An occupational divide is developing between jobs that demand excessive time commitments and jobs that may not offer sufficient time at work to meet workers' needs or preferences.

Long work weeks are most common among male professionals and managers. Almost 40 percent of men (37.2 percent, to be exact) who work in professional, technical, or managerial occupations work 50 hours or more per week, compared to one in five (21.3 percent) in other occupations. For women, the comparable figures are one in six for the professional and managerial positions versus less than one in fourteen for other occupations.

The changes in working time are connected to race as well, but to a smaller degree. And the race difference varies by gender. White men work two hours more per week on average than do Black, Hispanic or Asian-American men. These differences are most pronounced among those working 50 hours per week or more.[2]

For women, the story is reversed. Among women of similar ages, educational backgrounds, marital statuses, and occupational positions, White women work two hours less per week than Asian-American women and one hour less than Black women, and put in about the same number of hours per week on the job as do their Hispanic counterparts. Since they are more likely to be highly educated and to hold professional and managerial positions where working hours are longest, White women might be expected to work longer hours. Their higher participation in part-time work, however, offsets this effect and lowers their overall average.[3]

What factors are promoting the bifurcation of working time? At one end of the spectrum, employers have an incentive in encouraging long hours from salaried workers, who receive no additional earnings for the extra time they may be persuaded—or required—to work (see Landers, Rebitzer and Taylor, 1996). In addition, the segment of the labor force most at risk for these heavy time demands has grown markedly. When the Fair Labor Standards Act was passed in 1938, it hardly seemed necessary to protect the one in seven workers (or 14.8 percent of the labor) who were classified as professionals or managers. By 1995, however, that proportion had doubled to nearly two in seven (28.3 percent). The labor force now has a substantial number of workers who do not earn extra pay for "additional" time at work.

The costs of the most expensive fringe benefits, such as healthcare, are fixed for a full-time worker no matter how many hours he or she works. As the cost of these benefits has risen (especially as a proportion of total compensation), employers find it tempting to push full-time workers toward longer working hours. For all these reasons, employers face rising incentives to pressure salaried workers to put in more than the once obligatory forty-hour work week and to use working time as a measure of work commitment and a basis for promotions and raises.

Once long hours become the expected norm, informal rules develop that change the meaning of working time. More than just a way to earn a living, working time becomes suffused with moral meaning, and employers begin to equate time at work with career commitment. Time on the job comes to represent work devotion and organizational loyalty, and long hours may persist even if they are not the most efficient way of organizing work (Blair-Loy, 2003). Those who choose to put in fewer hours then run the risk of being branded "deviants" who depart from accepted "time norms" and are thus not worthy of serious consideration for advancement (Epstein et al., 1999).

At the other end of the occupational spectrum, those who are paid by the hour face a different situation. Especially when additional working time produces a sharp increase in hourly pay (such as time-and-a-half payments for working more than a forty hour week), employers may be less likely to demand long work weeks.[4] The rising cost of benefits, which adds to the appeal of extracting long hours from salaried workers, also makes it attractive to employ part-time workers. Since part-time workers are rarely offered a benefits package, part-time employment can substantially reduce labor costs. The creation of part-time jobs with low pay and few benefits may, in turn, force many workers to take several jobs to stay afloat, ultimately lengthening their work weeks as well. The high cost of benefits thus tends to enhance the attraction of both long and short work weeks, depending on the type of occupation, without reducing the pressures on workers at either end.

Since the early 1980s, downsizing has become a common response to the growing pressures of international competition, as well as a speedy way to cut costs and increase profits. Yet rather than producing across-the-board increases in working time, downsizing has had different consequences for different levels of the occupational ladder. At the highest levels, the ranks of professionals and managers have often been trimmed, with those left behind expected to pick up the slack and put in more time. At lower levels, however, reducing jobs and outsourcing have superseded efforts to extend the work week. A general increase in the intensity of work thus does not automatically produce across-the-board increases in working time. A set of economic and social forces are encouraging the growth of jobs built on the premise of both long *and* short work weeks. While well-educated and highly trained workers who earn salaries may be facing increased pressure to put in long hours at the office, those with less secure jobs, such as hourly workers, part-time employees, and contingent workers, may have a difficult time getting the amount of work they desire, even though these workers may also face intensified pressures during the time they spend on the job. (See, for example, Pfeffer and Baron, 1988; Gordon, 1996; Ryan, this volume.)

Time demands, like other work-related opportunities and pressures, are not distributed equally across the labor force. The growing bifurcation into longer and shorter work weeks reminds us that the labor force consists of a diverse collection of workers. Any policy response needs to take account of the varying pressures, constraints, and contingencies attached to different jobs.

The Aspiration Divide and the Gap Between Ideals and Options

The increasing bifurcation of the labor force has engendered another time divide between the kinds of schedules workers desire and the options available to them. Especially at the extremes of the working time spectrum, the supply of jobs available neither reflects nor fits well with workers' preferences and needs. At both ends of this continuum, workers report a significant gap between their ideal and actual working conditions. Those putting in very long hours wish to work less, and those putting in relatively short hours wish to work more. While the drawbacks of long hours may be most obvious in the current climate, the drawbacks of short hours are equally significant. If current trends continue, we are likely to see a widening gap between those who would prefer to work less and those who wish to work more.

Whatever the benefits to employers, the personal and social costs of long work weeks are becoming increasing obvious. Certainly, they undermine a worker's ability to achieve a reasonable balance between work and home, public and private, earning a living and caring for both self and others. Beyond these personal and family costs, however, there are social costs as well. Robert Putnam (1996, 2000) has called attention to the declining engagement in volunteer groups, civic associations, and other forms of participation in public life. Long work weeks no doubt undermine participation in civil society, especially for those trying to balance jobs and the time-demanding work of rearing children, and as we discuss below, they also undermine the prospects for gender and parenting equality.[5]

At the opposite end of the working time divide, significant personal, familial, and social costs are also linked to overly brief work weeks. Often, these jobs signify underemployment, inadequate income, and financial insecurity. They may also lack the benefits that provide a safety net for workers with full-time jobs. While some part-time workers are making adjustments to meet their family's needs, even workers who spend less than full-time at work may have little flexibility to take needed time in the event of a personal or family illness or other emergency (Heymann, 2000).

Creating opportunities for a more equitable balance between paid work and the rest of life is thus not simply a private issue between employers and employees, but a matter of great public interest. The social need for greater balance can also be found in the personal ideals of workers, whose expressed desires belie the argument that the bifurcation in working time is merely a reflection of individual preferences. To the contrary, most workers aspire to a balance between home and work that eludes them. Many of those putting in very long hours would willingly forgo income and other benefits for the chance to work less and gain greater flexibility in how they use their time. Many of those with short working hours would gladly work longer if the opportunity arose. Workers' needs and desires are often out of sync with job structures and options. This suggests that the labor market, left to its own devices, has not produced the mix of jobs that matches the needs and preferences of the American workforce.[6]

The trend toward a bifurcation in working time neither reflects nor supports workers' desires for a balance between paid work and family time. Effective responses to this growing 'aspiration divide' must focus on establishing reasonable expectations and boundaries for how jobs are structured and rewarded. The public good and the welfare of families depend on creating public policies that promote a level playing field in which employers do not face incentives either to shorten or to extend the work week unduly.

The Gender Divide and the Persistence of Work and Parenting Inequality

The multifaceted time divides between work and family, long and short work weeks, and ideals and aspirations are converging to reinforce a "gender divide" between women and men. This divide takes several forms, all of which recreate older gender inequalities in new and problematic ways.

The bifurcation of the labor force, for example, is not gender neutral. Women are more likely to hold part-time jobs, which may not meet their families' financial needs or provide long-term opportunities for career development. Just as overly long work weeks erode the chances for parenting equality and men's equal family involvement, overly short work weeks—especially for women—can contribute to gender inequality at home and at work by placing pressure on women to take on more of the parenting and housework load. Women work about six hours less per week than men do, on average, and the proportion of women putting in very long hours trails the proportion of men by even more. And since the statistics most often cited on the gender gap in wages adjust for these differences, they capture only a portion of the gender gap in earnings that emerges from differences in working time. Crittenden (2001) endeavors to capture the full loss of wages resulting from motherhood due to reduced work weeks as well as years out of the labor force. She estimates that the cost of becoming a mother in terms of lost lifetime earnings can easily exceed half-a-million dollars for a middle-income woman and well over a million dollars for a woman with a college degree.

On the other side of the occupational divide, jobs requiring excessive time commitments also subvert gender equality. Certainly, the long hours expected of managers and other professionals contribute to the glass ceiling on women's mobility and women's relative absence in the highest echelons of management and the professions. What's more, we found that women holding highly demanding jobs with long working hours are less likely than their male peers to enjoy the flexibility and autonomy to meld heavy work commitments with life outside the office. Women who put in long hours at the workplace are less likely than men with similarly long work days to report that they can exercise a measure of control over their schedules.

It is often said that the imbalances between men and women at home and work are simply the result of their preferences. Men prefer to work long hours; women prefer to spend more time with their families. But we found that both women and men tend to prefer a flexible balance between home and the workplace.[7] While women may wish to work slightly less than men, on average, this small difference is overshadowed by the large diversity within gender categories and by a growing agreement among men and women about what would ease their work–family conflicts. There are many women—and men—who would prefer to blend a thirty- to forty-hour-a-week work career with a rich and committed life outside the office. This balance is unlikely to prove workable, however, in jobs and occupations where fifty to sixty hours is the norm and heavy costs accrue to working less. Workers across the gender divide worry that any time they take for family pursuits will undermine their credibility as committed workers and exact a heavy price in the long run. The new occupational structure allows choices, but for too many these are forced choices between unpalatable alternatives—either too much work or too little.

It is thus highly misleading to equate workers' actions with their preferences. Meyers and Gornick (2003, p. 22) point out that in today's highly constrained environment, "the meaningful question is neither 'What do women and men want?' nor 'What do families want?' but, instead: 'In a much changed world—one where women are fully valued as earners and men as carers, where employment arrangements enable workers to combine employment and parenting, where public policies provide critical supports and incentives for both women and men—would women and men choose differentiated engagements in earning and caring, up through and including their children's teenage years?' " We simply do not know the answer to this question, they conclude, and will not know until public policies supporting a gender-egalitarian society are adopted, implemented, and sustained over time. Only then might we "be able to uncover what it is that women and men—and families—'really want' in relation to earning and caring."

The Parenting Divide and the Penalties of Involved Parenthood

The final divide is the one that separates involved parents from other workers. When it comes to parenting, mothers and fathers alike continue to confront work structures that penalize parental involvement and reinforce parenting inequities. Fathers as well as mothers would like more family-supportive workplaces and would trade other work-related benefits to have them.

The principles of justice and fairness are reason enough to remedy the inequities that continue to divide workers by gender and parental status. Beyond its intrinsic merit, however, equal opportunities for balancing work and parenting are crucial for the welfare of new generations and for the common good. In an era of diverse and changing family arrangements, children increasingly depend on the earnings of women and need to be able to count on a wide net of caretakers, including fathers, mothers, and others. For single mothers, who often are left to provide the lion's share of both breadwinning and caretaking on their own, the need to create both work opportunities and child care support is even more pressing. The precipitous rise of single-parent families headed by fathers, which now account for over 10 percent of all single-parent families, contributes to men's growing desire and need for jobs that do not penalize parental involvement. (See Jacobs and Gerson, chapter 3 and also Fritsch, 2001.) Creating equal opportunities—for women as paid workers and for men as family caretakers—is thus an essential ingredient in the formulation of effective and just social policies.

WHERE DO WE GO FROM HERE?

Time, like money, is a scarce and unequally distributed resource. Although each day contains twenty-four hours and each week consists of seven days, institutional arrangements and personal responsibilities constrain the ways that time can be "spent." Yet today's social arrangements and economic trends pose time constraints and create time dilemmas in different ways for different social groups. In considering the future of family, work, and gender, we thus need to move beyond a focus on individual choices or values to consider the full range and social sources of our multifaceted time divides.

Our economy is producing too much work for some and too little work for others, leaving workers at both ends of the spectrum facing different, but equally severe, difficulties. Neither the structure of work nor the provision of public services has responded sufficiently to the widespread and deeply anchored changes taking place in our gender and family relationships. As a consequence, we face a growing divide not just between family and work, but also between overly-demanding and under-rewarded jobs, between women and men, between parents and other workers, and between workers' aspirations and the options they are offered. Any debate about the changing contours of time use needs to consider not just worker preferences in the context of forced choices but also the fundamental right of workers and parents to meet their own and their families' needs. Resolving our growing time dilemmas requires reconsidering the structure of work and the nature of community responsibility.

What are the implications of these time divides for developing effective social policies? Specific policy reforms will work best if they reflect a comprehensive, yet flexible vision of the goals we seek to achieve. These goals include a more equitable balance between work and family responsibilities, protection for parents and children and for the opportunities of all workers, and an array of genuine options for reducing the time divides separating home and work, women and men, the overworked and the underemployed. To reach these goals, we need to consider new and broader ways to restructure the workplace, to affirm the principle of equal opportunity as well as the rights of parents and workers, and to rethink the responsibilities of employers, communities, and public institutions.

There is, however, no "one size fits all" solution to the time divides of contemporary Americans. Beyond any one specific approach, work–family policies need to promote family-supportive working conditions without assuming or imposing a uniform vision on everyone. The new diversity in family arrangements and worker circumstances reminds us that social policies need to be sensitive to the myriad needs facing households with varying structures, incomes, and priorities. This means reducing time for the overworked and providing more work to the underemployed. It means establishing more flexibility in rigid job structures and creating institutional supports outside the workplace, such as community supports for childcare and child rearing. It means being attentive to the needs of workers contending with different economic resources, family circumstances, and gender arrangements. It means creating a range of policies that enable people to meet their work and family aspirations, as they define them and as they change over time. In short, workers need genuine options and social supports, not moralizing about the "choices" they have been forced to make. Indeed, creating a "culture of tolerance" that recognizes the diversity of needs among parents and workers may be the most important contribution a national debate can make.

In addition to discussing the place of work and family in our national culture, we need to consider three types of policy approaches: "work facilitating" and "family support" reforms that foster a better integration of family and paid work; "equal opportunity" reforms that insure the rights of all workers, regardless of their gender or family circumstances, to combine the pursuit of work opportunities with parental involvement; and "work regulating" reforms that provide more equitable and reasonable ways to structure—and limit—working time. Each of these policy approaches is part of a broad array of needed reforms, including new workplace regulations and worker protections, the provision of social services, and legislative initiatives. We focus on each policy arena, but pay most attention to the possibilities for reorganizing working time. Although it has received far less attention than policy approaches stressing family support, changing the way we structure and regulate time holds the potential to alter the entire range of options available to workers and their families.

FACILITATING WORK THROUGH FAMILY SUPPORT

Many worthwhile proposals to reduce work–family conflict are "work facilitating" because they help to reduce the barriers to participating in paid work, especially for dual-earning parents and employed mothers. Community-based and on-site childcare supports, for example, make it easier to combine work and family without necessarily reducing work commitments. Supports of this sort, while relatively undeveloped in the United States, are commonly available in other advanced industrial societies, where citizens are more likely to take such programs as daycare and parental leave for granted.

High quality childcare for young children is a central and, indeed, indispensable ingredient in any work-facilitating approach to work–family conflict. So, too, are well-developed after-school programs. Without such supports, parents are often forced to choose between providing for their children economically and providing for their children's psychological and emotional development. While these programs may seem out of reach, France's system of publicly funded, high quality preschools that are available to all makes it clear that universal childcare and after-school programs are not only worthy goals, but attainable ones. (See Gornick and Meyers, 2003, for a discussion of family-friendly policies in place in various European countries.)

In the United States, the lack of high quality, affordable childcare limits the ability of mothers to maintain their connection to the labor market after the birth of a child, and makes working full-time more difficult. Studies have found that some women report they would work more if childcare were more available (Hayes et al., 1990; Mason and Kuhlthau, 1992). Combined with parental leaves (Glass and Riley, 1998; Klerman and Leibowitz, 1999), childcare enables more mothers of young children to work. Thus, in these cases, addressing the concerns of working mothers has the potential for increasing the labor force and contributing to economic growth.

The dilemmas created by our collective resistance to creating high-quality childcare options are perhaps best—and most painfully—exemplified by the situation facing poor, single mothers. It is beyond ironic that poor mothers with meager childcare supports are being pushed into the least satisfying and most poorly paid jobs while middle-class mothers with better jobs face criticism for securing high-quality care for their children. These contradictions in our policies and perceptions surrounding work and family issues reveal more than just a deep ambivalence about the nature of social change; they point to the class and gender inequalities in how this ambivalence is expressed.[8] Childcare thus raises one set of issues for poor, single mothers and another for affluent parents. Yet all children, regardless of their economic and family circumstances, need quality care, and good social policy needs to recognize the collective stake we all have in providing it. Whether support is offered in the form of subsidies for kin networks and neighborhood efforts or for the direct provision of care, we need a variety of approaches that speak to the needs of parents and children facing different obstacles and possessing differing resources. In Sweden, for example, mothers and fathers alike can take up to 16 months of paid parental leave, with legal assurances that the time they take to be with their children will not exact an undue toll on their careers when they return to the workplace.

Providing income supports to those in need is one of the most straightforward ways to support working families (Sklar et al., 2001). For those holding jobs at the bottom of the economic ladder, just staying afloat typically requires working two (or more) jobs and overtime. These jobs are often as personally unrewarding as they are economically unrewarded. Like those in high-paying and high-pressure professions, workers with more modest jobs, whether women or men, also generally seek a balance between work time and family time. But they also need to provide for the economic well-being of their families. Work–family policies should thus include efforts to insure that all workers are able to earn a decent standard of living—and, at the least, avoid falling into poverty—at a forty-hour-a-week job. With such income guarantees, some will surely continue to pursue over-time and supplemental jobs, but others will have the option of working less. At the least, a national minimum wage should guarantee that all full-time workers are paid enough to support their families without falling into poverty.

INSURING EQUAL OPPORTUNITY AND PROTECTING PARENTAL RIGHTS

Unless "family friendly" and "work facilitating" supports are intertwined with equal opportunity policies that insure the rights of workers regardless of gender or parental status, involved parents—who are more likely to be women, but increasingly include men as well—will have to sacrifice career opportunities for the sake of care, and committed workers will be forced to sacrifice family involvement for the sake of career and even financial security. In an economy that depends on the contributions of women as well as men, mothers as well as fathers, and parents as well as childless workers, we cannot afford to force people into such zero-sum choices.

Providing such protections will require legislative measures comparable to the rights gained by workers during the nineteenth and twentieth centuries. These legislative measures should outlaw discrimination against parents, provide equal work opportunities for women, and protect the rights of all parents to care for their children without incurring undue costs at the workplace. Just as the minimum wage and the forty-hour work week were legislative achievements that once seemed out of reach but are now taken for granted, securing parental rights and gender-equal opportunities at work need to be seen as an integral aspect of the restructuring of work and family in the twenty-first century. And just as earlier movements for workers' rights once seemed overly intrusive but are now deemed essential to a productive and humane economy, insuring the rights of women and parents to care for their families without facing penalties at work also promises to enhance our social fabric as well as our private lives.

The costs now attached to taking some time from work to provide domestic care, for example, are not an inherent feature of work, but rather a socially constructed arrangement that is subject to social redefinition. Just as men who served in the military in the Second World War were not penalized for the time they spent serving their country, the time parents, and especially women, take to care for children need not be unduly penalized. As adults live longer and spend more years engaged in paid work, there should be protections for taking time for parental caretaking, especially for the relatively brief period when family responsibilities are at their peak. Without such opportunities for women and involved parents, many will find the price of care too high and those who do not will be penalized for their "sacrifices."[9]

FAMILY SUPPORT THROUGH WORK FLEXIBILITY AND SOCIAL POLICY

Even if families could routinely rely on high quality childcare, widely available after-school programs, and income supports for the working poor, another crucial set of reforms would still be needed to give workers greater flexibility at the workplace, so that they have more options in deciding how to weave their public and private commitments. The Family and Medical Leave Act, for example, gives more private time to parents and those with ill or elderly dependents. These reforms increase the scope of the flexibility provided to workers and begin to redress the imbalance between work demands and family needs. By legislating the rights of workers across a broad range of work settings, these reforms provide a needed floor of *minimal* supports for new parents and others with heavy, but temporary family responsibilities. Studies of the impact of this legislation indicate that it has resulted in more workers being covered by this protection than had previously been the case (Waldfogel, 1999).

Despite these demonstrable achievements, the United States still has a long way to go to catch up with many of our peers in the industrialized world. Europeans, for example, routinely enjoy four to six weeks of yearly vacation time. Recent legislation prohibits discrimination against part-time workers. In addition, access to a national health system gives most European workers the leeway to choose jobs and working hours without regard to their own or their family's health insurance needs.

In a world where dual-earners and single parents are the clear majority of workers, a thirty-five hour work week not only makes sense but takes on a new urgency. Even this slight reduction in the standard would ease the time crunch on working parents, provide more time for caretaking, create the possibility of more gender equity in parenting and paid work, and allow workers in all types of families to participate more fully in their communities. Just as the forty hour work week has never been mandatory for everyone, the thirty-five hour work week would not be required of all. It would, however, become an expected standard that helps articulate the ideals, values, and norms of our society.[10] It would set expectations for employers and employees alike, promote coordination and efficiency within and among firms, and foster greater cooperation among workplaces, families, and communities.

The thirty-five hour work week may appear to be a radical idea, but the forty hour week seemed equally revolutionary before collective social action made it the standard. More important, the alternatives are less attractive. The most obvious alternative is to take no action and leave conditions as they are—that is, with the onus of responsibility on individual workers to cope as best they can. This scenario means leaving parents to face continuing and probably mounting pressure and allowing employers to presume fifty to sixty hour work weeks until these workers either burn out, retire early, or simply relinquish the hope of having a life outside of work. The next alternative is to emphasize individual flexibility and choice, but to ignore the structure of work in which such choices are made. Such an approach may help some workers find a better balance but only at the expense of equal opportunity and gender equity.

BRIDGING OUR TIME DIVIDES

The underlying demographic shifts and economic trends that have created our overlapping time divides have left few Americans untouched. As these demographic changes continue to make work and family issues more pressing, they are bound to gain political momentum. Some political observers, including Theda Skocpol (1999), Stanley Greenberg (1996), and Mona Harrington

(1999) have thus proposed to make support for "working families" the compelling rubric for advancing a progressive political agenda. Not simply a disparate collection of fanciful ideas, family-friendly policies are becoming increasingly central to the needs of families and to the nation's political agenda. What ordinary Americans need and increasingly want is not utopia, but rather a reasonable set of supports and options for managing work and family conflicts.

The policies we have suggested represent only a few of the myriad of possible approaches to address the problems of work and family change. Effective policies, whatever their form, can only emerge from a national debate that rejects a framework of parental blame to reconsider workplace organization and the structure of opportunities confronting workers and their families.

Hours matter in the balance people are able to strike in their lives, but solutions to modern family dilemmas most involve more than just tackling the problem of overwork. For the "over-worked Americans" concentrated in the professional and managerial occupations, job flexibility and genuine formal and informal support for family life matter as much as, and possibly more than, actual hours. For the "underworked," who are concentrated in the less rewarded and less demanding jobs, security and opportunity are paramount for their own welfare and that of their children.

One facet of change, however, spans the occupational and class structure: the emergence of women as a large and committed group of workers. They need and have a right to expect the same opportunities afforded men, and their families' well-being depends on their ability to gain these opportunities. We have found significant points of convergence between women and men in their commitment to work and their desire for family supports. However, we have also found that women workers, and especially those putting in long hours at professional jobs, have less job flexibility and do not enjoy the same level of support from supervisors and employers as do their male counterparts. Principles of justice as well as the new realities of families suggest that gender equity needs to be integral to any policy initiatives aimed at easing the conflicts between family and work.

At the broadest level, our discovery of multiple and intertwined time divides suggests that reform efforts should uphold two important principles: equality of opportunity for women and men and generous support for all involved parents, regardless of gender. We cannot afford to build work-family policies on old, outdated stereotypes, in which women are seen as less committed to work than men. Yet we can also not afford to build our policies on new stereotypes, in which working mothers and, to a lesser extent, fathers are depicted as avoiding their families and neglecting their children.

These images place all too many workers in a difficult bind, in which work commitment is defined as family neglect and family involvement is defined as a lack of work commitment. These are inaccurate images that offer untenable choices. If our findings are a guide, what workers need most is flexible, satisfying, and economically rewarding work in a supportive setting that offers them a way to integrate work and family life. With these supports, contemporary workers and the generations to follow will be able to bridge the time divides they face.

NOTES

1. For a full listing of our sources, see Jacobs and Gerson (2004).
2. The differences between White men and their Black and Hispanic counterparts narrow roughly by one hour per week when education, age, occupation, and marital and parental status are taken into account, but these differentials in working time are not completely erased.

3. Interesting and important differences by race, marital status, and other factors are too numerous to discuss in detail here. For example, the longer working hours of African-American women are not simply a matter of their lower marriage rate, since married African-American women work about 3 hours longer per week than do White women.

4. Some situations may lead employers to prefer a smaller number of workers putting in overtime despite the added costs. In cyclical industries, for example, where expected downturns mean periodic layoffs and union contracts may require employers to assist those experiencing layoffs, firms may prefer a smaller workforce. And despite the increase in hourly pay, there are no additional benefits costs associated with requiring a smaller pool of workers to put in overtime. Nonetheless, analysis of national survey data indicate that those eligible for overtime tend to work fewer hours than those who are not eligible (Jacobs and Gerson, 1997).

5. See also Skocpol, 1999, for a discussion of the complexities of the issue of civic participation.

6. We recognize that one strand of economic theory suggests that an efficient labor market should produce just the type of jobs that workers want. In other words, if employers offered jobs that were too far out of line from what workers want, they would be forced to pay an extra "compensating differential" to attract an adequate staff. The evidence presented thus far, as well as findings on shift differentials for evening and night work discussed in Chapter 16, suggest that the labor market does not operate in this way. For a more detailed discussion of this issue, see Jacobs and Steinberg (1990) and Wax (2002).

7. To explain how contemporary women and men are experiencing the vast changes taking place at the workplace, in the home, and in the conflicts between them, we draw on findings from *The National Study of the Changing Workforce* (Bond, Galinsky, and Swanberg, 1998).

8. In another irony of the debate over childcare, affluent families, including those with nonworking mothers, routinely rely on nursery schools and "early childhood education programs" to give their children an educational head start. Yet "early education" becomes "childcare" when the focus turns to critiques of employed mothers.

9. For economic analyses of the benefits of equality in parenting and work, see Folbre (2001) and Gornick and Meyers (2003). Crittenden (2001) offers a critique of the myriad economic penalties attached to caring for children, as also noted in Jacons and Gerson, chapter 6.

10. As Epstein et al. (1999), point out, the current normative standard for professional workers now extends well beyond the forty hour week, which is defined as "part-time" in law and other highly pressured occupations. These writers call for a fundamental restructuring of the "time norms" that equate work success with all-consuming commitment.

REFERENCES

Bond, James T., Ellen Galinksy, and Jennifer E. Swanberg. 1998. *The National Study of the Changing Workforce.* New York: Families and Work Institute.

Blair-Loy, Mary. 2003. *Competing Devotions: Career and Family among Women Executives.* Cambridge, MA: Harvard University Press.

Crittenden, Ann. 2001. *The Price of Motherhood: Why the Most Important Job in the World is Still the Least Valued.* New York: Metropolitan Books.

Epstein, Cynthia Fuchs, Carroll Seron, Bonnie Oglensky, and Robert Saute. 1999. *The Part-Time Paradox : Time Norms, Professional Lives, Family, and Gender.* New York: Routledge.

Folbre, Nancy. 2001. *The Invisible Heart: Economics and Family Values.* New York: New Press.

Fritsch, Jane. 2001. "A Rise in Single Dads." *New York Times,* May 20.

Glass, Jennifer L. and Lisa Riley. 1998. "Family Responsive Policies and Employee Retention Following Childbirth." *Social Forces* 76(4): 1401–1435.

Gordon, David. M. 1996. *Fat and Mean: The Corporate Squeeze of Working Americans and the Myth of Managerial "Downsizing".* New York: Free Press.

Gornick, Janet C., and Marcia K. Meyers. 2003. *Earning and Caring: What Government Can Do to Reconcile Motherhood, Fatherhood, and Employment.* New York: Russell Sage Foundation Press.

Greenberg, Stanley. 1996. *Middle Class Dreams: The Politics and Power of the New American Majority.* New Haven, CT: Yale University Press.

Harrington, Mona. 1999. *Care and Equality: Inventing a New Family Politics.* New York: Knopf.

Hayes, Cheryl D., John L. Palmer and Martha J. Zaslow, eds., 1990. *Who Cares for America's Children: Child Care Policy for the 1990s.* Washington, DC: National Academy Press.

Heymann, Jody. 2000. *The Widening Gap. Why America's Working Families Are in Jeopardy and What Can Be Done About It.* New York: Basic Books.

Jacobs, Jerry A. and Kathleen Gerson. 1997. *The Endless Day or the Flexible Office? Working Time, Work-Family Conflict, and Gender Equity in the Modern Workplace.* Report to the Alfred P. Sloan Foundation.

Jacobs, Jerry A. and Kathleen Gerson. 2004. *The Time Divide: Work, Family, and Gender Inequality.* Cambridge, MA: Harvard University Press.

Jacobs, Jerry A. and Ronnie Steinberg. 1990. "Compensating Differentials and the Male–Female Wage Gap: Evidence from the New York State Comparable Worth Study," *Social Forces* 69(2): 439–468.

Klerman, Jacob A. and Arleen Leibowitz. 1999. "Job Continuity Among New Mothers." *Demography* 36(2): 145–155.

Landers, Renee M., James B. Rebitzer and Lowell J. Taylor. 1996. "Rat Race Redux: Adverse Selection in the Determination of Work Hours in Law Firms." *The American Economic Review* 86(3): 329–348.

Mason, Karen O. and Karen Kuhlthau. 1992. "The Perceived Impact of Child Care Costs on Women's Labor Supply and Fertility." *Demography* 29(4): 523–543.

Meyers, Marcia K. and Janet C. Gornick. 2003. "Public or Private Responsibility? Early Childhood Education and Care, Inequality and the Welfare State." *Journal of Comparative Family Studies* 34(3): 379–411.

Pfeffer, Jeffrey and James N. Baron. 1988. "Taking the Workers Back Out: Recent Trends in the Structuring of Employment." *Research in Organizational Behavior* 10: 257–303.

Putnam, Robert. 2000. *Bowling Alone: The Collapse and Revival of American Community*. New York: Simon and Schuster.

Putnam, Robert. 1996. "The Strange Disappearance of Civic America." *The American Prospect* 24: Winter: 34–48.

Sklar, Holly, Laryssa Mykyta, and Susan Wefald. 2001. *Raise the Floor: Wages and Policies That Work for All of Us*. New York: Ms. Foundation for Women.

Skocpol, Theda. 1999. "Associations without Members." *The American Prospect* 45: July–August: 66–73.

Waldfogel, Jane. 1999. "Family Leave Coverage in the 1990s." *Monthly Labor Review* 122(10): 13–21.

Wax, Amy. 2002. "Economic Models of the 'Family-Friendly' Workplace: Making the Case for Change." Unpublished Manuscript, University of Pennsylvania Law School.

Selected Bibliography of Recent Sources

Compiled for the first edition by Maya Parson and revised for the second edition by Gabrielle Raley

Almeida, Rhea V., Lynn Parker and Kenneth Dolan-Del Vecchio. *Transformative Family Therapy: Just Families in a Just Society*. (Allyn & Bacon, 2007).

Amott, Teresa L., and Julie Mattaei. *Race, Gender, and Work: A Multicultural Economic History of Women in the United States*. (Boston, MA: South End Press, 1991).

Anderson, Margaret L., and Patricia Hill Collins, eds. *Race, Class, and Gender: An Anthology*. Third edition. (Belmont, CA: Wadsworth, 1998).

Aswad, Barbara C., and Barbara Bilge, eds. *Family and Gender among American Muslims: Issues Facing Middle-Eastern Immigrants and Their Descendents*. (Philadelphia: Temple University Press, 1996).

Auhagen, Ann E., and Maria von Salisch. *The Diversity of Human Relationships*. (Cambridge, MA: Cambridge University Press, 1996).

Beam, Cris. *Transparent: Love, Family, and Living the T With Transgender Teenagers*. (Orlando, FL: Harcourt, 2007).

Berry, Mary Frances. *The Politics of Parenthood: Child Care, Women's Rights, and the Myth of the Good Mother*. (New York: Viking, 1993).

Bettie, Julie. *Women Without Class: Girls, Race, and Identity*. (Berkeley: University of California Press, 2003).

Boris, Eileen, and Elisabeth Priigl, eds. *Homeworkers in Global Perspective: Invisible No More*. New (York: Routledge, 1996).

Bowman, Phillip J. "Coping with Provider Role Strain: Adaptive Cultural Resources among Black Husband-Fathers." *The Journal of Black Psychology*, 16 (Spring 1990): 1–21.

Boydston, Jeanne. *Home and Work: Housework, Wages, and the Ideology of Work in the Early Republic*. (New York: Oxford University Press, 1990).

Braman, Donald. *Doing Time on the Outside: Incarceration and Family Life in Urban America*. (Ann Arbor: University of Michigan Press, 2004).

Brewer, Rose. "Theorizing Race, Class, and Gender: The New Scholarship of Black Feminist Intellectuals and Black Women's Labor." In *Theorizing Black Feminisms: The Visionary Pragmatism of Black Women*, eds. Stanlie M. James and Abena P. A. Busia, pp. 13–30. (London: Routledge, 1993).

Carrington, Christopher. *No Place Like Home: Relationships and Family Life among Lesbians and Gay Men*. (Chicago: University of Chicago Press, 1999).

Chang, Hedy Nai-Lin, Amy Muckelroy, and Dora Pulido-Tobiassen. *Looking In, Looking Out: Redefining Child Care and Early Education in a Diverse Society*. (San Francisco: California Tomorrow, 1996).

Chase-Lansdale, P. Lindsay, and Jeanne Brooks-Gunn, eds. *Escape from Poverty: What Makes a Difference for Children?* (Cambridge, MA: Cambridge University Press, 1995).

Chee, Maria W. L. *Taiwanese American Transnational Families: Women and Kin Work*. (New York: Routledge, 2005).

Chow, Esther Ngan-Ling, and Catherine White Berheide. *Women, the Family, and Policy: A Global Perspective*. (Albany, NY: State University of New York Press, 1994).

Chow, Esther Ngan-Ling, Doris Wilkinson, and Maxine Baca Zinn, eds. *Race, Class, and Gender: Common Bonds, Different Voices*. Gender in Society Reader. Published in Cooperation with Sociologists for Women in Society. (Thousand Oaks, CA: Sage Publications, 1996).

Cobble, Dorothy Sue. *The Sex of Class: Women Transforming American Labor*. (Ithaca, NY: ILR Press, 2007).

Cole, Jennifer and Deborah Durham, eds. *Generations and Globalization: Youth, Age, and Family in the New World Economy*. (Bloomington: Indiana University Press, 2007).

Collins, Patricia Hill. *Black Feminist Thought: Knowledge, Consciousness, and the Politics of Empowerment*. Tenth Anniversary Edition. (New York: Routledge, 2000).

—— *Black Sexual Politics: African Americans, Gender, and the New Racism*. (New York: Routledge, 2004).

Comas-Diaz, Lillian, and Beverly Greene, eds. *Women of Color: Integrating Ethnic and Gender Identities in Psychotherapy*. (New York: Guilford Press, 1994).

Congress, Elaine P., and Manny J. Gonzales, eds. *Multicultural Perspectives in Working with Families*. Second Edition. (New York: Springer, 2005).

Coontz, Stephanie. *The Way We Never Were: American Families and the Nostalgia Trap*. (New York: Basic Books, 1992).

—— *The Way We Really Are: Coming to Terms with America's Changing Families*. (New York: Basic Books, 1997).

—— "Historical Perspectives on Family Studies." *Journal of Marriage and Family*, Vol. 62, No. 2 (2000): 283–297.

—— *Marriage, A History: From Obedience to Intimacy or How Love Conquered Marriage*. (New York: Viking, 2005).

DaCosta Nunez, Ralph. *The New Poverty: Homeless Families in America*. (New York: Insight Books, 1996).

DeVault, Marjorie L. *Feeding the Family: The Social Organization of Caring as Gendered Work*. (Chicago: University of Chicago Press, 1991).

Dickerson, Bette J., ed. *African-American Single Mothers: Understanding Their Lives and Families*. Sage Series on Race and Ethnic Relations, Volume 10. (Thousand Oaks, CA: Sage Publications, 1995).

Dill, Bonnie Thornton, Maxine Baca Zinn, and Sandra Patton. "Feminism, Race, and the Politics of Family Values." *Report from the Institute for Philosophy & Public Policy*, 13 (Summer 1993): 13–18.

Duncan, Greg J., and Jeanne Brooks-Gunn, eds. *Consequences of Growing Up Poor*. (New York: Russell Sage Foundation, 1997).

Duncan, Greg J., and P. Lindsay Chase-Lansdale, eds. *For Better and For Worse: Welfare Reform and the Well-Being of Children and Families*. (New York: Russell Sage Foundation, 2001).

Dunn, Dana, ed. *Workplace/Women's Place: An Anthology*. (Los Angeles: Roxbury Publishing Company, 1997).

Durr, Marlese, and Shirley A. Hill, eds. *Race, Work, and Family in the Lives of African Americans*. (Lanham, MD: Rowman & Littlefield, 2006).

Dykeman, Cass, J. Ron Nelson, and Valerie Appleton. "Building Strong Working Alliances with American Indian Families." *Social Work in Education*, 17:3 (July 1995): 148–158.

Edelman, Peter B., and Joyce A. Ladner, eds. *Adolescence and Poverty: Challenge for the 1990s*. (Washington, DC: Center for National Policy Press, 1991).

Edin, Kathryn, and Laura Lein. *Making Ends Meet: How Single Mothers Survive Welfare and Low Wage Work*. (Russell Sage Foundation, 1997).

Edin, Kathryn, and Maria Kefalas. *Promises I Can Keep: Why Poor Women Put Motherhood Before Marriage*. (Berkeley: University of California Press, 2005).

Ehrenreich, Barbara, and Arlie Russell Hochschild, eds. *Global Woman: Nannies, Maids, and Sex Workers in the New Economy*. (New York: Metropolitan Books, 2003).

England, Paula, and Kathryn Edin. *Unmarried Couples with Children*. (New York: Russell Sage, 2007).

Espiritu, Yen Le. *Asian American Women and Men: Labor, Laws, and Love*. The Gender Lens Series. (Thousand Oaks, CA: Sage Publications, 1996).

Farley, Reynolds, ed. *State of the Union: America in the 1990s*. (New York: Russell Sage Foundation, 1995).

Ferguson, Susan J. "Challenging Traditional Marriage: Never Married Chinese American and Japanese American Women." *Gender & Society*, 14:1 (2000): 136–159.

Folbre, Nancy. *Who Pays for the Kids? Gender and the Structures of Constraint*. (London: Routledge, 1994).

—— *The Invisible Heart: Economics and Family Values*. (New York: New Press, 2001).

Franklin, Donna. *Ensuring Inequality: The Structural Transformation of the African-American Family*. (New York: Oxford University Press, 1997).

Gabaccia, Donna R., and Vicki L. Ruiz. *American Dreaming, Global Realities: Rethinking U.S. Immigration History*. (Urbana: University of Illinois Press, 2006).

Gillis, John R. *A World of Their Own Making: Myth, Ritual, and the Quest for Family Values*. (New York: Basic Books, 1996).

Glenn, Evelyn Nakano. "Gender and the Family." In *Analyzing Gender: A Handbook of Social Science Research*, eds. Beth B. Hess and Myra Marx Ferree. (Newbury Park, CA: Sage Publications, 1987, 348–380).

Glenn, Evelyn Nakano, Grace Chang, and Linda Rennie Forcey, eds. *Mothering: Ideology, Experience, and Agency*. Perspectives on Gender. (New York: Routledge, 1994).

Gonzalez-Mena, Janet. *Multicultural Issues in Child Care*. Second edition. (Mountain View, CA: Mayfield Publishing Company, 1997).

Greene, Beverly A. "What Has Gone Before: The Legacy of Racism and Sexism in the Lives of Black Mothers and Daughters." *Women and Therapy*, 9:1/2 (1990): 207–230.

—— *Ethnic and Cultural Diversity Among Lesbians and Gay Men*. Psychological Perspectives on Lesbian and Gay Issues, Volume 3. (Thousand Oaks, CA: Sage Publications, 1997).

Hansen, Karen. *Not So Nuclear Families: Class, Gender, and Networks of Care*. (New Brunswick, NJ: Rutgers University Press, 2005).

Hardy, Kenneth. "The Theoretical Myth of Sameness: A Critical Issue in Family Therapy Training and Treatment." *Journal of Psychotherapy and the Family*, 6 (1989): 17–33.

Harvard Project on American Indian Economic Development. *The State of the Native Nations: Conditions under U.S. Policies of Self-Determination*. (New York: Oxford University Press, 2008).

Hertz, Rosanna. *Single by Chance, Mothers by Choice: How Women are Choosing Parenthood without Marriage and Creating the New American Family*. (New York: Oxford University Press, 2006).

Hertz, Rosanna and Nancy L. Marshall. *Working Families: The Transformation of the American Home*. (Berkeley; Los Angeles: University of California Press, 2001).

Heymann, Jody, and Christopher Beem, eds. *Unfinished Work: Building Equality and Democracy in an Era of Working Families*. (New York: W.W. Norton & Co., 2005).

Higginbotham, Elizabeth, and Mary Romero, eds. *Women and Work: Exploring Race, Ethnicity, and Class.* Women and Work, Volume 6. (Thousand Oaks: Sage Publications, 1997).

Hill, Robert B. *The Strengths of African-American Families: Twenty-five Years Later.* (Washington, DC: R & B Publishers, 1997).

Hill, Shirley A. *Black Intimacies: A Gender Perspective on Families and Relationships.* (Walnut Creek, CA: AltaMira Press, 2005).

Hing, Bill Ong. *Making and Remaking Asian Americans through Immigration Policy, 1850–1990.* (Stanford, CA: Stanford University Press, 1993).

Hirsch, Jennifer S. *A Courtship After Marriage: Sexuality and Love in Mexican Transnational Communities.* (Berkeley: University of California Press, 2003).

Hondagneu-Sotelo, Pierrette. "Overcoming Patriarchal Constraints: The Reconstruction of Gender Relations among Mexican Immigrant Women and Men." *Gender and Society,* 6 (September 1992): 393–415.

—— ed. *Gender and U.S. Immigration: Contemporary Trends.* (Berkeley: University of California Press, 2003).

Ingoldsby, Bron B., and Suzanna D. Smith, eds. *Families in Global and Multicultural Perspective.* (Thousand Oaks, CA: Sage Publications, 2006).

Ishwaran, K. *Family and Marriage: Cross-Cultural Perspectives.* Revised edition. (Toronto: Thompson Educational Publishing, 1992).

Jacobs, Jan et al. "Gender, Race, Class, and the Trend Toward Early Motherhood: A Feminist Analysis of Teen Mothers in Contemporary Society." *Journal of Contemporary Ethnography,* 22:4 (January 1994): 442.

Jacobs, Jerry A., and Kathleen Gerson. *The Time Divide: Work, Family, and Social Policy in the 21st Century.* (Cambridge, MA: Harvard University Press, 2004).

Jencks, Christopher. *Rethinking Social Policy: Race, Poverty, and the Underclass.* (New York: HarperPerennial, 1993).

Kamerman, Sheila B. "Gender Role and Family Structure Changes in the Advanced Industrialized West: Implications for Social Policy." In *Poverty, Inequality, and the Future of Social Policy: Western States in the New World Order,* eds. Katherine McFate, Roger Lawson, and William Julius Wilson, pp. 231–256. (New York: Russell Sage Foundation, 1995).

Kaplan, Lisa, and Judith Girard. *Strengthening High-Risk Families: A Handbook for Practitioners.* (New York: Lexington Books; Toronto: Maxwell Macmillan, 1994).

Katz, Jane, ed. *Messengers of the Wind: Native American Women Tell Their Life Stories.* (New York: Ballantine, 1995).

Kennedy, Cynthia M. *Braided Relations, Entwined Lives: The Women of Charleston's Urban Slave Society.* (Bloomington: Indiana University Press, 2005).

Kozol, Jonathan. *The Shame of the Nation: The Restoration of Apartheid Schooling in America.* (New York: Crown Publishers, 2005).

Laird, Joan, and Robert-Jay Green. *Lesbians and Gays in Couples and Families: A Handbook for Therapists.* (San Francisco: Jossey-Bass Publishers, 1996).

Lamont, Michèle. *The Dignity of Working Men: Morality and the Boundaries of Race, Class, and Immigration.* (New York: Russell Sage Foundation; Cambridge, MA: Harvard University Press, 2000).

Lamphere, Louise, Patricia Zavella, and Felipe Gonzalez, with Peter B. Evans. *Sunbelt Working Mothers: Reconciling Family and Factory.* (Ithaca, NY: Cornell University Press, 1993).

Laosa, Luis M. "Ethnicity and Single Parenting in the United States." In *Impact of Divorce, Single Parenting, and Stepparenting on Children,* eds. E. Mavis Hetherington and Josephine D. Arasteh, pp. 23–49. (Hillsdale, NJ: Lawrence Erlbaum Associates, Publishers, 1988).

Lee, Jennifer, and Min Zhou, eds. *Asian American Youth: Culture, Identity, and Ethnicity.* (New York: Routledge, 2004).

Leong, Russell, ed. *Asian American Sexualities: Dimensions of the Gay and Lesbian Experience.* (New York: Routledge, 1996).

Levine, James A., and Edward W. Pitt. *New Expectations: Community Strategies for Responsible Fatherhood.* (New York: Families and Work Institute, 1995).

Lobo, Susan, ed. *Native American Voices: A Reader.* (New York: Longman, 1998).

Logan, Sadye L., ed. *The Black Family: Strengths, Self-Help, and Positive Change.* (Boulder, CO: Westview Press, 1996).

Lott, Juanita Tomayo. *Common Destiny: Filipino American Generations.* (Lanham, MD: Rowman & Littlefield, 2006).

Luker, Kristin. *Dubious Conceptions: The Politics of Teenage Pregnancy.* (Cambridge, MA: Harvard University Press, 1996).

Lynn, Laurence K., and Michael G. H. McGeary, eds. *Inner-City Poverty in the United States.* (Washington, DC: National Academy Press, 1990).

Maffi, Mario. *Gateway to the Promised Lands: Ethnic Cultures on New York's Lower East Side.* (New York: New York University Press, 1995).

Malley-Morrison, Kathleen, and Denise A. Hines. *Family Violence in a Cultural Perspective: Defining, Understanding, and Combating Abuse.* (Thousand Oaks, CA: Sage Publications, 2004).

Marsiglio, William, ed. *Fatherhood: Contemporary Theory, Research, and Social Policy.* Research on Men and Masculinities, Volume 7. (Thousand Oaks, CA: Sage Publications, 1995).

May, Elaine Tyler. *Homeward Bound: American Families and the Cold War Era.* (New York: BasicBooks, 1988).

McAdoo, Harriette Pipes, ed. *Black Families.* Fourth edition. (Thousand Oaks, CA: Sage Publications, 2007).

—— *Family Ethnicity: Strength in Diversity.* (Newbury Park, CA: Sage Publications, 1993).

McGoldrick, Monica, ed. *Re-Visioning Family Therapy: Race, Culture, and Gender in Clinical Practice.* (New York: Guilford Press, 1998).

McGoldrick, Monica, Joe Giordano, and Nydia Garcia-Preto. *Ethnicity and Family Therapy*. Third Edition. (New York: Guilford Press, 2005).

Miles, Tiya. *Ties That Bind: The Story of an Afro-Cherokee Family in Slavery and Freedom*. (Berkeley: University of California Press, 2005).

Mink, Gwendolyn. *The Wages of Motherhood: Inequality in the Welfare State, 1917–1942*. (Ithaca, NY: Cornell University Press, 1995).

Mintz, Steven, and Susan Kellogg. *Domestic Revolutions: A Social History of American Family Life*. (New York: The Free Press, 1988).

Mitra, Kalita S. *Suburban Sahibs: Three Immigrant Families and Their Passage from India to America*. (New Brunswick, NJ: Rutgers University Press, 2003).

Moran, Rachel. *The Regulation of Race and Romance*. (Chicago: University of Chicago Press, 2001).

Newman, Katherine S. *Falling From Grace: The Experience of Downward Mobility in the American Middle Class*. (New York: The Free Press, 1988).

—— *A Different Shade of Gray: Midlife and Beyond in the Inner City*. (New York: W.W. Norton, 2003).

Ngai, Mae M. *Impossible Subjects: Illegal Aliens and the Making of Modern America*. (Princeton, NJ: Princeton University Press, 2004).

Okun, Barbara F. *Understanding Diverse Families: What Practioners Need to Know*. (New York: Guilford Press, 1996).

Oliver, Melvin L., and Thomas M. Shapiro. *Black Wealth/White Wealth: A New Perspective on Racial Inequality*. Tenth anniversary edition. (New York: Routledge, 2006).

Ong, Paul, Edna Bonacich, and Lucie Cheng, eds. *The New Asian Immigration in Los Angeles and Global Restructuring*. (Philadelphia: Temple University Press, 1994).

Parreñas, Rhacel Salazar. *Servants of Globalization: Women, Migration, and Domestic Work*. (Stanford, CA: Stanford University Press, 2001).

Pesquera, Beatriz M. "In the Beginning He Wouldn't Even Lift a Spoon: The Division of Household Labor." In *Building With Our Hands: New Directions in Chicana Studies*, eds. Adela de la Torre and Beatriz M. Pesquera. (Berkeley: University of California Press, 1993).

Peters, Virginia Bergman. *Women of the Earth Lodges: Tribal Life on the Plains*. (North Haven, CT: Archon, 1995).

Polakow, Valerie. *Who Cares For Our Children?: The Child Care Crisis in the Other America*. (New York: Teachers College Press, 2007).

Presser, Harriet B. *Working in a 24/7 Economy: Challenges for American Families*. (New York: Russell Sage Foundation, 2003).

Quadagno, Jill S. *The Color of Welfare: How Racism Undermined the War on Poverty*. (New York: Oxford University Press, 1994).

Rank, Mark R. *Living on the Edge: The Realities of Welfare in America*. (New York: Columbia University Press, 1994).

Reich, Jennifer A. *Fixing Families: Parents, Power, and the Child Welfare System*. (New York: Routledge, 2005).

Risman, Barbara J. *Gender Vertigo: American Families in Transition*. (New Haven, CT: Yale University Press, 1998).

Ritterhouse, Jennifer. *Growing Up Jim Crow: How Black and White Southern Children Learned Race*. (Chapel Hill: University of North Carolina Press, 2006).

Roberts, Dorothy. *Killing the Black Body: Race, Reproduction, and the Meaning of Liberty*. (New York: Vintage, 1997).

Robertson, Claire. "Africa into the Americas? Slavery and Women, the Family and the Gender Division of Labor." In *More than Chattel: Black Women and Slavery in the Americas*, eds. David Barry Gaspar and Darlene Clark Hine. (Bloomington: Indiana University Press, 1996).

Robson, Ruthann. "Resisting the Family—Repositioning Lesbians in Legal Theory." *Signs*, 19 (Summer 1994): 975–996.

Romero, Mary. " 'I'm Not Your Maid I Am the Housekeeper': The Restructuring of Housework and Work Relationships in Domestic Service." In *Color, Class, and Country: Experiences of Gender*, eds. Gay Young and Bette J. Dickerson, pp. 71–83. (London: Zed Books, 1994).

Romero, Mary, Pierette Hondagneu-Sotelo, and Vilma Ortiz, eds. *Challenging Fronteras: Structuring Latina and Latino Lives in the U.S.: An Anthology of Readings*. (New York: Routledge, 1997).

Root, Maria P.P. *Love's Revolution: Interracial Marriage*. (Philadelphia, PA: Temple University Press, 2001).

—— ed. *The Multiracial Experience: Racial Borders* as the New Frontier. (Thousand Oaks, CA: Sage Publications, 1996).

Roschelle, Ann R. *No More Kin: Exploring Race, Class, and Gender in Family Networks*. Understanding Families Series. (Thousand Oaks, CA: Sage Publications, 1997).

Rosenblatt, Paul C., Terri A. Karis, and Richard D. Powell. *Multiracial Couples: Black and White Voices*. Understanding Families, Volume 1. (Thousand Oaks, CA: Sage Publications, 1995).

Rothman, Barbara Katz. *Weaving a Family: Untangling Race and Adoption*. (Boston: Beacon Press Books, 2005).

Ruiz, Vicki. *Cannery Women, Cannery Lives: Mexican Women, Unionization, and the California Food Processing Industry, 1930–1950*. (Albuquerque: University of New Mexico Press, 1987).

Ruiz, Vicki L., and Ellen Carol DuBois, eds. *Unequal Sisters: A Multicultural Reader in U.S. Women's History*. Fourth Edition. (New York: Routledge, 2007).

Rumbaut, Ruben and Alejandro Portes, eds. *Ethnicities: Children of Immigrants in America*. (Berkeley: University of California Press; New York: Russell Sage Foundation, 2001).

Schneider, Barbara, and Linda J. Waite. *Being Together, Working Apart: Dual-Career Families and the Work–Life Balance*. (Cambridge, UK; New York: Cambridge University Press, 2005).

Schorr, Lisbeth B. *Common Purpose: Strengthening Families and Neighborhoods to Rebuild America*. (New York: Doubleday, 1997).

Segura, Denise A., and Patricia Zavella. *Women and Migration in the U.S.-Mexico Borderlands: A Reader*. (Durham: Duke University Press, 2007).

Shelton, Beth Anne, and Daphne John. "Ethnicity, Race, and Difference: A Comparison of White, Black, and Hispanic Men's Household Labor Time." In *Men, Work, and Family*. Research on Men and Masculinities Series, Volume 4, ed. Jane Hood, pp. 131–150. (Thousand Oaks, CA: Sage Publications, 1993).

Sidel, Ruth. *Keeping Women and Children Last: America's War on the Poor*. (New York: Penguin Books, 1996).

—— *Unsung Heroines: Single Mothers and the American Dream*. (Berkeley: University of California Press, 2006).

Skocpol, Theda. *The Missing Middle: Working Families and the Future of American Social Policy*. (New York: W.W. Norton, 2000).

Skolnick, Arlene S., and Jerome H. Skolnick, eds. *Family in Transition*. Twelfth edition. (Boston: Allyn and Bacon, 2003).

Snipp, C. Matthew. *American Indians: The First of This Land*. (New York: Russell Sage Foundation, 1989). [For the National Committee for Research on the 1980 Census]

Sokoloff, Natalie J., and Christina Pratt, eds. *Domestic Violence at the Margins: Readings on Race, Class, Gender, and Culture*. (New Brunswick, NJ: Rutgers University Press, 2005).

Solinger, Rickie. *Wake Up Little Susie: Single Pregnancy and Race Before Roe v. Wade*. (New York: Routledge, 1992).

—— *Pregnancy and Power: A Short History of Reproductive Politics in America*. (New York: New York University Press, 2005).

Spain, Daphne, and Suzanne M. Bianchi, eds. *Balancing Act: Motherhood, Marriage, and Employment among American Women*. (New York: Russell Sage Foundation, 1996).

Stacey, Judith. *Brave New Families: Stories of Domestic Upheaval in Late Twentieth-Century America*. (Berkeley: University of California Press, 1998).

Stacey, Judith and Timothy J. Biblarz. "(How) Does the Sexual Orientation of Parents Matter?" *American Sociological Review*, Vol. 66, No. 2 (2001): 159–183.

Stack, Carol B. *Call to Home: African Americans Reclaim the Rural South*. (New York: Basic Books, 1996).

Stavig, Ward. " 'Living in Offense of Our Lord': Indigenous Sexual Values and Marital Life in the Colonial Crucible." *Hispanic American Historical Review*, 75 (1995).

Stevenson, Brenda E. *Life in Black and White: Family and Community in the Slave South*. (New York: Oxford University Press, 1996).

Sullivan, Maureen. *The Family of Woman: Lesbian Mothers, Their Children, and the Undoing of Gender*. (Berkeley: University of California Press, 2004).

Tamura, Eileen. *Americanization, Acculturation, and Ethnic Identity: The Nisei Generation in Hawaii*. (Urbana: University of Illinois Press, 1994).

Taylor, Amy Murrell. *The Divided Family in Civil War America*. (Chapel Hill: University of North Carolina Press, 2005).

Taylor, Robert J., James M. Jackson, and Linda M. Chatters, eds. *Family Life in Black America*. (Thousand Oaks, CA: Sage Publications, 1997).

Taylor, Ronald L., ed. *African-American Youth: Their Social and Economic Status in the United States*. (Westport, CT: Praeger Publications, 1995).

—— ed. *Minority Families in the United States: A Multicultural Perspective*. Third Edition. (Upper Saddle River, NJ: Prentice Hall, 2002).

Thompson, Charis. *Making Parents: The Ontological Choreography of Reproductive Technologies*. (Cambridge, MA: MIT Press, 2005).

Thorne, Barrie, with Marilyn Yalom. *Rethinking the Family: Some Feminist Questions*. Revised edition. (Boston: Northeastern University Press, 1992).

Tienda, Marta and William Julius Wilson, eds. *Youth in Cities: A Cross-National Perspective*. (Cambridge, UK; New York: Cambridge University Press, 2002).

Toliver, Susan D. *Black Families in Corporate America*. Understanding Families Series. (Thousand Oaks, CA: Sage Publications, 1998).

Toro-Morn, Maura. "Gender, Class, Family, and Migration: Puerto Rican Women in Chicago." *Gender and Society*, 9:6 (1995): 712–726.

Townsend, Nicholas W. *The Package Deal: Marriage, Work, and Fatherhood in Men's Lives*. (Philadelphia: Temple University Press, 2002).

Tung, May Pao-May. *Chinese Americans and Their Immigrant Parents: Conflict, Identity, and Values*. (New York: Haworth Clinical Practice Press, 2000).

Vecchio, Diane C. *Merchants, Midwives, and Laboring Women: Italian Migrants in Urban America*. (Urbana: University of Illinois Press, 2006).

Voydanoff, Patricia, and Linda C. Majka, eds. *Families and Economic Distress: Coping Strategies and Social Policy*. (Newbury Park, CA: Sage Publications, 1988).

Waite, Linda J. and Christine Bachrach, eds. *The Ties That Bind: Perspectives on Marriage and Cohabitation*. (New York: Aldine de Gruyter, 2000).

Waller, Maureen. *My Baby's Father: Unmarried Parents and Paternal Responsibility*. (Ithaca, NY: Cornell University Press, 2002).

Walsh, Froma, ed. *Normal Family Processes: Growing Diversity and Complexity.* Third Edition. (New York: Guilford Press, 2003).

Way, Niobe, and Judy Y. Chu, eds. *Adolescent Boys: Exploring Diverse Cultures of Boyhood.* (New York: New York University Press, 2004).

Wilkerson, Margaret B., and Jewell Handy Gresham. "Sexual Politics of Welfare: The Racialization of Poverty." *The Nation* (July 24/31, 1989): 126–132.

Williams, Walter L. *The Spirit and the Flesh: Sexual Diversity in American Indian Culture.* (Boston: Beacon Press, 1992).

Wilson, William Julius. *When Work Disappears: The World of the New Urban Poor.* (New York: Knopf, 1996).

Wong, Bernard P. *The Chinese in Silicon Valley: Globalization, Social Networks, and Ethnic Identity.* (Lanham: Rowman & Littlefield, 2006).

Yoshikawa, Hirokazu, Thomas S. Weisner, and Edward D. Lowe, eds. *Making It Work: Low-Wage Employment, Family Life, and Child Development.* (New York: Russell Sage Foundation, 2006).

Zavella, Patricia. *Women's Work in Chicano Families: Cannery Workers of the Santa Clara Valley.* Anthropology of Contemporary Issues. (Ithaca, NY: Cornell University Press, 1987).

Zambrana, Ruth, ed. *Understanding Latino Families: Scholarship, Policy, and Practice.* (Thousand Oaks, CA: Sage Publications, 1995).

Zinn, Maxine Baca, D. Stanley Eitzen, and Barbara Wells. *Diversity in Families.* Eighth Edition. (Boston: Pearson/Allyn and Bacon, 2008).

Zinn, Maxine Baca. "Family, Feminism, and Race in America." *Gender and Society.* 4:1 (1990): 68–82.

Zinn, Maxine Baca and Melissa Riba, "Childbearing Among Latina Youth." *Sage Race Relations Abstracts*, Vol. 24, No. 1 (1999).

Permission Acknowledgments

The following essays were previously published. Permission to reprint is gratefully acknowledged here.

Bonnie Thornton Dill, "Fictive Kin, Paper Sons, and *Compadrazgo*: Women of Color and the Struggle for Family Survival." Reprinted from *The Journal of Family History*, Vol. 13, No. 4 (1988), pp. 415–431. Reprinted by permission of Sage Publications, Inc.

David Wallace Adams, excerpts from *Education for Extinction: American Indians and the Boarding School Experience, 1875–1928* by David Wallace Adams, 1988. Reprinted by permission of the University Press of Kansas.

Norrece T. Jones Jr., excerpts from *Born a Child of Freedom, Yet a Slave: Mechanisms of Control and Strategies of Resistance in Antebellum South Carolina* by Norrece T. Jones, 1991. Reproduced by permission of the Wesleyan University Press.

Evelyn Nakano Glenn, "Split Household, Small Producer, and Dual Wage Earner: An Analysis of Chinese-American Family Strategies." Reprinted from *Journal of Marriage and the Family*, Vol. 45, No. 1 (1983), pp. 35–46. Copyright © 1983 by the National Council on Family Relations, 3989 Central Avenue, N.E., Suite 550, Minneapolis, MN 55421. Reprinted by permission of Blackwell Publishing.

Stephen Mintz, excerpts from *Huck's Raft: A History of American Childhood*, 2004. Copyright © 2004 by the President and Fellows of Harvard College. Reprinted by permission of the Harvard University Press.

George J. Sanchez, excerpts from *Becoming Mexican American: Ethnicity, Culture, and Identity in Chicano Los Angeles, 1905–1945*, by George J. Sanchez, 1993. Reprinted by permission of Oxford University Press.

Rachel Moran, excerpts from *Interracial Intimacy: The Regulation of Race and Romance* by Rachel Moran, 2001. Copyright © 2001 by the University of Chicago. Reproduced by permission of the University of Chicago Press.

Donna L. Franklin, excerpt from *Ensuring Inequality: The Structural Transformation of the African-American Family* by Donna L. Franklin, 1997. Reprinted by permission of Oxford University Press.

Patricia Hill Collins, "Shifting the Center: Race, Class, and Feminist Theorizing About Motherhood." Reprinted from *Mothering: Ideology, Experience, and Agency*, edited by Evelyn Nakano

Glenn, Grace Chang, and Linda Rennie Forcey (1994), pp. 45–65. Reprinted by permission of Routledge and the author.

Rayna Rapp, "Family and Class in Contemporary America: Notes Toward an Understanding of Ideology." Reprinted from *Science and Society*, Vol. 42 (1978), pp. 278–300. Reprinted by permission of the Guilford Press.

Karen Brodkin Sacks, "Toward a Unified Theory of Class, Race, and Gender." Reprinted from *American Ethnologist*, Vol. 16, No. 3 (August 1989), pp. 534–550. Reprinted by permission of the American Anthropological Association. Not for further reproduction.

Karen Pyke, "Immigrant Families in the US," from the *Blackwell Companion to the Sociology of Families*, eds J. Scott, J. Treas, and M. Richards, 2004. Reprinted by permission of Blackwell Publishing.

Maxine Baca Zinn and Barbara Wells, "Diversity Within Latino Families: New Lessons for Family Social Science," from *Handbook of Family Diversity*, eds David H. Demo, Katherine R. Allen, and Mark A. Fine, 1999. Reprinted by permission of Oxford University Press.

Lillian B. Rubin, excerpts from *Families on the Fault Line: America's Working Class Speaks About the Family, the Economy, Race, and Ethnicity* by Lillian B. Rubin, 1994. Copyright © 1994 by Lillian B. Rubin. Reprinted by permission of HarperCollins Publishers, Inc.

Rhacel Salazar Parreñas, "Migrant Filipina Domestic Workers and the International Division of Reproductive Labor," from *Gender & Society* 14 (August 2000) pp. 560–580. Reprinted by Permission of Sage Publications, Inc.

Min Zhou and Jennifer Lee, excerpts from *Asian American Youth: Culture, Identity and Ethnicity*, "The Making of Culture, Identity, and Ethnicity among Asian American Youth" by Min Zhou and Jennifer Lee, 2004. Reprinted by permission of Routledge, a division of Taylor & Francis Books.

Pierrette Hondagneu-Sotelo and Michael A. Messner, "Gender Displays and Men's Power: 'The New Man' and the Mexican Immigrant Man." Reprinted from *Theorizing Masculinities*, edited by Harry Brod and Michael Kauhan, pp. 200–218. Reprinted by permission of Sage Publications, Inc.

Nazli Kibria, "Migration and Vietnamese American Women: Remaking Ethnicity." Reprinted from *Women of Color in U.S. Society*, edited by Maxine Baca Zinn and Bonnie Thornton Dill (1994), pp. 247–261. Copyright © 1994 by Temple University Press. Reprinted by permission of Temple University Press.

Kevin Roy and Linda Burton, "Mothering through Recruitment: Kinscription of Nonresidential Fathers and Father Figures in Low Income Families," *Family Relations*, v 56 (January 2007), pp. 24–39. Reprinted by Permission of Blackwell Publishing.

Alison J. Pugh, "Windfall Child-Rearing," *Journal of Consumer Culture*, 4 (2) (2004), pp. 229–249. Reprinted by permission of Sage Publications, Inc.

David Cotter, Paula England, and Joan Hermsen, "Moms and Jobs: Trends in Mothers' Employment and Which Mothers Stay Home." Reprinted by permission of the Council on Contemporary Families.